Explore the World of Management:
HOW A MODULE WORKS

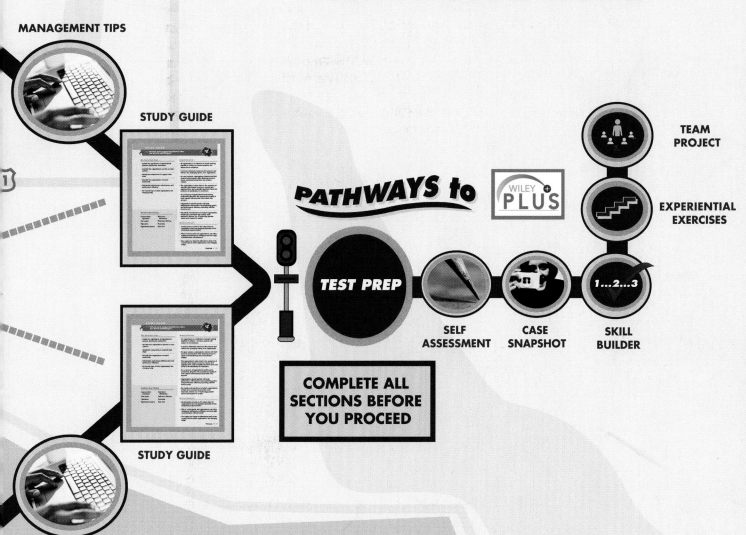

MANAGEMENT TIPS

STUDY GUIDE

STUDY GUIDE

MANAGEMENT TIPS

PATHWAYS to

WILEY PLUS

TEST PREP

COMPLETE ALL SECTIONS BEFORE YOU PROCEED

SELF ASSESSMENT

CASE SNAPSHOT

SKILL BUILDER

1...2...3

TEAM PROJECT

EXPERIENTIAL EXERCISES

THE WILEY BICENTENNIAL—KNOWLEDGE FOR GENERATIONS

*E*ach generation has its unique needs and aspirations. When Charles Wiley first opened his small printing shop in lower Manhattan in 1807, it was a generation of boundless potential searching for an identity. And we were there, helping to define a new American literary tradition. Over half a century later, in the midst of the Second Industrial Revolution, it was a generation focused on building the future. Once again, we were there, supplying the critical scientific, technical, and engineering knowledge that helped frame the world. Throughout the 20th Century, and into the new millennium, nations began to reach out beyond their own borders and a new international community was born. Wiley was there, expanding its operations around the world to enable a global exchange of ideas, opinions, and know-how.

For 200 years, Wiley has been an integral part of each generation's journey, enabling the flow of information and understanding necessary to meet their needs and fulfill their aspirations. Today, bold new technologies are changing the way we live and learn. Wiley will be there, providing you the must-have knowledge you need to imagine new worlds, new possibilities, and new opportunities.

Generations come and go, but you can always count on Wiley to provide you the knowledge you need, when and where you need it!

WILLIAM J. PESCE
PRESIDENT AND CHIEF EXECUTIVE OFFICER

PETER BOOTH WILEY
CHAIRMAN OF THE BOARD

FOR INSTRUCTORS

Wiley**PLUS** is built around the activities you perform in your class each day. With Wiley**PLUS** you can:

Prepare & Present

Create outstanding class presentations using a wealth of resources such as PowerPoint™ slides, image galleries, interactive simulations, and more. You can even add materials you have created yourself.

Create Assignments

Automate the assigning and grading of homework or quizzes by using the provided question banks, or by writing your own.

Track Student Progress

Keep track of your students' progress and analyze individual and overall class results.

Now Available with WebCT and Blackboard!

"It has been a great help, and I believe it has helped me to achieve a better grade."

Michael Morris,
Columbia Basin College

FOR STUDENTS

You have the potential to make a difference!

WileyPLUS is a powerful online system packed with features to help you make the most of your potential and get the best grade you can!

With Wiley**PLUS** you get:

- A complete online version of your text and other study resources.

- Problem-solving help, instant grading, and feedback on your homework and quizzes.

- The ability to track your progress and grades throughout the term.

For more information on what *WileyPLUS* can do to help you and your students reach their potential, please visit www.wiley.com/college/*wileyplus*.

76% of students surveyed said it made them better prepared for tests. *

*Based on a survey of 972 student users of *WileyPLUS*

Exploring Management

→ **IN MODULES**

Exploring
Management

IN MODULES

John R. Schermerhorn, Jr.

BICENTENNIAL
1807
WILEY
2007
BICENTENNIAL

John Wiley & Sons, Inc.

VICE PRESIDENT AND PUBLISHER	Susan Elbe
ASSOCIATE PUBLISHER	Judith Joseph
SENIOR ACQUISITIONS EDITOR	Jayme Heffler
SENIOR DEVELOPMENT EDITOR	Leslie Kraham
SENIOR PRODUCTION EDITOR	Valerie A. Vargas
ASSOCIATE EDITOR	Jennifer Conklin
EXECUTIVE MARKETING MANAGER	Christopher Ruel
CREATIVE DIRECTOR	Harry Nolan
INTERIOR DESIGN	Brian Salisburg
COVER DESIGN	Harry Nolan
PRODUCTION MANAGEMENT SERVICES	Ingrao Associates
SENIOR ILLUSTRATION EDITOR	Anna Melhorn
SENIOR PHOTO EDITOR	Hilary Newman
PHOTO RESEARCHER	Ramon Rivera-Moret
EDITORIAL ASSISTANT	Carissa Marker
MEDIA EDITOR	Allison Morris
FRONT COVER PHOTO	**Top left:** PhotoDisc, Inc./Getty Images. **Top and center:** Darren Robb/Getty Images. **Top right:** Masterfile. **Bottom:** C Squared Studios/PhotoDisc, Inc./Getty Images.
BACK COVER PHOTO	**Left:** IT Stock Free/Age Fotostock America, Inc. **Center:** Image Source/Getty Images, Inc. **Right:** Age Foto Stock/SUPERSTOCK.

This book was set in 10.5/12 Garamond by Prepare, Inc. Printed and bound by Courier-Kendallville, Inc. The cover was printed by Courier-Kendallville, Inc.

To order books or for customer service, please call 1-800-CALL WILEY (225-5945).

ISBN-13: 978-0471-73460-4
ISBN-10: 0-471-73460-8

Printed in the United States of America

10 9 8 7 6 5 4 3 2 1

*I dedicate this book to the person
who lovingly helps me explore
and appreciate life's wonders:
My wife, Ann.*

About the Author

Dr. John R. Schermerhorn, Jr. is the Charles G. O'Bleness Professor of Management in the College of Business at Ohio University, where he teaches graduate and undergraduate courses in management. Dr. Schermerhorn earned a Ph.D. in organizational behavior from Northwestern University, an MBA (with distinction) in management and international business from New York University, and a BS in business administration from the State University of New York at Buffalo. He has taught at Tulane University, the University of Vermont, and Southern Illinois University at Carbondale, where he also served as Head of the Department of Management and Associate Dean of the College of Business Administration.

Highly dedicated to serving the needs of practicing managers, Dr. Schermerhorn continually focuses on bridging the gap between the theory and practice of management in both the classroom and in his textbooks. Because of his commitment to instructional excellence and curriculum innovation, Ohio University has named Dr. Schermerhorn a University Professor. This is the university's highest campus-wide honor for excellence in undergraduate teaching.

Dr. Schermerhorn's international experience also adds a unique global dimension to his teaching and textbooks. He holds an honorary doctorate from the University of Pécs in Hungary. He has also served as a Visiting Professor of Management at the Chinese University of Hong Kong, as on-site Coordinator of the Ohio University MBA and Executive MBA programs in Malaysia, and as Kohei Miura visiting professor at the Chubu University of Japan. Presently he is Adjunct Professor at the National University of Ireland at Galway, a member of the graduate faculty at Bangkok University in Thailand, and advisor to the Lao-American College in Vientiane, Laos.

An enthusiastic scholar, Dr. Schermerhorn is a member of the Academy of Management, where he served as chairperson of the Management Education and Development Division. In addition, educators and students alike know him as author of *Management 8e* (Wiley, 2005) and senior co-author of *Organizational Behavior 9/e* (Wiley, 2005), and *Core Concepts of Organizational Behavior* (Wiley, 2004). Finally, Dr. Schermerhorn has also published numerous articles, such as in the *Academy of Management Journal, Academy of Management Review, Academy of Management Executive, Organizational Dynamics, Journal of Management Education*, and the *Journal of Management Development*.

Dr. Schermerhorn serves as a guest speaker at colleges and universities, lecturing on developments in higher education for business and management, as well as on manuscript development, textbook writing, and instructional approaches and innovations.

Dear Reader:

My career path as a management educator began over 30 years ago. Since then, my journey has evolved into one of continuous exploration and tremendous learning through both my work in the classroom and with students and colleagues around the world.

Indeed, I believe the study of management is an exploration, a daily one, whether we are instructors or students. After all, management is part of our everyday lives—at work, at school, at home, and even at leisure. It is ever present as we sort through the challenges of multiple directions, distant horizons, constantly changing opportunities, great possibilities, and the wonders of a diverse global community. Perhaps these words from T. S. Eliot's poem, *Little Gidding*, best sum up the quest that we all share:

> *We shall not cease from exploration*
> *And the end of all our exploring*
> *Will be to arrive where we started*
> *And know the place for the first time.*

The study of management is a lot like this. It is an ongoing journey, one full of exploration. But in the end we return to application, trying to use what we have learned through experience to better our lives and those of others. That's really what this book, **Exploring Management**, is all about.

Take a minute to look at the book's cover and the test art interspersed throughout the pages. Does the art inspire you to laugh and think about the wonders of nature and our global society? Does it tease you a bit, opening your thoughts as you consider not only what's ahead in the book and in your management course, but also in your own life?

I hope so. Because after all, how well we manage our lives, careers, and organizations can make a big difference in our increasingly complex world. So please join me in using **Exploring Management** as a learning opportunity. I believe you'll find the experience rich with the potential for useful learning of lasting personal and professional value.

John Schermerhorn

Charles G. O'Bleness Professor of Management
College of Business, Ohio University

What makes *Exploring Management* different?

I have written *Exploring Management* to help students embrace management in the context of their everyday lives, career aspirations, and personal experiences. It is designed to meet students in their personal spaces, using lots of examples, applications, visual highlights, thought questions, and learning aids to convey the essentials of management. My goal is that *Exploring Management* will help to enrich the learning experiences designed and led by committed management educators.

Exploring Management offers a more flexible, topic-specific presentation.

The first thing you'll notice is that I wrote this book as a series of "modules" – 23 to be exact. Each module is presented as a topical area with a subtitle that conveys a theme or storyline to guide the student. The modules, shorter than traditional chapters, "chunk" material in ways to make it easier for students to read and study. This is in response to my classroom experiences, where I, and my students, find the typical book chapters increasingly cumbersome and awkward to handle in the context of alternative course designs. The modular approach appeals to the comfort level of many of today's students who are more used to reading short bits of material, such as Internet news reports.

What a modular approach means for you, the instructor, is that topics now appear as easily assignable modules or module segments, sized just right for a class session or to ground a class discussion. Note in the example how the module titles and components are posed as questions and answers. This is to help students frame their reading in a context of relevancy. A module can be assigned in its entirety or as subsections that are focused and self-contained as learning units. It all depends on what fits best with your course design, learning approaches, and class session objectives.

Finally, I hope you find that I organized the modules in a convenient, but unrestrictive order. There are many options available for courses of different types, lengths, and meeting schedules, including distance learning formats.

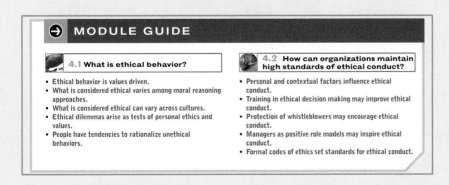

Exploring Management presents an integrated learning design.

Exploring Management offers an integrated pedagogy. Every module opens with a clear visual presentation that communicates the basic organization and content, helping students understand material right from the beginning. The internal module features are displayed to create a sense of direction and application for the reader, as well as to arouse enthusiasm for learning.

An Opening Example next highlights an issue or issues relevant to the module and its subtitle, while presenting a brief report on real organizations and people. The two-page opening layout ends with the question-and-answer style module guide discussed previously. This shows each section of the module as an intact reading and learning assignment. As a result, students can focus on one topic in one sitting and reach initial closure in terms of learning outcomes.

An integrated **Study Guide** at the end of each section is visually set up to provide a one-page checkpoint for learning and test preparation, all tied to the reading "chunk" that has just been completed. This helps student pause, consolidate, and check learning before moving on to the next section. The study guide elements include:

- *Be Sure You Can*—a checkpoint of major learning outcomes for mastery
- *Rapid Review*—bullet-list summary of concepts and points relevant to the section question
- *Define the Terms*—glossary quiz for vocabulary development
- *Reflect/React*—questions to stimulate further thinking and prompt questions for class discussions

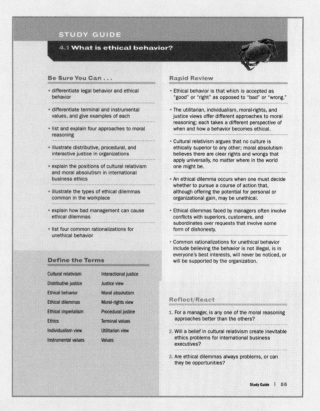

How will *Exploring Management* motivate students to learn about management?

Perhaps you have found, like I have, that many of today's students continuously deal with a number of conflicting demands and distractions. As I explore and learn about their world, I find that my teaching methods must constantly evolve, as well as my instructional materials. That's why I have taken special care to complement the modular approach with a student-friendly style and an appealing design to the book's pages. I hope you'll agree that I am writing and presenting material in ways that come closer to meeting our students in their spaces—rich, varied, colorful, and even digital as it is, rather than forcing them into ours.

Exploring Management relates concepts to students' experiences and interests.

PACESETTERS

I Simply Love What I Do

When John A. Byrne, now at *Business Week*, took over as editor of *Fast Company* magazine, he was already used to hard work. But with every new issue published, he felt the extra rush of accomplishment from a highly demanding job. His "Letter from the Editor" is an insightful look at top management work. In the letter he says it's a "thrill" doing such a challenging job. He talks about extreme hours—8 A.M. to 10 P.M. is the norm. He admits to leaving the office "exhausted." Yet he also points out that "rarely do I leave thinking I've wasted a day doing something that I didn't want to do. More often than not, I walk out feeling immensely proud of the people I work with and of the amazing things we have achieved together." Byrne even jokes that his job sometimes reminds him of being in college and pulling all-nighters on major projects. And in final recognition that being a manager is highly meaningful, Byrne answers the question "Why do I work so hard?" this way: "Frankly, it's not for my company, or for anyone else. I do it for me—because I'm enriched by the learning and personal growth that come from doing a job that I love."

NEWSLINE

Days of the "Imperial" CEO Are Over At least, so says Bill Parrett, chief executive of Deloitte, one of the world's largest financial advisory firms. Parrett was being interviewed in Ireland where he stopped on a tour of Deloitte's worldwide offices. As part of a staff briefing on the firm's strategy and business directions, he talked about a new "intensity of responsibility" for accountants in an age when business fraud is a major societal concern. Parrett uses these types of briefings to give others a chance to speak out and express themselves. Instead of the "imperial CEO," he operates with a management style that encourages discussion and even challenges to the CEO's strategy, even when running a firm with some 120,000 employees and offices in 150 countries.

Reflect: What special skills will Parrett['s] chosen management style? Start thinking ab[out] you want to work for. List the criteria that will b[e]

I want students to embrace management in the context of their everyday lives, career aspirations, and personal experiences. To make this easier, **Exploring Management** includes a number of special features that provide additional and timely content reference points in a visually appealing and meaningful way. Each module offers:

• A **Pacesetters** box introducing a real person's experience with issues being discussed. Examples include Meg Whitman of eBay, Anne Mulcahy of Xerox, and Ron Shaich of Panera Bread.

• A **Newsline** box highlighting an actual news story and posing questions in reaction to it. Examples include "International Agency Promotes Labor Rights Worldwide" and "Why Peter Drucker's Management Advice Still Matters."

• A **Management** box *Tips* offering short reminders and suggestions for how to apply module content - things like "New Workplace Survival Skills" and "How to Succeed in a Telephone Interview."

• A **Stay Informed** box briefly summarizing survey data and facts that stimulate critical inquiry on things like "Worker Attitudes in the Government" and "Hourly Wages Outside of the U.S."

MANAGEMENT TIPS

Checklist for dealing with ethical dilemmas

Step 1. Recognize the ethical dilemma.
Step 2. Get the facts.
Step 3. Identify your options.
Step 4. Test each option: Is it legal? Is it right? Is it beneficial?
Step 5. Decide which option to follow.
Step 6. Ask the "Spotlight Questions": to double check your decision.

"How would I feel if my family found out about my decision?"
"How would I feel if the local newspaper printed my decision?"

Step 7. Take action.

STAY INFORMED

What we know from job satisfaction studies:

• Majority of American workers at least somewhat satisfied with jobs.

• About 14% are "very satisfied."

• Job satisfaction declined 9% from 1995 to 2005.

• Job satisfaction higher in smaller firms (<50 employees) than larger ones (>5000).

• Job satisfaction and life satisfaction tend to run together.

Exploring Management uses a conversational and interactive writing style.

When writing *Exploring Management*, I knew that to engage today's students, I needed to break away from the textbook norm of communicating as the "sage on stage." Instead, I wanted to actually speak with students the way I do in the classroom—conversationally, interactively, and in a nondidactic fashion.

I hope you notice this writing style right from the module opener, through the content presentation, and in all the examples and special features offered for student enrichment. Although it may seem odd to have an author speaking as a person, my goal in doing this is to approach the spirit of what Ellen Langer calls *mindful learning*.[1] She describes this as engaging students from a perspective of active inquiry rather than as consumers of facts and prescriptions. I view it as a way of trying to move textbook writing in the same direction we are moving our teaching—being less didactic and much more interactive, trying to involve students in a dialog around meaningful topics, questions, examples, and even dilemmas; I want students to actively question and engage the world around them; I want them to be informed; I want them to take ownership of the principles and insights of our discipline. Don't you want the same, and more?

[1] Ellen J. Langer, *The Power of Mindful Learning* (Reading, MA: Perseus, 1997).

Exploring Management visually enhances the content presentation to appeal to visual learners.

I'm convinced that our students are very visual in orientation, a reflection of trends in popular culture. They watch movies, play video games, chat, communicate, and read online. All this has to make a difference in how they approach their courses. This is why I have chosen to visually enhance the presentation of module content in two significant ways.

First, I periodically supplement the text presentation with a visual highlight. Whether an **Exhibit** that briefly lists important points, a **Boxed Highlight** that summarizes a key point or theory, or a **Mini-figure** that schematically summarizes a concept under discussion, everything is designed to fit into and flow naturally with the text. I want the visual accents and reminders to be informative parts of a wholistic reading experience, much as we engage when reading magazines, newspapers, and Internet content.

> **Intellectual Capital = Competency × Commitment**

Second, when offering a *Major-figure* (such as Figure 2.3 in the example), I present the caption as a question. I then answer that question both in a short narrative summary and in the figure drawing. I call these "talking figures."

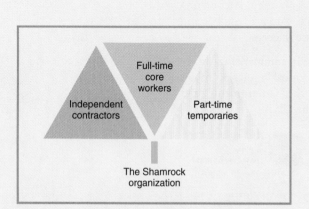

The Shamrock organization

Full-time core workers
Independent contractors
Part-time temporaries

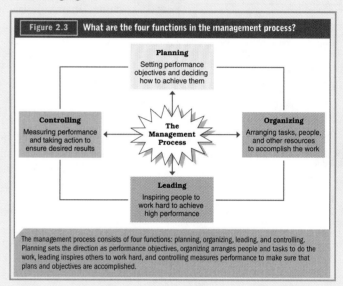

Figure 2.3 What are the four functions in the management process?

Planning Setting performance objectives and deciding how to achieve them

Controlling Measuring performance and taking action to ensure desired results

The Management Process

Organizing Arranging tasks, people, and other resources to accomplish the work

Leading Inspiring people to work hard to achieve high performance

The management process consists of four functions: planning, organizing, leading, and controlling. Planning sets the direction as performance objectives, organizing arranges people and tasks to do the work, leading inspires others to work hard, and controlling measures performance to make sure that plans and objectives are accomplished.

How will *Exploring Management* ensure that students understand management concepts and practices?

I believe that good things, like the field of management itself, grow from strong foundations. As instructors, we need to help our students gain those strong foundations. We're sending them into a world where the most innovative companies look to increase their intellectual capital by investing in employees with established capacities for growth, continuous learning, and good old-fashioned hard work.

Exploring Management includes a carefully selected set of end-of-module learning activities.

The end-of-module activities are designed to keep students moving in the direction of active learning. Keeping in mind what often matters most to students—grades—my first priority is to help them prepare for quizzes and tests, and to earn the best possible grades in their course. **Test Prep** asks students to answer multiple choice, short response, and integration and application questions to provide a good starting point for testing success. When coupled with the additional interactive test versions available on the book's student companion website, they should serve as a substantial learning resource.

But we want students to move beyond pure test readiness, don't we? Don't we want them to understand that there are no "one best ways" or guaranteed solutions out there, and to realize that we need to craft much of what we do in work and with our lives to fit the moment? Don't we want them to willingly seek out problems and opportunities, search for answers, gather information, and work cooperatively with others, just as they will likely have to do in the workplace?

To pursue these personal development directions, each module offers a **Self-Assessment** chosen to complement the subject matter just discussed. Examples include Learning Tendencies, Internal/External Locus of Control, and Managerial Assumptions. Students score and interpret the assessments to encourage greater self-reflection and personal exploration.

Further, a *Pathways to WileyPLUS* section includes recommended active-learning activities (located in full online via WileyPLUS). These include a timely **Case** presented in the format of a magazine article and allowing students to explore module material in a timely real-life context; a **Skill Builder**—another activity that helps students to further explore their managerial skills, tendencies, and personal characteristics; **Experiential Exercises**—for class activities and teamwork relating to the module content; and a **Team Project**—an active-learning group assignment that requires research, writing and presentation on a current topic or issue.

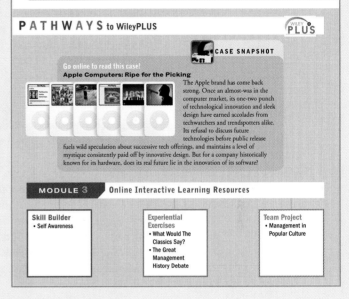

Exploring Management provides a portfolio of comprehensive learning cases.

The cases for *Exploring Management* are, I hope, more than just the standard set of textbook cases. Instead, we carefully developed these cases to help fulfill this book's goals and objectives as a comprehensive learning instrument. They were developed to be timely and compelling; they are designed and presented as magazine articles to stimulate involvement. I believe that the cases will actively engage students through content, writing style, and visual presentation, while being timely and representative of the range of organizations and people that are in today's news. They offer high versatility and should fit a variety of course applications and uses.

To provide maximum flexibility, I include "long", "medium", and "short" cases. The "long cases" appear in the format of a magazine article. And as with most magazine articles, within each long case is a sidebar. This sidebar not only focuses on a person or organization that relates to the subject for the longer case, it also becomes a "short case" of its own. For example, the case on *Electronic Arts* contains a sidebar on *Take2Interactive*, the case on *Dunkin Donuts* contains a sidebar on *Starbucks*, and the case on *New Balance* contains a sidebar on *Nike*.

There are also "medium cases" that represent shorter and quicker-hitting magazine articles. They, too, contain sidebars that can be used as stand-alone cases. Among the medium cases, you'll find *Mozilla* and a sidebar on the *Red Cross,* and a sidebar on founders *Anderson and DeWolfe,* and *Kate Spade, Inc.* with a sidebar on *Kate and Andy Spade.*

There are 25 cases for this book, all available exclusively within WileyPlus, with one suggested for each module. To encourage their use, I've included a **Case Snapshot** at the end of each module. These snapshots will hopefully draw in students so that they will read the case in its entirety.

What additional special materials does *Exploring Management* offer to both instructors and students?

When it comes to support packages, it's always helpful to have a lot of substantive material available. With that in mind, I worked closely with Wiley and my colleagues in designing materials, for both instructors and students, which will reflect, and extend, the goals of this book. On the next two pages, you'll find just a sampler of these additional materials that you can use to enrich your course.

• **Companion Website**

The Companion Website for *Exploring Management in Modules*, at **http://www.wiley.com/college/schermerhorn**, contains a myriad of tools and links to aid both teaching and learning, including nearly all of the resources described in this section.

• **Instructor's Resource Guide**

Prepared by Charles Foley, Columbus State Community College, the Instructor's Resource Guide includes a Conversion Guide, for moving from a chapter format to a modular format; Module Outlines; Module Objectives; Teaching Notes on how to integrate and assign special features; and suggested answers for all quiz and test questions found in the text. A series of Lecture Notes are included to help integrate the various resources available. The Instructor's Resource Guide also includes additional discussion questions and assignments that relate specifically to the cases, as well as case notes, self-assessments, and team exercises.

• **Test Bank**

This Test Bank consists of over 40 true/false, multiple-choice, and short-answer questions per module. Dr. John B. Stark, California State University, Bakersfield, specifically designed the questions to vary in degree of difficulty, from straightforward recall to challenging, to offer instructors the most flexibility when designing their exams. Adding more flexibility is the *Computerized Test Bank,* which requires a PC running Windows. The Computerized Test Bank, which contains all the questions from the manual version, includes a test-generating program that allows instructors to customize their exams.

• **PowerPoint Slides**

Prepared by Vincent Lutheran, University of North Carolina, Wilmington, this set of interactive PowerPoint slides includes lecture notes to accompany each slide. This resource provides another visual enhancement and learning aid for students, as well as additional talking points for instructors. Instructors can access the PowerPoint slides and lecture notes on the instructor portion of the book's website.

• **Personal Response System**

Elnora Farmer, Clayton State University, designed this set of Personal Response System questions (PRS or "Clicker" content) for each module, to spark additional discussion and debate in the classroom. For more information on PRS, please contact your local Wiley sales representative.

• **Web Quizzes**

This resource, available on the student portion of the *Exploring Management in Modules* companion website, offers online quizzes, with questions varying in level of difficulty, designed to help students evaluate their individual progress through a module. Each module's quiz includes 10 questions. These review questions, developed by the Test Bank author, were created to provide the most effective and efficient testing system. Within this system, students have the opportunity to "practice" the type of knowledge they'll be expected to demonstrate on the exam.

- **Pre- and Post-Lecture Quizzes**

  Prepared by Michael W. Wakefield, Colorado State University-Pueblo, the Pre- and Post-Lecture Quizzes, found in WileyPLUS, consist of 10–15 questions (multiple choice and true/false) per module, varying in level of detail and difficulty, but all focusing on that module's key terms and concepts. This resource allows instructors to quickly and easily evaluate their students' progress, by monitoring their comprehension of the material from before the lecture to after it.

- **Videos**

  This set of short video clips provides an excellent starting point for lectures or for general classroom discussion. Please contact your local Wiley representative for more information about the Management Video Program.

- **Movies and Music**

  Interested in integrating pop culture into your management course? Looking for ways to integrate the humanities (movies and music) into your classroom? Robert L. Holbrook, Ohio University, provides *Art Imitates Life*, a supplement rich with innovative teaching ideas for integrating these ideas into your classroom experience. This instructor's supplement is available exclusively for adopters. Please contact your local Wiley representative.

- **MP3 downloads**

  These mini-lectures, one for each module, cover the main concepts and key points of each module. Each 2-4 minute audio file is a perfect tool for student review and can be downloaded to student computers or personal mp3 players.

- **Business Simulations**

  These simulations, available exclusively on WileyPLUS, allow students to reinforce their understanding of management concepts through interactive role-playing and problem-solving scenarios. Every simulation provides learners with rich and complete feedback and can be used to stimulate classroom discussion.

- **Cases**

  This resource, exclusively available on WileyPLUS, contains cases linked to each module of the text. Ranging in length, these featured companies, selected specifically to appeal to students, include Kate Spade, Nike, Apple, and MySpace. Longer cases include sidebar discussions to illustrate different viewpoints. A set of discussion questions accompanies each case, with suggested answers found in the Instructor's Resource Guide.

- **Business Extra Select**

  Wiley has launched this online program, found at **http://www.wiley.com/college/bxs**, to provide instructors with millions of content resources, including an extensive database of cases, journals, periodicals, newspapers, and supplemental readings. This courseware system lends itself extremely well to integrating real-world content within the management course, thereby enabling instructors to convey the relevance of the course to their students.

WileyPLUS:

WileyPLUS is a powerful online tool that provides instructors and students with an integrated suite of teaching and learning resources, including an online version of the text, in one easy-to-use website. To learn more about WileyPLUS, and view a demo, please visit www.wiley.com/college/WileyPLUS.

- **WileyPLUS Tools for Instructors**

  WileyPLUS enables instructors to:

  - Assign automatically graded homework, practice, and quizzes from the end of chapter and test bank.
  - Track students' progress in an instructor's gradebook.
  - Access all teaching and learning resources including an online version of the text, and student and instructor supplements, in one easy-to-use website. These include teaching tips, full color PowerPoint slides, and in-class activities.
  - Create class presentations using Wiley-provided resources, with the ability to customize and add your own materials.

- **WileyPLUS Resources for Students**

  WileyPLUS provides students with a variety of study tools:
  - mp3 downloads—audio overviews of each module
  - team evaluation tools
  - experiential exercises
  - self-assessments
  - flashcards of key terms, and more!

Acknowledgments

This isn't the typical "book" project that most publishers deal with, that is, developed from a neat proposal. Instead, *Exploring Management* is a "concept" book, which began, grew, and found life and form over the course of many telephone conversations, conference calls, e-mail exchanges, and face-to-face meetings. There wouldn't be an *Exploring Management* without the support, commitment, creativity, and dedication of the following members of the Wiley team. It's a team with which I am most proud to be associated. My thanks travel now to you all: Jayme Heffler; *Senior Acquisitions Editor*; Leslie Kraham, *Senior Development Editor*, Judy Joseph, *Associate Publisher*; Susan Elbe, *Vice President and Publisher*; Jennifer Conklin, *Associate Editor*; Carissa Marker, *Editorial Assistant*; Chris Ruel, *Executive Marketing Manager*, Terry Ann Kremer, *Freelance Development Editor*; Valerie A. Vargas, *Senior Production Editor*; Harry Nolan, Director, *Creative Group* Hilary Newman, *Photo Manager*; Ramon Rivera-Moret, *Photo Researcher*; Anna Melhorn, *Illustration Editor.*

I also want to thank the many individuals who took the time to read and evaluate the draft manuscript prior to production. These reviewers generously provided their expertise to help me ensure the book's accuracy, clarity, and focus on the needs of today's management instruction. Without their many, many helpful comments, the book would not be what it is today. Thank you to all the following, for your invaluable contributions:

Focus Group Participants:

Maria Aria, *Camden County College*
Ellen Benowitz, *Mercer County Community College*
John Brogan, *Monmouth University*
Lawrence J. Danks, *Camden County College*
Matthew DeLuca, *Baruch College*
David Fearon, *Central Connecticut State University*
Stuart Ferguson, *Northwood University*
Eugene Garaventa, *College of Staten Island*
Scott Geiger, *University of South Florida, St. Petersburg*
Larry Grant, *Bucks County Community College*
Fran Green, *Pennsylvania State University, Delaware County*
F.E. Hamilton, Ph.D., *Eckerd College*
Don Jenner, *Borough of Manhattan Community College*
John Podoshen, *Franklin and Marshall College*
Neuman Pollack, *Florida Atlantic University*
David Radosevich, *Montclair State University*
Moira Tolan, *Mount Saint Mary College*

Virtual Focus Group Participants:

George Alexakis, *Nova Southeastern University*
Steven Bradley, *Austin Community College*
Paula Brown, *Northern Illinois University*
Elnora Farmer, *Clayton State University*
Paul Gagnon, *Central Connecticut State University*
Eugene Garaventa, *College of Staten Island*
Larry Garner, *Tarleton State University*
Wayne Grossman, *Hofstra University*
Dee Guillory, *University of South Carolina, Beaufort*
Julie Hays, *University of St. Thomas*
Kathleen Jones, *University of North Dakota*
Marvin Karlins, *University of South Florida*
Al Laich, *University of Northern Virginia*
Vincent Lutheran, *University of North Carolina, Wilmington*

Douglas L. Micklich, *Illinois State University*
David Oliver, *Edison College*
Jennifer Oyler, *University of Central Arkansas*
Kathleen Reddick, *College of Saint Elizabeth*
Terry L. Riddle, *Central Virginia Community College*
Roy L. Simerly, *East Carolina University*
Frank. G. Titlow, *St. Petersburg College*
David Turnipseed, *Indiana University – Purdue University, Fort Wayne*
Michael Wakefield, *Colorado State University, Pueblo*
George A. (Bud) Wynn, *University of Tampa*

Reviewers:
Peter Geoffrey Bowen, *University of Denver*
Kenneth G. Brown, *University of Iowa*
Beverly Bugay, *Tyler Junior College*
Robert Cass, *Virginia Wesleyan College*
Susan Davis, *Claflin University*
Matthew DeLuca, *Baruch College*
Valerie Evans, *Lincoln Memorial University*
Paul Ewell, *Bridgewater College*
Elnora Farmer, *Clayton State University*
Larry Garner, *Tarleton State University*
Dee Guillory, *University of South Carolina, Beaufort*
Debra Hunter, *Troy University*
Gary S. Insch, *West Virginia University*
Robert Klein, *Philadelphia University*
John Knutsen, *Everett Community College*
Al Laich, *University of Northern Virginia*
Susan Looney, *Delaware Technical & Community College*
Vincent Lutheran, *University of North Carolina, Wilmington*
John Markert, *Wells College*
Brenda McAleer, *Colby College*
Gerald McFry, *Coosa Valley Technical College*
Diane Minger, *Cedar Valley College*
Michael Monahan, *Frostburg State University*
Joelle Nisolle, *West Texas A&M University*
Penny Olivi, *York College of Pennsylvania*
Jennifer Oyler, *University of Central Arkansas*
Kathy Pederson, *Hennepin Technical College*
Joseph C. Santora, *Essex County College*
Howard Stanger, *Canisius College*
David Turnipseed, *Indiana University – Purdue University, Fort Wayne*
Robert Turrill, *University of Southern California*
Michael Wakefield, *Colorado State University, Pueblo*
Daniel Wubbena, *Western Iowa Tech Community College*

Student Focus Group Participants, Baruch College:

Farhana Alam; Laureen Attreed; Sarah Bohsali; Susanna Eng; Dino Genzano; Annie Gustave; Andrew Josefiak; Diana Pang; Vidushi Parmar; Dulari Ramkishun; Vicky Roginskaya; Jessica Scheiber; Ruta Skarbauskaite; Darren Smith

Brief Contents

Contents

Module 4   Ethics and Ethical Behavior
Character doesn't stay home when we go to work **48**

Part 2   Management and Society

Module 5   Social Responsibility and Governance
Organizations have ethics too **64**

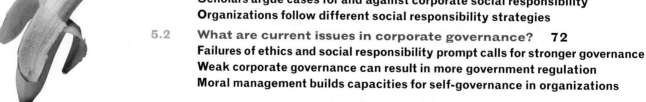

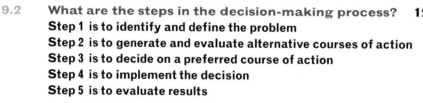

Part 3   Management Processes, Structures, and Systems

Module 11   Controls and Control Systems
What gets measured happens **152**

Module 12   Strategic Management
Insights and hard work deliver results **166**

Part 4   Managers in Action

Module 20   Motivational Dynamics
Money isn't everything; the job counts too **286**

Module 21   Teams and Teamwork
Two heads can be better than one **300**

Special Features

Pacesetters

Management Tips

Newsline

Self-Assessment

Case Snapshot

This is no time

Our New Workplace

For most people, a day at work is an experience full of opportunities and rewards. What about you? Do you view work, or the prospect of working, as a source of learning and experience, or just a means to a paycheck? And what about the future? What is your ideal job? Are your skills and competencies competitive? Will you be able to balance career demands with personal responsibilities? What about other people; do you understand their needs and aspirations? [1]

for complacency

As you ponder these and related questions, take time to browse *Fortune* magazine's online list of "100 Best Companies to Work For."

The Container Store is one example, built with an idea (help people streamline their lives by selling them great containers at good prices) and a set of values (respect all those who contribute to making the company a success).[2] CEO Kip Tindell says: "We are so proud to foster a place where people enjoy getting up and coming to work every morning, working alongside great people—truly making a difference every single day."

The Container Store seems to walk the talk. It's known for treating its employees well—training, good pay, equal treatment, and the opportunity for input.

Wouldn't you like to work in this type of environment? And if you were to start your own company someday, shouldn't this respect for people be part of your business model?

> **What to Expect from Employees of the Future**
>
> - More loyal to themselves than to employers
> - Change jobs often during a career
> - Like more time off for personal affairs and community service
> - Use more flexible work approaches, including working remotely from home
> - Value employers that nurture quality of life and personal development
> - High expectations for ethics and morality by employers

MODULE GUIDE

 1.1 What issues and concerns complicate the new workplace?

- Failures of ethics and corporate governance are troublesome.
- Globalization and job migration are changing the world of work.
- Diversity and discrimination are continuing social priorities.
- Talent and intellectual capital drive high-performance organizations.
- Career success requires skills and a capacity for self-management.

 1.2 What are organizations like as work settings?

- Mission statements express the purposes of organizations.
- Organizations are open systems that interact with their environments.
- Organizations create value for customers and clients.
- Productivity is a measure of organizational performance.
- Organizations are changing as society changes.

You might already have noticed that this text may differ from others you've read. I'm going to ask you a lot of questions, and try to expose you to different viewpoints and possibilities. This process of active inquiry begins with recognition that we live and work at a time of great changes, ones that are likely to increase, not decrease, in number, intensity, and complexity in the future.

Are you ready to meet the challenges ahead? Are you informed about the issues and concerns that complicate our new workplace? Are you willing to admit that this is no time for complacency?

• Failures of Ethics and Corporate Governance Are Troublesome

Ethics set moral standards of what is "good" and "right" behavior.

We have recently been exposed to sensational ethical failures in business, including the WorldCom and Enron debacles. If you don't follow and think about these cases, you should. When Enron collapsed, the results were devastating. Loyal employees who had invested their retirement savings in company stock saw the value fall to virtually zero. Outside stockholders suffered large losses on their investments. How would you recover if this happened to you?

In response, our society is becoming much stricter in expecting businesses, other social institutions, and the people who run and work in them to operate with high moral standards.[3] The U.S. government has even passed legislation, the Sarbanes-Oxley Act of 2002, to make it easier to prosecute corporate executives for financial misconduct.[4] But external regulation can only do so much. At the end of the day, we depend on individual people, working at all levels of organizations, to act ethically.

Corporate governance is oversight of a company's management by a board of directors.

Ethics is a code of moral principles that sets standards of conduct for what is "good" and "right" as opposed to "bad" or "wrong." Given all the scandals, you might be cynical about ethical behavior in organizations. But even though ethical failures get most of the publicity, there is still a lot of good happening in the world of work. Look around. You should find that many people and organizations exemplify a new ethical reawakening, one that places high value on personal integrity and ethical leadership. You should find concerns for sustainable development and protection of the natural environment, product safety and fair practices, and protection of human rights in all aspects of society, including employment.[5] And you should find organizations declaring their values, such as this example from the Johnson & Johnson credo.[6]

We are responsible to the communities in which we live and work and to the world community as well. We must be good citizens—support good works and charities and bear our fair share of taxes. We must encourage civic improvements and better health and education. We must maintain in good order the property we are privileged to use, protecting the environment and natural resources.

One of the positive results from the recent rash of business ethics failures is renewed attention on the role of **corporate governance**, the active oversight of management decisions, corporate strategy, and financial reporting by boards of directors.[7] Typical responsibilities of corporate and nonprofit board members include overseeing decisions on

NEWSLINE

Social responsibility begins with building a great workplace In a book entitled *The Transparent Leader*, former CEO of Dial Corporation, Herb Baum, argues that integrity is a major key to leadership success. He also believes that the responsibility to set the tone for leadership integrity begins at the top. He tries to walk the talk—no reserved parking place, straight talking, open door, honest communication, careful listening, and hiring good people. Believing that most CEOs are overpaid, he once gave his annual bonus to the firm's lowest paid workers. He also tells the story of an ethical role model—a rival CEO, Reuben Mark of Colgate Palmolive. Mark called him one day to say that a newly hired executive had brought with him to Colgate a disk containing Dial's new marketing campaign. Rather than read it, he returned the disk to Baum—an act Baum called "the clearest case of leading with honor and transparency I've witnessed in my career."

Reflect: What acts of personal integrity have you encountered in your work and student activities? Can you think of any situation where you disappointed yourself by failing to display integrity?

hiring, firing, and compensating senior executives, assessing strategies and their implementation, and verifying financial records.

Because weak corporate governance undoubtedly contributes to ethics failures in organizations, there is more emphasis today on holding boards accountable for what happens in the organizations they oversee. Former board members of bankrupted World-Com, Inc., found this out the hard way. They paid personal fines of $18 million for failing to spot fraudulent behavior by the firm's top managers.[8]

• Globalization and Job Migration Are Changing the World of Work

Do you know where your favorite athletic shoes or the parts for your computer and cell phone were manufactured? Can you go to the store and buy a toy or piece of apparel that is really "Made in America"? And whom do you speak with when calling a service center with computer problems, trying to track a missing package, or seeking information on retail store locations? Don't be surprised if the person serving you is on the phone from India, the Philippines, Ireland, or even Ghana.

Welcome to the global economy of the twenty-first century.[9] Japanese management consultant Kenichi Ohmae calls this a "borderless world," suggesting the disappearance of national boundaries in world business.[10] Take the example of Hewlett-Packard.[11] It operates in 178 countries and most of its 140,000+ employees work outside of the United States. It is the largest technology company in Europe, the Middle East, and Russia. Although headquartered in Palo-Alto, California, is HP an American company any more?

What we are talking about is **globalization**, the worldwide interdependence of resource flows, product markets, and business competition.[12] In the global economy, businesses sell goods and services to customers around the world. They also search the world to buy the things they need for the lowest price. Many businesses actively engage in **global outsourcing** by hiring workers and contracting for supplies and services in other countries. The firms save money and gain efficiency by manufacturing things and getting jobs done in countries with lower costs of labor. Doesn't it make perfect business sense for Ohio-based Rocky Boots to outsource when a shoe that costs $12 to make in the United States can be made in China for 40 cents?[13] Or is there more to the story?

One controversial side effect to global outsourcing is **job migration**, the shifting of jobs from one country to another. At present, the U.S. economy is a net loser to job migration. In one three-month period, global outsourcing caused 3 out of every 10 layoffs.[14] By contrast, countries like China, India, Philippines, and Russia are net gainers. And they aren't just sources of unskilled labor; they are now able to offer highly trained workers—engineers, scientists, accountants—for as little as one-fifth the cost of an equivalent U.S. worker.

Politicians and policymakers regularly debate how to best deal with the high costs of job migration, as local workers lose their jobs and their communities lose economic vitality. One side looks for new government policies to stop job migration by protecting the jobs of U.S. workers. The other side calls for patience, believing that the national economy will strengthen in the long run as it readjusts and creates new jobs for U.S. workers. Which side are you on?

• Diversity and Discrimination Are Continuing Social Priorities

In 1987, the Hudson Institute, a public policy research center, published the report *Workforce 2000: Work and Workers for the 21st Century*. It created an immediate stir in business circles, among government policymakers, and in the public eye.[15] The report called attention to the slow growth of the U.S. workforce, as well as its changing demographics—fewer younger workers and more older ones, as well as more women, minorities, and immigrants.[16]

A follow-up report, *Workforce 2020*, provided "a wake-up call for American workers, corporations, educators, parents and government officials."[17] It focused on

Globalization is the worldwide interdependence of resource flows, product markets, and business competition.

Global outsourcing involves contracting for work that is performed by workers in other countries.

Job migration occurs when global outsourcing shifts from one country to another.

STAY INFORMED

- Women are 47% of the U.S. workforce and hold 50.3% of managerial jobs.
- African-Americans are 13.8% of the workforce and hold 6.5% of managerial jobs.
- Hispanics are 11.1% of the workforce and hold 5% of managerial jobs.
- Women hold 14.7% of board seats at *Fortune* 500 companies; women of color hold 3.4%.
- For each $1 earned by men, women earn 76 cents; African-American women earn 64 cents; Hispanic women earn 52 cents.

Workforce diversity describes difference among workers in gender, race, age, ethnic culture, able-bodiness, religious affiliation, and sexual orientation.

workforce diversity, which describes the composition of a workforce in terms of differences among the members, such as gender, age, race, ethnicity, religion, sexual orientation, and able-bodiness.[18]

U.S. laws strictly prohibit the use of demographic characteristics in human resource management decisions, such as hiring, promotion, and firing.[19] But laws are one thing, actions are yet another. One study revealed that resumes with names like "Brett" received 50 percent more responses from potential employers than ones with identical credentials but with names such as "Kareem."[20] And, do you ever wonder why women and minorities hold few top jobs in large companies?[21] One explanation is a subtle form of discrimination known as the **glass ceiling effect**. It occurs when an invisible barrier or "ceiling" prevents members of diverse populations from advancing to high levels of responsibility in organizations.[22]

The **glass ceiling effect** is an invisible barrier limiting career advancement of women and minorities.

Prejudice is the display of negative, irrational attitudes toward women or minorities.

There is little doubt that women and minorities still face special work and career challenges in our society at large. Although progress is being made, diversity bias still exists in too many of our work settings.[23] This bias begins with **prejudice**, the holding of negative, irrational attitudes regarding people who are different from us. Prejudice becomes active **discrimination**, like that revealed in the resume study, when people in organizations treat minority members unfairly and deny them full membership benefits.

Discrimination actively denies women and minorities the full benefits of organizational membership.

Scholar Judith Rosener suggests that employment discrimination of any form comes at a high cost—not just to the individuals involved, but also to society. The organization's loss for any discriminatory practices, she says, is "undervalued and underutilized human capital."[24]

• Talent and Intellectual Capital Drive High-Performance Organizations

A values statement on the website of Herman Miller, the innovative manufacturer of designer furniture, reads: "Our greatest assets as a corporation are the gifts, talents and abilities of our employee-owners. . . . When we as a corporation invest in developing people; we are investing in our future."

We shouldn't find prejudice and discrimination at Herman Miller. Rather, we should find a work environment that respects all employees, raises their confidence, and inspires them to achieve high performance and find self-fulfillment. Hopefully, this also describes the organization in which you work, will work and, perhaps, even will someday lead.

After studying high-performing companies, management scholars Charles O'Reilly and Jeffrey Pfeffer conclude that they do better because they get extraordinary results from the people working for them. "These companies have won the war for talent," they say, "not just by being great places to work—although they are that—but by figuring out how to get the best out of all of their people, every day."[25]

Intellectual capital is the collective brainpower or shared knowledge of a workforce.

O'Reilly and Pfeffer are talking about an organization's **intellectual capital**, the collective brainpower or shared knowledge of its workforce.[26] For you, intellectual capital can be a personal asset—a package of brains, skills, and capabilities that differentiates you from others and that makes you valuable to potential employers. And as you think about it, consider the two foundations of intellectual capital—competency and commitment.[27]

Competency represents our talents or job-relevant capabilities; commitment represents our willingness to work hard in applying them to important tasks. Obviously both

> ➜ **Intellectual Capital = Competency × Commitment**

are essential; one without the other is not enough to meet anyone's career needs or any organization's performance requirements. Max DePree, former CEO of Herman Miller, puts it this way: "We talk about the difference between being successful and being exceptional. Being successful is meeting goals in a good way—being exceptional is reaching your potential."[28]

Knowledge workers use their minds and intellects as critical assets to employers.

When it comes to human potential, the new workplace is well into the *information age* dominated by **knowledge workers**. These are persons whose minds, not just their physical capabilities, are critical assets.[29] But things are not standing still. Futurist Daniel Pink says that we are already moving into a new *conceptual age* in which intellectual capital rests with people who are both "high concept" (creative and good with ideas) and "high touch" (joyful and good with relationships).[30] He says the future will belong to those of us with "whole mind" competencies, ones that combine left-brain analytical thinking with right-brain intuitive thinking.

• Career Success Requires Skills and a Capacity for Self-Management

No matter how you look at it, the future poses a complex setting for career success. And if current trends continue it will be more and more of a **free-agent economy**. Like professional athletes, many of us will be changing jobs more often and even working on flexible contracts with a shifting mix of employers over time.[31] British scholar and consultant Charles Handy uses the analogy of the **shamrock organization** to describe the implications.[32]

Each leaf in the shamrock organization represents a different group of workers. The first leaf is a core group of permanent, full-time employees with critical skills, who follow standard career paths. The second leaf consists of workers hired on short- and long-term contracts. They provide the organization with specialized skills and talents that support the needs of the core workers. The third leaf is a group of temporary part-timers, hired as the needs of the business grow and let go when business falls.

Full-time core workers

Independent contractors

Part-time temporaries

The Shamrock organization

As you might guess, today's college graduates must be prepared to succeed in the second and third leaves of Handy's Shamrock organization, not just the first. And to achieve success, Handy advises everyone to maintain a portfolio of skills that is always up-to-date and attractive to potential employers, regardless of where in the shamrock your goals may center.

Former IBM CEO Lou Gerstner describes a similar concept. He says we must set a goal of "lifetime employability" and we must accept personal responsibility for its achievement. This places a premium on your capacity for **self-management**, realistically assessing yourself and actively managing your personal development. It means exercising initiative, accepting responsibility for accomplishments and failures, and continually seeking new learning opportunities and experiences.

The fact is that what happens from this point forward in your career is largely up to you. Would you agree that there is no better time than the present to start taking charge? Picture yourself in an interview situation. The person sitting across the table asks the question, "What can you do for us?" How do you reply?

A good answer to the interviewer's question describes your "personal brand"—a unique and timely package of skills and capabilities of real value to a potential employer. Management consultant Tom Peters advises that your brand should be "remarkable, measurable, distinguished, and distinctive" relative to the competition—others who want the same career opportunities that you do.[33]

Have you thought about what employers want, and about your brand? Does your personal portfolio include new workplace survival skills like those shown in Management Tips?[34]

In a **free-agent economy** people change jobs more often, and many work on independent contracts with a shifting mix of employers.

A **shamrock organization** operates with a core group of full-time long-term workers supported by others who work on contracts and part-time.

Self-management is the ability to understand oneself, exercise initiative, accept responsibility, and learn from experience.

MANAGEMENT TIPS

New workplace survival skills

- *Mastery:* You must be good at something, to contribute something of value to your employer.
- *Contacts:* You must get to know the people who can help you get things done.
- *Entrepreneurship:* You must be willing to take risks, spot opportunities, and step out to engage them.
- *Love of technology:* You must embrace technology, and be willing and able to fully utilize IT.
- *Marketing:* You must create a positive impression, and communicate well your successes and progress.
- *Passion for renewal:* You must learn and change continuously, to update yourself for the future.

STUDY GUIDE

1.1 What issues and concerns complicate the new workplace?

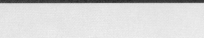

Be Sure You Can . . .

- describe how corporate governance influences ethics in organizations

- explain how globalization and job migration are changing the economy

- differentiate prejudice, discrimination, and the glass ceiling effect

- state the intellectual capital equation

- discuss career opportunities in the Shamrock organization

- explain the importance of self-management to career success in the new economy

Define the Terms

Corporate governance	Intellectual capital
Discrimination	Job migration
Ethics	Knowledge workers
Free-agent economy	Prejudice
Glass ceiling effect	Self-management
Global outsourcing	Shamrock organization
Globalization	Workforce diversity

Rapid Review

- Society increasingly expects organizations and their members to perform with high ethical standards and in socially responsible ways.

- Globalization is bringing increased use of global outsourcing by businesses and concern for the adverse effects of job migration.

- Organizations operate with diverse workforces and each member should be respected for her or his talents and capabilities.

- Work in the new economy is increasingly knowledge-based, relying on people with the capacity to bring valuable intellectual capital to the workplace.

- Careers in the new economy are becoming more flexible, requiring personal initiative to build and maintain skill portfolios that are always up-to-date and valued by employers.

Reflect/React

1. To what extent are current concerns for ethics in business, globalization, and changing careers addressed in your courses and curriculum?

2. How can people of color can avoid being hurt by prejudice, discrimination, and the glass ceiling effect in their careers?

3. In what ways can the capacity for self-management help you to prosper in a free-agent economy?

In the article "The Company of the Future," University of California Professor and former U.S. Secretary of Labor Robert Reich says: "Everybody works for somebody or something—be it a Board of Directors, a pension fund, a venture capitalist, or a traditional boss. Sooner or later you're going to have to decide who you want to work for."[35] Are you ready to make this decision? Do you understand the nature of organizations well enough to evaluate them when making career choices?

• Mission Statements Express the Purposes of Organizations

Any **organization**, large or small, public or private, can be described as a collection of people working together to achieve a common purpose.[36] Think about the implications of this definition. It applies to virtually all of our social institutions—banks, hospitals, large and small businesses, multinational corporations, government agencies, churches, voluntary associations, and more. And importantly, it also suggests that all organizations play unique roles in society, enabling their members to accomplish far more by working together collectively than alone.

When things work right, the power of collective action energizes the **organizational purpose**, its reason for existence as a social institution. Just as with people, a clear and compelling purpose sets a good direction for an organization and its members. In fact, researchers believe that organizations gain strength and perform better when their purposes are clearly tied to quality products and customer satisfaction.[37]

Google's stated purpose is: "To organize the world's information and make it universally accessible."[38] Do you believe it is well stated? Could this sense of purpose be one of the reasons why Google has been successful and is constantly innovating to stay so? And by the way, can you think of an organization that doesn't seem to have a clear purpose, or that doesn't act consistent with its stated purpose?

You can learn a lot about an organization from its *mission statement*, which typically describes not only the purpose but also goals, values, and even priorities.[39] Consider, for example, the excerpts from the unique three-part mission statement of Ben & Jerry's Homemade, Inc.[40] The statement shows a firm that is publicly committed not only to making the highest quality ice creams, but also to respecting its employees, protecting the natural environment, and being a good citizen of society. It's quite a statement, but also a lot to live up to.

> An **organization** is a collection of people working together in a division of labor to achieve a common purpose.

> The **organizational purpose** is usually to provide society with useful goods or services.

→ Ben & Jerry's Mission Statement

Product Mission
To make, distribute, and sell the finest quality all natural ice cream . . . promoting business practices that respect the earth and the environment.

Social Mission
To initiate innovative ways to improve the quality of life locally, nationally, and internationally.

Economic Mission
To increase value for our stakeholders and expand opportunities for development and career growth for our employees.

• Organizations Are Open Systems that Interact with Their Environments

You can see in Ben & Jerry's mission statement a clear linkage between the firm and its external environment. This illustrates how organizations act as **open systems** in a continuous input–transformation–output cycle (see Figure 1.1). They interact with their

> An **open system** transforms resource inputs from the environment into product outputs.

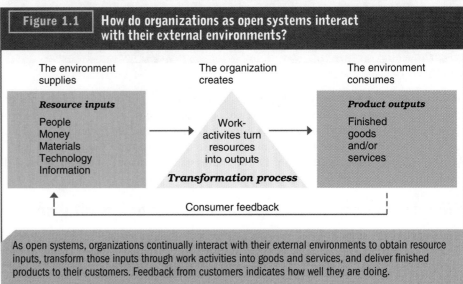

Figure 1.1 | How do organizations as open systems interact with their external environments?

The environment supplies

Resource inputs
People
Money
Materials
Technology
Information

The organization creates

Work-activites turn resources into outputs

Transformation process

The environment consumes

Product outputs
Finished goods and/or services

Consumer feedback

As open systems, organizations continually interact with their external environments to obtain resource inputs, transform those inputs through work activities into goods and services, and deliver finished products to their customers. Feedback from customers indicates how well they are doing.

environments to obtain resources (e.g., people, technology, information, money, and supplies) that are transformed through work activities into goods and services for their customers and clients. Google, Ben & Jerry's, your college or university, and the local bookstore can all be described in this manner.

This concept also helps explain why there is so much emphasis today on **customer-driven organizations**. These are organizations that try hard to focus their resources, energies, and goals on continually satisfying the needs of their customers and clients. Look again at Figure 1.1 and you should recognize the logic. Can you see how customers hold the keys to the long-term prosperity and survival of a business, like an auto manufacturer? Their willingness to buy products or use services provides the revenues needed to obtain resources and keep the cycle in motion. And as soon as the customers balk or start to complain, someone should be listening. This feedback is a warning that the organization needs to change and do things better in the future.

> **Customer-driven organizations** focus their resources, energies, and goals on satisfying the needs of customers.

• Organizations Create Value for Customers and Clients

The sequence of activities through which organizations actually create value for their customers and clients is called the **value chain**. The process of value creation begins with obtaining resources. It continues as the organization combines and transforms these resources to create finished goods or services. The value chain ends when customers and clients are well served.

Organizational success can be evaluated from a value creation perspective. If it adds value to the original cost of resource inputs, then a business organization earns a profit. It is able to sell its products for more than the cost of making them. If it adds value to the original cost of resource inputs, a nonprofit organization adds wealth to society. It is able to provide a public service, such as community fire protection, that is worth more than its cost.

Of course, the value chain works well only when all parts of the organization, people and processes, work well together.[41] In fact, one of the ways consultants and managers try to improve organizations is to carefully describe the parts of the value creation process, analyze each part, examine relationships among the parts, and then make changes to streamline the value chain for better performance.

> A **value chain** is a sequence of activities through which organizations transform inputs into outputs.

Resources Acquired from Environment

Resources Received and Organized for Use

People and Technology Create Goods and Services

Goods and Services Distributed as Final Products

Customers and Clients Are Served

The organization's value chain

• Productivity Is a Measure of Organizational Performance

To rate the overall performance of organizations it is common to use some measure of **productivity**—the quantity and quality of work accomplished relative to resources used. In simplest terms you can think of this as a ratio: outputs/inputs. At Southwest Airlines, for example, productivity is measured and tracked year-to-year in such terms as operating profit per passenger, expenses per passenger, and average monthly passengers per employee.[42]

The performance of organizations can also be described in terms of efficiency and effectiveness, as shown in Figure 1.2. **Performance efficiency** is an input measure of the cost of resources consumed. A common efficiency measure is cost of labor; others include equipment utilization, facilities maintenance, and supplies or materials expenses. **Performance effectiveness** is an output measure of goal accomplishment. It indicates the extent to which things are done right, ideally in terms of both quantity and quality of work performed.

You can see from the figure that true productivity results from a combination of performance efficiency and performance effectiveness. But one of the realities of organizational life is that efficiency and effectiveness get involved in trade-offs; sometimes organizations emphasize one over the other.

Have you ever considered, for example, why so much customer service is now handled electronically? The answer is efficiency, the drive to reduce business costs by replacing personal contact with computer assistance.[43] You see examples of this everywhere—from self-checkouts at the grocery store, to ATM machines, to online order tracking.

All of this added efficiency is often great for us, the customers, as well as for the organization. But you have to admit that it can sometimes go too far, hurting effectiveness through customer dissatisfaction. How do you react when those highly efficient, computer-assisted or automated transactions fail to meet your service needs? And what about those times when a voice mail menu of options is not only tedious, but doesn't offer the choices you need?

STAY INFORMED

Cost of handling customer service inquiries:

- $9.50—in person
- $2.50—by personal e-mail
- $1.10—by interactive voice response
- $ .50—through website
- $ .25—by automated e-mail response

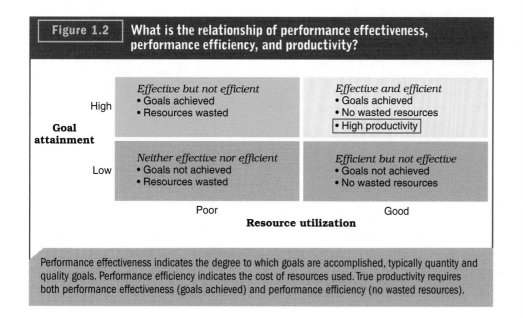

| Figure 1.2 | What is the relationship of performance effectiveness, performance efficiency, and productivity? |

Goal attainment

High — *Effective but not efficient*
- Goals achieved
- Resources wasted

High — *Effective and efficient*
- Goals achieved
- No wasted resources
- High productivity

Low — *Neither effective nor efficient*
- Goals not achieved
- Resources wasted

Low — *Efficient but not effective*
- Goals not achieved
- No wasted resources

Poor ——— **Resource utilization** ——— Good

Performance effectiveness indicates the degree to which goals are accomplished, typically quantity and quality goals. Performance efficiency indicates the cost of resources used. True productivity requires both performance effectiveness (goals achieved) and performance efficiency (no wasted resources).

Key Transitions in Organizations

Less "command-and-control" Traditional top-down ways are proving inadequate. The old "do as I say" bosses are giving way to new "how I can help you" ones.

Belief in human capital The new economy rewards high involvement and participatory work settings. The goals are to rally knowledge, experience, and commitment of all workers.

Commitment to teamwork Today's organizations are less vertical and more horizontal in focus. They are more driven by teamwork, pooling talents for creative problem solving.

Emphasis on technology Changes in computer and information technology bring continuous opportunities. Technology keeps changing the ways organizations operate and people work.

New workforce expectations A new generation of workers is more informal and less tolerant of hierarchy. The new generation tends to value performance merit over status and seniority.

Concern for work–life balance As society changes, life gets more complicated for individuals and families. Organizations gain by actively helping people balance work and personal affairs.

• Organizations Are Changing as Society Changes

When interviewed by *Business Week*, consultant Tom Peters was asked to describe how organizations would operate in the future. He responded this way:[44]

. . .we will be working with an eclectic mix of contract teammates from around the globe, many of whom we'll never meet face-to-face. Every project will call for a new team, composed of specially tailored skills. . . . Every player on this team will be evaluated—pass-by-pass, at-bat by at-bat, for the quality and uniqueness and timeliness and passion of her or his contribution.

Predicting the future is never easy. But Peters was right on; the future is now. As most everyone realizes, organizations are already asking people to work together in new and different ways. And if you compare what is taking place with what might be considered traditional practices in the past, you may be surprised.

Exciting trends are unfolding. In the new workplace there is less command and control, and more freedom and self-direction. There is more emphasis on respecting people as valuable assets to be nurtured and developed, not as costs to be controlled. In executive boardrooms, management conversations, and the business literature, themes of "respect," "participation," "empowerment," "involvement," "teamwork," and "ethical behavior" are common when organization and management practices are being discussed.

Many forces drive these and other organizational transitions. Look at the Exhibit: *Key Transitions in Organizations*.[45] Take the time to read through it twice. The first time, think about how different organizations probably were when your parents started their careers. Could these differences have affected their progress, satisfactions, and lives overall? On the second reading, think about what the transitions mean for you, for your future. What are the opportunities and the potential risks? And, are you well prepared for them?

Things are different in our new century and post-9/11 world; sometimes they can be downright scary. *New York Times* columnist and author Thomas Friedman spends a lot of time thinking and writing about world events and globalization.[46] He recognizes the challenges ahead, and believes we can flourish in the future. But, he says, you and I, and our children, must be "strategic optimists" who have the "right imagination and the right motivation." And he says we have to be willing to wake up every day and not just imagine that things can be better, but be willing to act on that imagination.

As we now move together to explore management through the pages of this book, there's no doubt that the new workplace is here. And it is shaping up to be very different from those of the past. But it's also still a work in progress. Imagine what it can be in the future.

PACESETTERS

At Xerox, Anne Mulcahy's high-performance leadership is based on valuing people.

When faced with a crisis—basically to change dramatically or go out of business—the Xerox Corporation Board of Directors turned to an experienced insider for leadership. Their choice was Anne Mulcahy, a company veteran who had worked her way to the top over a 27-year career. Her charismatic and hands-on style of leadership focused on communicating with customers and employees. Facing what she considered an "unsustainable business model," one of her first steps was to fly around the world to personally visit employees in all Xerox locations. Her goals were to communicate face-to-face the realities associated with the company's problems, yet still raise morale and motivation by refocusing attention away from past failures and toward future possibilities. Considered one of the most respected and powerful women in the world of business, Mulcahy says: "People have to feel engaged, motivated and feel they are making a contribution to something that is important."

Anne Mulcahy, CEO, Xerox

1.2 What are organizations like as work settings?

Be Sure You Can . . .

- explain the significance of organizational purpose and mission statements

- describe how organizations operate as open systems

- identify the components in a typical value chain

- describe how organizations measure productivity

- differentiate performance effectiveness and performance efficiency

- list several ways in which organizations are changing today

Define the Terms

Customer-driven organization	Performance effectiveness
Open system	Performance efficiency
Organization	Productivity
Organizational purpose	Value chain

Rapid Review

- An organization is a collection of people working together to achieve a common purpose, the reason for its existence.

- A mission statement expresses the purpose and reflects the underlying values of an organization.

- As open systems, organizations interact with their external environments while obtaining resource inputs and transforming them into product outputs.

- The organization's value chain is the sequence of activities that acquire resources, receive and organize them, and eventually transform them into products for distribution to customers.

- As a measure of organizational performance, productivity describes the quantity and quality of work outputs with resource costs taken into account.

- Organizations should operate with both performance effectiveness (accomplishing goals), and performance efficiency (operating with the lowest costs).

- Key trends and transitions in today's organizations include less command and control, more teamwork, intense use of technology, greater speed, and respect for people.

Reflect/React

1. At what point or points in the value chain do organizations have the greatest potential to find productivity improvements?

2. Why is it that people and organizations can often emphasize performance efficiency and lose sight of performance effectiveness?

3. How might your future be affected by each of the several ways in which organizations are changing today?

MODULE

1

TEST PREP
Take the complete set of Module 1 quizzes online!

Multiple Choice

1. The Sarbanes-Oxley Act of 2002, which makes it easier to prosecute corporate executives for financial misconduct, was prompted by a lack of _____ displayed by some corporate leaders.
(a) self-management **(b)** ethics **(c)** customer orientation **(d)** intellectual capital

2. _____ is the active oversight by boards of directors of top management decisions in such areas as corporate strategy and financial reporting.
(a) value chain analysis **(b)** productivity **(c)** outsourcing **(d)** corporate governance

3. When a manager denies promotion to a qualified worker simply because of a personal dislike for the fact that she is Hispanic, this is an example of _____.
(a) discrimination **(b)** workforce diversity **(c)** self-management **(d)** a free-agent economy

4. Information and technology would be considered _____ in the open systems view of organizations.
(a) inputs **(b)** outputs **(c)** transformations **(d)** feedback

5. If performance effectiveness means doing the "right things," performance efficiency means doing these things _____.
(a) at low cost **(b)** with high quality **(c)** in a timely manner **(d)** with high job satisfaction

6. When an apparel manufacturer buys its cloth in one country, has designs made in another country, sews the garments in another country, and sells the finished product in yet other countries, it is actively engaging in the practice of _____.
(a) job migration **(b)** performance effectiveness **(c)** value creation **(d)** global outsourcing

7. The analogy of the _____ describes organizations that hire fewer full-time employees, and hire more part-timers and independent contractors.
(a) open system **(b)** conceptual age **(c)** shamrock **(d)** information age

8. The intellectual capital equation states that: Intellectual Capital = _____ × commitment.
(a) diversity **(b)** confidence **(c)** competency **(d)** communication

9. By reading an organization's mission statement you should be able to learn about the organization's purpose and _____.
(a) glass ceiling **(b)** values **(c)** productivity **(d)** governance

10. The first step in the value chain for most organizations would be _____.
(a) serving customers **(b)** acquiring resources **(c)** creating goods and services **(d)** distributing products for sale

Short Response

11. What is the difference between prejudice and discrimination in the workplace?

12. Why is job migration often associated with an increase in global outsourcing?

13. How is the emergence of a "free-agent economy" changing career and work opportunities?

14. Why isn't any open system automatically a customer-driven organization?

Integration & Application

15. Choose an organization with which you are familiar—perhaps where you work, a place where you do business, or a voluntary organization.

Questions: What is the organization's purpose? How would you describe the organization as an open system? What are the elements in its value chain? Are there areas where you might suggest improvements in the chain? Does the organization operate consistent with a customer-driven orientation, and with what implications for its performance?

SELF-ASSESSMENT
21st-Century Manager

INSTRUCTIONS *Use this scale to rate yourself on the following list of personal characteristics.*

S = Strong, I am very confident with this one.
G = Good, but I still have room to grow.
W = Weak, I really need work on this one.
U = Unsure, I just don't know.

1 *Resistance to stress:* The ability to get work done even under stressful conditions.
2 *Tolerance for uncertainty:* The ability to get work done even under ambiguous and uncertain conditions.
3 *Social objectivity:* The ability to act free of racial, ethnic, gender, and other prejudices or biases.
4 *Inner work standards:* The ability to personally set and work to high performance standards.
5 *Stamina:* The ability to sustain long work hours.
6 *Adaptability:* The ability to be flexible and adapt to changes.
7 *Self-confidence:* The ability to be consistently decisive and display one's personal presence.

8 *Self-objectivity:* The ability to evaluate personal strengths and weaknesses and to understand one's motives and skills relative to a job.
9 *Introspection:* The ability to learn from experience, awareness, and self-study.
10 *Entrepreneurism:* The ability to address problems and take advantage of opportunities for constructive change.

SCORING
Give yourself 1 point for each S, and 1/2 point for each G. Do not give yourself points for W and U responses. Total your points and enter the result here [**PMF =** _____].

INTERPRETATION
This assessment offers a self-described *profile of your management foundations* (PMF). Are you a perfect 10, or something less? There shouldn't be too many 10s around. Ask someone else to also assess you on this instrument. You may be surprised at the results, but the insights are well worth thinking about. The items on the list are skills and personal characteristics that should be nurtured. Success as a twenty-first-century manager may well depend on a willingness to continually strengthen these basic management foundations throughout one's career.

P A T H W A Y S to WileyPLUS

CASE SNAPSHOT

Go online to read this case!
New Balance: No Heroes, Just Sneakers
In an era in which *outsourcing* is a dirty word to every one except manufacturers, New Balance seems to have done what so many of its competitors couldn't: maintain quality and price control while keeping much of its manufacturing in the United States. To do so, they've invested in manufacturing advances to cut costs and energy, and yet still pay their U.S. workers more than the competition. New Balance has a sizeable cultural following in the United States; can it beat Nike on its own track?

MODULE 1 — Online Interactive Learning Resources

Skill Builder
• Diversity Maturity

Experiential Exercises
• Future Workplace
• Organizational Metaphors

Team Project
• Service Learning in Management

Everyone becomes a

The Management Process

It wasn't too long ago that my son called home to announce that he was taking a new job with a popular e-commerce firm, as a software development engineer. Although great news, what really makes the story interesting is that he made the initial contact through Monster.com! As a leading global online career site, Monster.com began just like many other successful businesses—with creativity, talent, and a willingness to take risk. Its founder, Jeff Taylor, says: "One morning I woke up at 4 A.M., and wrote an idea down on a pad of paper I keep next to my bed. I had this dream that I created a bulletin board called the Monster Board. That became the original name for the company. When I got up, I went to a coffee shop,

manager someday

and from 5:30 A.M. until about 10:00 A.M., I wrote the user interface for what today is Monster.com."

Today, Monster.com is a top destination, but there are other good choices among the many online career websites. You might take a look at competing "big board" sites like HotJobs.com, CollegeGrad.com and CareerBuilder.com, among others. And in the specialty areas, Dice.com focuses on tech jobs, AfterCollege.com focuses on first jobs post graduation, and TheLadders.com deals with professional earning $100,100+. You should be able to find many others without much effort.[1]

Is it time for you to sign up with these and other placement services? With initiative and a solid resume, you'll gain access to many new and exciting opportunities. But you'll also most likely encounter competition; the really great jobs are in high demand.

What is on the list of skills and personal characteristics that helps set you apart from other job applicants? Does the list include your managerial potential?[2]

> **→ What Employers Look for in Job Candidates**
>
> - Communication and interpersonal skills
> - Ability to work well in teams
> - Personal ethics and integrity
> - Analytical and problem-solving skills
> - Leadership potential
> - Fit with corporate culture
> - Strategic thinking

→ MODULE GUIDE

 2.1 What does it mean to be a manager?

- Organizations have different types and levels of managers.
- Accountability is a cornerstone of managerial performance.
- Effective managers help others achieve high performance and satisfaction.
- Managers must meet multiple and changing expectations.

 2.2 What do managers do?

- Managerial work is often intense and demanding.
- Managers plan, organize, lead, and control.
- Managers enact informational, interpersonal, and decisional roles.
- Managers pursue action agendas and engage in networking.
- Managers use a variety of technical, human, and conceptual skills.
- Managers learn from experience.

A **manager** is a person who supports and is responsible for the work of others.

First-line managers supervise people who perform nonmanagerial duties.

You find them everywhere, in small and large businesses, voluntary associations, government agencies, schools, hospitals, and wherever people work together for a common cause. Even though the job titles vary from team leader to department head, project leader, president, administrator, and more, the people in these jobs all share a common responsibility—helping others do their best work. We call them **managers**—persons who directly supervise, support, and help activate work efforts to achieve the performance goals of individuals, teams, or even an organization as a whole. In this sense, I think you'll agree with the chapter subtitle; we all are presently, or will be someday be, managers.

• Organizations Have Different Types and Levels of Managers

Figure 2.1	What are the typical job titles and levels of management in organizations?

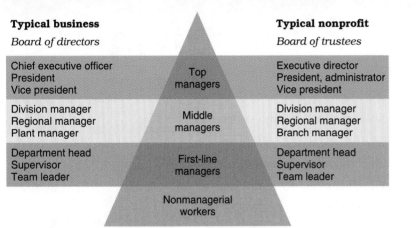

The traditional organization is structured as a pyramid. The top manager, typically a CEO, President, or Executive Director, reports to a Board of Directors (business) or Board of Trustees (nonprofit organization). Middle managers report to top managers while first-line managers report to middle managers. Nonmanagerial workers report to first-line managers.

"I've just never worked on anything that so visibly, so dramatically changes the quality of someone's life. Some days you wake up, and if you think about all the work you have to do it's so overwhelming, you could be paralyzed." These are the words of Justin Fritz as he described her experiences leading a 12-member team to launch a new product at Medtronics, a large Minnesota-based medical products company. About the challenge of managerial work, she says: "You just have to get it done."[3]

Look at Figure 2.1, which describes an organization as a series of layers, each of which represents different levels of work and managerial responsibilities.[4] See where Justin would fit as a **first-line manager**—someone who leads a group of people who perform nonmanagerial duties. Common job titles for first-line managers include department head, team leader, and supervisor.[5]

Look again at Figure 2.1 to see where Justin may be headed in her career. At the next level above team leader we find **middle managers**—persons in charge of relatively large departments or divisions consisting of several smaller work units or teams. Middle managers usually supervise several first-line managers. Examples might include clinic directors in hospitals; deans in universities; and division managers, plant managers, and regional sales managers in businesses. Because of their position "in the middle," these managers must be able to work well with people from all parts of the organization—higher, lower, and side-to-side. Obviously, as you or Justin move up the career ladder to middle management there will be more pressure and challenges to face. But there should also be rewards and satisfaction.

Some middle managers advance still higher in the organization, earning job titles such as chief executive officer (CEO), president, or vice president. These **top managers** are responsible for the performance of an organization as a whole or for one of its larger parts. They are expected to be alert to trends and developments in the external environment, recognize potential problems and opportunities, and lead the organization to long-term success. The best of them are future-oriented strategic thinkers able

Middle managers oversee the work of large departments or divisions.

Top managers guide the performance of the organization as a whole or of one of its major parts.

to make good decisions under highly competitive and uncertain conditions. And, they communicate an inspiring vision that motivates and keeps organization members focused on important objectives.[6]

The Pacesetters feature on John Byrne offers an interesting look into what it's like to be a top manager. But while you are reading about him, someone who seems responsible and successful, think also about those top managers who are just the opposite. We have to admit that some slack off, don't live up to expectations, and even take personal advantage of their positions, perhaps to the point of abusing them and commiting illegal acts. If top managers really are at the top of organizations, who or what keeps them focused and high performing?

Governance is the answer, based on our discussion in the first module. Figure 2.1 is a reminder that even the CEO or president of an organization reports to a higher-level boss. In business corporations this is a **Board of Directors** whose members are elected by stockholders to represent their ownership interests. In nonprofit organizations, such as a hospital or university, top managers report to a *Board of Trustees*. These board members may be elected by local citizens, appointed by government bodies, or invited to serve by existing members.

In both business and the public sector, the basic responsibilities of a board are the same. The members are supposed to oversee the affairs of the organization and the performance of its top management. In other words, they are supposed to make sure that the organization is always being run right.

Members of a **Board of Directors** are elected by stockholders to represent their ownership interests.

• Accountability Is a Cornerstone of Managerial Performance

Just one week before she was fired as CEO of Hewlett-Packard, Carly Fiorina, once described as America's most powerful businesswoman, told reporters that her relationship with the HP board was "excellent."[7] But board members soon acted to hold her accountable for what they considered to be HP's unacceptable performance results.

Throughout the workplace, not just at the top, the term **accountability** describes the requirement of one person to answer to a higher authority for performance achieved in his or her area of work responsibility. This notion of accountability is an important aspect of managerial performance. In the traditional organizational pyramid accountability flows upward. Team members are accountable to a team leader; the team leader is accountable to a middle manager; the middle manager is accountable to a top manager; and, as in the case of Carly Fiorina at HP, the top manager is accountable to a Board of Directors.

Of course, it is also important to recognize the unique challenges of accountability and dependency in managerial performance. At the same time that any manager is being held accountable by a higher level for the

Accountability is the requirement to show performance results to a supervisor.

Accountability and dependency in managerial performance

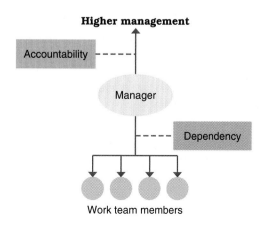

Higher management

Accountability

Manager

Dependency

Work team members

performance results of her or his area of supervisory responsibility, the manager is dependent on others to do the required work. In fact, we might say that a large part of the study of management is all about learning how to best manage the dynamics of accountability and dependency.

• Effective Managers Help Others Achieve High Performance and Satisfaction

This discussion of performance accountability and related challenges may make you wonder: What exactly is an effective manager? Most people, perhaps you, would reply that an effective manager is someone who helps people and organizations perform. That's a fine starting point, but I like to go one step further. I define an **effective manager** as someone who successfully helps others achieve both high performance and satisfaction in their work.

This concern for not just performance but also satisfaction is a central theme in the new workplace. It brings to our attention **quality of work life** (QWL) issues. This term describes the overall quality of human experiences in the workplace. Have you experienced a "high QWL" environment? Most people would describe it as a place where they are respected and valued by their employer; a place where they have fair pay, safe work conditions, opportunities to learn and use new skills, room to grow and progress in a career, and protection of individual rights; a place where members take pride in their work and the organization.

Are you willing to work anywhere other than in a high QWL setting? Would you, as a manager, be pleased with anything less than knowing you excel at helping others achieve not just high performance, but also job satisfaction?[8] Sadly, the real world of work doesn't always live up to these expectations. Talk to people at work, your parents, and friends. You might be surprised. Many people today still encounter difficult, sometimes even hostile and unhealthy, work environments—low QWL to be sure![9]

> An **effective manager** successfully helps others achieve high performance and satisfaction in their work.

> **Quality of work life** is the overall quality of human experiences in the workplace.

• Managers Must Meet Multiple and Changing Expectations

Like everything else in our lives, the work of managers constantly evolves along with changes in our society and organizations. It is common today to hear managers referred to as "coordinators" and "coaches." These labels certainly contrast with the more traditional notion of managers as "order-givers" and "directors." Just their use gives a very different impression of the manager's job. And the fact is that most organizations need more than managers who simply sit back and tell others what to do.

Take a moment to jot down a few notes on the behaviors and characteristics of the *best* managers you've ever had. My students describe theirs as leading by example, willing to do any job, treating others as equals and with respect, acting approachable, being enthusiastic and challenging, and helping others grow. They talk about managers that often work alongside those they supervise, spending most of their time providing advice and support so that others can perform to the best of their abilities, and with satisfaction. How does this listing compare with your experiences?

Figure 2.2 uses the notion of an *upside-down pyramid* to describe a new mindset for managers—a real expression of what it means to act as a coach rather than an order-giver. Prominent at the top of the upside-down pyramid are nonmanagerial workers, people who interact directly with customers and clients, or produce products and services for them. Managers are shown a level below. Their attention is concentrated on supporting these workers so they can best serve the organization's customers.

In the upside-down pyramid view there is no doubt that the organization exists to serve its customers. And, it is clear that managers are there to help and support the people whose work makes that possible. Doesn't that sound like the way things should be?

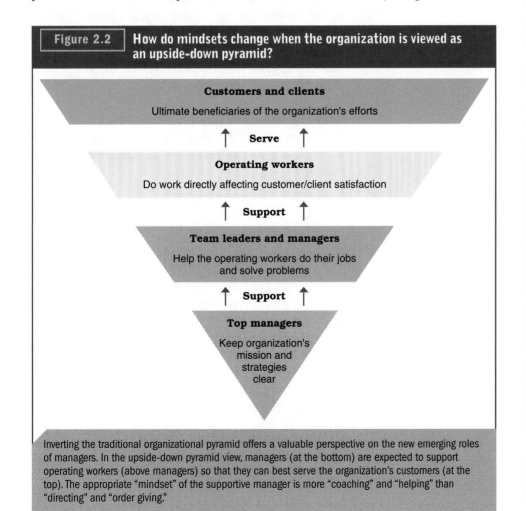

Figure 2.2 | **How do mindsets change when the organization is viewed as an upside-down pyramid?**

Customers and clients
Ultimate beneficiaries of the organization's efforts

↑ **Serve** ↑

Operating workers
Do work directly affecting customer/client satisfaction

↑ **Support** ↑

Team leaders and managers
Help the operating workers do their jobs and solve problems

↑ **Support** ↑

Top managers
Keep organization's mission and strategies clear

Inverting the traditional organizational pyramid offers a valuable perspective on the new emerging roles of managers. In the upside-down pyramid view, managers (at the bottom) are expected to support operating workers (above managers) so that they can best serve the organization's customers (at the top). The appropriate "mindset" of the supportive manager is more "coaching" and "helping" than "directing" and "order giving."

Be Sure You Can . . .

- explain how managers contribute to organizations

- describe the activities of managers at different levels

- explain how accountability operates in organizations

- describe the goals of an effective manager

- list several ways the work of managers is changing from the past

- explain the role of managers in the upside-down pyramid

Define the Terms

Accountability	Manager
Board of Directors	Middle managers
Effective manager	Quality of work life
First-line manager	Top managers

Rapid Review

- Managers support and facilitate the work efforts of other people in organizations.

- Top managers scan the environment and pursue long-term goals; middle managers coordinate activities among large departments or divisions; first-line managers like team leaders supervise and support nonmanagerial workers.

- Everyone in organizations is accountable to a higher level manager for their performance accomplishments; at the highest level, top managers are held accountable by boards of directors.

- Effective managers help others achieve both high performance and high levels of job satisfaction.

- New directions in managerial work emphasize "coaching" and "supporting", rather than "directing" and "order-giving."

- In the upside-down pyramid view of organizations, the role of managers is to support nonmanagerial workers who serve the needs of customers at the top.

Reflect/React

1. Other than at work, in what situations do you expect to be a manager during your lifetime?

2. Why should a manager be concerned about the quality of work life in an organization?

3. In what ways does the upside-down pyramid view of organizations offer advantages over the traditional view of the top-down pyramid?

The managers we have been discussing are indispensable to organizations; their efforts bring together resources, technology, and human talents to get things done. Some of the tasks are fairly routine, done day after day. Many others, however, are challenging and novel, often appearing as unexpected problems and opportunities. But regardless of the task at hand, managers are expected to make things happen in ways that best serve the goals of the organization and the interests of its members.

The **management process** is planning, organizing, leading, and controlling the use of resources to accomplish performance goals.

• Managerial Work Is Often Intense and Demanding

Although this description of what managers are supposed to do may seem straightforward, putting it in practice can be much more complicated. In his classic book, *The Nature of Managerial Work*, Henry Mintzberg describes the daily work of corporate chief executives as: "There was no break in the pace of activity during office hours. The mail . . . telephone calls . . . and meetings . . . accounted for almost every minute from the moment these executives entered their offices in the morning until they departed in the evenings."[10] Today, we might add the ever-full e-mail and voice-mail inboxes to Mintzberg's list of executive preoccupations.[11]

Planning is the process of setting objectives and determining what should be done to accomplish them.

Can you imagine a day filled with these responsibilities? The managers Mintzberg observed had little free time because unexpected problems and continuing requests for meetings consumed almost all the time that became available. Their workdays were intense, hectic, and fast paced; the pressure for continuously improving performance was all-encompassing. Says Mintzberg:

The manager can never be free to forget the job, and never has the pleasure of knowing, even temporarily, that there is nothing else to do. . . . Managers always carry the nagging suspicion that they might be able to contribute just a little bit more. Hence they assume an unrelenting pace in their work.[12]

> **➔ Managerial Work According to Mintzberg**
>
> - **Managers work long hours.**
> - **Managers work at an intense pace.**
> - **Managers work at fragmented and varied tasks.**
> - **Managers work with many communication media.**
> - **Managers work largely through relationships.**

• Managers Plan, Organize, Lead, and Control

There is little doubt that managerial work can be busy, demanding, and stressful not just for chief executives in large businesses, but for managers at all levels of responsibility in any organization.[13] If you are ready to perform as a manager or to get better as one, a good starting point is Figure 2.3. It shows the four functions in the **management process**—planning, organizing, leading, and controlling. The belief is that all managers, regardless of title, level, and organizational setting, are responsible for doing each of them well.[14]

In management, **planning** is the process of setting performance objectives and determining what actions should be taken to accomplish them. When managers plan, they set goals and objectives, and select ways to achieve them.

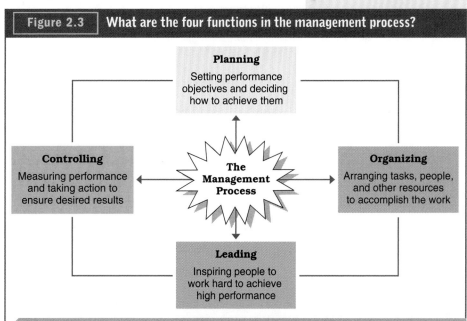

Figure 2.3 What are the four functions in the management process?

Planning
Setting performance objectives and deciding how to achieve them

Controlling
Measuring performance and taking action to ensure desired results

The Management Process

Organizing
Arranging tasks, people, and other resources to accomplish the work

Leading
Inspiring people to work hard to achieve high performance

The management process consists of four functions: planning, organizing, leading, and controlling. Planning sets the direction as performance objectives, organizing arranges people and tasks to do the work, leading inspires others to work hard, and controlling measures performance to make sure that plans and objectives are accomplished.

There was a time, for example, when Ernst & Young's top management grew concerned about the firm's retention rates for women.[15] Why? Turnover rates at the time were much higher than among men, running some 22 percent per year and costing the firm about 150 percent of each person's annual salary to hire and train a replacement. Chairman Philip A. Laskawy responded to the situation by setting a planning objective to reduce turnover rates for women.

Organizing is the process of assigning tasks, allocating resources, and coordinating work activities.

Even the best plans will fail without strong implementation. Success begins with **organizing**, the process of assigning tasks, allocating resources, and coordinating the activities of individuals and groups. When managers organize they bring people and resources together to put plans into action.

At Ernst & Young, Laskawy organized to meet his planning objective by convening and personally chairing a Diversity Task Force of partners. He also established a new Office of Retention and hired Deborah K. Holmes to head it. As retention problems were identified in various parts of the firm, Holmes created special task forces to tackle them and recommend location-specific solutions.

Leading is the process of arousing enthusiasm and inspiring efforts to achieve goals.

The management function of **leading** is the process of arousing people's enthusiasm to work hard and inspiring their efforts to fulfill plans and accomplish objectives. When managers lead they build commitments to plans and influence others to do their best work in implementing them.

Deborah Holmes actively pursued her leadership responsibilities at Ernst & Young. She noticed that, in addition to the intense work at the firm, women often faced more stress because their spouses also worked. She became a champion of improved work-life balance and pursued it relentlessly. She started "call-free holidays" where professionals did not check voice mail or e-mail on weekends and holidays. She also started a "travel sanity" program that limited staffers' travel to four days a week so that they could get home for weekends. And, she started a Woman's Access Program to provide mentoring and career development.

STAY INFORMED

Top reasons for leaving jobs

Reason	Women	Men
Family time	1	5
Earn degree, training	2	2
Work not enjoyable	3	3
Moved away	4	–
Change careers	5	1
Lost interest in field	–	4

Controlling is the process of measuring performance and taking action to ensure desired results.

Controlling is the process of measuring work performance, comparing results to objectives, and taking corrective action as needed. As you have surely experienced, things don't always go as planned. When managers control, they stay in contact with people as they work, gather and interpret information on performance results, and use this information to make adjustments.

At Ernst & Young, Laskawy and Holmes regularly measured retention rates for women at the firm and compared them to the rate that existed when their new programs were started. By comparing results with plans and objectives, they were able to track changes in work-life balance and retention rates, and pinpoint where they needed to make further adjustments in their programs. Over time, turnover rates for women were reduced at all levels in the firm.[16]

• Managers Enact Informational, Interpersonal, and Decisional Roles

When you consider the four management functions, don't be unrealistic. The functions aren't always performed one at a time or step-by-step. Remember the manager's workday as earlier described by Mintzberg—intense, fast-paced, stressful. The reality is that managers must plan, organize, lead and control continuously while dealing with the numerous events, situations, and problems of the day.

To describe how managers actually get things done, Mintzberg identified three sets of roles that he believed all good managers enact successfully.[17]

Interpersonal roles	Informational roles	Decisional roles
How a manager interacts with other people • Figurehead • Leader • Liaison	How a manager exchanges and processes information • Monitor • Disseminator • Spokesperson	How a manager uses information in decision making • Entrepreneur • Disturbance handler • Resource allocator • Negotiator

Mintzberg's 10 managerial roles.

A manager's *informational roles* focus on the giving, receiving, and analyzing of information. The *interpersonal roles* reflect interactions with people inside and outside the work unit. The *decisional roles* involve using information to make decisions to solve problems or address opportunities.[18] It is through these roles, so to speak, that managers fulfill their planning, organizing, leading, and controlling responsibilities.

• Managers Pursue Action Agendas and Engage in Networking

While we are speaking about realities, consider this description of just one incident from the workday of a general manager.[19]

> On the way to a scheduled meeting, a general manager met a staff member who did not report to him. They exchanged "hellos" and in a two-minute conversation the manager: (a) asked two questions and received helpful information; (b) reinforced his relationship with the staff member by sincerely complimenting her on recent work; and, (c) enlisted the staff member's help on another project.

Can you see the pattern here? In just two short minutes, this general manager accomplished a lot. In fact, he demonstrated excellence with two activities that management consultant and scholar John Kotter considers critical to succeeding with the management process—agenda setting and networking.[20]

Through *agenda setting* managers develop action priorities. These agendas may be incomplete and loosely connected in the beginning. But over time, as the manager utilizes information continually gleaned from many different sources, the agendas become more specific. Kotter believes that the best managers keep their agendas always in mind so they can quickly recognize and take advantage of opportunities to advance them. In the example above, what might have happened if the manager had simply nodded "hello" to the staff member and continued on to his meeting?

Through *networking* managers build and maintain positive relationships with other people, ideally those whose help might be useful someday. These networks create the opportunities through which many agenda items can be fulfilled. Much of what needs to be done is beyond a manager's capabilities alone; the support and contributions of other people often make the difference between success and failure.

In the present example, our manager needed help from someone who did not report directly to him. Although he wasn't in a position to order the staff person to help him out, this wasn't a problem. Because of the working relationship they maintained through networking, she wanted to help when asked.

Most managers maintain extensive networks with peers, members of their work teams, higher-level executives, and people at various points elsewhere in the organization at the very least. Many are expected to network even more broadly, such as with customers, suppliers, and community representatives.

How do you rate your agenda-setting and networking capabilities? Are your To-Do lists too long, filled with minor rather than major things? Do you engage in or avoid opportunities to network with other people whose support and assistance might be helpful someday?

Lower level managers	Middle level managers	Top level managers

Conceptual skills—The ability to think analytically and achieve integrative problem solving

Human skills—The ability to work well in cooperation with other persons; emotional intelligence

Technical skills—The ability to apply expertise and perform a special task with proficiency

Katz's essential managerial skills.

• Managers Use a Variety of Technical, Human, and Conceptual Skills

The discussion of roles, agendas, and networking is but a starting point for inquiry into your personal portfolio of management skills. Another step forward is available through the work of Harvard scholar Robert L. Katz. He has classified the essential skills of managers into three categories—technical, human, and conceptual, with the relative importance of each varying by level of managerial responsibility.[21]

A **technical skill** is the ability to use a special proficiency or expertise to perform particular tasks. Accountants, engineers, market researchers, financial planners, and systems analysts, for example, possess obvious technical skills. Other baseline technical skills for any college graduate today include such things as written and oral communication, computer literacy, and math and numeracy.

In Katz's model, technical skills are very important at career entry levels. So how do you get them? Formal education is an initial source for learning these skills, but continued training and job experiences are important in further developing them. Why not take a moment to inventory your technical skills, the ones you have and the ones you still need to learn for your future career? Katz tells us that the technical skills are especially important at job entry and early career points. Surely, you want to be ready the next time a job interviewer asks the bottom-line question: "What can you really do for us?"

The ability to work well with others is a **human skill**, and it is a foundation for managerial success. How can we excel at networking, for example, without an ability and willingness to relate well with other people? A manager with good human skills will have a high degree of self-awareness and a capacity to understand or empathize with the feelings of others. You would most likely observe this person working with others in a spirit of trust, enthusiasm, and genuine involvement.

A manager with good human skills is also likely to be high in **emotional intelligence**.[22] Discussed in Module 16 as an important leadership attribute, "EI" is defined by scholar and consultant Daniel Goleman as the "ability to manage ourselves and our relationships effectively."[23]

Given the highly interpersonal nature of managerial work, it is easy to see why human skills and emotional intelligence are so helpful. As shown in the previous figure, Katz believes they are consistently important across all the managerial levels.

The ability to think critically and analytically is a **conceptual skill**. It involves the capacity to break down problems into smaller parts, see the relations between the parts, and recognize the implications of any one problem for others. While all managers should have the ability to view situations broadly and to solve problems to the benefit of everyone concerned, Katz believes that the conceptual skills actually grow in importance as one moves up to higher management responsibilities. At each higher level, the problems managers face often become more ambiguous and have many complications with longer-term consequences.

A **technical skill** is the ability to use expertise to perform a task with proficiency.

A **human skill** is the ability to work well in cooperation with other people.

Emotional intelligence is the ability to manage ourselves and our relationships effectively.

A **conceptual skill** is the ability to think analytically and solve complex problems.

→ Five Facets of Emotional Intelligence

1. Self awareness—understanding moods, emotions
2. Self regulation—thinking before acting, controlling disruptive impulses
3. Motivation—working hard and persevering
4. Empathy—understanding emotions of others
5. Social skills—gaining rapport and building good relationships

• Managers Learn from Experience

Functions, roles, agendas, networks, skills! How can anyone develop and be consistently good at all of these things? How can the capacity to do them all well be developed and maintained for long-term career success?

This book can be a good starting point, a foundation for the future. Take some time and give thought when answering the questions that I ask as you read. Consider also how you might apply what you are learning to your current situations—school, work, and personal. And then ask what you can learn from these situations in turn. It is well recognized that successful managers do this all the time. We call it learning from experience.

The challenge for all of us is to be good at **lifelong learning**—the process of continuously learning from our daily experiences and opportunities. Consider this point by State Farm CEO Ed Rust:

> *I think the whole concept of lifelong learning is more relevant today than ever before. It's scary to realize that the skill sets we possess today are likely to be inqadequate five years from now, just due to the normal pace of change. As more young people come into the workforce, they need a deeper, fundamental understanding of the basic skills—not just to get a job, but to grow with the job as their responsibilities change over their lifetimes.*[24]

EXHIBIT

The Six Critical Managerial Skills

Teamwork Able to work effectively as team member and leader; strong on team contributions, leadership, conflict management, negotiation, consensus building.

Self-management Able to evaluate self, modify behavior, and meet obligations; strong on ethical reasoning, personal flexibility, tolerance for ambiguity, performance responsibility.

Leadership Able to influence and support others to perform complex and ambiguous tasks; strong on diversity awareness, project management, strategic action.

Critical thinking Able to gather and analyze information for problem solving; strong on information analysis and interpretation, creativity and innovation, judgment and decision making.

Professionalism Able to sustain a positive impression and instill confidence in others; strong on personal presence, initiative, and career management.

Communication Able to express self well in communication with others; strong on writing, oral presentation, giving and receiving feedback, technology utilization.

Does Rust's assessment sound daunting? Or, is it a challenge you are confident in meeting? Do you agree that this is an accurate description of today's career environment? If you do, and I believe you should, you'll also have to admit that learning, learning, and more learning is a top priority in our lives.

The Exhibit *Six Critical Managerial Skills* builds from earlier discussion to highlight areas for you to consider for continued professional advancement and career success. Why not use this as a preliminary checklist for assessing your managerial learning and career readiness? With it as a starting point, the rest of this book should be even more meaningful for your personal development.

Finally, one more question is worth asking: Given all the hard work and challenges that it involves, why would anyone want to be a manager? Beyond the often-higher salaries, there is one very compelling answer to this question: pride. As pointed out by management theorist Henry Mintzberg, being a manager is an important and socially responsible job:[25]

> *No job is more vital to our society than that of the manager. It is the manager who determines whether our social institutions serve us well or whether they squander our talents and resources. It is time to strip away the folklore about managerial work, and time to study it realistically so that we can begin the difficult task of making significant improvement in its performance.*

Lifelong learning is continuous learning from daily experiences.

Be Sure You Can . . .

- describe the intensity and pace of a typical workday for a manager

- give examples of each of the four management functions

- list the three managerial roles identified by Mintzberg

- explain how managers use agendas and networks in their work

- give examples of a manager's technical, human, and conceptual skills

- explain how these skills vary in importance across management levels

- explain the importance of experience as a source of managerial learning

Rapid Review

- The daily work of managers is often intense and stressful, involving long hours and continuous performance pressures.

- In the management process, planning sets the direction, organizing assembles the human and material resources, leading provides the enthusiasm and direction, and controlling ensures results.

- Managers perform interpersonal, informational, and decision-making roles while pursuing high-priority agendas and engaging in successful networking.

- Managers rely on a combination of technical skills (ability to use special expertise), human skills (ability to work well with others), and conceptual skills (ability to analyze and solve complex problems).

- Everyday experience is an important source of continuous lifelong learning for managers.

Define the Terms

Conceptual skill	Lifelong learning
Controlling	Management process
Emotional intelligence	Organizing
Human skill	Planning
Leading	Technical skill

Reflect/React

1. Is Mintzberg's view of the intense and demanding nature of managerial work realistic and, if so, why would you want to do it?

2. If Katz's model of how different levels of management use the essential managerial skills is accurate, what are its career implications for you?

3. Why is emotional intelligence an important component of one's human skills?

Multiple Choice

1. If a sales department supervisor is held accountable by a middle manager for the department's performance, who is the department supervisor dependent upon to make this performance possible?
   (a) Board of Directors **(b)** top management **(c)** customers or clients **(d)** department sales persons

2. The management function of _____ is being activated when a retail manager measures daily sales in the DVD section and compares them with daily sales targets.
   (a) planning **(b)** agenda setting **(c)** controlling **(d)** delegating

3. The research of Henry Mintzberg and others concludes that managers _____.
   (a) work at a leisurely pace **(b)** use a lot of private time for planning **(c)** are rarely free from the pressures of performance responsibility **(d)** benefit from short workweeks

4. The process of building and maintaining good working relationships with others who may someday help a manager implement his or her work agendas is called _____.
   (a) governance **(b)** networking **(c)** emotional intelligence **(d)** entrepreneurship

5. According to thinking by Robert Katz, _____ skills are more likely to be emphasized by top managers than by first-line managers.
   (a) human **(b)** conceptual **(c)** informational **(d)** technical

6. A dean in the university and a branch manager for a regional bank would be considered _____ managers.
   (a) first-line **(b)** top **(c)** middle **(d)** command-and-control

7. The book's definition for an effective manager is someone who helps others to achieve high levels of both _____ and _____.
   (a) pay/satisfaction **(b)** performance/satisfaction **(c)** performance/pay **(d)** pay/quality of work life

8. Which management function is most directly concerned with setting performance targets and standards?
   (a) planning **(b)** motivating **(c)** controlling **(d)** organizing

9. When managers use information gathered from other people to make decisions and solve problems, they are performing which of Mintzberg's roles?
   (a) networking **(b)** agenda setting **(c)** conceptual **(d)** decisional

10. All managers have access to at least one very important means for continuously developing their job and career skills. What is it?
    (a) Studying for a master's degree. **(b)** Learning from a great boss. **(c)** Learning from experience. **(d)** Participating in employer-sponsored training programs.

Short Response

11. If the direction in managerial work today is away from command and control, what is it toward?

12. How does planning differ from controlling in the management process?

13. What are the common characteristics of a *low* quality of work life environment?

14. In what ways will the job of a top manager typically differ from that of a first-line manager?

Integration & Application

15. Suppose you have been hired as the new supervisor of an audit team for a national accounting firm. With four years of auditing experience, you feel technically well prepared. However, it is your first formal appointment as a manager. The team has 12 members of diverse demographic and cultural backgrounds, and varying work experience. The workload is intense and there is lots of performance pressure.

Questions: In order to be considered *effective* as a manager, what goals will you set for yourself in the new job? What skills will be important to you, and why, as you seek success as the audit team supervisor?

SELF-ASSESSMENT
Learning Tendencies

INSTRUCTIONS *Distribute 10 points between the two statements in each pair to best describe how you like to learn. For example:*

3 (a) I like to read.
7 (b) I like to listen to lectures.

1. _____ (a) I like to learn through working with other people and being engaged in concrete experiences.
_____ (b) I like to learn through logical analysis and systematic attempts to understand a situation.

2. _____ (a) I like to learn by observing things, viewing them from different perspectives, and finding meaning in situations.
_____ (b) I like to learn by taking risks, getting things done, and influencing events through actions taken.

SCORING

Place "dots" on the following graph to record the above scores: "Doing"=2b. "Watching"=1b. "Feeling"=1a. "Thinking"=2a. Connect the dots to plot your learning tendencies.

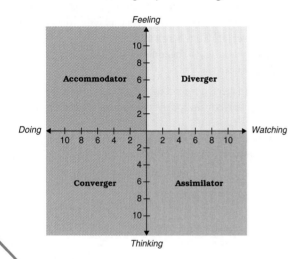

INTERPRETATION

This activity provides a first impression of your tendencies on four learning styles—convergers, accommodators, divergers, and assimilators. Consider the following descriptions for their accuracy in describing you. For more insights on your learning tendencies, ask several others to complete questions 1 and 2 for you. Then, compare how their results match your own perceptions.

Convergers—combined tendencies toward abstract conceptualization (thinking) and active experimentation (doing). They like to learn in practical situations, deal with technical issues, and solve problems systematically. They are good at experimentation, finding new ways of doing things, making decisions.

Accommodators—combine concrete experience (feeling) with active experimentation (doing). They like to learn from hands-on experience. They prefer "gut" responses to problems rather than systematic analysis. They are good at influencing others, committing to goals, seeking opportunities.

Divergers—combine concrete experience (feeling) with reflective observation (watching). They like to learn from observation. They enjoy brainstorming and imaginative information gathering. They are good at listening, imagining, and being sensitive to feelings.

Assimilators—combine abstract conceptualization (thinking) with reflective observation (watching). They like to learn through information. They prefer ideas and concepts, and value logical reasoning. They are good at organizing information, building models, and analyzing data.

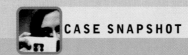

CASE SNAPSHOT

Go online to read this case!
Meg Whitman: Cautious, Conservative, Capitalist
A disciplined growth strategy has cultivated long-term success for eBay CEO Meg Whitman. The traditionally educated and trained leader has aimed for and achieved lasting success in the still-evolving e-commerce industry, unlike many offbeat or less astute contemporaries from the late 1990s, who faded away after erratic growth. She has managed the brand conservatively, not letting it get away from her. How has Whitman managed to maintain such a consistent strategy in the face of unpredictable market conditions?

MODULE 2 — Online Interactive Learning Resources

Self-Assessment
- Emotional Intelligence

Skill Builder
- Learning Style

Experiential Exercises
- My Best Manager
- What Managers Do

Team Project
- Managing Millenials

Good things grow from

Management Learning

There is no doubt that the world of work is changing today, and fast. We've already talked about some of the new practices and viewpoints that are starting to replace more traditional ones. And there's a lot more to come in this book. But we have to be careful in the rush toward an exciting future. Let's not sell history short. In management, as in life, there is a lot to be gained from insights that come to us from the past.[1]

strong foundations

A good example is Mary Parker Follett, considered a "prophet" of management.[2] Although writing in the 1920s, her ideas still offer the wisdom of history. She advocated social responsibility, respect for workers, and better cooperation throughout organizations; she warned against the dangers of too much hierarchy and called for visionary leadership.

Doesn't this sound familiar? Many of these themes are still central to management theory, even though we describe them by terms like "empowerment," "involvement," "flexibility," "self-management," and "transformational leadership."

And what about executive success today?[3] I wonder what Follett would say?

→ Thoughts on the Twenty-First-Century Executive

- **Inspiring leader**—attracts talented people, motivates them with a setting where everyone can do their best work
- **Ethical role model**—acts ethically, sets high ethical standards, infuses ethics throughout the organization
- **Global strategist**—understands linkages among nations of the world, their economies, cultures, and peoples
- **Master of technology**—comfortable with technology, uses it well, always informed about trends and developments
- **Active doer**—makes things happen, focuses on right things and making sure that they really get done

→ MODULE GUIDE

3.1 What can we learn from classical management thinking?

- Taylor's scientific management sought efficiency in job performance.
- Weber's bureaucratic organization is supposed to be efficient and fair.
- Administrative principles describe managerial duties and practices.

3.2 What is unique about the behavioral management approaches?

- The Hawthorne studies focused attention on the human side of organizations.

- Maslow described a hierarchy of human needs with self-actualization at the top.
- McGregor believed managerial assumptions create self-fulfilling prophecies.
- Argyris suggests that workers treated as adults will be more productive.

3.3 What are the foundations of the modern management approaches?

- Organizations operate as complex networks of cooperating subsystems.
- Contingency thinking recognizes there is no one best way to manage.
- Learning organizations continually adapt to new circumstances.

Historians trace management as far back as 5000 B.C., when ancient Sumerians used written records to assist in governmental and commercial activities.[4] Management contributed to the construction of the Egyptian pyramids, the rise of the Roman Empire, and the commercial success of fourteenth-century Venice. During the Industrial Revolution in the 1700s, great social changes helped to prompt a leap forward in the manufacture of basic staples and consumer goods. Adam Smith's ideas of efficient production through specialized tasks and the division of labor further accelerated industrial development.

By the turn of the twentieth century, Henry Ford and others were making mass production a mainstay of the emerging economy.[5] What we now call the classical school was launching a path of rapid and continuing development in the science and practices of management.[6]

Classical approaches
Assumption: People are rational

Scientific management	Bureaucratic organization	Administrative principles
Frederick Taylor	Max Weber	Henry Fayol Mary Parker Follett

Major branches in the classical approach to management.

Scientific management emphasizes careful selection and training of workers and supervisory support.

• Taylor's Scientific Management Sought Efficiency in Job Performance

In 1911 Frederick W. Taylor stated the following in his book *The Principles of Scientific Management*: "The principal object of management should be to secure maximum prosperity for the employer, coupled with the maximum prosperity for the employee."[7] Taylor had noticed that many workers did their jobs in their own way—perhaps haphazard, and without consistent supervision. And it seemed to him that a lack of clear and uniform methods caused workers to lose efficiency and perform below their true capacities. As a result, their organizations also underperformed.

To correct this problem, Taylor believed that jobs should be studied to identify their basic steps and motions, and determine the most efficient ways of doing them. Once this job "science" was defined, workers could be trained to follow it, and supervisors could be trained to best support and encourage workers to perform to the best of their abilities. This approach became known as **scientific management**.

Are you clear about the principles of scientific management? Think about what happens when a top coach trains a group of soccer players. If the coach teaches players the techniques of their positions and how the positions fit into the overall team strategy, the team will probably do better in its games, right? In the same way, Taylor hoped to improve the productivity of workers and organizations. With a stopwatch and notebook in hand, he analyzed tasks and motions to describe the most efficient ways to perform them.[8] He then linked these requirements with job training, monetary incentives for performance success, and better direction and assistance from supervisors.

If you really look, you will find that Taylor's ideas are still influential (see Management Tips). For example, calibrated productivity standards

→ Taylor's Four Principles of Scientific Management

1. Develop a "science" for each job—rules of motion, standard work tools, proper work conditions.
2. Hire workers with the right abilities for the job.
3. Train and motivate workers to do their jobs according to the science.
4. Support workers by planning and assisting their work by the job science.

carefully guide workers at the United Parcel Service (UPS). After analyzing delivery stops on regular van routes, supervisors generally know within a few minutes how long a driver's pickups and deliveries will take. Industrial engineers devise precise routines for drivers, who save time by knocking on customers' doors rather than looking for the doorbell. Handheld computers further enhance delivery efficiencies. At UPS, savings of seconds on individual stops add up to significant increases in productivity. Wouldn't Taylor be pleased?

• Weber's Bureaucratic Organization Is Supposed to Be Efficient and Fair

Max Weber was a late-nineteenth-century German intellectual whose insights have made a significant impact on the field of management and the sociology of organizations. Like Taylor, his ideas developed somewhat in reaction to what he considered to be poor performance by the organizations of his day. He was especially concerned that people were in positions of authority not because of their job-related capabilities, but because of their social standing or "privileged" status in German society. Haven't you seen the same problem today—people who rise to positions of major responsibility not because of their competencies but because of whom they know or what families they belong to?

At the heart of Weber's proposal for correcting such problems was a specific form of organization he called a **bureaucracy**.[9] When staffed and structured along the lines listed in the Exhibit *Characteristics of an Ideal Bureaucracy*, he believed organizations could be both highly efficient and very fair in treating their members and clients. In Weber's own words, the bureaucratic organization is described as:

> . . . *capable of attaining the highest degree of efficiency. . . . It is superior to any other form in precision, in stability, in the stringency of its discipline, and in its reliability. It thus makes possible a particularly high degree of calculability of results for the heads of the organization and for those acting in relation to it. It is finally superior both in intensive efficiency and in the scope of its operations and is formally capable of application to all kinds of administrative tasks.*[10]

A bureaucracy works well, in theory at least, because of its reliance on logic, order, and legitimate authority, as well as promotions based on competency and demonstrated performance. But if it is so good, why do we so often hear the terms "bureaucracy" and "bureaucrat" used negatively? That's because bureaucracies don't always live up to Weber's expectations.

Think of the last time you were a client of a traditional bureaucracy, perhaps a government agency or the registrar at your school. Would you agree that they are sometimes slow in handling problems, making changes, and adapting to new customer or client needs? As a customer have you sometimes encountered employees who seem impersonal, resistant to change, even apathetic?

These and other disadvantages are among the reasons why the bureaucratic model isn't always the best choice for organizations; it works well sometimes, but not all of the time. In fact, a major challenge for research on organizational design is to identify when and under what conditions bureaucratic features work well, and what the best alternatives are when they don't. Later in the module we'll call this type of problem solving "contingency thinking."

A **bureaucracy** is a rational and efficient form of organization founded on logic, order, and legitimate authority.

EXHIBIT

Characteristics of an Ideal Bureaucracy

Clear division of labor Jobs are well defined, and workers become highly skilled at performing them.

Clear hierarchy of authority Authority and responsibility are well defined, and each position reports to a higher-level one.

Formal rules and procedures Written guidelines describe expected behavior and decisions in jobs; written files are kept for historical record.

Impersonality Rules and procedures are impartially and uniformly applied; no one gets preferential treatment.

Careers based on merit Workers are selected and promoted on ability and performance; managers are career employees of the organization.

1. **Foresight**—complete a plan of action for the future.
2. **Organization**—provide and mobilize resources to implement plan.
3. **Command**—lead, select, and evaluate workers.
4. **Coordination**—fit diverse efforts together, ensure information is shared and problems solved.
5. **Control**—make sure things happen according to plan, take necessary corrective action.

• Administrative Principles Describe Managerial Duties and Practices

Another branch in the classical approaches to management includes attempts to document and understand the experiences of successful managers, as well as to analyze organizations in their social context. Two prominent writers in this realm are Henri Fayol and Mary Parker Follett.

In 1916, after a career in French industry, Henri Fayol published *Administration Industrielle et Générale*.[11] The book outlines his views on the proper management of organizations and the people within them. It identifies five "rules" or "duties" of management in respect to foresight, organization, command, coordination, and control. Looking at Fayol's duties, do you see how they closely resemble the four functions of management that we talk about today—planning, organizing, leading, and controlling?

We've already talked about Mary Parker Follett in the module opener. Working just a bit later than Fayol, she made significant contributions to the development of management thinking. In fact, she was eulogized as "one of the most important women America has yet produced in the fields of civics and sociology."[12] Follett's work is a reminder that good things really do grow from strong foundations.

In Follett's view, groups were important aspects of organizations; they provided the means that allowed individuals to combine their talents for a greater good. She described organizations as "communities" in which managers and workers should labor in harmony, without one party dominating the other and with the freedom to talk over and truly reconcile conflicts and differences. And she believed that managers should help people in organizations cooperate with one another and achieve an integration of interests.

Even though Follett's ideas were expressed more than 80 years ago, many would consider them very far sighted indeed.[13] She suggested that making every employee an owner in the business would create feelings of collective responsibility. Today, we address the same issues as "employee ownership," "profit sharing," and "gain-sharing plans." Follett believed that business problems involve a wide variety of factors that must be considered in relationship to one another. Today, we talk about "systems" when describing the same phenomenon. Follett viewed businesses as services, organizations that should always consider making profits vis-à-vis the public good. Today, we pursue the same issues as "managerial ethics" and "corporate social responsibility."

> *If an organization becomes too hierarchical, ideas that bubble up from younger people aren't going to be heard.*
>
> **Nandan M. Nilekani, CEO, INFOSYS**

3.1 What can we learn from classical management thinking?

Be Sure You Can . . .

- list the principles of Taylor's scientific management

- list key characteristics of bureaucracy

- explain why Weber considered bureaucracy an ideal form of organization

- list possible disadvantages of bureaucracy

- describe how Fayol's "duties" overlap with the four functions of management

- explain why Follett's ideas were quite modern in concept

Define the Terms

Bureaucracy

Scientific management

Rapid Review

- Taylor's principles of scientific management focused on the need to carefully select, train, support, and reward workers in their jobs.

- Weber considered bureaucracy, with its clear hierarchy, formal rules, well-defined jobs, and competency-based staffing, as a form of organization that is efficient and fair.

- Fayol suggested that managers learn and fulfill duties we now call the management functions of planning, organizing, leading, and controlling.

- Follett's ideas on groups, human cooperation, and organizations that served social purposes foreshadowed current management themes.

Reflect/React

1. How did Taylor and Weber differ in the approaches they took to improving the performance of organizations?

2. Should Weber's concept of the bureaucratic organization be scrapped, or does it still have potential value today?

3. What are the risks of accepting the "lessons of experience" offered by successful executives such as Fayol?

During the 1920s, Follett's emphasis on the human side of the workplace influenced the emergence of behavioral management approaches. They include the famous Hawthorne studies and Maslow's theory of human needs, as well as theories generated from the work of Douglas McGregor and Chris Argyris. The underlying assumption is that people are social and self-actualizing, and that workers seek satisfying social relationships, respond to group pressures, and search for personal fulfillment. Does that sound like you?

Hawthorne studies	Human resource approaches	Theory X and Theory Y
Elton Mayo	*Assumption:* People are social and self-actualizing	Douglas McGregor
Theory of human needs		Personality and organization
Abraham Maslow		Chris Argyris

Foundations in the behavioral or human resource approaches to management.

• The Hawthorne Studies Focused Attention on the Human Side of Organizations

In 1924, the Western Electric Company commissioned a study of individual productivity at the Hawthorne Works of the firm's Chicago plant.[14] The initial "Hawthorne studies," with a research team headed by Elton Mayo of Harvard University, sought to determine how economic incentives and the physical conditions of the workplace affected the output of workers. But their results were perplexing. After failing to find that better lighting in the manufacturing facilities would improve productivity, they concluded that unforeseen "psychological factors" somehow interfered with their study. Yet, similar results occurred when they conducted further tests.

After isolating six relay-assembly workers in a special room, Mayo and his team measured the effect on outputs of various rest pauses, and lengths of workdays and workweeks. They found no direct relationship between changes in physical working conditions and performance; productivity increased regardless of the changes made. The researchers concluded that these results were caused by the new "social setting" in the test room. The six workers in the test room shared pleasant social relations with one another and received more attention from the researchers than they got from supervisors in their usual jobs. As a result, they tried to do what they thought the researchers wanted them to do—a good job.

This tendency to try to live up to expectations became known as the **Hawthorne effect**. And, one of its major implications is the possibility that people's performance will be affected by the way they are treated by their managers. Have you noticed in your experience that people given special attention will tend to perform as expected? Could the Hawthorne effect explain why some students, perhaps you, do better in smaller classes or for instructors who pay more attention to them in class?

The Hawthorne Studies continued until the economic conditions of the Depression forced their termination in 1932. By then, interest in the human factor had broadened to include employee attitudes, interpersonal relations, and group relations. For example, over 21,000 employees were interviewed to learn what they liked and disliked about their work environment. "Complex" and "baffling" results led the researchers to conclude that the same things that satisfied some workers—such as work conditions or wages, led to dissatisfaction for others. And in a final study in the bank wiring room at Western Electric, a "surprise" finding was that people would restrict their output in order to avoid the displeasure of the group, even if it meant sacrificing increased pay. Mayo and his team had recognized first-hand what most of us realize already; that groups can have strong negative, as well as positive, influences on the behaviors of their members.

The **Hawthorne effect** is the tendency of persons singled out for special attention to perform as expected.

 Hawthorne Effect:

People given special attention are likely to perform as expected.

Scholars have criticized the Hawthorne studies for poor research design, weak empirical support for the conclusions drawn, and overgeneralized findings.[15] And there is no doubt that management research has moved on from this point of departure with greater care in the use of scientific methods. Yet, the Hawthorne studies were significant turning points in the evolution of management thought. They helped shift the attention of managers and management researchers away from just the technical and structural concerns of the classical approaches, and toward social and human concerns as important potential keys to workplace productivity.

• Maslow Described a Hierarchy of Human Needs with Self-Actualization at the Top

The work of psychologist Abraham Maslow in the area of human needs emerged as a key component of the new direction in management thinking.[16] He began with the notion of the human **need**, a physiological or psychological deficiency that a person feels compelled to satisfy. Why, you might ask, is this a significant concept for managers? The answer is because needs create tensions that can influence a person's work attitudes and behaviors.

What needs, for example, are important to you? How do they influence your behavior, the way you study and the way you work? Maslow described the five levels of human needs shown in Figure 3.1. From lowest to highest in order, they are physiological, safety, social, esteem, and self-actualization needs.

According to Maslow, people try to satisfy the five needs in sequence, moving step by step from lowest up to the highest. He calls this the *progression principle*—a need at any level becomes activated only after the next-lower-level need is satisfied. Once a need is

A **need** is a physiological or psychological deficiency that a person wants to satisfy.

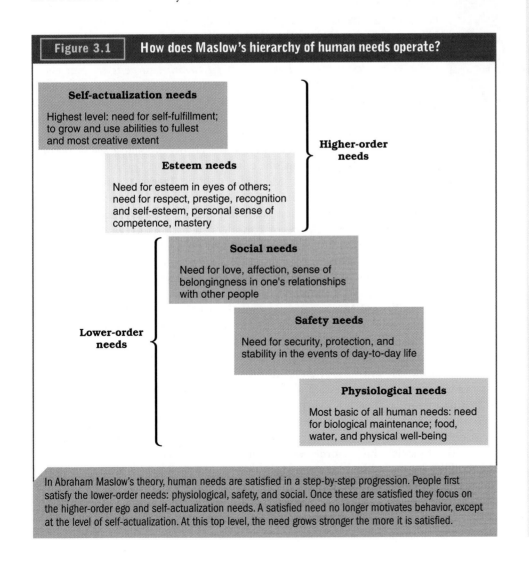

| Figure 3.1 | How does Maslow's hierarchy of human needs operate? |

Self-actualization needs

Highest level: need for self-fulfillment; to grow and use abilities to fullest and most creative extent

Esteem needs

Need for esteem in eyes of others; need for respect, prestige, recognition and self-esteem, personal sense of competence, mastery

Higher-order needs

Social needs

Need for love, affection, sense of belongingness in one's relationships with other people

Safety needs

Need for security, protection, and stability in the events of day-to-day life

Lower-order needs

Physiological needs

Most basic of all human needs: need for biological maintenance; food, water, and physical well-being

In Abraham Maslow's theory, human needs are satisfied in a step-by-step progression. People first satisfy the lower-order needs: physiological, safety, and social. Once these are satisfied they focus on the higher-order ego and self-actualization needs. A satisfied need no longer motivates behavior, except at the level of self-actualization. At this top level, the need grows stronger the more it is satisfied.

activated, it dominates attention and determines behavior until it is satisfied. Maslow calls this the *deficit principle*—people act to satisfy needs for which a satisfaction deficit exists; a satisfied need doesn't motivate behavior. Only at the highest level of self-actualization do the deficit and progression principles cease to operate. The more this need is satisfied, the stronger it grows.

Maslow's theory can help us to better understand people's needs and help find ways to satisfy them through their work. Of course this is easier said than done. If it were easy we wouldn't have so many cases of workers going on strike against their employers, complaining about their jobs, or quitting to find better ones. Consider also the case of volunteers working for the local Red Cross, community hospital, or youth soccer league. Our society needs volunteers; most nonprofit organizations depend on them. But what needs do they pursue? How can one keep volunteers involved and committed in the absence of pay?

• McGregor Believed Managerial Assumptions Create Self-Fulfilling Prophecies

Maslow's work along with the Hawthorne studies surely influenced another prominent management theorist, Douglas McGregor. His classic book, *The Human Side of Enterprise*, suggests that managers should pay more attention to the social and self-actualizing needs of people at work.[17] He framed his argument as a contrast between two opposing views of human nature: a set of negative assumptions he called "Theory X" and a set of positive ones he called "Theory Y."

Managers holding **Theory X** assumptions expect people to generally dislike work, lack ambition, act irresponsibly, resist change, and prefer to follow rather than to lead. McGregor considers such thinking wrong, believing that **Theory Y** assumptions are more appropriate and consistent with human potential. Managers holding Theory Y assumptions expect people to be willing to work, capable of self-control and self-direction, responsible, and creative.

Can you spot differences in how you behave or react when treated in a Theory X way or a Theory Y way? McGregor strongly believed that these assumptions create **self-fulfilling prophecies**. That is, as with the Hawthorne effect, people end up behaving consistent with the assumptions. Managers holding Theory X assumptions are likely to act in directive "command-and-control" ways, often giving people little say over their work. This in turn often creates passive, dependent, and reluctant subordinates who do only what they are told to do. Have you ever encountered a manager or instructor with a Theory X viewpoint?

Managers with Theory Y assumptions behave quite differently. They are more "participative," likely giving others more control over their work. This creates opportunities to satisfy higher-order esteem and self-actualization needs. In response, the workers are more likely to act with initiative, responsibility, and high performance. The self-fulfilling prophecy occurs again, but this time it is a positive one. You should find Theory Y thinking reflected in a lot of the ideas and developments discussed in this book, such as valuing diversity, employee involvement, job enrichment, empowerment, and self-managing teams.[18]

Theory X assumes people dislike work, lack ambition, are irresponsible, and prefer to be led.

Theory Y assumes people are willing to work, accept responsibility, are self-directed, and are creative.

A **self-fulfilling prophecy** occurs when a person acts in ways that confirm another's expectations.

• Argyris Suggests that Workers Treated as Adults Will Be More Productive

Ideas set forth by the well-regarded scholar and consultant Chris Argyris also reflect the belief in human nature advanced by Maslow and McGregor. In his book *Personality and Organization*, Argyris contrasts the management practices found in traditional and hierarchical organizations with the needs and capabilities of mature adults.[19]

Argyris clearly believes that when problems such as employee absenteeism, turnover, apathy, alienation, and low morale plague organizations, they may be caused by a mismatch between management practices and the adult nature of their workforces. His basic point is that no one wants to be treated like a child, but that's just the way many organizations treat their workers. The result, he suggests, is a group of stifled and unhappy workers who underperform.

Does Argyris seem to have a good point? For example, scientific management assumes that people will work more efficiently on better-defined tasks. Argyris would likely disagree, believing that limits opportunities for self-actualization in one's work. In a Weberian bureaucracy, typical of many of our government agencies, people work in a clear hierarchy of authority, with higher levels directing and controlling the work of lower levels.[20] This is supposed to be an efficient way of doing things. Argyris would worry that workers lose initiative and end up being less productive. Also, Fayol's administrative principles assume that efficiency will increase when supervisors plan and direct a person's work. Argyris might suggest that this sets up conditions for psychological failure; psychological success is more likely when people define their own goals.

> *"Attracting and holding talent have become two of the central tasks of management."*
>
> **Peter Drucker,** LATE MANAGEMENT AUTHOR AND CONSULTANT

STUDY GUIDE

3.2 What is unique about the behavioral management approaches?

Be Sure You Can . . .

- summarize findings of the Hawthorne studies

- explain and illustrate the "Hawthorne effect"

- explain Maslow's deficit and progression principles

- distinguish between McGregor's Theory X and Theory Y assumptions

- explain the self-fulfilling prophecies created by Theory X and Theory Y

- explain Argyris's concern that traditional organizational practices are inconsistent with mature adult personalities.

Rapid Review

- The Hawthorne studies suggested that social and psychological forces influence work behavior, and that good human relations may gain improved work performance.

- Maslow's hierarchy of human needs suggested the importance of self-actualization and the potential for people to satisfy important needs through their work.

- McGregor criticized negative Theory X assumptions about human nature and advocated positive Theory Y assumptions that view people as independent, responsible, and capable of self-direction in their work.

- Argyris pointed out that people in the workplace are mature adults who may react negatively when management practices treat them as if they were immature.

Reflect/React

1. How did insights from the Hawthorne studies bridge the gap between the classical and modern management approaches?

2. If Maslow's hierarchy of needs theory is correct, how can a manager use it to become more effective?

3. Where and how do McGregor's notions of Theory X and Theory Y overlap with Argyris's ideas regarding adult personalities?

Define the Terms

Hawthorne effect   Theory X

Need   Theory Y

Self-fulfilling prophecies

The next step in the timeline of management history sets the stage for a stream of new developments that are continuing to this day. Loosely called the modern management approaches, they share the assumption that people and organizations are complex, growing and changing over time in response to new problems and opportunities in their environments. Three building blocks of modern management are recognition of the inherent complexity of organizations as systems, rejection of the search for universal management principles, and respect for the capacity of people and organizations to grow, adapt, and learn over time.

• Organizations Operate as Complex Networks of Cooperating Subsystems

Think back to our earlier discussions of organizations as open systems, continuously interacting with their environments as they transform inputs into outputs. Formally defined, a **system** consists of interrelated parts that function together to achieve a common purpose. In other words, it is a complex network of **subsystems** or smaller components whose activities individually and collectively support the work of the larger system.[21]

Figure 3.2 shows the importance of cooperation among organizational subsystems.[22] In the figure, for example, the operations and service management systems serve as a central point. They provide the integration among other subsystems, such as purchasing, accounting, sales, and information, that are essential to the work, and the success, of the organization. But, the reality is that the cooperation is often imperfect and could be improved upon. Just how to achieve this, of course, is a major management challenge.

A **system** is a collection of interrelated parts working together for a purpose.

A **subsystem** is a smaller component of a larger system.

Contingency thinking tries to match management practices with situational demands.

• Contingency Thinking Believes There Is No One Best Way to Manage

Rather than try to find the one best way to manage in all circumstances, modern management adopts **contingency thinking**. That is, it recognizes organizational complexities and attempts to identify practices that best fit with the unique demands of different situations.

Consider again the concept of bureaucracy. Weber offered it as an ideal form of organization. But from a contingency perspective, the strict bureaucratic form is only one possible way of organizing things. What turns out to be the best structure in any given situation will depend on many factors, including environmental uncertainty, available technology, staff competencies, and more. Contingency thinking recognizes that the structure that works well for one organization may not work well for another in different circumstances. Also, what works well at one point in time may not work as well in the future if things have changed.[23]

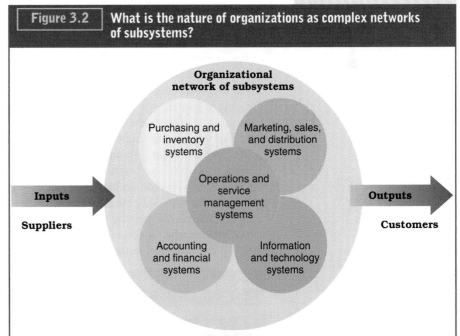

| Figure 3.2 | What is the nature of organizations as complex networks of subsystems? |

Externally, organizations interact with suppliers and customers in their environments. Internally, many different subsystems must interact and work well together so that high quality inputs are transformed into products satisfying customers' needs. Common subsystems of a business include purchasing, information technology, operations management, marketing and sales, distribution, human resources, and accounting and finance.

PACESETTERS

Google's Founders Accept Nothing Less Than Excellence.

"Googol" is a mathematical term that describes the number 1 followed by 100 zeros. That's a really big number. It also symbolizes the reach of the popular Web search engine Google. Google's origins trace to 1995, when Larry Page and Sergey Brin met as students at Stanford University. Their conversations led to collaboration on a search engine they called BackRub. It became so popular on campus that they kept refining and expanding the service in Larry's dormitory room. They hatched Google, Inc. in 1998 with the goal "to organize the information overload of the Internet in a transparent and superior way." It hasn't stopped running, or growing, since. How does Google differ from other search engines? How did it gain such runaway popularity? The answer is performance excellence based on speed, accuracy, and ease of use. The founders wanted to create a "perfect search engine" that "understands exactly what you mean and gives you back exactly what you want," says Page. And in the continuing search for innovation, the firm sticks to its historical roots—an informal culture with a small-company feel. At Google, creative and satisfied employees, diverse in backgrounds, skills, and interests, come together to build this ever-changing and ever-better company. The company website describes its approach to talent this way: "Google's hiring policy is aggressively non-discriminatory, and favors ability over experience."

Larry Page and Sergey Brin, *Founders, Google, Inc.*

A **learning organization** continuously changes and improves, using the lessons of experience.

You should find a lot of contingency thinking in this book. Its implications extend to all of the management functions—from planning and controlling for diverse environmental conditions, to organizing for diverse workforces and multiple tasks, to leading in different performance situations. And this is a good reflection of everyday realities. Don't you use a lot of contingency thinking when solving problems and otherwise going about your personal affairs?

• Learning Organizations Continually Adapt to New Circumstances

Speaking of life, one message most of us have heard from the time we were children is the importance of "learning from our mistakes." The same philosophy applies equally well in our adulthood, and to our organizations. Only this time the focus in both cases is on learning from experience. This notion was first introduced in the previous module where we talked about lifelong learning. Modern management essentially recognizes the emergence of a similar commitment at the level of the organization as a whole.

We now talk about **learning organizations**, ones that strive to continually learn from and adapt to new circumstances.[24] In his book *The Fifth Discipline*, consultant Peter Senge describes learning organizations as work settings that are exceptionally good at encouraging and helping all of their members to learn continuously. They emphasize information sharing, teamwork, empowerment, and participation as keys to learning. And importantly, the leaders of learning organizations set an example for others by embracing change and communicating enthusiasm for solving problems and growing with new opportunities.

This notion of the learning organization is an ideal concept. But, at the very least, you should be able to find examples that fit parts of the description. And you should notice that some organizations really are better than others at learning from experience.

It's no secret, for example, that many newspapers and news organizations get criticized for lack of accuracy in their reporting. The *New York Times* is no exception.[25] After one of its reporters was caught falsifying news stories, he was fired and the newspaper apologized; the same happened after its reporting on weapons of mass destruction in Iraq was found to be in error. Many organizations would stop there; situation handled, problem resolved. But the *Times* went further and you can see in its responses evidence of a learning organization. Top management not only admitted mistakes; it probed and studied to learn from them. Then it made staff and organizational changes designed to strengthen the organization in the future. A new position of Public Editor was even created and given the freedom to publish columns critical of the newspaper itself, when it is in the wrong.

While maybe not perfect, the *Times* does seem to be an organization moving in the right direction when it comes to learning. Just as management thought has developed historically, organizational learning is a never-ending process of continuous improvement.

➔ Peter Senge's Core Ingredients of Learning Organizations

1. **Mental models**—everyone sets aside old ways of thinking.
2. **Personal mastery**—everyone becomes self-aware and open to others.
3. **Systems thinking**—everyone learns how the whole organization works.
4. **Shared vision**—everyone understands and agrees to a plan of action.
5. **Team learning**—everyone works together to accomplish the plan.

3.3 What are the foundations of the modern management approaches?

Be Sure You Can . . .

- use the terms system and subsystem to describe how an organization operates

- explain how contingency thinking might influence a manager's decision to use or not use a bureaucratic structure

- list the characteristics of a learning organization

Define the Terms

Contingency thinking	System
Learning organization	Subsystem

Rapid Review

- The systems view depicts organizations as complex networks of subsystems that must interact and cooperate with one another if the organization as a whole is to accomplish its goals.

- Contingency thinking avoids "one best way" arguments, recognizing instead that managers need to understand situational differences and respond appropriately to them.

- In learning organizations the leadership and internal environment encourage continuous learning from experience to improve work methods and processes.

Reflect/React

1. Can you use the concepts of system and subsystem to describe the operations of an organization in your community?

2. In addition to the choice of organization structures, in what other areas of management decision making do you think contingency thinking plays a role?

3. Is a learning organization something that comes about because of the actions of managers, workers, or both?

Multiple Choice

1. A management consultant who advises managers to study jobs, carefully train workers to do those jobs with the most efficient motions, and offer financial incentives tied to job performance would most likely be using ideas from _____.
   (a) scientific management (b) contingency thinking (c) Henri Fayol (d) Theory Y

2. The Hawthorne studies were important in management history because they raised awareness about the importance of _____ as possible influences on productivity.
   (a) organization structures (b) human factors (c) physical work conditions (d) pay and rewards

3. If Douglas McGregor heard an instructor complaining that her students were lazy, didn't want to come to class, lacked creativity, and were irresponsible, he would worry that she might _____.
   (a) fail to use scientific management (b) spend too much time worrying about their need satisfactions (c) create a negative self-fulfilling prophecy (d) miss the chance to create a bureaucratic class organization

4. If your local bank or credit union is a complex system, then the loan-processing department of the bank would be considered a _____.
   (a) subsystem (b) closed system (c) learning organization (d) bureaucracy

5. When a manager puts Kwabena in a customer relations job because he has strong social needs and gives Sherrill lots of daily praise because she has strong ego needs, the manager is displaying _____ in his management approach.
   (a) systems thinking (b) Theory X (c) contingency thinking (d) administrative principles

6. In the learning organization, described by Peter Senge you would expect to find _____.

   (a) emphasis on following rules and procedures (b) promotions based on seniority (c) willingness to set aside old thinking and embrace new ways (d) a strict hierarchy of authority

7. When the registrar of a university deals with students by an identification number rather than a name, which characteristic of bureaucracy is being displayed and what is its intended benefit?
   (a) division of labor/competency (b) merit-based careers/productivity (c) rules and procedures/efficiency (d) impersonality/fairness

8. One of the conclusions from the Hawthorne studies was that _____.
   (a) motion studies could improve performance (b) groups can sometimes restrict productivity of their members (c) people respond well to monetary incentives (d) supervisors should avoid close relations with their subordinates

9. If an organization was performing poorly and Henri Fayol was called in as a consultant, what would he most likely advise as a way to improve things?
   (a) teach managers to better plan, organize, lead, and control (b) teach workers more efficient job methods (c) promote to management only the most competent workers (d) find ways to increase corporate social responsibility

10. When a worker has a family, makes car payments, has a mortgage, and is active in supporting community organizations, how might Argyris explain her poor performance at work?
    (a) management practices don't treat her as an adult (b) managers use too many Theory Y assumptions (c) there are inefficient subsystems in the organization (d) she doesn't work in a learning organzation

Short Response

11. Give an example of how principles of scientific management can apply in organizations today.

12. How do the defecit and progression principles operate in Maslow's hierarchy?

13. Compare the Hawthorne effect with McGregor's notion of self-fulfilling prophecies.

14. Explain by example several ways a manager might use contingency thinking in the management process.

Integration & Application

15. Enrique Temoltzin is the new manager of your local college bookstore. He wants to do a good job for the owner and therefore decides to operate the store according to Weber's concept of bureaucracy.

    Questions: Is the bureaucracy a good management approach for Enrique to follow? What are the potential advantages and disadvantages? How could Enrique use contingency thinking in this situation?

SELF-ASSESSMENT
Managerial Assumptions

INSTRUCTIONS *Use the space in the left margin to write "Yes" if you agree with the statement, or "No" if you disagree with it. Force yourself to take a "yes" or "no" position for every statement.*

1 Are good pay and a secure job enough to satisfy most workers?
2 Should a manager help and coach subordinates in their work?
3 Do most people like real responsibility in their jobs?
4 Are most people afraid to learn new things in their jobs?
5 Should managers let subordinates control the quality of their work?
6 Do most people dislike work?
7 Are most people creative?
8 Should a manager closely supervise and direct the work of subordinates?
9 Do most people tend to resist change?
10 Do most people work only as hard as they have to?
11 Should workers be allowed to set their own job goals?
12 Are most people happiest off the job?
13 Do most workers really care about the organization they work for?
14 Should a manager help subordinates advance and grow in their jobs?

SCORING

Count the number of "yes" responses to items 1, 4, 6, 8, 9, 10, 12; write that number here as [**X**=_____].
Count the number of "yes" responses to items 2, 3, 5, 7, 11, 13, 14; write that score here as [**Y**=_____].

INTERPRETATION

This assessment examines your orientation toward Douglas McGregor's Theory X (your "X" score) and Theory Y (your "Y" score) assumptions. Consider how your X/Y assumptions might influence how you behave toward other people at work. What self-fulfilling prophecies are you likely to create?

PATHWAYS to WileyPLUS

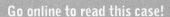

CASE SNAPSHOT

Go online to read this case!
Apple Computers: Ripe for the Picking

The Apple brand has come back strong. Once an almost-was in the computer market, its one-two punch of technological innovation and sleek design have earned accolades from techwatchers and trendspotters alike. Its refusal to discuss future technologies before public release fuels wild speculation about successive tech offerings, and maintains a level of mystique consistently paid off by innovative design. But for a company historically known for its hardware, does its real future lie in the innovation of its software?

MODULE 3 | Online Interactive Learning Resources

Skill Builder
- Self Awareness

Experiential Exercises
- What Would the Classics Say?
- The Great Management History Debate

Team Project
- Management in Popular Culture

Character doesn't stay at

Ethics and Ethical Behavior

Does learning about bad business behavior shock and dismay you? Consider this headline: "Former Worldcom CEO sentenced to 25 years in prison." A jury had convicted Bernie Ebbers for what CNN called "the biggest accounting fraud in corporate history."[1] The crimes included incorrectly reporting $11 billion of revenues and expenses. Here's another headline: "Two Tyco Executives Found Guilty of Stealing $150M." This story reported on the conviction of former Tyco CEO Dennis Kozlowski for 22 counts of grand larceny, fraud, conspiracy, and falsifying business records.[2]

home when we go to work

Scandals like these occur too often. And rather than incompetence, many are caused by personal failures such as greed.[3] It's understandable that some people, perhaps a lot of them, are left feeling cynical, pessimistic, and even helpless regarding the state of organizational leadership in our society.[4] What about you?

So, what can be done? For starters, would you say that it is time to get serious about the moral aspects and social implications of behavior in and by organizations? Can we agree here that, in your career and for any manager, the goal should always be to achieve performance objectives through ethical and socially responsible actions?

As you think about these questions, keep in mind this advice from Desmond Tutu, archbishop of Capetown, South Africa, and winner of the Nobel Peace Prize:

You are powerful people. You can make this world a better place where business decisions and methods take account of right and wrong as well as profitability. . . . You must take a stand on important issues: the environment and ecology, affirmative action, sexual harassment, racism and sexism, the arms race, poverty, the obligations of the affluent West to its less-well-off sisters and brothers elsewhere.[5]

→ MODULE GUIDE

 4.1 What is ethical behavior?

- Ethical behavior is values driven.
- What is considered ethical varies among moral reasoning approaches.
- What is considered ethical can vary across cultures.
- Ethical dilemmas arise as tests of personal ethics and values.
- People have tendencies to rationalize unethical behaviors.

 4.2 How can organizations maintain high standards of ethical conduct?

- Personal and contextual factors influence ethical conduct.
- Training in ethical decision making may improve ethical conduct.
- Protection of whistleblowers may encourage ethical conduct.
- Managers as positive role models may inspire ethical conduct.
- Formal codes of ethics set standards for ethical conduct.

It is tempting to say that any behavior that is legal can also be considered ethical. But, this is too easy; the "letter of the law" does not always translate into what others would consider as ethical actions.[6] For example, U.S. laws once allowed slavery, permitted only men to vote, and allowed young children to work full-time jobs. Today we consider such actions unethical.

Ethics is defined as the code of moral principles that sets standards of good or bad, or right or wrong, in our conduct.[7] Thus, personal ethics are guides for behavior, helping people make moral choices among alternative courses of action. Most typically, we use the term **ethical behavior** to describe what we accept as "good" and "right" as opposed to "bad" or "wrong."

Ethics sets standards of good or bad, or right or wrong, in our conduct.

Ethical behavior is "right" or "good" in the context of a governing moral code.

STAY INFORMED

The Wall Street Journal reports:

- 36% of workers calling in sick are lying.
- 35% keep quiet about co-worker misconduct.
- 12% of job resumes contain falsehoods.
- Managers are more likely than other workers to report wrongdoing.
- Managers with 0–3 years experience feel most pressure to violate personal ethics.

• Ethical Behavior Is Values Driven

It's one thing to look back and make ethical judgments; it is a bit harder to make them in real time. Is it truly ethical for an employee to take longer than necessary to do a job?; to make personal telephone calls on company time?; to call in sick and go on holiday instead? While not strictly illegal, many people would consider any one or more of these acts to be unethical. How about you? How often and in what ways have you committed or observed acts that could be considered unethical in your school?[8]

Many ethical problems arise at work when people are asked to do or find themselves about to do something that violates their personal beliefs. For some, if the act is legal, they proceed with confidence and consider their behavior ethical. For others, the ethical test goes beyond legality and extends to personal **values**—the underlying beliefs and judgements regarding what is right or desirable and that influence individual attitudes and behaviors.

The psychologist Milton Rokeach distinguishes between "terminal" and "instrumental" values.[9] **Terminal values** focus on desired ends, such as the goal of lifelong learning. Examples of terminal values considered important by managers include self-respect, family security, freedom, inner harmony, and happiness. **Instrumental values** concern the means for accomplishing these ends, such as the role of intellectual curiosity in lifelong learning. Instrumental values held important by managers include honesty, ambition, courage, imagination, and self-discipline.

Although terminal and instrumental values tend to be quite enduring for any one individual, they can vary considerably from one person to the next. Such values contrasts might help to explain why different people respond quite differently to the same situation. Although two people might share the terminal value of career success, they might disagree on how to balance the instrumental values of honesty and ambition in accomplishing it.

Test this point. Talk with some of your friends or classmates about terminal values (what you and they want to achieve) and instrumental values (how you and they are willing to do it). Don't be surprised to find values differences, and don't be surprised to find that these differences create conflicts. Some of the disagreements, furthermore, may rest on significant differences in what behaviors are and are not considered ethical.

Values are broad beliefs about what is appropriate behavior.

Terminal values are preferences about desired end states.

Instrumental values are preferences regarding the means to desired ends.

• What Is Considered Ethical Varies among Moral Reasoning Approaches

Figure 4.1 shows four different philosophical views of ethical behavior, with each representing an alternative approach to moral reasoning.[10] The **utilitarian view** considers ethical behavior as that which delivers the greatest good to the greatest number of people. Founded in the work of nineteenth-century philosopher John Stuart Mill, this results-oriented view tries to assess the moral implications of our actions in terms of their consequences. Business executives, for example, might use profits, efficiency, and other performance criteria to judge what decision is best for the most people. An example is the manager who decides to cut 30 percent of a plant's workforce in order to keep the plant profitable and save the remaining jobs, rather than lose them all to business failure.

An appeal to the **individualism view** of ethical behavior would focus on the long-term advancement of self-interests. People supposedly become self-regulating as they strive for individual advantage over time; ethics are maintained in the process. For example, just suppose that you might think about cheating on your next test. But you also realize that this quest for short-term gain might lead to a long-term loss if you get caught and expelled. This reasoning should cause a quick rejection of the original idea.

Not everyone, as you might expect, agrees that self-regulation will always promote honesty and integrity. One complaint is that individualism in business practice too often results in a "pecuniary ethic." This has been described by one executive as the tendency to "push the law to its outer limits" and "run roughshod over other individuals to achieve one's objectives."[11]

The **justice view** of moral reasoning considers a behavior ethical when people are treated impartially and fairly, according to legal rules and standards. It judges the ethical aspects of any decision on the basis of how equitable it is for everyone affected.[12] Researchers now like to speak about three aspects of justice in the workplace—procedural, distributive, and interactional.

Procedural justice involves the fair administration of policies and rules. For example, does a sexual harassment charge levied against a senior executive receive the same full hearing as one made against a first-level supervisor? **Distributive justice** involves the allocation of outcomes without respect to individual characteristics, such as those based on ethnicity, race, gender, or age. For example, does a woman with the same qualifications

In the **utilitarian view** ethical behavior delivers the greatest good to the most people.

In the **individualism view** ethical behavior advances long-term self-interests.

In the **justice view** ethical behavior treats people impartially and fairly.

Procedural justice focuses on the fair application of policies and rules.

Distributive justice focuses on treating people the same regardless of personal characteristics.

Figure 4.1	How do alternative moral reasoning approaches view ethical behavior?

Individualism view

Does a decision or behavior promote one's long term self-interests?

Moral-rights view

Does a decision or behavior maintain the fundamental rights of all human beings?

Utilitarian view

Does a decision or behavior do the greatest good for the most people?

Justice view

Does a decision or behavior show fairness and impartiality?

People often differ in the approaches they take toward moral reasoning, and they may use different approaches at different times and situations. Four ways to reason through the ethics of a course of action are utilitarianism, individualism, moral rights, and justice. Each approach can justify an action as ethical, but the reasoning will differ from that of the other views.

Interactional justice is the degree to which others are treated with dignity and respect.

In the **moral-rights view** ethical behavior respects and protects fundamental rights.

Cultural relativism suggests there is no one right way to behave; cultural context determines ethical behavior.

and experience as a man receive the same consideration for hiring or promotion? **Interactional justice** focuses on the treatment of others with dignity and respect. For example, does a bank loan officer take the time to fully explain to an applicant why he or she was turned down for a loan?[13]

Finally, a **moral-rights view** considers behavior as ethical when it respects and protects the fundamental rights of people. Based on the teachings of John Locke and Thomas Jefferson, this view considers inviolate the rights of all people to life, liberty, and fair treatment under the law. In organizations, this translates into protecting the rights of employees to privacy, due process, free speech, free consent, health and safety, and freedom of conscience.

As our nation and others grapple with the complexities of global society, one of the issues we often hear raised and debated is human rights. Even though the United Nations stands by the Universal Declaration of Human Rights passed by the General Assembly in 1948, business executives, representatives of activist groups, and leaders of governments still argue and disagree over human rights issues in various circumstances.[14] And without doubt, one of the areas where human rights can be most controversial is the arena of international business.

• What Is Considered Ethical Can Vary across Cultures

Does culture influence what is considered ethical behavior? Absolutely. Former Levi's CEO Robert Haas once said that any ethical concern "becomes even more difficult when you overlay the complexities of different cultures and values systems that exist throughout the world."[15] It would probably be hard to find a corporate leader or business person engaged in international business who would disagree. Put yourself in their positions. How would you deal with an issue such as child labor in a factory owned by one of your major suppliers?

Figure 4.2 offers one framework for dialogue with yourself and others on the thorny ethical aspects of international business dealings. It is based on the work of scholar and ethicist Thomas Donaldson, who points out two extremes in ethical positioning across cultures-cultural relativism and moral absolutism.

Have you ever heard the saying: "When in Rome, do as the Romans do"? Broadly, it suggests to us that we try to "go with the flow" when we are in someone else's home or territory. Donaldson takes this a step further and links the saying with the ethical position of **cultural relativism**.[16] The relativist believes that cultural context alone determines ethical behavior; in other words, if something is considered acceptable in a foreign

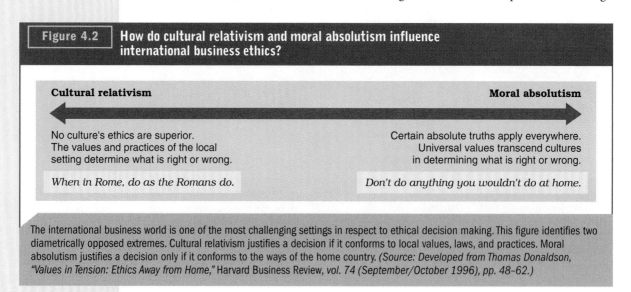

Figure 4.2 How do cultural relativism and moral absolutism influence international business ethics?

Cultural relativism ←———————————————→ Moral absolutism

No culture's ethics are superior. The values and practices of the local setting determine what is right or wrong.

When in Rome, do as the Romans do.

Certain absolute truths apply everywhere. Universal values transcend cultures in determining what is right or wrong.

Don't do anything you wouldn't do at home.

The international business world is one of the most challenging settings in respect to ethical decision making. This figure identifies two diametrically opposed extremes. Cultural relativism justifies a decision if it conforms to local values, laws, and practices. Moral absolutism justifies a decision only if it conforms to the ways of the home country. *(Source: Developed from Thomas Donaldson, "Values in Tension: Ethics Away from Home,"* Harvard Business Review, *vol. 74 (September/October 1996), pp. 48–62.)*

country, it is ethical. A U.S. business executive guided by rules of cultural relativism, for example, might agree that it is ethical to contract with a foreign supplier who uses child labor. The justification is that it is accepted practice according to the local culture's laws and customs.

Donaldson contrasts cultural relativism with the opposite extreme of **moral absolutism**. Someone who takes this perspective believes that certain values and practices are universally good and bad. Thus, it doesn't make any difference where in the world you might be; if something is wrong at home, it's wrong everywhere. The absolutist position uses the values and laws of the home country to set the standards for behavior everywhere else. In our example, the American executive using an absolutist position would refuse to do business with the foreign supplier. The reasoning is that child labor is bad; it is not acceptable at home so it is not acceptable anywhere.

How do these two alternatives sit with you? Actually, Donaldson finds problems with both. The relativist position is too easy, making it possible to justify anything that serve's ones best interests. But the absolutist position becomes a form of **ethical imperialism**, externally imposing one's own ethical standards on others.

In attempting to reconcile these problems, Donaldson argues that we should be able to act in ways that preserve certain fundamental rights and ethical standards in tricky international situations, while still respecting values and traditions of the local cultures.[17] He describes an ethical threshold of core values that should be universal—things like human dignity, basic rights, and good citizenship. If these core values are violated, there is no ethical excuse for doing business under such conditions. But once the threshold is satisfied, international businesses should be able to find ways to work within local and regional cultural contexts.[18]

• Ethical Dilemmas Arise as Tests of Personal Ethics and Values

It's all well and good to discuss ethical behavior in theory and in the safety of the college classroom. The real personal test, however, occurs when we encounter a real-life situation that challenges our ethical beliefs and standards. And sooner or later, we all will. Often ambiguous and unexpected, these ethical challenges are inevitable. Project ahead to your next job search. Suppose you have accepted an offer, only to get a better one from another employer two weeks later. Should you come up with an excuse to back out of the first job so that you can accept the second one instead?

An **ethical dilemma** is a situation requiring a decision about a course of action that, although offering potential benefits, may be considered unethical. As a further complication, there may be no clear consensus on what is "right" and "wrong." In these circumstances, one's personal values are often the best indicators that something isn't right. An engineering manager speaking from experience sums it up this way: "I define an unethical situation as one in which I have to do something I don't feel good about."[19]

Take a look at the Exhibit – *common situations for unethical behavior at work*.[20] Have you been exposed to anything like this? Are you ready to deal with these situations and any ethical dilemmas that they may create?

In a survey of *Harvard Business Review* subscribers, managers report that many of their ethical dilemmas arise out of conflicts with superiors, customers, and subordinates.[21] The most frequent issues involved dishonesty in advertising and in communications with top management, clients, and government agencies. The survey also revealed ethics problems in dealing with special gifts, entertainment expenses, and

Moral absolutism suggests ethical standards apply absolutely across all cultures.

Ethical imperialism attempts to impose ethical standards on other cultures.

An **ethical dilemma** is a situation that although offering potential benefit or gain is also unethical.

EXHIBIT

Common Situations for Unethical Behavior at Work

Discrimination Denying people a promotion or job because of their race, religion, gender, age, or another reason that is not job-relevant

Sexual harassment Making a coworker feel uncomfortable because of inappropriate comments or actions regarding sexuality; or by requesting sexual favors in return for favorable job treatment

Conflicts of interest Taking bribes, kickbacks, or extraordinary gifts in return for making decisions favorable to another person

Customer confidence Giving someone privileged information regarding the activities of a customer

Organizational resources Using official stationery or a business e-mail account to communicate personal opinions or to make requests from community organizations

Unethical Pressures from Bad Bosses

- Meet unrealistic performance goals
- Distort, withhold information
- Support incorrect viewpoints
- Sign false documents
- Overlook boss's wrongdoings
- Do business with boss's friends

kickbacks. And significantly, the managers reported that their bosses were a common cause of ethical dilemmas. They felt pressured at times, for example, to support incorrect viewpoints, sign false documents, overlook the boss's wrongdoings, and do business with the boss's friends.

At the top of any list of bad boss behaviors is holding people accountable for unrealistically high performance goals.[22] When individuals feel extreme performance pressures, they sometimes act incorrectly and engage in questionable practices in attempting to meet these expectations. Scholar Archie Carroll says: " . . . otherwise decent people start cutting corners on accuracy or quality, or start covering up incidents, lying or deceiving customers."[23] The lesson is to be realistic and supportive in what you request of others. In Carroll's words again, "Good management means that one has to be sensitive to how pressure to perform might be perceived by those who want to please the boss."[24]

• People Have Tendencies to Rationalize Unethical Behaviors

What happens after someone commits an unethical act? Most of us generally view ourselves as "good" people. When we do something that is or might be "wrong," therefore, it leaves us doubtful, uncomfortable, and anxious. A common response is to rationalize the questionable behavior to make it seem acceptable in our minds.

You might observe in yourself and others tendencies toward four rationalizations that are used to justify ethical misconduct.[25] First, a rationalizer might say, *It's not really illegal.* This implies that the behavior is acceptable, especially in ambiguous situations. When dealing with shady or borderline situations in which you may not be able to precisely determine right from wrong, stop and reconsider. When in doubt about the ethics of a decision, don't do it.

A rationalizer might also say: *It's in everyone's best interests.* This response suggests that just because someone might benefit from the behavior, it becomes justifiable. To overcome this "ends justify the means" rationalization, we need to look beyond short-run results to address longer-term implications. Sometimes rationalizers use a third excuse: *No one will ever know about it.* The argument implies that only upon discovery is a crime committed. Lack of accountability, unrealistic pressures to perform, and a boss who prefers "not to know" can all reinforce such thinking. In today's world of great transparency, such thinking seems very hard to justify.

Finally, rationalizers may proceed with a questionable action because they believe that *the organization will stand behind me.* This is misperceived loyalty. The individual be-

Four Ways to Rationalize Unethical Behavior

1. "What I'm doing is not really illegal."
2. "My behavior is in everyone's best interests."
3. "Nobody will ever find out what I've done."
4. "The organization will protect me."

lieves that the organization's best interests stand above all others. In return, the individual believes that top managers will condone the behavior and protect the individual from harm. But if caught doing something wrong, would you want to count on the organization going to bat for you? And when you read about people who have done wrong and then try to excuse it by saying "I only did what I was ordered to do," how sympathetic are you?

Be Sure You Can . . .

- differentiate legal behavior and ethical behavior

- differentiate terminal and instrumental values, and give examples of each

- list and explain four approaches to moral reasoning

- illustrate distributive, procedural, and interactive justice in organizations

- explain the positions of cultural relativism and moral absolutism in international business ethics

- illustrate the types of ethical dilemmas common in the workplace

- explain how bad management can cause ethical dilemmas

- list four common rationalizations for unethical behavior

Define the Terms

Cultural relativism	Interactional justice
Distributive justice	Justice view
Ethical behavior	Moral absolutism
Ethical dilemmas	Moral-rights view
Ethical imperialism	Procedural justice
Ethics	Terminal values
Individualism view	Utilitarian view
Instrumental values	Values

Rapid Review

- Ethical behavior is that which is accepted as "good" or "right" as opposed to "bad" or "wrong."

- The utilitarian, individualism, moral-rights, and justice views offer different approaches to moral reasoning; each takes a different perspective of when and how a behavior becomes ethical.

- Cultural relativism argues that no culture is ethically superior to any other; moral absolutism believes there are clear rights and wrongs that apply universally, no matter where in the world one might be.

- An ethical dilemma occurs when one must decide whether to pursue a course of action that, although offering the potential for personal or organizational gain, may be unethical.

- Ethical dilemmas faced by managers often involve conflicts with superiors, customers, and subordinates over requests that involve some form of dishonesty.

- Common rationalizations for unethical behavior include believing the behavior is not illegal, is in everyone's best interests, will never be noticed, or will be supported by the organization.

Reflect/React

1. For a manager, is any one of the moral reasoning approaches better than the others?

2. Will a belief in cultural relativism create inevitable ethics problems for international business executives?

3. Are ethical dilemmas always problems, or can they be opportunities?

As quick as we are to recognize the bad news and problems about ethical behavior in organizations, we shouldn't forget that there is a lot of good news, too. There are many organizations out there whose leaders and members set high ethics standards for themselves and others, and engage in a variety of methods to encourage consistent ethical behaviors.

⊙ Personal and Contextual Influences on Ethical Behavior at Work

INDIVIDUAL AS A PERSON	ORGANIZATION AND ACTION CONTEXT
Family influences	Behaviors of supervisors, peers
Religious beliefs	Rules, policies, codes of conduct
Personal values	Societal norms, expectations
Past experiences	Laws and government regulations

Ethical frameworks are well-thought-out personal rules and strategies for ethical decision making.

• Personal and Contextual Factors Influence Ethical Conduct

There are many possible influences on our personal ethics and how we apply them at work. One set traces to who we are as a person, what might be called our "character." This is what we represent and stand for in terms of family influences, religious beliefs, personal standards, personal values, and even past experiences.

Character shouldn't stay home when we go to work, but it isn't always easy to stand up for what you believe. This problem grows when we are exposed to extreme pressures, get contradictory or just plain bad advice, and when our career is at stake. "Do this or lose your job!" That's a terribly intimidating message. So it may be no surprise that 56 percent of U.S. workers in one survey reported feeling pressured to act unethically in their jobs.[26] Sadly, the same survey also revealed that 48 percent of respondents had themselves committed questionable acts within the past year.

Such problems become more manageable when we have solid **ethical frameworks**, or well-thought-out personal rules and strategies for ethical decision making. Taking the time to think through our ethical anchors can help us to act consistently and confidently. By giving high priority to such virtues as honesty, fairness, integrity, and self-respect, the process provides ethical anchors that can help us make correct decisions even under the most difficult conditions.

The organization and action context also influence workplace ethics. And, quite frankly, you will probably find that some settings create more positive ethical influences than others. Whether the ethical climate of an organization is good or bad, it probably reflects to some extent the behaviors, expectations, and examples set by its managers—top to bottom. At the work unit level the ethical climate will also reflect the expectations and reinforcements provided by a person's co-workers. And whatever the source, the more ethical the expectations, the more likely that individuals will try to act ethically. Unfortunately, the reverse case holds equally well.

Finally, we should also understand that organizations and their members are influenced by conditions in the external environment. This includes government laws and regulations, and social norms and values. Laws interpret social values to define appropriate behaviors for organizations and their members. Regulations help governments monitor these behaviors and keep them within acceptable standards.

NEWSLINE

Values drive student commitments to social entrepreneurship Most of us know how devastated Afghanistan was after the fall of the Taliban. Sarah Takesh has done more than just admit the existence of the situation, she has acted on it. As an MBA student at the University of California at Berkeley, she conceived of a business plan to help Afghan women, by hiring them to sew "beautiful"

clothes for sale. She says: "I wanted to blend my love for fashion with a social element." Her business, Tarsian & Blinkley, is up and running, and helping to make a difference in that country. Now shift to Ghana. Romeo Tetteh-Jones, as a student at the University of Ghana in Legon, started his company to provide safe and economical drinking water to the population. Tetteh-Jones hopes products from his new firm, African Filtration Systems Limited, will reduce infant mortality caused by unsanitary drinking water.

Reflect: How might ethics and personal values influence your career decisions? Will you become involved in community service? Will you only work for employers that strive to "do good while doing business"?

When Enron and Arthur Andersen collapsed in a terrible scandal and great financial loss to employees, owners, and customers, it led to new legislation being passed. The *Sarbanes-Oxley Act* of 2002 was the government's attempt to substitute for an apparent lack of ethical leadership in our nation's businesses. This law makes it easier to try and sentence corporate executives for financial misconduct. However, one still has to ask a tough question: Can laws and regulations alone guarantee ethical behavior in organizations?

• Training in Ethical Decision Making May Improve Ethical Conduct

It would be nice if everyone had access through their employers to **ethics training** that helps them understand and best deal with ethical aspects of decision making. Although not everyone will have this opportunity, more and more are getting it, including most college students. Most business schools, for example, now offer required and elective courses on ethics or integrate ethics into courses on other subjects.[27]

In college or in the workplace, however, we should keep ethics training in perspective. It won't work for everyone; it won't provide sure-fire answers to all ethical dilemmas; it won't guarantee ethical behavior throughout an organization. But, it does help. An executive at Chemical Bank once put it this way: "We aren't teaching people right from wrong—we assume they know that. We aren't giving people moral courage to do what is right—they should be able to do that anyhow. We focus on dilemmas."[28]

MANAGEMENT TIPS

Checklist for dealing with ethical dilemmas

Step 1. Recognize the ethical dilemma.
Step 2. Get the facts.
Step 3. Identify your options.
Step 4. Test each option: Is it legal? Is it right? Is it beneficial?
Step 5. Decide which option to follow.
Step 6. Ask the "Spotlight Questions" to double check your decision.

"How would I feel if my family found out about my decision?"
"How would I feel if the local newspaper printed my decision?"

Step 7. Take action.

One of the biggest differences between facing an ethical dilemma in a training seminar or in class, is pressure. Many times we must, or believe we must, move fast. Management tips is a reminder that it often helps to pause and double-check important decisions before taking action in uncomfortable circumstances. It presents a seven-step checklist that is used in some corporate training workshops. Would you agree that the most powerful is Step 6? This is what some call the test of the **Spotlight Questions**. You might think of this as the risk of public disclosure for your actions. Asking and answering the questions about how you would feel if family, friends, and acquaintances learn of your actions is a powerful way to test whether a decision is consistent with your ethical standards.

• Protection of Whistleblowers May Encourage Ethical Conduct

Agnes Connolly pressed her employer to report two toxic chemical accidents. Dave Jones reported that his company was using unqualified suppliers in the construction of a nuclear power plant. Margaret Newsham revealed that her firm was allowing workers to do personal business while on government contracts. Herman Cohen charged that the ASPCA in New York was mistreating animals. Barry Adams complained that his hospital followed unsafe practices.[29]

Who are these people? They are whistleblowers, persons who expose organizational misdeeds in order to preserve ethical standards and protect against wasteful, harmful, or illegal acts.[30] All were also fired from their jobs.

It shouldn't be too surprising to you that whistleblowers take significant career risks when they expose wrongdoing in organizations. Although there are federal and state laws that offer whistleblowers some defense against "retaliatory discharge," the protection is still inadequate overall. Laws vary from state to state, and the federal laws mainly protect government workers. Furthermore, even with legal protection, there are other reasons why potential whistleblowers might hesitate.

Have you ever encountered a student cheating on an exam or homework assignment? If so, did you blow the whistle by informing the instructor? A survey by the Ethics Resource Center reports that some 44 percent of U.S. workers fail to report the wrongdoings they observe at work. The top reasons for not reporting are "the belief that no corrective action would be taken, and the fear that reports would not be kept confidential."[31]

The very nature of organizations as power structures creates potential barriers to whistleblowing. A *strict chain of command* can make it hard to bypass the boss if he or she is the one doing something wrong. *Strong work group identities* can discourage whistleblowing and encourage loyalty and self-censorship. And, *ambiguous priorities* can make it hard sometimes to distinguish right from wrong.[32]

In the attempt to remove these and other obstacles to the exposure of unethical behaviors, organizations are trying new approaches. Some are formally appointing staff members to serve as *ethics advocates*. Others are experimenting with *moral quality circles*, small groups of workers meeting together to share commitments to work at their moral best.[33]

• Managers as Positive Role Models May Inspire Ethical Conduct

Gabrielle Melchionda, a young entrepreneur in Portland, Maine, started Mad Gab's Inc., an all-natural skin-care business, while a college student. After her sales had risen to over $300,000, an exporter offered to sell $2 million of her products abroad. She turned it down. Why? The exporter also sold weapons, which contradicted her values. Her values guide all business decisions, from offering an employee profit-sharing plan, to hiring disabled adults, to using only packaging designs that minimize waste.[34]

Don't you think Gabrielle's example would be an inspiration to those who work for and with her? The way top managers approach ethics can make a big difference in what happens in their organizations. They have a lot of power to shape an organization's policies and set its moral tone. Some of this power works through the attention given to policies that set high ethics standards, and to their enforcement. Another and significantly large part of this power works through the personal examples top managers set. In order to have a positive impact on ethical conduct throughout an organization, those at the top must walk the talk.

Of course it's not just managers at the top who have this power and the responsibility to use it well. Managers at all levels in organizations probably have more power than they realize to influence the ethical behavior of others. Again, part of this power is walking the talk; setting the example; acting as an ethical role model. Another part is just practicing good management; keeping goals and performance expectations reasonable. Some 64 percent of 238 executives in one study, for example, reported feeling so stressed to achieve company goals that they considered compromising personal standards. A *Fortune* survey also reported that 34 percent of its respondents felt a company president can help to create an ethical climate by setting reasonable goals "so that subordinates are not pressured into unethical actions."[35]

PACESETTERS

Living by personal values makes business sense.

You don't need to leave your personal values at home when you go to work or own your own business. Just look at the example set by Aaron Feurstein. Many said he was crazy when he kept some 1,000 workers on the payroll after his apparel factory burned down. But, after Malden Mills of Lawrence, Massachusetts, got back in business producing Polartec and Polarfleece knits, owner, president, and CEO Feurstein couldn't have been prouder. He had paid his jobless employees over $15 million during the several months it took to rebuild the plant. He also retained and gained a loyal workforce dedicated to customers. According for Feurstein his decision was just "common sense." When praised for his corporate decency, he said that he hopes other CEOs believe "that there's a moral imperative that they must answer to as well."

Aaron Feurstein, owner president, and CEO, Malden Mills.

• Formal Codes of Ethics Set Standards for Ethical Conduct

Many organizations today have a **code of ethics** that formally states the values and ethical principles members are expected to display. Some employers even require new hires to sign and agree to the code as a condition of employment. Don't be surprised if you encounter this someday.

A **code of ethics** is a formal statement of values and ethical standards.

Ethics codes can get specific to the point of offering guidelines on how to behave in situations susceptible to ethical dilemmas—how sales representatives and purchasing agents should handle giving and receiving gifts, for example. Ethics codes might also specify consequences for bribes and kickbacks, dishonesty of books or records, and confidentiality breaches of corporate information.

> ### → Excerpts from the Gap's Code of Vendor Conduct in Global Manufacturing
>
> - **Discrimination**—"Factories shall employ workers on the basis of their ability to do the job, not on the basis of their personal characteristics or beliefs."
> - **Forced labor**—"Factories shall not use any prison, indentured or forced labor."
> - **Working conditions**—"Factories must treat all workers with respect and dignity and provide them with a safe and healthy environment."
> - **Freedom of association**—"Factories must not interfere with workers who wish to lawfully and peacefully associate, organize or bargain collectively."

Ethics codes are increasingly common in the complex world of international business, where problems dealing with foreign suppliers and contractors are prevalent.[36] Corporate executives realize that their customers and society at large hold them accountable for the actions of their foreign suppliers. They have become much stricter in policing their international operations. Leading firms like the Gap, Inc., use codes of conduct to anchor their international business dealings and communicate clear expectations to their business partners.[37]

Still, don't be surprised if you read about some future scandal at an organization with a strong code of ethical conduct. Although these codes can be helpful, they can't guarantee results for everyone. Ultimately, the value of any ethics code still rests on the human resource foundations of the organization. There is no replacement for effective hiring practices that staff organizations with honest and moral people. And there is no replacement for leadership by committed managers who set positive examples and always act as ethical role models.

> *Ethics in a corporation is like water—it flows downhill.*
>
> **Professor Thomas Donaldson, OF THE WHARTON SCHOOL AT THE UNIVERSITY OF PENNSYLVANIA**

4.2 How can organizations maintain high standards of ethical conduct?

Be Sure You Can . . .

- explain how ethical behavior is influenced by both a person's character and the organizational context

- explain the term whistleblower

- list three organizational barriers to whistleblowing

- compare and contrast ethics training, codes of ethical conduct, and ethical role models as ways for encouraging ethical behavior in organizations

- state two "Spotlight" Questions for checking the ethics of a decision

Define the Terms

Code of ethics   Spotlight Questions

Ethical frameworks   Whistleblowers

Ethics training

Rapid Review

- Ethical behavior at work is influenced by an individual's character, represented by values, beliefs, and family background; and the organizational context, including expectations set by management and by co-workers.

- Ethics training can help people better understand how to make decisions involving ethical dilemmas in the workplace.

- The Spotlight Questions require decision makers to confront the ethics risks from public disclosure of their actions.

- Whistleblowers expose the unethical acts of others in organizations.

- Top management sets an ethical tone for the organization as a whole, but all managers are responsible for acting as positive models of ethical behavior.

- Written codes of ethical conduct formally state what an organization expects of its employees or business partners regarding ethical conduct.

Reflect/React

1. Is it right for organizations to require ethics training of employees?

2. Should whistleblowers have complete protection under the law?

3. Should all managers be evaluated on how well they serve as ethical role models?

Multiple Choice

1. A business owner makes a decision to reduce a plant's work-force by 10 percent in order to cut costs and be able to save jobs for the other 90 percent of employees. This decision could be justified as ethical using the _____ approach to moral reasoning.
   (a) utilitarian **(b)** individualism **(c)** justice **(d)** moral-rights

2. If a manager fails to enforce a late-to-work policy for all workers, that is, by allowing favored employees to arrive late without penalties, this would be considered a violation of _____ .
   (a) human rights **(b)** personal values **(c)** distributive justice **(d)** Sarbanes-Oxley law

3. According to research on ethics in the workplace, _____ is/are often a major and frequent source of pressures that create ethical dilemmas for people in their jobs.
   (a) declining morals in society **(b)** long work hours **(c)** low pay **(d)** requests or demands from bosses

4. Someone who exposes the ethical misdeeds of others in an organization is usually called a/an _____.
   (a) whistleblower **(b)** ethics advocate **(c)** ombudsman **(d)** stakeholder

5. Two employees are talking about ethics in their workplaces. Sean says that ethics training and codes of ethical conduct are worthless; Maura says they are the only ways to ensure ethical behavior by all employees. Who is right and why?
   (a) Sean—no one cares. **(b)** Maura—only the organization can influence ethical behavior. **(c)** Neither Sean nor Maura—training and codes can encourage but never guarantee ethical behavior. **(d)** Neither Sean nor Maura—only the threat of legal punishment will make people act ethically.

6. Which ethical position has been criticized as a source of "ethical imperialism?"
   (a) individualism **(b)** absolutism **(c)** utilitarianism **(d)** rationalism

7. If a manager takes a lot of time explaining to a subordinate why he did not get a promotion and sincerely listens to his concerns, this is an example of an attempt to act ethically according to _____.
   (a) utilitarian reasoning **(b)** individualism **(c)** interactional justice **(d)** moral rights

8. Things like family influences, religious beliefs, and personal values can be the source of strong _____ that can help individuals better deal with the ethical dilemmas they encounter at work.
   (a) moral quality circles **(b)** ethical frameworks **(c)** codes of ethical conduct **(d)** ethics training

9. In respect to the link between bad management and ethical behavior, research shows that _____.
   (a) unrealistic goals can cause unethical behavior **(b)** most whistleblowers just want more pay **(c)** only top management behavior really makes a difference **(d)** codes of ethics make up for any management deficiencies

10. A person's desires for a comfortable life and family security represent _____ values, while his or her desires to be honest and hard working represent _____ values.
    (a) terminal/instrumental **(b)** instrumental/terminal **(c)** universal/individual **(d)** individual/universal

Short Response

11. How does distributive justice differ from procedural justice?

12. What are the spotlight questions for double-checking the ethics of a decision?

13. In what specific ways can "bad bosses" cause unethical behavior?

14. If someone commits an unethical act, how can he or she rationalize it to make it seem right?

Integration & Application

A small outdoor clothing company in Georgia has just received an attractive proposal from a business in Tanzania to manufacture the work gloves that it sells. Accepting the offer from the Tanzanian firm would allow for substantial cost savings compared to the current supplier. However, the outdoor clothing firm's manager has recently read reports that some businesses in Tanzania are forcing people to work in unsafe conditions in order to keep their costs down. The manager seeks your help in clarifying the ethical aspects of this opportunity.

Questions: How would you describe the manager's alternatives in terms of cultural relativism and absolutism? What would be the major issues and concerns in terms of the cultural relativism position versus the absolutist position?

SELF-ASSESSMENT
Terminal Values Survey

INSTRUCTIONS *Rate each of the following values in terms of its importance to you. Think about each value in terms of its importance as a guiding principle in your life. As you work, consider each value in relation to all the other values listed in the survey.* Use this scale for each item:

1	2	3	4	5	6	7
Of lesser importance				Of greater importance		

TERMINAL VALUES

1 A comfortable life	1	2	3	4	5	6	7
2 An exciting life	1	2	3	4	5	6	7
3 A sense of accomplishment	1	2	3	4	5	6	7
4 A world at peace	1	2	3	4	5	6	7
5 A world of beauty	1	2	3	4	5	6	7
6 Equality	1	2	3	4	5	6	7
7 Family security	1	2	3	4	5	6	7
8 Freedom	1	2	3	4	5	6	7
9 Happiness	1	2	3	4	5	6	7
10 Inner harmony	1	2	3	4	5	6	7
11 Mature love	1	2	3	4	5	6	7
12 National security	1	2	3	4	5	6	7
13 Pleasure	1	2	3	4	5	6	7
14 Salvation	1	2	3	4	5	6	7
15 Self-respect	1	2	3	4	5	6	7
16 Social recognition	1	2	3	4	5	6	7
17 True friendship	1	2	3	4	5	6	7
18 Wisdom	1	2	3	4	5	6	7

INTERPRETATION AND SCORING

Terminal values reflect a person's preferences concerning the ends to be achieved. They are the goals individuals would like to achieve in their lifetimes. Multiply your score for each item times a "weight"—e.g., (#3 × 5)=your new question 3 score.

1. Calculate your Personal Values Score as:
   (#1×5)+(#2×4)+(#3×4)+(#7)+(#8)+(#9×4)+ (#10×5)+(#11×4)+(#13×5)+(#14×3)+(#15×5) +(#16×3)+(#17×4)+(#18×5).

2. Calculate your Social Values Score as:
   (#4 × 5) +(#5×3)+(#6×5)+(#12×5).

3. Calculate your Terminal Values Score as:
   Personal Values−Social Values.

Go online to read this case!

Nike: Making and Mastering Markets

Nike is a huge worldwide brand with an enormous ad budget, yet it has a relatively small domestic headquarters (most nonexecutive work is outsourced). It has run afoul with international suppliers and labor and copyright laws. Once you own the athletic shoe market, where do you go from there?

MODULE 4 — Online Interactive Learning Resources

Skill Builder
• Personal Character

Self-Assessment
• Instrumental Values

Experiential Exercise
• Confronting Ethical Dilemmas

Team Project
• Cheating on Campus

Organizations

Social Responsibility and Governance

Former U.S. Secretary of Labor Robert Reich wrote in his book "The Future of Success:" "The emerging economy is offering unprecedented opportunities, an ever-expanding choice of terrific deals, fabulous products, good investments, and great jobs for people with the right talents and skills. Never before in human history have so many had access to so much so easily."[1]

In these terms, the present outlook couldn't be better for organizations and career seekers. But Reich also goes on to say that to survive in this economy "all organizations must dramatically and continuously improve— cutting costs, adding value, creating new products."[2] What Reich might have added to this list was earning respect from society at large.

have ethics too

Look around; consider the organizations that you do business with. How many really earn your respect? Are there any that you would describe as "pursuing profits with principles"?

Some might argue that this is hardly possible. But Tom and Kate Chappell would very much disagree. At their business, Tom's of Maine, a core philosophy guides the sale of an ever-expanding range of all-natural personal care products: "to do what is right for our customers, employees, communities, and environment."[3]

Founded in Kennebunkport, Maine, in 1970 and now part of Colgate-Palmolive, the firm has been described by the Council of Economic Priorities as one of the "saints of social responsibility." And, yes, profits with principles is at the heart of the matter. Tom says: "I believe we have been able to expand upon the historical point of view that business is just for making money to a broader view that business is about doing good for others in the process of getting financial gain."

→ MODULE GUIDE

 5.1 What should we know about organizational environments and social responsibility?

- Organizations operate within conditions set by the general environment.
- The specific environment includes an organization's stakeholders.
- Social responsibility is an organization's obligation to best serve society.
- Social performance by organizations can be evaluated in different ways.
- Scholars argue cases for and against corporate social responsibility.
- Organizations follow different social responsibility strategies.

 5.2 What are current issues in corporate governance?

- Failures of ethics and social responsibility prompt calls for stronger governance.
- Weak corporate governance can result in more government regulation.
- Moral management builds capacities for self-governance in organizations.

5.1 What Should We Know about Organizational Environments and Social Responsibility?

Tom and Kate Chappell obviously have a well-thought-out view of their business and its role in society—to be a contributor, not a taker. And when Tom's customers buy and its employees help make their toothpaste, or cleansers or deodorants, they are all participating in that vision. Wouldn't it be nice if many more organizations would act with similar vision and commitments? Like people, shouldn't organizations have ethics, too?

• Organizations Operate within Conditions Set by the General Environment

The **general environment** consists of all background conditions that establish the organization's context for action. The examples given in the Exhibit – *Environments of Organizations*, include economic, sociocultural, legal-political, technological, and natural environmental conditions. All, in one way or another, make a significant difference in how organizations operate and how successful they become.

Consider the natural environment. Have you noticed that Japanese automakers seem to have an advantage over U.S. companies in selling cars that are more environmentally friendly? The Sierra Club did. It gave awards to both Honda and Toyota for excellence in environmental engineering; their hybrid cars are leading the industry. Why weren't the U.S. automakers on the podium? Why did their Japanese competitors stick with investments in hybrids even before customers were ready to buy them in large numbers? Could it have been, in part at least, a greater willingness to value the natural environment and factor it into their new product developments?

Consider also the sociocultural environment. Do you recognize subtle trends in values, demographic profiles, and social trends in our society? When managers stay informed they are often able to better relate their organizations with their customers. For example, American parents are now spending more money on decorating their children's rooms. Recognizing the trend, Pottery Barn quickly expanded its line of furniture and accessories to include Pottery Barn Kids and PB Teen.

Differences in general environment conditions may be most noticeable internationally. Think, for example, how your lifestyle varies from that of someone living in an African country like Tanzania or Niger. Think also about how political systems vary, say between the United States, China, Venezuela, and France. Large global corporations like McDonalds, Procter & Gamble, Dell, and Apple depend for their success on having executives who understand such environmental differences and know how to best deal with them. The pharmaceutical giant Merck, for example, uses things like alliances with local companies, research with local partners, and consultations with local governments on legal matters to stay in touch with business conditions in Europe.

• The Specific Environment Includes an Organization's Stakeholders

Whereas the general environment represents background conditions, the **specific environment** consists of the actual organizations, groups, and persons with whom an organization interacts and conducts business. The members of the specific environment for any one organization are

> The **general environment** consists of cultural, economic, legal-political, and educational conditions.

> The **specific environment** includes the people and groups with whom an organization interacts.

EXHIBIT

Environments of Organizations

Economic conditions   Health of the economy in terms of inflation, income levels, gross domestic product, unemployment, and job outlook

Sociocultural conditions   Norms, customs, and social values on such matters as human rights, trends in education and related social institutions, as well as demographic patterns in society

Legal-political conditions   Prevailing philosophy and objectives of the political party or parties running the government, as well as laws and government regulations

Technological conditions   Development and availability of technology, including scientific advancements

Natural environment conditions   Nature and conditions of the natural environment, including levels of public concern expressed through environmentalism

known as its **stakeholders** because they have a direct "stake" or interest in its performance. Figure 5.1 shows just how complex the field of organizational stakeholders can become. Perhaps the most recognizable among them are the organization's customers, suppliers, competitors, regulators, investors/owners, as well as employees.

When it comes to the performance of an organization, stakeholders can have rather different interests. Customers, for example, typically want value prices and quality products; owners are interested in realizing profits as returns on their investments; suppliers are interested in long-term business relationships; communities are interested in corporate citizenship and support for public services; employees are interested in good wages, benefits, security, and satisfaction in their work.

You can probably see from this discussion, and even another look at the figure, that satisfaction of multiple and possibly conflicting stakeholder interests can become difficult at times. Also, there may be a tendency for the interests of owners and customers to dominate those of other stakeholders. When asked what a business firm's top priority should be, 75 percent of MBA students in one recent study indicated it was "maximizing shareholder value"; 71 percent said "satisfying customers." Only 25 percent included "creating value for communities" as a top priority, and only 5 percent listed "concern for environmentalism" at the top.[4]

Do you agree with the priorities in this sample of MBAs? Or, do you view the relationship between business and its stakeholders somewhat differently?

| Figure 5.1 | Who are the stakeholders of organizations? |

Federal, state, local governments · Educational institutions · Employees · Competitors · Suppliers · Political parties · **Business firm** · Court and legal institutions · Labor unions · Customers · Stockholders · Public-interest groups · Financial institutions

Stakeholders are the individuals, groups, and other organizations that have a direct interest in how well an organization performs. A basic list of stakeholders for any organization would begin with the employees and contractors who work for the organization, customers and clients who consume the goods and services produced, suppliers of needed resources, owners who invest capital, regulators in the form of government agencies, and special interest groups such as community members and activists.

Stakeholders are people and institutions most directly affected by an organization's performance.

Corporate social responsibility is the obligation of an organization to serve its own interests and those of its stakeholders.

• Social Responsibility Is an Organization's Obligation to Best Serve Society

The way organizations behave in relationship with their stakeholders is a good indicator of their underlying ethical characters.[5] There is quite a difference, for example, between the "profits with principles" approach of Tom's of Maine and the "profits and personal gain" ways that seemed to drive Enron Corporation before its notorious collapse.[6]

When we talk about the "good" and the "bad" in business and society relationships, **corporate social responsibility** is at issue. It is defined as an obligation of the organization to act in ways that serve both its own interests and the interests of its stakeholders, representing society at large.[7] And even though *irresponsibility* seems to get most of the media's attention, we can't forget that there is a lot of responsible behavior taking place.

Not too long ago, Deloitte & Touche, one of the world's largest accounting firms, all but closed its doors for a day. Instead of working, many of the firm's employees volunteered over 240,000

PACESETTERS

Businessman believes Africa can solve its own problems

"Trade not aid" is a common, if not controversial, expression these days. But for Andrew Rugasira it is a message that resonates. Educated in London, the Ugandan businessman is a strong believer that African countries can solve their own problems if given access to markets in the developed countries. He says that African countries need to "trade their ways out of economic underdevelopment." His contributions began with a food and commodity trading company, VR Promotions. His latest venture is the Rwenzori Coffee Company. It buys from over 10,000 small producers at prices above the market and then returns one-half of its profits to the growers and their communities. Corruption, admits Rugasira, is one of the big problems of the African business environment. But, he also says: "The only way you get around corruption in the long term is to build a community of stakeholders. The more Africans get trading, earning incomes, buying houses, owning property, the less willing they will be to tolerate corruption."

Andrew Rugasira, Rwenzori Coffee Company.

hours of community service in cities throughout the United States.[8] IBM has a program to help retiring workers with science and math skills to become certified teachers; Google set up a philanthropic foundation to be funded by 1 percent of its equity and profits; Procter & Gamble invests in venture capital funds for minority businesses.[9] Each of Timberland Company's full-time employees gets 40 hours of paid time per year for community volunteer work. One person that turned down a higher-paying job elsewhere says: "Timberland's motto is 'when you come to work in the morning, don't leave your values at the door.' "[10]

The list of socially responsible examples can go on. Look for examples of your own and check out Management Tips. When it does come to social irresponsibility, organizations today are finding it harder to hide from public scrutiny. Their activities anywhere in the world are increasingly transparent in our technology-driven information age. The media is quick to find and publicize cases of misbehavior; activist groups and governments pressure organizations to respect and protect everything from human rights to the natural environment; some large investment groups will only buy shares in companies that meet special criteria of social responsibility.

And when you do consider the responsibility practices of organizations, dig a bit deeper than the surface of the examples. You may notice that some firms and organizations seem to act in socially responsible ways out of pure *compliance*—that is, with the desire to avoid adverse consequences. But sometimes, perhaps in the examples just cited, organizations seem to act out of *conviction*—that is, with the desire to create positive impact.[11] Quite obviously, conviction would seem to put an organization higher up on the social responsibility scale than compliance.

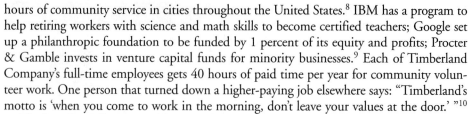

A **social responsibility audit** assesses an organization's accomplishments in areas of social responsibility.

• Social Performance by Organizations Can Be Evaluated in Different Ways

Management scholar Archie Carroll suggests that the social performance of organizations can be assessed using a **social responsibility audit**, much as the IRS audits income tax returns to ensure compliance with tax regulations.[12] The basic framework for such an audit might start with the following four questions, with each probing a bit higher on the compliance–commitment scale of social responsibility.

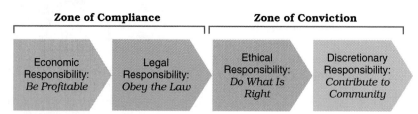

Zone of Compliance		Zone of Conviction	
Economic Responsibility: *Be Profitable*	Legal Responsibility: *Obey the Law*	Ethical Responsibility: *Do What Is Right*	Discretionary Responsibility: *Contribute to Community*

Criteria for evaluating corporate social performance.

Question 1 asks: Is the organization's *economic responsibility* met? According to Carroll, an organization meets its economic responsibility when it earns a profit by providing goods and services desired by customers. Question 2 asks: Is the organization's *legal responsibility* met? That is, does it obey the law? An organization fulfills its legal responsibility when it operates within the law and according to the requirements of any government regulations.

Question 3 asks: Is the organization's *ethical responsibility* met? Is it doing the right things? An organization meets its ethical responsibility when its actions voluntarily conform not just to minimum legal expectations, but to the broader values and moral expectations of society. Question 4 asks: Is the organization's *discretionary responsibility* met?

Does it contribute to the broader community? At this highest level of social performance, the organization voluntarily moves beyond basic economic, legal, and ethical expectations to provide leadership in advancing the well-being of individuals, communities, and society as a whole.

Carroll's questions are a good outline for a basic social responsibility audit. However, we could probably create additional ones that get even more specific. Why not ask how well a firm performs in respect to environmental protection, truth in lending, product safety, consumer protection, corporate philanthropy, aid to education, and so on? Wouldn't it be good, for example, to assess an organization's employee benefit schemes, diversity practices, labor relations practices, and service to communities?

• Scholars Argue Cases for and against Corporate Social Responsibility

You may or may not be surprised to learn that not everyone agrees that organizations should make social responsibility a top business goal. Two contrasting views of corporate social responsibility, the classical view and the socioeconomic view, have stimulated quite a bit of debate in academic and public policy circles.[13]

The *classical view* holds that management's only responsibility in running a business is to maximize profits, and thereby shareholder value. In other words: "The business of business is business." Milton Friedman, a respected economist and Nobel Laureate, supports this view. He says: "Few trends could so thoroughly undermine the very foundations of our free society as the acceptance by corporate officials of social responsibility other than to make as much money for their stockholders as possible."[14]

The *socioeconomic view* holds that management of any organization should be concerned for the broader social welfare, not just corporate profits. Paul Samuelson, another distinguished economist and also a Nobel Laureate, supports this perspective. He states: "A large corporation these days not only may engage in social responsibility, it had damn well better try to do so."[15] And, management theorist Keith Davis once responded to critics of social responsibility with this statement:[16]

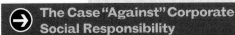

The Case "Against" Corporate Social Responsibility

- **Reduces business profits**
- **Creates higher business costs**
- **Dilutes business purpose**
- **Gives too much social power to business**

> *Society wants business as well as all other major institutions to assume significant social responsibility. Social responsibility has become the hallmark of a mature, global organization. . . . The business which vacillates or chooses not to enter the arena of social responsibility may find that it gradually will sink into customer and public disfavor.*

The Case "in Favor of" Corporate Social Responsibility

- **Increases long-run profits**
- **Improves public image**
- **Helps avoid government regulation**
- **Businesses have resources and ethical obligations to act responsibly**

At the very least, the argument that commitments to social responsibility will hurt the "bottom line" of businesses is getting harder to defend. The worst-case scenario seems to be that social responsibility has no adverse financial impact. And even though there is no guarantee that it will pay off in better bottom lines, some research has linked social responsibility with strong financial performance.[17] There is also some evidence for the existence of a **virtuous circle** in the social responsibility and performance relationship.[18] This occurs when corporate social responsibility leads to improved financial performance that, in turn, leads to more socially responsible actions in the future.

The **virtuous circle** is when corporate social responsibility leads to improved financial performance that leads to more social responsibility.

• Organizations Follow Different Social Responsibility Strategies

Even though you might find Davis's statement and the concept of the virtuous circle appealing, the reality is that organizations still vary widely in how they deal with social responsibility issues. Figure 5.2 shows a continuum of four corporate social responsibility strategies. Notice that the commitment to social responsibility is lowest with the "obstructionist" strategy and highest with the "proactive" strategy.[19]

When an organization follows an **obstructionist strategy**, "Fight the social demands," it puts economic priorities ahead of everything else. The organization resists doing anything outside of its perceived self-interests. If criticized for wrongdoing, it is likely to deny the claims; the official response might even be "It didn't happen."[20] When you next hear of a business fighting court orders to clean up waste dumped in a landfill or to remove

An **obstructionist strategy** avoids social responsibility and reflects mainly economic priorities.

Proactive strategy
"Take leadership in social initiatives"
Meet economic, legal, ethical, *and* discretionary responsibilities

Accommodative strategy
"Do minimum ethically required"
Meet economic, legal, and ethical responsibilities

Defensive strategy
"Do minimum legally required"
Meet economic and legal responsibilities

Obstructionist strategy
"Fight social demands"
Meet economic responsibilities

Commitment to corporate social responsibilities

Organizations approach their social responsibilities in different ways. The least committed ones pursue obstructionist strategies that actively fight against social demands. At the next higher levels come defensive strategies (do the minimum to meet legal requirements), and accommodative strategies (do the ethical minimum). The most committed organizations pursue proactive strategies that show active leadership in pursuing social initiatives.

a chemical ingredient from a product, these are good indicators of an obstructionist approach to social responsibility.

One step up from acting in obstructionist ways is the **defensive strategy**, "Do the minimum *legally* required." The organization tries to protect itself and satisfy critics by doing only what the law requires, and perhaps waiting for lawsuits or new laws before changing its behavior. Corporate decision making at this level is likely to be driven by competitive market pressures or outside scrutiny by the legal system and activist groups. When criticized, "It's not our fault" may be a common cry.[21]

Some organizations pursue an **accommodative strategy**, "Do the minimum *ethically* required." In social audits we would expect them to satisfy Carroll's economic, legal, and ethical criteria of social performance. But their behavior may still be prompted by outside pressures. For example, it was after, not before, Starbucks was criticized for paying low prices to coffee growers in developing countries that the firm took action. Then it went full bore, opening its books to activists, buying more "fair trade" coffee from environmentally friendly farmers, and helping fund health clinics and schools for the coffee farmers' children.[22]

The **proactive strategy**, "Take leadership in social initiatives," tries to meet all of Carroll's criteria of social performance, including discretionary performance. Socially responsible behavior at this level is internally driven and the firm shows active leadership in identifying and using its resources to respond to emerging social issues. You could argue that social responsibility becomes part of the basic business model.[23] Intel, for example, won the *Business Ethics* CSR Management Award for its proactivity in combating supply chain management problems, such as sweatshop operations. Dave Stangis, Intel's director of corporate responsibility, said: " . . . we decided to band together with other companies and take a leadership position on the issue." This resulted in the Electronics Industry Code of Conduct.[24]

A **defensive strategy** seeks protection by doing the minimum legally required.

An **accommodative strategy** accepts social responsibility and tries to satisfy economic, legal, and ethical criteria.

A **proactive strategy** meets all the criteria of social responsibility, including discretionary performance.

STUDY GUIDE

5.1 What should we know about organizational environments and social responsibility?

Be Sure You Can . . .

- list key elements in the general environments of organizations

- differentiate the general and specific environments

- describe the stakeholders for a business in your local community

- identify where interests of different stakeholders might be conflicting

- explain the concept of social responsibility

- summarize arguments for and against corporate social responsibility

- illustrate how the virtuous circle of corporate social responsibility might work

- identify four criteria for measuring corporate social performance

- give examples of four social responsibility strategies used by organizations

Define the Terms

Accommodative strategy

Corporate social
  responsibility

Defensive strategy

General environment

Obstructionist strategy

Proactive strategy

Social responsibility
  audit

Specific environment
  stakeholders

Virtuous circle

Rapid Review

- The general environment includes background economic, sociocultural, legal-political, technological, and natural environment conditions.

- The specific environment consists of suppliers, customers, competitors, regulators, and other stakeholders with whom an organization interacts.

- Corporate social responsibility is an obligation of the organization to act in ways that serve both its own interests and the interests of its stakeholders.

- Criteria for evaluating corporate social performance include how well it meets economic, legal, ethical, and discretionary responsibilities.

- The argument against corporate social responsibility says that businesses should focus on making profits; the argument for corporate social responsibility says that businesses should use their resources to serve broader social concerns.

- Businesses follow different social responsibility strategies, including obstruction, defense, accommodation, and proaction.

Reflect/React

1. If the interests of an organization's investors/owners conflict with those of community stakeholders, whose interests should be taken care of first?

2. Choose an organization in your community; what questions would you include on a social audit of its operations?

3. Is the logic of the virtuous circle a convincing argument in favor of corporate social responsibility?

Corporate governance is the oversight of top management by a board of directors.

When we admit that organizations and their leaders can have different approaches toward social responsibility, it raises an issue first discussed in Module 1: governance. We have been using the term **corporate governance** to describe oversight of the top management of an organization by its board of directors. Active governance typically involves hiring, firing, and compensating the CEO; assessing business strategy; verifying financial records; and, more generally making sure that the firm operates in the best interests of the owners and shareholders. One board member describes his governance responsibilities this way: "It's really about setting and maintaining high standards."[25]

• Failures of Ethics and Social Responsibility Prompt Calls for Stronger Governance

It is tempting to think that corporate governance is a clear-cut way to ensure that organizations behave with social responsibility and that their leaders behave ethically. But every new case of business irresponsibility or ethical failures by corporate executives is a reminder that governance is ineffectual in some cases and nonexistent in others. And the issues don't have to be sensational for us to call governance into question.

Consider a topic that we will discuss again in a later module on motivation and rewards—CEO performance and compensation. Have you read about CEOs who receive big raises and financial rewards even when their firms perform poorly, or receive big "buyouts" when their employment is terminated? Where is governance in these cases?

When Morgan Stanley's board voted to pay Philip Purcell $113 million to oust him from the company, many investors were enraged. Although we might applaud the directors for removing him, don't you wonder why they agreed to pay him so much to leave?

In another case, the former CEO of Boeing was allowed to receive $600,000 a year, even though he stepped down due to an extramarital affair that violated the firm's code of conduct—a code he helped to write.[26] Was this good governance?

Examples like these are reminders about both the needs for and the complexities of governance in any organization, business or nonprofit. Would you join in calls for board members to step up and rigorously fulfill their governance responsibilities and make sure that top managers perform up to expectations? And among these expectations, would you include standards of ethics and social responsibility, not just financial performance, as top priorities?

• Weak Corporate Governance Can Result in More Government Regulation

When governance is weak and corporate scandals occur, you will sometimes see government stepping in to try and correct things for the future. Laws are passed and regulating agencies are put in place in an attempt to better control and direct business behavior. The **Sarbanes-Oxley Act**, discussed briefly in the previous module, is one example. Passed by Congress in 2002 in response to public

NEWSLINE

Nonprofit supports social accountability worldwide Among nonprofit organizations, Social Accountability International (SAI) stands tall for its dedication to workers and their communities around the world. The organization describes its mission as "setting standards for a just world." In practice, this involves the organization's commitment to improving workplaces and combating sweatshops through the expansion and further development of the international workplace standards known as SA8000 and S8000. Nine categories of social accountability are measured: child labor, forced labor, health and safety, freedom of association and the right to collective bargaining, discrimination, discipline, working hours, remuneration, and management systems. Certification is voluntary, but unions and nongovernmental organizations (NGOs) highly regard it. There are SAI certified firms in more than 30 countries and industries.

Reflect: How much impact can organizations like SAI have in a world with such great differences between rich and poor nations? Is there a role for an organization to perform a similar social accountability mission in your state or even local community?

outcries over major ethics and business scandals, its goal is to ensure that top managers properly oversee the financial conduct of their organizations. Although the jury is still out on the Act's effectiveness, a *Wall Street Journal* survey suggests that business executives are starting to embrace corporate governance reform. They also see its value in terms of enhanced corporate reputations.[27]

Government regulation of businesses and other organizations extends well beyond the territory of Sarbanes-Oxley. For example, in the area of *worker safety and health*, the Occupational Safety and Health Act (OSHA) of 1970 firmly established the federal government's interest in protecting employee health and safety on the job. Even though some complain that the regulations are still too weak, the Act does influence the concerns of employers and government policymakers for worker safety. In respect to *fair labor practices*, a variety of legislation is designed to prohibit discrimination in labor practices. For example, the Equal Employment Opportunity (EEO) Act of 1972 and related regulations help to reduce barriers to employment based on race, gender, age, national origin, and marital status.

STAY INFORMED

Senior executives identify benefits of positive corporate reputations:

- Easier to recruit and retain employees
- Able to generate additional sales
- Facilitates strategic transactions and partnerships
- Able to charge premium prices
- Better stock price performance
- Better public and government relations

Consumer protection is another area of regulatory interest. The Consumer Product Safety Act of 1972 gives government the authority to examine and force a business to withdraw from sale any product that it feels might harm the consumer, such as children's toys and flammable fabrics. And in respect to *environmental protection*, the Air Pollution Control Act of 1962 is but one of many examples. It was passed with the goal of eliminating careless pollution of the air, water, and land, something you might think would be avoided if corporate governance did its job right in the first place.

Although this was just a sampling of the complex legal environment surrounding business today, such laws demonstrate that weak governance does not go unnoticed by our lawmakers. Of course we often hear business executives complaining about the burdens imposed by the increased regulations. And they do have a point. But the fact is we wouldn't need the laws and have the regulators if all organizations were socially responsible and all of their leaders were highly ethical in the first place.

• Moral Management Builds Capacities for Self-Governance in Organizations

When it comes to ethical leadership in organizations, Archie Carroll makes a distinction between amoral, immoral, and moral managers.[28] The **immoral manager** chooses to behave unethically. He or she does something purely for personal gain, and intentionally disregards the ethics of the action or situation. The **amoral manager** also disregards the ethics of an act or decision, but does so unintentionally. This manager simply fails to consider the ethical consequences of his or her actions. In contrast to both prior types, the **moral manager** considers ethical behavior as a personal goal. He or she makes decisions and acts always in full consideration of ethical issues.

Immoral manager chooses to behave unethically.

Amoral manager disregards the ethics of an act or decision, but does so unintentionally.

Moral manager considers ethical behavior as a personal goal.

Chooses to behave unethically	Fails to consider ethics	Makes ethical behavior a personal goal
Immoral manager	Amoral manager	Moral manager

Which of these three types of managers do you believe is most common in the real world of work? Which might best describe you, not just as a manager but in your

Leadership impact on ethics mindfulness

Amoral leadership, "Negative shift"

Moral leadership, "Virtuous shift"

Organizational ethics center of gravity

People with high levels of ethics mindfulness are always considering ethical aspects of decisions. Moral leaders are ethically mindful. They become role models that influence and help others to develop ethics mindfulness. Through positive example, communication, and inspiration they help shift the ethics center of gravity for an organization in a positive direction. When leaders are amoral or immoral, however, their influence on others can create a negative shift in the ethics center of gravity.

(Source: Terry Thomas, John R. Schermerhorn, Jr., and John W. Dinehart, "Strategic Leadership of Ethical Behavior in Business," Academy of Management Executive, Vol. 18 (May 2004, pp. 56–66.)

Ethics mindfulness is enriched awareness that leads to consistent ethical behavior.

approach to day-to-day living? As much as it might surprise you, Carroll actually suggests that most of us act amorally. Although well intentioned, we remain mostly uninformed or undisciplined in considering the ethical aspects of our behavior.

Now, put yourself at the top of an organization and ask the question of what difference moral management can make. In answer, Figure 5.3 shows how leaders can influence the "ethics center of gravity" of the organization as a whole.[29] The key is **ethics mindfulness**—a state of enriched awareness that causes a person to behave ethically from one situation to the next. Moral managers are leaders with ethics mindfulness. And by communicating ethical values and serving as ethics role models they can help move the ethics center of gravity of the whole organization in a positive direction, contributing to a virtuous shift. Of course amoral and immoral leaders can be just as influential, but their impact on the ethics center of gravity is largely negative rather than positive.

If you buy into the notions of ethics mindfulness and an ethics center of gravity for organizations, it raises the possibility that organizations have the capacity to become self-governing. This would occur when governance becomes a shared responsibility at all levels of management and among all members of the organization, not just something that Boards of Directors are expected to do.

Although you might find this idealistic, why can't we get to the point where the right things happen because people throughout an organization act morally as a matter of routine? Why can't we expand the "bottom line" of performance accountability at any level, individual, group, or organizational, to include achieving performance objectives in ethical and socially responsible ways?

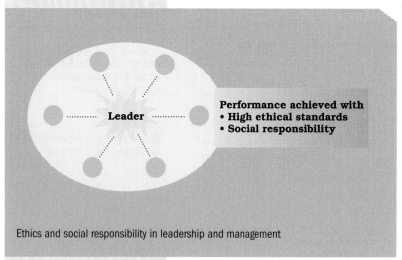

Leader

Performance achieved with
• High ethical standards
• Social responsibility

Ethics and social responsibility in leadership and management

5.2 What are current issues in corporate governance?

Be Sure You Can . . .

- explain the role of governance in business and nonprofit organizations

- illustrate how governments use legislation to influence business behavior

- describe how moral management can shift an organization's ethics center of gravity

- define ethics mindfulness

- explain a team leader's performance accountability in a way that includes the notion of self-governance

Define the Terms

Amoral manager	Moral manager
Corporate governance	Sarbanes-Oxley Act
Ethics mindfulness	
Immoral manager	

Rapid Review

- There are many pressures to strengthen corporate governance as active oversight of management decisions, corporate strategies, and financial performance by organizations.

- Governments sometimes enact laws to regulate business behavior and make up for weak governance; an example is the Sarbanes-Oxley Act.

- Immoral managers choose to behave unethically; amoral managers fail to consider ethics; moral managers make ethics a personal goal.

- Moral management by top leaders can shift the ethics center of gravity in organizations in a positive direction, thus strengthening capacities for self-governance.

- Managers at all levels should accept their responsibilities for achieving performance objectives in ways that are ethical and socially responsible.

Reflect/React

1. Does the concept of governance differ between businesses and nonprofit organizations?

2. Should government play a stronger role in making up for weak corporate governance?

3. Can amoral and moral managers lead organizations equally well?

MODULE

5

TEST PREP
Take the complete set of Module 5 quizzes online!

Multiple Choice

1. The general environment of a business firm includes such things as _____.
(a) social values (b) regulating agencies (c) competitors (d) customers

2. From a value creation standpoint, the stakeholders with the most direct interest in a firm's profits and losses are the _____.
(a) employees (b) local communities (c) owners and investors (d) suppliers

3. A proponent of the classical view of corporate social responsibility would most likely agree with which of these statements?
(a) Social responsibility improves the public image of business. (b) The primary responsibility of business is to maximize profits. (c) By acting responsibly, businesses avoid government regulation. (d) Businesses should do good while they are doing business.

4. The criterion of _____ responsibility identifies the highest level of conviction by an organization to operate in a responsible manner.
(a) economic (b) legal (c) ethical (d) discretionary

5. An organization that demonstrates leadership in addressing emerging social issues is trying to be _____ in its corporate social responsibility strategy.
(a) accommodative (b) obstructionist (c) defensive (d) proactive

6. An organization that always tries to satisfy its economic, legal, and ethical responsibilities can described as following a/an _____ social responsibility strategy.
(a) accommodative (b) obstructionist (c) defensive (d) proactive

7. The U.S. Equal Opportunity Act of 1972 is an example of government regulation of business in the area of _____.
(a) fair labor practices (b) consumer protection (c) environmental protection (d) occupational safety and health

8. Which well-known economist is most associated with the case against corporate social responsibility?
(a) Paul Samuelson (b) Milton Friedman (c) Alan Greenspan (d) Kofi Annan

9. A manager that displays ethics mindfulness is most likely to be _____.
(a) amoral (b) mindful of the penalties for unethical behavior (c) continually thinking about ethical aspects of decisions (d) a top manager rather than a first-line manager

10. A manager contributes to an organization's self-governance when he or she always tries to achieve performance objectives in ways that are_____.
(a) consistent with the ethics center of gravity (b) cost efficient (c) quality oriented (d) ethical and socially responsible

Short Response

11. What is the major case against corporate social responsibility?

12. What is the virtuous circle of corporate social responsibility?

13. What decisions should a Board of Directors oversee in order to fulfill its governance responsibilities?

14. What is the difference between an amoral and an immoral manager?

Integration & Application

Not too long ago Kraft Foods announced that it was going to ban some food ads to children.[30] A U.S. government study had linked advertising to childhood obesity, which placed Kraft at risk for criticism. Soon after the study was publicized, Kraft announced that it was going to stop some advertising to young kids. The move caught Kraft's competitors by surprise, put some of Kraft's sales at risk, and was praised by lawmakers.

Questions: If you were to conduct a social audit of Kraft Foods, at which of Carroll's four levels of social responsibility would you place the firm based on this set of circumstances? What appears to be Kraft's social responsibility strategy? How do you justify your answers based on the limited information provided?

SELF-ASSESSMENT
Turbulence Tolerance

INSTRUCTIONS *How would you like to have a job with these characteristics?*

0 = This feature would be very unpleasant for me.
1 = This feature would be somewhat unpleasant for me.
2 = I'd have no reaction to this feature one way or another.
3 = This would be enjoyable and acceptable most often.
4 = I would enjoy this very much; it's completely acceptable.

1 I spend 30–40 percent of my time in meetings.
2 Eighteen months ago my job did not exist, and I have been essentially inventing it as I go along.
3 At any given moment in my job, I have on the average about a dozen phone calls to be returned.
4 There seems little relation between my performance and my pay.
5 My job brings me into contact with people of many races, ethnic groups, and nationalities, and of both sexes.
6 I report to three different bosses for different aspects of my job.
7 About a third of my time is spent on emergencies.
8 I am out of town at least one night per week.
9 During my time here, we have reorganized every year or so.
10 While I anticipate promotions I have no realistic chance of getting to the top of the company.

SCORING AND INTERPRETATION

Add your scores and divide by 10. This is your "Turbulence Tolerance" (TT) score.

It may be interpreted much like a grade point average in which 4.0 is a perfect "A."

PATHWAYS to WileyPLUS

CASE SNAPSHOT

Go online to read this case!
BURT'S BEES: DOING GOOD, DOING BUSINESS

Homespun and proud of it, Burt's Bees stays environmentally conscious while maintaining strong growth. Could growing pains challenge the company's ethical progress? And how long can the skin-care giant stay independent *and* profitable?

MODULE 5 — Online Interactive Learning Resources

Skill Builder
• Professionalism

Experiential Exercise
• Stakeholder Maps

Team Project
• Corporate Social Responsibility

There are new faces

Diversity and Global Cultures

The facts are not refutable: we live and work in a diverse and global society.[1] And one of the firms praised by Working Mother magazine as among America's best employers for women of color is Hewlett-Packard. VP of Culture and Diversity, Emily Duncan, says: " . . .our culture . . .is all about creating a workplace that gives employees the tools and resources to work to their best potential."[2]

But the story doesn't stop there, or in America. Hewlett-Packard isn't just a business; it's a global giant.

Around the world HP's management is made up of 20 percent women, yet in Japan the figure is only 4 percent. These numbers don't meet HP's diversity standards. A new mentoring program has been started in HP

in the neighborhood

Japan with the goal of increasing the number of female managers. Aikio Dawai, the head of this program, says: "We had to do something." She also notes that when Japanese women are able to network with successful female executives they realize that " . . .rising to the top is not an impossible dream but something they can actually do themselves."[3]

Knowing all this, would it surprise you that HP is also highly regarded for its social responsibility practices? *Forbes* magazine gives it "A's" for approaches to diversity, community, and the environment.[4] It might be that the "best" firms try to be the best in all areas of performance, serving the interests of all stakeholders.

Why not do your own research? Start with the top 10 firms on *The Black Collegian's* list of best diversity employers: BMW, Johnson & Johnson, Goldman Sachs, IBM, Microsoft, Citigroup, McKinsey & Company, Deloitte, Coca-Cola, and JPMorganChase. Check also *Fortune's* "50 Best Companies for Minorities" and *Working Mother's* "100 Best Companies for Working Mothers." Such comparisons are not only information, they are a good way to start thinking about the qualities you expect from employers now and in your future career.

➜ Diversity Trends in U.S. Workforce

- People of color increasing percent of workforce
- Hispanics fastest-growing minority group in workforce
- Minorities highly represented in lower-wage service-sector jobs
- More workers from nontraditional families
- Average age of workers rising
- Religious diversity of workers increasing
- More women working

➜ MODULE GUIDE

 6.1 What should we know about diversity in the workplace?

- There is a business case for diversity.
- Inclusive organizational cultures value and support diversity.
- Organizational subcultures can create diversity challenges.
- Minorities and women suffer diversity bias in many situations.
- Managing diversity should be top leadership priority.

 6.2 What should we know about diversity among global cultures?

- Culture shock comes from discomfort in cross-cultural situations.
- Cultural intelligence is the capacity to adapt to foreign cultures.
- The "silent" languages of cultures include context, time, and space.
- Hofstede identifies five value differences among national cultures.
- Project GLOBE identifies ten country clusters displaying cultural differences.

Diversity describes race, gender, age, and other individual differences.

In Module 1 we first discussed diversity in respect to age, race, ethnicity, gender, physical ability, and sexual orientation. A broad definition of workplace **diversity** would also include differences in such areas as religious beliefs, education, experience, family status, national cultures, and perhaps more.[5] In his book *Beyond Race and Gender*, diversity consultant R. Roosevelt Thomas, Jr., goes so far as to say that "diversity includes everyone . . . white males are as diverse as their colleagues."[6]

• There Is a Business Case for Diversity

One of Thomas's main points is that diversity is good for organizations, that it is a potential source of competitive advantage. Picture an organization whose diverse employees reflect a mixture of talents and perspectives, and are representative of the firm's customers and clients. Wouldn't this be good for business?

Lou Gerstner, former CEO of IBM, thinks so. He once said that at IBM: "We made diversity a market-based issue . . . it's about understanding our markets which are diverse and multicultural."[7] Reports from IBM attribute the growth in its sales to minority- and women-owned smaller businesses with the increased presence of women and minorities in its management ranks.[8] Also, the New York research group Catalyst reports that companies with a greater percentage of women on their boards outperform those whose boards have the lowest female representation.[9] All of this points toward what some call a strong "business case for diversity."[10]

> ### Arguments in the Business Case for Diversity
>
> - Cultural diversity builds strength for dealing with global markets.
> - Ethnic diversity builds strength for dealing with diverse customers.
> - Diverse work teams are high in creativity and innovation.
> - Diverse workforces attract new highly talented members.

But just having a diverse workforce doesn't necessarily guarantee organizational success. If all members of this workforce are not fully respected by management and one another, and if they are not actively engaged in day-to-day affairs, it is highly unlikely that any diversity benefits will be realized. In fact, Thomas Kochan and his colleagues at MIT found in their research that it is only when managers leverage diversity through training and supportive human resource practices that they gain the hoped-for advantages.[11] They advise:

To be successful in working with and gaining value from diversity requires a sustained, systemic approach and long-term commitment. Success is facilitated by a perspective that considers diversity to be an opportunity for everyone in an organization to learn from each other how better to accomplish their work and an occasion that requires a supportive and cooperative organizational culture as well as group leadership and process skills that can facilitate effective group functioning.

• Inclusive Organizational Cultures Value and Support Diversity

Just how do managers go about leveraging diversity in the workplace? Many organizations seem to be good or relatively good at attracting new employees of diverse backgrounds to join, but they aren't always successful in keeping them for the long term. This problem of high employee turnover among minorities and women has been called the "revolving door" syndrome.[12] It can reflect a lack of **inclusivity** in the employing organizations—that is, the degree to which they are open to anyone who can perform a job, regardless of race, sexual preference, gender, or other diversity attribute.[13]

Inclusivity is how open the organization is to anyone who can perform a job

Look around; think about how people are treating those who differ from themselves. What about your experiences at school and at work? Are you always treated with respect and inclusion? Or, do you sense at times disrespect and exclusion?

When an organization is truly inclusive, its internal climate or **culture** is rich in beliefs, values, and expectations that respect and empower the full potential of a diverse workforce. The model for inclusivity is the **multicultural organization** that displays commitments to diversity like those in the Exhibit – *Characteristics of a Multicultural Organization*.[14]

• Organizational Subcultures Can Create Diversity Challenges

We have to be realistic in facing up to the challenges in creating truly multicultural organizations; it isn't always easy to get the members of a workforce to really respect and work well with one another. One of the reasons is the existence of **organizational subcultures**. These are informal groupings of persons with shared identities.

Organizational subcultures can form around such things as gender, age, race and ethnicity, and even job functions. And they can create diversity challenges. People can get so caught up in their subcultures that they often identify and interact mostly with others who are like themselves. They may develop tendencies toward **ethnocentrism**, acting in ways that suggest that their ways are superior to all others. All of this generally makes it harder for people from different organizational subcultures to work well together.

Consider, for example, the subcultures that form around our *occupational identities*. Some employees may consider themselves "systems people" who are very different from "those marketing people" and even more different still from "those finance people." Even at school, in course project groups, have you noticed how students tend to identify themselves by their majors? Don't some students look down on others who they consider as pursuing "easy" majors, or seem to view their own majors as the most superior ones?

Whereas this discussion may have caused you to think for the first time about occupational subcultures, you don't need a reminder that cultures vary around the world. We'll be discussing these global cultural dimensions later in this module. For now, though, how familiar are you with the cultures of our neighborhoods, communities, and workplaces? How much do you know about African-American or Latino or Anglo or Asian or Islamic cultures?[15] Many corporations are quick to invest in cross-cultural training of workers to help improve their global businesses. But how much is invested in helping people understand the racial and ethnic subcultures they come into contact with every day?

And while speaking about subcultures, we shouldn't forget age. The *Harvard Business Review* reports that today's teenagers, the "Millennial" generation, are highly ambitious and prefer job mobility;[16] Harris and Conference Board polls report younger workers tend to be more dissatisfied than older workers.[17] They are also described as more short-term oriented, giving higher priority to work-life balance, and expecting to hold at least five jobs during their careers.[18] Imagine the possible conflicts that can occur when a member of the Millennial generation leaves college and goes to work for a manager from the Baby Boomer generation who started working in the late 1960s or early 1970s. As suggested in Management Tips, each may have to take special steps in order to work really well with the other.[19]

EXHIBIT

Characteristics of a Multicultural Organization

Pluralism Members of minority and majority cultures influence key values and policies.

Structural integration Minority-culture members are well represented at all levels and in all responsibilities.

Informal network integration Mentoring and support groups assist career development of minority-culture members.

Absence of prejudice and discrimination Training and task force activities support goal of eliminating culture-group biases.

Minimum intergroup conflict Members of minority and majority cultures avoid destructive conflicts.

Culture is a shared set of beliefs, values, and patterns of behavior common to a group of people.

A **multicultural organization** is based on pluralism and operates with inclusivity and respect for diversity.

Organizational subcultures are groupings of people based on shared demographic and job identities.

Ethnocentrism is the belief that one's membership group or subculture is superior to all others.

MANAGEMENT TIPS

Tips for working with members of different generations

With Baby Boomers:
• Show respect—let them know you're willing to learn from them.
• Use face-to-face conversations to be more personal.
• Give full attention when trying to communicate.
• Be diplomatic; workplace politics are a fact of life.
• Show respect for the past; find out what's happened before.

With Millennials:
• Challenge them—give meaningful work.
• Reward them with responsibility and recognition for accomplishments.
• Ask their opinions, avoid command-and-control approaches.
• Link them with an older mentor.
• Give timely feedback; they're used to instantaneous gratification.

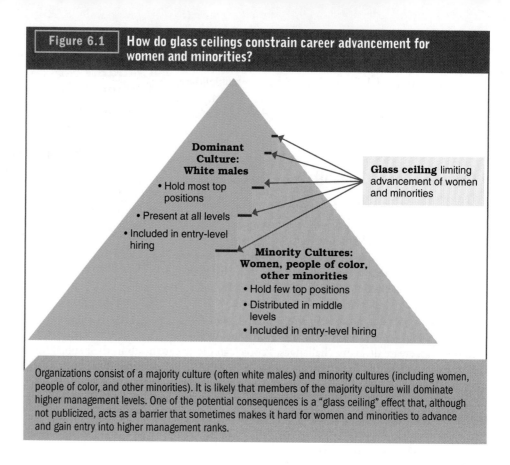

Figure 6.1 How do glass ceilings constrain career advancement for women and minorities?

Dominant Culture: White males
- Hold most top positions
- Present at all levels
- Included in entry-level hiring

Glass ceiling limiting advancement of women and minorities

Minority Cultures: Women, people of color, other minorities
- Hold few top positions
- Distributed in middle levels
- Included in entry-level hiring

Organizations consist of a majority culture (often white males) and minority cultures (including women, people of color, and other minorities). It is likely that members of the majority culture will dominate higher management levels. One of the potential consequences is a "glass ceiling" effect that, although not publicized, acts as a barrier that sometimes makes it hard for women and minorities to advance and gain entry into higher management ranks.

• Minorities and Women Suffer Diversity Bias in Many Situations

The term "diversity" basically means the presence of differences, and that's both important and potentially challenging in its own right. But diversity issues in organizations are further complicated because such differences are often distributed unequally in the power structure. Let's be honest. Most senior executives in large businesses are still older, white, and male; there is more diversity among lower and middle levels of most organizations than at the top. And for some women and minority workers, the **glass ceiling** depicted in Figure 6.1 is a real barrier to career advancement.[20]

Jesse Spaulding experienced the glass ceiling while working as a regional manager for a restaurant chain owned by Shoney's. He says that the firm used to operate on the "buddy system," which "left people of color by the wayside" when it came to promotions. Fortunately, things changed when new leadership took over. Their commitments to diversity provided Spaulding with new opportunity. And *Fortune* magazine went on to include Shoney's in its list of America's 50 Best Companies for Minorities.[21]

Minorities and women can face work challenges that range from misunderstandings, to lack of sensitivity, to glass ceiling limitations, to outright job discrimination and harassment. One senior executive reports her surprise upon finding out that the top performer in her work group, an African-American male, was paid 25 percent less than anyone else. His pay increases over time had always trailed those given to white co-workers.[22]

The **glass ceiling** is a hidden barrier to the advancement of women and minorities.

STAY INFORMED

The Conundrum of the Glass Ceiling

In 1995
- Women held 45.7% of America's jobs.
- Women held .7% of CEO jobs.
- Women held 5% of top management jobs.
- Women managers earned 68% the pay of males.

In 2005
- Women held 46.5% of America's jobs.
- Women held .7% of CEO jobs.
- Women held 8% of top management jobs.
- Women managers earned 72% the pay of males.

People respond to bad treatment at work in different ways. Some may challenge the system by filing complaints, pursuing harassment and discrimination charges, taking legal action. Some may quit to look for better positions elsewhere, or to pursue self-employment opportunities. Some may try to "fit in," to adapt through **biculturalism** by displaying majority culture characteristics that seem necessary to succeed in the work environment. For example, gays and lesbians might hide their sexual orientation; an African-American or Hispanic manager might avoid using words or phrases at work that white colleagues would consider subculture slang; a woman might use football or baseball metaphors in conversations to gain acceptance into male-dominated networks.

Biculturalism is when minority members adopt characteristics of majority cultures in order to succeed.

• Managing Diversity Should Be Top Leadership Priority

What can leaders and managers do so that people are treated inclusively and don't need to fall back on these types of adaptive behaviors? The process begins with a willingness to recognize that, regardless of their backgrounds, most workers want the same things. They want respect for their talents; they want to be fairly treated; they want to be able to work to the best of their abilities; they want to achieve their full potential. Meeting these expectations requires the best in diversity leadership.

R. Roosevelt Thomas describes a continuum of leadership approaches to diversity.[23] At one end is *affirmative action*. Here, leadership commits the organization to hiring and advancing minorities and women. You might think of this as advancing diversity by increasing the representation of diverse members in the organization's workforce. But this is only a partial solution, and the revolving door syndrome may even negate some of its positive impact. Thomas says that the "assumption is that once you get representation, people will assimilate. But we're actually seeing that people are less willing to assimilate than ever before."[24]

Affirmative Action
Create upward mobility for minorities and women

Valuing Differences
Build quality relationships with respect for diversity

Managing Diversity
Achieve full utilization of diverse human resources

Leadership approaches to diversity

A step beyond affirmative action is what Thomas calls *valuing diversity*. Here, a leader commits the organization to education and training programs designed to help people better understand and respect individual differences. The goal is to teach people of diverse backgrounds more about one another, and how to work well together. Thomas says this training should help us deal with "similarities, differences and tensions." And, it should help us answer a fundamental question: "Can I work with people who are qualified that are not like me."[25]

The final step in Thomas's continuum is **managing diversity**. A leader who actively manages diversity is always seeking ways to make an organization truly multicultural and inclusive, and keep it that way. Eastman Kodak might be a good example. The firm is praised by *Business Ethics* magazine for "leading-edge anti-discrimination policies toward gay, bisexual, and transgender employees." It has also received a perfect score from the Human Rights Campaign for its efforts to end sexual discrimination.[26]

According to Thomas, leaders have a performance incentive to embrace managing diversity.[27] A diverse workforce offers a rich pool of talents, ideas, and viewpoints that can help solve complex problems; a diverse workforce aligns well with needs and expectations of diverse customers and stakeholders.[28] A racially and ethnically inclusive workplace can also be good for morale.[29] Michael R. Losey, president of the Society for Human Resource Management (SHRM), agrees. He says: "Companies must realize that the talent pool includes people of all types, including older workers; persons with disabilities; persons of various religious, cultural, and national backgrounds; persons who are not heterosexual; minorities; and women."[30]

Managing diversity is building an inclusive work environment that allows everyone to reach his or her potential.

STUDY GUIDE

6.1 What should we know about diversity in the workplace?

Be Sure You Can . . .

- identify major diversity trends in American society

- explain the business case for diversity

- explain the concept of inclusivity

- list characteristics of multicultural organizations

- identify subcultures common to organizations

- discuss the types of employment problems faced by minorities and women

- explain Thomas's concept of managing diversity

Define the Terms

Biculturalism	Inclusivity
Diversity	Managing diversity
Ethnocentrism	Multicultural organization
Glass ceiling	Organizational subcultures

Rapid Review

- Workforce diversity can improve business performance by expanding the talent pool of the organization and establishing better understandings of customers and stakeholders.

- Inclusivity is a characteristic of multicultural organizations that value and respect diversity of their members.

- Organizational subcultures, including those based on occupational, functional, ethnic, racial, age, and gender differences, can create diversity challenges.

- Minorities and women can suffer diversity bias in such forms as job and pay discrimination, sexual harassment, and the glass ceiling effect.

- A top leadership priority should be managing diversity to develop an inclusive work environment within which everyone is able to reach their full potential.

Reflect/React

1. Why don't current demographic trends and conditions make it easy to create truly multicultural organizations?

2. What are some of the things organizations and leaders can do to reduce diversity bias faced by minorities and women in the workplace?

3. What does the existence of an affirmative action policy say about an organization's commitment to diversity?

6.2 What Should We Know about Diversity among Global Cultures?

A trip to the grocery store, a day spent at work, a visit to our children's schools—all are possible opportunities for us to have cross-cultural experiences. And you have to admit, there's a lot of new faces in the neighborhood. At my university even a walk across campus can be a trip around the world, but we have to be willing to take it. How about you? Do you greet, speak with, and actively engage people of other cultures? Or are you shy, hesitant, and even inclined to avoid them?[31]

• Culture Shock Comes from Discomfort in Cross-Cultural Situations

Maybe it is a bit awkward to introduce yourself to an international student or foreign visitor to your community. Maybe the appearance of a Muslim woman in a head scarf, or a Nigerian man in a long overblouse is un-usual to the point of being intimidating. Maybe, too, when we do meet or work with someone from another culture we experience something well known to international travelers as **culture shock**. This is feelings of confusion and discomfort when in or dealing with an un-familiar culture.

International businesses are concerned about culture shock because they need their employees to be successful as they travel and work around the world. Management Tips summarizes a model they can use to help employees heading abroad to recognize and better deal with culture shock.[32] Perhaps some of these ideas might also be applied to our everyday cross-cultural experiences.

> **Culture shock** is the confusion and discomfort that a person experiences when in an unfamiliar culture.

MANAGEMENT TIPS

Stages of adjustment to a new culture

- *Confusion*—First contacts with the new culture leave you anxious, uncomfortable, and in need of information and advice.
- *Small victories*—Continued interactions bring some "successes," and your confidence grows in handling daily affairs.
- *Honeymoon*—A time of wonderment, cultural immersion, and even infatuation, with local ways viewed positively.
- *Irritation and anger*—A time when the "negatives" overwhelm the "positives," and the new culture becomes a target of your criticism.
- *Reality*—A time of rebalancing; you are able to enjoy the new culture while accommodating its less desirable elements.

• Cultural Intelligence Is the Capacity to Adapt to Foreign Cultures

A U.S. businessman once went to meet a Saudi Arabian official. He sat in the office with crossed legs and the sole of his shoe exposed, an unintentional sign of disrespect in the local culture. He passed documents to the host using his left hand, which Muslims consider unclean. He declined when coffee was offered, suggesting criticism of the Saudi's hospitality. What was the price for these cultural miscues? A $10 million contract was lost to a Korean executive better versed in Arab ways.[33]

Some might say that this American's behavior was ethnocentric, so self-centered that he ignored and showed no concern for the culture of his Arab host. Others might excuse him as suffering culture shock. Maybe he was so uncomfortable upon arrival in Saudi Arabia that all he could think about was offering his contract and leaving as quickly as possible. Still others might give him the benefit of the doubt. It could have been that he was well intentioned, but didn't have time to learn about Saudi culture before making the trip.

Regardless of the possible reasons for the cultural miscues, however, they still worked to his disadvantage. And there is little doubt that he failed to show **cultural intelligence**—the ability to adapt and adjust to new cultures.[34] People with cultural intelligence have high cultural self-awareness and are flexible in dealing with cultural differences. In cross-cultural situations they are willing to learn from what is

> **Cultural intelligence** is the ability to adapt to new cultures.

Low-context cultures emphasize communication via spoken or written words.

High-context cultures rely on nonverbal and situational cues as well as spoken or written words in communication.

In **monochronic cultures** people tend to do one thing at a time.

In **polychronic cultures** people accomplish many different things at once.

unfamiliar; they modify their behaviors to act with sensitivity to another culture's ways. In other words, someone high in cultural intelligence views cultural differences not as threats but as learning opportunities.

Cultural intelligence is probably a good indicator of someone's capacity for success in international assignments, and in relationships with persons of different cultures. How would you rate yourself? Could cultural intelligence be one of your important personal assets?

• The "Silent" Languages of Cultures Include Context, Time, and Space

It is easy to recognize differences in the spoken and written languages used by people around the world. And foreign language skills can open many doors to cultural understanding.[35] But anthropologist Edward T. Hall points out that there are other "silent" languages of culture that are very significant, too.[36] They are found in the culture's approach to communication context, time, and space.

If we look and listen carefully, Hall believes we should recognize how cultures differ in the ways their members use language in communication.[37] In **low-context cultures** most communication takes place via the written or spoken word. This is common in the United States, Canada, and Germany, for example. As the saying goes: "We say (or write) what we mean, and we mean what we say."

In **high-context cultures** things are different. What is actually said or written may convey only part, and sometimes a very small part, of the real message. The rest must be interpreted from nonverbal signals and the situation as whole, things like body language, physical setting, and even past relationships among the people involved. Dinner parties and social gatherings in high-context cultures allow potential business partners to get to know one another. Only after the relationships are established and a context for communication exists is it possible to make business deals.

Hall also notes that the way people approach and deal with time varies across cultures. He describes a **monochronic culture** as one in which people tend to do one thing at a time. This is typical of the United States, where most business people schedule a meeting for one person or group to focus on one issue for an allotted time.[38] And if someone is late for one of those meetings, or brings an uninvited guest, we tend not to like it.

Members of a **polychronic culture** are more flexible toward time and who uses it. They often try to work on many different things at once, perhaps not in any particular order. An American visitor (monochronic culture) to an Egyptian client (polychronic culture) may be frustrated, for example, by continued interruptions as the client greets and deals with people continually flowing in and out of his office.

Finally, Hall points out that most Americans like and value their own space, perhaps as much space as they can get. We like big offices, big homes, big yards; we get uncomfortable in tight spaces and when others stand too close to us in lines. When someone "talks right in our face," we don't like it; the behavior may even be interpreted as an expression of anger.

Members of other cultures can view all of these things quite differently. Hall describes these cul-

tural tendencies in terms of **proxemics**, or how people use interpersonal space to communicate. If you could visit Japan you would notice the difference in proxemics very quickly. Space is precious in Japan; its use is carefully planned and it is respected. Small, tidy homes, offices, shops are the norm; gardens are tiny but immaculate; public spaces are carefully organized for most efficient use.

• Hofstede Identifies Five Value Differences among National Cultures

As companies expand operations around the world, they need managers with global viewpoints, open to new experiences, and strong on cultural appreciation. Understanding the silent languages just discussed is a good place to start, but cultures are still more complex. Geert Hofstede, a Dutch scholar and international management consultant, explores this complexity in respect to value differences among national cultures.

STAY INFORMED

The Glass Ceiling in the Global Workplace

- *France*: Five percent of "well heeled" executives are women.
- *Britain*: Number of female executive directors' of FTSE100 companies increased from 11 in 2000 to 17 in 2004.
- *Japan*: Women are 41 percent of workforce and majority of college graduates, but hold few top posts.

After studying employees of a U.S.-based corporation operating in 40 countries, Hofstede identified the four cultural dimensions of power distance, uncertainty avoidance, individualism–collectivism, and masculinity–femininity.[39] Later studies resulted in the addition of a fifth dimension, time orientation.[40] Figure 6.2, on the next page, uses the examples of Japan, the United States, and other countries to show how national cultures varied in his research. Can you see why these cultural dimensions can be significant in business and management?

PACESETTERS

Pernille Spiers-Lopez sells a lifestyle at IKEA North America.

Business Week magazine claims that IKEA, the huge Swedish retailer, is fast becoming a "global cult brand." With 226 stores worldwide and more than 400 million customers, the firm is a global model of retail success. But when IKEA opened in the United States, it had trouble touching base with customers. That's now turned around in part, due to the leadership of Pernille Spiers-Lopez, president of North American operations. She shares the values of IKEA's founder, Ingvar Kamprad, sometimes called Sweden's Sam Walton—commitment to the environment, children, and employees. She received *Working Mother* magazine's Family Champion Award for her support of worker-friendly policies, and she is constantly alert to employee problems that she can help solve. Pernille-Spiers's IKEA career began as sales manager; from there, she worked her way to the top. What advice does she offer today's college students? Find employers that share your values, for one. And give priority to your family, for another. About her leadership style, she says: "I am authentic, and I am open. And I am not trying to be someone else."

Pernille Spiers-Lopez, president, IKEA North America.

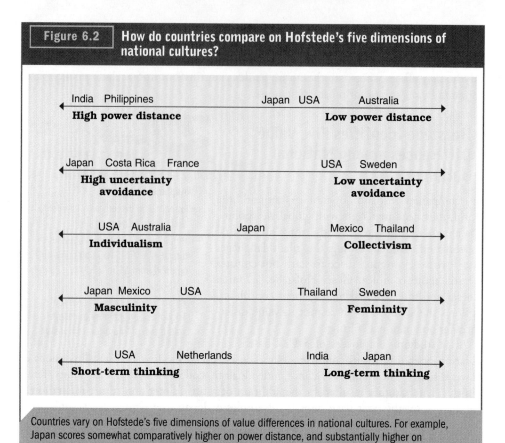

Figure 6.2 | **How do countries compare on Hofstede's five dimensions of national cultures?**

India Philippines   Japan USA   Australia
← **High power distance**   **Low power distance** →

Japan Costa Rica France   USA Sweden
← **High uncertainty**   **Low uncertainty**
    avoidance   **avoidance** →

    USA Australia   Japan   Mexico Thailand
← **Individualism**   **Collectivism** →

Japan Mexico   USA   Thailand Sweden
← **Masculinity**   **Femininity** →

        USA   Netherlands   India Japan
← **Short-term thinking**   **Long-term thinking** →

Countries vary on Hofstede's five dimensions of value differences in national cultures. For example, Japan scores somewhat comparatively higher on power distance, and substantially higher on uncertainty avoidance and masculinity; the United States is much more individualistic and short-term oriented. The implications of such cultural differences can be significant. Imagine what they might mean when international business executives try to make deals around the world, or when representatives of national governments try to work out problems.

Power distance is the degree to which a society accepts unequal distribution of power.

Uncertainty avoidance is the degree to which a society tolerates risk and uncertainty.

Individualism-collectivism is the degree to which a society emphasizes individuals and their self-interests.

Power distance is the degree to which a society accepts or rejects the unequal distribution of power among people in organizations and the institutions of society. In high power distance cultures like Japan we would expect to find great respect for age, status, and titles. Could this create problems for an American visitor used to the informalities of a more moderate power distance culture, and perhaps accustomed to first names and casual dress in the office?

Uncertainty avoidance is the degree to which a society tolerates or is uncomfortable with risk, change, and situational uncertainty. In high uncertainty avoidance cultures, like France, one would expect to find a preference for structure, order, and predictability. Could this be one of the reasons why the French seem to favor employment practices that provide job security? Could this explain why Hong Kong Chinese, from a low uncertainty avoidance culture, are considered very entrepreneurial in business affairs?

Individualism–collectivism is the degree to which a society emphasizes individual accomplishments and self-interests, or collective accomplishments and the interests of groups. In Hofstede's data the United States had the highest individualism score of any country. Think about it; don't you find the "I" and "me" words used a lot in our conversations and meetings? I'm always surprised, for example, how often they occur when students are making team presentations in class. This may reflect our cultural tendency toward individualism. But what are the implications when we try to work with people from more collectivist national cultures? How, for example, are individualistic Americans perceived in Mexico or Thailand?

Masculinity-femininity is the degree to which a society values assertiveness and materialism, versus feelings, relationships, and quality of life.[41] You might think of it as a tendency to emphasize stereotypical masculine or feminine traits. It also reflects attitudes toward gender roles. Visitors to Japan, with the highest masculinity score in Hofstede's research, may be surprised at how restricted career opportunities can be for women.[42] The *Wall Street Journal* comments: "In Japan, professional women face a set of socially complex issues—from overt sexism to deep-seated attitudes about the division of labor." One female Japanese manager says: "Men tend to have very fixed ideas about what women are like." [43]

Time orientation is the degree to which a society emphasizes short-term or long-term goals and gratifications.[44] Americans are notorious for impatience and desires for quick, even instantaneous, gratifications. Even our companies are expected to achieve short-term results; those failing to meet quarterly financial targets often suffer immediate stock price declines. Many Asian cultures are quite the opposite, valuing persistence and thrift, being patient and willing to work for long-term success. Maybe this helps explain why Japan's auto executives were willing to invest in hybrid technologies, and stick with them even though market demand was very low at first.

Although Hofstede's ideas are insightful, his five value dimensions offer only a ballpark look at national cultures, a starting point at best. And Hofstede himself warns that we must avoid the **ecological fallacy**.[45] This is acting with the mistaken assumption that a generalized cultural value, such as individualism in American culture or masculinity in Japanese culture, applies always and equally to all members of the culture.

Masculinity-femininity is the degree to which a society values assertiveness and materialism.

Time orientation is the degree to which a society emphasizes short-term or long-term goals.

The **ecological fallacy** assumes that a generalized cultural value applies equally well to all members of the culture.

• Project GLOBE Identifies Ten Country Clusters Displaying Cultural Differences

In project GLOBE, short for Global Leadership and Organizational Behavior Effectiveness, a team of international researchers and led by Robert House convened to study leadership, organizational practices and diversity among world cultures.[46] So far they have collected data from 170,000 managers in 62 countries. They also discovered that these countries fall into *ten culture clusters*, with societal culture practices more similar among countries within a cluster than across them.

As shown in Figure 6.3, on the next page, GLOBE researchers use nine dimensions to

Sample Countries in GLOBE's Ten Culture Clusters

LATIN AMERICA	ANGLO	LATIN EUROPE	NORDIC EUROPE	GERMANIC EUROPE
Brazil	Australia	France	Denmark	Germany
Ecuador	England	Italy	Finland	Netherlands
Mexico	U.S.A.	Spain	Sweden	Switzerland
EASTERN EUROPE	**CONFUCIAN ASIA**	**SOUTHERN ASIA**	**SUB-SAHARAN AFRICA**	**MIDDLE EAST**
Greece	China	India	Nigeria	Egypt
Hungary	Japan	Malaysia	South Africa	Kuwait
Russia	Singapore	Philippines	Zambia	Turkey

explore and describe cultures.[47] Two are rather direct fits with Hofstede: *power distance*—higher in Confucian Asia and lower in Nordic Europe, and *uncertainty avoidance*—high Germanic Europe and low in the Middle East.

Three other dimensions are quite similar with Hofstede's. *Gender Egalitarianism* is the degree to which a culture minimizes gender inequalities; similar to Hofstede's masculinity/femininity. It is high in the cultures of Eastern and Nordic Europe and low in those of the Middle East. *Future Orientation* is the degree to which members of a culture are willing to look ahead, delay gratifications and make investments in the expectation of longer-term payoffs; similar to Hofstede's time orientation. Germanic and Nordic Europe are high on future orientation; Latin America and the Middle East are low. *Institutional Collectivism* is the extent to which the organizations of a society emphasize and reward group action and accomplishments versus individual ones; similar to Hofstede's individualism/collectivism. Confucian Asia and Nordic Europe score high in institutional collectivism, while Germanic and Latin Europe score low.

The remaining four of GLOBE's dimensions offer additional cultural insights. *In-Group Collectivism* is the extent to which people take pride in their families and organizational memberships, acting loyal and cohesive regarding them. This form of collectivism runs high in Latin America and the Middle East, and tends to be low in Anglo and Germanic Europe cultures. *Assertiveness* is described as the extent to which a culture emphasizes competition and assertiveness in social relationships, valuing behavior that is tough and confrontation as opposed to showing modesty and tenderness. Cultures in Eastern and Germanic Europe score high in assertiveness; those in Nordic Europe and Latin America score low.

Performance Orientation is the degree of emphasis on performance excellence and improvements. Anglo and Confucian Asia cultures tend to be high in performance orientation. Countries in these clusters can be expected to reward performance accomplishments and invest in training to encourage future performance gains. *Humane Orientation* reflects tendencies in a society for people to emphasize fairness, altruism, generosity and caring as they deal with one another. It tends to be high in Southern Asia and Sub-Saharan Africa, and to be low in Latin and Germanic Europe.

The GLOBE research offers a timely, systematic and empirical look at culture across a large sample of countries. Its results are also being analyzed extensively for their management and leadership implications. Yet as with other cross-cultural research, the GLOBE project is insightful but not definitive. Given all of the complexity surrounding societal cultures, perhaps the best thing is to always integrate the many insights. Do you see how the ideas and findings of Hall, Hofstede, Trompenaars, the GLOBE researchers, and others, can be useful as we try to better understand the diversity of global cultures?[48]

Figure 6.3	How does Project GLOBE classify societal cultures?		
Power distance	Nordic Europe	Sub-Saharan Africa	—
Uncertainty avoidance	Latin America	Southern Asia	Germanic Europe
Gender egalitarianism	Middle East	Anglo	Eastern Europe
Future orientation	Eastern Europe	Latin Europe	Nordic Europe
Institutional collectivism	Latin America	Anglo	Confucian Asia
In-group collectivism	Anglo	Latin Europe	Middle East
Assertiveness	Nordic Europe	Confucian Asia	Germanic Europe
Performance orientation	Eastern Europe	Southern Asia	Confucian Asia
Humane orientation	Germanic Europe	Middle East	Sub-Saharan Africa
	Low-score clusters	**Mid-score clusters**	**High-score clusters**

A large team of international researchers collaborated in Project GLOBE to examine societal cultures using the nine cultural dimensions shown in the figure. When results from extensive empirical studies were analyzed for 62 countries, they were found to fall into ten culture clusters. Countries within a cluster share many societal cultural practices; countries tend to differ significantly across clusters in their cultural practices.

6.2 What should we know about diversity among global cultures

Be Sure You Can . . .

- explain culture shock and how people may respond to it

- differentiate low-context and high-context cultures, monochronic and polychromic cultures

- list Hofstede's five dimensions of value differences among national cultures

- contrast America culture with that of other countries on each dimension

- explain the insights of project GLOBE for cross-cultural understanding

Define the Terms

Cultural intelligence	Masculinity–femininity
Culture	Monochronic culture
Culture shock	Polychronic culture
Ecological fallacy	Power distance
High-context culture	Proxemics
Individualism–collectivism	Time orientation
Low-context culture	Uncertainty avoidance

Rapid Review

- People can experience culture shock due to the discomfort experienced in cross-cultural situations.

- Cultural intelligence is an individual capacity to understand, respect, and adapt to cultural differences.

- Hall's "silent" languages of culture include the role of context in communication, time orientation, and use of interpersonal space.

- Hofstede's five dimensions of value differences in national cultures are: power distance, uncertainty avoidance, individualism–collectivism, masculinity–femininity, and time orientation.

- Project GLOBE groups countries into ten clusters, with cultures similar within clusters and different across them on nine cultural dimensions.

Reflect/React

1. Should religion be included on Hall's list of the silent languages of culture?

2. Which of Hofstede's, or project GLOBE's cultural dimensions might pose the greatest challenges to U.S. managers working in Asia, the Middle East, or Latin America?

3. Even though cultural differences are readily apparent around the world, is the trend today for cultures to converge and become more like one another?

Multiple Choice

1. Demographic trends in the United States today show that _____.
   (a) fewer women are working (b) more workers come from traditional families (c) Hispanics are a growing percentage of the workforce (d) the average age of workers is falling

2. When members of minority cultures feel that they have to behave similar to the ways of the majority culture, this tendency is called _____.
   (a) biculturalism (b) particularism (c) the glass ceiling effect (d) multiculturalism

3. The beliefs that older workers are not creative and mostly desire routine, low-stress jobs are examples of stereotypes that might create bad feelings among members of different _____ subcultures in organizations.
   (a) gender (b) generational (c) functional (d) ethnic

4. Among the three leadership approaches to diversity identified by Thomas, which one is primarily directed at making sure that minorities and women are hired by the organization?
   (a) equal employment opportunity (b) affirmative action (c) valuing diversity (d) managing diversity

5. In _____ cultures, members tend to do one thing at a time; in _____ cultures, members tend to do many things at once.
   (a) monochronic/polychronic (b) universal/particular (c) collectivist/individualist (d) neutral/affective

6. Hofstede's study of national cultures found that the United States is the most highly _____ culture of any countries in his sample.
   (a) individualistic (b) collectivist (c) feminine (d) long-term oriented

7. When a foreign visitor to India attends a dinner, and criticizes as "primitive" a local custom of eating with one's fingers, he or she can be described as acting _____.
   (a) diffuse (b) sequentially (c) monochronic (d) enthnocentric

8. In a high-context culture like that characteristic of Egypt, we would expect to find _____.
   (a) low uncertainty avoidance (b) belief in achievement (c) an inner-directed orientation toward nature (d) emphasis on nonverbal as well as verbal communication

9. It is common in Malaysian culture for people to value teamwork and to display great respect for authority. Hofstede would describe this culture as high in both _____.
   (a) uncertainty avoidance and feminism (b) universalism and particularism (c) collectivism and power distance (d) long-term orientation and masculinity

10. In the Project GLOBE framework, someone from a culture high in _____ would be expected to take a lot of pride in their families and act loyal in their group memberships.
    (a) in group collectivism (b) Humane Orientation (c) Institutional collectivism (d) Future orientation

Short Response

11. What is the difference between valuing diversity and managing diversity?

12. How can subculture differences create diversity challenges in organizations?

13. In what ways can the power-distance dimension of national culture become an important issue in management?

14. Why would a global corporation be interested in training its managers to understand cultural differences in what project GLOBE calls "assertiveness"?

Integration & Application

A friend of mine in West Virginia owns a small manufacturing firm employing about 50 workers. His son spent a semester in Japan as an exchange student. Upon return he said to his Dad: "Boy, the Japanese really do things right; everything is organized in teams; decisions are made by consensus, with everyone participating; no one seems to disagree with anything the bosses say. I think we should immediately start more teamwork and consensus decision making in our factory."

Questions: My friend has asked you for advice. Using insights from Hofstede's framework, what would you say to him? What differences in the Japanese and American cultures should be considered in this situation, and why?

INSTRUCTIONS *Indicate "O" for often, "S" for sometimes, and "N" for never in response to each of the following questions as they pertain to where you work or go to school.*

1 How often have you heard jokes or remarks about other people that you consider offensive?

2 How often do you hear men "talk down" to women in an attempt to keep them in an inferior status?

3 How often have you felt personal discomfort as the object of sexual harassment?

4 How often do you work or study with African Americans or Hispanics?

5 How often have you felt disadvantaged because members of ethnic groups other than yours were given special treatment?

6 How often have you seen a woman put in an uncomfortable situation because of unwelcome advances by a man?

7 How often does it seem that African Americans, Hispanics, Caucasians, women, men, and members of other minority demographic groups seem to "stick together" during work breaks or other leisure situations?

8 How often do you feel uncomfortable about something you did and/or said to someone of the opposite sex or a member of an ethnic or racial group other than yours?

9 How often do you feel efforts are made in this setting to raise the level of cross-cultural understanding among people who work and/or study together?

10 How often do you step in to communicate concerns to others when you feel actions and/or words are used to the disadvantage of minorities?

INTERPRETATION

There are no correct answers for the Diversity Awareness Checklist. The key issue is the extent to which you are sensitive to diversity issues in the workplace or university. Are you comfortable with your responses? How do you think others in your class responded? Why not share your responses with others and examine different viewpoints on this important issue?

PATHWAYS to WileyPLUS

WILEY PLUS

CASE SNAPSHOT

Go online to read this case!

MySpace.com: The Kids Are Online

Social networking is heavily influencing today's younger generation. How is MySpace.com affecting the way the next generation interacts? How will its recent acquisition by News Corporation change its array of services, if at all? Could it become a portal to rival Yahoo!?

MODULE 6 — Online Interactive Learning Resources

Self-Assessment
• Time Orientation

Skill Builder
• Cultural Awareness

Experiential Exercise
• What Do You Value in Work?

Team Project
• Diversity Lessons

The world isn't just

Globalization and International Business

This is a shopping test: What do Victoria's Secret, Express, Bath & Body Works, The White Barn Candle Co., and Henri Bendel have in common? Answer: Their roots all trace to 1963 and a small woman's clothing store in Columbus, Ohio. That single store has grown into a company with one of the best fashion names in the world—Limited Brands, Inc., headed by founder, chairman, and CEO Leslie Wexner. For anyone interested in retailing Wexner has been called a "pioneer of specialty brands" and someone with unique retailing "vision and focus." A member of the CEO's retail all-star team, he also knows international business.

This is a global economy test: Where does the Limited shop to stock its stores? Answer: It shops around the world—anywhere and everywhere it

for travelers

can get quality products at the best prices.[1] But it also has to be careful. Although it finds high-quality materials products at good prices from many reliable foreign partners, it also risks getting entangled with some whose lack of ethics and bad behavior could reflect poorly on its brands.

To protect its image as an international business, The Limited uses its "What We Stand For" policy to guide its relationships with suppliers and subcontractors. The policy states:

> *We will not do business with individuals or suppliers that do not meet our standards. We expect our suppliers to promote an environment of dignity, respect and opportunity; provide safe and healthy working conditions; offer fair compensation through wages and other benefits; hire workers of legal age, who accept employment on a voluntary basis; and maintain reasonable working hours.[2]*

How does Limited Brands do as it travels the world seeking business partners and products? For its role in helping to expand the apparel manufacturing industry in sub-Saharan Africa to over $1 billion in sales, Limited Brands was given the Special Recognition Award for Business Enterprise in Africa from the Africa-America Institute. And in respect to business success, Wexner says: "Better brands. Best brands. I don't believe bigger is better. I believe better is better. Period."

Hourly Labor Costs for Textile Workers

- France—$19.82
- Italy—$18.63
- U.S.—$15.78
- Slovakia—$3.27
- Turkey—$3.05
- Bulgaria—$1.14
- Egypt—$0.88
- China—$0.49

⊙ MODULE GUIDE

 7.1 What is the nature of international business?

- Globalization creates international business opportunities.
- International business is done by global sourcing, import/export, licensing, and franchising.
- International business is done by joint ventures and wholly owned subsidiaries.
- International business is complicated by different legal and political systems.

 7.2 What are multinational corporations and how do they work?

- Multinational corporations do substantial business in several countries.
- Multinational corporations can be controversial at home and abroad.
- Multinational corporations face a variety of ethical challenges.
- Planning and controlling are complicated in multinational corporations.
- Organizing is complicated in multinational corporations.
- Leading is complicated in multinational corporations.

In the **global economy**, resources, markets, and competition are worldwide in scope.

Globalization is the process of growing interdependence among elements of the global economy.

Limited Brands is a good example of what is happening on the outsourcing side of our **global economy**, one among many possible examples of how resource supplies, product markets, and business competition are now worldwide rather than local or national in scope.[3] The term we use to describe all this is **globalization**, introduced in Module 1 as a set of forces driving the growing interdependence among the many components in the global economy.[4]

Regardless of your work or your career plans, do you have a good idea of how much globalization affects your life? Travel to Ohio and you'll find almost 1 out of every 20 persons employed in the private sector working for foreign firms.[5] These are *insourced jobs*; at last count there were more than 5 million of them in the U.S. economy. Perhaps you are or will someday be holding one, working in America for a foreign employer.

Globalization also means to me that most of the clothing that we buy is foreign made. It means Japanese investors own 7-Eleven, Inc. It means that Chrysler's PT Cruiser is assembled in Mexico for a German parent company, DaimlerChrysler. It means that Honda, Nissan, and Toyota get as much as 80 to 90 percent of their profits from auto sales in North America. And it also means that I worry about the stability of my sons' new jobs, about their future careers, and about the way the world will look when they reach my age.

John Chambers, CEO of Cisco Systems, Inc., pretty much lays it on the line for all of us when he says: "I will put my jobs anywhere in the world where the right infrastructure is, with the right educated workforce, with the right supportive government."[6]

NEWSLINE

Get ready, your next job may be with a foreign employer

People were skeptical when Honda opened its first U.S. automobile plant in Marysville, Ohio, in 1982. People worried that U.S. workers could not adapt to the Japanese firm's production methods, technology, and style. But not only did American consumers embrace the firm's products—local workers did, too.

As Allen Kinzer, the first U.S. manager whom Honda hired in its Marysville plant, says: "It wasn't easy blending the cultures; anyone who knew anything about the industry at the time would have to say it was a bold move." Bold move indeed! Honda now employs over 13,000 people in its multiple U.S. plants, which produce over 500,000 cars per year. It is only one among hundreds of foreign firms offering employment opportunities to U.S. workers.

Reflect: Does it make a difference to you if you work for an "American" employer or not? Would you expect problems, either personal or work-related, if working at home for Honda or another foreign employer?

An **international business** conducts commercial transactions across national boundaries.

• Globalization Creates International Business Opportunities

Cisco Systems, Limited Brands, and other firms like them are **international businesses**. They do business by conducting for-profit transactions of goods and services across national boundaries. Such businesses, from small exporters and importers to the huge multinational corporations (MNCs), form the foundations of the global economy. And, they all "go international" for good reasons.

International business can be a source of greater profits through expansion, more customers through new markets, and more capital from international investors. It can create access to better suppliers in terms of quality and costs, and lower costs for both unskilled and highly talented labor.

• International Business Is Done by Global Sourcing, Import/Export, Licensing, and Franchising

In **global sourcing**, firms purchase materials or services around the world for local use.

Not only is there more than one reason for getting into international business, there are several ways of doing it. And, getting started can be relatively easy. A common first step is **global sourcing** as described in the opening example of Limited Brands. Through global sourcing a business purchases materials, manufacturing components, or services from around the world. This is basically taking advantage of international wage gaps by contracting for goods and services in low-cost foreign locations.

In automobile manufacturing, for example, global sourcing may mean designs from Italy, windshields and instrument panels from Mexico, antilock braking systems from Germany, and electronics from Malaysia. In services, it may mean setting up customer-support call centers in the Philippines, contracting for computer software engineers in Russia, or having medical x-rays read by physicians in India. If you follow the news, you'll find many more examples; the global sourcing trend shows little signs of slowing down.[7]

A second form of international business involves **exporting**—selling locally made products in foreign markets, and/or **importing**—buying foreign-made products and selling them in domestic markets. Because the growth of export industries creates local jobs, governments often support these business initiatives. Franklin Jacobs is the founder of a commercial furniture company, St. Louis–based Falcon Products, Inc. While on a tour through Europe, he says, "I discovered that my products were a lot better and a lot cheaper." With the help of the U.S. government, he rented exposition space in London, showcased his furniture, and landed over US$200,000 in orders. He then built an export program that added jobs at his St. Louis firm.[8]

International business is also conducted through licensing and franchising. In a **licensing agreement**, a foreign firm pays for the rights to make or sell another company's products in a specified region. The license typically grants access to a unique manufacturing technology, special patent, or trademark. Walt Disney, Inc., for example, licenses rights for companies around the world to use Disney characters in a wide range of products, from tee shirts to toys to jewelry. In **franchising**, a foreign firm buys the rights to use another's name and operating methods in its home country. When companies like McDonalds or Starbucks franchise internationally, they sell facility designs, equipment, product ingredients, recipes, and management systems to foreign investors. They also typically retain certain product and operating controls to protect their brand's image.

• International Business Is Done by Joint Ventures and Wholly Owned Subsidiaries

Sooner or later, some firms that are active in international business decide to make costly direct investments in operations in foreign countries. One common way to do this is through a **joint venture**. This is a co-ownership arrangement in which the foreign and local partners agree to pool resources, share risks, and jointly operate the new business. Sometimes the joint venture is formed when a foreign partner buys part ownership in an existing local firm; in other cases it is formed as an entirely new operation that the foreign and local partners start up together.

International joint ventures are **global strategic alliances** in which each partner hopes to achieve through cooperation things they couldn't do or would have a hard time doing alone. In return for its investment, for example, the outside or foreign partner may hope to gain both access to a new market and the expert assistance of a local partner who understands it. This is the strategy followed in China by most of the world's large automakers. Recognizing the local complexities, they decided it was better to cooperate with local partners than try to enter the Chinese market on their own.

In return for its side of the investment, the local joint venture partner often hopes to gain new technologies and opportunities for its employees to learn new skills. This is a reason why Chinese firms were so willing to partner with General Motors, Ford, Toyota, DaimlerChrysler, and other foreign automakers. Of course, and as we will discuss shortly, there are no guarantees for success on either side of joint venture deals (see Management Tips).[9]

In **exporting**, local products are sold abroad.

Importing is the process of acquiring products abroad and selling them in domestic markets.

> **→ Five Reasons to Pursue International Business**
> 1. **Expanded profit potential**
> 2. **More customers**
> 3. **More capital**
> 4. **Lower cost suppliers**
> 5. **Lower costs of labor**

In **licensing,** one firm pays a fee for rights to make or sell another company's products.

In **franchising,** a firm pays a fee for rights to use another company's name and operating methods.

A **joint venture** operates in a foreign country through co-ownership with local partners.

In a **global strategic alliance** each partner hopes to achieve through cooperation things they couldn't do alone.

> **MANAGEMENT TIPS**
>
> **Criteria for choosing a partner for successful joint ventures**
>
> • Familiar with your firm's major business
> • Employs a strong local workforce
> • Values its customers
> • Has potential for future expansion
> • Has strong local market for its own products
> • Has good profit potential
> • Has sound financial standing

A **foreign subsidiary** is a local operation completely owned by a foreign firm.

In contrast to the international joint venture, which is a cross-border partnership, a **foreign subsidiary** is a local operation completely owned and controlled by a foreign firm. It might be a local firm that was purchased in its entirety; it might be a brand new operation built up as a start-up, or "green field," venture. Quite often, the decision to set up a foreign subsidiary is made only after the foreign firm has gained experience in the local environment through earlier joint ventures.

Foreign subsidiaries can involve very large financial investments. Can you see why some firms might be willing to take this risk? Even though this commits a firm to the highest level of involvement in international operations, a foreign subsidiary can make good business sense. When Nissan opened a new plant in Canton, Mississippi, its expectation was to produce 400,000 cars a year. An auto analyst for a Japanese brokerage firm said: "It's a smart strategy to shift production to North America. They're reducing their exposure through building more in their regional markets, as well as being able to meet consumers' needs more quickly."[10]

• International Business Is Complicated by Different Legal and Political Systems

When it comes to risk in international business, some of the biggest complications come from differences in legal and political systems. When firms conduct business abroad they are expected to abide by local laws, some of which may be unfamiliar. In the United States, for example, executives of foreign-owned companies must comply with antitrust issues that prevent competitors from regularly talking to one another, something that they may not be used to at home. They also must deal with a variety of laws regarding occupational health and safety, equal employment opportunity, sexual harassment, and other matters. These, again, may be different from the legal environments they are used to at home.

As you might imagine, the more home- and host-country laws differ, the more difficult and complex it is for international businesses to adapt to local ways. Common legal problems faced by international businesses involve incorporation practices and business ownership; negotiating and implementing contracts with foreign parties; handling foreign exchange; and intellectual property rights—patents, trademarks, and copyrights.

The issue of intellectual property is particularly sensitive these days. You might know this best in terms of concerns about movie and music downloads, photocopying of books and journals, and sale of fake designer fashions. Many Western businesses know it as lost profits due to their products or designs being copied and sold as imitations by foreign firms. Starbucks recently won a case in Chinese courts. A local firm was using Starbucks' Chinese name, "Xingbake" (*Xing* means "star" and *bake* is pronounced "bah kuh"), and was also copying its café designs.[11]

The **World Trade Organization** is a global institution to promote free trade and open markets around the world.

General Motors, too, has had problems in China. Not long ago, its executives noticed that a new car from a fast-growing local competitor, partially owned by GM's Chinese joint venture partner, looked very similar to one of its models. GM claims its design was copied. The competitor denies it, and even has plans to export the cars, called "Cherys," for sale in the United States. Who knows? Perhaps you'll be driving one someday.[12]

When international businesses believe they are being mistreated in foreign countries, or when local companies believe foreign competitors are disadvantaging them, their respective governments might take the cases to the **World Trade Organization (WTO)**. This global institution was established to promote free trade and open markets around the world. Its 140 members give one another *most favored nation status*—the most favorable treatment for imports and exports. They also agree to work together within the WTO framework to try and resolve some international business problems. But, controversies are still inevitable.

PACESETTERS

Global woman to watch— Izumi Kobayashi.

When the *Wall Street Journal* did a special feature on "50 women to watch," the goal was to identify the growing number of women having an impact at the highest levels of corporate leadership. One of them is Izumi Kobayashi, President of Merrill Lynch Japan Securities. The firm is one of the most profitable in Japan; but it wasn't always that way. In fact, before Kobayashi took over as president it was a money loser and facing major operating problems. She came in with the goal of earning the trust of the firm's employees while helping to turn things around. "We told our people that it was not just about cutting for the present," she says, "but about strengthening the company for the future." And that's the way she has run her own life and career. After finding herself stereotyped by male colleagues and limited to largely clerical work in her first job after graduating college, she eventually left to join Merrill. Since then it has been a steady rise to the top to become the first Japanese and the first woman to head the firm's Japan operations.

Izumi Kobayashi, President, Merrill Lynch Japan Securities

Be Sure You Can . . .

- explain how globalization impacts our lives

- list five reasons that companies pursue international business opportunities

- describe and give examples of how firms do international business by global sourcing, exporting/importing, franchising/licensing, joint ventures, and foreign subsidiaries

- discuss how differences in legal environments can affect businesses operating internationally

- explain the purpose of the WTO

Define the Terms

Exporting	Globalization
Foreign subsidiary	Importing
Franchising	International business
Global economy	Joint venture
Global sourcing	Licensing agreement
Global strategic alliance	World Trade Organization (WTO)

Rapid Review

- The forces of globalization create international business opportunities to pursue profits, customers, capital, and low-cost suppliers and labor in different countries.

- The least costly ways of doing business internationally are to use global sourcing, exporting and importing, and licensing and franchising.

- Direct investment strategies to establish joint ventures or wholly owned subsidiaries in foreign countries represent substantial commitments to international operations.

- Environmental differences, particularly in legal and political systems, can complicate international business activities.

- The World Trade Organization (WTO) is a global institution to promote free trade and open markets around the world.

Reflect/React

1. Why would a government want to prohibit a foreign firm from owning more than 49 percent of a local joint venture?

2. Are joint ventures worth the risk of being taken advantage of by foreign partners, as with GM's "Chery" case in China?

3. What aspects of the U.S. legal environment might prove complicating for a Russian firm starting new operations in the U.S.

7.2 What Are Multinational Corporations and How Do They Work?

Although many international businesses exist, they don't all pursue worldwide missions and strategies or earn substantial revenues abroad. There is quite a difference between Nike, which earns over 60 percent of its profit outside of the United States, for example, and the small St. Louis furniture maker that exports to foreign customers when the opportunity arises.

• Multinational Corporations Do Substantial Business in Several Countries

A **multinational corporation (MNC)** is a business with extensive international operations in more than one foreign country.

A **multinational corporation (MNC)** has extensive international operations in several foreign countries, and derives a substantial portion of its sales and profits from international sources.[13] You can find lists of the world's largest MNCs regularly published by the *Wall Street Journal*, *Fortune*, *Business Week* and other news media. Many firms on the lists will be household names—Wal-Mart, BP, Toyota.

Most MNCs retain strong national identifications even while operating around the world. Is there any doubt in your mind that Wal-Mart and Dell are "American" firms while Honda and Sony are "Japanese"? Most likely not; but that may not be the way their executives would like the firms viewed.

Top managers of many multinationals are trying to move their firms toward becoming **transnational corporations**. That is, they would like to operate worldwide and without being identified with one national home.[14] Nestlé is a good example. When you buy the firm's products do you have any idea that it is a registered Swiss company? Executives at Nestlé , like any true transnational, view the entire world as their domain for acquiring resources, locating production facilities, marketing goods and services, and establishing brand image. They seek total integration of global operations, try to make major decisions from a global perspective, distribute work among worldwide points of excellence, and employ senior executives from many different countries.

A **transnational corporation** is an MNC that operates worldwide on a borderless basis.

• Multinational Corporations Can Be Controversial at Home and Abroad

Have you ever thought about how much power multinational corporations wield in the world economy? The United Nations reports that they hold one-third of the world's productive assets and control 70 percent of world trade. Furthermore, more than 90 percent of these MNCs are based in the Northern Hemisphere. While this economic power is undoubtedly good for the business leaders and investors, it can be threatening to small and less-developed countries and their domestic industries.

Ideally, global corporations and the countries that host their foreign operations should all benefit. But, as Figure 7.1 shows, things can go both right and wrong in MNC–host country relationships.

Figure 7.1	What can go right and wrong in relationships between MNCs and their host countries?

MNC host-country relationships

What should go right

Mutual benefits

Shared opportunities with potential for
- Growth
- Income
- Learning
- Development

MNC host-country relationships

What can go wrong

Host-country complaints about MNCs

- Excessive profits
- Economic domination
- Interference with government
- Hires best local talent
- Limited technology transfer
- Disrespect for local customs

MNC complaints about host countries

- Profit limitations
- Overpriced resources
- Exploitative rules
- Foreign exchange restrictions
- Failure to uphold contracts

When things go right, both the MNC and its host countries gain. The MNC gets profits or resources, and the host country often sees increased job opportunities, tax revenues, and technology transfers. But when things go wrong, each can blame the other. MNCs may complain that the host country bars it from taking profits out of country, overprices local resources, and enforces restrictive government rules. Host countries may accuse the MNCs of hiring the best local talent, failing to respect local customs, making too much profit, and failing to transfer really useful technology.

The potential benefits that MNCs bring to host countries include larger tax bases, increased employment opportunities, technology transfers, the introduction of new industries, and the development of local resources. Complaints from host countries are that MNCs sometimes take out excessive profits, dominate the local economy, interfere with the local government, ignore local customs and laws, fail to help domestic firms develop, hire the most talented of local personnel, and fail to share their most advanced technologies.[15] And they may also use unfair practices, such as below-cost pricing, to drive local competitors out of business. This is one of the arguments in favor of **protectionism**, the use of laws and political tariffs to protect a country's domestic businesses from foreign competitors.

MNCs can also run into difficulties in their home or headquarters countries. If a multinational cuts local jobs and then moves or outsources the work to another country, local government and community leaders will quickly criticize the firm for its lack of social responsibility. After all, they will say, shouldn't you be creating local jobs and building the local economy? Perhaps you might agree with this view. But can you see why business executives might disagree?

Protectionism is a call for tariffs and special treatment to protect domestic firms from foreign competition.

• Multinational Corporations Face a Variety of Ethical Challenges

When it comes to ethics, another criticism of international business and MNCs is that their employees sometimes get involved in **corruption**.[16] That is, they resort to illegal practices, such as bribes, to further their business interests in foreign countries.

In the United States, the Foreign Corrupt Practices Act makes it illegal for U.S. firms and their representatives to engage in corrupt practices overseas. This prevents them from paying bribes or excessive commissions to foreign officials in return for business favors. Such a ban makes sense, but critics claim that it fails to recognize the realities of business as practiced in many foreign nations. They believe it puts U.S. companies at a competitive disadvantage because they can't offer the same "deals" as businesses from other nations—deals that the locals may regard as standard business practices.

Corruption involves illegal practices to further one's business interests.

STAY INFORMED

Transparency International gives these countries its poorest corruption scores:
- Indonesia
- Tajikistan
- Paraguay
- Myanmar
- Nigeria
- Bangladesh
- Haiti

Sweatshops employ workers at very low wages, for long hours, and in poor working conditions.

Child labor is the full-time employment of children for work otherwise done by adults.

Sustainable development meets the needs of the present without hurting future generations.

Currency risk is possible loss because of fluctuating exchange rates.

What do you think? Should U.S. legal standards apply to American companies operating abroad? Or should they be allowed to practice business in whatever way the local setting considers acceptable? A case in point involves countries with weak employment laws. International businesses may end up working with local firms best described as **sweatshops**, places in which employees work at low wages for long hours and in poor, even unsafe, conditions.[17] They may also work with those using **child labor**, the full-time employment of children for work otherwise done by adults.[18] As you might guess, the owners of such places might be in a good position to offer low prices to foreign companies buying their products. But just because the factory is legal by local standards, does this justify doing business with its owners?

Even if your answer to the question is a resounding "No!," the fact is that even well-intentioned MNCs can end up in troublesome relationships with their suppliers. Nike, Inc., for example, contracts with hundreds of manufacturing sites around the world. When problems with employee treatment at some of them came to light, Nike was threatened with consumer boycotts. The firm now lists on its website all countries it does business in and who its suppliers are, as well as results from social audits of its international labor practices.[19]

MNCs are also expected to respect and protect the natural environment. Industrial pollution of cities, hazardous waste disposal, depletion of natural resources, and related issues are now worldwide concerns. Yet, we also want the products and economic development that comes from utilizing environmental resources—everything from timber, to ore and minerals, to oil. You might hear this dilemma debated as an issue of **sustainable development**—defined by The International Institute of Sustainable Development as "development that meets the needs of the present without compromising the ability of future generations to meet their own needs." While some might consider this concept idealistic, would you be willing to consider it a worthwhile guide for international business activities?

• Planning and Controlling Are Complicated in Multinational Corporations

Setting goals, making plans, controlling results—all of these standard management functions can become quite complicated in the international arena. Picture a home office somewhere in the United States, say, Chicago. The MNC's foreign operations are scattered in Asia, Africa, South America, and Europe. Somehow, planning and controlling must span all locations, meeting home office needs and those of foreign affiliates. Today's sophisticated information and communications technologies surely help. Global communication networks and secure Web portals most likely allow home and field offices to share databases, electronically transfer documents, hold virtual conferences, and make group decisions without face-to-face meetings. But what are some of the potential complications in this planning environment?

One of the risks of international business is **currency risk**, or fluctuations in foreign exchange rates. Companies like Dell and IBM, for example, make a lot of sales abroad. These sales are in foreign currencies; eventually, a good part of the revenues must be converted into dollars. But as exchange rates vary, the dollar value of sales revenues goes up and down over time. Companies have to plan for these eventualities—the risk of exchange rate fluctuations affecting business profits.

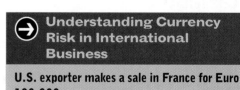

Understanding Currency Risk in International Business

U.S. exporter makes a sale in France for Euro 100,000.

Scenario 1: **Weak dollar**
 .95 Euros = 1 $US
 Take home revenue = $105,263

Scenario 2: **Strong dollar**
 1.25 Euros = 1 $US
 Take home revenue = $80,000

When the dollar is weak against the euro, for example, you get more when trading in euros earned abroad for dollars. This is good for companies making lots of sales in euros. It is also good for American exporters. They can sell more to Euro-zone customers because their euros have more purchasing power for products priced in dollars. But suppose the dollar strengthens and the euro is worth less; what happens then?

Another risk of international business is **political risk**, the potential loss in value of an investment in or managerial control over a foreign asset because of instability and political changes in the host country. The major threats of political risk today come from terrorism, civil wars, armed conflicts and military disruptions, shifting government systems through elections or forced takeovers, and new laws and economic policies. Although such things can't be prevented, they can be anticipated. MNCs use a planning technique called **political-risk analysis**. It tries to forecast the probability of disruptive events that can threaten the security of a foreign investment. Given the world we now live in, can you see the high stakes of such analysis?

Political risk is the possible loss of investment in or control over a foreign asset because of instability and political changes in the host country.

Political-risk analysis forecasts how political events may impact foreign investments.

• Organizing Is Complicated in Multinational Corporations

Even with plans in place, it isn't easy to organize for international operations. When just starting international activities, businesses often appoint a vice president or other senior manager to oversee them. But as global business expands, a more complex arrangement is usually necessary. One possible choice is the *global area structure* shown in Figure 7.2. It arranges production and sales functions into separate geographical units and assigns a top manager to oversee them. This allows activities in major areas of the world to be run by executives with special local expertise.[20]

| Figure 7.2 | How can multinational corporations organize for global operations? |

Some firms initially organize for international business by adding a new senior management position, such as head of international operations, to the existing structure. When the international side of the business grows, the structure often gets more sophisticated. One approach is a global area structure that assigns senior managers to oversee all product operations in major parts of the world. Another is the global product structure in which area specialists advise other senior managers on business practices in their parts of the world.

Another organizing option is the *global product structure*, also shown in the figure. It gives worldwide responsibilities to product group managers, for example, a global sales and marketing group, who are assisted by area specialists on the corporate staff. These specialists provide expert guidance on the unique needs of various countries or regions.

• Leading Is Complicated in Multinational Corporations

An **expatriate** lives and works in a foreign country.

No organizational structure can work without the right people in place. And one of a business leader's most important jobs anywhere is to ensure that the firm is staffed with a talented workforce. When it comes to international operations, an often-heard rule of thumb is: "Hire competent locals, use competent locals, and listen to competent locals." Yet, in addition to hiring locals, many MNCs also employ **expatriate workers**. These are employees who live and work in foreign countries on short- or long-term assignments.[21]

Not only do expatriate assignments offer the individuals challenging work experiences, they also help the firms develop a pool of culturally aware managers with global horizons and interpersonal networks of global contacts. Of course, not everyone performs well in an overseas assignment. The risk of failure can sometimes be reduced when employers provide predeparture training and cultural orientation, extra support in the foreign environment, special attention to the needs of an expatriate's family members, and extra assistance on the return home.[22]

Does expatriate work sound appealing to you? Take a look at the list of personal attributes linked with success in an expatriate assignment. There is no doubt the growth of international businesses is creating a need for more **global managers**, ones aware about international developments and competent in working across cultures.[23] In fact, the *Wall Street Journal* calls it a business imperative, saying that global companies need managers who "understand different countries and cultures" and "intuitively understand the markets they are trying to penetrate."[24]

A **global manager** is culturally aware and informed on international affairs.

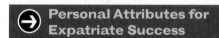

Personal Attributes for Expatriate Success

- High degree of self-awareness
- Cultural sensitivity
- Desire to live and work abroad
- Family flexibility and support
- Technical job competence

Are you willing to admit that the world isn't just for traveling anymore, and to embrace it as a career opportunity? Is it possible that you might stand out to a potential employer as someone with the skills to excel as a global manager?

> *Like it or not, we are in a global economy and a global political world... the responsibility is huge.*
>
> **A.G. Lafley, CEO, PROCTER & GAMBLE**

STUDY GUIDE

7.2 What are multinational corporations and how do they work?

Be Sure You Can . . .

- differentiate a multinational corporation from a transnational corporation

- list common host-country complaints and three home-country complaints about MNC operations

- explain the challenges of corruption, sweatshops, and child labor for MNCs

- discuss the implications of political risk for MNCs

- differentiate the global area structure and global product structure

- discuss the challenges of expatriate work

- list competencies of a global manager

Define the Terms

Child labor

Corruption

Currency risk

Expatriate workers

Global manager

Multinational corporation (MNC)

Political risk

Political-risk analysis

Protectionism

Sustainable development

Sweatshop

Transnational corporation

Rapid Review

- A multinational corporation (MNC) is a business with extensive operations in several foreign countries; a transnational corporation attempts to operate without national identity and with a worldwide mission and strategies.

- MNCs can benefit host countries by paying taxes, bringing in new technologies, and creating employment opportunities; MNCs can also hurt host countries by interfering with local government and politics, extracting excessive profits, and dominating the local economy.

- The Foreign Corrupt Practices Act prohibits representatives of U.S. international businesses from engaging in corrupt practices abroad.

- Planning and controlling in MNCs must take into account such things as currency risk and political risk in changing environmental conditions.

- Organizing for multinational operations often involves use of a global product structure or a global area structure.

- Leading in MNCs involves staffing the firm with talented local employees, and with expatriates and global managers who are capable of working in different cultures and countries.

Reflect/React

1. Should becoming a transnational corporation be the goal of all MNCs?

2. Is there anything that MNCs and host governments can do to avoid conflicts and bad feelings with one another?

3. Are laws such as the Foreign Corrupt Practices Act unfair to American companies trying to compete around the world?

MODULE

7

TEST PREP
Take the complete set of Module 7 quizzes online!

Multiple Choice

1. When Rocky Brands decided to increase its international operations by buying 70 percent ownership of a manufacturing company in the Dominican Republic, Rocky was engaging in which form of international business?
   (a) import/export **(b)** licensing **(c)** foreign subsidiary **(d)** joint venture

2. When Limited Brands buys cotton in Egypt and has pants sewn from it in Sri Lanka according to designs made in Italy for sale in the United States, this is a form of international business known as _____.
   (a) licensing **(b)** importing **(c)** joint venturing **(d)** global sourcing

3. If a new government comes into power and seizes all foreign assets in the country without any payments to the owners, the loss to foreign firms is considered a _____ risk of international business.
   (a) franchise **(b)** political **(c)** currency **(d)** corruption

4. A joint venture is a form of _____ in which each of the partners expects to gain something of value from working with the other.
   (a) global strategic alliance **(b)** green field venture **(c)** sustainable development **(d)** protectionism

5. When a Hong Kong firm makes an agreement with The Walt Disney Company to legally make jewelry in the shape of Disney cartoon characters, Disney is engaging in a form of international business known as _____.
   (a) exporting **(b)** licensing **(c)** joint venturing **(d)** franchising

6. One major difference between an international business and a transnational corporation is that the transnational tries to operate _____.
   (a) without a strong national identity **(b)** in at least six foreign countries **(c)** with only expatriate managers at the top **(d)** without corruption

7. The Foreign Corrupt Practices Act makes it illegal for _____.
   (a) U.S. businesses to work with subcontractors running foreign sweatshop operations **(b)** foreign businesses to pay bribes to U.S. government officials **(c)** U.S. businesses to make "payoffs" abroad to gain international business contracts **(d)** foreign businesses to steal intellectual property from U.S. firms operating in their countries

8. If an international business firm has separate vice presidents in charge of its Asian, African, and European divisions, it is most likely using a global _____ structure.
   (a) product **(b)** functional **(c)** area **(d)** matrix

9. The athletic footwear maker New Balance recently discovered that exact copies of its running shoe designs were on sale in China under the name "New Barlun." This is an example of a/an _____ problem in international business.
   (a) most favored nation **(b)** global strategic alliance **(c)** joint venture **(d)** intellectual property rights

10. A person who is sent overseas by his or her employer to work for an extended period of time in a foreign subsidiary is called a/an _____.
    (a) expatriate employee **(b)** global manager **(c)** transnational manager **(d)** foreign worker

Short Response

11. What is the difference between a joint venture and wholly owned subsidiary?

12. List three reasons why host countries sometimes complain about MNCs.

13. What does it mean in an international business sense if a U.S. Senator says she favors "protectionism"?

14. What is the difference between currency risk and political risk in international business?

Integration & Application

Picture yourself sitting in a discussion group at the local bookstore and proudly signing copies of your newly published book, *Business Transitions in the New Global Economy*. A book buyer invites a comment from you by stating: "I am interested in your point regarding the emergence of transnational corporations. But, try as I might, a company like Ford or Procter & Gamble will always be 'as American as Apple pie' for me."

Questions: How would you respond in a way that both (a) clarifies the difference between a multinational and a transnational corporation, and (b) explains reasons why Ford or P&G may wish not to operate as or be viewed as "American" companies?

SELF-ASSESSMENT
Global Readiness Index

INSTRUCTIONS *Rate yourself on each of the following items as an indicator of your readiness to participate in the global work environment. Use this scale:*

1 = Very Poor   2 = Poor   3 = Acceptable   4 = Good
5 = Very Good

1 I understand my own culture in terms of its expectations, values, and influence on communication and relationships.

2 When someone presents me with a different point of view, I try to understand it rather than attack it.

3 I am comfortable dealing with situations where the available information is incomplete and the outcomes unpredictable.

4 I am open to new situations and am always looking for new information and learning opportunities.

5 I have a good understanding of the attitudes and perceptions toward my culture as they are held by people from other cultures.

6 I am always gathering information about other countries and cultures and trying to learn from them.

7 I am well informed regarding the major differences in government, political, and economic systems around the world.

8 I work hard to increase my understanding of people from other cultures.

9 I am able to adjust my communication style to work effectively with people from different cultures.

10 I can recognize when cultural differences are influencing working relationships and adjust my attitudes and behavior accordingly.

SCORING AND INTERPRETATION

The goal is to score as close to a perfect "5" as possible.

Items (1+2+3+4)/4 = ___ Global Mindset Score
Items (5+6+7)/3 = ___ Global Knowledge Score
Items (8+9+10)/3 = ___ Global Work Skills Score

A *global mindset* is receptive to and respectful of cultural differences; *global knowledge* includes the continuing quest to know and learn more about other nations and cultures; *global work skills* allow you to work effectively across cultures.

PATHWAYS to WileyPLUS

CASE SNAPSHOT

Go online to read this case!

Toyota: Sometimes Money Is Best Left on the table

Sometimes Money Is Best Left on the Table. What is Toyota doing right? Rather, what *isn't* Toyota doing right? The company is succeeding financially both in the United States and worldwide. Toyota has demonstrated a willingness to invest in positive relationships with suppliers over the long term; how has this improved its production capability? How has its philosophy of *kaizen* shaped its drive for quality?

MODULE 7 | Online Interactive Learning Resources

Skill Builder
• Global Mindset

Experiential Exercise
• American Football

Team Project
• Globalization Pros and Cons

It's nice to be

Entrepreneurship and Small Business

When Anita Santiago moved to the United States from Venezuela, she thought: "I'll never be able to land a job." But she did, in the advertising business. Four years later she started Anita Santiago Advertising, Inc. to focus on the Latin community and help communicate her culture to large companies. *Que gran idioma tengo* (What a great language I have) reads the front page of her website, quoting Chilean poet Pablo Neruda. "I can see culture from both sides," says Santiago. "You can't learn that from a book."[1]

This is a success story—a person with a great idea, taking the risk, starting a business. Could this be you someday? Perhaps, but you also need to be realistic. There's a very high failure rate for start-up small

your own boss

businesses. Each year there are many people with good ideas who can't find the resources to turn them into reality, or don't implement well because they don't have good business skills.

A good percentage of those starting small businesses are women, and they can face special challenges. Nell Merlino, creator of Take Our Daughters to Work Day, points out, "Women own 38 percent of all businesses in this country, but still have far less access to capital than men because of today's process."

Along with Iris Burnett, Merlino founded Count-Me-In for Women's Economic Independence to help female entrepreneurs get started.[2] Geneva Francais got a $1500 loan to support her homemade cooking sauce—"Geneva's Spash." She says: "A bank would not lend a woman money when she is 65 years old. It's as simple as that." Heather McCartney was also an early client. She received a $5,000 loan to expand "Ethnic Edibles," a line of African-motif cookies and cookie cutters.

Don't you think more people, women and men, should have this type of chance? Shouldn't everyone be "counted in" for economic independence?

→ MODULE GUIDE

 8.1 What is entrepreneurship and who are entrepreneurs?

- Entrepreneurs are risk takers that spot and pursue opportunities.
- Entrepreneurs often share similar personal characteristics.
- Women and minority entrepreneurs are growing in numbers.
- Social entrepreneurs seek novel solutions to social problems.

 8.2 What should we know about small business, and how can you start one?

- Small businesses are mainstays of the economy.
- Most small businesses fail within five years.
- Family-owned businesses can face unique challenges.
- A small business should start with a sound business plan.
- There are different forms of small business ownership.
- There are different ways of financing a small business.

Entrepreneurship is dynamic, risk-taking, creative, growth-oriented behavior.

An **entrepreneur** is willing to pursue opportunities in situations that others view as problems or threats.

A **first-mover advantage** comes from being first to exploit a niche or enter a market.

Anita Santiago, Heather McCartney, Iris Burnett, and Nell Merlino share a personal quality that is much valued in today's challenging economic times: **entrepreneurship**. Each showed original thinking and then acted upon it to create something new for society – an advertising agency, a cookie company, and a venture capital firm. They are **entrepreneurs**, persons who are willing to take risks to pursue opportunities that others either fail to recognize, or view as problems or threats.

• Entrepreneurs Are Risk Takers that Spot and Pursue Opportunities

H. Wayne Huizenga, former owner of Blockbuster Video and a member of the Entrepreneurs' Hall of Fame, describes being an entrepreneur this way: "An important part of being an entrepreneur is a gut instinct that allows you to believe in your heart that something will work even though everyone else says it will not." You say, "I am going to make sure it works. I am going to go out there and make it happen."[3] In business we talk about this as an entrepreneur's skill at gaining **first-mover advantage**, moving faster than competitors to spot, exploit, and enter a new market or an unrecognized niche in an existing one.

Management Tips starts our discussion by debunking some of the common myths about entrepreneurs.[4] With that out of the way, let's meet some real ones, people that built successful long-term businesses from good ideas and hard work.[5] As you read about these creative and confident individuals, think about how you might apply their experiences to your own life and career. After all, it could be very nice to be your own boss someday.

MARY KAY ASH

After a career in sales, Mary Kay "retired" in 1963. She then started to write a book to help women compete in the male-dominated business world. However, she soon realized she was actually writing a business plan instead. From that plan arose Mary Kay Cosmetics, with the goal "to help women everywhere reach their full potential." Launched on $5,000, the company now operates worldwide. It has been named one of the best companies to work for in the United States.

MANAGEMENT TIPS

Challenging the myths about entrepreneurs

- *Entrepreneurs are born, not made.*
  Not true! Talent gained and enhanced by experience is a foundation for entrepreneurial success.
- *Entrepreneurs are gamblers.*
  Not true! Entrepreneurs are risk takers, but the risks are informed and calculated.
- *Money is the key to entrepreneurial success.*
  Not true! Money is no guarantee of success. There's a lot more to it than that; many entrepreneurs start with very little.
- *You have to be young to be an entrepreneur.*
  Not true! Age is no barrier to entrepreneurship; with age often comes experience, contacts, and other useful resources.
- *You have to have a degree in business to be an entrepreneur.*
  Not true! But, it helps to study and understand business fundamentals.

RICHARD BRANSON

Want to start an airline? Many try but not too many succeed. Richard Branson did both, calling his venture Virgin Atlantic. His entrepreneurship began in his native England with a student literary magazine and small mail-order record business. Now he's built Virgin into one of the world's most recognized brand names. Today, the Virgin Group is a business conglomerate employing some 25,000 people around the globe. It holds over 200 companies, including Virgin Mobile, Virgin Records, and even Virgin Cola. It's all very creative and ambitious. But that's Branson. "I love to learn things I know little about," he says.

EARL GRAVES

With a vision and a $175,000 loan, Earl Graves started *Black Enterprise* magazine in 1970. That success grew into the diversified business information company Earl G. Graves, Ltd., including BlackEnterprise.com. Today the business school at his college alma mater, Baltimore's Morgan State University, is named after him. Graves says: "I feel that a large part of my role as publisher of *Black Enterprise* is to be a catalyst for black economic development in this country."

DAVID THOMAS

Have you had your Wendy's today? A lot of people have, and there's quite a story behind it. The first Wendy's restaurant opened in Columbus, Ohio, in November 1969. It's still there, although there are also about 5,000 others now operating around the world. What began as founder David Thomas's dream to own one restaurant grew into a global enterprise. He went on to become one of the world's best-known entrepreneurs: "the world's most famous hamburger cook." But there's more to Wendy's than profits and business performance. The company strives to help its communities, with a special focus on schools and schoolchildren. In 1992, Dave, an adopted child himself, founded the Dave Thomas Foundation for Adoption.

• Entrepreneurs Often Share Similar Personal Characteristics

Although we might think of all entrepreneurs as founding a new business that achieves large-scale success, many operate on a smaller and less public scale. Entrepreneurs also include those who buy a local Subway Sandwich franchise, open a small retail shop, or start a self-employed service business. Entrepreneurs exist within larger organizations as well. Anyone who assumes responsibility for introducing a new product or changing the organization in significant ways is also demonstrating entrepreneurship.

But what makes entrepreneurs different? Do you see any common patterns in the prior examples? Researchers tell us that most entrepreneurs are very self-confident, determined, self-directing, resilient, adaptable, and driven by excellence.[6] A report in the *Harvard Business Review* suggests that they have strong interests in both "creative production" and "enterprise control." They like to start things. This is creative production; they enjoy working with the unknown and finding unique solutions to problems. They like to run things. This is enterprise control; they enjoy making progress toward a goal.[7]

Test yourself. Look at the personality traits and characteristics in the Exhibit – *Profiles of Entrepreneurial Characteristics*.[8] Is there an entrepreneur lurking within you, perhaps just waiting for the right setting before emerging?

• Women and Minority Entrepreneurs Are Growing in Numbers

Sometimes it takes an outside stimulus or a special set of circumstances to awaken one's entrepreneurial tendencies. When economists speak about entrepreneurs they differentiate between those who are driven by the quest for new opportunities and those who are driven by absolute need.[9] Those in the latter group pursue **necessity-based entrepreneurship**. They start new ventures because they see no other employment options or they find career doors closed, perhaps due to hitting glass ceilings.

Necessity-based entrepreneurship is when people start new ventures because they have few or no other employment options.

EXHIBIT

Profile of Entrepreneurial Characteristics

Internal locus of control   Believe in control of own destiny; self-directing and likes autonomy

High energy level   Persistent, hard working, willing to exert extraordinary efforts to succeed

High need for achievement   Motivated to accomplish challenging goals; thrives on performance feedback

Tolerance for ambiguity   Risk taker; tolerates situations with high degrees of uncertainty

Self-confidence   Feels competent, believes in themselves, willing to make decisions

Action orientation   Try to act ahead of problems; want to get things done and not waste time

Self-reliance   Want independence; want to be their own boss, not work for others

Flexibility   Willing to admit problems and errors, to change course when plans aren't working

The National Foundation for Women Business Owners reports that women own over 9 million businesses in the United States, some 38 percent of all U.S. businesses.[10] Entrepreneurship offers women opportunities to strike out on their own and gain economic independence, providing a pathway for career success that may be blocked otherwise.[11] Having employers that failed to recognize or value them and seeing others promoted ahead of them, for example, are among the top motivations toward entrepreneurship given by women of color.[12]

Career difficulties may help explain why minority entrepreneurship is one of the fastest-growing sectors of our economy. Businesses created by minority entrepreneurs employ over 4 million U.S. workers and generate over $500 billion in annual revenues. And the trend is upward. In the last census of small businesses, those owned by African Americans grew by 45%, by Hispanics 31%, and by Asians 24%. During this same time small businesses owned by women also grew by 24%.[13]

• Social Entrepreneurs Seek Novel Solutions to Social Problems

Housing and job training for the homeless; bringing technology to poor families; improving literacy among disadvantaged youth; making small loans to start minority-owned businesses. What do these examples have in common? They are all targets for **social entrepreneurship**, a unique form of entrepreneurship that seeks novel ways to solve pressing social problems, at home and abroad.[14]

Social entrepreneurship seeks novel ways to solve pressing social problems.

Social entrepreneurs share many characteristics with other entrepreneurs, but also have one unique difference: a social mission drives them.[15] Their personal quests are for innovations that help solve social problems, or at least to help make lives better for people who are disadvantaged.

John Wood is a social entrepreneur. Once comfortably immersed in his career as a Microsoft executive, he found inspiration while on a vacation to the Himalayas of Nepal. Wood was shocked at the lack of schools! And he discovered a passion that determined what he calls the "second chapter" in his life: to provide the lifelong benefits of education to children in the developing world.

Wood quit his Microsoft job and started a nonprofit organization called Room to Read. So far, the organization has built nearly 200 schools and established over 2,500 libraries in Cambodia, India, Sri Lanka, Nepal, Vietnam, and Laos.

Noting that one-seventh of the global population can't read or write, Wood says: "I don't see how we are going to solve the world's problems without literacy." The Room to Read model is so efficient that it can build schools for as little as $10,000. *Time* magazine has honored Wood as an "Asian Hero," and *Fast Company* magazine awarded Room to READ with its Social Capitalist Award for three consecutive years.[16]

What do you think of Wood's model? Could you see yourself doing something like this someday? And, are there social entrepreneurs already active in your community and to whom you might lend a helping hand?

Be Sure You Can . . .

- explain the concept of entrepreneurship

- explain the concept of first-mover advantage

- explain why people like Mary Kay Ash and Earl Graves are entrepreneurs

- list personal characteristics often associated with entrepreneurs

- explain trends in entrepreneurship by women and minorities

- explain what makes social entrepreneurs unique

Define the Terms

Entrepreneur

Entrepreneurship

First-mover advantage

Necessity-based entrepreneurship

Social entrepreneurship

Rapid Review

- Entrepreneurship is original thinking that creates value for people, organizations, and society.

- Entrepreneurs take risks to pursue opportunities others may fail to recognize.

- Entrepreneurs like Mary Kay Ash, Richard Branson, Earl Graves, and Anita Roddick can be a source of learning and inspiration for others.

- Entrepreneurs tend to be creative people who are self-confident, determined, resilient, adaptable, and driven to excel; they like to be masters of their own destinies.

- Women and minorities are well represented among entrepreneurs, with some of this being driven by necessity or the lack of alternative career options.

- Social entrepreneurs apply their energies to create innovations that help to solve important problems in society.

Reflect/React

1. Does an entrepreneur always need to have first-mover advantage in order to succeed?

2. Are there any items on the list of entrepreneurial characteristics that are essential "must haves" for someone to succeed in any career, not just entrepreneurship?

3. Could necessity-driven entrepreneurship be an indicator of some deeper problems in our society?

A **small business** has fewer than 500 employees, is independently owned and operated, and does not dominate its industry.

The SBA defines a **small business** as one with 500 or fewer employees, with the number varying a bit by industry. The SBA also views a small business as one that is independently owned and operated and that does not dominate its industry.[17] Almost 99 percent of U.S. businesses meet this definition. Some 87 percent employ fewer than 20 persons.

• Small Businesses Are Mainstays of the Economy

Most nations rely on their small business sector. Why? Among other things, small businesses offer major economic advantages. In the United States, for example, small businesses employ some 52 percent of private workers, provide 51 percent of private-sector output, receive 35 percent of federal government contract dollars, and provide as many as 7 out of every 10 new jobs in the economy.[18] Smaller businesses are especially prevalent in the service and retailing sectors of the economy. Higher costs of entry make them less common in other industries such as manufacturing and transportation.

And then there's the Internet. Have you looked at the action on eBay recently? Can you imagine how many people might now be running small trading businesses from their homes? If you're one of them, you're certainly not alone. The SBA believes that some 85 percent of small firms are already conducting business over the Internet.[19] Even established "bricks-and-mortar" small retailers are finding the Internet ripe with opportunities.

That's what happened to Rod Spencer and his S&S Sports Cards store in Worthington, Ohio. In fact, he closed the store not because business was bad, but because it was really good. When his Internet sales greatly exceeded in-store sales, Spencer decided to follow the world of e-commerce. He now works from home, saving the cost of renting retail space and hiring store employees. "I can do less business overall," Ron says, "and make a higher profit."[20]

PACESETTERS

African-American entrepreneurs lead the way.

In 1956, at a small brick church in Montgomery, Alabama, Martin Luther King, Jr., told African-Americans to "work within the framework of democracy to bring about a better distribution of wealth." And indeed they have. "The history of black Americans has always been self-employment and entrepreneurship," says John Butler, professor of business at the University of Texas at Austin. Among those starting businesses in the United States, African-Americans help lead the way. In fact, there are three start-ups of African-American–owned companies for each headed by someone of another ethnicity. Gwen Day Richardson started cushcity.com, an online bookstore selling African-American merchandise. Fred Terrell started the venture capital fund Provender Capital. He believes that having more African-American–owned venture capital funds makes it easier for black entrepreneurs to get started.

Gwen Day Richardson, Founder, Cushcity.com.
Fred Terrell Provender Capital.

• Most Small Businesses Fail within Five Years

Figure 8.1 describes the typical progression in the life of a small business.[21] The new firm begins with the *birth stage*—where the entrepreneur struggles to get the new venture established and survive long enough to really test the marketplace. The firm then passes into the *breakthrough stage*—where the business model begins to work well, growth takes place, and the complexity of the business expands significantly. Next comes the *maturity stage*—where the entrepreneur experiences market success and financial stability, but also has to face competitive challenges in a dynamic environment.

Doesn't it all sound good, making the prospects of starting your own small business attractive? It should, but a word of caution is called for as well. The figure doesn't show a very common event in the life cycle of a small business: it's failure.

Figure 8.1 What are the stages in the life cycle of an entrepreneurial firm?

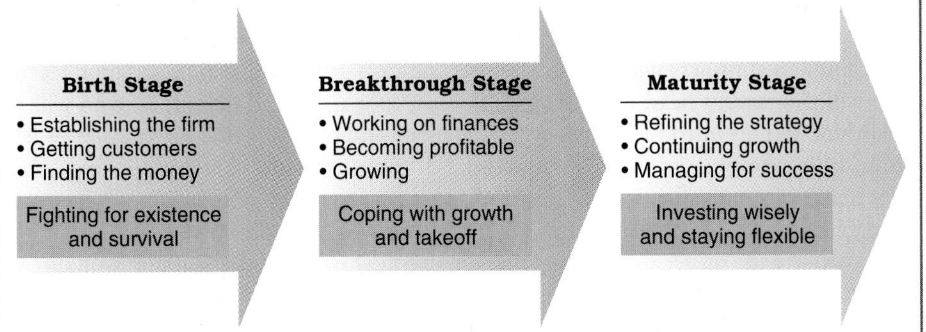

Birth Stage
- Establishing the firm
- Getting customers
- Finding the money

Fighting for existence and survival

Breakthrough Stage
- Working on finances
- Becoming profitable
- Growing

Coping with growth and takeoff

Maturity Stage
- Refining the strategy
- Continuing growth
- Managing for success

Investing wisely and staying flexible

It is typical for small businesses to move through three life cycle stages. During the *birth* stage, the entrepreneur focuses on getting things started—bringing a product to market, finding initial customers, and earning enough money to survive. *Breakthrough* is a time of rapid growth when the business model really starts working well. Growth often slows in the *maturity* stage where financial success is realized, but also where the entrepreneur often needs to make adjustments to stay successful in a dynamic marketplace.

Small businesses have a scarily high failure rate. The SBA reports that as many as 60 to 80 percent of new businesses fail in their first five years of operation.[22] Part of this might be explained as a "counting" issue, since the government counts as a "failure" any business that closes, whether it is due to the death or retirement of an owner, sale to someone else, or the inability to earn a profit.[23] Nevertheless, the fact remains: a lot of small business start-ups don't make it.

Look at the Exhibit – *Common Causes of Small Business Failures*.[24] Most of the failures result from poor judgment and management mistakes made by entrepreneurs and owners. So if you decide to launch your own venture someday, you'll need to learn from these mistakes. This is just as important as studying success stories.

• Family-Owned Businesses Can Face Unique Challenges

Among the reasons given for getting started in small businesses, you'll find the owners saying they were motivated to be their own bosses, be in control of their own futures, fulfill dreams, and become part of a family-owned business.[25] Indeed, **family businesses**, those owned and financially controlled by family members, represent the largest percentage of businesses operating worldwide. The Family Firm Institute reports that family businesses account for 78 percent of new jobs created in the United States, and provide 60 percent of the nation's employment.[26]

Family businesses must master the same challenges as other small or large businesses, such as devising strategy, achieving competitive advantage, and ensuring operational excellence. When everything goes right, the family firm can be an ideal situation. Everyone works together, sharing values and a common goal: working together to support the family. But things don't always turn out this way or stay this way, especially as a business changes hands over successive generations.

"Okay, Dad, so he's your brother. But does that mean we have to put up with inferior work and an erratic schedule that we would never tolerate from anyone else in the business?"[27] This conversation introduces a problem that can lead to small business failure, the **family business feud**. The

EXHIBIT

Common Causes of Small Business Failures

Lack of experience Not having sufficient know-how to run a business in the chosen market or area

Lack of expertise Not having expertise in the essentials of business operations, including finance, purchasing, selling, and production

Lack of strategy Not taking the time to craft a vision and mission, nor to formulate and properly implement strategy

Poor financial control Failing to track the numbers and to control business finances

Growing too fast Not taking the time to consolidate a position, fine-tune the organization, and systematically meet the challenges of growth

Insufficient commitment Not devoting enough time to the requirements of running a competitive business

Ethical failure Falling prey to the temptations of fraud, deception, and embezzlement

feud can be about jobs and who does what, business strategy, operating approaches, finances, or other matters. It can be between spouses, among siblings, between parents and children. It really doesn't matter. Unless family business feuds are resolved satisfactorily, the firm may not survive.

A survey of small and midsized family businesses indicated that 66 percent planned on keeping the business within the family.[28] The management question is: Upon leaving, how will the current head of the company distribute assets and determine who will run the business? This introduces the **succession problem**, how to handle the transfer of leadership from one generation to the next. The data on succession are eye opening. About 30 percent of family firms survive to the second generation; 12 percent survive to the third generation; only 3 percent are expected to survive beyond that.[29]

If you were the owner of a successful family business, what would you do? Wouldn't you want to have a **succession plan** that clearly spells out how leadership transition and related matters, including financial ones, are to be handled when the time for changeover occurs?

• A Small Business Should Start with a Sound Business Plan

When people start new businesses, or even start new units within existing ones, they can greatly benefit from another type of plan—a sound **business plan**. This plan describes the goals of the business and the way it intends to operate, ideally in ways that can help obtain any needed start-up financing.[30]

Banks and other financiers want to see a business plan before they loan money or invest in a new venture. Senior managers want to see a business plan before they allocate scarce organizational resources to support a new entrepreneurial project. You should also want a small business plan. It helps sort out your ideas, map strategies, and pin down your business model; this detailed and disciplined thinking can increase the likelihood of success. Says Ed Federkeil, who founded a small business called California Custom Sport Trucks: "It gives you direction instead of haphazardly sticking your key in the door every day and saying—'What are we going to do?' "[31]

Although there is no single template for a successful business plan, most would agree on the general framework presented in Management Tips.[32] Any business plan should include an executive summary, cover certain business fundamentals, be well organized with headings, be easy to read, and be relatively short. In addition to advice available in books and magazines, you should also be able to find many online resources for the development of a business plan.

MANAGEMENT TIPS

What to include in a business plan

- *Executive summary*—business purpose; highlights of plan
- *Industry analysis*—nature of industry, economic trends, legal or regulatory issues, risks
- *Company description*—mission, owners, legal form
- *Products and services*—major goods or services, uniqueness vis-à-vis competition
- *Market description*—size, competitor strengths and weaknesses, five-year sales goals
- *Marketing strategy*—product characteristics, distribution, promotion, pricing
- *Operations description*—manufacturing or service methods, suppliers, controls
- *Staffing*—management and worker skills needed and available, compensation, human resource systems
- *Financial projection*—cash flow projections 1-5 years, breakeven points
- *Capital needs*—amount needed, amount available, amount being requested
- *Milestones*—timetable for completing key stages of new venture

• There Are Different Forms of Small Business Ownership

One of the important choices when starting a new venture is the legal form of ownership. There are a number of alternatives, each with respective advantages and disadvantages.

A **sole proprietorship** is simply an individual or a married couple that pursues business for a profit. The business often operates under a personal name, such as "Tiana Lopez Designs." Because a sole proprietorship is simple to start, run, and terminate, it is the most common form of U.S. small business ownership. If you were to choose this for

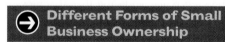

Different Forms of Small Business Ownership

- Sole proprietorship
- General partnership
- Limited partnership
- Corporation
- Limited liability corporation

your small business, however, you have to remember that any owner of a sole proprietorship is personally liable for all business debts and claims.

A **partnership** is formed when two or more people agree to contribute resources to start and operate a business together. Most partnerships are set up with legal and written agreements that document what each party contributes in resources and skills, and how profits and losses are to be shared. You would be ill advised to enter into a serious partnership without such an agreement. But the choice of partnership type is important also.

In a **general partnership**, the simplest and most common form, the owners share management responsibilities. Each is supposed to be directly involved in day-to-day operations. This differs from a **limited partnership** consisting of a general partner and one or more "limited" partners. The general manager runs the business; the limited partners do not participate in its day-to-day management. All partners share in profits, but their losses are limited to the amounts of their investments. This limit to one's liabilities is a major advantage. In fact, you'll notice that many professionals, such as accountants and attorneys, join in *limited liability partnerships* because they limit the liability of one partner in case of negligence by any others.

A **corporation**, commonly identified by the "Inc." designation in a name, is a legal entity that exists separately from its owners. Corporations are legally charted by the states in which they are registered, and they can be for-profit, such as Microsoft Inc., or not-for-profit, such as Count-Me-In, Inc. There are two major advantages in choosing to incorporate a small business: (1) it grants the organization certain legal rights (for example, to engage in contracts), and (2) the corporation is responsible for its own liabilities. This gives the firm a life of its own and separates the owners from personal liability. The major disadvantages rest with the legal costs of forming the corporation, and the complexity of documentation required to operate as one.

Recently, the **limited liability corporation (LLC)** has gained popularity. It combines the advantages of sole proprietorship, partnership, and corporation. For liability purposes, it functions like a corporation, protecting the assets of owners against claims made against the company. For tax purposes, it functions as a partnership in the case of multiple owners, and as a sole proprietorship in the case of a single owner.

> A **partnership** is when two or more people agree to contribute resources to start and operate a business together.
>
> In a **general partnership**, owners share management responsibilities.
>
> A **limited partnership** consists of a general partner that manages the business one or more limited partners.
>
> A **corporation** is a legal entity that exists separately from its owners.
>
> A **limited liability corporation (LLC)** is a hybrid business form combining advantages of the sole proprietorship, partnership, and corporation.

NEWSLINE

Chamber of Commerce connects businesses across borders Through a special program called "Wiring the Border," the United States–Mexico Chamber of Commerce is helping border companies tap the e-commerce marketplace. The Chamber's

president, Albert C. Zapanta, says: "This initiative will help small businesses reach the international marketplace and compete effectively around the world." Major U.S. and Mexican corporations, including IBM and TelMex, are helping to sponsor the program by contributing Web-enabling components. The member small businesses will be joined in a virtual network stretching from San Diego/Tijuana to Brownsville/Matamoros. All will utilize e-commerce to increase sales, profits, and employment. Zapanta says: "Communities along the border have not shared in the economic growth enjoyed by most Americans the past several years, but they have borne a disproportionate share of the burden." Through Wiring the Border, the Chamber and its partners hope to bring positive change to both sides of the border.

Reflect: What role can small business development along the U.S.-Mexican border play in helping both nations deal with the problem of illegal cross-border workers? Could a similar approach help rural small businesses elsewhere to prosper and grow?

• There Are Different Ways of Financing a Small Business

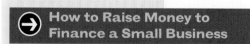

Starting a new venture takes money. Unless you possess personal wealth that you are willing to risk, that money has to be raised. The two most common ways to raise it are through debt financing and equity financing.

Debt financing involves borrowing money from another person, a bank, or a financial institution. This loan must be paid back over time with interest. A loan also requires collateral that pledges business assets or personal assets, such as a home, to secure the loan in case of default. This is the same type of financing that you probably use when purchasing a home or a car; you borrow money with a promise to repay both the loan amount and interest.

Equity financing gives ownership shares to outsiders in return for their financial investments. And in important contrast to debt financing, this money does not need to be paid back. Instead, the investor assumes the risk of potential gains and losses based on the performance of the business. But in return for taking that risk, the equity investor gains something—part of your original ownership. The amount of ownership and control given up is represented in the number and proportion of ownership shares transferred to the equity investors.

When businesses need equity financing in fairly large amounts, from the tens of thousands to the millions of dollars, they often turn to **venture capitalists.** These are individuals and companies that make money by pooling capital to invest in new ventures. Their hope is that their equity stakes rise in value and can be sold for a profit when the business becomes successful. Sometimes they can be quite aggressive in wanting active management roles to make sure the business grows in value as soon as possible. Then, this value is tapped by an **initial public offering (IPO)**. This is when shares in the business are sold to the public at large, most likely beginning to trade on a major stock exchange.

When an IPO is successful, the market bids up the share prices, thus increasing the value of the original shares held by the venture capitalist and the entrepreneur. When Google's IPO went public, the stock opened at $85 per share; by the end of the day it was already above $100, and it has risen dramatically since. This has been a great return for the founders and original venture capital investors. Check out the current price for a GOOG share on the NASDAQ today and you'll find it worth considerably more. Wouldn't it have been nice to be in on that original IPO?

Entrepreneurs may try to find an **angel investor** when venture capital isn't available or isn't yet interested. This is a wealthy individual who invests in return for equity in a new venture. Angel investors are especially helpful in the late birth and early breakthrough stages of a new venture. Once they jump in it can raise the confidence and interests of venture capitalists, thus making it easier to attract even more funding. For example, when Liz Cobb wanted to start her sales compensation firm, Incentive Systems, she contacted 15 to 20 venture capital firms. Only 10 interviewed her, and all of those turned her down. However, after she located $250,000 from two angel investors, the venture capital firms renewed their interest, allowing her to obtain her first $2 million in financing. Her firm grew to employ over 70 workers.[33] This isn't quite a Google story, but it's still a good one.

Venture capitalists make large investments in new ventures in return for an equity stake in the business.

An **initial public offering (IPO)** is an initial selling of shares of stock to the public at large.

An **angel investor** is a wealthy individual willing to invest in return for equity in a new venture.

STUDY GUIDE

8.2 What should we know about small business, and how can you start one?

Be Sure You Can . . .

- state the SBA definition of small business

- illustrate opportunities for entrepreneurship on the Internet

- list the life-cycle stages of a small business

- list several reasons why many small businesses fail

- discuss the succession problem in family-owned businesses

- list the major elements in a business plan

- differentiate the common forms of small business ownership

- differentiate debt financing and equity financing

- explain the roles of venture capitalists and angel investors in new venture financing

Define the Terms

Angel investor	Limited partnership
Business plan	Limited liability corporation (LLC)
Corporation	
Debt financing	Partnership
Equity financing	Small business
Family business	Sole proprietorship
Family business feud	Succession plan
General partnership	Succession problem
Initial public offering (IPO)	Venture capitalists

Rapid Review

- Small businesses constitute the vast majority of businesses in the United States and create 7 out of every 10 new jobs in the economy.

- Small businesses have a high failure rate; as many as 60 to 80 percent of new businesses fail in their first five years of operation.

- Family businesses that are owned and financially controlled by family members can suffer from the succession problem of transferring leadership from one generation to the next.

- A business plan describes the intended nature of a proposed new business, how it will operate, and how it will obtain financing.

- Proprietorships, partnerships, and corporations are different forms of business ownership, with each offering advantages and disadvantages.

- New ventures can be financed through debt financing in the form of loans, and through equity financing, which exchanges ownership shares in return for outside investment.

- Venture capitalists and angel investors invest in new ventures in return for an equity stake in the business.

Reflect/React

1. Given the high economic importance of small businesses, what could local, state, and federal governments do to make it easier for them to prosper?

2. If you were asked to join a small company, what would you look for in its business plan as potential success indicators?

3. Why should the owner of a small but growing business want to be careful when accepting big investments from venture capitalists?

Multiple Choice

1. Someone who thrives on uncertainty and risk-taking displays an entrepreneurial characteristic known as a/an _____.
   (a) high tolerance for ambiguity **(b)** internal locus of control **(c)** need for achievement **(d)** action orientation

2. Almost _____ percent of U.S. businesses meet the definition of "small business" used by the Small Business Administration.
   (a) 40 **(b)** 99 **(c)** 75 **(d)** 81

3. A small business owner who is concerned about passing the business on to other family members after retirement or death is advised to prepare a _____ plan that documents his or her wishes.
   (a) retirement **(b)** succession **(c)** partnership **(d)** liquidation

4. One of the most common reasons that new small business start-ups often fail is because _____.
   (a) the owner lacks experience and business skills **(b)** there is too much government regulation **(c)** the owner tightly controls money and finances **(d)** the business grows too slowly

5. A pressing problem faced by a small business in the birth or start-up stage is _____.
   (a) gaining acceptance in the marketplace **(b)** finding partners for expansion **(c)** preparing the initial public offering **(d)** bringing professional skills into the management team

6. A venture capitalist that receives an ownership share in return for investing in a new business is providing _____ financing.
   (a) debt **(b)** equity **(c)** limited **(d)** corporate

7. In _____ financing, the business owner borrows money as a loan that must eventually be paid along with agreed-upon interest to the lender.
   (a) debt **(b)** equity **(c)** partnership **(d)** limited

8. If an entrepreneur wants to start a small business, avoid losing any more than the amount of his or her original investment, and avoid costly legal fees for setting up the company, a _____ form of ownership would be a good choice.
   (a) sole proprietorship **(b)** general partnership **(c)** limited partnership **(d)** corporation

9. The first element in a good business plan is usually _____.
   (a) an industry analysis **(b)** a marketing strategy **(c)** an executive summary **(d)** a set of performance milestones

10. Data on current trends in U.S. small business ownership would most likely show that _____.
    (a) the numbers of businesses owned by women and minorities are growing **(b)** very few small businesses conduct some business by Internet **(c)** large businesses create more jobs than small businesses **(d)** very few small businesses are family owned

Short Response

11. What is the relationship between diversity and entrepreneurship?

12. What major challenges do business owners face at each stage in the life cycle of an entrepreneurial firm?

13. What are the advantages of choosing a limited partnership form of small business ownership?

14. What is the difference, if any, between a venture capitalist and an angel investor?

Integration & Application

Assume that you have a great idea for a potential Internet-based start-up business. In discussing the idea with a friend, she advises you to clearly link your business idea to potential customers, and then describe it well in a business plan. "After all," she says, "you won't succeed without customers and you'll never get a chance to succeed if you can't attract financial backers through a good business plan."

Questions: This sounds like good advice. What questions will you ask and answer to ensure that you are customer-focused in this business? What are the major areas that you would address in your initial business plan?

SELF-ASSESSMENT
Entrepreneurship Orientation

1 What portion of your college expenses did you earn (or are you earning)?
(a) 50 percent or more (b) less than 50 percent (c) none

2 In college, your academic performance was/is
(a) above average. (b) average. (c) below average.

3 What is your basic reason for considering opening a business?
(a) I want to make money. (b) I want to control my own destiny. (c) I hate the frustration of working for someone else.

4 Which phrase best describes your attitude toward work?
(a) I can keep going as long as I need to; I don't mind working for something I want. (b) I can work hard for a while, but when I've had enough, I quit. (c) Hard work really doesn't get you anywhere.

5 How would you rate your organizing skills?
(a) superorganized (b) above average (c) average (d) I do well to find half the things I look for.

6 You are primarily a(n)
(a) optimist. (b) pessimist. (c) neither.

7 You are faced with a challenging problem. As you work, you realize you are stuck. You will most likely
(a) give up. (b) ask for help. (c) keep plugging; you'll figure it out.

8 You are playing a game with a group of friends. You are most interested in
(a) winning. (b) playing well. (c) making sure that everyone has a good time. (d) cheating as much as possible.

9 How would you describe your feelings toward failure?
(a) Fear of failure paralyzes me. (b) Failure can be a good learning experience. (c) Knowing that I might fail motivates me to work even harder. (d) "Damn the torpedoes! Full speed ahead."

10 Which phrase best describes you?
(a) I need constant encouragement to get anything done. (b) If someone gets me started, I can keep going. (c) I am energetic and hard-working—a self-starter.

11 Which bet would you most likely accept?
(a) a wager on a dog race (b) a wager on a racquetball game in which you play an opponent (c) Neither. I never make wagers.

12 At the Kentucky Derby, you would bet on
(a) the 100-to-1 long shot. (b) the odds-on favorite. (c) the 3-to-1 shot. (d) none of the above.

SCORING

Give yourself 10 points each for answers 1a, 2a, 3c, 4a, 5a, 6a, 7c, 8a, 9c, 10c, 11b, 12c; total the scores and enter the result here [I = _____]. Give yourself 8 points each for answers 3b, 8b, 9b; enter total here [II = _____]. Give yourself 6 points each for answers 2b, 5b; enter total here [III = _____]. Give yourself 5 points for answer 1b; enter result here [IV = _____]. Give yourself 4 points for answer 5c; enter result here [V = _____]. Give yourself 2 points each for answers 2c, 3a, 4b, 6c, 9d, 10b, 11a, 12b; enter total here [VI = _____]. Any other answers are worth 0 points. Total your summary scores for I + II + III + IV + V + VI and enter the result here [EP = _____].

INTERPRETATION

This assessment offers an impression of your *entrepreneurial profile (EP)*. It compares your characteristics with those of typical entrepreneurs, according to this profile: 100+ = Entrepreneur extraordinaire; 80–99 = Entrepreneur; 60–79 = Potential entrepreneur; 0–59 = Entrepreneur in the rough.

PATHWAYS to WileyPLUS

CASE SNAPSHOT

Go online to read this case!
Zappos.com: Steps Ahead of the Competition
Unlike Amazon.com, which has been pursuing a department store strategy, Zappos is taking an alternate approach: They're focusing on one line of product, going as deep into that product line as possible. Is this strategy – staying true to the original brand focus – stronger than Amazon's? Or are both strategies viable, considering the companies?

MODULE 8 — Online Interactive Learning Resources

Skill Builder
• Self-Confidence

Experiential Exercise
• Entrepreneurs among Us

Team Project
• Community Entrepreneurs

Decide first,

Managers as Decision Makers

Whenever one talks about decision making these days, it's hard not to think about how people and organizations dealt with Hurricane Katrina.

New Orleans was devastated; people lost homes, fortunes, and lives; organizations lost reputations for failures in their response capabilities. And in retrospect, it is clear that a lot could have been done differently and better. But when things are happening in "real time" it's not easy to do all the right things; mistakes get made, and well-intended decisions go wrong or prove inadequate to the task.

Fred Sawyers was there, in New Orleans, managing a Hilton hotel. But in what he describes as "the most harrowing week of his life," he exceled. Using common sense, quick perception, and dogged hard work, he moved

then act

from decision to decision motivating staff, keeping the damaged hotel as safe as possible, and feeding and sheltering 4500 persons from the storm.

The *Business Week* article carrying Sawyers's story led with the headline: "They don't teach this in B-School."[1] We might disagree a bit. Anyone who studies management knows that decision making is part of the job. They also know that not all decisions are going to be easy ones; some will always have to be made under tough conditions. All of those case studies, experiential exercises, class discussions, and even essay exam questions are intended to engage students in the complexities of managerial decision making, the potential problems and pitfalls, and even the pressures of crisis situations.

From the classroom forward, however, it's all up to you. Only you can determine whether you step forward like Sawyers and make the best out of very difficult circumstances, or collapse under pressure.

> *"The significant problems we face cannot be solved at the same level of thinking we were at when we created them."*
>
> **Albert Einstein**

→ MODULE GUIDE

 9.1 How do managers use information to make decisions and solve problems?

- Managers deal with problems posing threats and offering opportunities.
- Managers can be problem avoiders, problem solvers, or problem seekers.
- Managers display systematic and intuitive problem-solving styles.
- Managers make decisions under conditions of certainty, risk, and uncertainty.
- Managers solve problems with programmed and nonprogrammed decisions.

 9.2 What are the steps in the decision-making process?

- Step 1 is to identify and define the problem.
- Step 2 is to generate and evaluate alternative courses of action.
- Step 3 is to decide on a preferred course of action.
- Step 4 is to implement the decision.
- Step 5 is to evaluate results.

9.3 What are some practicalities of managerial decision making?

- Judgmental heuristics and other biases may cause decision-making errors.
- Group decision making has both advantages and disadvantages.
- Managers must be prepared for crisis decision making.
- Managers should always check the ethics of their decisions.

Problem solving is the process of identifying a discrepancy between an actual and desired state of affairs, and then taking action to resolve it. The context for managerial problem solving is depicted in Figure 9.1. It clearly shows why managers fit our earlier definition of *knowledge workers*, persons whose value to organizations rests with their intellectual, not physical, capabilities.[2] All managers continually solve problems as they gather, give, receive, and process information from many sources.[3] In fact, one of your most critical skills might be described as **information competency**—the ability to locate, retrieve, evaluate, organize, and analyze information to make decisions that solve problems.

• Managers Deal with Problems Posing Threats and Offering Opportunities

The most obvious problem solving situation for managers, or anyone for that matter, is a **performance threat**. This occurs as an actual or potential performance deficiency: something is wrong, or is likely to be wrong in the near future. Hurricane Katrina is a ready example. There were lots of warnings, but many underestimated or were either lazy or overconfident in preparing for it. They weren't ready when Katrina hit and a high price was paid for their errors.

Problem solving involves identifying and taking action to resolve problems.

Information competency is the ability to gather and use information to solve problems.

A **performance threat** is a situation where something is wrong or likely to be wrong.

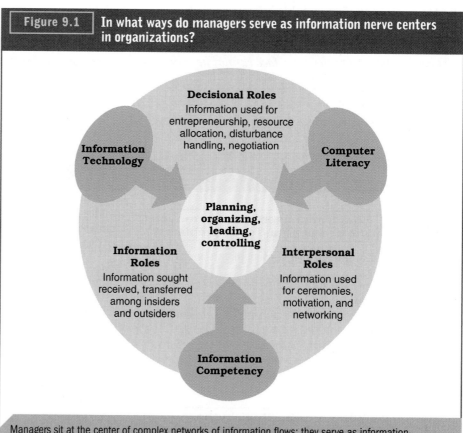

Figure 9.1 | **In what ways do managers serve as information nerve centers in organizations?**

Managers sit at the center of complex networks of information flows; they serve as information-processing hubs or nerve centers. Each of the management functions—planning, organizing, leading, and controlling—requires the gathering, use, and transfering of information in these networks. Managers must have the information competencies needed to perform well in these roles.

Let's not forget, however, that problem solving often involves, or should involve, a **performance opportunity**.[4] This is a situation that offers the possibility of a better future, if the right steps are taken now. Suppose that a regional manager notices that sales at one retail store are unusually high. Does she just say "Great," and go on about her business? That's an opportunity missed. If she says, "Wait a minute, there may be something happening here that I could learn from and possibly transfer to other stores; I had better find out what's going on," that's an opportunity gained.

• Managers Can Be Problem Avoiders, Problem Solvers, or Problem Seekers

What do you do when you receive a lower grade than expected on an exam or assignment? Do you get the grade, perhaps complain a bit to yourself or friends, and then forget it? Or do you get the grade, recognize that a problem exists, and try to learn from it so that you can do better in the future? Managers are just like you and me. They approach problem solving in different ways, and realize different consequences.

Some managers are *problem avoiders* who ignore information that would otherwise signal the presence of a performance threat or opportunity. They are not active in gathering information, preferring not to make decisions or deal with problems.

Other managers are *problem solvers* who will make decisions and try to solve problems when required. They are reactive, gathering information and responding to problems when they occur, but not before. These managers may deal reasonably well with performance threats, but they are likely to miss many performance opportunities.

Still other managers, perhaps the better ones, are *problem seekers* who are always looking for problems to solve or opportunities to explore. True problem seekers are proactive information gatherers, and they are forward thinking. They anticipate threats and opportunities, and they are eager to take action to gain the advantage in dealing with them.

PACESETTERS

Sometimes a problem can become the opportunity of a lifetime.

That's true, but getting a good *grip* on the problem can really help. In fact, grips were the solution to a problem faced by Caryl Parker. An ex-IBM employee who had left the firm some 10 years ago to raise a family, Parker was looking for a way to get back into the workforce. But she wanted it on her terms: flexible hours, time with her family, and a good income. This problem became opportunity when she noticed a big market for tennis racket "overgrips" that had some style. Working at home, she made some samples and after a year's worth of trial and error hit the market with a successful Hawaiian design. Now her Hipgrips are hot items in tennis shops around the country, and her employment problem has been solved in a unique and financially rewarding way. But it took hard work, a cooperative family, lots of mistakes, and a willingness to see her problem as an opportunity in the making. Now she says: "When you start your own company you're much more passionate about what you do."

Caryl Parker, entrepreneur, Hipgrips.

• Managers Display Systematic and Intuitive Problem-Solving Styles

Again like you and me, managers also differ in their use of "systematic" and "intuitive" thinking. In **systematic thinking** a person approaches problems in a rational, step-by-step, and analytical fashion. You might recognize this when someone you are working with tries to break a complex problem into smaller components that can be addressed one by one. We might expect systematic managers to make a plan before taking action, and to search for information and proceed with problem solving in a step-by-step fashion.

Someone using **intuitive thinking** is more flexible and spontaneous than the systematic thinker; the person may also be quite creative.[5] You might observe this pattern as someone who always seems to come up with an imaginative response to a problem, often based on a quick and broad evaluation of the situation. Intuitive managers often tend to deal with many aspects of a problem at once, jump quickly from one issue to another, and act on hunches from experience or on spontaneous ideas.

Systematic thinker solves problems step-by-step.

Intuitive thinker solves problems imaginatively.

• Managers Make Decisions under Conditions of Certainty, Risk, and Uncertainty

It's not just personal styles that differ in problem solving; the environment counts too. Figure 9.2 shows three different conditions or problem environments in which managers make decisions—certainty, risk, and uncertainty. As you might expect, the levels of risk and uncertainty in problem environments tends to increase the higher one moves in management ranks. You might think about this each time you hear about Coca-Cola or Pepsi launching a new flavor or product. Are the top executives making these decisions *certain* that the results will be successful; or, are they taking *risks* in market situations that are *uncertain* as to whether the new flavor or product will be positively received by customers?

It would be nice if we could all make decisions and solve problems in the relative predictability of a **certain environment**. This is an ideal decision situation where factual information exists for the possible alternative courses of action and their consequences. All a decision maker needs to do is study the alternatives and choose the best solution. It isn't easy to find examples of decision situations with such certain conditions. One possibility is a decision to take out a student loan; at least you can make the decision knowing future interest costs and repayment timetables.

As you might expect, managers more often face **risk environments** where information and facts are incomplete. Alternative courses of action and their consequences can be discussed and analyzed only as *probabilities* (e.g., 4 chances out of 10) of occurrence. One way of dealing with risk is by gathering as much information as possible, perhaps in different ways. In the case of a new product, such as Zero Coke or even a college textbook like this, it is unlikely that marketing executives would make go-ahead decisions without getting positive reports from multiple focus groups that tested the product in the sample stage.

When facts are few and information is so poor that managers have a hard time even assigning probabilities to things, an **uncertain environment** exists. This is the most difficult decision condition.[6] Responses to uncertainty depend greatly on intuition, judgment, informed guessing, and hunches—all of which leave considerable room for error. This is one reason why groups are often used for this type of problem solving. By bringing more information, perspectives, and creativity to bear on the situation, the chances for a good decision are often improved.

A **certain environment** offers complete information on possible action alternatives and their consequences.

A **risk environment** lacks complete information but offers probabilities of the likely outcomes for possible action alternatives.

An **uncertain environment** lacks so much information that it is difficult to assign probabilities to the likely outcomes of alternatives.

| Figure 9.2 | What are the differences between certain, risk, and uncertain decision-making environments? |

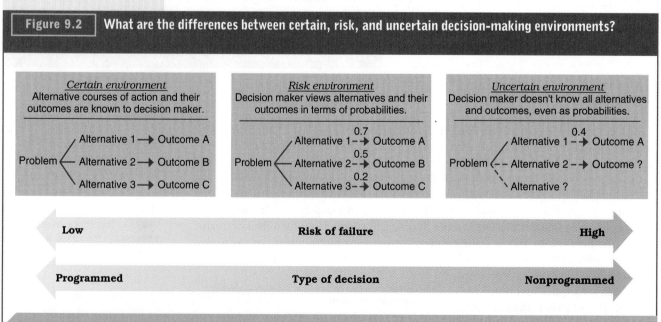

Managers rarely face a problem where they can know all the facts, identify all alternatives and their consequences, and chart a clear course of action. Such *certainty* is more often than not replaced by problem environments involving risk and uncertainty. *Risk,* is where alternatives are known but their consequences can be described in terms of probabilities. *Uncertainty,* is where all alternatives are not known and their consequences are highly speculative.

• Managers Solve Problems with Programmed and Nonprogrammed Decisions

So far in this discussion we have used the word *decision* rather casually. From this point forward, though, let's agree that a **decision** is a choice among possible alternative courses of action. Let's also admit that decisions can be made in different ways, with some approaches working better than others in various circumstances.

Some management problems are routine and repetitive. They can be addressed through **programmed decisions** that apply preplanned solutions based on the lessons of past experience. Such decisions work best for structured problems that are familiar, straightforward, and clear with respect to information needs. In human resource management, for example, decisions always have to be made on things like vacations and holiday work schedules. Forward-looking managers can use past experience and plan ahead to make these decisions in programmed, not spontaneous, ways.

Other management problems, many in fact, arise as new or unusual situations full of ambiguities and information deficiencies. These problems require **nonprogrammed decisions** that craft novel solutions to meet the unique demands of a situation. The module opening example showed Fred Sawyers involved in a lot of nonprogrammed decisions. Even though his hotel had evacuation plans that were programmed or preset, the enormity and speed of the Katrina disaster made them largely unusable. To meet an ever-changing mix of problems, he was crafting solutions as best he could under the cirumstances. These were nonprogrammed decisions that solved unstructured problems in highly uncertain conditions.

A **decision** is a choice among possible alternative courses of action.

A **programmed decision** applies a solution from past experience to a routine problem.

A **nonprogrammed decision** applies a specific solution crafted for a unique problem.

NEWSLINE

Middle manager meets Hurricane Katrina and gets the job done Hurricane Katrina may have met her match in Jeff McCracken, a chief engineer for the Norfolk Southern Railroad. McCracken anticipated that the storm would cause big problems and positioned himself and repair equipment to be ready when needed.

After the storm passed, he moved quickly, taking 100 men to try and repair five miles of track that had been torn from a bridge over Lake Ponchartrain. Without the bridge, the railroad lost its East-West linkage. Two alternatives were on the table: rebuild using new tracks (taking weeks), or rebuild with old track salvaged from the lake (very risky and never done before). After extensive consultations he decided to salvage the old track. He brought together a team of 350+ people and worked 24 hours a day— the job was done in less than a week. McCracken called it a "colossal job" and said the satisfaction came from "working with people from all parts of the company and getting the job done without anyone getting hurt."

Reflect: Can you find examples of really good decision making in your local news? What about in your personal experience? How would you describe the major differences between decisions that turned out right and wrong?

STUDY GUIDE

9.1 How do managers use information to make decisions that solve problems?

Be Sure You Can . . .

- explain the notion of problem solving

- describe different ways managers approach and deal with problems

- discuss the differences between systematic and intuitive thinking

- explain the challenges of decision making under conditions of certainty, risk, and uncertainty environments

- differentiate programmed and nonprogrammed decisions

Define the Terms

Certain environment	Performance threat
Decision	Problem solving
Information competency	Programmed decision
Intuitive thinking	Risk environment
Nonprogrammed decision	Systematic thinking
Performance opportunity	Uncertain environment

Rapid Review

- A problem can occur as a threat or an opportunity, and involves an existing or potential discrepancy between an actual and a desired state of affairs.

- Managers deal with problems in different ways, with some being problem avoiders, others being reactive problem solvers, and still others being proactive problem finders.

- Managers using systematic thinking approach problems in a rational step-by-step fashion; managers using intuitive thinking approach them in a more flexible and spontaneous way.

- The problems that managers face occur in environments of certainty, risk, and uncertainty.

- Managers can deal with structured and routine problems using programmed decisions; novel and unique problems require special solutions developed by nonprogrammed decisions.

Reflect/React

1. Can a manager be justified for acting as a problem avoider in certain situations?

2. Would an organization be better off with mostly systematic or mostly intuitive thinkers?

3. Is it possible to develop programmed decisions for use in conditions of risk and uncertainty?

The **decision-making process** involves a straightforward series of steps: identify and define the problem, generate and evaluate alternative solutions, decide on a preferred course of action and do an ethics double-check, implement the decision, and then evaluate results.[7] When General Motors announced it was closing nine plants in North America and laying off 30,000 workers, it was a blow to workers, their families, and communities.[8] The following case isn't quite as sensational, but it's equally real. Let's use it to follow how the decision-making steps apply to real situations.

The decision-making process begins with identification of a problem and ends with evaluation of implemented solutions.

The Ajax Case. On December 31, the Ajax Company decided to close down its Murphysboro plant. Market conditions were forcing layoffs, and the company hadn't been ablt to find a buyer for the plant. Of 172 employees, some had been with the company as long as 18 years, others as little as 6 months. Ajax needed to terminate all of them. Under company policy they would be given severance pay equal to one week's pay per year of service.

Decision-Making Process

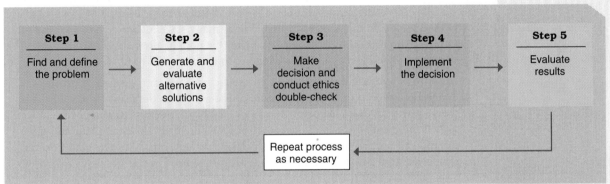

This case reflects how competition, changing times, and the forces of globalization can take their toll on organizations, the people that work for them, and the communities in which they operate. How would you feel—as one of the affected employees, as the mayor of this small town, as a corporate executive having to make the tough decisions?

• Step 1 Is to Identify and Define the Problem

The first step in decision making is to identify and define the problem. This is a stage of information gathering, information processing, and deliberation.[9] It is also where goals are clarified to specify exactly what a decision should accomplish. The more specific the goals, the easier it is to evaluate results after implementing the decision.

Three mistakes are common in this critical first step in decision making. First, we may define the problem too broadly or too narrowly. To take a classic example, instead of stating the problem as "Build a better mousetrap" we define it as "Get rid of the mice." Ideally, problems are defined in ways that give them the best possible range of problem-solving options.

Second, we may focus on symptoms instead of causes. Symptoms only indicate that problems may exist; they aren't the problems themselves. Of course, managers need to be good at spotting problem symptoms (e.g., a drop in performance). But instead of just treating symptoms (such as simply encouraging higher performance), they need to seek out and address their root causes (e.g., discovering the worker's need for training in the use of a complex new computer system).

Third, we may choose the wrong problem to deal with. This can easily happen when we are rushed and time is short, or when there are many

Common Mistakes When Identifying Problems

1. Defining problem too broadly or too narrowly
2. Dealing with symptoms, not real causes
3. Focusing on wrong problem to begin with

things happening at once. Instead of just doing something, it's important to do the right things. This means setting priorities and dealing with the most important problems first.

Back to the Ajax Case. Closing the plant will result in a loss of jobs for a substantial number of people from the small community of Murphysboro. The unemployment created will negatively impact these individuals, their families, and the community as a whole. The loss of the Ajax tax base will further hurt the community. Ajax management therefore defines the problem as how to minimize the adverse impact of the plant closing on the employees, their families, and the community.

Cost-benefit analysis involves comparing the costs and benefits of each potential course of action.

• Step 2 Is to Generate and Evaluate Alternative Courses of Action

After the problem is defined, the next step in decision making is to assemble the needed facts and information. Here managers must be clear on exactly what they know and what they need to know. Extensive information gathering should identify alternative courses of action, as well as their anticipated consequences. It's a time to identify key stakeholders in the problem and consider the effects of each possible course of action on them. In the case of GM's plant closings and layoffs, for example, a union negotiator said: "While GM's continuing decline in market share isn't the fault of workers or our communities, it is these groups that will suffer."[10]

Most managers use some form of **cost-benefit analysis** to evaluate alternatives. This compares what an alternative will cost with its expected benefits. At a minimum, benefits should exceed costs. In addition, an alternative should be timely, acceptable to as many stakeholders as possible, and ethically sound. Of course, the better the pool of alternatives and the better the analysis, the more likely that a good decison will result.

> **⊙→ Criteria for Evaluating Alternatives**
>
> - **Cost and benefits:** Are expected benefits greater than costs?
> - **Timeliness:** How long before the benefits occur?
> - **Acceptability:** Is it acceptable to key stakeholders?
> - **Ethical soundness:** Does it satisfy ethical standards?

Back to the Ajax Case. Ajax will definitely close the plant; keeping it open is no longer an option. These alternatives are considered: close the plant on schedule and be done with it; delay the plant closing and try again to sell it to another firm; offer to sell the plant to the employees and/or local interests; close the plant and offer transfers to other Ajax plant locations; close the plant, offer transfers, and help the employees find new jobs in and around Murphysboro.

• Step 3 Is to Decide on a Preferred Course of Action

Management theory recognizes two quite different ways that alternatives get explored and decisions get made: the classical and behavioral models shown in Figure 9.3. The **classical decision model** views the manager as acting rationally and in a fully informed

The **classical decision model** describes decision making with complete information.

| Figure 9.3 | How does the classical model of managerial decision making differ from the behavioral model? |

Classical Model

- Structured problem
- Clearly defined
- Certain environment
- Complete information
- All alternatives and consequences known

Optimizing Decision
Choose absolute best among alternatives

Rationality
Acts in perfect world

Manager as decision maker

Bounded rationality
Acts with cognitive limitations

Behavioral Model

- Unstructured problem
- Not clearly defined
- Uncertain environment
- Incomplete information
- Not all alternatives and consequences known

Satisficing Decision
Choose first "satisfactory" alternative

The classical model views decision makers as having complete information and making optimum decisions that are the absolute best choices to resolve problems. The behavioral model views decision makers as having limited information processing capabilities. They act with incomplete information and make satisficing decisions, choosing the first satisfactory alternative that comes to their attention.

manner. The problem is clearly defined, all possible action alternatives are known, and each of their consequences are clear. As a result, he or she makes an **optimizing decision** that gives the absolute best solution to the problem.

Although this sounds ideal, it's a bit too good to be true, at least most of the time. Because there are limits to our information processing capabilities, something called *cognitive limitations*, it is hard to be fully informed and make perfectly rational decisions in all situations.[11] Recognizing this, the **behavioral decision model** assumes that people act only in terms of their perceptions, which are frequently imperfect. Furthermore, armed with only partial knowledge about the available action alternatives and their consequences, decision makers are likely to choose the first alternative that appears satisfactory to them. Herbert Simon, who won a Nobel Prize for his work, calls this the tendency to make **satisficing** decisions. What do you think? Does this seem accurate in describing how we make a lot of decisions?

> **Back to the Ajax Case.** Ajax executives decide to close the plant, offer employees transfers to company plants in another state, and offer to help displaced employees find new jobs in and around Murphysboro.

An **optimizing decision** chooses the alternative giving the absolute best solution to a problem.

The **behavioral decision model** describes decision making with limited information and bounded rationality.

A **satisficing decision** chooses the first satisfactory alternative that presents itself.

• Step 4 Is to Implement the Decision

Once a preferred course of action is chosen, managers must take action to fully implement it. Until they do, nothing new can or will happen to solve the problem. This not only requires the determination and creativity to arrive at a decision, it also requires the ability and personal willingness to act. And, most likely, it requires the support of many other people. More often than you might realize, it is insufficient support that sabotages the implementation of otherwise perfectly good decisions.

Managers fall prey to *lack-of-participation error* when they don't include in the decision making process those persons whose support is necessary for implementation. When managers use participation wisely, by contrast, they get the right people involved from the beginning. This not only gains their inputs and insights, it helps build commitments to support the decision and make sure it works as intended. Remember the module subtitle: Decisions, when implemented, solve problems.

> **Back to the Ajax Case.** Ajax management ran an ad in the local and regional newspapers for several days that announced an "Ajax skill bank" composed of "qualified, dedicated, and well-motivated employees with a variety of skills and experiences." The ad urged interested employers to contact Ajax for further information.

• Step 5 Is to Evaluate Results

What good is a decision if it doesn't achieve the desired results, or if undesired side effects occur? Not much, and this is why the decision-making process is not complete until results are evaluated. This is a form of control. It involves gathering data to measure performance results against initial goals, examining both positive and negative outcomes. If the original decision appears inadequate, it also means reassessing things and perhaps redoing earlier steps in the decision-making process.

> **Back to the Ajax Case.** How effective was Ajax's decision? Well, we don't know. After Ajax ran the advertisement for 15 days, the plant's industrial relations manager said: "I've been very pleased with the results." However, we really need a lot more information for a true evaluation. How many employees got new jobs locally? How many transferred to other Ajax plants? How did the local economy perform in the following months? Probably you can add to this list questions of your own. And by the way, don't forget to follow the General Motors situation. On the day its layoffs and plant closures were announced, analysts were already criticizing the decision as not what was needed to restore the firm to long-term profitability.

Be Sure You Can . . .

- list the steps in the decision-making process

- apply these steps to a sample decision-making situation

- explain cost-benefit analysis

- compare and contrast the classical and behavioral decision models

- illustrate "optimizing" and "satisficing" in your personal decision-making experiences

Define the Terms

Behavioral decision model

Classical decision model

Cost-benefit analysis

Decision-making process

Optimizing decision

Satisficing decision

Rapid Review

- The steps in the decision-making process are:
  (1) identify and define the problem
  (2) generate and evaluate alternatives
  (3) decide on the preferred course of action
  (4) implement the decision
  (5) evaluate the results

- A cost-benefit analysis compares the expected costs of a decision alternative with its expected results.

- In the classical model, an optimizing decision chooses the absolute best solution from a known set of alternatives.

- In the behavioral model, cognitive limitations lead to satisficing decisions that choose the first satisfactory alternative to come to attention.

Reflect/React

1. Do the steps in the decision-making process have to be followed in order?

2. Do you see any problems or pitfalls for managers using the behavioral decision model?

3. How can you make sure that a problem is correctly identified?

9.3 What Are Some Practicalities of Managerial Decision Making?

Once you accept the fact that each of us is likely to make imperfect decisions at least some of the time, it makes sense to probe even further into the how's and why's of decision making in organizations. Among the practicalities are possible causes of decision bias and error, advantages and disadvantages of group decision making, crisis decision making, and the foundations for ethical decision making.

• Judgmental Heuristics and Other Biases May Cause Decision-Making Errors

Faced with limited information, time, and even energy, people often use simplifying strategies for decision making. But these strategies, known as *heuristics*, can cause decision-making errors.[12]

The **availability heuristic** occurs when people use information "readily available" from memory as a basis for assessing a current event or situation. You may decide, for example, not to buy running shoes from a company if your last pair didn't last long. The potential bias is that the readily available information may be fallible and irrelevant. Even though your present running shoes are worn out, you may have purchased the wrong model for your needs or used them in the wrong conditions.

The **representativeness heuristic** occurs when people assess the likelihood of something occurring based on its similarity to a stereotyped set of occurrences. An example is deciding to hire someone for a job vacancy simply because he or she graduated from the same school attended by your last and most successful new hire. Using the representative stereotype may mask the truly important factors relevant to the decision, the real abilities and career expectations of the new job candidate.

The **anchoring and adjustment heuristic** involves making decisions based on adjustments to a previously existing value, or starting point. For example, a manager may set a new salary level for a current employee by simply raising the prior year's salary by a percentage increment. But this increment is anchored in the existing salary level, and that may be much lower than the employee's true market value. Rather than being pleased with a raise, the employee may start looking for another, higher-paying, job.

In addition to heuristic biases, **framing error** can influence one's decisions. Framing occurs when managers evaluate and resolve a problem in the context in which they perceive it—either positive or negative. Suppose that marketing data show that a new product has a 40 percent market share. What does this really mean? A negative frame views the product as deficient because it is missing 60 percent of the market. Discussion and problem solving within this frame would likely focus on: "What are we doing wrong?" If the marketing team used a positive frame and considered a 40 percent share as a success, the conversation might be quite different: "How can we do even better?" And by the way, we are constantly exposed to framing in the world of politics; the word used to describe it is *spin*.

While we are talking about politics, another decision-making trap should come to mind; **escalating commitment** to a previously chosen course of action. It is a tendency to increase effort and perhaps apply more resources to pursue a course of action that signals indicate is not working.[13] Perhaps you have experienced an inability to call it quits, even when the facts suggest this is the best decision under the circumstances. Ego and the desire to avoid being associated with a mistake or bad decision can play a big role in escalation. Are you disciplined enough to minimize this risk in the future? Management tips offers advice on how to avoid getting trapped in escalating commitments.

The **availability heuristic** uses readily available information to assess a current situation.

The **representativeness heuristic** assesses the likelihood of an occurrence using a stereotyped set of similar events.

The **anchoring and adjustment heuristic** adjusts a previously existing value or starting point to make a decision.

Framing error is solving a problem in the context perceived.

Escalating commitment is the continuation of a course of action even though it is not working.

MANAGEMENT TIPS

How to avoid the escalation trap

- Set advance limits on your involvement and commitment to a particular course of action; stick with these limits.
- Make your own decisions; don't follow the lead of others, since they are also prone to escalation.
- Carefully determine just why you are continuing a course of action; if there are insufficient reasons to continue, don't.
- Remind yourself of the costs of a course of action; consider saving these costs as a reason to discontinue.
- Watch for escalation tendencies; be on guard against their influence on both you and others involved in the course of action.

Potential Advantages and Disadvantages of Group Decision Making

Why group decisions are often good:

More information   More information, expertise, and viewpoints are available to help solve problems.

More alternatives   More alternatives are generated and considered during decision making.

Increased understanding   There is increased understanding and greater acceptance of decision by group members.

Greater commitment   There is increased commitment of group members to work hard and support the decision.

Why group decisions can be bad:

Conformity with social pressures   Some members feel intimidated by others and give in to social pressures to conform.

Domination by a few members   A minority dominates; some members get railroaded by small coalition of others.

Time delays   More time is required to make decisions when many people try to work together.

A **crisis** is an unexpected problem that can lead to disaster if not resolved quickly and appropriately.

• Group Decision Making Has Both Advantages and Disadvantages

Sometimes the most important decisions we make involve choosing whether to make them alone or with the participation of others. And it really shouldn't be an either-or question. Effective managers and team leaders typically switch back and forth between individual and group decision making, trying to use the best methods for the problems at hand. To do this well, however, they need to understand the implications of the Exhibit – *Potential Advantages and Disadvantages of Group Decision Making*.[14]

In respect to advantages, group decisions can be good because they bring greater amounts of information, knowledge, and expertise to bear on a problem. They often expand the number and even the creativity of action alternatives examined. And as noted earlier, participation helps group members gain better understanding of any decisions reached. This increases the likelihood that they will both accept and work hard to help implement them.

In respect to disadvantages, we all know that it is sometimes difficult and time consuming for people trying to work together. There may be social pressure to conform in group situations. Some individuals may feel intimidated or compelled to go along with the apparent wishes of others. Minority domination might cause some members to feel forced or railroaded into a decision advocated by one vocal individual or a small coalition. Also, the more people involved, the longer it can take to reach a group decision.[15]

• Managers Must Be Prepared for Crisis Decision Making

The module opening example involved one of the most challenging of all decision situations, the **crisis**. This is an unexpected problem that can lead to disaster if not resolved quickly and appropriately. The ability to handle crises could well be the ultimate test of any manager's decision-making capabilities. But unfortunately, research indicates that we sometimes react to crises by doing exactly the wrong things.

Managers err in crisis situations when they isolate themselves and try to solve the problem alone or in a small, closed group.[16] This denies them access to crucial information at the very time that they need it the most. It not only sets them up for poor decisions, it may create even more problems. This is why many organizations are developing formal crisis management programs. They train managers in crisis decision making, assign people ahead of time to crisis management teams, and develop crisis management plans to deal with various contingencies.

Just as police departments and community groups plan ahead and train to best handle civil and natural disasters, so, too, can managers and work teams plan ahead and train to best deal with organizational crises.[17] This only makes sense, doesn't it, in our post-9/11 world?

• Managers Should Always Check the Ethics of Their Decisions

Ethics, ethical decisions, and ethical behavior have been part of this book right from the beginning. And if you look back at Step 3 in the decision-making process, you'll be reminded once again of the importance of conducting an ethics double-check.

Previously, we discussed the ethics double-check in respect to two spotlight questions: "How would I feel if my family found out about this decision?" and "How would I feel if the local newspaper published this decision?" The Josephson Institute model for ethical decision making suggests that a third question can further strengthen the ethics double-check: "Think of the person you know or know of (in real life or fiction) who has the strongest character and best ethical judgment. Then ask yourself—what would that person do in your situation?"[18]

Although it adds time to decision making, any ethics double-check helps to ensure the proper consideration of the ethical aspects of a problem. It is also consistent with the demanding moral standards of modern society.[19]

STUDY GUIDE

9.3 What are some practicalities of managerial decision making?

Be Sure You Can . . .

- explain the availability, representativeness, and anchoring and adjustment heuristics

- illustrate framing error and escalating commitment in decision making

- explain and give an example of escalating commitment

- list potential advantages and disadvantages of group decision making

- describe what managers can do to prepare for crisis decisions

- list three questions that can be asked to double check the ethics of a decision

Define the Terms

Anchoring and adjustment heuristic

Availability heuristic

Crisis

Escalating commitment

Framing error

Representativeness heuristic

Rapid Review

- Judgmental heuristics such as availability, anchoring and adjustment, and representativeness can bias decisions by oversimplifying the situation.

- Framing errors influence decisions by placing them in either a negative or positive situational context.

- Escalating commitment occurs when one sticks with a course of action even though evidence indicates that it is not working.

- Group decisions offer the potential advantages of more information, greater understanding, and expanded commitments; a major disadvantage is that they are often time consuming.

- A crisis problem occurs unexpectedly and can lead to disaster if managers fail to handle it quickly and properly.

- Taking time for the ethics double-check is a useful way for managers to make sure their decisions always meet ethical standards.

Reflect/React

1. How can you avoid being hurt by anchoring and adjustment in your annual pay raises?

2. What are some real-world examples of escalating commitment in decision making?

3. Is it possible that the ethics double-check questions might fail to ensure an ethical decision?

Multiple Choice

1. A manager who is reactive and works hard to address problems after they occur is described as a/an _____.
   (a) problem seeker **(b)** problem solver **(c)** rational thinker **(d)** strategic opportunist

2. A problem is a discrepancy between a/an _____ situation and a desired situation.
   (a) unexpected **(b)** risk **(c)** actual **(d)** uncertain

3. If a manager approaches problems in a rational and analytical way, trying to solve them in step-by-step fashion, he or she is well described as a/an _____.
   (a) systematic thinker **(b)** intuitive thinker **(c)** problem seeker **(d)** behavioral decision maker

4. The first step in the decision-making process is to _____.
   (a) generate a list of alternatives **(b)** assess costs and benefits of each alternative **(c)** find and define the problem **(d)** perform the ethics double-check

5. When the members of a special task force are asked to develop a proposal for increasing the international sales of an existing product, this problem most likely requires _____ decisions.
   (a) routine **(b)** programmed **(c)** crisis **(d)** nonprogrammed

6. Costs, benefits, timeliness, and _____ are among the recommended criteria for evaluating alternative courses of action in the decision-making process.

7. _____

(a) ethical soundness **(b)** past history **(c)** availability **(d)** simplicity

7. The _____ decision model views managers as making optimizing decisions, whereas the _____ decision model views them as making satisficing decisions.
   (a) behavioral/judgmental heuristics **(b)** classical/behavioral **(c)** judgmental heuristics/ethical **(d)** crisis/routine

8. When a manager makes a decision about someone's annual pay raise only after looking at the person's current salary, the risk is that the decision will be biased because of _____.
   (a) a framing error **(b)** escalating commitment **(c)** anchoring and adjustment **(d)** strategic opportunism

9. One of the reasons why certainty is the most favorable environment for problem solving is that it can be addressed through _____ decisions.
   (a) satisficing **(b)** optimizing **(c)** programmed **(d)** intuitive

10. A common mistake by managers facing crisis situations is _____.
    (a) trying to get too much information before responding **(b)** relying too much on group decision making **(c)** isolating themselves to make the decision alone **(d)** forgetting to use their crisis management plan

Short Response

11. How does an optimizing decision differ from a satisficing decision?

12. What is the difference between a risk environment and an uncertain environment in decision making?

13. How can you tell from people's behavior if they tend to be systematic or intuitive in problem solving?

14. What is escalating commitment and how can it be avoided?

Integration & Application

As a participant in a new "mentoring" program between your university and a local high school, you have volunteered to give a presentation to a class of sophomores on the topic:

"Individual versus group decision making: Is one better than the other?"

Questions: What will you say to them, and why?

SELF-ASSESSMENT
Intuitive Ability

1 Do you prefer to
  (a) be given a problem and left free to do it?
  (b) get clear instructions how to solve a problem before starting?

2 Do you prefer to work with colleagues who are
  (a) realistic?   (b) imaginative?

3 Do you most admire
  (a) creative people?   (b) careful people?

4 Do your friends tend to be
  (a) serious and hard working?   (b) exciting and emotional?

5 When you ask for advice on a problem do you
  (a) seldom or never get upset if your basic assumptions are questioned?
  (b) often get upset with such questions?

6 When you start your day, do you
  (a) seldom make or follow a specific plan? (b) usually make and follow a plan?

7 When working with numbers do you make factual errors
  (a) seldom or never?   (b) often?

8 Do you
  (a) seldom daydream and really don't enjoy it?
  (b) often daydream and enjoy it?

9 When working on a problem, do you
  (a) prefer to follow instructions or rules?
  (b) often enjoy bypassing instructions or rules?

10 When trying to put something together, do you prefer
  (a) step-by-step assemble istructions?
  (b) a picture of the assembled item?

11 Do you find that people who irritate you most appear to be
  (a) disorganized?   (b) organized?

12 When an unexpected crisis comes up do you
  (a) feel anxious?
  (b) feel excited by the challenge?

SCORING
Total the "a" responses for 1, 3, 5, 6, 11; [A = _____]. Total the "b" responses for 2, 4, 7, 8, 9, 10, 12; score here [B = _____]. Your *intuitive score* = A + B, the highest score is 12.

PATHWAYS to WileyPLUS

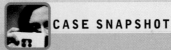

CASE SNAPSHOT

Go online to read this case!
Limited Brands, Inc.: A Brand for Every Occasion
Les Wexner's retailing Goliath has encountered immense success. Has the acquisition/development of supplementary brands (Limited Too, Structure) hurt or helped the original brand? Is the original Limited brand even relevant in today's marketplace?

MODULE 9 **Online Interactive Learning Resources**

Skill Builder
• Problem-Solving Style

Experiential Exercises
• Decision-Making Biases
• Lost at Sea

Team Project
• Dealing with Crisis

Goals and objectives

Plans and Planning Techniques

- **Pacesetters**
  Things moved a lot faster than planned for Skype's founders

- **Management Tips**

  How to manage your time

- **Newsline**

  Cisco is sold on India

- **Self-Assessment**

  Time Management Profile

- **Case Snapshot**

  eBay

The next time you visit a Kinko's copy center, look around and consider the operation. It all started in 1970 when Paul Orfalea, recently graduated from college, decided to put a photocopier, film-processing equipment, and a small selection of stationery supplies in a shop near the University of California at Santa Barbara. He called his business "Kinko's," a nickname given to him by friends.

The story is that Orfalea got the idea for Kinko's when he saw so many students lining up to use the photocopy machine in his university's library. Such insight is a critical management skill. So is timing, and his was perfect. He was so busy that he had to move the photocopier out into the street, where customers served themselves.

get you there faster

What began as a single small shop is now owned by Federal Express and self-proclaimed as "the world's leading provider of document solutions and business services." Kinko's employs over 20,000 "team members" in more than 1100 locations and nine countries.[1]

Orfalea's success was due to an ability to spot business opportunities, decide how to best deal with them, and then do it. He began with a good idea, started his firm, and never looked back–only forward. His original photocopy business was transformed many times in its march toward the future. And all the while, Orfelea never lost sight of his goal: Keep Kinko's growing and keep it getting better. These are planning skills we all need, managers included. But needing them is one thing; having them is another.

Think back to the example in the previous module of General Motors closing nine plants in North America and laying off 30,000 workers.[2] While GM was closing plants, Toyota was opening them; while GM was emphasizing large SUVs and pick-up trucks, Toyota was offering smaller, gas-friendly vehicles; while GM was losing money, Toyota was making money.

Maybe GM should have hired Paul Orfalea as a planning consultant.[3] Do you think he would have missed the market trends?

➡ MODULE GUIDE

 10.1 How and why do managers plan?

- Planning is one of the four functions of management.
- Planning sets objectives and identifies how to achieve them.
- Planning improves focus and action orientation.
- Planning improves coordination and control.
- Planning improves time management.

 10.2 What types of plans do managers use?

- Managers use short-range and long-range plans.
- Managers use strategic and operational plans.
- Organizational policies and procedures are plans.

- Plans are an essential part of project management.
- Budgets are plans that commit resources to activities.

 10.3 What are some useful planning tools and techniques?

- Forecasting tries to predict the future.
- Contingency planning creates back-up plans for when things go wrong.
- Scenario planning crafts plans for alternative future conditions.
- Benchmarking identifies best practices used by others.
- Staff planners provide special expertise in planning.
- Participatory planning improves implementation capacities.

Planning is a process of setting goals and objectives, and determining how to best accomplish them. Said a bit differently, planning involves looking ahead, identifying exactly what you want to accomplish, and deciding how to best go about it.

• Planning Is One of the Four Functions of Management

Among the four management functions, planning comes first. When done well, it sets the stage for the others: organizing—allocating and arranging resources to accomplish tasks; leading—guiding the efforts of human resources to ensure high levels of task accomplishment; and controlling—monitoring task accomplishments and taking necessary corrective action.

Planning is the process of setting objectives and determining how to accomplish them.

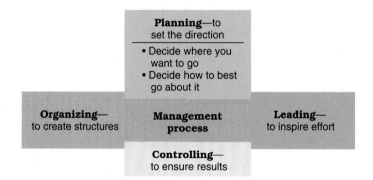

Objectives are specific results that one wishes to achieve.

In today's demanding organizational and career environments, effective planning is essential to staying one step ahead of the competition. An Eaton Corporation annual report, for example, once stated: "Planning at Eaton means taking the hard decisions before events force them upon you, and anticipating the future needs of the market before the demand asserts itself."[4]

You really should take these words to heart. But instead of a company, think about your personal situation. What hard decisions do you need to make? Where are the job markets going? Where do you want to be in 5 or 10 years?

• Planning Sets Objectives and Identifies How to Achieve Them

From experience alone you are probably familiar with the Exhibit – *Steps in The Planning Process* and its action implications. *Step 1* in planning is to define your **objectives**, to identify the specific results or desired goals you hope to achieve. This step is important enough to stop and reflect a moment. Whether you call them goals or objectives, they are targets; they point us toward the future and provide a frame of reference for evaluating progress. With them, as the module subtitle suggests, you should get where you want to go and get there faster.

But goals and objectives have to be good ones; they should push you to achieve substantial, not trivial, things.

Jack Welch, former CEO of GE, believed in what he called **stretch goals**—performance targets that we have to work extra hard and really stretch to reach.[5] Would you agree that Welch's concept of stretch goals adds real strength to the planning process, for organizations and for individuals?

Step 2 in planning is to compare where you are at present with the objectives. This establishes a baseline for performance; the present becomes a standard against which future progress can be gauged. *Step 3* is to formulate premises about future conditions. It is where one looks ahead trying to figure out what may happen. *Step 4* is to analyze the alternatives, choose one, and make an actual **plan**. This is a list of actions that must be taken in order to pursue the alternative and accomplish the objectives. *Step 5* is to implement the plan and evaluate results. This is where action takes place and measurement happens. Results are compared with objectives and, if needed, new plans are made to improve things in the future.

Don't consider this planning process just a textbook model; it's real. It is something we do at school, at work, and in our everyday lives. But we probably rarely stop to think about it so systematically. Have you thought about how well you plan and how you might do it better?

Managers should be asking the same question. They rarely get to plan while working alone in quiet rooms, free from distractions, and at regularly scheduled times. Quite the contrary. Because of the fast pace and complications of the typical workday, managerial planning is ongoing. It takes place even as one deals with a constant flow of problems in a sometimes hectic and demanding work setting.[6] Yet, it's all worth it: planning offers many benefits to people and organizations.[7]

• Planning Improves Focus and Action Orientation

Planning can help sharpen focus and increase flexibility, both of which can improve performance. An organization with focus knows what it does best and what it needs to do. Individuals with focus know where they want to go in a career or situation, and they keep the focus even when difficulties arise. An organization with flexibility is willing and able to change and adapt to shifting circumstances. An individual with flexibility adjusts career plans to fit new and developing opportunities.

 Good planning makes us:

- **Action oriented**—keeping a results-driven sense of direction
- **Priority oriented**—making sure the most important things get first attention
- **Advantage oriented**—ensuring that all resources are used to best advantage
- **Change oriented**—anticipating problems and opportunities so they can be best dealt with

Planning helps us avoid the trap of complacency, becoming lulled into inaction by successes or failures of the moment. Instead, planning keeps us looking toward the future. Management consultant Stephen R. Covey describes this as an action orientation that includes a clear set of priorities.[8] He points out that the most successful executives "zero in on what they do that adds value to an organization." They know what is important and they work first on the things that really count. They don't waste time by working on too many things at once.

Would Covey describe you as focused on priorities, or as flitting from one thing to another? Could you achieve more by getting your priorities straight and working hard on things that really count?

• Planning Improves Coordination and Control

Organizations consist of many people and subsystems doing many different things at the same time. But even as each pursues specific tasks and objectives, their accomplishments must add together meaningfully if the organization is to succeed. Good planning facilitates this by linking people and subsystems together in a **hierarchy of objectives**. This is a means–ends chain in which lower-level objectives (the means) lead to the accomplishment of higher-level ones (the ends). An example is the total quality management program shown in Figure 10.1

Stretch goals are performance targets that we have to work extra hard and stretch to reach.

A **plan** is a statement of intended means for accomplishing objectives.

In a **hierarchy of objectives**, lower-level objectives help to accomplish higher-level ones.

Figure 10.1 | **What is a sample hierarchy of objectives for a corporate total quality management program?**

Corporate quality objectives	Manufacturing division quality objectives	Plant quality objectives	Shift supervisor quality objectives
Deliver error-free products that meet customer requirements 100% of the time.	Become a preferred supplier by achieving 100% on-time delivery of all products.	Increase percent accepted by 16% to meet customer's delivery requirements.	Assess capabilities of machine operators and provide/arrange appropriate training.

A hierarchy of objectives identifies a means–ends chain through which lower-level objectives become the pathways for accomplishing higher-level ones. In the case of total quality management, the top-level objective (delivering error-free products that meet customer needs 100% of the time) moves step-by-step down the hierarchy until the point where a shift supervisor supports TQM with the objective of making sure that machine operators are trained well enough to do error-free work.

Good planning also provides an essential link with controlling in the management process. Without planning objectives it's hard to exercise control; without control, plans may fail because of a lack of follow-through. With both, it's a lot easier to spot when things aren't going well and make the necessary adjustments. For example, two years after launching a costly information technology upgrade, the CEO of McDonald's realized that the system couldn't deliver on its promises. He stopped the project, took a loss of $170 million, and refocused the firm's resources on projects with more direct impact on customers.[9]

• Planning Improves Time Management

One of the great benefits of planning is often better time management. Lewis Platt, former chairman of Hewlett-Packard, once described his workday as "a series of choices."[10] Each of us has to make choices that allocate our time among competing demands and possibilities. Platt says that he was "ruthless about priorities" and that you "have to continually work to optimize your time."

MANAGEMENT TIPS

How to manage your time

- *Do* say "No" to requests that divert you from what you really should be doing.
- *Don't* get bogged down in details that you can address later or leave for others.
- *Do* have a system for screening telephone calls, e-mails, and requests for meetings.
- *Don't* let drop-in visitors or instant messages use too much of your time.
- *Do* prioritize what you will work on in terms of importance and urgency.
- *Don't* become calendar bound by letting others control your schedule.
- *Do* follow priorities; work on the most important and urgent tasks first.

Surely you have experienced difficulties in balancing time-consuming commitments and requests. Indeed, it is all too easy to lose track of time and fall prey to what consultants identify as "time wasters" (see Management Tips). How often do you allow other people or nonessential activities to dominate your time?[11] Perhaps like many others you use To-Do lists as a way of staying on top of things. But while they can help, they aren't much good unless the lists contain the high-priority things. In daily living and in management we need to distinguish between things that we must do (top priority), should do (high priority), might do (low priority), and really don't need to do (no priority).

Be Sure You Can . . .

- explain the importance of planning as the first of four management functions

- list the steps in the formal planning process

- illustrate the benefits of planning for a business or organization familiar to you

- illustrate the benefits of planning for your personal career development

- list at least three things you can do now to improve your time management

Define the Terms

Hierarchy of objectives

Objectives

Plan

Planning

Stretch goals

Rapid Review

- Planning is the process of setting performance objectives and determining how to accomplish them.

- A plan is a set of intended actions for accomplishing important objectives.

- The steps in the planning process are:
  (1) define your objectives
  (2) determine where you stand vis-à-vis objectives
  (3) develop your premises regarding future conditions
  (4) make a plan to best accomplish objectives
  (5) implement the plan, and evaluate results

- The benefits of planning include better focus and action orientation, better coordination and control, and better time management.

- Planning improves time management by setting priorities and avoiding time wasters

Reflect/React

1. Should all employees plan, or just managers?

2. Which step in the planning process do you think is the hardest to accomplish?

3. How could better planning help in your personal career development?

Managers face different planning challenges in the flow and pace of activities in organizations. In some cases, the planning environment is stable and predictable. In others, it is more dynamic and uncertain. To meet these different needs, managers rely on a variety of plans.

• Managers Use Short-Range and Long-Range Plans

Short-range plans usually cover a year or less.

Long-range plans usually cover three years or more.

We live and work in a fast-paced world where planning horizons are becoming compressed. We now talk about planning in Internet time, where businesses are continually changing and updating plans. Even most top managers would likely agree that *long-range* planning is becoming shorter and shorter. A reasonable rule of thumb in this context is that **short-range plans** cover a year or less, while **long-range plans** look ahead three or more years into the future.[12]

Quite frankly, the advent of Internet time and shorter planning horizons might be an advantage for many of us. Management researcher Elliot Jaques found that very few people have the capacity to think long term.[13] He believes that most of us work comfortably with only three-month time spans; some can think about a year into the future; only about one person in several million can handle a 20-year time frame.

Do Jaques's conclusions match your experience? And if we accept his findings, what are their implications for managers and career development? Although a team leader's planning challenges may rest mainly in the weekly or monthly range, a chief executive needs to have a vision extending at least some years into the future. Career progress to higher management levels still requires the conceptual skills to work well with longer-range time frames.[14]

• Managers Use Strategic and Operational Plans

A **strategic plan** identifies long-term directions for the organization.

An **operational plan** identifies activities to implement strategic plans.

The plans used in organizations differ not only in time horizons but also in scope. **Strategic plans** set broad, comprehensive, and longer-term action directions. Strategic planning by top managers involves describing a vision of what and where the organization wants to be in the future, setting objectives that can make the vision a reality, and laying out the strategic plan for actions to achieve the objectives.

As the next module will describe, there is a lot of room for both success and error in strategic plans. You might see senior executives of some firms diversifying by buying businesses in unrelated areas. A successful oil firm might acquire an office products company, or a successful cereal manufacturer might acquire an apparel company. But these firms are moving outside of their areas of competency; these diversification strategies are risky and may prove unsuccessful.

Operational plans define what specific functions or work units need to do to implement strategic plans. You will find many types of operational plans in a typical business. *Production plans* deal with the methods and technology needed by people in their work. *Financial plans* deal with money required to support various operations. *Facilities plans* deal with facilities and work layouts. *Marketing plans* deal with the requirements of selling and distributing goods or services. *Human resource plans* deal with the recruitment, selection, and placement of people into various jobs.

PACESETTERS

Things moved a lot faster than planned for Skype's founders.

It was just three years from founding that Skype was bought by eBay for $2.6 billion and a promise of $1.5 billion in four years if certain performance targets are hit. Wow, that's quite a payoff for Skype's investors and the firm's founders, Niklas Zennstrom and Janus Friis. And it wasn't in their plan to just start the company, move it fast, and sell quickly to the highest bidder. Says Zennstrom: "Our objective was to build the business." But once started, Skype took off to gain 54 million users, and the suitors soon appeared—among them Yahoo!, News Corp., and even Google. But eBay got the prize after Niklas and Janus had a breakthrough meeting with eBay's CEO Meg Whitman. According to Zennstrom, it was an *Aha*! experience. "We went crazy on the whiteboard, mapping out ideas." The rest is business history; a plan that worked so well it moved even faster than Skype's founder's ever anticipated.

Niklas Zennstrom and Janus Friis, founders, Skype.

• Organizational Policies and Procedures Are Plans

In addition to strategic and operational plans, organizations also need plans that provide members with day-to-day guidance on such things as attendance, hiring practices, ethical behavior, privacy, trade secrets, and more. This is often provided in the form of organizational policies and procedures. We call them *standing-use plans*, ones designed to be used over and over again until changed.

A **policy** communicates broad guidelines for making decisions and taking action in specific circumstances. For example, human resource policies address such matters as employee hiring, termination, performance appraisals, pay increases, promotions, and discipline. **Procedures**, or *rules*, describe exactly what actions to take in specific situations. They are often found stated in employee handbooks or manuals as SOPs (standard operating procedures).

Whereas a policy sets broad guidelines, procedures define specific actions to be taken. A sexual harassment policy, for example, should be backed with procedures that spell out how to file a sexual harassment complaint, as well as the steps through which any complaint will be handled.[15] When Judith Nitsch started her own engineering consulting business, for example, she defined a sexual harassment policy, took a hard line in its enforcement, and designated both a male and a female employee for others to talk with about sexual harassment concerns.[16]

• Plans Are an Essential Part of Project Management

Organizations also need *single-use plans* designed to meet the needs of specific situations and timetables. For example, a lot of work takes the form of **projects**, one-time activities that, although potentially very complex, have clear beginning and end points. Examples include the completion of a new student activities building on a campus, the development of a new computer software program, or the implementation of a new advertising campaign for a sports team. These are guided by **project plans** that define specific task objectives, link activities to due dates, and identify the amounts and timing of resource requirements. And just as with any group project done in school, good **project management** ensures that the required activities happen on time and according to plans.

• Budgets Are Plans that Commit Resources to Activities

A **budget** is a plan that commits resources to activities, programs, or projects. It is a powerful tool that allocates scarce resources among multiple and often competing uses. Managers typically negotiate with their bosses to obtain budgets that support the needs of their work units or teams. They are also expected to achieve performance objectives while keeping within their budgets.

You will find many kinds of budgets in most organizations. A *fixed budget* allocates a set amount of resources for a specific purpose. For example, a manager may have a $25,000 budget for equipment purchases in a given year. A *flexible budget* allows the allocation of resources to vary in proportion with various levels of activity. For example, a manager may have flexibility to hire extra temporary workers when and if the workload moves above a predetermined threshold.

One of the problems with budgeting in some organizations is that resource allocations get *rolled over* from one time period to the next without any real performance review. A **zero-based budget** deals with this problem by approaching each new budget period as if it were brand new. No guarantee exists for renewing any past funding. Instead, all proposals compete for available funds at the start of each new budget cycle. This helps eliminate wasting scarce resources on outdated or unimportant activities. And you might be surprised by how much waste there is in some carryover budgets. In a major division of Campbell Soups, managers using zero-based budgeting once discovered that 10 percent of the marketing budget was being spent on sales promotions that were totally irrelevant.

→ **Excerpts from a Sample Sexual Harassment Policy**

Sexual harassment is specifically prohibited by this organization. Any employee found to have violated the policy against sexual harassment will be subject to immediate and appropriate disciplinary action including but not limited to possible suspension or termination.

A **policy** is a standing plan that communicates broad guidelines for decisions and action.

A **procedure** or rule precisely describes actions to take in specific situations.

Projects are one-time activities that have clear beginning and end points.

Project plans specify activities, resources, and timetables for completing projects.

Project management ensures the timely and correct accomplishment of project activities.

A **budget** is a plan that commits resources to projects or activities.

A **zero-based budget** allocates resources as if each budget was brand new.

Be Sure You Can . . .

- differentiate short-range and long-range plans

- differentiate strategic and operational plans

- explain how strategic and operational plans complement one another

- differentiate policies and procedures, and give examples of each

- explain project plans and project management

- explain the benefits of a zero-based budget

Define the Terms

Budget	Project management
Long-range plan	Project plan
Operational plan	Short-range plan
Policy	Strategic plan
Procedures	Zero-based budget
Project	

Rapid Review

- Short-range plans tend to cover a year or less, while long-range plans extend up to five years or more.

- Strategic plans set critical long-range directions; operational plans are designed to support and help implement strategic plans.

- Policies, such as a sexual harassment policy, are plans that set guidelines for the behavior of organizational members.

- Procedures are plans that describe actions to take in specific situations, such as how to report a sexual harassment complaint.

- Budgets are plans that allocate resources to activities or projects.

- A zero-based budget allocates resources as if each new budget period is brand new; no "roll over" resource allocations allowed without new justifications.

Reflect/React

1. Is there any need for long-range plans in today's fast-moving environment?

2. What types of policies do you believe are essential for any organization?

3. Are there any possible disadvantages to zero-based budgeting?

The benefits of planning are best realized when plans are built from strong foundations. The useful planning tools and techniques include forecasting, contingency planning, scenarios, benchmarking, participatory planning, and the use of staff planners.

• Forecasting Tries to Predict the Future

Forecasting is the process of predicting what will happen in the future.[17] Most plans involve forecasts of some sort. Periodicals such as *Business Week*, *Fortune*, and *The Economist* regularly report forecasts of industry conditions, interest rates, unemployment trends, and national economies, among other issues.[18] Some rely on qualitative forecasting, which uses expert opinions to predict the future. Others involve quantitative forecasting, which uses mathematical models and statistical analysis of historical data and surveys.

Any forecast should be used with caution. They are planning aids, not planning substitutes. It is said that a music agent once told Elvis Presley: "You ought to go back to driving a truck because you ain't going nowhere." That's the problem with forecasts; they always rely on human judgment, and that can be wrong.

• Contingency Planning Creates Back-Up Plans for When Things Go Wrong

Things often go wrong, as you well know. It is highly unlikely that any plan will ever be perfect. Changes in the environment will occur sooner or later, as will crises and emergencies. And when they do, the best managers and organizations have contingency plans ready to go.

Contingency planning identifies alternative courses of action that can be implemented to meet the needs of changing circumstances. A really good contingency plan will even contain "trigger points" to indicate when to activate preselected alternatives. Given the uncertainties of our day, this is really an indispensable tool for managerial and personal planning.

• Scenario Planning Crafts Plans for Alternative Future Conditions

A long-term version of contingency planning, called **scenario planning**, involves identifying several alternative future scenarios or states of affairs. Managers then make plans to deal with each, should it actually occur.[19]

Scenario planning began years ago at Royal Dutch/Shell when top managers asked themselves a perplexing question: "What would Shell do after its oil supplies ran out?" Although recognizing that scenario planning can never be inclusive of all future possibilities, a Shell executive once said that it helps "condition the organization to think" and better prepare for "future shocks." For Shell this has meant planning for such issues as climate change, sustainable development, human rights, and biodiversity.[20]

• Benchmarking Identifies Best Practices Used by Others

All too often managers and planners become too comfortable with the ways things are going. They become trapped by habits and overconfident that the past is a good indicator of the future. Planning helps us deal with such tendencies by challenging the status quo and reminding us not to always

Forecasting attempts to predict the future.

Contingency planning identifies alternative courses of action to take when things go wrong.

Scenario planning identifies alternative future scenarios and makes plans to deal with each.

NEWSLINE

Cisco is sold on India Cisco Systems is already a global networking giant. But it plans to grow a lot more in the future, and a lot of that growth is going to come from its investments overseas. It wasn't too long ago that China was the big target in Asia. It still is a big one, but "big" got smaller when Cisco's planners analyzed their planning premises and projected future scenarios for both India and China. It turns out that they found a lot to like about India going forward, and some major things to worry about in China.

What Cisco Likes about India	What Cisco Worries about in China
Excellence in software design	Centrally planned economy
Need for Cisco's products	Government favors local companies
Weak local competition	Poor intellectual property protection

Reflect: Would you agree with Cisco's international planning premises? Could a similar "balance sheet" comparison help sort out your career alternatives? Why not take the time to make two lists: ("What I like about [career fields A, B, etc.]" and "What worries me about [career fields A, B, etc.]")?

accept things as they are. One way to do this is through **benchmarking**, a planning technique that makes use of external comparisons to better evaluate current performance.[21] It is a way of learning from the successes of others.

Managers use benchmarking to find out what other people and organizations are doing well, and plan how to incorporate these ideas into their own operations. They search for **best practices** inside and outside of the organization, and among competitors and noncompetitors alike. These are things that others are doing and that help them to achieve superior performance. Xerox, for example, has benchmarked L.L. Bean's warehousing and distribution methods, Ford's plant layouts, and American Express's billing and collections. There's little doubt that sports stars benchmark one another; scientists and scholars do it; executives and managers do it. Could you be doing it too?

• Staff Planners Provide Special Expertise in Planning

As organizations grow, they often need to increase the sophistication of their planning systems. In some cases they employ staff planners who are specialists in all steps of the planning process, as well as up to date on the latest planning tools and techniques.

Staff planners can help bring focus, expertise, and energy to important planning tasks. But one of the risks is that a communication gap develops between the planners and the rest of the organization; plans end up getting made in a vacuum. Not only might the plans end up off the mark, there might be little commitment in the workforce to their implementation.

• Participatory Planning Improves Implementation Capacities

When it comes to implementation, *participation* can be a very important word in the planning process. **Participatory planning** (as shown in Figure 10.2) includes people whose ideas and inputs can benefit the plans and whose support is needed for implementation. It has all the advantages of group decision making discussed in Module 9.

Participatory planning can increase the creativity and information available; it can increase understanding and acceptance of plans; it can build stronger commitments to a plan's success. When 7-Eleven executives planned for new upscale products and services, such as selling fancy meals-to-go, they learned this lesson the hard way. Although their ideas sounded good at the top, franchise owners and managers balked at the shop level. The executives belatedly realized the value of taking time to involve them in planning new directions for the stores.[22]

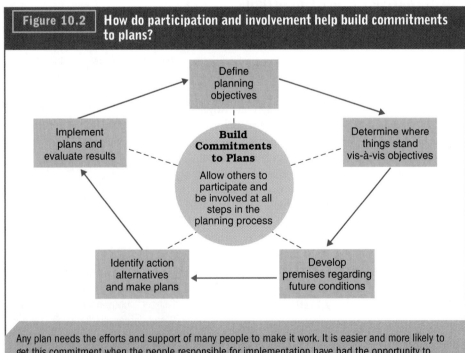

Figure 10.2 **How do participation and involvement help build commitments to plans?**

Define planning objectives

Determine where things stand vis-à-vis objectives

Develop premises regarding future conditions

Identify action alternatives and make plans

Implement plans and evaluate results

Build Commitments to Plans

Allow others to participate and be involved at all steps in the planning process

Any plan needs the efforts and support of many people to make it work. It is easier and more likely to get this commitment when the people responsible for implementation have had the opportunity to participate in developing the plans in the first place. When managers use participatory planning and allow others to become involved in the planning process, it leads to better plans, a deeper understanding of the plans, and a strengthened commitment to fully implementing the plans.

10.3 What are some useful planning tools and techniques?

Be Sure You Can . . .

- differentiate among forecasting, contingency planning, scenario planning, and benchmarking

- explain the importance of contingency planning

- explain why staff planners sometimes don't succeed

- describe the benefits of participatory planning as a special case of group decision making

Define the Terms

Benchmarking

Best practices

Contingency planning

Forecasting

Participatory planning

Scenario planning

Rapid Review

- Forecasting, which attempts to predict what might happen in the future, is a planning aid but not a planning substitute.

- Contingency planning identifies alternative courses of action to implement if and when circumstances change and an existing plan fails.

- Scenario planning analyzes the implications of alternative versions of the future.

- Benchmarking utilizes external comparisons to identify best practices and possibly desirable actions.

- Participation and involvement open the planning process to valuable inputs from people whose efforts are essential to the effective implementation of plans.

Reflect/React

1. If forecasting is going to be imperfect, why bother with it?

2. Shouldn't all planning provide for contingency plans?

3. Will members of today's workforce like participatory planning?

MODULE
10

TEST PREP
Take the complete set of Module 10 quizzes online!

Multiple Choice

1. Planning is best described as the process of _____ and _____.
   (a) developing premises about the future/evaluating them
   (b) measuring results/taking corrective action
   (c) measuring past performance/targeting future performance **(d)** setting objectives/deciding how to accomplish them

2. The benefits of planning should include _____.
   (a) improved focus **(b)** lower labor costs **(c)** more accurate forecasts **(d)** increased business profits

3. In order to help implement her firm's strategic plans, the CEO of a business firm would most likely want marketing, manufacturing, and finance executives to develop _____.
   (a) means-ends chains **(b)** operational plans **(c)** flexible budgets **(d)** project management

4. _____ planning identifies alternative courses of action that can be taken if problems occur with the original plan.
   (a) Benchmark **(b)** Participatory **(c)** Staff
   (d) Contingency

5. A "No Smoking" rule and a sexual harassment policy are examples of _____ that are types of _____ in organizations.
   (a) long-range plans/policies **(b)** single-use plans/means–ends chains **(c)** policies/standing-use plans
   (d) operational plans/short-range plans

6. When a manager is asked to justify a new budget proposal on the basis of projected activities rather than as an incremental adjustment to the prior year's budget, this is an example of _____.
   (a) zero-based budgeting **(b)** strategic planning
   (c) operational planning **(d)** contingency planning

7. One of the expected benefits of participatory planning is _____.
   (a) faster planning **(b)** less need for forecasting **(c)** greater attention to contingencies **(d)** more commitment to implementation

8. When managers use the benchmarking approach to planning they usually try to _____.
   (a) use flexible budgets **(b)** identify best practices used by others **(c)** find the most accurate forecasts that are available **(d)** use expert staff planners to set objectives

9. The planning process isn't complete until _____.
   (a) future conditions have been identified **(b)** stretch goals have been set **(c)** plans are implemented and results evaluated **(d)** budgets commit resources to plans

10. In a hierarchy of objectives, the ideal situation is for plans at lower levels to act as _____ for accomplishing higher-level plans.
    (a) means **(b)** ends **(c)** scenarios **(d)** benchmarks

Short Response

11. List the five steps in the planning process, and give examples of each.

12. How does planning facilitate controlling?

13. What is the difference between contingency planning and scenario planning?

14. Why is participation good for the planning process?

Integration & Application

My friends Curt and Rich own a local bookstore. They are very interested in making plans for improving the store and better dealing with competition from the other bookstores that serve college students in our town. I once heard Curt saying to Rich: "We should be benchmarking what some of the successful coffee shops, restaurants, and novelty stores are doing." Rich replied: "I don't see why; we should only be interested in bookstores. Why don't we study the local competition and even look at what the best bookstores are doing in the big cities?"

Questions: Who is right? If you were hired by Curt and Rich as a planning consultant, what would you suggest as the best way to utilize benchmarking as a planning technique to improve their bookstore?

INSTRUCTIONS *Indicate "Y" (yes) or "N" (no) for each item. Be frank; let your responses describe an accurate picture of how you tend to respond to these kinds of situations.*

1 When confronted with several items of similar urgency and importance, I tend to do the easiest one first.

2 I do the most important things during that part of the day when I know I perform best.

3 Most of the time I don't do things someone else can do; I delegate this type of work to others.

4 Even though meetings without a clear and useful purpose upset me, I put up with them.

5 I skim documents before reading them and don't complete any that offer a low return on my time investment.

6 I don't worry much if I don't accomplish at least one significant task each day.

7 I save the most trivial tasks for that time of day when my creative energy is lowest.

8 My workspace is neat and organized.

9 My office door is always "open"; I never work in complete privacy.

10 I schedule my time completely from start to finish every workday.

11 I don't like "to-do" lists, preferring to respond to daily events as they occur.

12 I "block" a certain amount of time each day or week that is dedicated to high-priority activities.

SCORING AND INTERPRETATION

Count the number of "Y" responses to items 2, 3, 5, 7, 8, 12. [Enter that score here _____.] Count the number of "N" responses to items 1, 4, 6, 9, 10, 11. [Enter that score here _____.] Add together the two scores.

The higher the total score, the closer your behavior matches recommended time management guidelines. Reread those items where your response did not match the desired one. Why don't they match? Are there reasons for your action tendencies? Think about what you can do to be more consistent with time management guidelines.

P A T H W A Y S to WileyPLUS

WILEY
PLUS

CASE SNAPSHOT

Go online to read this case!

This Phone Call Brought to You by . . . eBay?

Is e-Bay getting too big? The online auction giant has taken a well-paced approach to growth, and has otherwise been a solid market-maker. But with its recent purchase of Skype, some critics wonder if it is diversifying too much. Or, like Amazon.com, is it reaching a new point of product/service diversification within its brand?

MODULE 10 Online Interactive Learning Resources

Skill Builder
- Time Management

Experiential Exercise
- Beating the Time Wasters

Team Project
- Affirmative Action Directions

What gets measured

Controls and Control Systems

People in the ever-changing technology industry know that CEO T. J. Rodgers of Cypress Semiconductor Corp. values both performance and accountability. Cypress employees work with clear and quantified work goals, which they help set. Rodgers believes that this system helps find problems before they interfere with performance. He says: "Managers monitor the goals, look for problems, and expect people who fall behind to ask for help before they lose control of or damage a major project."[1]

Rodgers is all about planning—setting goals, and control—keeping things on track to accomplish them. And control is important for any organization; it adds performance discipline and facilitates learning.

happens

Consider the *after-action review* pioneered by the U.S. Army and now used in many businesses. It is a formal review of lessons learned and results accomplished when a project or special operation is completed. Participants answer questions like: "What was the intent?" "What actually happened?" "What did we learn?"[2] After-action reviews not only help make continuous improvements in an organization's performance, they encourage everyone to take responsibility for his or her own performance and its consequences.

But don't let the Cyprus and U.S. Army organizational examples mislead you; each of us practices a lot of control quite naturally. Think of fun things you do—playing golf or tennis or Frisbee, reading, dancing, driving a car, or riding a bike. You may be surprised to know that through them you've already become quite expert in the control process. How did you learn to ride a bike or swim? Most probably with an objective in mind, always checking how well you were doing, and making continuous adjustments until you got it perfect.

This is the control process in a nutshell. The trick is carrying these natural capabilities into the workplace.

→ MODULE GUIDE

 11.1 What is important to know about the control process?

- Controlling is one of the four management functions.
- Control begins with objectives and standards.
- Control measures actual performance.
- Control compares results with objectives and standards.
- Control takes corrective action as needed.
- Control focuses on work inputs, throughputs, and outputs.

 11.2 What are some organizational control systems and techniques?

- Management by objectives integrates planning and controlling.
- Employee discipline is a form of managerial control.
- Quality control is a foundation for total quality management.
- Purchasing and inventory controls help save costs.
- Breakeven analysis shows where revenues will equal costs.

Controlling is the process of measuring performance and taking action to ensure desired results.

Managers understand **controlling** as a process of measuring performance and taking action to ensure desired results. Its purpose is straightforward—to make sure that plans are achieved and that actual performance meets or surpasses objectives. Like any aspect of decision-making, the foundation of control is information. Henry Schacht, former CEO of Cummins Engine Company, once discussed control in terms of what he called "friendly facts." He stated, "Facts that reinforce what you are doing . . . are nice, because they help in terms of psychic reward. Facts that raise alarms are equally friendly, because they give you clues about how to respond, how to change, where to spend the resources."[3]

• Controlling Is One of the Four Management Functions

How does control fit in with the other management functions? Planning sets the directions. Organizing arranges people and resources for work. Leading inspires people toward their best efforts. Controlling sees to it that the right things happen, in the right way, and at the right time. And if things go wrong, control helps get things back on track.

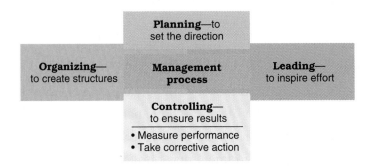

• Control Begins with Objectives and Standards

The control process begins with setting performance objectives and standards for measuring them. It can't start any other way. This is the planning part: setting the performance objectives against which results can eventually be compared. Measurement standards are important too. It isn't always easy to set them, but they are essential.

Standards for measuring business performance that we often hear about are things like earnings per share, sales growth, and market shares. Others include quantity and quality of production, costs incurred, service or delivery time, and error rates. But how about other types of organizations, like a symphony orchestra? When the Cleveland Orchestra wrestled with performance standards, the members weren't willing to rely on vague generalities like "we played well," "the audience seemed happy," "not too many mistakes were made." Rather, they decided to track standing ovations, invitations to perform in other countries, and how often other orchestras copied their performance styles.[4]

An **output standard** measures performance results in terms of quantity, quality, cost, or time.

These have all been examples of **output standards** that measure actual outcomes or work results. Businesses use many output standards; we have already discussed a couple. Just based on your experience at work and as a customer you can probably come up with even more examples. When Allstate Corporation launched a new diversity initiative, it created a "diversity index" to quantify performance on diversity issues. The standards included how well employees met the goals of bias-free customer service, and how well managers met the firm's diversity expectations.[5] When GE became concerned about managing ethics in its 320,000 member global workforce, it created measurement standards to track compliance. Each business unit now reports quarterly on how many of its members attended ethics training sessions and what percentage signed the firm's "Spirit and Letter" ethics guide.[6]

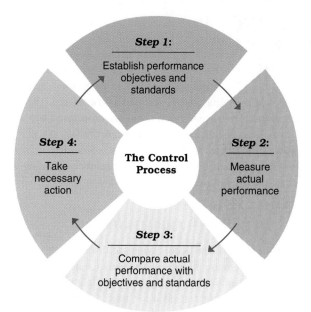

The control process also uses **input standards** to measure work efforts. These are often used in situations where outputs are difficult or expensive to measure. Examples of input standards for a college professor might be the existence of an orderly course syllabus, meeting all class sessions, and returning exams and assignments in a timely fashion. Of course, as this example might suggest, measuring inputs doesn't mean that outputs, such as high-quality teaching and learning, are necessarily achieved. Other examples of input standards in the workplace include conformance with rules and procedures, efficiency in the use of resources, and work attendance or punctuality.

An **input standard** measures work efforts that go into a performance task.

• Control Measures Actual Performance

The second step in the control process is to measure actual performance using agreed-upon standards. Accurate and timely measurement is essential in order to spot differences between what is really taking place and what was originally planned. Unless we are willing to measure, very little control is possible. And as the module subtitle indicates, a willingness to measure has its rewards: what gets measured tends to happen.

When IBM appointed Linda Sanford head of its sales force, she came with an admirable performance record earned during a 22-year career with the company. Notably, Sanford grew up on a family farm, where she developed an appreciation for measuring results. "At the end of the day, you saw what you did, knew how many rows of strawberries you picked." This experience carried over into her work at IBM. She earned a reputation for walking around the factory just to see "at the end of the day how many machines were going out of the back dock."[7]

• Control Compares Results with Objectives and Standards

The third step in the control process is to compare actual results with objectives and standards. You might remember its implications by this control equation: Need for action = Desired performance − Actual performance. But as with any other problem solving, don't forget that the need for action can point you in two possible directions. It can point toward the need to deal with a performance threat or deficiency (when actual is less than desired) or to explore a performance opportunity (when actual is more than desired).

The question of what constitutes desired performance plays an important role in the control equation and its implications. Ideally this is clarified when the original objectives and standards are set, such as in the earlier example of ethics at GE. But there are other approaches available. Some organizations use *engineering comparisons*. An example is UPS. The firm carefully measures the routes and routines of its drivers to establish the times expected for each delivery. When a delivery manifest is scanned as completed, the driver's time is registered in an electronic performance log that is closely monitored by supervisors.

Organizations, just as we, make use of *historical comparisons* as well. These use past experience as a basis for evaluating current performance. Similarly, *relative comparisons* are also common. These benchmark our performance against that being achieved by other people, work units, or organizations.

• Control Takes Corrective Action as Needed

Management by exception focuses attention on substantial differences between actual and desired performance.

The final step in the control process occurs when action is taken to correct performance deficiencies or make improvements based on performance opportunities. You might hear the term **management by exception** used in this regard. It is the practice of giving attention to situations that show the greatest need for action. Managing by exception can save valuable time, energy, and other resources by focusing our attention on high-priority problems or opportunities.

• Control Focuses on Work Inputs, Throughputs, and Outputs

You should recall discussions in earlier modules of how organizations operate as open systems that interact with their environments in an input-throughput-output cycle. Figure 11.1 now shows how three types of managerial controls—feedforward, concurrent, and feedback—apply to each phase.[8]

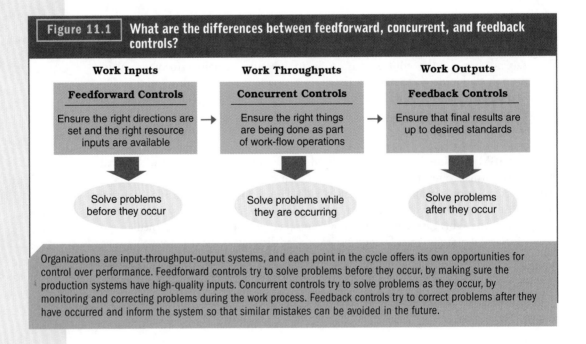

| Figure 11.1 | What are the differences between feedforward, concurrent, and feedback controls? |

Work Inputs

Feedforward Controls

Ensure the right directions are set and the right resource inputs are available

↓

Solve problems before they occur

Work Throughputs

Concurrent Controls

Ensure the right things are being done as part of work-flow operations

↓

Solve problems while they are occurring

Work Outputs

Feedback Controls

Ensure that final results are up to desired standards

↓

Solve problems after they occur

Organizations are input-throughput-output systems, and each point in the cycle offers its own opportunities for control over performance. Feedforward controls try to solve problems before they occur, by making sure the production systems have high-quality inputs. Concurrent controls try to solve problems as they occur, by monitoring and correcting problems during the work process. Feedback controls try to correct problems after they have occurred and inform the system so that similar mistakes can be avoided in the future.

Feedforward control ensures clear directions and needed resources before the work begins.

Feedforward controls, also called *preliminary controls*, take place before work begins. Their goal is to prevent problems before they occur. This is a forward-thinking and proactive approach to control, one that we should all try to follow whenever we can. A good example is the area of quality control, where the adage might be: quality in, quality out.

At McDonald's, preliminary control of food ingredients plays an important role in the firm's quality program. The company requires that suppliers of its hamburger buns produce them to exact specifications, covering everything from texture to uniformity of color. Even in overseas markets, the firm works hard to develop local suppliers that can supply it with ingredients of dependable quality.[9]

Concurrent controls focus on what happens during the work process; they take place while people are doing their jobs. The goal is to solve problems as they occur. Sometimes called *steering controls*, they make sure that things are always going according to plan. The ever-present shift leaders at McDonald's restaurants are a good example of how this happens through direct supervision. They constantly observe what is taking place, even while helping out with the work. They also intervene immediately to correct things on the spot. The question continually being asked is: "What can we do to improve things right now?"

By the way, how often do you hear this question in your courses? Most student course evaluations are examples of **feedback controls** done not during, but at the end of a course. All such *post-action controls* take place after a job or project is completed. Most course evaluation systems ask you "Was this a good learning experience?" only when the class is almost over; servers ask us "Was everything okay?" after we finish our meals; probably the last question a computer maker asks before your machine is shipped from the factory floor is: "Does it work?"

Although these are all good questions, they show how feedback controls focus mainly on the quality of finished products. This type of control may prevent you from receiving a defective computer, but it may not help you much in the restaurant or at school. However, if carried a step further into the organizational learning phase, feedback controls can help make sure that identified problems won't happen again in the future.

Concurrent control focuses on what happens during the work process.

Feedback control takes place after completing an action.

> *All the pleasure of life is in general ideas. But all the use of life is in specific solutions ... reached by insight, tact, and specific knowledge.*
>
> **Oliver Wendell Holmes**

STUDY GUIDE

11.1 What is important to know about the control process?

Be Sure You Can . . .

- explain the role of controlling in the management process

- list the steps in the control process

- explain how planning and controlling work together in management

- differentiate output standards and input standards

- illustrate the use of feedforward, concurrent, and feedback controls

- state the control equation and explain management by exception

Define the Terms

Concurrent control

Controlling

Feedback control

Feedforward control

Input standards

Management by exception

Output standards

Rapid Review

- Controlling is the process of measuring performance and taking corrective action as needed.

- The control process begins when performance objectives and standards are set; both input standards for work efforts and output standards for work results can be used.

- The second step in control is to measure actual performance; the third step compares these results with objectives and standards to determine the need for corrective action.

- The final step in the control process involves taking action to resolve problems and improve things in the future.

- Feedforward controls try to make sure things are set up right before work begins; concurrent controls make sure that things are being done correctly; feedback controls assess results after an action is completed.

- The control equation states: Need for Action = Desired Performance – Actual Performance.

- Management by exception focuses attention on the greatest need for action.

Reflect/React

1 What performance standards should guide a hospital emergency room or fire department?

2 Can one control performance equally well with input standards and output standards?

3 What are the possible downsides to management by exception?

11.2 What Are Some Organizational Control Systems and Techniques?

Most organizations use a variety of comprehensive and system-wide controls. On the human resources side you are likely to encounter management by objectives and employee discipline. On the operations side you should be familiar with quality control, purchasing and inventory controls, and the use of breakeven analysis.

• Management by Objectives Integrates Planning and Controlling

A useful technique for integrating planning and controlling in human resource practice is **management by objectives (MBO)**. This is a structured process of regular communication in which a supervisor or team leader and a subordinate or team member both jointly set performance objectives and review accomplished results.[10]

As Figure 11.2 shows, MBO creates an agreement between the two parties regarding performance objectives for a given time period, plans for accomplishing them, standards for measuring them, and procedures for reviewing them. After reaching an agreement on these matters, both parties are supposed to work closely together to fulfill its terms.

MBO is a process of joint objective setting between a superior and subordinate.

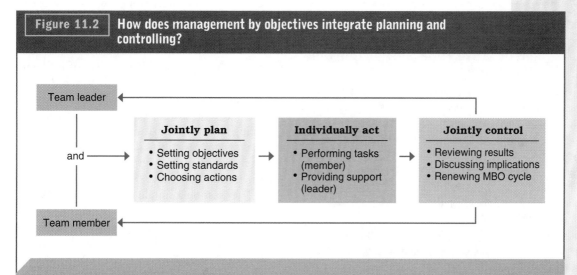

Figure 11.2 How does management by objectives integrate planning and controlling?

Management by objectives is a structured process of communication between a supervisor and subordinate, or team leader and team members. Planning is accomplished when both parties communicate to identify the subordinates' performance objectives. This is a form of participatory planning, and the goal is agreement. Informed by the objectives, the supervisor provides support for the subordinate as work progresses. Controlling is accomplished when the two parties meet at scheduled times to jointly discuss progress and results, and make new plans setting future performance objectives.

How people describe and establish objectives can influence the success of MBO. Two types of objectives are most common. *Improvement objectives* document intentions for improving performance in a specific way. An example is "to reduce quality rejects by 10 percent." *Personal development objectives* focus on personal growth activities, often those resulting in expanded job knowledge or skills. An example is "to learn the latest version of a computer spreadsheet package."

Whatever the objectives, one of the most important aspects of MBO is the need to state them specifically and as quantitatively as possible. Ideally, this involves agreement on a *measurable end product*, for example, "to reduce housekeeping supply costs by 5 percent by the end of the fiscal year." But this can be hard to do for some jobs.

For example, how could you measure the performance objective "To improve communications with my team members"? Rather than abandon MBO in such cases, performance objectives can often be stated as *verifiable work activities*. In this example, the team leader can commit to holding weekly team meetings as a means for achieving better communications.

You might already be wondering if MBO works, or if it can become too complicated a process. It is actually one of the most talked about management concepts.[11] Critics note that problems can arise when MBO links objectives to pay, focuses too much attention on easy accomplishments, involves excessive paperwork, and ends up with supervisors telling subordinates their objectives.

But the advantages of MBO are also clear. It can focus workers on the most important tasks and priorities, while focusing supervisors on the best ways to help them meet agreed-upon objectives. Because the process involves direct face-to-face communication, MBO can lead to better interpersonal relationships. And by increasing employees' participation in decisions that affect their work, it also encourages self-management.[12] Would you be surprised to learn that research shows that participation in goal setting helps increase a person's motivation to perform as expected?[13]

• Employee Discipline Is a Form of Managerial Control

MANAGEMENT TIPS

"Hot stove rules" of employee discipline

- *Issue a reprimand immediately.* A hot stove burns the first time you touch it.
- *Direct a reprimand toward someone's actions, not their personality.* A hot stove doesn't hold grudges, humiliate people, or accept excuses.
- *Apply a reprimand consistently.* A hot stove burns anyone who touches it, and it does so every time.
- *Provide an informative reprimand.* A hot stove lets a person know what to do to avoid getting burned again: "Don't touch."
- *Give the reprimand within a supportive setting.* A hot stove conveys warmth but with an inflexible rule: "Don't touch."
- *Support a reprimand with the relevant rules.* The Don't-touch-a-hot-stove rule isn't a power play, a whim, or an emotion of the moment; it is a necessary rule of reason.

Discipline is the act of influencing behavior through reprimand.

Progressive discipline ties reprimands to the severity and frequency of misbehavior.

ISO certification verifies an organization meets international quality standards.

Absenteeism, tardiness, sloppy work; the list of undesirable work conduct can go on to even more extremes—falsifying records, sexual harassment, embezzlement. Managers address such problems through **discipline**, the act of influencing behavior through reprimand. When done in a fair, consistent, and systematic manner, discipline is a useful form of managerial control.

Acting fairly and consistently as a disciplinarian, however, is not easy; just ask any parent or teacher. Yet these are essential management and life skills. Consider the "hot stove rules" in Management Tips. They rest on a simple understanding: "When a stove is hot, don't touch it." Everyone knows that when you violate this rule, you get burned—immediately, consistently, but usually not beyond the possibility of repair.[14]

What is known as **progressive discipline** is a system that ties reprimands to the severity and frequency of the employee's misbehavior. The goal is to achieve compliance with organizational expectations through the least extreme reprimands possible. For example, the ultimate penalty of *discharge* would be reserved for the most severe behaviors (e.g., any felony crime) or for repeated infractions of a less severe nature (e.g., being continually late for work or failing to respond to a series of written reprimands).

• Quality Control Is a Foundation for Total Quality Management

If managing for high performance is a theme of the day, *quality control* is one of its most important watchwords. In fact, businesses that want to compete as world-class companies are now expected to have **ISO certification** by the International Standards Organization in Geneva, Switzerland. Any organization that is ISO certified has undergone a rigorous assessment by outside auditors to verify that it meets international quality standards.

You will also often hear the term **total quality management (TQM)**, used to describe operations that make quality an everyday performance objective and strive to always do things right the first time.[15] A foundation of TQM is the quest for *continuous improvement*, meaning that one is always looking for new ways to improve on current performance.[16] The notion is that you can never be satisfied; something always can and should be improved on. See, for example, the *Exhibit – Four Absolutes of Quality Control*.[17]

Something else that you might hear discussed in conversations about quality control is the **quality circle**. This is a small group of workers that meets regularly to discuss ways of improving the quality of their products or services.[18] Members of a quality circle are expected to use their collective expertise and creativity to ensure quality outcomes. Here are some comments from persons taking part in quality circles: "This is the best thing the company has done in 15 years"; "The program proves that supervisors have no monopoly on brains"; "It gives me more pride in my work."[19]

• Purchasing and Inventory Controls Help Save Costs

Cost control ranks right up there with quality control as an important performance concern. And a very good place to start is with purchasing. Like any individual, organizations should know how much they pay for what they buy and what they are getting for their money. The goal of **purchasing control** is to buy what is needed at the right quality, at a good price, and for on-time delivery.

A lot of organizations today are trying to control purchasing costs through **supply chain management**. This is the use of information technology and special relationships to link suppliers and purchasers in the most cost-efficient ways. As you might expect, nobody is better at this than Wal-Mart.[20] The firm's supply chain is a continuing target for the cost savings that allow customers to buy at low prices. A current initiative is expanding the use of new *RFID* technologies (radio frequency identification microchips). Top Wal-Mart suppliers are required to ship all products with RFID tags so that computers can track them from point of manufacture, throughout distribution, right into the stores. From there the process continues as sales are logged into customer purchasing databases that control orders sent to manufacturers for new supplies.

The Wal-Mart story is also a reminder about how important it is to control the costs of inventories, the amount of materials or products kept in storage. The goal of **inventory control** is to make sure that any inventory is only big enough to meet one's immediate performance needs. This is greatly facilitated today when the use of RFID chips and other computer technologies enable advanced forms of a more traditional inventory control method known as the **economic order quantity**. This *EOQ* method automatically orders a fixed number of items every time an inventory level falls to a predetermined point. The order sizes are mathematically calculated to minimize costs of inventory. The best example is your local supermarket. It routinely makes hundreds of daily orders on an economic order quantity basis.

Finally, Wal-Mart's investments in supply chain management also enable another approach to inventory control known as **just-in-time scheduling (JIT)**. First made popular by the Japanese, these systems reduce costs and improve workflow by scheduling materials to arrive at a workstation or facility *just in time for use*. Because JIT nearly eliminates the carrying costs of inventories, it is an important business productivity tool. When a major hurricane was predicted to hit Florida, Wal-Mart's computer database anticipated high demand for, of all things, strawberry Pop-Tarts. It's JIT system delivered them to the stores just in time for the storm.[21]

Total quality management (TQM) commits to quality objectives, continuous improvement, and doing things right the first time.

A **quality circle** is a small group that meets regularly to discuss ways of improving work quality.

Purchasing control means buying what is needed at the right quality, at a good price, and for on-time delivery.

Supply chain management uses information technology to link suppliers and purchasers in cost-efficient ways.

Inventory control ensures that inventory is only big enough to meet immediate needs.

The **economic order quantity** method places new orders when inventory levels fall to predetermined points.

Just-in-time scheduling routes materials to workstations just in time for use.

• Breakeven Analysis Shows Where Revenues Will Equal Costs

When business executives are deliberating new products or projects, a frequent control question is: "What is the **breakeven point**?" A breakeven point is computed using this formula: Breakeven Point = Fixed Costs − (Price − Variable Costs). The graph in Figure 11.3 shows this as the point where revenues just equal costs. You can also think of it as the point where losses end and profit begins.

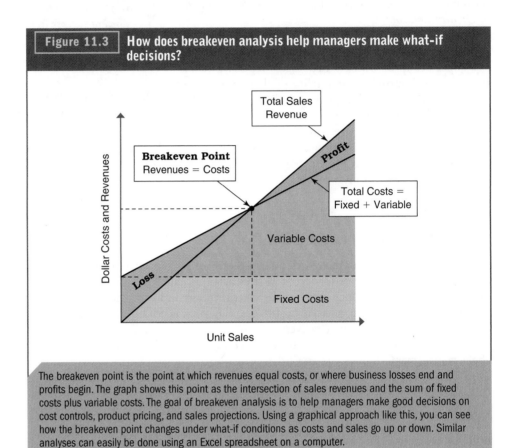

| Figure 11.3 | How does breakeven analysis help managers make what-if decisions? |

The breakeven point is the point at which revenues equal costs, or where business losses end and profits begin. The graph shows this point as the intersection of sales revenues and the sum of fixed costs plus variable costs. The goal of breakeven analysis is to help managers make good decisions on cost controls, product pricing, and sales projections. Using a graphical approach like this, you can see how the breakeven point changes under what-if conditions as costs and sales go up or down. Similar analyses can easily be done using an Excel spreadsheet on a computer.

Managers rely on **breakeven analysis** to perform "what-if" calculations under different projected cost and revenue conditions. See if you can calculate some breakeven points. Suppose the proposed target price for a new product is $8 per unit, fixed costs are $10,000, and variable costs are $4 per unit. What sales volume is required to break even? (*Answer:* Breakeven at 2500 units). What happens if you are good at cost control and can keep variable costs to $3 per unit? (*Answer:* Breakeven at 2000 units). Now, suppose you can only produce 1000 units in the beginning and at the original costs. At what price must you sell them to break even? (*Answer:* $14). These are exactly the types of cost control analyses that business executives perform every day.

STUDY GUIDE

11.2 What are some organizational control systems and techniques?

Be Sure You Can . . .

- illustrate how MBO might operate between a team leader and a team member

- explain what makes a discipline system progressive

- explain how supply chain management helps organizations control purchasing costs

- explain two common approaches to inventory cost control

- explain the role of continuous improvement in TQM

- state the equation used to calculate a breakeven point

- explain breakeven analysis

Define the Terms

Breakeven analysis

Breakeven point

Discipline

Economic order quantity

Inventory control

ISO certification

Just-in-time scheduling

Management by objectives

Progressive discipline

Purchasing control

Quality circle

Supply chain management

Total quality management(TQM)

Rapid Review

- Management by objectives is a process through which team leaders work with team members to "jointly" set performance objectives and review performance results.

- Discipline is the process of influencing behavior through reprimand; progressive discipline bases reprimands on the severity of infractions.

- Supply chain management helps save purchasing costs by using information technology and special relationships to link with suppliers in cost efficient ways.

- Economic order quantities and just-in-time deliveries are common approaches to inventory cost control.

- The breakeven equation is Breakeven Point = Fixed Costs − (Price − Variable Costs).

- Breakeven analysis identifies the points where revenues will equal costs under different pricing and cost conditions.

Reflect/React

1. Can MBO work when there are problems in the relationship between a team leader and a team member?

2. What might cause a progressive discipline system to fail?

3. Can a firm, like Wal-Mart, ever go too far in controlling its purchasing and inventory costs?

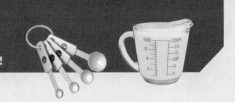

Multiple Choice

1. After objectives and standards are set, what step comes next in the control process?
   (a) Measure results. **(b)** Take corrective action.
   (c) Compare results with objectives. **(d)** Modify standards to fit circumstances.

2. When a soccer coach tells her players at the end of a losing game, "You really played well and stayed with the game plan," she is using a/an _____ as a measure of performance.
   (a) input standard **(b)** output standard **(c)** historical comparison **(d)** relative comparison

3. When an automobile manufacturer is careful to purchase only the highest-quality components for use in production, this is an example of an attempt to ensure high performance through _____ control.
   (a) concurrent **(b)** statistical **(c)** inventory
   (d) feedforward

4. Management by exception means _____.
   (a) managing only when necessary **(b)** focusing attention where the need for action is greatest **(c)** the same thing as concurrent control **(d)** the same thing as just in time delivery

5. A total quality management program is most likely to be associated with _____.
   (a) EOQ **(b)** continuous improvement **(c)** RFID
   (d) breakeven analysis

6. A manager following the "hot stove rules" of progressive discipline would _____.

   (a) avoid giving too much information when reprimanding someone **(b)** reprimand at random
   (c) focus the reprimand on actions, not personality
   (d) delay reprimands until something positive can also be discussed.

7. When MBO is done right, who does the review of a team member's performance accomplishments?
   (a) the team member **(b)** the team leader **(c)** both the team member and team leader **(d)** the team leader, the team member, and a lawyer

8. A good performance objective is written in such a way that it _____.
   (a) has a flexible timetable **(b)** is general and not too specific
   (c) is impossible to accomplish **(d)** can be easily measured

9. A manager is not living up to the concept of MBO if he or she _____.
   (a) sets performance objectives for subordinates **(b)** stays in touch and tries to support subordinates in their work
   (c) jointly reviews performance results with subordinates
   (d) keeps a written record of subordinates' performance objectives

10. Supply chain management is most likely to be concerned with _____.
    (a) cost control through efficient purchasing
    (b) profitability through increased sales **(c)** generating cash to pay bills **(d)** maximizing return on investments

Short Response

11. What type of control is being exercised in the U.S. Army's after-action review?

12. How do quality circles contribute to a TQM program?

13. How does a progressive discipline system work?

14. How can a just-in-time system reduce inventory costs?

Integration & Application

Put yourself in the position of a management consultant who specializes in MBO. The local Small Business Enterprise Association has asked you to be the speaker for its luncheon next week. The president of the association says that the group would like to learn more about the topic: "How to Use Management by Objectives for Better Planning and Control."

Questions: Your speech will last 15 to 20 minutes. What is the outline for your speech? How will you explain the potential benefits of MBO to this group of small business owners?

INSTRUCTIONS *Circle either "a" or "b" to indicate the item you most agree with in each pair of the following statements.*

1 (a) Promotions are earned through hard work and persistence.
(b) Making a lot of money is largely a matter of breaks.

2 (a) Many times the reactions of teachers seem haphazard to me.
(b) In my experience I have noticed that there is usually a direct connection between how hard I study and the grades I get.

3 (a) The number of divorces indicates that more and more people are not trying to make their marriages work.
(b) Marriage is largely a gamble.

4 (a) It is silly to think that one can really change another person's basic attitudes.
(b) When I am right I can convince others.

5 (a) Getting promoted is really a matter of being a little luckier than the next guy.
(b) In our society an individual's future earning power is dependent on his or her ability.

6 (a) If one knows how to deal with people, they are really quite easily led.
(b) I have little influence over the way other people behave.

7 (a) In my case the grades I make are the results of my own efforts; luck has little or nothing to do with it.
(b) Sometimes I feel that I have little to do with the grades I get.

8 (a) People like me can change the course of world affairs if we make ourselves heard.
(b) It is only wishful thinking to believe that one can really influence what happens in society at large.

9 (a) Much of what happens to me is probably a matter of chance.
(b) I am the master of my fate.

10 (a) Getting along with people is a skill that must be practiced.
(b) It is almost impossible to figure out how to please some people.

SCORING
Give yourself 1 point for 1b, 2a, 3a, 4b, 5b, 6a, 7a, 8a, 9b, 10a. Check your total against this rubric: 8–10 = high *internal* locus of control, 6–7 = moderate *internal* locus of control, 5 = *mixed* locus of control, 3–4 = moderate *external* locus of control, 0–2 = high *external* locus of control.

INTERPRETATION
This instrument offers an impression of your tendency toward an *internal locus of control or external locus of control.* Persons with a high internal locus of control tend to believe they have control over their own destinies. They may be most responsive to opportunities for greater self-control in the workplace. Persons with a high external locus of control tend to believe that what happens to them is largely in the hands of external people or forces. They may be less comfortable with self-control and more responsive to external controls in the workplace.

PATHWAYS to WileyPLUS

 CASE SNAPSHOT

Go online to read this case!

Take-Two Interactive: How Far is Too Far?
Still recovering from the PR fiasco of having embedded bawdy bits in a very successful video game, how does a company with an edgy reputation manage to cross the line, recover, and still maintain its attitude? How can you know where the line is, and what to do when it's crossed?

MODULE 11 | **Online Interactive Learning Resources**

Skill Builder
• Risk Taking

Experiential Exercises
• The MBO Contract
• Defining Quality

Team Project
• Fringe Benefits Costs

Insights and hard

Strategic Management

Starbucks probably claims the most valuable brand name in its industry. The question is: How long can Starbucks keep brewing a better cup of coffee?

"Forever," might answer Howard Schultz, chairman and chief global strategist of the company.[1] When he joined Starbucks in 1982 as director of retail operations, the firm was a small coffee retailer in Seattle. But his vision was much bigger: to have a national chain of stores offering the finest coffee drinks and "educating consumers everywhere about fine coffee."

Today Starbucks is found around the world. But it has also become more than just another coffee retailer. Visit a store or go online, and you'll

work deliver results

find it selling tea, chocolates, ice cream, luncheon sandwiches, specialty apparel, gift cards, a variety of other gift items, and music. It's all part of a global quest for growth. But even a top-notch firm like Starbucks can't pause and rest on its past laurels. Success today is no guarantee of success tomorrow.[2]

Henry Ford once said of his Model T's: "The customer can have any color he wants as long as it's black."[3] Back then the firm, quite literally, was in the driver's seat. Not so now; an environment of soaring gasoline prices has changed the rules of the game.

Today's businesses must deal with much more demanding customer tastes and markets. Stephen Haeckel, director of strategic studies at IBM's Advanced Business Institute, describes the shift this way: "It's a difference between a bus, which follows a set route, and a taxi, which goes where customers tell it to go."[4]

Starbucks is quite obviously taking the taxi, and growing like crazy. Ford recently announced major layoffs and plant closings; is it riding the bus?[5]

➡ MODULE GUIDE

 12.1 What types of strategies are used by organizations?

- Strategy is a comprehensive plan for achieving competitive advantage.
- Organizations use strategy at the corporate, business, and functional levels.
- Growth and diversification strategies focus on expansion.
- Restructuring and divestiture strategies focus on consolidation.
- Global strategies focus on international business initiatives.
- E-business strategies focus on using the Internet for business transactions.

 12.2 How are strategies formulated and implemented in strategic management?

- Strategy formulation begins with the organization's mission and objectives.
- SWOT analysis identifies strengths, weaknesses, opportunities, and threats.
- Porter's five forces model examines industry attractiveness.
- Porter's competitive strategies model examines business or product strategies.
- Portfolio planning examines strategies across multiple businesses or products.
- Strategic leadership activates organizations for strategy implementation.

A **strategy** is a comprehensive plan guiding resource allocation to achieve long-term organization goals.

Strategic intent focuses organizational energies on achieving a compelling goal.

The bus–taxi analogy could be applied to your career strategy. Will you be acting like the bus following the set route, or the taxi following opportunities? Don't be afraid to move back and forth between the worlds of business strategy and personal strategy as our discussions in this module develop. The applications go both ways. And just like you and your career progress, success in the business world requires leaders with the abilities to move their organizations forward strategically. "If you want to make a difference as a leader," says *Fast Company* magazine, "you've got to make time for strategy."[6]

• Strategy Is a Comprehensive Plan for Achieving Competitive Advantage

A **strategy** is a comprehensive action plan that identifies long-term direction for an organization and guides resource utilization to accomplish its goals. Strategy focuses leadership attention on the competitive environment. It represents a "best guess" about what to do to be successful in the face of rivalry and changing conditions.

A good strategy also provides leaders with a plan for allocating and using resources with consistent **strategic intent**. Think of this as having all organizational energies directed toward a unifying and compelling target or goal.[7] Coca-Cola, for example, describes its strategic intent as "To put a Coke within 'arm's reach' of every consumer in the world."

Ultimately, a good strategy helps an organization achieve **competitive advantage**. This means that it is able to outperform rivals. In fact, the best strategies provide *sustainable* competitive advantage. This means that they operate in ways that bring success and that competitors cannot easily imitate.

Wal-Mart, for example, is well-known for its abilities to save costs through highly efficient supply chain management. This is made possible by a competitive advantage in information technology utilization. The firm's computer databases hold more information than all of the Internet's fixed pages combined—and some say its computer system rivals the Department of Defense's in size.[8] This is a tough act for other retailers, even Target, to follow. It's one of the things that helps keep Wal-Mart almost always a step ahead of its competitors.

PACESETTERS

eBay Inc.'s Meg Whitman has proven to be one of a kind.

As president and CEO of eBay Inc., Margaret C. (Meg) Whitman has made her mark on global business. While helping build the firm into the world's premier e-commerce site, she has earned a reputation as a most savvy and talented strategic leader. Under her guidance eBay has grown from an emergent dot-com to a $3 billion company that serves some 100 million buyers and sellers each week. This is 25% of all e-commerce. And through all the rapid growth she's kept the firm on track even while expanding and taking new risks. With some sense that the online auction business may be flattening out, Whitman has been making acquisitions. One of her most recent and controversial was paying $2.5 billion for Skype Technologies, the Internet telephony company. Although some analysts wonder if this moves eBay too far from its core business areas, Whitman says: "In the end we'll be judged on the results, whether this vision turned out to be the right one." Now she's investing $100 million in China.[29]

Meg Whitman, *President and CEO, eBay, Inc.*

A **competitive advantage** means operating in successful ways that are difficult to imitate.

A **corporate strategy** sets long-term direction for the total enterprise.

A **business strategy** identifies how a division or strategic business unit will compete in its product or service domain.

• Organizations Use Strategy at the Corporate, Business, and Functional Levels

You can identify strategies at three levels in most organizations. At the top level, **corporate strategy** provides direction and guides resource allocations for the organization as a whole. The *strategic question* at the corporate strategy level is: In what industries and markets should we compete? In large, complex organizations, like PepsiCo, IBM, and General Electric, decisions on corporate strategy identify how the firm intends to compete across multiple industries, businesses, and markets.

	Corporation	

Corporate strategy
What businesses are we in?

Business strategy
How do we compete in each of our major businesses?

Functional strategy
How do we best support each of our business strategies?

Business Division A

Business Division B

Business Division C

Finance

Human resources

Manufacturing

Marketing

A **functional strategy** guides activities within one specific area of operations.

A **growth strategy** involves expansion of the organization's current operations.

Growth through **concentration** means expansion within an existing business area.

In **diversification**, expansion occurs by entering new business areas.

Business strategy focuses on the strategic intent for a single business unit or product line. The *strategic question* at the business strategy level is: How are we going to compete for customers within this industry and in this market? Typical business strategy decisions include choices about product and service mix, facilities locations, new technologies, and the like. For smaller, single-business enterprises, business strategy is the corporate strategy.

Functional strategy guides activities to implement higher-level business and corporate strategies. This level of strategy unfolds within a specific functional area such as marketing, manufacturing, finance, and human resources. The *strategic question* for functional strategies is: How can we best utilize resources within the function to support implementation of the business strategy? Answers to this question involve a wide variety of practices and initiatives to improve things like operating efficiency, product quality, customer service, or innovativeness.

• Growth and Diversification Strategies Focus on Expansion

At the levels of corporate and business strategy you will often read and hear about organizations trying to get bigger.[9] They are pursuing **growth strategies** to increase the size and scope of current operations. In some industries, such as fast food, companies view growth as necessary for long-run profitability. You should probably question this assumption and probe deeper right from the start. Is growth always the best path? And if the choice is to grow, how should it be accomplished?

A strategy of growth through **concentration** seeks expansion within an existing business area, one in which the firm has experience and presumably expertise. You don't see McDonald's trying to grow by getting involved in bookstores or gasoline stations; it keeps opening more restaurants at home and abroad. You don't see Wal-Mart trying to grow by buying a high-end department store chain or even opening Wal-Mart convenience stores; it keeps opening new stores at the rate of 500+ per year. These are classic growth by concentration strategies.

A distinctly different strategy is growth through **diversification**. In this case expansion occurs by entering new business areas. As you might expect,

NEWSLINE

It may be American Standard, but it's made in Bulgaria No business strategy is risk free. And in business some would say that when American Standard went to Bulgaria in 1992, bought a local company, and set up manufacturing it was taking extraordinary risk. The country was just emerging from decades of Soviet domination; the economy was bad and the infrastructure very poor. But American Standard needed to ramp up its European production of bathroom fixtures and its executives saw Bulgaria as a strategic opportunity. And they were right; Bulgaria is hot now as it prepares to join the EU. Foreign investment is running high as others join American Standard in trying to tap the country's low wage rates, highly skilled labor, and proximity to the rest of Europe. CEO Frederic Poses says the Sarajevo operation is "very competitive to what we do in Asia."

Reflect: Asia and Eastern Europe are often in the news as high-payoff international business locations. But will they stay that way for long? Where else in the world could a manufacturer go to get in ahead of the crowd—the Middle East, Southern or West Africa, or . . .?

there is more risk to diversification because the firm may be moving outside its existing areas of competency. One way to moderate the risk is to grow through *related diversification,* expanding into similar or complementary new businesses areas. PepsiCo did this when it purchased Tropicana. Although Tropicana's fruit juices were new to Pepsi, the business is related to its expertise in the beverages industry.

But firms also get involved in *unrelated diversification* that pursues growth in entirely new business areas. Did you know, for example, that Exxon once owned Izod? Does that make sense? Can you see why growth through unrelated diversification might cause problems? In fact, research is quite clear that business performance may decline with too much unrelated diversification.[10]

Diversification can also take the form of **vertical integration**. This is where a business acquires its suppliers (*backward vertical integration*), or its distributors (*forward vertical integration*). Backward vertical integration has been a historical pattern in the automobile industry as firms purchased parts suppliers, although you'll find that recent trends are to reverse this. In beverages, both Coca-Cola and PepsiCo have pursued forward vertical integration by purchasing some of their major bottlers.

• Restructuring and Divestiture Strategies Focus on Consolidation

When organizations run into problems, perhaps brought about by too much growth and diversification, these problems have to be solved. A **retrenchment strategy** seeks to correct weaknesses by making radical changes to current ways of operating. Its most extreme form is **liquidation**, where a business closes down and sells its assets to pay creditors.

A less extreme and more common form of retrenchment is **restructuring**. This involves making major changes to reduce the scale and/or mix of operations. The goals of restructuring are to cut costs and gain short-term efficiencies, as well as buy time to develop new strategies to improve future success.

One of the restructuring approaches you will often hear about is **downsizing**, cutting down the size of operations and reducing the workforce.[11] When you learn of organizations reducing budgets or staffs by across-the-board cuts, however, you might be a bit skeptical. Research has shown that downsizing is more successful when cutbacks are done selectively, in ways that focus on key performance objectives.[12]

Finally, restructuring by **divestiture** involves selling parts of the organization to refocus on core competencies, cutting costs, and improving operating efficiency. This type of retrenchment often occurs when organizations have become overdiversified. General Motors did this when it sold off its major parts supplier, Delphi.

• Global Strategies Focus on International Business Initiatives

International business offers a variety of growth opportunities, but they can be engaged in quite different ways.[13] A firm pursuing a **globalization strategy** tends to view the world as one large market. With that in mind, it tries to advertise and sell standard products for use everywhere. For example, Gillette sells and advertises its latest razors around the world.

Firms pursuing a *multidomestic strategy* try to customize products and advertising to fit local cultures and needs. Bristol Myers, Procter & Gamble, and Unilever, for example, all vary their products according to consumer preferences in different countries and cultures.

A third approach is the *transnational strategy,* which seeks a balance between efficiencies in global operations and responsiveness to local markets. You should recall that a transnational firm tries to operate without a strong national identity,

STAY INFORMED

Hourly wages outside of United States:

Country	Factory	Engineer
Poland	$3.07	$ 4.32
Germany	18.80	38.90
China	.80	3.50
India	.43	2.40

Growth through **vertical integration** is by acquiring suppliers or distributors.

A **retrenchment strategy** changes operations to correct weaknesses.

Liquidation is where a business closes and sells its assets to pay creditors.

Restructuring reduces the scale or mix of operations.

Downsizing decreases the size of operations.

Divestiture sells off parts of the organization to refocus attention on core business areas.

A **globalization strategy** adopts standardized products and advertising for use worldwide.

hoping to blend instead with the global economy.[14] In a transnational strategy firms try to fully utilize business resources and tap customer markets worldwide. Ford, for example, draws upon design, manufacturing, and distribution expertise all over the world to build car platforms. These are then modified within regions to build cars that meet local tastes.

• E-Business Strategies Focus on Using the Internet for Business Transactions

Without a doubt, one of the most frequently asked questions these days for the business executive is: "What is your **e-business strategy**?" This is the strategic use of the Internet to gain competitive advantage.[15] The *Exhibit – Web-based Business Models* lists some of common options that are available, along with examples of each.[16]

Among the terms you will hear used in this regard are B2B (business-to-business) and B2C (business-to-customer) applications. **B2B business strategies** use IT and Web portals to vertically link organizations with members of their supply chains. For example, Dell Computer sets up special website services that allow its major corporate customers to manage their accounts online. Wal-Mart links its suppliers to the firm's information systems so they can manage inventories for their own products electronically.

As individuals, we often do business with firms using **B2C business strategies**, using IT and Web portals to link with customers. Whenever you buy a music download from Apple's iTunes Store, order a book from Amazon.com, or shop online for a new Dell notebook PC, you are the "C" in a B2C strategy. And if you are looking for benchmarking standards for excellence, these firms are good starting points.

EXHIBIT

Web-Based Business Models

Advertising model   Providing free information or services to generate revenues from advertising (e.g., Yahoo!, Google)

Brokerage model   Bringing buyers and sellers together for online business transactions (e.g., CarsDirect, eBay, Priceline)

Infomediary model   Providing free service in exchange for collecting information on users for sale to other businesses (e.g., NetZero, ePinions)

Merchant model   E-tailing, selling products or services direct to customers through the Web (e.g., Amazon, Flowers Direct)

Referral model   Providing free service and getting referral fees from online merchants for directing potential customers to them (e.g., Shopzilla, PriceGrabber)

Subscription model   Selling access to high value content through a subscription web site (e.g., *Wall Street Journal* Interactive, Consumer Reports)

An **e-business strategy** strategically uses the Internet to gain competitive advantage.

A **B2B business strategy** uses IT and Web portals to link organizations vertically in supply chains.

A **B2C business strategy** uses IT and Web portals to link businesses with customers.

> *Always play to win. Anybody who's not managing for profitable, sustainable growth risks becoming defensive and, over time, arrogant.*
>
> Ram Charan, **PROFESSOR AND ADVISOR TO CEOs**

12.1 What types of strategies are used by organizations?

Be Sure You Can . . .

- differentiate strategy, strategic intent, and competitive advantage

- differentiate corporate, business, and functional levels of strategy

- list and explain major types of growth and diversification strategies

- list and explain restructuring and divestiture strategies

- explain alternative global strategies

- differentiate B2B and B2C as e-business strategies

Define the Terms

B2B business strategy	Functional strategy
B2C business strategy	Globalization strategy
Business strategy	Growth strategy
Competitive advantage	Liquidation
Concentration	Restructuring
Corporate strategy	Retrenchment strategy
Diversification	Strategic intent
Divestiture	Strategy
Downsizing	Vertical integration
E-business strategy	

Rapid Review

- A strategy is a comprehensive plan that sets long-term direction for an organization and guides resource allocations to achieve sustainable competitive advantage, being able to operate in ways that outperform the competition.

- Corporate strategy sets the direction for an entire organization; business strategy sets the direction for a large business unit or product division; functional strategy sets the direction within business functions.

- Organizations follow growth strategies that expand existing business areas through concentration, or pursue new ones by related or unrelated diversification.

- Organizations follow retrenchment strategies that allow periods of consolidation where operations are streamlined for better performance through restructuring and divestiture.

- Global strategies take advantage of international business opportunities, by both multidomestic and transnational approaches.

- E-business strategies use information technology and the Internet to pursue competitive advantage, with popular forms being B2B and B2C.

Reflect/React

1. With things changing so fast today, is it really possible to achieve "sustainable" competitive advantage?

2. Why is growth such a popular business strategy?

3. Is it good news or bad news for investors when a business announces that it is restructuring?

12.2 How Are Strategies Formulated and Implemented in Strategic Management?

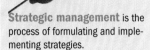

The late and great management guru Peter Drucker once said: "The future will not just happen if one wishes hard enough. It requires decision—now. It imposes risk—now. It requires action—now. It demands allocation of resources, and above all, of human resources—now. It requires work—now."[17] That fits squarely with the module subtitle: Insights and hard work deliver results. Let's talk a bit more about the hard work of strategic management.

Figure 12.1 shows **strategic management** as the process of formulating and implementing strategies to accomplish long-term goals and sustain competitive advantage. **Strategy formulation** is the process of crafting strategy. It involves assessing the organization and environment to plan new strategies to deliver future competitive advantage. **Strategy implementation** is the process of putting strategies into action. It involves leading and activating the entire organization to put strategies to work.

Strategic management is the process of formulating and implementing strategies.

Strategy formulation is the process of creating strategies.

Strategy implementation is the process of putting strategies into action.

Figure 12.1	What are the steps in the strategic management process?

The strategic management process involves responsibilities for both formulating and implementing organizational strategies. The process begins by analyzing mission and objectives to set a baseline for strategy formulation. Then organizational resources and capabilities are analyzed, and strategies are crafted at corporate, business, and functional levels. Finally, the strategies must be put into action. This requires strategic leadership to ensure that all organizational resources and systems fully support strategy implementation.

Can you see that both activities are necessary, that success is only possible when strategies are both well formulated and well implemented? Competitive advantage in business or success in a career doesn't just happen; it is created when great strategies are implemented to full advantage.

• Strategy Formulation Begins with the Organization's Mission and Objectives

Strategy formulation begins with review and clarification of organizational mission and objectives.[18] You should remember from Module 1 that the **mission** describes the purpose of an organization, its reason for existence in society.[19] The best organizations have clear missions that communicate a sense of direction and motivate members to work hard in their behalf.[20] They also link these missions with well-chosen **operating objectives** that serve as short-term guides to performance.[21]

The **mission** is the organization's reason for existence in society.

Operating objectives are specific results that organizations try to accomplish.

A sampling of typical business operating objectives includes: profitability, cost efficiency, market share, product quality, innovation, and social responsibility. When mission and objectives are clear, a strategic planning baseline is established. From here, the next step in strategy formulation is to understand how well the organization is currently positioned to fulfill its mission and objectives.

• SWOT Analysis Identifies Strengths, Weaknesses, Opportunities, and Threats

A **SWOT analysis** involves a detailed examination of organizational *strengths* and *weaknesses*, and environmental *opportunities* and *threats*. As Figure 12.2 shows, the results of this examination can be portrayed in a straightforward and very useful planning matrix.

A **SWOT analysis** examines organizational strengths and weaknesses and environmental opportunities and threats.

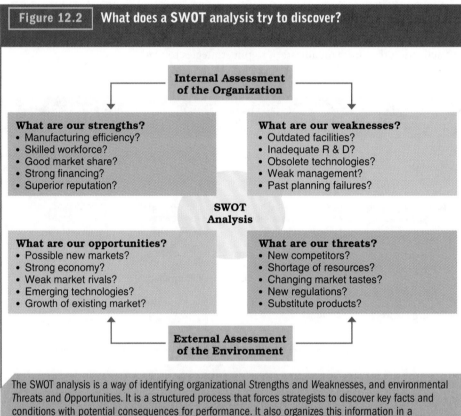

Figure 12.2 | **What does a SWOT analysis try to discover?**

The SWOT analysis is a way of identifying organizational *Strengths* and *Weaknesses*, and environmental *Threats* and *Opportunities*. It is a structured process that forces strategists to discover key facts and conditions with potential consequences for performance. It also organizes this information in a structured manner that is useful for making strategy decisions. Managers using a SWOT analysis should be looking for organizational strengths that can be leveraged as core competencies to make future gains, as well as environmental opportunities that can be exploited.

A **core competency** is a special strength that gives an organization a competitive advantage.

When looking at the organization's strengths, one goal is to find among them **core competencies**. These are special strengths that the organization has or does exceptionally well in comparison with its competitors. When an organization's core competencies are unique and costly for others to imitate, they become potential sources of competitive advantage.[22]

Organizational weaknesses, of course, are the flip side of the picture. Although it might take some extra discipline to do it, they must also be investigated and understood to develop a realistic perspective on the organization's capabilities. The same discipline holds when examining conditions in the environment. It's not only the opportunities that count—such as new markets, a strong economy, weak competitors, and emerging technologies. The threats must be considered also—perhaps the emergence of new competitors, resource scarcities, changing customer tastes, and new government regulations.

And again, don't forget the career planning implications. If you were to analyze your strategic readiness for career advancement right now, what would your SWOT look like?

• Porter's Five Forces Model Examines
Industry Attractiveness

Harvard scholar and consultant Michael Porter says, "A company without a strategy is willing to try anything."[23] With a good strategy in place, by contrast, the organization can focus its entire resources on its overall goal. Porter goes on to suggest that managers must craft strategy with a good understanding of the industry within which they are competing. He offers a "five forces" model for doing this, with a focus on what he calls industry attractiveness.

Force 1 is: *industry competitors*—intensity of rivalry among firms in the industry. Force 2 is: *new entrants*—threats of new competitors entering the market. Force 3 is: *suppliers*—the bargaining power of suppliers. Force 4 is: *customers*—the bargaining power of buyers. Force 5 is: *substitutes*—threats of substitute products or services.[24]

Can you recognize how Porter's five forces influence industry attractiveness?

Porter's Five Forces

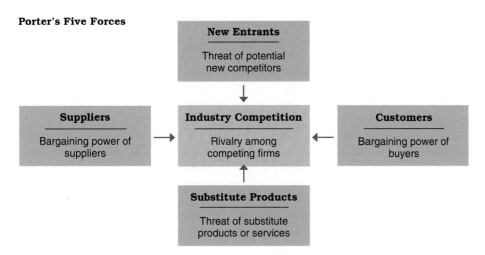

An unattractive industry will have intense competitive rivalries, substantial threats in the form of possible new entrants and substitute products, and powerful suppliers and buyers who dominate any bargaining with the firm. As you might expect, this is a very challenging environment for strategy formulation.

A very attractive industry will have little existing competition, few threats from new entrants or substitutes, and low bargaining power among suppliers and buyers. Obviously, strategy formulation under these conditions should be less of a problem.

• Porter's Competitive Strategies Model Examines Business
or Product Strategies

Once industry forces are understood, Porter's attention shifts to how a business or its products can be strategically positioned relative to competitors. He believes that competitive strategies can be built around differentiation, cost leadership, and focus.

A **differentiation strategy** seeks competitive advantage through uniqueness. Organizations try to develop goods and services that are clearly different from those of the competition. The strategic objective is to attract customers who stay loyal to the firm's products and lose interest in its competitors.

Success with a differentiation strategy depends on customer perceptions of product quality and uniqueness. This requires organizational strengths in marketing, research and development, and creativity. An example is Polo Ralph Lauren, retailer of upscale classic fashions and accessories. In Ralph Lauren's words, "Polo redefined how American style and quality is perceived. Polo has always been about selling quality products by creating worlds and inviting our customers to be part of our dream."[25] If you've seen any Polo ads in magazines or television, you'll know that the company aggressively markets this perception.

A **differentiation strategy** offers products that are unique and different from the competition.

→ **Porter's Competitive Strategies**

- **Differentiation**—make products that are unique and different.
- **Cost leadership**—produce at lower cost and sell at lower price.
- **Focused differentiation**—use differentiation and target needs of a special market.
- **Focused cost leadership**—use cost leadership and target needs of a special market.

A **cost leadership strategy** seeks to operate with lower costs than competitors.

A **focused differentiation strategy** offers a unique product to a special market segment.

A **focused cost leadership strategy** seeks the lowest costs of operations within a special market segment.

A **cost leadership strategy** seeks competitive advantage by operating with lower costs than competitors. This allows organizations to make profits while selling products or services at low prices their competitors can't match. The objective is to continuously improve the operating efficiencies of production, distribution, and other organizational systems.

Success with the cost leadership strategy requires tight cost and managerial controls, as well as products or services that are easy to create and distribute. This is what might be called the "Wal-Mart" strategy: do everything you can to keep costs so low that you can offer customers the lowest prices and still make a reasonable profit. You can see this strategy in many places. In financial services, for example, the Vanguard Group keeps costs low so it can offer mutual funds to customers with minimum fees. Its website proudly proclaims that Vanguard leads the industry in the lowest average expense ratios.

Porter's generic *focus strategy* concentrates attention on a special market segment, with the objective of serving its needs better than anyone else. It can be pursued in two forms. In the **focused differentiation strategy**, the organization concentrates on one special market segment and tries to offer customers in that segment a unique product. In the **focused cost leadership strategy**, the organization concentrates on one special market segment and tries in that segment to be the provider with lowest costs. Low-fare airlines, for example, offer heavily discounted fares and "no frills" service for customers who want to travel point-to-point for the lowest prices.

Can you apply these four competitive strategies to an actual situation, say alternative sodas in the soft-drink industry? Porter would begin by asking and answering two questions for each soda: What is the market scope—is the target market for the drink broad or narrow? What is the potential source of competitive advantage—is it in a lower price or in product uniqueness?

Figure 12.3 shows how answers to these questions might strategically position some soft drinks with which you might be familiar. The makers of Coke and Pepsi follow a differentiation strategy. They spend billions on advertising to convince consumers that their products are high quality and uniquely desirable. Big K Kola, a Kroger product, sells as a cheaper alternative. In order to make a profit at the lower selling price, Kroger must follow a cost leadership strategy.

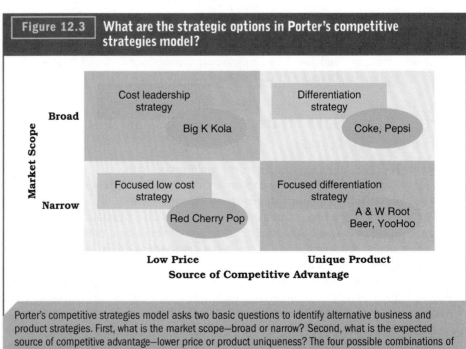

Figure 12.3 | **What are the strategic options in Porter's competitive strategies model?**

Porter's competitive strategies model asks two basic questions to identify alternative business and product strategies. First, what is the market scope—broad or narrow? Second, what is the expected source of competitive advantage—lower price or product uniqueness? The four possible combinations of answers result in differentiation, cost leadership, focused differentiation, and focused cost leadership strategies. The figure uses examples from the soft drink industry to show how these strategies can be used for different products.

What about a can of A&W Root Beer or a can of Vanilla Coke? In Porter's model they represent a strategy of focused differentiation—products with unique tastes for customers wanting quality brands. This is quite different from the strategy behind your local convenience store's version of "Cheap Cherry Pop." This is a classic case of focused cost leadership—a product with a unique taste for customers who want a low price.

• Portfolio Planning Examines Strategies across Multiple Businesses or Products

As you might expect, strategic management gets quite complicated for companies that operate multiple businesses selling many different products and services. A good example is the global conglomerate General Electric. The firm owns a portfolio of diverse businesses ranging from jet engines, to capital services, to medical systems, to power systems, and even more. CEO Jeffrey Immelt faces a difficult strategic question all the time: How should GE's resources be allocated across this mix, or portfolio, of businesses?[26]

If you think about it, Immelt's strategic management problem at GE is similar to what we face with managing our personal assets. How, for example, do you manage a mix of cash, stocks, bonds, and real estate investments? What do you increase, what do you sell, and what do you hold? These are the same questions that Immelt and other executives ask; they are *portfolio-planning* questions, and they have major strategic implications. Shouldn't they be made systematically, rather than haphazardly?[27]

The Boston Consulting Group has proposed a strategic planning approach shown in Figure 12.4 and known as the **BCG Matrix**. This portfolio-planning framework asks managers to analyze business and product strategies based on the industry or market growth rate, and the market share held by the firm.[28]

Stars in the BCG Matrix have high-market-shares in high-growth markets. They produce large profits through substantial penetration of expanding markets. The preferred strategy for stars is growth; the BCG Matrix recommends making further resource investments in them. Stars are not only high performers in the present, they offer future potential to do the same or even more so.

The **BCG Matrix** analyzes business opportunities according to market growth rate and market share.

| Figure 12.4 | In what ways is the BCG Matrix useful in strategic planning? |

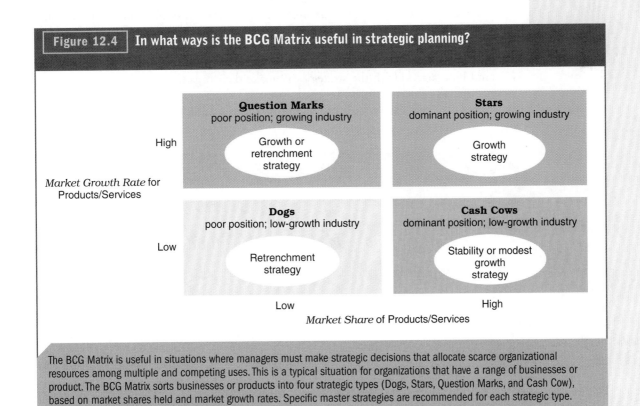

The BCG Matrix is useful in situations where managers must make strategic decisions that allocate scarce organizational resources among multiple and competing uses. This is a typical situation for organizations that have a range of businesses or product. The BCG Matrix sorts businesses or products into four strategic types (Dogs, Stars, Question Marks, and Cash Cow), based on market shares held and market growth rates. Specific master strategies are recommended for each strategic type.

Cash cows have high-market-shares in low-growth markets. They produce large profits and a strong cash flow, but with little upside potential. Because the markets offer little growth opportunity, the preferred strategy for cash cows is stability or modest growth. Like real dairy cows, the BCG Matrix advises firms to "milk" these businesses to generate cash for investing in other more promising areas.

Question marks have low-market shares in high-growth markets. Although they may not generate much profit at the moment, the upside potential is there because of the growing markets. Question marks make for difficult strategic decision making. The BCG Matrix recommends targeting only the most promising question marks for growth, while retrenching those that are less promising.

Dogs have low-market shares in low-growth markets. They produce little if any profit, and they have low potential for future improvement. The preferred strategy for dogs is straightforward: retrenchment by divestiture.

• Strategic Leadership Activates Organizations for Strategy Implementation

The rest of *Exploring Management* is really all about strategy implementation. In order to successfully put strategies into action, the entire organization with all of its people, resources, and systems must be activated in support of them. This requires good organization structures, strong organizational cultures, and the right staffing. And above all, it requires effective leadership.

In our dynamic and often-uncertain environment, in fact, the premium is on **strategic leadership**—the capability to inspire people to successfully engage in a process of continuous change, performance enhancement, and implementation of organizational strategies.[29] And even though it may make sense to think first about strategic leadership as a top management responsibility, it really should be shared by managers at all levels.

As you try to digest this concept, think of it this way.[30] A strategic leader has to be the *guardian of trade-offs*, making sure that resources are allocated in ways always consistent with strategy. A strategic leader needs to *create a sense of urgency*, not allowing the people to grow slow and complacent even when things are going well. A strategic leader needs to *make sure that everyone understands the strategy* so that daily tasks and efforts have a clear sense of purpose. A strategic leader must *be a teacher*, someone who builds understanding of the strategy and makes it a "cause." Finally, a strategic leader must *be a great communicator*, someone who makes everyone understand how success with the strategy will make their organization significantly different from all others.

Now, isn't that good food for thought to end this module?

> **Strategic leadership** inspires people to implement organizational strategies.

> *A strategy is no good if people don't fundamentally believe in it.*
>
> **Robert Haas, FORMER CEO, LEVI-STRAUSS**

STUDY GUIDE

12.2 How are strategies formulated and implemented in strategic management?

Be Sure You Can . . .

- describe the strategic management process

- explain Porter's five forces model

- explain Porter's competitive strategies model

- describe the purpose and use of the BCG Matrix

- explain the responsibilities of strategic leadership

Define the Terms

BCG Matrix	Operating objectives
Core competencies	Strategic management
Cost leadership strategy	Strategic leadership
Differentiation strategy	Strategy formulation
Focused cost leadership strategy	Strategy implementation
	SWOT analysis
Focused differentiation strategy	
Mission	

Rapid Review

- Strategic management is the process of formulating and implementing strategies to achieve sustainable competitive environment.

- A SWOT analysis sets a foundation for strategy formulation by systematically assessing organizational strengths and weaknesses, and environmental opportunities and threats.

- Porter's five forces model analyzes industry attractiveness in terms of competitors, new entrants, substitute products, and the bargaining powers of suppliers and buyers.

- Porter's competitive strategies model examines how business and product strategies are created around differentiation (distinguishing one's products from the competition), cost leadership (minimizing costs relative to the competition), and focus (concentrating on a special market segment).

- The BCG Matrix is a portfolio-planning approach that classifies businesses or product lines as stars, cash cows, question marks, or dogs, and associates each with a suggested master strategy.

- Strategic leadership is the responsibility for activating people and all organizational resources and systems to continually pursue and fully accomplish strategy implementation.

Reflect/React

1. Can an organization have a good strategy but a poor sense of mission?

2. Would a monopoly receive a perfect score for industry attractiveness in Porter's five forces model?

3. Does the BCG Matrix oversimplify a complex strategic management problem?

MODULE 12

TEST PREP
Take the complete set of Module 12 quizzes online!

Multiple Choice

1. Which is the best first question to ask when starting the strategic management process?
   (a) "What is our mission?" **(b)** "How well are we currently doing?" **(c)** "How can we get where we want to be?" **(d)** "Why aren't we doing better?"

2. The ability of a firm to consistently outperform its rivals is called _____.
   (a) vertical integration **(b)** competitive advantage **(c)** strategic intent **(d)** core competency

3. General Electric is a complex conglomerate that owns both NBC Universal and GE Healthcare, firms operating in very different industries. The strategies pursued for each of these units within GE would best be called _____-level strategies.
   (a) corporate **(b)** business **(c)** functional **(d)** transnational

4. An organization that is downsizing by cutting staff to reduce costs can be described as pursuing a _____ strategy.
   (a) liquidation **(b)** divestiture **(c)** retrenchment **(d)** stability

5. When you buy music downloads online, the firm selling them to you is engaging in which type of e-business strategy?
   (a) B2C **(b)** B2B **(c)** HTTP **(d)** WWW

6. A _____ in the BCG Matrix would have a high-market share in a low-growth market.
   (a) dog **(b)** cash cow **(c)** question mark **(d)** star

7. In Porter's five forces model, which of the following conditions is most favorable from the standpoint of industry attractiveness?
   (a) many competitive rivals **(b)** many substitute products **(c)** low bargaining power of suppliers **(d)** few barriers to entry

8. If Google's top management were to announce that the firm was going to buy Federal Express, this would indicate a strategy of _____.
   (a) diversification **(b)** concentration **(c)** horizontal integration **(d)** vertical integration

9. The alliances that link together firms in supply chain management relationships are examples of how businesses try to use _____ strategies.
   (a) B2C **(b)** growth **(c)** cooperation **(d)** concentration

10. Among the global strategies that international businesses might pursue, the _____ strategy is the one that most tries to tailor products to fit local needs and cultures in different countries.
    (a) concentration **(b)** globalizaton **(c)** e-business **(d)** multidomestic

Short Response

11. What is the difference between corporate strategy and functional strategy?

12. Why is a cost leadership strategy so important when one wants to sell products at lower prices than competitors?

13. What strategy should be pursued for a "question mark" in the BCG Matrix, and why?

14. What is "strategic leadership"?

Integration & Application

Kim Harris owns and operates a small retail store, selling the outdoor clothing of an American manufacturer to a predominately college-student market. Lately, a large department store outside of town has started selling similar but lower-priced clothing manufactured in China, Thailand, and Bangladesh. Kim is starting to lose business to this store. She has asked your instructor to have a student team analyze the situation and propose some strategic alternatives to best deal with this threat. You are on the team.

Questions: Why would a SWOT analysis be helpful in addressing Kim's strategic management problem? How could Porter's competitive strategies model be helpful as well?

SELF-ASSESSMENT
Facts and Inferences

INSTRUCTIONS *Read the following report. Then, indicate whether you think the observations are true, false, or doubtful. Write T if the observation is definitely true, F if the observation is definitely false, and ? if the observation may be either true or false. Judge each observation in order. Do not reread the observations after you have indicated your judgment, and do not change any of your answers.*

A well-liked college instructor had just completed making up the final examinations and had turned off the lights in the office. Just then a tall, broad figure with dark glasses appeared and demanded the examination. The professor opened the drawer. Everything in the drawer was picked up, and the individual ran down the corridor. The president was notified immediately.

1 The thief was tall, broad, and wore dark glasses.
2 The professor turned off the lights.
3 A tall figure demanded the examination.
4 The examination was picked up by someone.
5 The examination was picked up by the professor.
6 A tall, broad figure appeared after the professor turned off the lights in the office.
7 The man who opened the drawer was the professor.
8 The professor ran down the corridor.
9 The drawer was never actually opened.
10 Three persons are referred to in this report.

SCORING

The correct answers in reverse order (starting with 10) are: ?, F, ?, ?, T, ?, ?, T, T, ?. Your instructor may have additional information on these correct answers.

INTERPRETATION

To begin, ask yourself if there was a difference between your answers and those of the group for each item. If so, why? Why do you think people, individually or in groups, may answer these questions incorrectly? Good planning depends on good decision making by the people doing the planning. Being able to distinguish "facts" and understand one's "inferences" are important steps toward improving the planning process. Involving others to help do the same can frequently assist in this process.

PATHWAYS to WileyPLUS

CASE SNAPSHOT

Go online to read this case!
Dunkin Donuts: Go West (Life Is Caffeinated There)
Dunkin' Donuts has long been a staple on the East Coast. But the brand is now on an aggressive campaign to move into previously uncharted territory, attempting to capture market share and new dominance in new regions. It has taken a risk by adding many nontraditional menu items. Will customers bite, or is Dunkin' Donuts diluting its brand?

MODULE 12 Online Interactive Learning Resources

Skill Builder
- Critical Thinking

Experiential Exercises
- Strategic Scenarios
- Personal Career Planning

Team Project
- Saving Legacy Companies

It's all about

Organization Structures

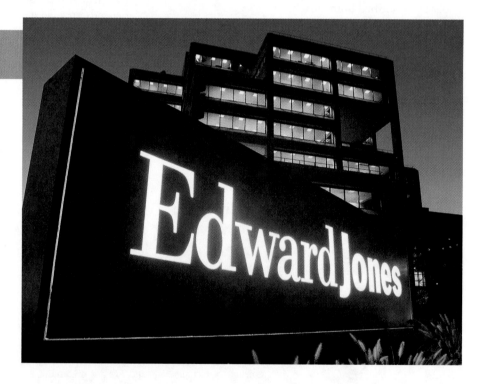

When St. Louis–based brokerage firm Edward Jones was called "the Wal-Mart of Wall Street" by Peter Drucker, he didn't mean low-wage employees, global supply chains, and controversies with local retailers. He did mean that the firm had a clear strategy that was well supported by an innovative organizational structure.

Edward Jones operates with a strong center surrounded by largely independent satellites. Drucker described it as a "confederation of highly autonomous entrepreneurial units bound together by a highly centralized core of values and services." The business strategy is face-to-face and customer-oriented brokerage; individual brokers have the freedom to deal with customers in their own ways in their local settings.

working together

Managing Partner John Bachman believes that his firm thrives by being different. He says: "I'm comfortable with our strategy. There's a difference between being part of a market and being the total market. We're the leader in what we do." Once called "America's Main Street Broker" by *Forbes* magazine and ranked by *Fortune* magazine as one of the best companies to work for, Edward Jones also appeared in *Working Mother* magazine's list of the best firms for working mothers.[1]

Of course, the approach taken by Edward Jones is only one of many options for achieving business success. You'll often find news reports of firms changing structures as they try to perform best under new circumstances. And you'll also see many alternatives being put into play; no one structure suits all.

But even so, researchers have found some consistent patterns and themes among the best-run organizations.[2] They emphasize empowerment, support for employees, responsiveness to client or customer needs, flexibility in dynamic environments, and continual attention to quality. And, they have structures that fit well with their strategies.

→ MODULE GUIDE

 13.1 What is organizing as a managerial responsibility?

- Organizing is one of the management functions.
- Organization charts describe the formal structures of organizations.
- Organizations also operate with important informal structures.
- Informal structures have good points and bad points.

 13.2 What are the most common types of organization structures?

- Functional structures group together people using similar skills.
- Divisional structures group together people by products, customers, or locations.
- Matrix structures combine the functional and divisional structures.
- Team structures use many permanent and temporary teams.
- Network structures extensively use strategic alliances and outsourcing.

Like most things, it is much easier to talk about high-performing organizations than to actually create them. In true contingency fashion there is no one best way to do things; no one organizational form meets the needs of all circumstances. Furthermore, what works well at one moment in time can quickly become outdated, even dysfunctional, in another. This is why you often read and hear about organizations making changes and reorganizing in an attempt to improve their performance.

But in organizational settings where nothing is constant, at least not for long, management scholar Henry Mintzberg points out that people often have problems.[3] Whenever job assignments and reporting relationships change, whenever mergers take place or new work units are created, whenever old ways of doing things are reconfigured, people naturally struggle to understand the new ways of working. And perhaps even more importantly, they will worry about the implications for their jobs and careers.

• Organizing Is One of the Management Functions

Most of us like to be organized—at home, at work, when playing games. We tend to get uncomfortable and anxious when things are disorganized. It shouldn't surprise you, therefore, that people in organizations need answers to such questions as: "Where do I fit in?" "How does my work relate to that of others?" "Who runs things?" "How do I get problems answered?"[4] They need these answers when they first join, when they take new jobs, and whenever things are substantially changed.

Organizing arranges people and resources to work toward a goal.

Organizing—
to create structures
• Divide up the work
• Arrange resources
• Coordinate activities

Planning—
to set the direction

Management process

Controlling—
to ensure results

Leading—
to inspire effort

Organization structure is a system of tasks, reporting relationships, and communication linkages.

This is where and why **organizing** comes into play as one of the four functions of management. It is the process of arranging people and resources to work together to accomplish the goals. Planning sets the goals; through organizing managers begin to carry them out.[5]

• Organization Charts Describe the Formal Structures of Organizations.

When managers organize things, they arrange people and jobs into meaningful working relationships. They clarify who is to do what, who is in charge of whom, and how different people and work units are supposed to cooperate with one another. This creates what we call the **organization structure**, a formal arrangement that links the various parts of an organization to one another.

An **organization chart** describes the arrangement of work positions within an organization.

You probably know the concept of structure best in terms of an **organization chart**. This is a diagram of positions and reporting relationships within an organization.[6] A typical organization chart identifies major job titles and shows the hierarchy of authority and communication that links them together. It should give the viewer a sense of the organization's **division of labor**—people and groups performing different jobs, ideally ones for which they are well skilled. It should also indicate how the various parts are linked together so that everyone's work contributes to a common purpose.

The **division of labor** is people and groups performing different jobs.

**Organization charts show
the formal structure**

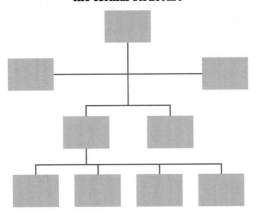

Check *Exhibit – What You Can Learn from an Organization Chart*. You can learn a lot. But, only in respect to the **formal structure**, the "official" structure, the way things are supposed to operate. At best this is just a starting point for organizational understanding. Things may well have changed since the chart was made. And, realities of any organization are usually much more complicated than what any chart alone can describe.

• Organizations Also Operate with Important Informal Structures

Behind every formal structure also lies an **informal structure**. You might think of this as a "shadow" organization made up of unofficial, but often critical, working relationships between organizational members. Like any shadow, the shape of the informal structure will be blurry and possibly shifting. You may have to work hard to understand its full complexities.

Even if you could draw the informal structure of your organization, you would find relationships cutting across levels and moving from side to side. Some would be work-related, reflecting how people have found it best to get their jobs done. Many others would be personal, reflecting who meets for coffee, stops in for office chats, meets together in exercise groups, and spends time together as friends, not just co-workers.[7]

Formal structure is the official structure of the organization.

EXHIBIT

What You Can Learn from an Organization Chart

Division of work   Positions and titles show work responsibilities.

Supervisory relationships   Lines between positions show who reports to whom in the chain of command.

Span of control   The number of persons reporting to a supervisor.

Communication channels   Lines between positions show routes for formal communication flows.

Major subunits   Which job titles are grouped together in work units, departments, or divisions.

Staff positions   Staff specialists that support other positions and parts of the organization.

Levels of management   The number of management layers from top to bottom.

Informal structure is the set of unofficial relationships among an organization's members.

**Informal structures create a
"shadow" organization**

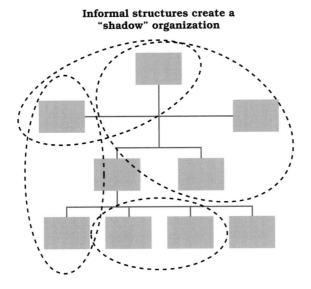

Organizations can be structured for informal learning

When the Center for Workforce Development conducted a study at a Siemens factory in North Carolina, the focus was on informal learning. They found that the cafeteria was a "hotbed" of learning, as workers shared ideas, problems, and solutions with one another over snacks and meals. The Director of Training for Siemens said: "The assumption was made that this was chit chat, talking about the golf game. But there was a whole lot of work activity." For Siemens and other organizations, the lesson is to mobilize informal learning opportunities as a resource for continuous organizational improvement.

Reflect: Think about space design when you walk around your workplace or college. Most facilities use space in ways that tend to keep people apart. What physical changes in your organization would encourage people to spend more time talking and learning together?

• Informal Structures Have Good Points and Bad Points

Let's start with the good points. Through the emergent and spontaneous relationships of informal structures, people can easily find help getting things done when necessary. One of the first things you probably learned in college was that knowing secretaries and departmental assistants is a very good way to get into classes that are "closed" or find out about new courses that will be offered. Think about all the different ways you use informal structures to get things done; most people in most organizations do the same.

The relationships available in the informal structure can play important roles in helping people learn their jobs and solve problems while doing them. This occurs as people assist one another not because the structure requires it, but because they know and like one another. The relationships also provide a lot of social and emotional support. Informal structures give people access to friendships, conversations, and advice that can help make the normal workday pleasant and a bad workday less troublesome.

For these reasons and possibly more, you can argue that informal structures are essential for any organization to succeed. They fill gaps missing in the formal structure and help compensate for its inadequacies, both task-related and people-related.

Yet, let's not forget the potential bad points to informal structures. Because they exist outside the formal system, things that happen in them may work against the best interests of the organization as a whole. Informal structures can be susceptible to rumor, carry inaccurate information, breed resistance to change, and even distract members from their work efforts. And if you happen to end up as an "outsider" rather than an "insider," you may feel less a part of things. Some U.S. managers of Japanese firms, for example, have complained about being excluded from what they call the "shadow cabinet," an informal group of Japanese executives who hold the real power and sometimes act to the exclusion of others.[8]

> *If an institution wants to be adaptive, it has to let go of some control and trust that people will work on the right things in the right way.*
>
> Robert Shapiro, **CEO MONSANTO**

Be Sure You Can . . .

- explain the importance of organizing as a management function

- differentiate formal and informal structures

- discuss potential good and bad points about informal structures

Define the Terms

Division of labor

Formal structure

Informal structure

Organization chart

Organization structure

Organizing

Rapid Review

- Organizing is the process of arranging people and resources to work toward a common goal.

- Structure is the system of tasks, reporting relationships, and communication that links people and positions within an organization.

- Organization charts describe the formal structure, how an organization should ideally work.

- The informal structure of an organization consists of the unofficial relationships that develop among its members.

- Informal structures create relationships for social support and task assistance, but can be susceptible to rumors.

Reflect/React

1. Why is organizing such an important management function?

2. If organization charts are imperfect, why bother with them?

3. Could an organization consistently perform well without the help of its informal structure?

A traditional principle of organizing is that performance improves with a good division of labor whose parts are well coordinated. The process of trying to arrange this is called **departmentalization**, and it can take different forms.[9] The most basic ones are the functional, divisional, matrix, team, and network structures. As you read about each don't forget, organizations rarely use only one type of structure. Most often they will use a mixture, with different parts and levels having different structures because of their unique needs.

Departmentalization is the process of grouping together people and jobs into work units.

• Functional Structures Group Together People Using Similar Skills

A **functional structure** groups together people with similar skills who perform similar tasks.

Take a look at Figure 13.1. What organizing logic do you see? In these **functional structures** people with similar skills and performing similar tasks are grouped together into formal work units. In business, for example, typical functions include marketing, finance, accounting, production, management information systems, and human resources. The assumption is that if the functions are well chosen and each does its

| Figure 13.1 | What does a typical functional structure look like? |

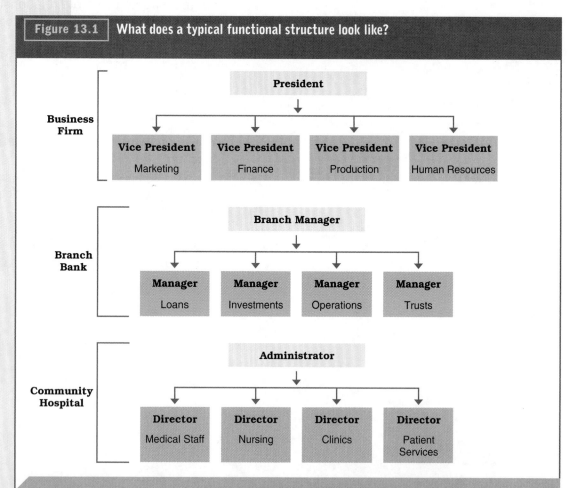

Functional structures are common in organizations of all types and sizes. In a typical business you might have vice presidents or senior managers heading the traditional functions of accounting, human resources, finance, manufacturing, marketing, and sales. In a bank, they may head such functions as loans, investments, and trusts. In a hospital, managers or administrators are usually in charge of functions like nursing, clinics, and patient services.

work properly, the business should operate successfully. Functional structures are not limited to businesses, and the figure also shows how other types of organizations such as banks and hospitals may use them.

Functional structures work well for small organizations that produce only one or a few products or services. They also tend to work best for organizations, or parts of organizations, dealing with relatively stable environments where the problems are predictable and demands for change are limited. And they offer benefits to individuals. Within a given function, say marketing, people share technical expertise, interests, and responsibilities. They also can advance in responsibilities and pursue career paths within the function. Perhaps you work or plan to work someday in this type of setup.

Although functional structures have a clear logic, there are some potential downsides as well. When an organization is divided up into functions it is sometimes hard to pinpoint responsibilities for things like cost containment, product or service quality, and innovation.

With everyone focused on meeting functional goals, the sense of overall performance accountability may get lost. This tendency may be reinforced when employee training emphasizes functional needs and neglects broader organizational issues, values and objectives. And, people may find that they get trapped in functional career niches that are hard to break out of to gain experiences in other areas.

Another significant concern is something that you might hear called the **functional chimneys problem**. Sometimes called the problem of *functional silos*, this is when performance suffers due to a lack of communication, coordination, and problem solving across functions. Instead of cooperating with one another, members of functions sometimes end up either competing or selfishly focusing on functional goals rather than broader organizational objectives. When problems occur across functions, they often get sent up to higher levels for resolution rather than being addressed at lower levels. This slows decision making and can mean that problems persist rather than being solved.

Ford Motor Company faced this problem when it acquired the British automaker Jaguar. There were lots of quality problems, and many were traced to what the firm called "excessive compartmentalization." The different functional departments did very little talking and working with one another as they built the cars; responsibility for quality of finished Jaguars became lost. What was Ford's response? The company's management pushed for more interdepartmental coordination and consensus decision making.[10]

The **functional chimneys problem** is a lack of communication and coordination across functions.

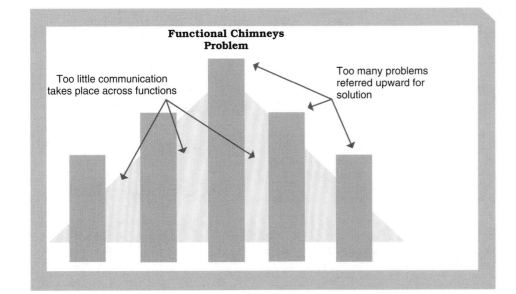

Functional Chimneys Problem

Too little communication takes place across functions

Too many problems referred upward for solution

A **divisional structure** groups together people working on the same product, in the same area, or with similar customers.

A **product structure** groups together people and jobs working on a single product or service.

A **geographical structure** groups together people and jobs performed in the same location.

A **customer structure** groups together people and jobs that serve the same customers or clients.

• Divisional Structures Group Together People by Products, Customers, or Locations

A second organizational alternative is the **divisional structure** shown in Figure 13.2. It groups together people who work on the same product, serve similar customers, and/or are located in the same area or geographical region.[11]

Product structures group together jobs and activities devoted to a single product or service. They identify a common point of managerial responsibility for costs, profits, problems, and successes in a defined market area. An expected benefit is that the product division will be able to respond quickly and effectively to changing market demands and customer tastes. For example, when taking over as H.J. Heinz's new CEO, William R. Johnson became concerned about the company's international performance. He decided that a change to global products divisions might improve things. Brand managers in the new structure were given worldwide responsibilities for their product lines.

Geographical structures, or *area structures*, group together jobs and activities conducted in the same location or geographical region. Companies typically use geographical divisions when they need to focus attention on the unique product tastes or operating requirements of particular regions. As UPS operations expanded worldwide, for example, the company announced a change from a product to geographical organizational structure. The company created two geographical divisions—the Americas and Europe/Asia, with each area responsible for its own logistics, sales, and other business functions.

Customer structures group together jobs and activities that serve the same customers or clients. The major appeal of customer divisions is the ability to best serve the special needs of the different customer groups. This is a common structure for

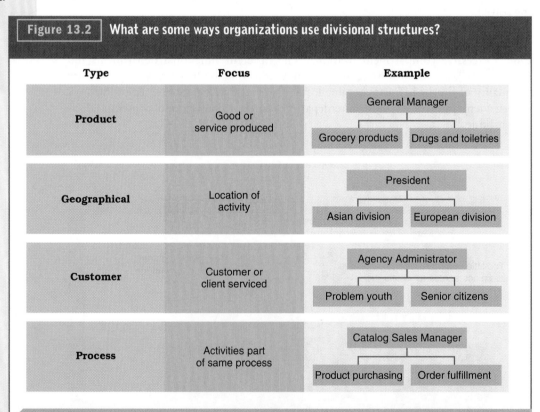

Figure 13.2 | **What are some ways organizations use divisional structures?**

Type	Focus	Example
Product	Good or service produced	General Manager → Grocery products, Drugs and toiletries
Geographical	Location of activity	President → Asian division, European division
Customer	Customer or client serviced	Agency Administrator → Problem youth, Senior citizens
Process	Activities part of same process	Catalog Sales Manager → Product purchasing, Order fulfillment

In product structures, divisions are based on the product or service provided—such as consumer products and industrial products. In geographic structures, divisions are based on geography or territories—such as an Asia-Pacific division and North American division. In customer structures, divisions are based on customers or clients served—such as graduate students and undergraduate students in a university.

complex businesses in the consumer products industries. 3M Corporation, for example, structures itself to focus on such diverse markets as consumer and office, specialty materials, industrial, health care, electronics and communications, transportation, graphics, and safety. Customer structures are also useful in service companies and social agencies. Banks, for example, use them to give separate attention to consumer and commercial customers for loans; government agencies use them to focus on different client populations.

Divisional structures are supposed to avoid some of the major problems of functional structures, including functional chimneys. But, as with any structural alternative, they, too, have potential disadvantages. They can be costly when economies of scale get lost through the duplication of resources and efforts across divisions. They can also create unhealthy rivalries between divisions that end up competing with one another for scarce resources, prestige, or special top management attention.

• Matrix Structures Combine the Functional and Divisional Structures

A **matrix structure** combines functional and divisional approaches to emphasize project or program teams.

The **matrix structure**, often called the *matrix organization*, combines the functional and divisional structures to try to gain the advantages of each. This is accomplished by setting up permanent teams that operate across functions to support specific products, projects, or programs.[12] Workers in a typical matrix structure, like Figure 13.3, belong to at least two formal groups at the same time—a functional group, and a product, program, or project team. They also report to two bosses—one within the function and the other within the team.

→ Potential Advantages of Matrix Structures

- Performance accountability rests with program, product, or project managers.
- Better communication across functions.
- Teams solve problems at their levels.
- Top managers spend more time on strategy.

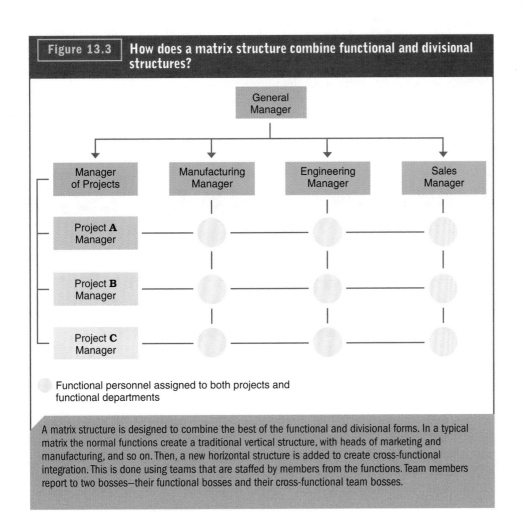

| Figure 13.3 | How does a matrix structure combine functional and divisional structures? |

Functional personnel assigned to both projects and functional departments

A matrix structure is designed to combine the best of the functional and divisional forms. In a typical matrix the normal functions create a traditional vertical structure, with heads of marketing and manufacturing, and so on. Then, a new horizontal structure is added to create cross-functional integration. This is done using teams that are staffed by members from the functions. Team members report to two bosses—their functional bosses and their cross-functional team bosses.

The matrix structure has gained a strong foothold in the workplace, with applications in such diverse settings as manufacturing (e.g., aerospace, electronics, pharmaceuticals), service industries (e.g., banking, brokerage, retailing), professional fields (e.g., accounting, advertising, law), and the nonprofit sector (e.g., government agencies, hospitals, universities).

The use of permanent **cross-functional teams** in matrix structures creates several potential advantages. These are teams whose members come together from different functional departments, to work on a common task. Everyone, regardless of their departmental affiliation, are required to work closely with others on the cross-functional team—no functional chimneys tendencies allowed. They share expertise and information to solve problems at the team level and make sure that their programs or projects get accomplished in the best ways possible.

Still, matrix structures aren't perfect; they can't overcome all disadvantages of their functional and divisional parents. The two-boss system of the matrix can lead to power struggles if functional supervisors and team leaders make confusing or conflicting demands on team members. Matrix structures can be costly because they require a whole new set of managers, the leaders who run the cross-functional teams.[13] And as you might guess, team meetings in the matrix can be time consuming.

A **cross-functional team** brings together members from different functional departments.

• Team Structures Use Many Permanent and Temporary Teams

Some organizations are adopting **team structures** that extensively use permanent and temporary teams to solve problems, complete special projects, and accomplish day-to-day tasks.[14] As Figure 13.4 shows, these teams are often formed across functions and staffed with members whose talents match team tasks.[15] The goals are to reduce the functional chimneys problem, tap the full benefits of group decision making, and gain as much creativity in problem solving as possible.

At Polaroid Corporation a research team developed a new medical imaging system in three years, when most had predicted it would take six. As one Polaroid executive noted, "Our researchers are not any smarter, but by working together they get the value of each other's intelligence almost instantaneously."[16]

Things don't always work this well in team structures, however, since the complexities of teams and teamwork can create other problems. As with the matrix, team

A **team structure** uses permanent and temporary cross-functional teams to improve lateral relations.

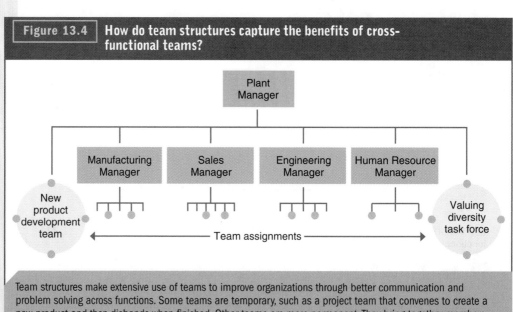

Figure 13.4 | **How do team structures capture the benefits of cross-functional teams?**

Team structures make extensive use of teams to improve organizations through better communication and problem solving across functions. Some teams are temporary, such as a project team that convenes to create a new product and then disbands when finished. Other teams are more permanent. They bring together members from different functions to work together on standing issues and common problems, such as quality control, diversity management, labor-management relations, or health care benefits.

members sometimes have to deal with conflicting loyalties between their team and functional assignments. Teamwork always takes time. And like any team situation, the quality of results often depends on how well the team is managed and how well team members gel as a group. This is why you'll most likely find organizations with team structures, like Polaroid, investing heavily in team building and team training.

• Network Structures Extensively Use Strategic Alliances and Outsourcing

Another development in organizational structures dramatically reduces the need for full-time staff by making extensive use of strategic alliances and outsourcing. Shown by example in Figure 13.5, a **network structure** links a central core with "networks" of relationships with outside contractors and partners that supply essential services.[17] The potential advantages are lower costs, more speed, and greater flexibility in dealing with changing environments.

Instead of doing everything for itself with full-time employees, the network organization employs a minimum staff and contracts out as much work as possible. It makes use of **strategic alliances** by cooperating with other firms to pursue business activities of mutual interest. Some are *outsourcing alliances* in which they contract to purchase important services from another organization. Others may be *supplier alliances* that link businesses in preferred supplier-customer relationships that guarantee a smooth and timely flow of quality supplies among the partners.

The example in the figure shows a network structure for a company that sells lawn and deck furniture over the Internet and by mail order. The firm employs only a few full-time "core" employees. Other business requirements are met through a network of alliances and outsourcing relationships. A consultant creates product designs; suppliers produce them at low-cost sites around the world. A supply chain management firms gets products shipped to and distributed from a rented

A **network structure** uses IT to link with networks of outside suppliers and service contractors.

In a **strategic alliance** organizations join together in partnership to pursue an area of mutual interest.

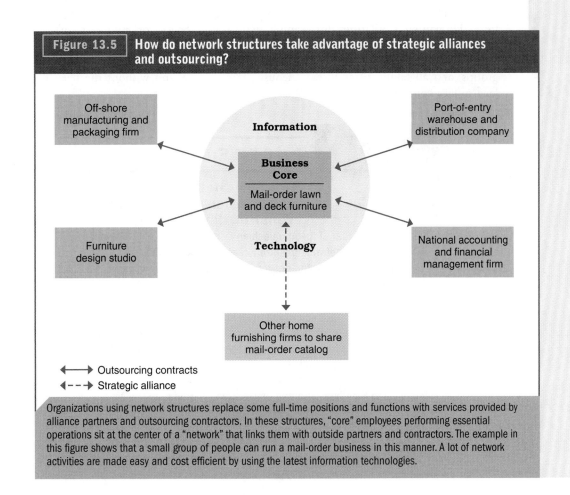

| Figure 13.5 | How do network structures take advantage of strategic alliances and outsourcing? |

Organizations using network structures replace some full-time positions and functions with services provided by alliance partners and outsourcing contractors. In these structures, "core" employees performing essential operations sit at the center of a "network" that links them with outside partners and contractors. The example in this figure shows that a small group of people can run a mail-order business in this manner. A lot of network activities are made easy and cost efficient by using the latest information technologies.

warehouse. A quarterly catalog is mailed as part of a strategic alliance with two other firms that sell different home furnishings. Accounting services are outsourced. Even the company website that supports customer and network relationships is maintained by an outside contractor.

This may sound a bit radical, but it isn't. It is an increasingly common arrangement that might even raise some entrepreneurial opportunities for you. Could the growing popularity of network organization concepts make it easier for you to start your own business someday?

If network structures are highly streamlined, efficient, and adaptable, don't you wonder why even more organizations aren't adopting them? Part of the answer may lie in inertia, simply being caught up in old ways and finding it very hard to change. Another reason is the management complication of having to deal with a vast and sometimes shifting network of contracts and alliances. If one part of the network breaks down or fails to deliver, the entire system may suffer the consequences. Also, there is concern that overly aggressive outsourcing might actually harm a firm. Management Tips lists "seven deadly sins" of outsourcing that were discovered through research.[18]

As information technology continues to evolve, a variation of the network structure is appearing. Called the **virtual organization**, it uses information technologies to operate a constantly shifting network of alliances.[19] The goal is to use virtual networks to eliminate boundaries that traditionally separate a firm from its suppliers and customers, and its internal departments and divisions from one another. The intense use of IT allows virtual relationships to be called into action as needed; when the work is done they are disbanded or left idle until next needed.

If you really think about it, each of us is probably already a part of virtual organizations. Do you see similarities, for example, with the MySpace communities? Isn't the virtual organization concept similar to how we manage our relationships online — signing on, signing off, getting things done as needed with different people and groups, and all taking place instantaneously, temporarily, and without the need for face-to-face contacts?

A **virtual organization** uses information technologies to operate as a shifting network of alliances.

PACESETTERS

Nonprofit network organization improves rural economic development.

June Holley, founder of the Appalachian Center for Economic Networks (ACEnet), applies network organization concepts to support rural economic development. The not-for-profit organization's mission is described as: "ACEnet links small businesses and micro-enterprises in rural Appalachian Ohio, to develop new business initiatives." When Holley started ACEnet she wanted to tap local ingenuity and resources for economic development, believing that rural Appalachia suffered not from lack of talents but from lack of connections. The pathway to progress was networking—bringing people into contact with one another. Holley believes that economic growth can be unlocked by helping people find one another and then by supporting their skills and products. She says: "Poverty is due to isolation." By breaking the isolation, ACEnet's networking model of organization for rural economic development has provided a valuable community service for over 20 years.

June Holley, *founder, Appalachian Center for Economic Networks (ACEnet)*.

13.2 What are the most common types of organization structures?

Be Sure You Can . . .

- compare the functional, divisional, and matrix structures

- draw charts to show how each structure might be used in a business

- list advantages and disadvantages of each structure

- explain the functional chimneys problem

- describe how cross-functional and project teams operate in team structures

- illustrate how an organization familiar to you might operate as a network structure

- list advantages and disadvantages of the network approach to organizing

Rapid Review

- Functional structures group together people using similar skills to perform similar activities.

- Divisional structures group together people who work on a similar product, work in the same geographical region, or serve the same customers.

- A matrix structure uses permanent cross-functional teams to try to gain the advantages of both the functional and divisional approaches.

- Team structures make extensive use of permanent and temporary teams, often cross functional, to improve communication, cooperation, and problem solving.

- Network structures maintain a staff of core full-time employees and use contracted services and strategic alliances to accomplish many business needs.

Define the Terms

Customer structure	Matrix structure
Departmentalization	Product structure
Divisional structure	Cross-functional teams
Functional chimneys problem	Network structure
	Strategic alliance
Functional structure	Team structure
Geographical structure	Virtual organization

Reflect/React

1. Why use functional structures if they are prone to functional chimneys problems?

2. Could a matrix structure improve performance for an organization familiar to you?

3. How can the disadvantages of group decision making hurt team structures?

Multiple Choice

1. The main purpose of organizing as a management function is to _____.
   (a) make sure that results match plans **(b)** arrange people and resources to accomplish work **(c)** create enthusiasm for the needed work **(d)** link strategies with operational plans

2. An organization chart is most useful for _____.
   (a) mapping informal structures **(b)** eliminating functional chimneys **(c)** showing designated supervisory relationships **(d)** describing the shadow organization

3. Rumors and resistance to change are potential disadvantages often associated with _____.
   (a) virtual organizations **(b)** informal structures **(c)** functional chimneys **(d)** cross-functional teams

4. When an organization chart shows vice presidents of marketing, finance, manufacturing, and purchasing all reporting to the president, top management is using a _____ structure.
   (a) functional **(b)** matrix **(c)** network **(d)** product

5. The "two-boss" system of reporting relationships is both a potential source of problems and one of the key aspects of _____ structures.
   (a) functional **(b)** matrix **(c)** network **(d)** product

6. A manufacturing business with a functional structure has recently acquired two other businesses with very different product lines. The president of the combined company might consider using a _____ structure to allow a better focus on the unique needs of each product area.
   (a) virtual **(b)** team **(c)** divisional **(d)** network

7. An organization using a _____ structure should expect more problems to be solved at lower levels and that top managers will have more time free to engage in strategic thinking.
   (a) virtual **(b)** matrix **(c)** functional **(d)** product

8. The functional chimneys problem occurs when people in different functions _____.
   (a) fail to communicate with one another **(b)** try to help each other work with customers **(c)** spend too much time coordinating decisions **(d)** focus on products rather than functions

9. An organization that employs just a few "core" or essential full-time employees and outsources a lot of the remaining work shows signs of using a _____ structure.
   (a) functional **(b)** divisional **(c)** network **(d)** team

10. Which organization structure is likely to have better managerial accountability for product or service delivery?
    (a) virtual **(b)** functional **(c)** area division **(d)** matrix

Short Response

11. Why should an organization chart be trusted "only so far"?

12. In what ways can informal structures be good for organizations?

13. How does a product divisional structure differ from a geographical divisional structure?

14. Exactly how does a matrix structure combine functional and divisional forms?

Integration & Application

Be a consultant to your university or college president. The assignment is: Make this organization more efficient without sacrificing our educational goals. Although the president doesn't realize it, you are a specialist in network structures. You are going to suggest building a network organization, and your ideas are going to be radical and provocative.

Questions: What would be the core of the network—is it the faculty who teach the various courses, or is it the administration that provides the infrastructure that students and faculty use in the learning experience? What might be outsourced— grounds and facilities maintenance, food services, security, recreation programs, even registration? What types of alliances might prove beneficial—student recruiting, faculty, even facilities?

SELF-ASSESSMENT
Cosmopolitan/Local

INSTRUCTIONS *Answer the following questions using this scale for each:*

Strongly disagree 1 2 3 4 5 Strongly agree

1 You believe it is the right of the professional to make his or her own decisions about what is to be done on the job.

2 You believe a professional should stay in an individual staff role regardless of the income sacrifice.

3 You have no interest in moving up to a top administrative post.

4 You believe that professionals are better evaluated by professional colleagues than by management.

5 Your friends tend to be members of your profession.

6 You would rather be known or get credit for your work outside rather than inside the company.

7 You would feel better making a contribution to society than to your organization.

8 Managers have no right to place time and cost schedules on professional contributors.

SCORING AND INTERPRETATION

Add your score for each item to get a total score between 8 and 40.

A score of 30–40 suggests a "cosmopolitan" work orientation, 10–20 a "local" orientation, and 20–30 a "mixed" orientation. A "cosmopolitan" is more likely to identify with the career profession, and a "local" tends to identify with the employing organization.

PATHWAYS to WileyPLUS

WILEY PLUS

 CASE SNAPSHOT

Go online to read this case!
Mozilla: Browse As You Please
Virtually by word-of-mouth, Mozilla's Firefox Web browser has gained unprecedented market share, quickly challenging Microsoft's dominance. How has this open-source *wunderkind* managed to attract such loyalty from a demanding tech audience?

MODULE 13 Online Interactive Learning Resources

Skill Builder
• Networking

Experiential Exercises
• Network "U"
• Contingency Workforce

Team Project
• Downsizing or Rightsizing?

Adaptability and

Organizational Design and Culture

The business is professional services; the name is KPMG International. Together, this combination proves irresistible to the many college graduates who seek positions with the firm. KPMG offers great hands-on training and experience for those who want to apply their education in audit, tax, and business advisory services.

KPMG is a top-rated international network of affiliated member firms, with locations in 148 countries and employing some 100,000 professional workers. And to stay at the top of its industry, KPMG organizes for high performance and staffs its affiliates with talented professionals committed to excellence.

values set the tone

Leadership at KPMG recognizes the design challenges of matching the career opportunities of the new workplace with the diversity of today's college graduates. It goes to great lengths to ensure that individual personalities and talents are a good fit with the organization's culture and jobs.

For a time, the section of the firm's website devoted to careers, KPMG Campus, asked prospective employees to "choose your shoes." The intent was to identify applicants' personal preferences and career inclinations, and then match them with KPMG opportunities.

Choose "hiking boots" and read about promoting from within, rewards, and advancement possibilities. Select "sandals" and read about the importance of volunteer opportunities and community responsibility. Click on "dress shoes" and read about hard work, dependability, and service to clients. And if you preferred "mountain climbing boots," the message was about KPMG's commitment to challenging you with high expectations.

Which shoes would you choose?

Top management at KPMG knows that "one style doesn't fit all." By valuing both diversity and a good person–organization fit, it aims to keep talent a main source of the firm's competitive advantage.[1]

→ MODULE GUIDE

 14.1 What are the trends in organizational design?

- Organizations are becoming flatter with fewer levels of management.
- Organizations are increasing decentralization and reducing staff.
- Organizations are increasing delegation and empowerment.
- Organizations are becoming more horizontal and adaptive.
- Organizations are reengineering work processes for greater efficiency.
- Organizations are using multiple means of subsystems integration.

 14.2 What is the nature of organizational culture?

- Organizational culture is the personality of the organization.
- Successful organizations tend to have strong and positive cultures.
- The observable culture is what you see and hear as an employee or customer.
- The core culture is found in the underlying values of the organization.

Organizational design is the process of configuring organizations to meet environmental challenges.

Span of Control is the number of persons directly reporting to a manager.

Centralization means top management keeps the power to make most decisions.

Just as organizations vary in size and type, so too do the variety of problems and opportunities they face.[2] This is why they use different ways of organizing—from the functional, divisional, and matrix structures, to the team and network structures reviewed in the previous module. Now it is time to probe further, recognizing that there is still more to the story of how managers try to align their organizations with the unique situations that they face.

This process of alignment is called **organizational design**. It deals with the choices managers make to configure their organizations to best meet the problems and opportunities posed by their environments.[3] And because every organization faces its own set of unique challenges, there is no "one fits all" best design. Like KPMG's shoes there are different designs available, and the styles change with time. Thus, organizational design is best thought of as a problem-solving activity where managers strive to always have the best possible configuration to meet current demands. Among today's developments, some recognizable design trends seem to have pretty common support.

• Organizations Are Becoming Flatter with Fewer Levels of Management

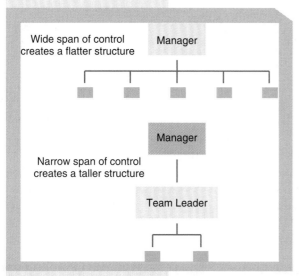

Wide span of control creates a flatter structure

Manager

Narrow span of control creates a taller structure

Manager

Team Leader

When organizations grow in size, they tend to get taller by adding more and more levels of management. This raises costs. It also increases the distance between top management and lower-levels, making it harder for the levels to communicate with one another. This increases the risks of decision-making delays and poorly informed decisions.

For these and other reasons, taller organizations are generally viewed as less efficient, less flexible, and less customer-sensitive.[4] You shouldn't be surprised that the trend is for organizations to get flatter. And as they do, one of the things often affected is **span of control**—the number of persons directly reporting to a manager. When span of control is narrow, a manager supervises only a few people; a manager with a wide span of control supervises many people. Flatter organizations tend to have wider spans of control that require fewer levels of management; taller organizations tend to have narrow spans of control and many levels of management.

• Organizations Are Increasing Decentralization and Reducing Staff

While we are talking about levels of management, the next question becomes: Should top management make the decisions and the lower levels just carry them out? The answer increasingly heard is "No," at least not for all decisions. When top management keeps the power to make most decisions, the setup is called **centralization**. When top management allows employees at lower levels to make decisions in their areas of responsibility and on those matters where they are best prepared or informed, the setup is called **decentralization**.

STAY INFORMED

CEOs rank changes to improve global businesses:

1. More focus on core business
2. Flatter organization
3. Mergers and acquisitions
4. Decentralization
5. Global business units
6. Centralized administration

Decentralization means top management allows lower levels to make many decisions.

If you had to choose right now, wouldn't you go for decentralization? Well you wouldn't be wrong, since it is a characteristic of the more progressive organizations.[5] But you would not be exactly right. Do you really want lower levels making major decisions and changing things whenever they see fit? You shouldn't. The reality is that there is no need for a trade-off between these two alternatives; you can have both. One of the unique opportunities of today's high-tech world is that top management can decentralize and still maintain centralized control. The key is using information technology to best advantage.

Computer networks and advanced information systems allow top managers to easily stay informed about day-to-day performance results at all levels throughout an organization. Because they have this information readily available, it is easier for them to allow more decentralizaton.[6] They can trust lower levels to make more decisions because the information systems allow them to quickly spot when things go wrong and exercise control.

It has also been quite traditional for top managers to get decision-making advice from persons holding *staff positions*, often a large number of them. But with decentralization, many are finding that they don't need the specialized staff. They can readily tap the expertise of people throughout the entire system, and save on costs by doing so. This is a classic case of finding out that you are able to do more with less, and many organizations are going for it. The trend is unmistakable; organizations are hiring and using fewer staff personnel.

> **Delegation** is the process of entrusting work to others.

> **Empowerment** gives people freedom to do their jobs as they think best.

◯→ Three Steps in Delegation

1. **Assign responsibility**—explain task and expectations to others.
2. **Grant authority**—allow others to act as needed to complete task.
3. **Create accountability**—require others to report back, complete task.

• Organizations Are Increasing Delegation and Empowerment

Decentralization brings with it another trend that is good for organizations and their members: increased delegation and empowerment. **Delegation** is the process of entrusting work to others by giving them the right to make decisions and take action. It is the foundation for decentralization.

Every manager really needs to know how and when to delegate. You should be good at it and probably looking for ways to get even better. Delegation involves deciding what work you should do yourself and what you should allow others to accomplish. It sounds easy, but there is skill to doing delegation right.[7]

A classical management principle states: Authority should equal responsibility when a supervisor delegates work to a subordinate. This principle warns managers not to delegate without giving the subordinate sufficient authority to perform. Can you think of a time when you were asked to get something done but didn't have the authority to do it? This was probably frustrating, perhaps it even caused you to lose respect for the manager who failed to understand the basic steps in delegation.

Unfortunately, some managers go even one step further; they fail to delegate at all. Whether because they are unwilling or unable to trust others or are too inflexible in how they want things done, the failure to delegate is more common than you might think. And it creates problems. A failure to delegate not only makes it hard for people to do their jobs, it overloads the manager with work that really should be done by others.

But let's remember that the trend is in the direction of more, not less, delegation. And when delegation is done well it leads to **empowerment**. This is the process of giving people the freedom to contribute ideas, make decisions, show initiative, and do their jobs in the best possible ways. Empowerment is the engine that powers decentralization;

N E W S L I N E

Family firm designs for a global future and customer service In the competitive arena of business strategy, Enterprise Rent-a-Car achieved success by pursuing a market that its rivals chose to ignore—renting cars to people whose cars are being serviced or are out of commission because of accidents. Started in St. Louis by Jack Taylor in 1957, the privately held company is now bigger than Hertz and Avis. Enterprise runs its 500,000-vehicle fleet through some 5000 offices with 50,000 employees spread around North America. It's now gaining ground in Europe as well. Current Chairman and CEO Andy Taylor says his father built the company around a culture devoted to customer service and satisfaction. The company reinforces this culture by careful employee selection and extensive training to put the right people in the field. And the Enterprise design ensures effectiveness by blending decentralization of operations with central control. Each branch gets a financial statement and customer satisfaction score every month. Says Taylor: "Our branch managers know exactly how well they did. They've got their bottom line."

Reflect: How do the cultures of the companies you deal with compare with that described for Enterprise? As you read and listen to the business news, what other examples of successful strong culture firms do you find?

it is the foundation from which organizations become faster, more flexible, and adaptable in today's dynamic environments.

• Organizations Are Becoming More Horizontal and Adaptive

You should remember our discussion of **bureaucracy** in Module 3. Its distinguishing features are clear-cut division of labor, strict hierarchy of authority, formal rules and procedures, and promotion based on competency. According to Max Weber, bureaucracies should be orderly, fair, and highly efficient.[8] Yet, the chances are your image of a bureaucracy is an organization bogged down with "red tape," which acts cumbersome and impersonal and is sometimes overcome to the point of inadequacy by rules and procedures.

Where, you might ask, is the decentralization, delegation, and empowerment that we have just been talking about? Well, researchers have looked into the question and arrived at some interesting answers. When Tom Burns and George Stalker investigated 20 manufacturing firms in England, they found that two quite different organizational forms could be successful.[9] The key was "fit" with challenges in the firm's external environment.

A more bureaucratic form of organization, which Burns and Stalker called the **mechanistic design**, thrived in stable environments. It was good at doing routine things in predictable situations. But in rapidly changing and uncertain situations, a much less bureaucratic form, called the **organic design**, performed best. It was adaptable and better suited to handle change and less predictable situations.

Figure 14.1 portrays these two approaches as opposite extremes on a continuum of organizational design alternatives. The figure points out that mechanistic organizations typically operate as "tight" structures of the traditional vertical and bureaucratic form.[10] They are good for production efficiency. A ready example is your local fast-food restaurant. On your next visit, why not look things over? Think about it also the next time you

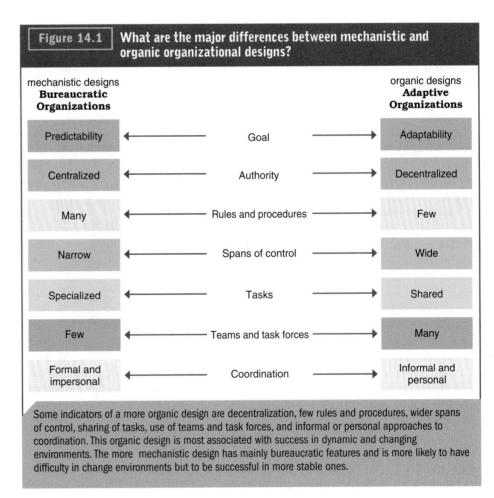

| **Figure 14.1** | **What are the major differences between mechanistic and organic organizational designs?** |

mechanistic designs
Bureaucratic Organizations

organic designs
Adaptive Organizations

Bureaucratic Organizations		Adaptive Organizations
Predictability	Goal	Adaptability
Centralized	Authority	Decentralized
Many	Rules and procedures	Few
Narrow	Spans of control	Wide
Specialized	Tasks	Shared
Few	Teams and task forces	Many
Formal and impersonal	Coordination	Informal and personal

Some indicators of a more organic design are decentralization, few rules and procedures, wider spans of control, sharing of tasks, use of teams and task forces, and informal or personal approaches to coordination. This organic design is most associated with success in dynamic and changing environments. The more mechanistic design has mainly bureaucratic features and is more likely to have difficulty in change environments but to be successful in more stable ones.

A **bureaucracy** emphasizes formal authority, rules, order, fairness, and efficiency.

Mechanistic designs are bureaucratic, using a centralized and vertical structure.

Organic designs are adaptive, using a decentralized and horizontal structure.

turn on your PC and "Microsoft" pops up. *Business Week* reports that the software giant is suffering from "bureaucratic red tape" and endless meetings that bog employees down and limit their abilities to be creative and on top of market demands.[11] *The Wall Street Journal* takes the case even further, suggesting that Microsoft should be broken into three smaller pieces to free the firm from "bureaucracy that's stifling entrepreneurial spirits."[12]

Does your experience as a Microsoft customer confirm these criticisms? Do you think the firm could perform better with a different configuration? One possibility is to create new and smaller components that operate with more organic designs—decentralization, flatter, wider spans of control, and fewer rules and procedures.

You might picture the organic organizational design as more horizontal and less vertical than its mechanistic counterpart. It operates with more emphasis on empowerment and teamwork, and gets a lot of work done through informal structures and interpersonal networks maintained by its members.[13] The result is an organization that is adaptive and flexible, and whose employees are allowed to be more creative and dynamic in dealing with changing markets and environments.[14] This type of design is good for creativity and innovation.

Harvard scholar and consultant Rosabeth Moss Kanter says these organic forms are just the types of organizations most likely to succeed today. Specifically, she states:

The organizations now emerging as successful will be, above all, flexible; they will need to be able to bring particular resources together quickly, on the basis of short-term recognition of new requirements and the necessary capacities to deal with them. . . . The balance between static plans—which appears to reduce the need for effective reaction—and structural flexibility needs to shift toward the latter.[15]

Mechanistic Designs

- Work efforts centrally coordinated.
- Standard interactions in well-defined jobs.
- Limited information-processing capability.
- Best at simple and repetitive tasks.
- Good for production efficiency.

Organic Designs

- Work efforts highly interdependent.
- Intense interactions in self-defined jobs.
- Expanded information-processing capability.
- More effective at complex and unique tasks.
- Good for innovation and creativity.

• Organizations Are Reengineering Work Processes for Greater Efficiency

Another development in subsystems design is **process reengineering**.[16] Consultant Michael Hammer defines this as the systematic and complete analysis of work processes and workflows, and the design of new and better ones. The goal in process reengineering is to increase efficiency by changing the way work is carried out; old habits are broken and replaced by better ways of doing things.[17]

Process reengineering begins by analyzing workflows and mapping them to describe how work moves from one point or subsystem to another.[18] When things are running smoothly, each process is done right, on time, and supportive of the next step. Once inefficiencies are pinpointed, changes can be made to streamline the process performance. Hammer once demonstrated his ideas at Aetna Life & Casualty Company. His initial analysis showed a complex system of customer-service tasks and processes that took as long as 28 days to accomplish.[19] Why? Because many different persons handled customer requests in a step-by-step fashion. After studying the workflow, Hammer redesigned it into a "one and done" format. In the new system, a single customer service provider handled each request from start to finish. After the change, one of Aetna's customer account managers said: "Now we can see the customers as individual people. It's no longer 'us' and 'them.' "

Process reengineering systematically analyzes work processes to design new and better ones.

• Organizations Are Using Multiple Means of Subsystems Integration

The work of Burns and Stalker set the stage for contingency thinking in organizational design, that is, matching designs with situations to achieve the best performance. Paul Lawrence and Jay Lorsch carried this notion further with their research on subsystems design and integration.[20] They found that subsystems in successful firms often had quite different designs. But, each could be successful as long as its design fit with the special problems and opportunities of its specific environment.

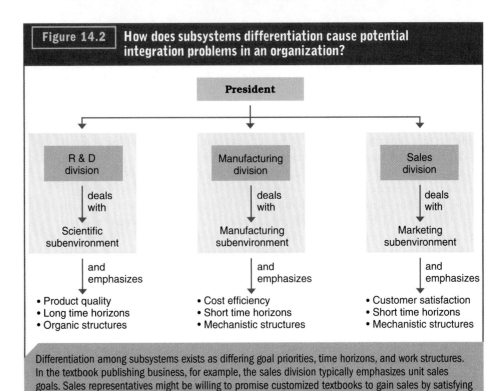

Figure 14.2 | How does subsystems differentiation cause potential integration problems in an organization?

Differentiation among subsystems exists as differing goal priorities, time horizons, and work structures. In the textbook publishing business, for example, the sales division typically emphasizes unit sales goals. Sales representatives might be willing to promise customized textbooks to gain sales by satisfying unique customer requests. But, the production division emphasizes cost efficiency goals. They prefer to produce one version of a book in large numbers to gain economies of scale. They might resist modifying production runs to customize products because it raises their costs.

Differentiation is the degree of difference between subsystems in an organization.

Integration is the level of coordination achieved between subsystems in an organization.

EXHIBIT

Ways for Achieving Subsystems Integration

Rules and procedures   Clearly specify required activities for each subsystem.

Hierarchical referral   Refer problems between subsystems upward to a common superior.

Planning   Set targets that keep each subsystem headed in the right direction.

Direct contact   Have subsystem managers coordinate directly with each other.

Liaison roles   Assign formal roles to persons whose job it is to handle subsystems relationships.

Task forces   Form temporary task forces to coordinate subsystems activities and solve problems.

Teams   Form permanent teams with the authority to coordinate subsystems activities and solve problems.

Matrix organizations   Create a matrix structure to improve coordination among subsystems involved in specific programs, projects, or products.

Figure 14.2 shows differences between research and development, manufacturing, and sales divisions in one of the firms studied by Lawrence and Lorsch. It illustrates **differentiation**, the presence of differences among the internal subsystems of the organization. It seems logical to expect that the greater the differentiation, the harder it will be for the subsystems to work together and the organization as a whole to perform well. But Lawrence and Lorsch found that subsystems in the successful firms worked well with one another even though they were highly differentiated. The reason was "integration."

The term **integration** describes the level of coordination that exists among an organization's internal subsystems. As you might expect again, the greater the integration, the better performing the organization as a whole. Although this is true, it isn't easy to accomplish, especially as differentiation increases. At the same time that more differentiation among subsystems creates the need for greater integration, it becomes harder to accomplish.

Lawrence and Lorsch found that successful firms dealt with this dilemma as shown in the Exhibit-*Ways for Achieving Subsystems Integration*. Integrating mechanisms that rely on vertical coordination and the use of authority work fine when differentiation is low. Integration is accomplished through rules and procedures, hierarchical referral, and planning. As differentiation gets more extreme, integrating mechanisms that emphasize horizontal coordination and improved lateral relations are needed.[21] They accomplish integration through direct contact between managers, liaison roles, task forces, teams, and matrix structures.

Be Sure You Can . . .

- illustrate the link between tall or flat organizations and spans of control

- explain the reasons for more decentralization and smaller staffs

- list the steps in delegation

- differentiate mechanistic and organic organizational designs

- explain the organizational design implications of the Burns and Stalker study

- explain subsystems design implications of the Lawrence and Lorsch study

- list several ways to improve subsystem integration

- explain the purpose of process reengineering

Define the Terms

Bureaucracy	Integration
Centralization	Mechanistic design
Decentralization	Organic design
Delegation	Organizational design
Differentiation	Process reengineering
Empowerment	Span of control

RAPID REVIEW

- Organizations are becoming flatter, with fewer management levels, operating with fewer staffpeople, using decentralization with centralization, and using more delegation and empowerment.

- Mechanistic organizational designs are vertical and bureaucratic; they perform best in stable environments with mostly routine and predictable tasks.

- Organic organizational designs are horizontal and adaptive; they perform best in change environments requiring adaptation and flexibility.

- As subsystems become more highly differentiated, they have a greater need for integration; but as differentiation increases, integration is harder to accomplish.

- Process reengineering seeks to increase operating efficiency by reducing unnecessary work steps and streamlining work processes.

Reflect/React

1. Which, if any, of the organizational trends are unlikely to persist in today's ever-changing economy?

2. Knowing your personality, will you fit in better with an organization that has a mechanistic or organic design?

3. As organizations grow larger in size, will subsystems differentiation inevitably cause performance problems?

Organizational culture is a system of shared beliefs and values guiding behavior.

You probably hear the word *culture* a lot these days. In today's global economy, how can we fail to appreciate the cultural differences between people or nations? However, you may not hear about another type of culture that can be just as important: the cultures of organizations. Noted scholar and consultant Edgar Schein defined **organizational culture** as the system of shared beliefs and values that develops within an organization and guides the behavior of its members.[22] Sometimes called the *corporate culture*, it is a key aspect of any organization and work setting.

• Organizational Culture Is the Personality of the Organization

Whenever someone speaks of "the way we do things here," he or she is talking about the organization's culture. You can think of this as the personality of the organization, something in the background that creates the atmosphere within which people work.

Management Tips suggests how you can learn to read and understand an organization's culture, whether as a job applicant, employee, or customer. Acquiring this important skill can guide you toward working for, and with, the organizations that best fit your career goals and personal preferences.

MANAGEMENT TIPS

SCORES—How to read an organization's culture

S—How tight or loose is the *structure*?
C—Are decisions *change* oriented or driven by the status quo?
O—What *outcomes* or results are most highly valued?
R—What is the climate for *risk taking*, innovation?
E—How widespread is *empowerment*, worker involvement?
S—What is the competitive *style*, internal and external?

• Successful Organizations Tend to Have Strong and Positive Cultures

Although culture is not the sole determinant of what happens in organizations, it does influence what they accomplish, and how. The internal culture has the potential to shape attitudes, reinforce beliefs, direct behavior, and establish performance expectations and the motivation to fulfill them. It helps set the organization's performance tone.

A widely discussed study of successful businesses concluded that organizational culture had a positive impact on long-term performance.[23] The cultures in these organizations provided for a clear vision that allowed people to rally around the goals and work hard to accomplish them.[24] The cultures discouraged dysfunctional work behaviors and encouraged positive ones, helping commit members to doing things for and with one another that are good for the organization. And they were also **strong cultures**— clear, well defined, and widely shared among members.[25] Honda is a good example. Its culture is tightly focused around "The Honda Way"—principles emphasizing ambition, respect for ideas, open communication, work enjoyment, harmony, and hard work.

Strong cultures are clear, well defined, and widely shared among members.

• The Observable Culture Is What You See and Hear as an Employee or Customer

Organizational culture can be understood at two levels, as shown in Figure 14.3—the "observable" culture and the "core" culture.[26] Strong culture organizations share many features that are quickly apparent to new members and visitors alike. This **observable culture** is what you see in people's behaviors and hear in their conversations. It includes how people dress at work, arrange their offices, speak to and behave toward one another, and talk about and treat their customers. You'll notice it not only as an employee, but also when being served as a customer or client.

Test this out the next time you go in a store, restaurant, or service establishment. How do people look, act, behave? How do they treat one another? How do they treat customers? What's in their conversations? Are they enjoying themselves? When you answer these questions you are starting to describe the observable culture of the organization.

The observable culture is also found in the stories, heroes, rituals, and symbols that are part of daily organizational life. In the university it includes the pagentry of graduation and honors ceremonies; in sports teams it's the pre-game rally and pep talk; in places like Apple, Hewlett-Packard, and Amazon, it's in the stories told about the founders and the firm's history; in the workplace it's the spontaneous celebration of an accomplishment or even a co-worker's birthday or wedding.

The presence or absence of such things, and the ways they are practiced, can say a lot about an organization's culture. They represent, communicate, and carry the culture over time, keeping it visible and clear in all members' eyes. New members learn the organization's culture through them; all members keep the culture alive by sharing and joining in them. And you have to admit, in some organizations this culture is far richer and more positive than in others.

The **observable culture** is what you see and hear when walking around an organization.

| Figure 14.3 | **What are the main components of organizational culture?** |

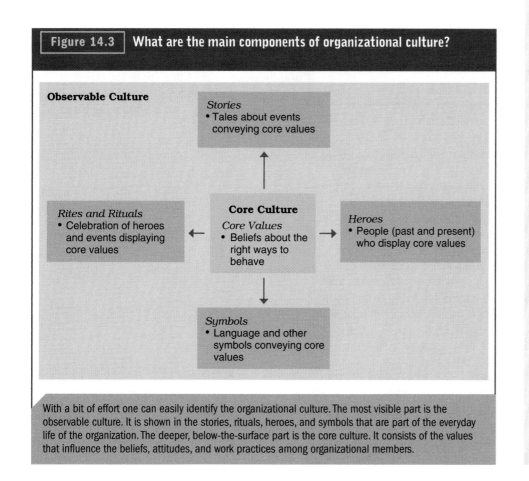

With a bit of effort one can easily identify the organizational culture. The most visible part is the observable culture. It is shown in the stories, rituals, heroes, and symbols that are part of the everyday life of the organization. The deeper, below-the-surface part is the core culture. It consists of the values that influence the beliefs, attitudes, and work practices among organizational members.

Core culture is found in the underlying values of the organization.

Core values are beliefs and values shared by organization members.

• The Core Culture Is Found in the Underlying Values of the Organization

The second and deeper level of organizational culture is called the **core culture**. It consists of the **core values** or underlying assumptions and beliefs that shape and guide people's behaviors.

Strong culture organizations typically operate with a small but enduring set of core values, ones that contribute to long-term success.[27] Values in some of the best companies, for example, emphasize performance excellence, innovation, social responsibility, integrity, worker involvement, customer service, and teamwork. Organizations often communicate their values on websites, in mission statements, and in executive speeches. Examples are: "Service above all else"—Nordstrom; "Science-based innovation"—Merck; "Fanatical attention to consistency and detail"—Disney.

→ **Characteristics of Successful and Strong Organizational Cultures**

- High-performance oriented.
- Emphasize teamwork.
- Allow and support risk taking.
- Encourage innovation.
- Make well-being of people a top management priority.

Don't be fooled, however, by value statements alone. It's easy to write them, post them on the Web, and talk about them. It's a lot harder to live up to them. But if the values are to have any positive effects, the entire organization from top to bottom must reflect the values. Managers have a special responsibility to "walk the values talk," and make them real. After all, how might you react if you found out that senior executives in your organization talked up values such as honesty and ethical behavior, but then acted quite differently—spending company funds on private parties and vacations?

Value-based management actively develops, communicates, and enacts shared values.

When managers do practice the core values, model them for others, and communicate and reinforce them in all that they do, this is called **value-based management**. It is managing with a commitment to actively help develop, communicate, and represent shared values within an organization. An incident at Tom's of Maine provides a good example. The incident involved the firm's founder and co-CEO Tom Chappell. After a big investment in a new deodorant, Tom was dismayed when he learned that customers were very dissatisfied with it. But he had founded the company on values that include fairness and honesty in all matters. He decided to reimburse customers and pull the product from the market, even though it cost the company a substantial amount of money. By doing what he believed was the right thing, Tom was living up to the full spirit of the company's values. And by doing so he set a very positive example for others to follow. This is what value-based management is all about.

PACESETTERS

A great communicator tries to change the culture at Sears.

The reports are that Aylwin B. Lewis has his hands full as the new CEO of the new Sears Holding Corp., a merger of Kmart and Sears. "Our worst stores are dungeons! Who wants to work in a dungeon? Who wants to shop in a dungeon?" was just part of his message at a meeting of Kmart managers. He talked for 25 minutes, no notes, and received cheers and applause when finished. But will it work? The goal is to get some 330,000 employees thinking and acting as if they are part of "a $55 billion startup." Lewis's style is described as being tough on objectives but also willing to help meet the targets, and he is acclaimed as "a great orator" with a knack for getting to the "heart of issues." One of the problems he faces is that the corporate cultures of both firms were not customer focused. Part of his tact for changing that is to require headquarters employees to spend a day working in a store, a new experience for many. He also visits stores regularly, and he also talks with the managers about sales goals and financial targets to make sure they are on top of things. High potential leaders of the new company are being given special training in a course entitled Sowing the Seeds of Our Culture.

Aylwin B. Lewis, *CEO, Sears Holding Corp.*

Be Sure You Can . . .

- explain organizational culture as the personality of an organization

- describe how strong cultures influence organizations

- distinguish between the observable and core cultures

- list sample core values of organizations

- explain the concept of value-based management

DEFINE THE TERMS

Core culture

Core values

Observable culture

Organizational culture

Strong cultures

Value-based management

Rapid Review

- Organizational culture is a system of shared values and beliefs that guides the behavior of members; it is an internal climate that creates the personality of the organization and also sets its performance tone.

- High-performing organizations tend to have strong cultures that are positive influences on employee behaviors, teamwork, and attitudes.

- The observable culture is found in the everyday rites, rituals, stories, heroes, and symbols of the organization.

- The core culture consists of the core values and fundamental beliefs on which the organization is based.

- Value-based management communicates, models, and reinforces core values throughout the organization.

REFLECT/REACT

1. Can an organization achieve success with a good organizational design but a weak organizational culture?

2. When you are in your local bank as a customer, what do you see and hear around you that identifies its observable culture?

3. What core values would you choose if you were creating a new organization and wanted to establish a strong performance-oriented culture?

Multiple Choice

1. A "tall" organization will likely have _____ spans of control than a "flat" organization with the same number of members. **(a)** wider **(b)** narrower **(c)** more ambiguous **(d)** less centralized

2. If a student in one of your course groups volunteers to gather information for a case analysis project and the other members agree while telling him to choose the information sources he believes is most important, the group is giving this student _____ to fulfill the agreed-upon task. **(a)** responsibility **(b)** accountability **(c)** authority **(d)** values

3. The current trend in the use of staff personnel in organizations is to _____. **(a)** give them more authority **(b)** reduce their numbers **(c)** distribute them among all levels of management **(d)** increase their efficiency with better use of IT

4. The bureaucratic organization described by Max Weber is similar to the _____ organization described by Burns and Stalker. **(a)** adaptive **(b)** mechanistic **(c)** organic **(d)** horizontal

5. Teamwork, task forces, and empowerment are common in _____ organizations. **(a)** mechanistic **(b)** organic **(c)** vertical **(d)** bureaucratic

6. Which organization would likely be a good fit for a dynamic and changing external environment? **(a)** vertical **(b)** centralized **(c)** organic **(d)** mechanistic

7. A basic paradox in subsystems design is that as differentiation among subsystems increases, the need for _____ also increases but is harder to accomplish. **(a)** cost efficiency **(b)** flexibility **(c)** integration **(d)** decentralization

8. An organization with a strong culture is most likely to have _____. **(a)** tight, bureaucratic structure **(b)** loose, flexible design **(c)** small staff size **(d)** clearly communicated mission

9. Planned and spontaneous ceremonies and celebrations of work achievements are examples of the _____ that can help build strong organizational cultures. **(a)** rites and rituals **(b)** heroes **(c)** value-based management **(d)** core values

10. Innovation, social responsibility, and customer service are examples of _____ which can be foundations for an organization's core culture. **(a)** rites and rituals **(b)** values **(c)** subsystems **(d)** integrating devices

Short Response

11. How can top management maintain centralized control while pursuing an active program of decentralization?

12. Why is an organic design likely to be quicker and more flexible in adapting to changes than a mechanistic design?

13. What integrating devices might work best for highly differentiated subsystems?

14. What is value-based management?

Integration & Application

You have been assigned to particpate in a debate on the relationship between organizational design trends and organizational performance in the new economy. Your team is taking the affirmative position. That is, your team will be arguing in support of the positive performance impact of new trends. In preparing for the debate you have been asked to specifically research and defend trends relating to both levels of management and delegation.

Questions: What will you be prepared to say in the debate, and why?

SELF-ASSESSMENT
Organizational Design Preference

INSTRUCTIONS *In the margin near each item, write the number from the following scale that shows the extent to which the statement accurately describes your views.*

5 = strongly agree
4 = agree somewhat
3 = undecided
2 = disagree somewhat
1 = strongly disagree

I prefer to work in an organization where:

1 Goals are defined by those in higher levels.
2 Work methods and procedures are specified.
3 Top management makes important decisions.
4 My loyalty counts as much as my ability to do the job.
5 Clear lines of authority and responsibility are established.
6 Top management is decisive and firm.
7 My career is pretty well planned out for me.
8 I can specialize.
9 My length of service is almost as important as my level of performance.
10 Management is able to provide the information I need to do my job well.
11 A chain of command is well established.
12 Rules and procedures are adhered to equally by everyone.
13 People accept the authority of a leader's position.
14 People are loyal to their boss.
15 People do as they have been instructed.
16 People clear things with their boss before going over his or her head.

SCORING AND INTERPRETATION

Total your scores for all questions. Enter the score here [_____]. This assessment measures your preference for working in an organization designed along "organic" or "mechanistic" lines. The higher your score (above 64), the more comfortable you are with a mechanistic design; the lower your score (below 48), the more comfortable you are with an organic design. Scores between 48 and 64 can go either way.

PATHWAYS to WileyPLUS

 **CASE SNAPSHOT**

Go online to read this case!

Virgin Group: The Man Who Would Say "Yes" and the Company that Follows Him

Though helmed by a maverick, this company has always stuck to a very corporate structure while maintaining its unique culture and competitive edge. Its holdings have grown increasingly diversified and complex; yet it still maintains a consistent brand culture. How much of Virgin's culture (and tendencies toward diversified, unpredictable holdings) comes from its owner?

MODULE 14   Online Interactive Learning Resources

Skill Builder
• Self Management

Experiential Exercise
• Which Culture Fits You?

Team Project
• Organizational Culture Survey

Nurturing turns potential

Human Resource Management

Any organization with high-performance aspirations must rank people as a top priority. Testimonials like these say it all: "*People* are our most important asset"; "It's *people* who make the difference"; "It's the *people* who determine whether our company thrives or languishes." Found on websites, in annual reports, and in executive speeches, such statements communicate respect for people and the talents they bring to organizations. Wouldn't you want to work for an organization that views its employees so positively?

Of course you would. And hopefully, with hard work and some good decisions, you'll always be there. But many people face another reality.

into performance

A Harris Poll of working adults reports that 33 percent feel they are in dead-end jobs. Another 42 percent feel that they are experiencing job burnout. And only 44 percent report that they are glad they chose their current employer over others.[1]

So what does it take to be a great employer? Make your list and, as you do, why not check out the Great Place to Work Institute.[2] It provides an annual listing of the "100 Best Companies to Work for in America." Firms are chosen on the basis of trust, pride, and camaraderie among their employees.

Another good source is *Working Mother* magazine.[3] It publishes annual listings of the "100 Best Companies for Working Mothers" and of "Best Companies for Women of Color."[4] To make these lists employers have to score high on employment practices and advancement opportunities. A recent report identified these top ten employers for women of color: Allstate, American Express, Anthem Blue Cross/Blue Shield, General Mills, Hewlett-Packard, JP Morgan Chase, Pricewaterhouse Coopers.

➔ MODULE GUIDE

 15.1 What is the purpose and legal context of human resource management?

- Human resource management attracts, develops, and maintains a talented workforce.
- Government legislation protects workers against employment discrimination.
- Employee rights and other issues complicate the legal environment of work.
- Labor relations and collective bargaining are closely governed by law.

 15.2 What are the essential human resource management practices?

- Human resource planning matches staffing with organizational needs.
- Recruitment and selection attract and hire qualified job applicants.
- Socialization and orientation integrate new employees into the organization.
- Training continually improves employee skills and capabilities.
- Performance management techniques appraise individual accomplishments.
- Retention and career development provide career paths and options.

15.1 What Are the Purpose and Legal Context of Human Resource Management?

The key to managing people in ways that lead to profit, productivity, innovation, and real organizational learning ultimately lies in how you think about your organization and its people. . . . When you look at your people, do you see costs to be reduced? . . . Or, when you look at your people do you see intelligent, motivated, trustworthy individuals— the most critical and valuable strategic assets your organization can have?

These comments are from Jeffrey Pfeffer's book, *The Human Equation: Building Profits by Putting People First.*[5] What is your experience? Do you find employers treating people as costs or as assets? And what difference does this seem to make? Pfeffer and his colleague, John F. Veiga, believe it does make a performance difference, a potentially big one. After reviewing the evidence they conclude: "There is a substantial and rapidly expanding body of evidence . . . that speaks to the strong connection between how firms manage their people and the economic results achieved."[6]

The core argument being advanced here is that organizations will perform better when they treat their members better.[7] And when it comes to how people are treated at work, we enter the territory of "human resource management."

• Human Resource Management Attracts, Develops, and Maintains a Talented Workforce

The process of **human resource management (HRM)** attracts, develops, and maintains a talented and energetic workforce. Its purpose is to ensure that an organization is always staffed with the best people available so that it gets important jobs done in the best possible ways. You might state the *goal of HRM* this way: To build organizational performance capacity through people.

When Robert Nardelli took over as new CEO of Home Depot, his first hire was a new executive vice president for human resources. The VP said: "CEOs and boards of directors are learning that human resources can be one of your biggest game-changers in terms of competitive advantage."[8] Have you considered a career in human resources? It is a growing field with an interesting mix of job responsibilities and career opportunities.

• Government Legislation Protects Workers against Employment Discrimination

If valuing people is at the heart of human resource management, **job discrimination** should be its enemy. It occurs when an organization denies someone employment or a job assignment or an advancement opportunity for reasons that are not performance relevant.

As Figure 15.1 indicates, there are a number of U.S. laws designed to protect workers from job discrimination. An important cornerstone of this legal protection is *Title VII of the Civil Rights Act of 1964*, amended by the *Equal Employment Opportunity Act of 1972* and the *Civil Rights Act (EEOA) of 1991*. These acts provide for **equal employment opportunity (EEO)**— the right to employment without regard to sex, race, color, national origin, or religion. It is illegal under Title VII to use any of these as criteria when making decisions about hiring, promoting, compensating, terminating, or otherwise changing someone's terms of employment.

The intent of equal employment opportunity is to ensure everyone the right to gain and keep employment based only on their ability and job performance. The Equal Employment Opportunity Commission (EEOC) enforces the legislation through its federal power to file civil lawsuits against organizations that do not provide timely resolution of any discrimination charges lodged against them. These laws generally apply to all public and private organizations that employ 15 or more people.

Title VII also requires organizations to show **affirmative action** in their efforts to ensure equal employment opportunity for members of *protected groups*, those historically underrepresented in the workforce. Employers are expected to analyze existing workforce demographics, compare them with those in the relevant labor markets, and set goals for

---

Human resource management (HRM) is the process of attracting, developing, and maintaining a high-quality workforce.

Basic Responsibilities of Human Resource Management

1. Attract a quality workforce—human resource planning, recruitment, and selection.
2. Develop a quality workforce—employee orientation, training, performance appraisal.
3. Maintain a quality workforce—retention and career development.

Discrimination occurs when someone is denied a job or job assignment for non-job-relevant reasons.

Equal employment opportunity is the right to employment and advancement without regard to race, sex, religion, color, or national origin.

Affirmative action is an effort to give preference in employment to women and minority group members.

Figure 15.1 | What are some of the U.S. laws that protect against employment discrimination?

Equal Pay Act of 1963	Requires equal pay for men and women performing equal work in an organization.
Title VII of the Civil Rights Act of 1964 (as amended)	Prohibits discrimination in employment based on race, color, religion, sex, or national origin.
Age Discrimination in Employment Act of 1967	Prohibits discrimination against persons over 40; restricts mandatory retirement.
Occupational Health and Safety Act of 1970	Establishes mandatory health and safety standards in workplaces.
Pregnancy Discrimination Act of 1978	Prohibits employment discrimination against pregnant workers.
Americans with Disabilities Act of 1990	Prohibits discrimination against a qualified individual on the basis of disability.
Civil Rights Act of 1991	Reaffirms Title VII of the 1964 Civil Rights Act; reinstates burden of proof by employer, and allows for punitive and compensatory damages.
Family and Medical Leave Act of 1993	Allows employees up to 12 weeks of unpaid leave with job guarantees for childbirth, adoption, or family illness.

Workers in the United States have many legal protections against employment discrimination. The foundation law is Title IV of the Civil Rights Act of 1964, as amended since, which gives everyone the right to employment without regard to race, color, national origin, religion, gender, age, or physical and mental ability. Additional laws offer protections in such areas as pay, health and safety, pregnancy, disabilities, and family and medical leave. Even with these legal protections in place, however, violations do occur.

correcting any underrepresentation that might exist. These goals are supported by *affirmative action plans* that are designed to ensure that an organization's workforce represents women and minorities in proportion to their labor market availability.[9]

You are likely to hear debates over the pros and cons of affirmative action. Criticisms tend to focus on the use of group membership, female or minority status, as a criterion in employment decisions.[10] The issues raised include claims of *reverse discrimination* by members of majority populations. White males, for example, may claim that preferential treatment given to minorities in a particular situation interferes with their individual rights.

As a general rule, the legal protections of EEO do not restrict an employer's right to establish **bona fide occupational qualifications**. These are criteria for employment that an organization can clearly justify as relating to a person's capacity to perform a job. However, the EEO bars the use of employment qualifications based on race and color under any circumstances; those based on sex, religion, and age are very difficult to support.[11]

You should stay up to date on the legal context of HRM. The available protection is extensive, but we should also be realistic. Although laws can help, they can't guarantee that no employment discrimination will exist or that you will never be affected by it. Just read the papers and listen to the news. You'll often find reports on people taking employers to court with claims that they have been discriminated against based on gender, race, age, or other personal characteristics.[12]

> **Bona fide occupational qualifications** are employment criteria justified by capacity to perform a job.

• Employee Rights and Other Issues Complicate the Legal Environment of Work

The legal environment of human resource management grows more complex almost everyday. Although we can't be exhaustive, here is a sampling of employee rights and other concerns that you will find often have legal implications.

Many employers work hard to retain services of older workers Changing demographics are really starting to assert themselves in the workplace. The number of workers over

age 55, including rock star Mick Jagger, is growing rapidly, creating a huge pool of potential retirees. And contrary to the stereotypes, these workers aren't necessarily less productive than their younger counterparts. In fact, they represent a vast storehouse of experience, knowledge, and relationships that many organizations can't afford to lose. Some employers are going to great lengths to try to keep older workers on board, at least part time, to tap their performance assets. Things like training to reduce age bias in the workplace, phased retirement options, portable jobs that are vacation and lifestyle friendly, part-time projects, and full benefits for part-time work are among the retention options being used.

Reflect: What do organizations lose when their senior employees retire? Do the retention programs featured here make sense?

Have you heard about **comparable worth**? This is the notion that persons performing jobs of similar importance should be paid comparable salaries. At issue is the *Equal Pay Act of 1963*, which provides for men and women to be equally paid for doing equal work in terms of skills, responsibilities, and working conditions.

Take an example. Should a long-distance truck driver receive higher pay than an elementary school teacher? They often do, and one has to wonder: "Why?" Is it because driving trucks is a traditionally male occupation and teaching elementary-age children a traditionally female occupation? Advocates of comparable worth argue that pay differences like these are sometimes due to a gender bias that is embedded in historical pay disparities for various occupations. What do you think?

Another issue that is increasingly important in our high-tech world of work is **workplace privacy**—the right of individuals to privacy on the job.[13] Employers, of course, should be able to monitor and assess the work performance and behavior of their employees. But monitoring can become invasive, sometimes crossing legal and ethical lines.

Are you prepared to deal with privacy issues at work? Most employers can monitor e-mails and Internet searches to track your use of the computer while on the job. Technology allows employers to identify who is called by telephone and how long conversations last; work performance in many jobs can be electronically documented moment to moment. All of this information and more can be stored in vast databases that may be used and even passed on to others without your permission. Until the legal status of high-tech surveillance is cleared up, one consultant says the best assumption to make is that we have "no privacy at work."[14]

The outsourcing, restructurings, and search for greater cost efficiencies that are taking place in business today have created another legal issue—the status of part-time and temporary workers. Don't be surprised if you are asked someday to work only "as needed," or to work as an **independent contractor**. This would mean that you are expected to work for an agreed-upon period or for an agreed-upon task and without becoming part of the permanent workforce.

Although offering both employment and perhaps attractive flexibility, these jobs can have their downsides. Many people find themselves caught up in a status known as *permatemp*; they are regularly employed but denied access to standard health care, pension, and other fringe benefits. This is a murky area under the law and it is attracting more public attention, including that of labor unions.

• Labor Relations and Collective Bargaining Are Closely Governed by Law

Labor unions are organizations to which workers belong and that deal with employers on the workers' behalf.[15] They act as a collective "voice" for their members, bringing them a power in dealing with their employers that wouldn't otherwise be available to them as individuals. Historically, this voice of the unions has played an important role in American society.[16]

As bargaining agents, unions negotiate legal contracts affecting many aspects of the employment relationship for their members.[17] These **labor contracts** typically specify the rights and obligations of employees and management with respect to wages, work hours, work rules, seniority, hiring, grievances, and other conditions of work.

Comparable worth holds that persons performing jobs of similar importance should receive comparable pay.

Workplace privacy is the right to privacy while at work.

Independent contractors are hired on temporary contracts and are not part of the organization's permanent workforce.

A **labor union** is an organization that deals with employers on the workers' collective behalf.

A **labor contract** is a formal agreement between a union and employer about the terms of work for union members.

The front line in the legal context of the labor–management relationship is **collective bargaining**, the process that brings management and union representatives together in negotiating, administering, and interpreting labor contracts. During a collective bargaining session, these parties exchange a variety of demands, proposals, and counterproposals. Several rounds of bargaining may take place before a contract is reached or a dispute resolved. Sometimes the process breaks down, and one or both parties walk away. The impasse can be short or lengthy, in some cases leading to labor actions that can last months and even years before agreements are reached.

When labor–management relations take on the adversarial character shown in Figure 15.2, the conflict can be prolonged and costly for both sides. That's not good for anyone, and there is quite a bit of pressure these days for more cooperative union–management relationships. Wouldn't it be nice if unions and management would work together in partnership, trying to address the concerns of both parties in ways that best meet the great challenges and competitive pressures of a global economy?

The trend, if you follow the news, does appear to be in the direction of more labor–management cooperation. The U.S. auto industry is a good example. The companies are in crisis due to foreign competition; their workers are in crisis as job losses threaten careers and lifestyles; their communities are in crisis as plant shutdowns create economic hardships. These problems are not easily solved, and any solutions are likely both to be long term and to require substantial compromises and changes on both sides.[18] You'll most probably note ups and downs, complaints and controversies, as the automakers and unions bargain back and forth. But it's also likely that you'll see each side bending a bit, over time, as they to try and work things out in the best ways possible.

> **Collective bargaining** is the process of negotiating, administering, and interpreting a labor contract.

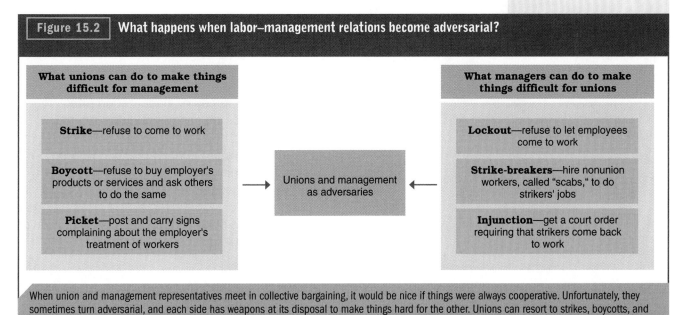

Figure 15.2 | **What happens when labor–management relations become adversarial?**

What unions can do to make things difficult for management

Strike—refuse to come to work

Boycott—refuse to buy employer's products or services and ask others to do the same

Picket—post and carry signs complaining about the employer's treatment of workers

Unions and management as adversaries

What managers can do to make things difficult for unions

Lockout—refuse to let employees come to work

Strike-breakers—hire nonunion workers, called "scabs," to do strikers' jobs

Injunction—get a court order requiring that strikers come back to work

When union and management representatives meet in collective bargaining, it would be nice if things were always cooperative. Unfortunately, they sometimes turn adversarial, and each side has weapons at its disposal to make things hard for the other. Unions can resort to strikes, boycotts, and picketing. Management can use lockouts, strikebreakers, and court injunctions to force strikers back to work.

15.1 What is the purpose and legal context of human resource management?

Be Sure You Can . . .

- explain the purpose of human resource management

- differentiate job discrimination, equal employment opportunity, and affirmative action

- identify the major laws protecting against employment discrimination

- explain the issues of comparable worth, workplace privacy, and independent contractors

- explain the role of labor unions and the process of collective bargaining

Define the Terms

Affirmative action

Bona fide occupational qualifications

Collective bargaining

Comparable worth

Equal employment opportunity

Human resource management (HRM)

Independent contractors

Job discrimination

Labor contract

Labor union

Workplace privacy

Rapid Review

- The human resource management process involves attracting, developing, and maintaining a quality workforce.

- Job discrimination occurs when someone is denied an employment opportunity for reasons that are not job relevant.

- Equal employment opportunity legislation guarantees people the right to employment and advancement without discrimination.

- Current legal issues in the work enviornment deal with comparable worth, workplace privacy, and rights of independent contractors, among other matters.

- Labor relations and collective bargaining are closely governed by law, and can be cooperative or adversarial in nature.

Reflect/React

1. How might the forces of globalization affect human resource management in the future?

2. Are current laws protecting American workers against discrimination in employment sufficient, or do we need additional ones?

3. What employee-rights issues and concerns would you add to those discussed here?

To attract and retain the right people to its workforce, an organization must first know exactly what it is looking for. It must have a clear understanding of the purpose and requirements of the jobs, and the talents that people need to do them well. And then, it must have the systems in place to fill the jobs with enthusiastic and high-performing workers.

• Human Resource Planning Matches Staffing with Organizational Needs

A marketing manager at Ideo, a Palo Alto–based industrial design firm, once said: "If you hire the right people . . . if you've got the right fit . . . then everything will take care of itself."[19] It really isn't quite that simple, but getting the right people on board is certainly a great starting point for success.

Human resource planning is the process of analyzing an organization's staffing needs and determining how to best fill them. The process begins with a review of organizational mission, objectives, and strategies to establish a baseline for forecasting human resource requirements. Once this is done, managers can assess the existing workforce and make recruiting, training, and career development plans to best meet future needs.

Human resource planning analyzes staffing needs and identifies actions to fill those needs.

Recruitment is a set of activities designed to attract a qualified pool of job applicants.

• Recruitment and Selection Attract and Hire Qualified Job Applicants

Recruitment is what organizations do to attract a qualified pool of applicants to an organization. **Selection** involves choosing to hire from this pool the persons who offer the greatest performance potential. You should already be familiar with both from the job applicant side, perhaps in collegiate recruiting for internships or full-time jobs.

The basic elements in the recruitment and selection processes are most typically: advertising job vacancies, preliminary contacts with job candidates, initial screening interview, formal application, in-depth interviews, employment testing, and reference checks. You need to be prepared to do well in all steps—both as an interviewer and interviewee. For example, are you ready for the increasingly common telephone interview?[20]

Steps in human resource planning

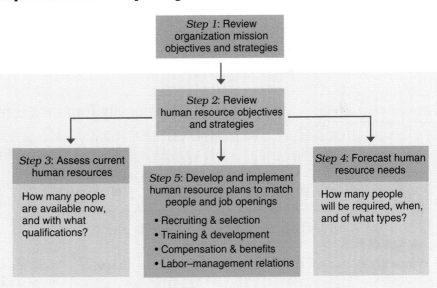

One thing to look and press for in an interview is a **realistic job preview**, one that gives you both the good points and the bad points of the job and organization.[21] You might be easily misled when the interviewer adopts a more traditional "tell and sell" approach, perhaps trying to hide or gloss over the potential negatives. It's far better to get a realistic and full picture of the situation before you decide to accept any offer, not after.

How can you tell if you are getting a realistic job preview? You need to listen for certain phrases such as: "Of course, there are some downsides. . . Something that you will want to be prepared for is. . . .We have found that some new hires had difficulty with. . . ." And if you don't hear these phrases, ask the tough questions yourself.

Selection is choosing whom to hire from a pool of qualified job applicants.

Realistic job previews provide job candidates with all pertinent information about a job and organization.

Reliability means a selection device gives consistent results over repeated measures.

Validity means scores on a selection device have demonstrated links with future job performance.

An **assessment center** examines how job candidates handle simulated work situations.

Work sampling evaluates applicants as they perform actual work tasks.

Socialization systematically influences the expectations, behavior, and attitudes of new employees.

Orientation familiarizes new employees with jobs, co-workers, and organizational policies and services.

Coaching occurs as an experienced person offers performance advice to a less-experienced person.

It's quite common that job candidates are asked to take employment tests. Some test job-specific knowledge and skills; others focus more on intelligence, aptitudes, personality, or general interests. Regardless of the intent, however, any employment test should be both reliable and valid. **Reliability** means that the test provides a consistent measurement, returning the same results time after time. **Validity** means that the test score is a good predictor of future job performance, with a high score associated with high job performance and vice-versa.

One of the popular developments in testing is use of **assessment centers**. This approach evaluates a person's job potential by observing his or her performance in experiential activities designed to simulate daily work. A related approach is **work sampling**, which asks you to work on actual job tasks while observers grade your performance. Google uses a form of this with its "Code Jams." These are essentially contests that the firm runs to find the most brilliant software coders. Google awards winners with financial prizes and job offers. Code Jams are held worldwide. A company spokesperson says: "Wherever the best talent is, Google wants them."[22]

• Socialization and Orientation Integrate New Employees into the Organization

Once hired, a new member of any organization has to "learn the ropes" and become familiar with "the way things are done." **Socialization** is the process of influencing the expectations, behavior, and attitudes of a new employee in a desirable way. It begins with the human resource management practice of **orientation**—a set of activities designed to familiarize new employees with their jobs, co-workers, and key values, policies, and other aspects of the organization as a whole.

For years, Disney has been considered a master at this. During orientation at its Disney World Resort in Buena Vista, Florida, new employees learn the corporate culture. They also learn that the company places a premium on personality and expects all employees—from entertainers to ticket sellers to groundskeepers—"to make the customer happy." A Disney HRM specialist notes: "We can train for skills. We want people who are enthusiastic, who have pride in their work, who can take charge of a situation without supervision."[23]

Obviously, a good orientation program like Disney's can go a long way toward setting the stage for high performance, job satisfaction, and work enthusiasm among new employees. Is this your experience?[24]

• Training Continually Improves Employee Skills and Capabilities

At this point you should probably be keeping a list of things to look for in your next employer. Here's another one: a willingness to invest in training so that you are continuously learning and updating your job skills.

We all need training, especially today when new knowledge and technologies quickly make so many of our existing skills obsolete. A great employer won't let this happen. Instead of trying to save costs, it willingly spends on training. It views training as an investment in human resources. In fact, you should probably ask questions about training opportunities in any job interview. And if the interviewer struggles for answers or evades the questions, you're getting a pretty good indication that the organization isn't likely to pass the "great employer" test.

A convenient and powerful training approach that you should be inquiring about is **coaching**. This is where an experienced person provides performance advice to someone else. Ideally, a new employee is assigned a coach who can model de-

MANAGEMENT TIPS

How to succeed in a telephone interview

- *Prepare ahead*—study the organization; list your relevant strengths and capabilities.
- *Minimize Distractions*—be in a quiet room, with privacy, without interruptions.
- *Dress professionally*—this increases confidence, sets your interview tone.
- *Practice your verbal skills*—what you say and how you sound affects your first impression.
- *Have materials handy*—have all supporting documents within easy reach.
- *Have questions ready*—be ready; don't hesitate; ask questions during the interview.
- *Ask what happens next*—ask how to follow up, what information you can provide.

sired work behaviors and otherwise help him or her to learn and make progress. Sometimes the best coach is the manager, other times is may be a co-worker. Always, the key is for the coach to be willing and able to show a newcomer by example how things should be done.

You should also be interested in **mentoring**. This is where a new or early-career employee is assigned as a protégé to someone senior in their area of expertise, perhaps a high-level manager. Good mentoring programs can be a great boost to a newcomer's career. Mentors are supposed to take an interest in the junior person, provide guidance and advice on skills and career progress, and otherwise inform them about how one gets ahead careerwise in the organization.

• Performance Management Techniques Appraise Individual Accomplishments

Once a person is hired and on the job, one of the important functions of HRM is performance management. This involves using various techniques of **performance appraisal** to formally assess and give feedback on someone's work accomplishments.[25] The purposes of performance appraisal are twofold: first, to evaluate and document performance for the record; second, to initiate a process of development that can improve performance in the future.[26]

In order for an appraisal method to have credibility it must satisfy reliability and validity criteria, just as with employment tests.[27] Any manager who hires, fires, or promotes based on performance appraisals, for example, may need to defend such actions in discrimination-based lawsuits. It is hard to make a defense if the performance appraisal method is faulted because of reliability or validity problems.

One of the most basic performance appraisal methods is a **graphic rating scale**. It is a checklist or scorecard for rating an employee on preselected personal traits or performance characteristics such as work quality, attendance, and punctuality. Athough simple, quick, and common, graphic rating scales have very questionable reliability and validity.

A more advanced approach to performance appraisal uses a **behaviorally anchored rating scale (BARS)**. This describes actual behaviors that exemplify various levels of performance achievement in a job. The example in Figure 15.3 shows a BARS for a customer service representative. "Extremely poor" performance is described with the behavioral anchor "rude or disrespectful treatment of a customer." Because the BARS relates performance assessments to specific descriptions of work behavior, it is more reliable and valid than the graphic rating scale. The behavioral anchors are also useful as benchmarks for training in job skills and objectives.

The **critical-incident technique** keeps an actual log of a person's effective and ineffective job behaviors. Using the case of the customer service representative again, a critical-incidents log might contain the following entries:

Positive example: "Took extraordinary care of a customer who had purchased a defective item from a company store in another city."

Mentoring assigns early career employees as protégés to more senior ones.

Performance appraisal is the process of formally evaluating performance and providing feedback to a job holder.

A **graphic rating scale** uses a checklist of traits or characteristics to evaluate performance.

A **behaviorally anchored rating scale (BARS)** uses specific descriptions of actual behaviors to rate various levels of performance.

The **critical-incident technique** keeps a log of someone's effective and ineffective job behaviors.

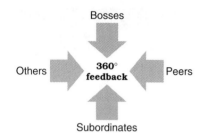

Bosses

Others → 360° feedback ← Peers

Subordinates

Negative example: "Acted rudely in dismissing the complaint of a customer who felt that we mistakenly advertised a sale item."

One of the current trends in performance appraisal is to move beyond the supervisor alone, and gather performance feedback from multiple sources. My guess is that you may well encounter a version of this known as **360° feedback**. This approach formally gathers inputs from the many people that work with and depend on the person being appraised. In a 360° feedback program you would most likely receive feedback from your immediate boss and possible higher level superiors, your subordinates, your peers, and others inside and outside of the organization with whom you directly work.[28] You would probably do a self-appraisal as well.

Finally, some performance management systems use **multiperson comparisons** to avoid the problem of everyone being rated "about the same." Instead, they make managers rate and rank people relative to one another.

Multiperson comparisons can be done by *rank ordering* people from top to bottom in order of performance achievement, with no ties allowed. They can be done by *paired comparisons* that first evaluate each person against every other, and then create a summary ranking based on the number of superior scores. Or it can be done by a *forced distribution* that places each person into a frequency distribution with fixed performance classifications—such as top 10 percent, next 40 percent, next 40 percent, and bottom 10 percent.

A **multiperson comparison** compares one person's performance with that of others.

Career development manages how a person grows and progresses in a career.

Career planning is the process of matching career goals and individual capabilities with opportunities for their fulfillment.

• Retention and Career Development Provide Career Paths and Options

After all the investments in recruitment, selection, orientation, training, and appraisal, an employer would be foolish to neglect efforts to retain the best employees for as long as possible. Of course there are many issues in retention, with compensation and benefits certainly of obvious importance. If one isn't willing to pay at or above market levels, with benefits to match, it goes without saying that the organization's investments in human resources may be lost as people leave for better jobs elsewhere.

Given a good compensation package, however, another significant retention issue becomes **career development**—the process of managing how a person grows and progresses in responsibility from one point in a career to the next. After initial entry, our career paths within organizations become subject to many considerations. Lots of choices will have to be made dealing with promotions, transfers, overseas assignments, mentors, higher degrees, even alternative employers and retirement. Ideally, the employer and the individual work closely together in making these choices.

With people changing jobs more often today, career development is becoming more and more a personal responsibility. This means that we each have to be diligent in **career planning**, the process of systematically matching career goals and individual capabilities with opportunities for their fulfillment. It involves answering such questions as "Who am I?," "Where do I want to go?," and "How do I get there?"

Some suggest that we should view a career as something that we should rationally plan and pursue in a logical step-by-step fashion. Others argue for much greater flexibility, allowing our career to progress in a somewhat random fashion as we respond to unexpected opportunities as they arise. My guess is that a well-managed career will probably include elements of each. A carefully thought-out career plan can point you in a general direction; an eye for opportunity helps fill in the details as you proceed along the way. Are you ready?

PACESETTERS

Visits to factory floor reflect people-oriented management style.

At Ariel Corp., a compressor manufacturing firm in central Ohio, CEO Karen Buchwald Wright has proven the skeptics wrong. "Several people said to me that there is no way I can run this company," she says. But four years into the job there aren't many doubters left. Working with over 800 employees she's made Ariel a turnaround story, taking it from marginal survival to double-digit growth rates. A mother of four with a degree in wildlife research, she took over the family firm more out of necessity than plan. Her success is self-described as based on the talents of the firm's loyal employees. She calls them the "brain trust" that deserve the credit, stating: "What I accomplished was to identify the people who needed to be empowered to allow the business to grow." And she believes motherhood is on her side in dealing with them. "You have to recognize what works for one won't for the other," she says. Even in the beginning when times were tough she did her best to retain workers, laying off as few as possible and putting others to work on anything available.

Karen Buchwald Wright, *CEO,* **Ariel Corp.**

STUDY GUIDE

15.2 What Are the essential human resource management practices?

Be Sure You Can . . .

- list steps in the recruitment process

- explain realistic job previews

- illustrate reliability and validity in employment testing

- illustrate how an assessment center might work

- explain the importance of socialization and orientation

- describe coaching and mentoring as training approaches

- discuss strengths and weaknesses of alternative performance appraisal methods

DEFINE THE TERMS

Assessment center	Multiperson comparison
Behaviorally anchored rating scale (BARS)	Orientation
Career development	Performance appraisal
Career planning	Realistic job preview
Coaching	Recruitment
Critical-incident technique	Reliability
Human resource planning	Selection
Graphic rating scale	Socialization
Mentoring	360° feedback
	Validity
	Work sampling

Rapid Review

- Human resource planning is the process of analyzing staffing needs and identifying actions that should be taken to satisfy them over time.

- Recruitment is the process of attracting qualified job candidates to fill vacant positions; realistic job previews try to provide candidates with accurate information on the job and organization.

- Assessment centers and work sampling are increasing common selection techniques; employment tests should meet the criteria of reliability and validity.

- Orientation is the process of formally introducing new employees to their jobs and socializing them with performance expectations.

- Training keeps workers' skills up to date and job relevant; important training approaches include coaching and mentoring.

- Performance appraisal methods include graphic rating scales, behaviorally anchored rating scales, critical incidents, 360° feedback, and multiperson comparisons; any appraisal method should meet the criteria of reliability and validity.

- Employee retention programs try to keep skilled workers in jobs and on career paths that are satisfying to them as well as making performance contributions for the employer.

Reflect/React

1. Is it realistic to expect that you can get a "realistic job preview" during the interview process?

2. Suppose a new employer doesn't formally assign someone to be your coach or mentor; what should you do?

3. What are some of the possible downsides to receiving 360° feedback?

Multiple Choice

1. Human resource management is the process of _____, developing, and maintaining a high-quality workforce.
   (a) attracting **(b)** compensating **(c)** appraising **(d)** selecting

2. A _____ is a criterion that organizations can legally justify for use in screening candidates for employment.
   (a) job description **(b)** bona fide occupational qualification **(c)** realistic job preview **(d)** BARS

3. _____ programs are designed to ensure equal employment opportunities for groups historically underrepresented in the workforce.
   (a) Realistic recruiting **(b)** Mentoring **(c)** Affirmative action **(d)** Coaching

4. An organization should replace an employment test that yields different results over time when taken by the same person because it lacks _____.
   (a) validity **(b)** reliability **(c)** realism **(d)** behavioral anchors

5. The assessment center approach to employee selection relies heavily on _____ to evaluate a candidate's job skills.
   (a) intelligence tests **(b)** simulations and experiential exercises **(c)** 360° feedback **(d)** formal one-on-one interviews

6. If a woman in a traditionally female occupation complains that a man in a traditionally male occupation is unfairly earning more pay even though the skill requirements for both jobs are equal, she is raising an issue known as _____.

   (a) equal employment opportunity **(b)** comparable worth **(c)** bona fide occupational qualification **(d)** reverse discrimination

7. Socialization of newcomers occurs during the _____ step of the staffing process.
   (a) orientation **(b)** recruiting **(c)** selecting **(d)** training existing workforce **(e)** review organizational mission, objectives, and strategies

8. Which phrase is most consistent with a recruiter offering a job candidate a realistic job preview?
   (a) "There are just no downsides to this job." **(b)** "No organization can be as good of an employer as this one." **(c)** "Don't ask me about negatives because there just aren't any." **(d)** "Let me tell you what you might not like once you start work."

9. The _____ purpose of performance appraisal is being addressed when a manager describes training options that might help an employee improve future performance.
   (a) development **(b)** evaluation **(c)** judgmental **(d)** legal

10. When a team leader must rate 10 percent of team members as "superior," 80 percent as "good," and 10 percent as "unacceptable" for their performance on a project, this is an example of the _____ approach to performance appraisal.
    (a) graphic **(b)** critical-incidents **(c)** behaviorally anchored rating scale **(d)** forced distribution

Short Response

11. Why is orientation important in the HRM process?

12. How does mentoring work as an on-the-job training approach?

13. When is an employment test or a performance appraisal method reliable?

14. How do the graphic rating scale and the BARS differ as performance appraisal methods?

Integration & Application

Sy Smith is not doing well in his job. The problems began to appear shortly after Sy's job changed from a manual to a computer-based operation. He has tried hard, but is just not doing well in learning how to use the computer to meet performance expectations. He is 45 years old, with 18 years with the company. He has been a great worker in the past and is both popular and influential among his peers. Along with his performance problems, you have also noticed that Sy is starting to sometimes "badmouth" the firm.

Questions: As Sy's manager, what options would you consider in terms of dealing with the issue of his retention in the job and in the company? What would you do and why?

SELF-ASSESSMENT
Performance Appraisal Assumptions

INSTRUCTIONS *In each of the following pairs of statements, check the one that best reflects your assumptions about performance evaluation.*

1. (a) a formal process that is done annually.
   (b) an informal process done continuously.
2. (a) a process that is planned for subordinates.
   (b) a process that is planned with subordinates.
3. (a) a required organizational procedure.
   (b) a process done regardless of requirements.
4. (a) a time to evaluate subordinates' performance.
   (b) a time for subordinates to evaluate their manager.
5. (a) a time to clarify standards.
   (b) a time to clarify the subordinate's career needs.
6. (a) a time to confront poor performance.
   (b) a time to express appreciation.
7. (a) an opportunity to clarify issues and provide direction and control.
   (b) an opportunity to increase enthusiasm and commitment.
8. (a) only as good as the organization's forms.
   (b) only as good as the manager's coaching skills.

INTERPRETATION

In general, the "a" responses show more (emphasis on the *evaluation* function) of performance appraisal. This largely puts the supervisor in the role of documenting a subordinate's performance for control and administrative purposes. The "b" responses show a stronger emphasis on the *counseling* or *development* function. Here, the supervisor is concerned with helping the subordinate do better and with learning from the subordinate what he or she needs to be able to do better.

PATHWAYS to WileyPLUS

CASE SNAPSHOT

Go online to read this case!

General Motors: A Former Giant Treads Lightly

Like many Americans companies, GM has demonstrated consistently short-term thinking that limits their ability to look to the future and innovate. Can its labor and personnel problems be overcome?

MODULE 15   Online Interactive Learning Resources

Skill Builder
- Giving/Receiving Feedback

Experiential Exercises
- You Be the Judge
- Contingency Workers

Team Project
- Future of Labor Unions

A leader lives in

Leadership

When asked about Southwest Airlines, most people think of reasonable prices, great service, and a company that thrives in a turbulent industry. How does Southwest manage all this? The answer traces back to one word: leadership.

The leadership of founder and retired CEO Herb Kelleher started things, and the leadership by current President Colleen C. Barrett helps keep things going. In an interview with *BizEd* magazine, Barrett says that the firm has three types of customers: employees, passengers, and shareholders. Among them she places the employees first! You have to wonder, why don't more CEOs say the same thing?

each of us

Although many might consider it strange and perhaps even wrong to define employees as an organization's most important customers, Barrett says: "If senior leaders regularly communicate with employees, if we're truthful and factual, if we show them that we care, and we do our best to respond to their needs, they'll feel good about their work environment and they'll be better at serving the passenger." She goes on: "We tell job applicants we're in the customer service business, we just happen to provide airline transportation."

Now that's a unique spin in an industry often known for customer complaints and dissatisfaction.

Everyone at Southwest is expected to be great at *TLC*—tender loving care for employees and customers. The company provides leadership classes and seminars, outside speakers, meetings with senior managers, roundtable discussions, and brown-bag meetings with employees.

When asked if he has any advice for Barrett and other would-be leaders, Kelleher says simply: "Ask your employees what's important to them. Ask your customers what is important to them. Then do it."[1]

→ MODULE GUIDE

 16.1 What are the foundations for effective leadership?

- Leadership is one of the four functions of management.
- Leadership relies on use of position power and personal power.
- Leadership traits and styles can influence leadership effectiveness.
- Fiedler's contingency model matches leadership styles with situational differences.
- House's path-goal theory matches leadership styles with task and follower characteristics.

 16.2 What are current issues and directions in leadership development?

- Transformational leadership inspires enthusiasm and extraordinary performance.
- Emotionally intelligent leadership handles emotions and relationships well.
- Interactive leadership emphasizes communication, listening, and participation.
- Moral leadership builds trust from a foundation of personal integrity.
- Servant leadership is follower centered and empowering.

A glance at the shelves in your local bookstore will quickly confirm that **leadership**—the process of inspiring others to work hard to accomplish important tasks, is one of the most popular management topics.[2] Consultant and author Tom Peters says that the leader is "rarely—possibly never?—the best performer."[3] They don't have to be; leaders thrive through and by the successes of others. But not all managers live up to these expectations. Warren Bennis, a respected scholar and consultant, claims that too many U.S. corporations are "over-managed and under-led." The late Grace Hopper, the first female admiral in the U.S. Navy, advised that "You manage things; you lead people."[4]

> **Leadership** is the process of inspiring others to work hard to accomplish important tasks.

• Leadership is One of the Four Functions of Management

Leadership is one of the four functions that make up the management process. Planning sets the direction and objectives; organizing brings together the resources to turn plans into action; *leading* builds the commitments and enthusiasm for people to apply their talents to help accomplish plans; and controlling makes sure things turn out right.

Where do you stand on leadership skills and capabilities?[5] If, as the module subtitle suggests, "A leader lives in each of us," what leader resides in you?

Leading—
to inspire effort
• Communicate the vision
• Build enthusiasm
• Motivate commitment, hardwork

Planning—
to set the direction

Controlling—
to ensure results

Management process

Organizing—
to create structures

• Leadership Relies on Use of Position Power and Personal Power

Are you surprised that our discussion of leadership starts with "power"? Harvard professor Rossabeth Moss Kanter once called it "America's last great dirty word."[6] She was concerned that too many people, managers among them, are not only uncomfortable with the concept, they don't realize how indispensable it is to leadership.

> **Power** is the ability to get someone else to do something you want done.

Power is the ability to get someone else to do something you want done; the ability to make things happen the way you want them to. Isn't that a large part of management? So, where and how do managers get power?

There are basically two sources of managerial power.[7] First is the power of the position, being "the manager." This power includes rewards, coercion, and legitimacy. Second is the power of the person, who you are and what your presence means in a situation. This power includes expertise and reference. Of course, some of us do far better than others at mobilizing and using power from these multiple sources.[8]

> **Reward power** achieves influence by offering something of value.

When it comes to position power, **reward power** is the capability to offer something of value as a means of influencing the behavior of other people. To use reward power, a manager says, in effect: "If you do what I ask, I'll give you a reward."

Very often the available rewards are things like pay raises, bonuses, promotions, special assignments, and verbal or written compliments. As you might expect, reward power can work well as long as people want the reward and the manager or leader makes it continuously available. But take the value of the reward or the reward itself away, and the power is quickly lost.

> **Coercive power** achieves influence by punishment.

Coercive power is the capability to punish or withhold positive outcomes as a way of influencing the behavior of other people. To mobilize coercive power, a manager is really saying: "If you don't do what I want, I'll punish you."

Managers have access to lots of possible punishments, including threatened or actual reprimands, pay penalties, bad job assignments, and even termination. How do you or would you feel when threatened in these ways? If you're like me, you'll most likely resent both the threat and the person making it. Sure, you might act as requested, or at least go through the motions. But you're unlikely to continue doing so once the threat no longer exists.

> **Legitimate power** achieves influence by formal authority.

Legitimate power is the capacity to influence through authority. It is the right by virtue of one's status as the manager, or person in charge, to exercise control over persons in subordinate positions. To mobilize legiti-

Power of the POSITION:
Based on things managers can offer to others.

Rewards: "If you do what I ask, I'll give you a reward."

Coercion: "If you don't do what I ask, I'll punish you."

Legitimacy: "Because I am the boss, you *must* do as I ask."

mate power, a manager is basically saying: "I am the boss; therefore you are supposed to do as I ask."

You might consider legitimate power in the context of your management course. When the instructor assigns homework, exams, and group projects, don't you most often do what is requested? Why? You do it because the requests seem legitimate in the context of the course. But if the instructor moves outside of the course boundaries, such as requiring you to attend a campus sports event, the legimacy is lost and your compliance is much less likely.

After all is said and done, we need to admit that position power alone isn't going to be sufficient for any manager. In fact, how much personal power you can mobilize through expertise and reference may well make the difference someday between success and failure in a leadership situation, and even a career.

Expert power is the ability to influence the behavior of others because of special knowledge and skills. When a manager uses expert power, the implied message is, "You should do what I want because of my special expertise or information."

Expert power achieves influence by special knowledge.

A leader's expertise may come from technical understanding or access to information relevant to the issue at hand. It can be acquired through formal education and evidenced by degrees and credentials. It is also acquired on the job, through experience, and by gaining a reputation as someone who is a high performer and really understands the work. Building expertise in these ways, in fact, may be one of your biggest early career challenges.

There's still more to personal power. Think of all the television commercials that show high-visibility athletes and personalities advertising consumer products. What's really going on here? The intent is to attract customers to the products through identification with the athletes and personalities. The same holds true in leadership. **Referent power** is the ability to influence the behavior of others because they admire and want to identify positively with you. When a manager uses referent power, the implied message is: "You should do what I want in order to maintain a positive self-defined relationship with me."

Referent power achieves influence by personal identification.

If referent power is so valuable, do you know how to get it? It is probably derived in large part from and maintained by good interpersonal relationships, ones that create admiration and respect for us in the eyes of others. My wife sums this up very simply, saying: "It's a lot easier to get people to do what you want when they like you, than when they dislike you." Doesn't this make sense? Isn't this good advice for how to approach your work and the people with whom you work every day?

> **Power of the PERSON:**
> *Based on how managers are viewed by others.*
>
> **Expertise**—as a source of special knowledge and information.
>
> **Reference**—as a person with whom others like to identify.

• Leadership Traits and Styles Can Influence Leadership Effectiveness

For centuries, people have recognized that some persons use power and perform very well as leaders, whereas others do not. You've certainly seen this yourself. How can such differences in leadership effectiveness be explained?

An early direction in leadership research tried to answer this question by identifying traits and personal characteristics shared by effective leaders.[9] Not surprisingly, results showed that physical characteristics such as height, weight, and physique make no difference. But a study of over 3400 managers found that followers rather consistently admired leaders who were honest, competent, forward-looking, inspiring, and credible.[10] Another comprehensive review is summarized in the *Exhibit – Traits Often Shared by Effective Leaders*.[11] You might use this list as a quick check of your leadership potential.

In addition to leadership traits, researchers have also studied how successful and unsuccessful leaders behaved when working with followers. Most of this research focused on two sets of behaviors: task-oriented behaviors and people-oriented behaviors. A leader high in concern for task generally plans and defines work goals, assigns task responsibilities, sets clear work standards, urges task completion, and monitors performance

EXHIBIT

Traits Often Shared by Effective Leaders

Drive Successful leaders have high energy, display initiative, and are tenacious.

Self-confidence Successful leaders trust themselves and have confidence in their abilities.

Creativity Successful leaders are creative and original in their thinking.

Cognitive ability Successful leaders have the intelligence to integrate and interpret information.

Business knowledge Successful leaders know their industry and its technical foundations.

Motivation Successful leaders enjoy influencing others to achieve shared goals.

Flexibility Successful leaders adapt to fit the needs of followers and demands of situations.

Honesty and integrity Successful leaders are trustworthy; they are honest, predictable, and dependable.

results. A leader high in concern for people acts warm and supportive toward followers, maintains good social relations with them, respects their feelings, shows sensitivity to their needs, and displays trust in them.

Leaders who show different combinations of task and people behaviors are often described as having unique **leadership styles**, such as you have probably observed in your own experiences. Someone who emphasizes task over people is often described as "autocratic."[12] An **autocratic leader** holds on to authority, delegates little, keeps information to himself or herself, and tends to act in a unilateral command-and-control fashion. Have you ever worked for someone fitting this description? How would you score their leadership effectiveness?

A leader who emphasizes people over task is often referred to as a **human relations leader**. This leader is interpersonally engaging, caring about others, sensitive to feelings and emotions, and tends to act in ways that emphasize harmony and good working relationships.

Interestingly, researchers at first believed that the human relations style was the most effective for a leader. However, after pressing further, the conclusion emerged that the most effective leaders were strong in both concerns for people and task.[13] Sometimes called a **democratic leader**, a person with this style shares decisions with subordinates, encourages participation, and supports the teamwork needed for high levels of task accomplishment.

One of the results of the early research on leader behaviors was the emergence of training programs designed to help people learn how to be good at both task-oriented and people-oriented behaviors needed for leadership success. How about you? Where do you fit on the leadership grid? What leadership training would be best for you? Hopefully you're not starting out with a **laissez-faire style**, low on both task and people concerns.

But as you consider your leadership style and tendencies, you should know that researchers eventually concluded that no one style always works best. Not even the democratic or "high-high" leader is successful all of the time. This finding led scholars to explore a *contingency* perspective on leadership success.

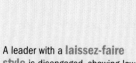

• Fiedler's Contingency Model Matches Leadership Styles with Situational Differences

One of the first contingency models of leadership was put forth by Fred Fiedler. He proposed that leadership success depends on achieving a proper match between your leadership style and situational demands.[14] And he believed that each of us has a predominant leadership style that is strongly rooted in our personalities. This is important because it suggests that a person's leadership style, yours or mine, is going to be quite enduring and difficult to change.

Fiedler uses an instrument called the *least-preferred co-worker scale (LPC)* to classify our leadership styles as either task motivated or relationship motivated. By the way, the LPC scale is available on this book's student website. Why not complete it and see how Fiedler would describe your style?

Leadership situations are analyzed in Fiedler's model for leader-member relations, task structure, and position power. Figure 16.1 shows that these three contingency variables can exist in eight different combinations, with each representing a different leadership challenge. The most-favorable situation provides high control for the leader (good leader-member relations, high task structure, strong position power); the least favorable situation provides low control for the leader (poor leader-member relations, low task structure, weak position power).

Fiedler's research revealed an interesting pattern when he studied the effectiveness of different styles in these leadership situations. As shown in the figure, a task-oriented leader is most successful in either very favorable (high-control) or very unfavorable (low-control) situations. In contrast, a relationship-oriented leader is more successful in situations of moderate control.

Don't let the apparent complexity of the figure fool you; Fiedler's logic is quite straightforward and, if on track, has some interesting career implications. It suggests that you should know yourself well enough to recognize your predominant leadership style. And you should seek out or create leadership situations for which this style is a good match, while avoiding those for which it is a bad match.

Let's do some quick examples. First, assume that you are the leader of a team of bank tellers. The tellers seem highly supportive of you,

Leadership style is the recurring pattern of behaviors exhibited by a leader.

A leader with an **autocratic style** acts in unilateral command-and-control fashion.

A leader with a **human relations** style emphasizes people over tasks.

A leader with a **democratic style** encourages participation with an emphasis on task and people.

A leader with a **laissez-faire style** is disengaged, showing low task and people concerns.

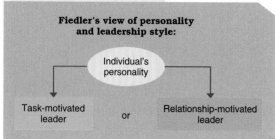

and their job is clearly defined. You have the authority to evaluate their performance and to make pay and promotion recommendations. This is a high-control situation consisting of good leader-member relations, high task structure, and high position power. By checking Figure 16.1 you can see that a task-motivated leader is recommended.

Now suppose you are chairperson of a committee asked to improve labor–management relations in a manufacturing plant. Although the goal is clear, no one knows exactly how to accomplish it—task structure is low. Further, not everyone believes that a committee is even the right way to approach the situation—poor leader-member relations are likely. Finally, committee members are free to quit any time they want—you have little position power. The figure shows that in this low-control situation a task-motivated leader should be most effective.

Finally, assume that you are the new head of a clothing section in a large department store. Because you won the job over one of the popular sales clerks you now supervise, leader-member relations are poor. Task structure is high since the clerk's job is well defined. But your position power is low because clerks work under a seniority system, with a fixed wage schedule. The figure shows that this moderate-control situation requires a relationship-motivated leader.

Figure 16.1 What are the best matches of leadership style and situation according to Fiedler's contingency model?

	High-control Situations			Moderate-control Situations			Low-control Situations	
Leader-member relations	Good			Good	Poor		Poor	
Task structure	High		Low	Low	High		Low	
Position power	Strong	Weak	Strong	Weak	Strong	Weak	Strong	Weak
	I	II	III	IV	V	VI	VII	VIII

Best Fit = Task-motivated Leader

Best Fit = Relationship-motivated Leader

Fiedler believes that leadership success requires the right style-situation match. He classifies leadership styles as either task-motivated or relationship motivated, and views them as strongly rooted in our individual personalities. He describes situations according to the leader's position power, quality of leader-member relations, and amount of task structure. In situations that are most favorable and unfavorable for leaders, his research shows the task-motivated style as a best fit. In more intermediate situations, the relationship-motivated style provides the best fit.

• House's Path-Goal Theory Matches Leadership Styles with Task and Follower Characteristics

Another contingency leadership approach is the path-goal theory advanced by Robert House.[15] This theory suggests that leaders are effective when they help followers move along paths through which they can achieve both work and personal goals. The best leaders create positive "path-goal" linkages, raising motivation by removing barriers and rewarding progress.

Like Fiedler's approach, House's path-goal theory seeks the right fit between leadership and situation. But unlike Fiedler, House believes that a leader can use four leadership styles: directive, supportive, achievement-oriented, and participative. When choosing among the different styles, furthermore, he suggests that the leader's job is to "add value" to a situation. This means acting in ways that contribute things that are missing, and not doing things that can otherwise take care of themselves.

For example, if you are the leader of a team whose members are expert and competent at their tasks, why would you need to be directive? They have the know-how to provide their own direction. More likely, the value you can add to this situation would be found in a participative leadership style that helps unlock the expertise of team members and apply it fully to the tasks at hand.

The details of path-goal theory provide a variety of research-based guidance of this sort to help leaders contingently match their styles with situational characteristics.[16] When job assignments are unclear, *directive leadership* helps to clarify task objectives and expected rewards. When worker self-confidence is low, *supportive leadership* can increase confidence by emphasizing individual abilities and offering needed assistance. When task challenge is insufficient in a job, *achievement-oriented leadership* helps to set goals and raise performance aspirations. When performance incentives are poor, *participative leadership* might clarify individual needs and identify appropriate rewards.

> **House's Four Path-Goal Leadership Styles**
>
> 1. "Directive leader" lets others know what is expected; gives directions, maintains standards.
> 2. "Supportive leader" makes work more pleasant; treats others as equals, acts friendly, shows concern.
> 3. "Achievement-oriented leader" sets challenging goals; expects high performance, shows confidence.
> 4. "Participative leader" involves others in decision making; asks for and uses suggestions.

Be Sure You Can . . .

- illustrate how managers use position and personal power

- list five traits of successful leaders

- describe the behaviors of high concern for task and high concern for people leaders

- explain Fiedler's contingency model for matching leadership style and situation

- describe the best use of directive, supportive, achievement-oriented, and participative leadership styles in House's path-goal theory

Define the Terms

Autocratic leader	Leadership
Coercive power	Leadership style
Democratic leader	Legitimate power
Expert power	Power
Human relations leader	Referent power
Laissez-faire leader	Reward power

Rapid Review

- Leadership, as one of the management functions, is the process of inspiring others to work hard to accomplish important tasks.

- Leaders use power, from two primary sources: position power that includes rewards, coercion, and legitimacy, and personal power that includes expertise and reference.

- Personal characteristics that have been associated with leadership success include drive, integrity, and self-confidence.

- Research on leader behaviors focused attention on concerns for task and concerns for people, with the leader high on both and using a democratic style considered most effective.

- Fiedler's contingency model describes how situational differences in task structure, position power, and leader-member relations may influence the success of task-motivated and relationship-motivated leaders.

- House's path-goal theory describes how leaders add value to situations by using supportive, directive, achievement-oriented, and/or participative styles as needed.

Reflect/React

1. When, if ever, is a leader justified in using coercive power?

2. How might a human relations leader get into difficulty trying to get things done in an organization?

3. What are the potential career development implications of Fiedler's contingency leadership model?

By now you should be thinking seriously about your leadership qualities, tendencies, styles, and effectiveness. You should also be thinking about continuing your personal development as a leader. And, in fact, if you look at what people say about leaders in their workplaces, you should be admitting that most of us have considerable room to grow in this regard.[17] Fortunately, leadership research continues to bring to our attention many interesting insights and possibilities.

• Transformational Leadership Inspires Enthusiasm and Extraordinary Performance

For a while now it has been popular to talk about "superleaders," persons whose visions and strong personalities have an extraordinary impact on others.[18] Some call them **charismatic leaders** because of their ability to inspire others in exceptional ways. We used to think charisma was limited to only a few lucky persons who were born with it. Today, it is linked with a broader set of personal qualities that most of us should be able to develop with foresight and practice.

Leadership scholars James MacGregor Burns and Bernard Bass have pursued this theme. They begin by describing the traditional leadership approaches we have discussed so far as **transactional leadership**.[19] You might picture the transactional leader engaging followers in a somewhat mechanical fashion, "transacting" with them by using power, employing behaviors and styles that seem to be the best choices at the moment for getting things done.

What is missing in the transactional approach, say Burns and Bass, is attention to things typically associated with charismatic superleaders—"enthusiasm" and "inspiration," for example. These are among the qualities that they associate with something called **transformational leadership**. Transformational leaders use their personalities to inspire followers, to get them so highly excited about their jobs and organizational goals that they strive for truly extraordinary performance accomplishments.[20] Sometimes the easiest way to spot a truly transformational leader is through their followers. They are likely to be enthusiastic about the leader and loyal and devoted to his or her ideas, and to work exceptionally hard together to support them.

Look at the Exhibit – *Characteristics of a Transformational Leader*.[21] Next, reconsider the "leader in you" question. How would you score on using charisma and related personal qualities to raise the aspirations of others and inspire them to high performance? This is what a transformational leader does, to the point that people end up accomplishing more than they originally expected to or may even have thought was possible.

A **charismatic leader** develops special leader-follower relationships and inspires followers in extraordinary ways.

Transactional leadership directs the efforts of others through tasks, rewards, and structures.

Transformational leadership is inspirational and arouses extraordinary effort and performance.

EXHIBIT

Characteristics of a Transformational Leader

Vision Has ideas and a clear sense of direction; communicates them to others; develops excitement about accomplishing shared "dreams."

Charisma Uses power of personal reference and emotion to arouse others' enthusiasm, faith, loyalty, pride, and trust in themselves.

Symbolism Identifies "heroes" and holds spontaneous and planned ceremonies to celebrate excellence and high achievement.

Empowerment Helps others grow and develop by removing performance obstacles, sharing responsibilities, and delegating truly challenging work.

Intellectual stimulation Gains the involvement of others by creating awareness of problems and stirring their imaginations.

Integrity Is honest and credible; acts consistently and out of personal conviction; follows through on commitments.

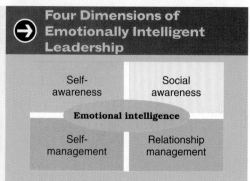

Four Dimensions of Emotionally Intelligent Leadership

Self-awareness	Social awareness
Emotional intelligence	
Self-management	Relationship management

Emotional intelligence (EI) is the ability to manage our emotions in social relationships.

• Emotionally Intelligent Leadership Handles Emotions and Relationships Well

The role of personality in transformational leadership raises another popular area of inquiry in leadership development—**emotional intelligence (EI)**. Popularized by the work of Daniel Goleman, and first discussed in Module 2, emotional intelligence is an ability to understand emotions in oneself and others, and use this understanding to handle one's relationships effectively.[22]

According to Goleman's research, emotional intelligence is an important influence on leadership success, especially in more senior management positions. In his words: "the higher the rank of the person considered to be a star performer, the more emotional intelligence capabilities showed up as the reason for his or her effectiveness."[23] This is a pretty strong endorsement for considering whether EI is one of your leadership assets. Important too is Goleman's belief that we can all learn basic emotional intelligence skills.[24]

To put Goleman's ideas into perspective, consider four primary emotional competencies.[25] *Self-awareness* is the ability to understand our own moods and emotions, and to understand their impact on our work and on others. *Social awareness* is the ability to empathize, to understand the emotions of others, and to use this understanding to better deal with them. *Self-management*, or self-regulation, is the ability to think before acting and to be in control of otherwise disruptive impulses. *Relationship management* is the ability to establish rapport with others in ways that build good relationships and influence their emotions in positive ways.

"Great leaders move us," say Goleman and his colleagues. "Great leadership works through emotions."[26] Think about it; is this the leader in you?

• Interactive Leadership Emphasizes Communication, Listening, and Participation

Sara Levinson, President of NFL Properties, Inc., of New York, once asked the all-male members of her management team: "Is my leadership style different from a man's?"[27] Would you be surprised to learn that they answered "Yes," telling her that just by asking the question she was providing evidence of the difference, they described her as a leader who emphasized communication, always gathering ideas and opinions from others. And when Levinson probed further by asking "Is this a distinctly 'female' trait?", they said it was.

This example poses an interesting question: Are there gender differences in leadership? Now, before you jump in with your own answer, let's be clear on two things. First, research largely supports the *gender similarities hypothesis*; that is, males and females are very similar to one another in terms of psychological properties.[28] Second, research leaves no doubt that both women and men can be effective leaders.[29]

What research on gender in leadership does show is that men and women are sometimes perceived as using somewhat different styles, perhaps arriving at leadership success from different angles.[30] And the perceived differences are quite interesting.

Some studies report male leaders being viewed as directive and assertive, using position power to get things done in traditional command-and-control ways.[31] Others report female leaders acting more participative, and being rated by peers, subordinates, and supervisors as strong on motivating others, persuading, fostering communication, listening to others, mentoring, and supporting high-quality work.[32]

This pattern of behaviors associated with female leaders has been called an **interactive leadership style**.[33] Interactive leaders are democratic, participative, and inclusive, often approaching problems and decisions through teamwork.[34] They focus on building consensus and good interpersonal relations through communication and involvement. They tend to get things done with personal power, seeking influence over others through support and interpersonal relationships.

Rosabeth Moss Kanter says, "Women get high ratings on exactly those skills required to succeed in the Global Information Age, where teamwork and partnering are so important."[35] But let's be careful. One of the risks in this discussion is falling prey to stereotypes that place men and women into leadership boxes in which they don't necessarily belong.[36]

Perhaps we should set gender issues aside for the moment, accept the gender similarities hypothesis, and focus instead on the notion of interactive leadership. The likelihood is that this style is a very good fit with the needs of today's organizations and workers.[37] And, furthermore, there seems every reason to believe that both men and women can do it equally well. What do you think?

Interactive leadership is strong on motivating, communicating, listening, and relating positively to others.

MANAGEMENT TIPS

How to empower others

- Get others involved in selecting their work assignments and the methods for accomplishing tasks.
- Create an environment of cooperation, information sharing, discussion, and shared ownership of goals.
- Encourage others to take initiative, make decisions, and use their knowledge.
- When problems arise, find out what others think and let them help design the solutions.
- Stay out of the way; give others the freedom to put their ideas and solutions into practice.
- Maintain high morale and confidence by recognizing successes and encouraging high performance.

• Moral Leadership Builds Trust from a Foundation of Personal Integrity

Would you be surprised that a Harris Poll found only 37 percent of U.S. adults in a survey willing to describe their top managers as acting with "integrity and morality"?[38] Based on that result, it may not surprise you that a *Business Week* survey found that just 13 percent of top executives at large U.S. firms rated "having strong ethical values" as a top leadership characteristic.[39] Don't you have to wonder: Where is the moral leadership that we so often hear talked about?

In contrast to the findings described in these surveys, there can be little doubt that society today is demanding more **ethical leadership** in our organizations. We want, even if we don't always have, leaders that practice high ethical standards of behavior, build and maintain an ethical organizational culture, and both help and require others to behave ethically in their work.[40] Hopefully, this theme has been well communicated throughout this book. Hopefully, too, you will agree that long-term success in work, and in life, can be built only on a foundation of solid ethical behavior.[41]

But where do we start when facing up to the challenge of building capacities for ethical leadership? Peter Drucker's answer would be: start with **integrity**! Start with honest, credible, and consistent behavior that puts your values into action. When a leader has integrity, he or she earns the trust of followers. And when followers believe that their leaders are trustworthy, they are more willing to try and live up to the leader's expectations.

There's a lot of power in this logic. Consider what Drucker calls "good old-fashioned leadership."[42] He doesn't use fancy words and build a complex theory. Instead he talks about integrity, trust, mission, goals, standards, and responsibility. As always his advice seems pretty solid.

Think also about Southwest Airlines again, and its leadership. The firm's CEO, Gary Kelly, seems to have gotten the message. He says: "Being a leader is about character . . . being straightforward and honest, having integrity, and treating people right." And there's a payoff; one of his co-workers says this about Kelly's leadership impact: "People are willing to run through walls for him."[43]

Ethical leadership has integrity and appears to others as "good" and "right" by moral standards.

Integrity in leadership is honesty, credibility, and consistency in putting values into action.

STAY INFORMED

Leadership surveys of U.S. workers report:

- 39% believe leaders most often act in best interest of organization.
- 22% see leaders as ready to admit mistakes.
- 46% believe their organizations give them freedom to do their jobs.
- 25% of women and 16% of men believe their organizations pick the best people for leadership.
- <33% of managers are perceived as "strong leaders."

• Servant Leadership Is Follower Centered and Empowering

When pondering leadership, don't gloss too quickly over Drucker's point that great leaders view leadership as a responsibility and not a rank. He was talking about coming to leadership not with expectations of privilege, but with expectations of service to others. His view is consistent with the concept of **servant leadership**. This is leadership firmly based on a commitment to serving others, to helping people use their talents to full potential while working together for organizations that benefit society.[44]

You might think of servant leadership with this question in mind: Who is most important in leadership, the leader or the followers? For those who believe in servant leadership, there is no doubt about the correct answer: the followers. Servant leadership is "other centered" and not "self-centered." And this raises interesting possibilities in our search for personal leadership development.

If one shifts the focus away from the self and toward others, what does that generate in terms of leadership directions and opportunities? **Empowerment** for one thing; this is the process through which managers give people job freedom and help them gain power to achieve influence within the organization (see Management Tips).

Servant leaders empower others by providing them with the information, responsibility, authority, and trust to make decisions and act independently. They know that when people feel empowered to act, they tend to follow through with commitment and high-quality work. They also realize that power in organizations is not a zero-sum quantity; rejecting the idea that in order for one person to gain power, someone else needs to give it up.[45] In this way servant leadership becomes empowering for everyone, making the whole organization more powerful in serving its cause or mission.

Max DePree of Herman Miller praises leaders who "permit others to share ownership of problems—to take possession of the situation."[46] Lorraine Monroe of the School Leadership Academy says: "The real leader is a servant of the people she leads. . . a really great boss is not afraid to hire smart people. You want people who are smart about things you are not smart about."[47] Robert Greenleaf, who is credited with coining the term servant leadership, says: "Institutions function better when the idea, the dream is to the fore, and the person, the leader is seen as servant to the dream."[48]

Reach back and take a good look. Is the leader in you capable of being a servant?

NEWSLINE

Why Peter Drucker's leadership advice still matters

When Peter Drucker died at the age of 95 in the year 2005, the former CEO of GE, Jack Welch, said: "The world knows he was the greatest management thinker of the last century." That could be an understatement. Drucker was renowned worldwide for his many books, consultancies, newspaper columns, and sage advice on matters of management, organizations, business and society, and executive leadership. Here's a sampler of his enduring advice:

- Good leaders have integrity; they mean what they say, earning and keeping the trust of followers.
- Good leaders define and establish a sense of mission; they set goals, priorities, and standards.
- Good leaders accept leadership as responsibility, not rank.
- Every decision is risky.
- Good leaders surround themselves with talented people.

Reflect: What does Drucker's advice mean to you? Can you translate each of his points into a "leadership lesson" of personal value?

STUDY GUIDE

16.2 What are current issues and directions in leadership development?

Be Sure You Can...

- differentiate transformational and transactional leadership

- list personal qualities of transformational leaders

- explain how emotional intelligence contributes to leadership success

- discuss research findings on interactive leadership

- list Drucker's three essentials of good old-fashioned leadership

- explain the role of integrity as a foundation for moral leadership

- explain the concept of servant leadership

Define the Terms

Charismatic leader

Emotional intelligence

Empowerment

Ethical leadership

Integrity

Interactive leadership style

Servant leadership

Transactional leadership

Transformational leadership

Rapid Review

- Transformational leaders use charisma and emotion to inspire others toward extraordinary efforts in support of change and performance excellence.

- Emotional intelligence, the ability to manage our emotions and relationships effectively, is an important leadership capability.

- The interactive leadership style, sometimes associated with women, emphasizes communication, involvement, and interpersonal respect.

- Moral or ethical leadership is built from a foundation of personal integrity, creating a basis for trust and respect between leaders and followers.

- A servant leader operates with a commitment to serving followers by empowering them and unlocking their personal talents in the quest for goals and accomplishments that help organizations best serve society.

Reflect/React

1. Should all managers be expected to excel at transformational leadership?

2. Do women lead differently than men?

3. Is servant leadership inevitably moral leadership?

Multiple Choice

1. When managers use offers of rewards and threats of punishments to try and get others to do what they want them to do, they are using which type of power?
(a) formal authority (b) position (c) referent (d) personal

2. When a manager says, "Because I am the boss, you must do what I ask," what power base is being put into play?
(a) reward (b) legitimate (c) moral (d) referent

3. The personal traits that are now considered important for managerial success include _____.
(a) self-confidence (b) gender (c) age (d) personality

4. In the research on leader behaviors, which style of leadership describes the preferred "high-high" combination?
(a) transformational (b) transactional (c) laissez-faire (d) democratic

5. In Fiedler's contingency model, both highly favorable and highly unfavorable leadership situations are best dealt with by a _____ leadership style.
(a) task-oriented (b) laissez-faire (c) participative (d) relationship-oriented

6. Which leadership theorist argues that one's leadership style is strongly anchored in personality and therefore very difficult to change?
(a) Daniel Goleman (b) Peter Drucker (c) Fred Fiedler (d) Robert House

7. Vision, charisma, integrity, and symbolism are all attributes typically associated with _____ leaders.
(a) people-oriented (b) democratic (c) transformational (d) transactional

8. In terms of leadership behaviors, someone who focuses on doing a very good job of planning work, setting standards, and monitoring results would be described as _____ .
(a) task oriented (b) servant oriented (c) achievement oriented (d) transformational

9. In the discussion of gender and leadership it was pointed out that some perceive women as having tendencies toward _____, a style that seems a good fit with developments in the new workplace.
(a) interactive leadership (b) use of position power (c) command-and-control (d) transactional leadership

10. In House's path-goal theory, a leader who sets challenging goals for others would be described as using the _____ leadership style.
(a) autocratic (b) achievement-oriented (c) transformational (d) directive

Short Response

11. Why are both position power and personal power essential in management?

12. Use Fiedler's terms to list the characteristics of situations that would be extremely favorable and extremely unfavorable to a leader.

13. Describe the situations in which path-goal theory would expect a participative leadership style and a directive leadership style to work best.

14. How do you sum up in two or three sentences the notion of servant leadership?

Integration & Application

When Marcel Henry took over as leader of a new product development team, he was both excited and apprehensive. "I wonder," he said to himself on the first day in his new assignment, "if I can meet the challenges of leadership." Later that day, Marcel shares this concern with you during a coffee break.

Questions: Based on the insights of this module, how would you describe to him the personal implications in this team setting of current thinking on transformational and moral leadership?

INSTRUCTIONS *For each of the following 10 pairs of statements, divide 5 points between the two according to your beliefs about which of the two statements characterizes you better. You cannot split the points equally (2— 1/2) between the two.*

1 (a) As leader I have a primary mission of maintaining stability.
(b) As leader I have a primary mission of change.

2 (a) As leader I must cause events.
(b) As leader I must facilitate events.

3 (a) I am concerned that my followers are rewarded equitably for their work.
(b) I am concerned about what my followers want in life.

4 (a) My preference is to think long range: What might be.
(b) My preference is to think short range: What is realistic.

5 (a) As a leader I spend considerable energy in managing separate but related goals.
(b) As a leader I spend considerable energy in arousing hopes, expectations, and aspirations among my followers.

6 (a) Although not in a formal classroom sense, I believe that a significant part of my leadership is that of teacher.
(b) I believe that a significant part of my leadership is that of facilitator.

7 (a) As leader I must engage with followers on an equal level of morality.
(b) As leader I must represent a higher morality.

8 (a) I enjoy stimulating followers to want to do more.
(b) I enjoy rewarding followers for a job well done.

9 (a) Leadership should be practical.
(b) Leadership should be inspirational.

10 (a) What power I have to influence others comes primarily from my ability to get people to identify with me and my ideas.
(b) What power I have to influence others comes primarily from my status and position.

SCORING AND INTERPRETATION

Circle your points for items 1b, 2a, 3b, 4a, 5b, 6a, 7b, 8a, 9b, 10a and add up the total points you allocated to these items; enter the score here [**T** = _____]. This gives an impression of your tendencies toward "transformational" leadership.

Next, add up the total points given to the uncircled items 1a, 2b, 3a, 4b, 5a, 6b, 7a, 8b, 9a, 10b; enter the score here [*T* = _____]. This gives an impression of your tendencies toward "transactional" leadership.

PATHWAYS to WileyPLUS

WILEY PLUS

CASE SNAPSHOT

Go online to read this case!

Richard Branson: Man on a Mission

This larger-than-life maverick billionaire has a very different personality than another billionaire who is more recognizable in the United States: Donald Trump. How have Branson's edginess, unpredictability, and sense of adventure shaped Virgin's development?

MODULE 16 — Online Interactive Learning Resources

Self-Assessments
• "T-P" Leadership
• LPC Scale

Skill Builder
• Empowerment

Experiential Exercises
• Sources of Power
• Leading by Participation

Team Project
• Gender and Leadership

Listening can be the key

Communication

If you really thought about leadership and leadership development in the previous module, you'll have to admit that "communication" deserves a top spot on the list of basic leadership skills. Indeed, how well we communicate and deal with others in interpersonal relationships is going to have a big impact on how we are perceived and received as leaders. But not everyone gets it right all the time; most of us probably get it right some of the time. All of us could do better. And sometimes we can improve with expert help.

The internationally regarded Center for Creative Leadership, in Greensboro, North Carolina, understands the importance of communication and interpersonal skills in leadership development. The center's mission is

to understanding

"to advance the understanding, practice and development of leadership for the benefit of society worldwide." One focus for that mission is active coaching for leadership development.

Richard Herlich came to the center after being recently promoted to be the director of marketing for his firm. "I thought I had the perfect style," he said. But in feedback sessions following role-playing exercises, he learned that wasn't how others saw him. Instead he was perceived as aloof and a poor communicator. Richard made it a point to go back to his job, meet with his marketing team, and discuss his personal style. And he ended up becoming more involved in their work projects.

Another participant, Robert Siddall, learned through feedback that he was too structured and domineering. He worked with instructors on how to develop more positive relationships and use more of a coaching style of management. After returning to his job, his performance ratings went up as his relationships with co-workers improved. He says, "If I start screaming and yelling, they say— 'Old Bob, old Bob.' "[1]

→ MODULE GUIDE

 17.1 What is communication and when is it effective?

- Communication is a process of sending and receiving messages with meanings attached.
- Communication is effective when the receiver understands the sender's message.
- Communication is persuasive when the receiver acts as the sender intends.
- Poor use of communication channels makes it hard to communicate effectively.
- Information filtering can bias communication between lower and higher levels.

 17.2 How can we improve communication with people at work?

- Active listening helps people say what they really mean.
- Constructive feedback is specific, timely, and relevant.
- Open communication channels build trust and improve upward communication.
- Office spaces can be designed to encourage interaction and communication.
- Appropriate technology can facilitate more and better communication.
- Sensitivity and etiquette can improve cross-cultural communication.

Communication is at the heart of the management process.[2] You might think of it as the glue that binds together the four functions of planning, organizing, leading, and controlling. Henry Mintzberg described managers as information nerve centers, continually gathering information, processing it, using it for problem solving, and sharing it with others.[3] John Kotter described effective general managers as entwined in complex webs of interpersonal networks through which they implement work priorities and agendas.[4] And from the firing line itself, Pam Alexander, as CEO of Ogilvy Public Relations Worldwide, says: "Relationships are the most powerful form of media. Ideas will only get you so far these days. Count on personal relationships to carry you further."[5]

Having read all this, would it surprise you that when the American Management Association asked members to rate the communication skills of their managers, only 22.1 percent rated them "high"?[6] The respondents also rated their bosses only slightly above average on transforming ideas into words, credibility, listening and asking questions, and written and oral presentations.[7] And even though communication skills regularly top the lists of characteristics looked for by corporate recruiters, why is it that 81 percent of college professors in one survey rated high school graduates as "fair" or "poor" in writing clearly?

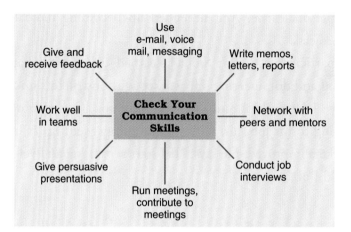

Strong communication skills could differentiate you from others wanting the same job or internship. How do you stand? Can you convince a recruiter that you have the communication skills necessary for success in your career field?

• Communication Is a Process of Sending and Receiving Messages with Meanings Attached

As you think about the prior questions, look at Figure 17.1. It describes **communication** as the interpersonal process of sending and receiving symbols with messages attached to them. Although it is simple and commonsense, there is a lot of room for error in the process. At each step things can be done well or poorly, with communication faring better or worse as a consequence.

In communication a *sender* encodes an intended message into meaningful symbols, both verbal and nonverbal. He or she sends the *message* through a *communication channel* to a *receiver*, who then decodes or interprets its meaning. This *interpretation* may or may not match the sender's original intentions. When present, *feedback* reverses the process and conveys the receiver's response back to the sender.

Communication is the process of sending and receiving symbols with meanings attached.

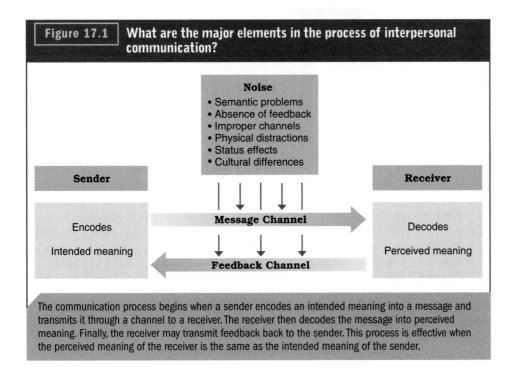

Figure 17.1 What are the major elements in the process of interpersonal communication?

Noise
- Semantic problems
- Absence of feedback
- Improper channels
- Physical distractions
- Status effects
- Cultural differences

Sender

Encodes

Intended meaning

Message Channel

Feedback Channel

Receiver

Decodes

Perceived meaning

The communication process begins when a sender encodes an intended meaning into a message and transmits it through a channel to a receiver. The receiver then decodes the message into perceived meaning. Finally, the receiver may transmit feedback back to the sender. This process is effective when the perceived meaning of the receiver is the same as the intended meaning of the sender.

• Communication Is Effective When the Receiver Understands the Sender's Message

Another way to describe the communication process is as a series of questions: "Who?" (sender) "says what?" (message) "in what way?" (channel) "to whom?" (receiver) "with what result?" (interpreted meaning). And in this context, an important question becomes: Do receiver and sender understand things the same ways?

Effective communication occurs when the receiver fully understands the sender's intended message; the intended meaning matches the received meaning. As you well know, this outcome can't be taken for granted; it just doesn't always happen. One reason is a trade-off between effectiveness and efficiency. **Efficient communication** occurs at minimum cost in terms of resources expended. And of these costs, time and convenience, in particular, often become very influential in how we choose to communicate.

Picture your instructor speaking individually, face-to-face, with each student about this module. This could be very effective, but it would certainly be inefficient in terms of the cost of his or her time. This is why we often send text messages, leave voice-mail messages, and use e-mail, rather than speak directly with other people. But although quick and easy, are they always effective? The next time you have something important to communicate, you might pause and consider the effectiveness–efficiency trade-offs.

• Communication Is Persuasive When the Receiver Acts as the Sender Intends

In life and in management we often want not just to be heard, but to be followed. That is, we want our communication to "persuade" the other party to believe or behave in a specific way that we intend. In communication, **persuasion** is getting someone else to accept, support, and act consistent with the sender's message.[8]

If you agree that managers get most things done through other people, you should also agree that managers must be very good at persuasive communication. Yet, scholar and consultant Jay Conger believes that many managers "confuse persuasion with bold stands and aggressive arguing." This sounds a lot like the so-called "debates" that we watch on television as advocates of different political viewpoints face off against one another. A lot is said, some of it quite aggressively, but little influence takes place. Conger believes that the approach can also raise questions about one's credibility.[9] And without

In **effective communication** the receiver fully understands the intended meaning.

Efficient communication occurs at minimum cost.

Persuasion is presenting a message in a manner that causes others to support it.

Layout and design can be a big boost in communicating for innovation

New products don't just appear from nowhere. They are created by people, often working together in teams with a simple but challenging charge: "Do something different, really different!" From Apple's Video

iPod to Motorola's Razr cellphone to the latest new toy or gadget, we're talking the same game. It's all about getting people together in a work environment that facilitates the free flow of ideas; a place that makes creativity and innovation easy. Fisher-Price Toys, part of Mattel, Inc., has such a place in a separate part of its headquarters. Called the "Cave," its not your typical office space. Picture bean-bag chairs, soft

lighting, casual chairs and couches. It's a place for brainstorming, where designers, marketeers, engineers, and others can meet and join in freewheeling to come up with the next great toy for preschoolers. Consultants recommend that such innovation spaces be separated from the normal workplace and be large enough for no more than 15 to 20 people.

Reflect: Look around. How often do you see people working in spaces that make communication harder, not easier? Is the model of the "Cave" transferable to workplaces where the issue may not be creativity per se, but just getting things done well with the help of other people?

Noise is anything that interferes with the communication process.

A **communication channel** is the medium used to carry a message.

Nonverbal communication takes place through gestures and body language.

credibility—trust, respect, and integrity in the eyes of others, he sees little chance for successful persuasion.

The late Sam Walton, Wal-Mart's founder, was considered a master of persuasive communication. Conger says this is a learned skill, one based on personal power of expertise and reference. Consider an example – classic Walton in action. Stopping once to visit a Memphis store, he called everyone to the front, saying: "Northeast Memphis, you're the largest store in Memphis, and you must have the best floor-cleaning crew in America. This floor is so clean, let's sit down on it." Picture Walton kneeling casually and wearing his Wal-Mart baseball cap. He congratulated the employees on their fine work. "I thank you. The company is so proud of you we can hardly stand it," he said. "But," he added, "you know that confounded Kmart is getting better, and so is Target. So what's our challenge?" Walton asked. "Customer service," he replied in answer to his own question. And everyone present took his message to heart.[10]

• Poor Use of Communication Channels Makes It Hard to Communicate Effectively

Noise, as previously shown in Figure 17.1, is anything that interferes with the effectiveness of the communication process. In international business, for example, one should be prepared to deal with language differences in communication. When Yoshihiro Wada was president of Mazda Corporation, he had to use interpreters when meeting with representatives of the firm's U.S. joint venture partner, Ford. He estimated that he lost 20 percent of his intended meaning in the exchange between himself and the interpreter, and another 20 percent between the interpreter and the Americans.[11]

Yoshihiro's problem is pretty easy to recognize, but many times the noise that interferes with communication is a lot more subtle. Problems can arise from a poor choice of **communication channel**, the medium used to carry the message.[12] Written channels such as memos, e-mails, and letters work well for conveying simple messages, and those that require extensive dissemination quickly. Spoken channels are more personal and can create a supportive, even inspirational relationship between sender and receiver. They work especially well face-to-face, when we need to convey complex or difficult messages and when we need immediate feedback.

Quality of *written or oral expression* is another potential sourse of noise. Consider this statement taken from a business report: "Consumer elements are continuing to stress the fundamental necessity of a stabilization of the price structure at a lower level than exists at the present time." If you're like me, you probably need to read it several times. Wouldn't it have been simpler to just say: "Consumers want prices to go down and stay down"?

We both know that written and oral communication require skill, that words need to be well chosen to express our intentions. It isn't easy to write a concise letter or report, or deliver a great oral presentation (see the *Exhibit – How to Make a Successful Presentation*).[13] In fact, it takes a lot of practice. There's no getting around it; good writing and good speaking are the products of plain old hard work. But it's well worth the investment. Are you willing to make it? Take the test: How many drafts do you write for memos, letters, reports; how often do you practice for an oral presentation?

The ways we use **nonverbal communication** can also work for or against our communication effectiveness. Hand movements, facial expressions, body posture, eye contact, and the use of interpersonal space are all important.[14] These nonverbals send both intentional and unintentional messages. A good listener, for example, knows how to read the body language of a speaker while listening to the words being spoken.

Sometimes our body may be talking even when we choose to remain silent; when we do speak, our body may say something quite different. This is called a **mixed message**, when a person's words communicate one thing while his or her nonverbals communicate something else.

Also, don't neglect the role of *physical distractions* in disrupting communication. Have you ever tried to talk with someone about an important matter, only to have that conversation interrupted by phone calls? Any number of distractions, from drop-in visitors to instant messages to ringing cell phones, can interfere with the effectiveness of a communication attempt. What can we do? One way to solve the problem is to plan ahead. If you have something important to say or hear, set aside adequate time, choose the right location, and take steps to avoid interruptions—including turning the cell phone off.

• Information Filtering Can Bias Communication between Lower and Higher Levels

The risk of ineffective communication may be highest when people are communicating upward in organizations, with the boss in particular. Haven't you heard people say things like this? "Criticize my boss? I'd get fired." "It's her company, not mine." "I can't tell him that; he'll just get mad at me."

We have to be realistic; the hierarchy of authority is a potential barrier to effective communication between lower and higher levels in organizations. This problem arises because of **filtering**—the intentional distortion of information to make it appear favorable to the recipient. You know this as "telling the boss or instructor what he or she wants to hear." And it's more common than many people think. Consultant Tom Peters calls it "Management Enemy Number 1."[15]

Whether caused by fear of retribution for bringing bad news, an unwillingness to identify personal mistakes, or just a general desire to please, the end result of filtering is the same. Lower levels "cleanse" the information sent to higher levels; the higher levels, although well intentioned, make poor decisions because their information is inaccurate or incomplete. And the consequences can be significant. Consider a "corporate cover-up" once discovered at an electronics company. Workers were predating product shipments and falsifying paperwork to artificially show that they were meeting unrealistic sales targets set by the president. At least 20 persons cooperated in the deception, and it was months before top management found out.

A **mixed message** results when words communicate one message while actions, body language, or appearance communicate something else.

Filtering is the intentional distortion of information to make it more favorable to the recipient.

Be Sure You Can . . .

- describe the communication process and identify its key components

- differentiate effective and efficient communication

- explain the role of credibility in persuasive communication

- list common sources of noise that interefere with effective communication

- explain how filtering operates in upward communication

Define the Terms

Communication

Communication channel

Effective communication

Efficient communication

Filtering

Mixed message

Noise

Nonverbal communication

Persuasion

Rapid Review

- Communication is the interpersonal process of sending and receiving symbols with messages attached to them.

- Effective communication occurs when the sender and the receiver of a message both interpret it in the same way; efficient communication occurs when the sender conveys the message at low cost.

- Persuasive communication results in the recipient acting as the sender intends.

- Credibility earned by expertise and good relationships is essential to persuasive communication.

- Noise interferes with the effectiveness of communication; it results from poor utilization of channels, including poor written or oral expression and the presence of physical distractions.

- Upward communication in organizations is sometimes compromised by filtering, intentional distortion of information to make a message as favorable as possible to higher levels.

Reflect/React

1. In what situations can you accept less communication effectiveness in order to gain communication efficiency?

2. Can persuasive communication occur without the sender having credibility?

3. What can a manager do to protect against filtering in communications received from subordinates?

With all the possible noise in the communication process, don't you wonder how we ever communicate effectively? Fortunately, there are a number of things we can do to overcome or minimize the effects of communication barriers as well as improve our communication behaviors.

• Active Listening Helps People Say What they Really Mean

When people talk, they are trying to communicate something. That "something" may or may not be what they are saying. **Active listening** is the process of taking action to help someone say what he or she really means. It requires being sincere while listening to someone, and trying to find the full meaning of a message. It also involves being disciplined, controlling one's emotions, and withholding premature evaluations or interpretations that can turn off rather than turn on the other party's willingness to communicate.

See the *Exhibit – Carl Rogers's Five Rules for Active Listening*.[16] You can get a flavor for it by contrasting the "passive" listener and "active" listener in the following samples of actual workplace conversations:

Question 1: "Don't you think employees should be promoted on the basis of seniority?"
Passive listener's response: "No, I don't!"
Active listener's response: "It seems to you that they should; did something happen to make you think about this?"

Question 2: "What does the supervisor expect us to do about these out-of-date computers?"
Passive listener's response: "Do the best you can, I guess."
Active listener's response: "It sounds like you're pretty disgusted with those machines; what do you think might be a first step in solving this problem?"

• Constructive Feedback Is Specific, Timely, and Relevant

When Lydia Whitfield, a marketing vice president at Avaya, asked one of her managers for feedback, she was surprised. He said: "You're angry a lot." Whitfield learned from the experience, saying: "What he and other employees saw as my anger, I saw as my passion."[17] **Feedback** is the process of telling other people how you feel about something they did or said, or about the situation in general.

The art of giving feedback is an indispensable skill for managers. When poorly given, critical feedback can easily come off as threatening and create more resentment than positive action. When the feedback is *constructive*, however, the receiver is more likely to listen and carefully consider the message, and even make some personal commitment to using it to best advantage.[18]

Take a look at the tips for giving constructive feedback in the box. Are there things you can learn to do better? Would you agree that constructive feedback is essential if performance appraisals are to be helpful for developmental purposes?

Active listening helps the source of a message say what he or she really means.

Feedback is the process of telling someone else how you feel about something that person did or said.

EXHIBIT

Carl Rogers's five rules for active listening

1. **Listen for message content**—Try to hear exactly what content the message is conveying.

2. **Listen for feelings**—Try to identify how the source feels about the content in the message.

3. **Respond to feelings**—Let the source know that you recognize her or his feelings.

4. **Note all cues**—Be sensitive to nonverbal and verbal messages; be alert for mixed messages.

5. **Paraphrase and restate**—State back to the source what you think you are hearing.

Managers using **MBWA** spend time out of their offices, meeting and talking with workers at all levels.

• Open Communication Channels Build Trust and Improve Upward Communication

Managers really can't afford to be on the receiving end of the filtering problem we discussed earlier. They need good information from the people who work for them if they are to make good decisions. One way of keeping channels open is **management by wandering around (MBWA)**. As the name implies, MBWA takes place when managers get out of their offices and simply spend time walking around and talking face-to-face with people.

MBWA is a way of breaking down status barriers and building relationships; it encourages people to share more and better information about themselves and their work. Patricia Gallup, CEO of PC Connection, became known for her interactive style of leadership and emphasis on communication. By making herself available by e-mail and spending as much time as possible out of her office, she made MBWA part of her style.[19]

There are other ways to open communication channels as well. Managers, like college professors, can get a lot of benefits from holding *open office hours*, setting aside time in their busy calendars to welcome walk-in visits. Today this approach can be easily expanded with information technologies; we have access to everything from e-mail to Instant Messaging to online chat rooms to Intranet discussion groups. All we have to do is open the channels and then use them well.

Holding regular *employee group meetings* is another helpful technique. Here, a rotating schedule of "shirtsleeve" meetings brings top managers into face-to-face contact with mixed employee groups throughout an organization. And again, the traditional face-to-face group meetings can be replaced by electronic ones powered by *computer conferencing* and *videoconferencing* to overcome time and distance limitations. Some organizations even use *employee advisory councils* whose members are elected by their fellow employees. Such councils meet with management on a regular schedule to discuss and react to new policies and programs that will affect employees.

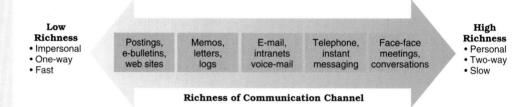

Low Richness
- Impersonal
- One-way
- Fast

| Postings, e-bulletins, web sites | Memos, letters, logs | E-mail, intranets voice-mail | Telephone, instant messaging | Face-face meetings, conversations |

High Richness
- Personal
- Two-way
- Slow

Richness of Communication Channel

Managers sometimes hire communication consultants to analyze communication practices and make recommendations for improvements. A consultant might interview or survey members to gather their views on communication and relationships, and then share the results with management. The process can be enlightening. Marc Brownstein, president of a public relations and advertising firm, was surprised when managers in an anonymous survey complained that he listened poorly and gave them insufficient feedback. They also said they were inadequately informed about the firm's financial health. His poor communication from the top was hurting staff morale. With help from consultants, Brownstein changed his style to hold more meetings and work more aggressively to share information and communicate regularly with the firm's employees.[20]

• Office Spaces Can Be Designed to Encourage Interaction and Communication

Proxemics is the study of the way we use space.

The way we use space, **proxemics**, is an important but sometimes neglected influence on communication.[21] We know that physical distance between people conveys varying intentions in terms of intimacy, openness, and status as they communicate with one another. But we might not be as sensitive to how the physical layout of an office can do the same things.

Think about your office and those of persons with whom you often visit. What messages do they send to visitors, just by the layouts and furnishings? And it's not only individual offices that count in this respect. Architects and consultants are helping executives

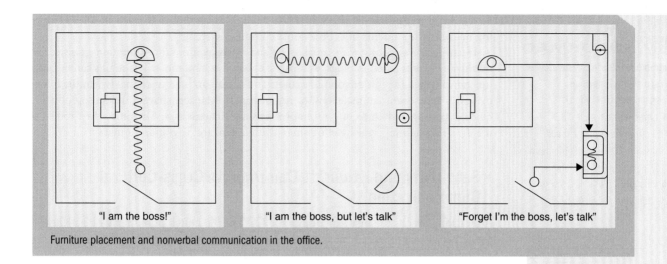

| "I am the boss!" | "I am the boss, but let's talk" | "Forget I'm the boss, let's talk" |

Furniture placement and nonverbal communication in the office.

build entire office spaces that are conducive to the intense, multilevel and cross-functional communications desired today. Sun Microsystems did this for a new facility in San Jose, California. Public spaces were designed to encourage communication among persons from different departments. The project relied on extensive suggestions from the employees. And the results seemed to justify the effort. One employee called it "the most productive workspace I have ever been in."[22]

• Appropriate Technology Can Facilitate More and Better Communication

IBM is known for technology leadership. But when the firm surveyed employees to find out how they learned what was going on at the company, executives got some good insights. They found out that co-workers were viewed as the most credible and useful information sources, and that information shared on the firm's intranet ranked equally high. In fact, IBM's internal websites were ranked higher than news briefs, company memos, and information provided by managers.[23]

The new age of communication is one of e-mail, voice mail, instant messaging, teleconferencing, online discussions, videoconferencing, virtual meetings, intranets, Web portals, and even blogs. But the technologies work for us only when they are used properly. Knowing how and when to use e-mail (see Management Tips) is a good case in point.[24] Intel once discovered that some of its employees faced up to 300 e-mail messages a day and spent some 2.5 hours per day dealing with them. The firm initiated a training program to improve e-mail utilization and efficiency.[25]

And don't forget that purpose and privacy are two big concerns with e-mail. Employers worry that too much work time gets spent handling personal e-mail; employees know that employers may eavesdrop on their e-mail messages. The advice first offered in Module 11 on controls and control systems is worth repeating. Find out the employer's policy on personal e-mail and follow it; don't ever assume that you have e-mail privacy at work.[26]

Communication technology also plays a role in the informal structures of organizations. It has created a new force to be reckoned with: the power of the *electronic grapevine*. Think of this example. The members of a sixth-grade class in Taylorsville, North Carolina (population 1566) sent out this e-mail message: "Hi! . . . We are curious to see where

MANAGEMENT TIPS

How to manage your e-mail

- Read items only once.
- Take action immediately to answer, move to folders, or delete.
- Purge folders regularly of useless messages.
- Send group mail and use "Reply to all" only when really necessary.
- Get off distribution lists without value to your work.
- Send short messages in subject line, avoiding a full-text message.
- Put large files on websites, instead of sending as attachments.
- Use Instant Messaging as an e-mail alternative.
- Double-check everything before hitting the "Send" button.
- Don't hit the "Send" button when angry; wait, take time to revise and rethink.
- Remember the iron rule of e-mail privacy: There isn't any.

Ethnocentrism is the tendency to consider one's culture superior to any and all others.

Cultural etiquette is use of appropriate manners and behaviors in cross-cultural situations.

in the world our e-mail will travel." Over a half-million replies flooded in, overwhelming not only the students but the school's computer system.[27]

Electronic messages fly with equal speed and intensity around organizations, assisted by informal networks based in blogs, webspaces, e-mail lists, and more. The results can be both functional (when the information is accurate and useful) and dysfunctional (when the information is false, distorted, malicious, or rumor based). Managers have to be on top of it all, quickly spotting and correcting misimpressions and inaccuracies. Of course they, too, can use the electronic grapevine by informing it with factual and relevant information.

• Sensitivity and Etiquette Can Improve Cross-Cultural Communication

After taking over as the first American to be CEO of the Dutch publisher Wolters Kluwer, Nancy McKinstry initiated major changes in strategy and operations—cutting staff, restructuring divisions, and investing in new business areas. She first described the new strategy as "aggressive" in speaking with her management team. But after learning the word wasn't well received by Europeans, she switched to "decisive." She says: "I was coming across as too harsh, too much of a results-driven American to the people I needed to get on board," says McKinstry, offering us a nice lesson in cross-cultural communication.[28]

When it comes to communicating, there is no doubt that cultural differences are a ready source of potential problems. And don't forget that you don't have be doing international business or taking a foreign vacation for this to be relevant. Just going to work and out to shop is a cross-cultural journey for most of us today. Furthermore, you should recall from Module 6 on diversity and global cultures that **ethnocentrism** is a major source of intercultural difficulties. It is the tendency to consider one's culture superior to any and all others.

Tendencies toward ethnocentrism can hurt cross-cultural communication in at least three ways. First, they may cause someone to not listen well to what others have to say. Second, they may cause someone to address or speak with others in ways that alienate them. And, third, they may involve use of inappropriate stereotypes.

Just recognizing tendencies toward ethnocentrism is a starting point for improving cross-cultural communication. You can spot it in conversations as arrogance in one's tone, manners, gestures, and words. But success in cross-cultural communication also takes sensitivity and a willingness to learn about how different people see, do, and interpret things. This involves a basic awareness of **cultural etiquette**, the use of appropriate manners and behaviors when communicating with people from other cultures. Cutural etiquette begins with recognition that the ways and customs of our culture, things we might naturally be inclined to use, do, or say, won't necessarily work in the same ways or mean the same things in another. Knowing the etiquette helps us avoid basic cross-cultural mistakes.

An example of at least an attempt at improving cultural etiquette took place when Atlanta was preparing to host the summer Olympic games in 1996. The organizing committee gathered and shared information about cultural sensitivity and manners in many common situations. This included these differences in how hand gestures communicate. The American "thumbs-up" sign is an insult in Ghana and Australia; signaling "OK" with thumb and forefinger circled together is not okay in parts of Europe; whereas we wave "hello" with an open palm, in West Africa it's an insult, suggesting the other person has five fathers.[29]

PACESETTERS

Top posts in foreign companies a real challenge for American CEOs.

It may be one of the toughest challenges in management, to be asked to lead a company headquartered in a foreign country. But that's starting to happen more often in today's global economy and with more corporations seeking "transnational" status. Here's an interesting one: Harold Stringer. He's not your average CEO for sure. Born in Wales, studied at Oxford, served in the U.S. Army, knighted by Queen Elizabeth II, and in a 30-year career at CBS is supposedly the one who brought in David Letterman to host CBS Latenight. And now he is CEO and Chairman of SONY Corporation, a firm facing a host of challenges in the global marketplace. Stringer is the first non-Japanese CEO of the firm and he faces not only the typical strategic leadership challenges, but also the cross-cultural ones. After taking over at SONY's headquarters in Japan, Stringer heard that one of the departments was concerned about poor communications with another. How did he respond? He did things the Japanese way. "I promised to throw them all a party to get to know each other," he says. And to keep the communication channels open, he works not from an isolated executive suite but from a mid-level office in the headquarters building, from which he stays in close contact with SONY's managers.

Herold Stringer, CEO, and Chairman, SONY Corporation

STUDY GUIDE

17.2 How can we improve communication with people at work?

Be Sure You Can . . .

- illustrate the practice of active listening

- list the rules for giving constructive feedback

- explain how MBWA can improve upward communication

- explain how space design influences communication

- identify ways technology utilization influences communication

- explain the concept of cultural etiquette

Define the Terms

Active listening

Cultural etiquette

Ethnocentrism

Feedback

Management by wandering around (MBWA)

Proxemics

Rapid Review

- Active listening, through reflecting back and paraphrasing, can help overcome barriers and improve communication.

- Interactive management through MBWA and use of structured meetings, suggestion systems, and advisory councils can improve upward communication.

- Organizations can design and use office architecture and physical space to improve communication.

- Information technology, such as e-mail, instant messaging, and intranets, can improve communication in organizations, but it must be well used.

- Ethnocentrism, feelings of cultural superiority, can interfere with the effectiveness of cross-cultural communication; with sensitivity and cultural etiquette such communication can be improved.

Reflect/React

1. Which rules for active listening do you think most people break?

2. Is MBWA a sure winner, or could a manager have problems with it?

3. How could you redesign your office space to make it more communication friendly?

Multiple Choice

1. A manager who uses paraphrasing and reflecting back of what someone else is saying in order to encourage them to say what they really mean is using a communication technique known as _____.
   (a) mixed messaging (b) active listening (c) constructive feedback (d) filtering

2. When the intended meaning of the sender and the interpreted meaning of the receiver are the same, communication is _____.
   (a) effective (b) persuasive (c) passive (d) efficient

3. One of the rules for giving constructive feedback is to make sure that it is always _____.
   (a) general rather than specific (b) indirect rather than direct (c) given in small doses (d) given at a time convenient for the sender

4. When a worker receives an e-mail memo from the boss with information about changes to his job assignment and ends up confused because he doesn't understand it, the boss has erred by making a bad choice of_____ for communicating the message.
   (a) words (b) channels (c) nonverbals (d) filters

5. _____ is a form of interactive management that helps improve upward communication.
   (a) Attribution (b) Mediation (c) MBWA (d) Proxemics

6. If a visitor to a foreign culture continues to make gestures that are commonly used at home even after learning that they are offensive to locals, the visitor can be described as _____.
   (a) a passive listener (b) ethnocentric (c) more efficient than effective (d) an active listener

7. In order to be truly and consistently persuasive when communicating in the workplace, a manager should build credibility by making sure _____.
   (a) rewards for compliance with requests are clear
   (b) penalties for noncompliance with requests are clear
   (c) everyone knows who is the boss (d) to have good relationships established with others

8. A manager who understands the importance of proxemics in communication is likely to _____.
   (a) avoid sending mixed messages (b) arrange work spaces so as to encourage interaction (c) be very careful choosing written and spoken words (d) send frequent e-mail messages to team members

9. When a person's words say one thing but his or her body language suggests something quite different, the person is said to be communicating _____.
   (a) a mixed message (b) noise (c) through the wrong channel (d) destructive feedback

10. The advice for managers to spend time out of the office every day, talking with and listening to people doing their jobs, is part of a communication approach known as _____.
    (a) active listening (b) cultural etiquette (c) MBWA (d) credibility

Short Response

11. What is the goal of active listening?

12. Why is it that well-intentioned managers sometimes make bad decisions based on information received from their subordinates?

13. What are four major errors a manager can make in trying to give someone else constructive feedback?

14. How does ethnocentrism influence cross-cultural communication?

Integration & Application

Glenn Pool was recently promoted to be the manager of a new store being opened by a large department store chain. Glenn wants to start out right, making sure that communications are always good between him, the six department heads, and the 50 full-time and part-time sales associates. He knows that he'll be making a lot of decisions in the new job and he wants to be sure that he is always well informed about store operations, and that everyone is always "on the same page" about important priorities. Put yourself in Glenn's shoes.

Questions: What steps should Glenn take right from the beginning to ensure that he and the department managers communicate well with one another? What can he do to open up and maintain good channels of communication with the sales associates?

SELF-ASSESSMENT
Assertiveness

INSTRUCTIONS *For each statement below, decide which of the following answers best fits you.*

1 = Never true; 2 = Sometimes true;
3 = Often true; 4 = Always true

1 I respond with more modesty than I really feel when my work is complimented.

2 If people are rude, I will be rude right back.

3 Other people find me interesting.

4 I find it difficult to speak up in a group of strangers.

5 I don't mind using sarcasm if it helps me make a point.

6 I ask for a raise when I feel I really deserve it.

7 If others interrupt me when I am talking, I suffer in silence.

8 If people criticize my work, I find a way to make them back down.

9 I can express pride in my accomplishments without being boastful.

10 People take advantage of me.

11 I tell people what they want to hear if it helps me get what I want.

12 I find it easy to ask for help.

13 I lend things to others even when I don't really want to.

14 I win arguments by dominating the discussion.

15 I can express my true feelings to someone I really care for.

16 When I feel angry with other people, I bottle it up rather than express it.

17 When I criticize someone else's work, they get mad.

18 I feel confident in my ability to stand up for my rights.

SCORING AND INTERPRETATION
Obtain your scores as follows:

Aggressiveness tendency score—Add items 2, 5, 8, 11, 14, and 17
Passiveness tendency score—Add items 1, 4, 7, 10, 13, and 16
Assertiveness tendency score—Add items 3, 6, 9, 12, 15, and 18

The maximum score in any single area is 24. The minimum score is 6. Try to find someone who knows you well. Have this person complete the instrument also as it relates to you. Compare his or her impression of you with your own score. What is this telling you about your behavior tendencies in social situations?

PATHWAYS to WileyPLUS

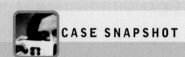
CASE SNAPSHOT

Go online to read this case!

Tom Anderson and Chris DeWolfe: From Rock 'n' Roll to Pot of Gold

The MySpace.com founders just want people to meet and get along, and they believe that budding relationships shouldn't be hindered by server issues and proprietary "friendship" limitations of Friendster. And since 2003, MySpace has become the number-one social networking site.

MODULE 17 | **Online Interactive Learning Resources**

Skill Builder
- Listening

Experiential Exercises
- Upward Appraisal
- How to Give and Take Criticism

Team Project
- How Words Count

There's beauty in

Individual Behavior

Herman Miller, Inc., is an innovative Michigan-based maker of office furniture. That in itself may not sound too exiciting. But, Max DePree, the firm's former chairperson and the son of its founder, is a well-known leadership thinker. He tells the story of a millwright who worked for his father. When the man died, DePree's father, wishing to express his sympathy to the family, went to their home. There he listened as the widow read some beautiful poems which, to his surprise, the millwright had written.

From that day forward, DePree says that his father often wondered, "Was the man a poet who did millwright's work, or a millwright who wrote poetry?" He summarizes the lesson of the story this way: "It is fundamental that leaders endorse a concept of persons."[1]

individual differences

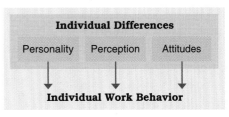

People are unique and there is beauty in that fact, as both this story and the module subtitle suggest. But how appreciative are we of the differences among us? Do we realize how personalities, perceptions, and attitudes affect behavior? And, are we aware of the tools and insights from psychology that can help us better understand them?

DePree's story tells of someone's very personal qualities. Were they hidden from DePree's father, or did he just fail to see them amid daily work routines?

We have talked a lot in this book about valuing and respecting people's abilities and performance potential. At issue now are individual differences, the personalities, perceptions, and attitudes that distinguish people and influence their behaviors. If we accept that each of us has the gift of uniqueness and are willing to explore it, perhaps that opens doors to leadership and managerial success that might have been as hidden as the poet in Max DePree's story.

Individual Differences

Personality	Perception	Attitudes
↓	↓	↓

Individual Work Behavior

→ MODULE GUIDE

 18.1 How do personalities influence individual behavior?

- The Big Five personality traits describe work-related individual differences.
- Additional personality traits can also influence work behavior.
- People with Type A personalities tend to stress themselves.
- Stress has consequences for work performance and personal health.

 18.2 How do perceptions influence individual behavior?

- Perceptual distortions can obscure individual differences.
- Perception sometimes causes attribution errors as we explain events and problems.

- Impression management is a way of influencing how others perceive us.

 18.3 How do attitudes influence individual behavior?

- Attitudes predispose people to act in certain ways.
- Job satisfaction is a positive attitude toward one's job and work experiences.
- Job satisfaction can predict absenteeism, turnover, and organizational citizenship.
- Job satisfaction has a complex relationship with job performance.

Personality is the profile of characteristics making a person unique from others.

Think of how many times you've complained about someone's "bad personality" or told a friend how much you like someone else because they had such a "nice personality." Well, the same holds true at work. Perhaps you have been part of or the object of conversations like these: "I can't give him that job. He's a bad fit; with a personality like that there's no way he can work with customers." Or, "Put Erika on the project; her personality is perfect for the intensity that we expect from the team."

In management we use the term **personality** to describe the combination or overall profile of enduring characteristics that makes each of us unique. And as the prior examples suggest, this uniqueness can have consequences for how we behave and how that behavior is regarded by others.

• The Big Five Personality Traits Describe Work-Related Individual Differences

EXHIBIT

How to Identify the Big Five Personality Traits

Extroversion   An extrovert is talkative, comfortable, and confident in interpersonal relationships; an introvert is more private, withdrawn, and reserved.

Agreeableness   An agreeable person is trusting, courteous, and helpful, getting along well with others; a disagreeable person is self-serving, skeptical, and tough, creating discomfort for others.

Conscientiousness   A conscientious person is dependable, organized, and focused on getting things done; a person who lacks conscientiousness is careless, impulsive, and not achievement oriented.

Emotional stability   A person who is emotionally stable is secure, calm, steady, and self-confident; a person lacking emotional stability is excitable, anxious, nervous, and tense.

Openness to Experience   A person open to experience is broad-minded, imaginative, and open to new ideas; a person who lacks openness is narrow-minded, has few interests, and resists change.

We all know that variations among personalities are both real and consequential in our relationships with everyone from family to friends to co-workers. To better understand their influence on work behavior, management scholars use a framework known as the *Big Five personality traits*. The Big Five are extroversion, agreeableness, conscientiousness, emotional stability, and openness to experience.[2] You can probably spot them pretty easily in people with whom you work, study, and socialize, as well as in yourself. Why not use the *Exhibit – How to Identify the Big Five Personality Traits* to take a quick check of your personality. Then ask: What are the implications for my interpersonal and working relationships?

In fact, the expectation is that people with more extroverted, agreeable, conscientious, emotionally stable, and open personalities will have more positive relationships and experiences in organizations.[3] Research indicates, in particular, that conscientious persons tend to be highly motivated in their work. Also, emotionally stable persons tend to handle change situations well. It's also likely that Big Five traits are implicit criteria used by managers when making judgments about people at work, handing out job assignments, building teams, and more. Psychologists even use the Big Five to steer people in the direction of career choices that may provide the best personality–job fits.

• Additional Personality Traits Can Also Influence Work Behavior

Locus of control is the extent to which one believes that what happens is within one's control.

In addition to the Big Five, Figure 18.1 shows a sampling of other personality traits that can influence how people behave and work together.[4] Among them, **locus of control** recognizes that some people believe they control their destinies while others believe what happens is beyond their control.[5] "Internals" are more self-confident and accept responsibility for their own actions; "externals" are prone to blaming others and outside forces when bad things happen. Interestingly, research suggests that internals tend to be more satisfied and less alienated from their work.

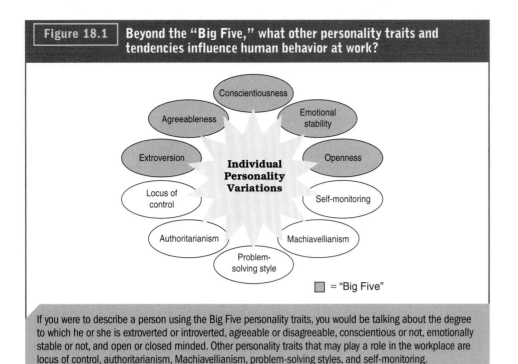

If you were to describe a person using the Big Five personality traits, you would be talking about the degree to which he or she is extroverted or introverted, agreeable or disagreeable, conscientious or not, emotionally stable or not, and open or closed minded. Other personality traits that may play a role in the workplace are locus of control, authoritarianism, Machiavellianism, problem-solving styles, and self-monitoring.

Authoritarianism is the degree to which a person defers to authority and accepts status differences.[6] Someone with an authoritarian personality might act rigid and control-oriented as a leader. Yet this same person is often subservient in a follower capacity. People with an authoritarian personality tend to obey orders. Of course this can create problems when their supervisors ask them to do unethical or even illegal things.

In his sixteenth-century book *The Prince*, Niccolo Machiavelli gained lasting fame for his advice on how to use power to achieve personal goals.[7] Today we use the term **Machiavellianism** to describe someone who is emotionally detached in using power or acts manipulatively. We usually view a "high-Mach" personality as exploitative and unconcerned about others, seemingly guided only by the rule that the end justifies the means. Those with "low-Mach" personality, by contrast, allow others to exert power over them.

The psychologist Carl Jung pointed out that people display significant differences in *problem-solving styles*.[8] People usually gather information by *sensation* (emphasizing details, facts, and routine) or by *intuition* (looking for the "big picture" and willing to deal with various possibilities). They evaluate information by *thinking* (using reason and analysis) or by *feeling* (responding to the feelings and desires of others).

When these differences are put together it creates the four problem-solving styles shown in the box. As you can see, people with the different styles approach things in quite different ways. Thus, it shouldn't surprise you that we all have difficulties at times in working with one another. Some organizations actually invest in training to help people understand their styles, spot the styles of others, and know better how to work with style differences. You might encounter training that uses the *Myers-Briggs Type Indicator*, a 100-question survey instrument, to measure problem-solving styles along these lines.

Finally, **self-monitoring** reflects the degree to which someone is able or unable to adjust and modify behavior in new situations.[9] This trait is an aspect of *emotional intelligence* as discussed in Module 16 on leadership. It involves the ability to recognize our emotions and behavioral tendencies, and to manage them for effectiveness in relationships with others.[10] Persons high in self-monitoring tend to be learners, comfortable with feedback, and both willing and able to change. Because they are flexible, however, others may perceive them as constantly shifting gears and hard to read. A person low in self-monitoring, by contrast, is predictable and tends to act consistently. But this consistency may not fit differing circumstances.

Authoritarianism is the degree to which a person defers to authority and accepts status differences.

Machiavellianism is the degree to which someone uses power manipulatively.

Self-monitoring is the degree to which someone is able to adjust behavior in response to external factors.

 Four Problem-Solving Styles

1. **"Sensation-Thinker"—approaches problems realistically; prefers facts, clear goals, certainty**
2. **"Intuitive-Thinker"—comfortable with abstraction and unstructured situations; tends to avoid details**
3. **"Intuitive-Feeler"—insightful, likes to deal with broad issues; values flexibility and relationships**
4. **"Sensation-Feeler"—emphasizes analysis using facts; open communicator, respects feelings and values**

• People with Type A Personalities Tend to Stress Themselves

Stress is a state of tension experienced by individuals facing extraordinary demands, constraints, or opportunities.[11] As you consider stress in your life and in your work, you might think about how your personality deals with it. Researchers describe the **Type A personality** as someone that is high in achievement orientation, impatience, and perfectionism. Type A's are likely to bring stress on themselves, even in circumstances that others find relatively stress-free.[12] Does this describe you?

The work environment has enough potential *stressors*, or sources of stress, without this added burden of a stress-prone personality. Some 34 percent of workers in one survey actually said that their jobs were so stressful that they were thinking of quitting.[13] The stress they were talking about comes from long hours of work, excessive e-mails, unrealistic work deadlines, difficult bosses or co-workers, unwelcome or unfamiliar work, and unrelenting change.[14]

As if this isn't enough for Type A's to deal with, there's the added kicker of stress in our personal lives. Things like family events (e.g., the birth of a new child), economics (e.g., a sudden loss of extra income), and personal issues (e.g., a preoccupation with a bad relationship) are all sources of potential emotional strain. Depending on how we deal with them, personal stressors can spill over to negatively affect our behavior at work. Of course the effects also hold in reverse; work stressors can have spillover impact on our personal lives.

• Stress Has Consequences for Work Performance and Personal Health

How does all of this add up as an influence on your work and life? It's tempting to view it all in the negative. But don't forget that stress can have its positive side as well.[15] Consider the analogy of a violin.[16] When a violin string is too loose, the sound produced by even the most skilled player is weak and raspy. When the string is too tight the sound gets shrill and the string might even snap. But when the tension on the string is just right, it creates a most beautiful sound. Just enough stress, in other words, may optimize performance.

In the workplace we talk about **constructive stress** that is energizing and performance enhancing.[17] You've probably felt this as a student. Don't you sometimes do better work "when the pressure is on," as we like to say? Moderate but not overwhelming stress can help us by encouraging effort, stimulating creativity, and enhancing diligence.

Just like tuning a violin string, however, achieving the right balance of stress for each person and situation is difficult. **Destructive stress** is dysfunctional when it is or seems to be so intense or long-lasting that it overloads and breaks down a person's physical and

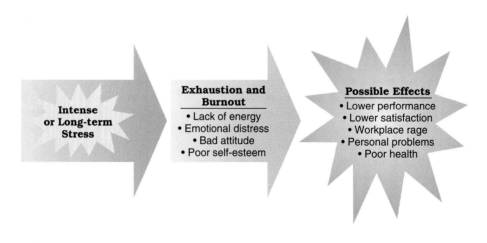

Intense or Long-term Stress

Exhaustion and Burnout
- Lack of energy
- Emotional distress
- Bad attitude
- Poor self-esteem

Possible Effects
- Lower performance
- Lower satisfaction
- Workplace rage
- Personal problems
- Poor health

mental systems. One of its outcomes is **job burnout**. This is a sense of physical and mental exhaustion that can be incapacitating both personally and professionally. Another is **workplace rage**—overly aggressive behavior toward co-workers, bosses, or customers.[18] Medical research also indicates that too much stress can reduce resistance to disease and increase the likelihood of physical and/or mental illness. It may contribute to health problems such as hypertension, ulcers, substance abuse, overeating, depression, and muscle aches.[19]

So what can we do about stress; how can it be managed? The best strategy is to prevent it from reaching excessive levels in the first place. If we can identify our stressors, whether work-related or personal, we can often take action to avoid or minimize their negative consequences.[20] And as managers, we can take steps to help others who are showing stress symptoms. Things like temporary changes in work schedules, reduced performance expectations, longer deadlines, and even reminders to take time off, can all help.

Finally, there is really no substitute for **personal wellness**. In management we use this term to describe the pursuit of a personal health-promotion program. This begins by taking personal responsibility for your physical and mental health. It means getting rest, exercise, and proper nutrition. It means dealing with things like smoking and alcohol or drug abuse. It means committing to a healthy lifestyle, one that helps you deal with stress and the demands of life and work.

Employers are really waking up to the value of personal wellness. Given the rates at which health-care costs are rising, more and more of them are sponsoring wellness programs—from exercise areas to stop-smoking assistance to health-risk appraisals to nutrition education to blood pressure screening to weight control, and more. And with time, some are getting even more extreme. As I'm writing this the Scotts Miracle-Grow Company has just announced that it won't hire or retain workers who smoke starting in late 2006.[21] What do you think of that?

STAY INFORMED

- 31% of college-educated people work 50+ hours per week.
- 40% of adults get less than 7 hours of sleep nightly during workweek.
- 60% of meals are rushed; 34% of lunches are eaten "on the run."
- 33% of workers feel dead-ended in their jobs.
- 47% of workers under 35 report having feelings of burnout versus 28% of those over 35.

Job burnout is physical and mental exhaustion from work stress.

Workplace rage is aggressive behavior toward co-workers or the work setting.

Personal wellness is the pursuit of a personal-health promotion program.

Overwork has become the big issue right now.

Brad Harrington, **EXECUTIVE DIRECTOR, BOSTON COLLEGE CENTER FOR WORK AND FAMILY**

Be Sure You Can . . .

- list the Big Five personality traits and give work-related examples of each

- list five more personality traits and give work-related examples for each

- identify common stressors in work and personal life

- describe the Type A personality

- differentiate constructive and destructive stress

- explain personal wellness as a stress management strategy

Define the Terms

Agreeableness	Machiavellianism
Authoritarianism	Openness
Conscientiousness	Personal wellness
Constructive stress	Personality
Destructive stress	Self-monitoring
Emotional stability	Stress
Extroversion	Type A personality
Job burnout	Workplace rage
Locus of control	

Rapid Review

- The Big Five personality factors are extroversion, agreeableness, conscientiousness, emotional stability, and openness.

- Additional personality dimensions of work significance are locus of control, authoritarianism, Machiavellianism, problem-solving style, and self-monitoring.

- Stress occurs as the tension accompanying extraordinary demands, constraints, or opportunities.

- For some people, having a Type A personality creates stress as a result of continual feelings of impatience and pressure.

- Stress can be destructive or constructive; a moderate level of stress typically has a positive impact on performance.

- Stress can be effectively managed through both prevention and coping strategies, including a commitment to personal wellness.

Reflect/React

1. Which personality trait would you add to the Big Five to make it six?

2. Do you think that most effective managers have a Type A personality?

3. How can someone turn destructive stress into constructive stress?

18.2 How Do Perceptions Influence Individual Behavior?

When people communicate with one another, everything passes through two silent but influential shields: the "perceptions" of the sender and the receiver. **Perception** is the process through which people receive and interpret information from the environment. It is the way we form impressions about ourselves, other people, and daily life experiences.

As suggested in Figure 18.2, you might think of perception as a bubble that surrounds us and influences significantly the way we receive, interpret, and process information received from our environments.[22] And because our individual idiosyncracies, backgrounds, values, and experiences influence our perceptions, this means that people can and do view the same things quite differently. These differences in perceptions influence how we communicate and behave in relationship to one another.

Perception is the process through which people receive and interpret information from the environment.

| Figure 18.2 | How does perception influence communication? |

Sender's perceptions

SENDER

Receiver's perceptions

RECEIVER

Message →

← Feedback

Perceptual Distortions
- Stereotypes
- Halo effects
- Selective perception
- Projection

Perception is the process of receiving and interpreting information from our environment. It acts as a screen or filter through which we interpret messages in the communication process. And, perceptions influence how we behave in response to information received. Because people often perceive the same things quite differently, perception is an important issue in respect to individual behavior at work. Perceptual distortions in the form of stereotypes, halo effects, projection, and selective perception can lead to inaccurate assumptions regarding other people and events.

• Perceptual Distortions Can Obscure Individual Differences

Given the complexity of the stimuli constantly flowing toward us from our environments, human beings use various means of simplifying and organizing their perceptions. One of the most common of these tendencies is the use of **stereotypes**. This occurs when you identify someone with a group or category, and then use the attributes associated with the group or category to describe the individual. Although this makes things easier by reducing the need to deal with unique individual characteristics, it is an oversimplification. By using the stereotype we end up missing the real individual.

Some of the most common stereotypes in the workplace, and in life in general, relate to such factors as gender, age, race, and physical ability. Consider how managers might use gender stereotyping to misconstrue work behavior. If they see men in a discussion, they might think they are discussing a new deal; if it's a group of women, they might perceive what they are doing as gossiping. And then there's the question of opportunity. Only a small proportion of U.S. managers sent on international assignments by their employers are women. Do you wonder why? A Catalyst study of women in global business blames gender stereotypes that place women at a disadvantage to men for international jobs. The perception seems to be that women lack the abilities or willingness for working abroad.[23]

A **halo effect** occurs when we use one characteristic of a person or situation to form an overall impression. You probably do this quite often, as do I. For example, when

A **stereotype** assigns attributes commonly associated with a group to an individual.

A **halo effect** uses one attribute to develop an overall impression of a person or situation.

At Panera the recipe for success is a positive attitude.

When Ron Shaich opened a cookie store in Boston in 1980, even he didn't know that he was on an entrepreneurial pathway to business success. It wasn't long before he joined forces with a local French bakery to expand his product line in a new venture named Au Bon Pain. Finding a niche with fresh breads and high-quality meats, Au Bon Pain grew rapidly through the mid-1990s and then leveled off. Shaich wanted more. Sensing opportunity in the St. Louis Bread Company, a recently acquired, small new chain now renamed Panera, he went to Au Bon Pain's board with a proposal: sell Au Bon Pain and focus on Panera. The board said they thought he might be "washed up," but he didn't give in. After nine months, they agreed. Panera took off like a rocket, growing to 500 stores in less than four years. People who know and work with Shaich describe him as "passionate" and "intense." One of the firm's vice presidents considers him a personal mentor, saying: "One of his greatest traits is that he is able to go from the very strategic to the very detailed, depending on the situation. That ability has had a big influence on me." With an ever-positive attitude toward opportunity, Shaich foresees more growth ahead for Panera.

Ron Shaich, *CEO and Chairman, Panera*.

Selective perception is the tendency to define problems from one's own point of view.

Projection assigns personal attributes to other individuals.

Fundamental attribution error overestimates internal factors and underestimates external factors as influences on someone's behavior.

meeting someone new, receiving a positive smile might create a halo effect that results in a positive overall impression. By contrast, the halo effect of an unfamiliar hairstyle or manner of dressing may create a negative impression.

Halo effects cause the same problems as do stereotypes; they obscure individual differences. The person who smiles might have a very negative work attitude; the person with the weird hair might be a top performer. Halo effects are especially significant in performance evaluations where one factor, such as a person's punctuality or lack of it, may become the halo that inaccurately determines the overall performance rating.

Selective perception is the tendency to single out for attention those aspects of a situation or person that reinforce or appear consistent with one's existing beliefs, values, or needs.[24] And what do we often do with information that conflicts with this perception? We simply screen it out. This happens in organizations when people from different departments or functions—such as marketing and manufacturing—tend to see things only from their own point of view. Like the other perceptual distortions, selective perception can bias our views of situations and individuals. One of the great benefits of teamwork and consultative decision making is the pooling of ideas and perceptions of many people, thus making it harder for selective perception to create problems.

Projection occurs when we assign our personal attributes to other individuals. Some call this the "similar-to-me" error. A classic projection error is to assume that other persons share our needs, desires, and values. Suppose, for example, that you enjoy a lot of responsibility and challenge in your work as a team leader. You might move quickly to increase responsibilities and challenges for team members, wanting them to experience the same satisfactions as you. But this involves projection. Instead of designing jobs to best fit their needs, you have designed their jobs to fit yours. In fact, an individual team member may be quite satisfied and productive doing his or her current job, one that seems routine to you. We can control projection errors through self-awareness and a willingness to communicate and empathize with other persons, that is, to try to see things through their eyes.

• Perception Sometimes Causes Attribution Errors as We Explain Events and Problems

One of the ways in which perception exerts its influence on behavior is through *attribution*. This is the process of developing explanations or assigning perceived causes for events. It is natural for people to try to explain what they observe and the things that happen to them. And one of the most significant places for this is the workplace. What happens when you perceive that someone else in a job or student group isn't performing up to expectations? How do you explain this? And, depending on the explanation, what do you do to try and correct things?

When someone else is the poor performer, the likelihood is for us to commit something called **fundamental attribution error**. This is a tendency to blame other people when things go wrong, whether or not this is really true. If I perceive that a student is doing poorly in my course, for example, this error pops up as a tendency to "blame" the student—perhaps perceiving a lack of ability or an unwillingness to study hard enough. But that perception may not be accurate, as you may well agree. Perhaps there's something about the course design, its delivery, or my actions as an instructor that are contributing to the problem; a deficiency in the learning environment, not the individual.

Consider another case. This time it's you having a performance problem—at school, at work, wherever. How do you explain it? Again, the likelihood of error is high, this time due to **self-serving bias**. This is the tendency for people to blame their personal failures or problems on external causes, and underestimate the role of personal responsibility. This is the "It's not my fault!" error. Of course the flip side is to claim personal responsibility for any successes—"It was me, myself, and I that did it!" This is also self-serving bias.

So what's the significance of these error tendencies? Actually, it is quite substantial. When we perceive things incorrectly we are likely to take the wrong actions, and miss solving a lot of problems in the process. When other people's performance is too quickly blamed on them, we may never realize that the real cause of the problem rested in the environment. While we are trying to correct things through training, motivation, or even replacement, the real opportunity for improving performance may be missed—clarifying goals, making more resources available, extending deadlines, for example. And when we too quickly blame the environment for our problems, we never, or rarely, face up to the personal responsibilities for making positive changes in our behavior.

Think about self-serving bias the next time you hear someone blaming your instructor for a poor course grade. And think about fundamental attribution error the next time you jump on a group member who didn't perform according to your standards. Our perceptions aren't always wrong, but they should always be double checked and tested for accuracy. There are no safe assumptions when it comes to the power of attributions.

Self-serving bias underestimates internal factors and overestimates external factors as influences on someone's behavior.

• Impression Management Is a Way of Influencing How Others Perceive Us

Richard Branson, CEO of the Virgin Group, may be one of the richest and most famous executives in the world. One of his early business accomplishments was the successful start-up of Virgin Airlines, now a major competitor of British Airways (BA). In a memoir, the former head of BA, Lord King, said: "If Richard Branson had worn a shirt and tie instead of a goatee and jumper, I would not have underestimated him."[25] This is an example of how much our impressions count—both positive and negative. Knowing this, scholars today emphasize the importance of **impression management**, the systematic attempt to influence how others perceive us.[26]

You might notice that we often do this as a matter of routine in everyday life. We dress, talk, act, and surround ourselves with things that reinforce a desireable self-image and help to convey that same image to other persons. When well done, impression management can help us to advance in jobs and careers, form relationships with people we admire, and even create pathways to group memberships.

Some basic tactics of impression management are worth remembering: dressing in ways that convey positive appeal in certain circumstances—for example, knowing when to dress up and when to dress down; using words to flatter other people in ways that generate positive feelings toward you; making eye contact and smiling when engaged in conversations to create a personal bond; and displaying a high level of energy suggestive of work commitment and initiative.[27]

Impression management tries to create desired perceptions in the eyes of others.

Be Sure You Can . . .

- describe how perception influences behavior

- explain how stereotypes, halo effects, selective perceptions, and projection operate in the workplace

- explain the concepts of attribution error and self-serving bias

- illustrate how we can use impression management for success in a job interview

Define the Terms

Fundametal attribution error

Halo effect

Impression management

Perception

Projection

Selective perception

Self-serving bias

Stereotype

Rapid Review

- Perception acts as a filter through which all communication passes as it travels from one person to the next.

- Different people may interpret the same message differently.

- Fundamental attribution error occurs when we blame others for performance problems while excluding possible external causes.

- Self-serving bias occurs when, in judging our own performance, we take personal credit for successes and blame failures on external factors.

- Stereotypes, projections, halo effects, and selective perception can distort perceptions and reduce communication effectiveness.

- Through impression management we influence the way that others perceive us.

Reflect/React

1. Are there times when a self-serving bias is actually helpful?

2. How do advertising firms use stereotypes in a positive way?

3. Does the notion of impression management contradict the idea of personal integrity?

At one time Challis M. Lowe was one of only two African-American women among the five highest-paid executives in over 400 U.S. corporations[28] She attained this success after a 25-year career that included several changes of employers and lots of stressors—working-mother guilt, a failed marriage, gender bias on the job, and an MBA degree earned part-time. Through it all she says: "I've never let being scared stop me from doing something. Just because you haven't done it before doesn't mean you shouldn't try." Would you agree that Lowe has what we often call a "can-do" attitude?

• Attitudes Predispose People to Act in Certain Ways

An **attitude** is a predisposition to act in a certain way toward people and environmental factors.[29] Challis Lowe seemed disposed to take risk and embrace challenges. This positive attitude influenced her behavior when dealing with the inevitable problems, choices, and opportunities of work and career.

To fully understand attitudes, positive or negative, you must recognize their three components. First is the *cognitive component*, which reflects a belief or value. You might believe, for example, that your management course is very interesting. Second is the *affective or emotional component*, which reflects a specific feeling. For example, you might feel very good about being a management major. Third is the *behavioral component*, which reflects an intention to behave consistently with the belief and feeling. Using the same example again, you might say to yourself: "I am going to work hard and try to get A's in all my management courses."

Have you noticed, however, that attitudes aren't always good predictors of behavior? Despite pledging to work hard as a student, you may not; despite wanting a more challenging job, you might stay with the current one because of family or other nonwork reasons. In these types of cases we fail to live up to our own expectations. Usually that's not a good feeling.

The psychological concept of **cognitive dissonance** describes the discomfort we feel in situations where our attitude is inconsistent with our behavior.[30] Most of us manage this dissonance by rethinking our attitude to make it seem to fit the behavior ("Oh well, work isn't really that important, anyway"), changing future behavior to fit the attitude (not putting extra time in at work; focusing more attention on leisure and personal hobbies), or rationalizing in ways that make the attitude and behavior seem compatible ("I'm in no hurry; there will be a lot of opportunities for new jobs in the future").

An **attitude** is a predisposition to act in a certain way.

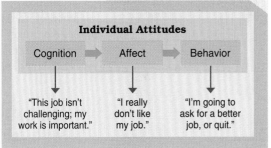

Individual Attitudes

Cognition ⟹ Affect ⟹ Behavior

"This job isn't challenging; my work is important." | "I really don't like my job." | "I'm going to ask for a better job, or quit."

Cognitive dissonance is discomfort felt when attitude and behavior are inconsistent.

• Job Satisfaction Is a Positive Attitude Toward One's Job and Work Experiences

People hold attitudes about many things in the workplace—bosses, each other, tasks, organizational policies, performance goals, paychecks, and more. A comprehensive work attitude is **job satisfaction**, the degree to which an individual feels positive or negative about various aspects of his or her job and work experiences.[31]

When researchers measure and people talk about job satisfaction, there are usually certain things at issue. Job satisfaction typically reflects attitudes toward the *job itself* (responsibility, interest, challenge), *quality of supervision* (task help, social support), *co-workers* (harmony, respect, friendliness), *opportunities* (promotion, learning, growth), *pay* (actual and perceived), *work conditions* (comfort, safety, support), and *security* (job and employment).

If you watch or read the news, you'll regularly find reports on the job satisfactions of U.S. workers. You'll also find lots of job satisfaction studies in the academic literature. The results don't always agree, but they usually fall within a common range.[32]

Job satisfaction is the degree to which an individual feels positive about a job and work experience.

Organizational citizenship behaviors are the extras people do to go the extra mile in their work.

• Job Satisfaction Can Predict Absenteeism, Turnover, and Organizational Citizenship

Back in Module 2 we identified two primary goals or concerns of an effective manager—to help others achieve high performance and experience job satisfaction. Surely you can agree that job satisfaction is important on quality-of-work-life grounds alone. Don't people deserve to have satisfying work experiences? Of course; but is job satisfaction important in other than a "feel good" sense?

Researchers tell us that there is a strong relationship between job satisfaction and *absenteeism*. Workers who are more satisfied with their jobs are absent less often than those who are dissatisfied. There is also a relationship between job satisfaction and *turnover*. Satisfied workers are more likely to stay, and dissatisfied workers are more likely to quit their jobs. The consequences of these withdrawal behaviors can be significant; absenteeism and excessive turnover are expensive. In fact, one study found that changing retention rates up or down results in magnified changes to corporate earnings. It also warns about the negative impact on corporate performance of declining employee loyalty and high turnover.[33]

Researchers also identify a relationship between job satisfaction and **organizational citizenship**.[34] This is a set of behaviors that basically represent a willingness to "go beyond the call of duty" or "go the extra mile" in one's work.[35] A person who is a good organizational citizen does things that, although not required, help advance the performance of the organization. You might observe this as a service worker who goes to extraordinary lengths to take care of a customer, a team member who is always willing to take on extra tasks, or a friend who is always working extra hours at no pay just to make sure things are done right for his employer.

• Job Satisfaction Has a Complex Relationship with Job Performance

The data on the job satisfaction and performance relationship, as you might expect, are somewhat complicated.[36] There are three different arguments available. One, is that job satisfaction causes performance; "a happy worker is a productive worker." The second is that performance causes job satisfaction. The third is that both job satisfaction and performance are intertwined, influencing one another, and mutually affected by other factors such as the availability of rewards. Can you make a case for each argument based on your personal experiences?

Although it was in doubt for quite some time, recent conclusions are that there is probably a modest link between job satisfaction and performance.[37] But, keep the stress on the word "modest" in the last sentence. We need to be careful before rushing to conclude that making people happy is a sure-fire way to improve their job performance. The reality is that some people will like their jobs, be very satisfied, and still not perform very well. That's just part of the complexity regarding individual differences. When you think of this, remember a sign that once hung in a tavern near a Ford plant in Michigan: "I spend 40 hours a week here, am I supposed to work too?"

The relationship between performance and satisfaction holds pretty much to the same pattern. High-performing workers are likely to feel satisfied. But again, a realistic position is probably best; not everyone is likely to fit the model. Some people may get their work done and even meet high performance expectations while still not feeling high job satisfaction. Perhaps you can come up with an example.

Finally, it is quite likely that job satisfaction and job performance influence one another. But the relationship is also most likely to hold under certain "conditions." Those conditions are the subject of a lot of research, particularly on the role of rewards. One of the more popular positions is that job performance that is followed by rewards that are valued and perceived as fair will create job satisfaction; this in turn will likely increase motivation to work harder to achieve high performance in the future.

Motivation! That's an issue that deserves a close look. Read on. The next two modules explore motivation theories that come to us from psychology and examine their practical applications at work.

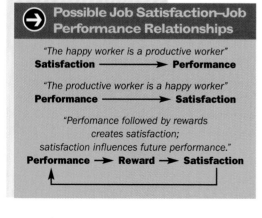

Possible Job Satisfaction–Job Performance Relationships

"The happy worker is a productive worker"
Satisfaction ⟶ Performance

"The productive worker is a happy worker"
Performance ⟶ Satisfaction

"Perfomance followed by rewards creates satisfaction; satisfaction influences future performance."
Performance ➔ Reward ➔ Satisfaction

Be Sure You Can . . .

- identify the three components of an attitude

- explain cognitive dissonance

- describe what one measures in job satisfaction

- explain the importance of job satisfaction for absenteeism, turnover, and citizenship

- list and describe three alternative explanations in the job satisfaction–performance relationship

Define the Terms

Attitude

Cognitive dissonance

Job satisfaction

Organizational citizenship

Rapid Review

- An attitude is a predisposition to respond in a certain way to people and things.

- Cognitive dissonance occurs when a person's attitude and behavior are inconsistent.

- Job satisfaction is an important work attitude, reflecting a person's evaluation of the job, co-workers, and other aspects of the work setting.

- Job satisfaction influences such behaviors as absenteeism, turnover, and organizational citizenship.

- Job satisfaction has a complex and reciprocal relationship with job performance.

Reflect/React

1. Is cognitive dissonance a good or bad influence on us?

2. How can a manager deal with someone who has high job satisfaction but is a low performer?

3. Should a manager be concerned about someone who is a high performer with low job satisfaction?

Multiple Choice

1. Among the Big Five personality traits, _____ indicates someone who tends to be responsible, dependable, and careful in respect to tasks.
   (a) authoritarian **(b)** agreeable **(c)** conscientious **(d)** emotionally stable

2. A person with a/an _____ personality would most likely act unemotional and manipulative when trying to influence others to achieve personal goals.
   (a) extroverted **(b)** sensation-thinking **(c)** self-monitoring **(d)** Machiavellian

3. When a person tends to believe that he or she has little influence over things that happen in life, this indicates a _____ personality.
   (a) low emotional stability **(b)** external locus of control **(c)** high self-monitoring **(d)** intuitive-thinker

4. A person with a _____ problem-solving style is most likely to be comfortable with abstraction and unstructured situations, and to avoid getting involved in details.
   (a) sensation-thinker **(b)** intuitive-thinker **(c)** sensation-feeler **(d)** intuitive-feeler

5. The similar-to-me error in perception occurs as a _____ error in that one's personal attributes are assigned to others.
   (a) halo effect **(b)** stereotyping **(c)** extroversion **(d)** projection

6. _____ is a form of attribution error that involves blaming the environment for problems that we may have caused ourselves.
   (a) Self-serving bias **(b)** Fundamental attribution error **(c)** Projection **(d)** Self-monitoring

7. The _____ component of an attitude is what indicates a person's belief about something, while the _____ component indicates a specific positive or negative feeling about it.
   (a) cognitive/affective **(b)** emotional/affective **(c)** cognitive/attributional **(d)** behavioral/attributional

8. The term used to describe the discomfort someone feels when his or her behavior turns out to be inconsistent with a previously expressed attitude is _____.
   (a) alienation **(b)** cognitive dissonance **(c)** job dissatisfaction **(d)** job burnout

9. Job satisfaction is known from research to be a very good predictor of _____.
   (a) job performance **(b)** job burnout **(c)** conscientiousness **(d)** absenteeism

10. Use of special dress, manners, gestures, and vocabulary words when meeting a prospective employer in a job interview are all examples of how someone can use _____.
    (a) projection **(b)** selective perception **(c)** impression management **(d)** self-serving bias

Short Response

11. What is the most positive profile of Big Five personality traits in terms of positive impact on work behavior?

12. What is the relationship between stress and performance?

13. How does the halo effect differ from selective perception?

14. If you were going to develop a job satisfaction survey, exactly what would you try to measure?

Integration & Application

When Scott Tweedy picked up a magazine article on "How to manage health-care workers," he was pleased to find some apparent advice. Scott was concerned about poor or mediocre performance by several of the respiratory therapists in his clinic. The author of the article said that the "best way to improve performance is to make your workers happy." Well, Scott was happy upon reading this and made a pledge to himself to start doing a much better job of this.

Questions: Should Scott be happy, or should he be concerned about this advice? What do we know about the relationship between job satisfaction and performance, and how can this apply to Scott's performance problems?

SELF-ASSESSMENT
Stress Test

INSTRUCTIONS *Complete the following questionnaire. Circle the number that best represents your tendency to behave on each bipolar dimension.*

Am casual about appointments	1 2 3 4 5 6 7 8	Am never late
Am not competitive	1 2 3 4 5 6 7 8	Am very competitive
Never feel rushed	1 2 3 4 5 6 7 8	Always feel rushed
Take things one at a time	1 2 3 4 5 6 7 8	Try to do many things at once
Do things slowly	1 2 3 4 5 6 7 8	Do things fast
Express feelings	1 2 3 4 5 6 7 8	"Sit on" feelings
Have many interests	1 2 3 4 5 6 7 8	Have few interests but work

SCORING

Total the numbers circled for all items, and multiply this by 3; enter the result here [_____].

POINTS	PERSONALITY TYPE
120+	A+
106–119	A
100–105	A−
90–99	B+
below 90	B

PATHWAYS to WileyPLUS

CASE SNAPSHOT

Go online to read
this case!

Electronic Arts: Fantasy Sports
Electronic Arts is a superpower in the video-game world. Despite dips in its stock, analysts still regard EA as a good buy. But as the level of detail in its games grows, so does the cost of producing top-rated sports titles. Can EA devise new streams of revenue to keep up? Or are they so far ahead of the competition that their rivals can only nibble at EA's leftovers?

MODULE 18 Online Interactive Learning Resources

Skill Builder
• Self-Monitoring

Experiential Exercise
• How to Give and Take Criticism

Team Project
• Difficult Personalities

Treat others as you

Motivation

Consider this. At the age of 83, Charlie Butcher finally sold his family firm to the S.C. Johnson Company. It was a good deal for Charlie and family—$18 million! But there's more to this story if we dig a bit deeper.

After selling the firm, Charlie shared the $18 million with the firm's employees. He handed out checks the day after the sale, written to an average of $55,000 per person. How did everyone react? The president, Paul P. McClaughlin, said the employees "just filled up with tears: They would just throw their arms around Charlie and give him a hug."

If you knew Charlie, they say, this wouldn't be a surprise. He always believed in people. This was just another chance to confirm the theory

would like to be treated

that he'd been practicing for years. If you treat talented people well they'll create business success. Charlie ties job satisfaction and performance, saying: "When people are happy in their jobs, they are at least twice as productive."[1] This is his answer to a perplexing question in social science: Why do some people work enthusiastically, while others hold back?

More answers are possible, and most begin with respect for people in all of their talents and diversity. Either you respect people, or you don't, and this makes a big difference in how they respond to you. The best managers already know this. Like Charlie Butcher, they lead with full awareness that "productivity through people" is the foundation for long-term success.

Why doesn't everyone get the message?

When people feel connected to something with a purpose greater than themselves, it inspires them to reach for levels they might not otherwise obtain.

George Zimmer, founder and CEO of Men's Wearhouse

It's part of a soundly designed strategy. . . . If you hire adults and treat them like adults, then they'll behave like adults.

Jim Goodnight, CEO of SAS Institute

⊙ MODULE GUIDE

 19.1 How do human needs influence motivation to work?

- Maslow described a hierarchy of needs topped by self-actualization.
- Alderfer's **ERG** theory focuses on existence, relatedness, and growth needs.
- Herzberg's two-factor theory focuses on higher-order need satisfaction.
- McClelland identified acquired needs for achievement, power, and affiliation.

 19.2 How do thought processes and decisions affect motivation to work?

- Equity theory explains how social comparisons can motivate individual behavior.

- Expectancy theory considers motivation = expectancy × instrumentality × valence.
- Goal-setting theory says that well chosen and well set goals can be motivating.

 19.3 What role does reinforcement play in motivation?

- Operant conditioning influences behavior by controlling its consequences.
- Positive reinforcement connects desirable behavior with pleasant consequences.
- Punishment connects undesirable behavior with unpleasant consequences.

Motivation accounts for the level, direction, and persistence of effort expended at work.

In management we use the term **motivation** to describe forces within the individual that account for the level, direction, and persistence of effort expended at work. Simply put, a highly motivated person works hard at a job; an unmotivated person does not. A manager who leads through motivation creates conditions that consistently inspire other people to work hard.

A highly motivated workforce is obviously indispensable. So how do we get there? One of the best starting points is to explore theories from psychology that deal with differences in individual **needs**—unfulfilled desires that stimulate people to behave in ways that will satisfy them. And as you might expect, there are different theories about human needs and how they may affect people at work.

A **need** is an unfulfilled physiological or psychological desire.

• Maslow Described a Hierarchy of Needs Topped by Self-Actualization

Abraham Maslow's *theory of human needs*, first discussed in Module 3, is an important foundation in the history of management thought. He described a hierarchy built on a foundation of **lower-order needs** (physiological, safety, and social concerns) and moving up to **higher-order needs** (esteem and self-actualization).[2] Whereas lower-order needs focus on physical well-being and companionship, the higher-order needs reflect psychological development and growth.

Lower-order needs are physiological, safety, and social needs in Maslow's hierarchy.

A key part of Maslow's thinking about how needs affect human behavior relies on two principles. The *deficit principle* states that a satisfied need is not a motivator of behavior. People act in ways that satisfy deprived needs, ones for which a "deficit" exists. For example, we eat because we are hungry; we call a friend when we are lonely; we seek approval from others when we are feeling insecure.

Higher-order needs are esteem and self-actualization needs in Maslow's hierarchy.

The *progression principle* states that people try to satisfy lower-level needs first, then move step-by-step up the hierarchy. This happens up until the level of self-actualization; the more these needs are satisfied, the stronger they will grow. According to Maslow, opportunities for self-fulfillment should continue to motivate a person as long as the other needs remain satisfied.

Although Maslow's theory has not been proven, it is still considered a good starting point for examining human needs and their potential influence on motivation. It seems to make sense, for example, that managers should try to understand the needs of people working with and for them. And isn't it a manager's job to help others find ways of satisfying their needs through work? Figure 19.1 gives some suggestions along these lines.

• Alderfer's ERG Theory Focuses on Existence, Relatedness, and Growth Needs

A well-regarded alternative to Maslow's work is the *ERG theory* proposed by Clayton Alderfer.[3] His theory collapses Maslow's five needs categories into three. *Existence needs* are desires for physiological and material well-being. *Relatedness needs* are desires for satisfying interpersonal relationships. *Growth needs* are desires for continued psychological growth and development.

ERG theory also rejects Maslow's deficit and progression principles. Instead, Alderfer suggests that any or all of the needs can influence individual behavior at any given time. His theory also suggests that a satisfied need doesn't lose its motivational impact. Instead, Alderfer describes a *frustration-regression principle* through which an already-satisfied lower-level need can become reactivated when a higher-level need cannot be satisfied. Perhaps this is why unionized workers frustrated by assembly line jobs (low growth need

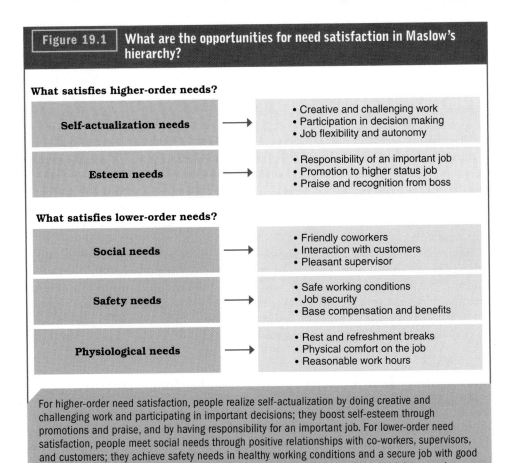

Figure 19.1 What are the opportunities for need satisfaction in Maslow's hierarchy?

What satisfies higher-order needs?

Self-actualization needs →
- Creative and challenging work
- Participation in decision making
- Job flexibility and autonomy

Esteem needs →
- Responsibility of an important job
- Promotion to higher status job
- Praise and recognition from boss

What satisfies lower-order needs?

Social needs →
- Friendly coworkers
- Interaction with customers
- Pleasant supervisor

Safety needs →
- Safe working conditions
- Job security
- Base compensation and benefits

Physiological needs →
- Rest and refreshment breaks
- Physical comfort on the job
- Reasonable work hours

For higher-order need satisfaction, people realize self-actualization by doing creative and challenging work and participating in important decisions; they boost self-esteem through promotions and praise, and by having responsibility for an important job. For lower-order need satisfaction, people meet social needs through positive relationships with co-workers, supervisors, and customers; they achieve safety needs in healthy working conditions and a secure job with good pay and benefits; and, they realize physiological needs by having reasonable work hours and comfortable work spaces.

satisfaction) give so much attention in labor negotiations to things like job security and wage levels (existence need satisfaction).

Don't be quick to reject either Maslow or Alderfer in favor of the other. Although questions can be raised about both theories, each adds value to our understanding of how individual needs can influence motivation.[4]

• Herzberg's Two-Factor Theory Focuses on Higher-Order Need Satisfaction

Frederick Herzberg's work on needs took a slightly different route. He began with extensive interviews of people at work, and then content analyzed their answers. The result is known as the *two-factor theory*.[5]

When questioned about what "turned them on," Herzberg found that his respondents mainly talked about the nature of the job itself. They were telling him about what they did. Herzberg called these **satisfier factors**, or *motivator factors*, and described them as part of *job content*. They include such things as a sense of achievement, feelings of recognition, a sense of responsibility, the opportunity for advancement, and feelings of personal growth. They are most consistent with the higher-order needs of Maslow and the existence needs of Alderfer.

When questioned about what "turned them off," Herzberg found that his respondents talked about quite different things. They were mostly telling him about where they worked, not about what they did. Herzberg called these **hygiene factors** and described them as part of *job context*. They include such things as working conditions, interpersonal relations, organizational policies and administration, technical quality of supervision, and base wage or salary. These seem more associated with Maslow's lower-order needs and Alderfer's existence and relatedness needs.

A **satisfier factor** is found in job content, such as a sense of achievement, recognition, responsibility, advancement, or personal growth.

A **hygiene factor** is found in the job context, such as working conditions, interpersonal relations, organizational policies, and salary.

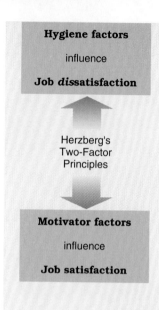

Hygiene factors

influence

Job *dissatisfaction*

Herzberg's
Two-Factor
Principles

Motivator factors

influence

Job satisfaction

The two-factor theory views hygiene factors as influencing high or low job *dissatis-*faction. By contrast, satisfier factors influence high or low job satisfaction. The distinction is important. Herzberg is saying that you can't increase job satisfaction by improving the hygiene factors. You will only get less dissatisfaction. And although you might agree that minimizing dissatisfaction is an important goal, you need to understand that Herzberg believes it won't deliver much by way of increased motivation. At least that's his theory.

The satisfier factors found in job content are the real keys to job satisfaction according to Herzberg. He believes that it's only by improving on them that we can expect more motivation and higher performance. And to create these high-content jobs he suggests the technique of *job enrichment*. Essentially, it involves building into a job more opportunities for people to manage themselves and exercise self-control over their work. We'll discuss this job design approach in more detail in the next module.

Although scholars have criticized Herzberg's theory as being method-bound and difficult to replicate, it makes us think about both job content and job context.[6] It cautions managers not to expect too much by way of motivational improvements from investments in things like special office fixtures and even high base salaries. And, it focuses attention on how the job itself can be designed to provide for responsibility, growth, and other sources of higher-order need satisfactions.

• McClelland Identified Acquired Needs for Achievement, Power, and Affiliation

In the late 1940s, David McClelland and his colleagues began experimenting with the Thematic Apperception Test (TAT) of human psychology.[7] The TAT asks people to view pictures and write stories about what they see. Researchers then analyzed the stories' contents, looking for themes that display individual needs.

From this research McClelland identified *three acquired needs* that he considers central to understanding human motivation. The **need for achievement** is the desire to do something better or more efficiently, to solve problems, or to master complex tasks. The **need for power** is the desire to control other people, to influence their behavior, or to be responsible for them. The **need for affiliation** is the desire to establish and maintain friendly and warm relations with other people.

Need for achievement is the desire to do something better, to solve problems, or to master complex tasks.

McClelland encourages managers to learn how to recognize the strength of each need in themselves and in other people. And because each need can be associated with a distinct set of work preferences, his insights offer helpful ideas for designing jobs and creating work environments that are rich in potential need satisfactions.

Consider someone high in the need for achievement. Do you, for example, like to put your competencies to work, take moderate risks in competitive situations, and often prefer to work alone? Need achievers are like this, and their work prefer-

ences usually follow a pattern. Persons high in need for achievement like work that offers challenging but achievable goals, feedback on performance, and individual responsibility. If you take one or more of these away, they are likely to become frus-

Need for power is the desire to control, influence, or be responsible for other people.

Work Preferences of a High Need Achiever

- **Challenging but achievable goals**
- **Feedback on performance**
- **Individual responsibility**

trated and their performance may suffer. As a manager, these preferences offer pretty straightforward insights for dealing with a high need achiever. And if you are that person, these are the things you should be talking about with your manager.

Insights are there for the other needs as well. People high in the need for affiliation prefer jobs offering companionship, social approval, and satisfying interpersonal relationships. People high in the need for power are motivated to behave in ways that have a clear impact on other people and events; they enjoy being in positions of control.

Importantly, McClelland distinguishes between two forms of the power need.[8] *The need for personal power* is exploitative and involves manipulation for the pure sake of personal gratification. As you might imagine, this type of power need is

Need for affiliation is the desire to establish and maintain good relations with people.

not respected in management. By contrast, the *need for social power* is the positive face of power. It involves the use of power in a socially responsible way, one that is directed toward group or organizational objectives rather than personal ones. This need for social power is essential to managerial leadership.

One of the interesting extensions of McClelland's work was an attempt to identify the need profiles of successful senior executives. His research found that they tended to have high needs for social power that in turn were higher than otherwise-strong needs for affiliation. Can you explain these results? It may be that managers high in the need for affiliation alone may let their desires for social approval and friendship interfere with business decisions. But with a higher need for power, they may be more willing to sometimes act in ways that other persons may disagree with. In other words, they'll do what is necessary and best for the organization even if it makes some people unhappy. Does this make sense?

As we leave the discussion of human needs, you should see similarities between McClelland's work and other theorists. Doesn't his need for achievement seem to fit with Maslow's higher order needs, Alderfer's growth needs, and Herberg's concepts of motivator factors? And regardless of the theory, don't forget to keep in mind the points made in the *Exhibit—Question and Answers on Individual Needs.*

EXHIBIT

Questions and Answers on Individual Needs

How many different individual needs are there? There isn't a perfect list of individual needs at work. But you can use the ideas of various theories to better understand the possible needs that people bring with them to work.

Can a work outcome or reward satisfy more than one need? Yes. Pay is an example. It can be a source of performance feedback for the high need achiever, as well as a source of personal security for someone with strong existence needs.

Is there a hierarchy of needs? It is more likely that human needs exist in a flexible hierarchy, such as in ERG theory. However, it is useful to distinguish between lower-order and higher-order needs.

How important are the various needs? Individuals vary widely in this regard. They may also value needs differently at different times, in different situations, at different ages, and during different career stages.

NEWSLINE

A company that tries to protect workers from burnout How would you like to work for a company that cares enough not to overwork you? Founded by Roger Greene, Ipswitch, Inc. is a software firm with a difference. Greene reminds employees about the need to take time for personal affairs—not missing vacation time or forgetting to use their personal days, for example. In an industry with high employee turnover, the Ipswitch culture pays off with turnover under 9 percent. Ipswitch pays higher salaries to keep attracting the best talent, rather than relying on the more risky stock options. As for the tendency of many people to work hard for 30 to 40 years and then retire to "have fun," Greene, says: "I'd much rather live life as it goes along and do neat things while you're working and enjoy every year of your life."

Reflect: Suppose a potential employer asks you to identify the things that you most want out of work. What will you say? In a job search, would you be willing to accept less pay to work in an environment like that of Ipswitch?

19.1 How do human needs influence motivation to work?

Be Sure You Can . . .

- describe work practices that can satisfy higher-order and lower-order needs in Maslow's hierarchy

- contrast Maslow's hierarchy with ERG theory

- describe hygiene factors and satisfier factors in Herzberg's theory

- explain needs for achievement, affiliation, and power in McClelland's theory

- differentiate the needs for personal and social power

- describe work preferences for a person with a high need for achievement

Define the Terms

Higher-order needs	Need for achievement
Hygiene factors	Need for affiliation
Lower-order needs	Need for power
Motivation	Satisfier factors
Need	

Rapid Review

- Motivation involves the level, direction, and persistence of effort expended at work; a highly motivated person can be expected to work hard.

- Maslow's hierarchy of human needs suggests a progression from lower-order physiological, safety, and social needs, up to higher-order ego and self-actualization needs.

- Alderfer's ERG theory identifies existence, relatedness, and growth needs.

- Herzberg's two-factor theory identifies satisfier factors in job content as influences on job satisfaction; hygiene factors in job context are viewed as influences on job dissatisfaction.

- McClelland's acquired needs theory identifies the needs for achievement, affiliation, and power, all of which may influence what a person desires from work.

Reflect/React

1. Was Maslow right in suggesting we each have tendencies toward self-actualization?

2. Is high need for achievement always good for managers?

3. Is there any situation where you would be happy working for or with someone high in the need for personal power?

19.2 How Do Thought Processes and Decisions Affect Motivation to Work?

Have you ever received an exam or project grade and felt good about it, only to get discouraged when you hear about someone who didn't work as hard getting the same or better grade? Or, have you ever suffered a loss of motivation when the goals set by your boss or instructor seem so high that you don't see any chance at all for meeting them?

My guess is that most of us have had these types of experiences, and perhaps fairly often.[9] They raise another question that those who study work motivation are very interested in answering: What influences people's decisions whether to work hard in various situations? The equity, expectancy, and goal-setting theories all offer insights into this quesiton.

• Equity Theory Explains How Social Comparisons Can Motivate Individual Behavior

The *equity theory of motivation* is best known in management through the work of J. Stacy Adams.[10] Based on the logic of social comparisons, it pictures us continually checking our situations against those of others. Any perceived inequities in these comparisons will motivate us to engage in behaviors that correct them. And as you might expect, an important work example is when people perceive that they have been unfairly treated.

STAY INFORMED

- In 2005 an average CEO earned 262 times the pay of an average worker.
- The average CEO took home about $11 million; the average worker $42,000.
- If the minimum wage increased as much as CEO pay since 1990, it would be $23.03/hour.

How have you reacted when your grade seems unfair compared with others? Did you reduce your efforts in the future? Drop the course? Rationalize that you really didn't work that hard either? Complain to the instructor and request a higher grade? All of these are ways to reduce the perceived grading inequity. And they are the same types of behaviors that perceived inequity can motivate people to pursue at work. Only instead of grades, the sources of inequity are more likely to be pay raises, job assignments, work schedules, office "perks" and the like. Pay, of course, is the really big one!

Research on equity theory has largely occurred in the laboratory. It is most conclusive with respect to the *perceived negative inequity* that we have just been discussing. People who feel underpaid, for example, experience a sense of anger. This causes them to try and restore perceived equity to the situation, such as by reducing current work efforts to compensate for the missing rewards or by even quitting the job.[11]

How to Deal with Perceived Negative Inequity

- Change inputs by putting in less effort.
- Change rewards by asking for better treatment.
- Change comparison points to make things seem better.
- Change situation by quitting or shifting jobs.

Interestingly, there is also some evidence for an equity dynamic among people who feel overpaid. This *perceived positive inequity* is associated with a sense of guilt. The individual becomes motivated to restore perceived equity by increasing the quantity or quality of work, taking on more difficult assignments, or working overtime.

Think about this finding for a minute. If valid, it suggests that managers, or instructors, might overreward individuals today in order to motivate them to work harder in the future. Do you think this really works? What if one of your instructors decides to inflate the grades of students on early assignments, thinking that perceived positive inequities will motivate them to study harder for the rest of the course. Would you work harder? Or, would you perhaps work even less hard?

Although there are no clear answers available in equity theory, there are some very good insights. The theory is a reminder that rewards perceived as equitable should positively affect satisfaction and performance; those perceived as inequitable may create dissatisfaction and cause performance problems. Probably the best advice is to anticipate potential equity problems whenever rewards of any type are being allocated, and punishments as well. We should also recognize that people may compare their situations with co-workers, workers elsewhere in the organization, and even persons employed by other organizations. And we should always understand that people behave according to their perceptions—a lesson from Module 18. If someone perceives inequity, it is likely to affect his or her behavior whether the manager sees the situation the same way or not.

• Expectancy Theory Considers Motivation = Expectancy × Instrumentality × Valence

Victor Vroom offers another approach to motivation. His *expectancy theory* asks: What determines the willingness of an individual to work hard at tasks important to the organization?[12] Vroom answers this question with an equation: *Motivation = Expectancy × Instrumentality × Valence.*

Expectancy is a person's belief that working hard will result in achieving a desired level of task performance (sometimes called *effort-performance expectancy*). **Instrumentality** is a person's belief that successful performance will lead to rewards and other potential outcomes (sometimes called *performance-outcome expectancy*). **Valence** is the value a person assigns to the possible rewards and other work-related outcomes.

The use of multiplication signs in the expectancy equation ($M = E \times I \times V$) has important implications. Mathematically speaking, a zero at any location on the right side of the equation will result in zero motivation. This means that we cannot neglect any of these factors—expectancy, instrumentality, or valence; each has an influence on motivation.

<table>
<tr><td>**Expectancy**</td><td>**Instrumentality**</td><td>**Valence**</td></tr>
<tr><td>"Can I achieve the desired level of task performance?"</td><td>"What work outcomes will be received as a result of the performance?"</td><td>"How highly do I value work outcomes?"</td></tr>
</table>

Are you ready to test this theory? Most of us assume that people will work hard to get promoted. But is this necessarily true? Expectancy theory predicts that motivation to work hard for a promotion will be low if any one or more of three conditions apply.

If *expectancy is low*, motivation suffers. The person feels that he or she cannot achieve the performance level necessary to get promoted. So why try? If *instrumentality is low*, motivation suffers. The person lacks confidence that high performance will actually result in being promoted. So why try? If *valence is low*, motivation suffers. The person doesn't want a promotion, preferring less responsibility in the present job. So, if it isn't a valued outcome, why work hard to get it?

Figure 19.2 summarizes the management implications of expectancy theory. It is a reminder that different people are likely to come up with different answers to the question: "Why should I work hard today?" Knowing this, Vroom's advice is to always try and build high expectancies that make people believe that if they try hard, they can perform. Managers should also build a sense of instrumentality that allows people to see what results from high performance. And they should make sure that valence is always high for these likely work outcomes.

• Goal-Setting Theory Says that Well Chosen and Well Set Goals Can Be Motivating

The *goal-setting theory* described by Edwin Locke recognizes another important influence on individuals at work: the motivational properties of task goals.[13] His basic premise is that task goals can be highly motivating, but only *if* they are the right goals and *if* they are set in the right ways.

Goals give direction to people in their work. Goals clarify the performance expectations between leaders and followers, among co-workers, and even across subunits in an organization. Goals establish a frame of reference for task feedback, and they provide a

Figure 19.2 | How can managers apply the insights of expectancy theory?

To Maximize Expectancy

| Make the person feel competent and capable of achieving the desired performance level | → | • Select workers with ability
• Train workers to use ability
• Support work efforts
• Clarify performance goals |

To Maximize Instrumentality

| Make the person confident in understanding which rewards and outcomes will follow performance accomplishments | → | • Clarify psychological contracts
• Communicate performance–outcome possibilities
• Demonstrate what rewards are contingent on performance |

To Maximize Valence

| Make the person understand the value of various possible rewards and work outcomes | → | • Identify individual needs
• Adjust rewards to match these needs |

Managers should act in ways that maximize expectancies, instrumentalities, and valences for others. To maximize expectancy, hire capable workers, train and develop them continuously, and communicate goals and confidence in their skills. To maximize instrumentality, clarify, and stand by performance-reward linkages. Finally, to maximize valence, understand individual needs and try to tie work outcomes to important sources of need satisfaction.

foundation for control and self-management.[14] In these and related ways, Locke believes goal setting is a very practical and powerful motivational tool.

But what is a motivational goal? Research by Locke and his associates indicates that managers and team leaders should focus on how specific and difficult goals are, and how likely it is that others will accept and commit to them.[15] As you might suspect, this is a tall order. It is no easy task for managers to work with others to set the right goals in the right ways. And as *Management Tips* recommends, an important key to the goal-setting process is participation. Goals are most motivating when the individual has participated in setting them.

The concept of management by objectives, described in Module 12 as an integrative approach to planning and controlling, can be a good example. When done well, MBO brings together team leaders and team members in a participative process of goal setting and performance review. Consistent with goal-setting theory, the positive impact of MBO is most likely when specific and difficult goals are set in ways that create mutual understanding and increase acceptance and commitment.

Although all this sounds ideal and good, we have to be realistic. We can't always choose our own goals; there are many times in work when goals come to us from above and we are expected to help accomplish them. Does this mean that the motivational properties of goal setting are lost? Not necessarily; even though the goals are set there may be opportunities to participate in how to best pursue them. Locke's research also suggests that workers will respond positively to externally imposed goals if they trust the supervisors assigning them and they believe the supervisors will adequately support them.

MANAGEMENT TIPS

How to make goal setting work for you

- *Set specific goals*—avoid more generally stated ones, such as "Do your best."
- *Set challenging goals*—when realistic and attainable, they motivate better than easy ones.
- *Build commitment*—people work harder for goals they accept and believe in.
- *Clarify priorities*—expectations should be clear on which goals to pursue first.
- *Provide feedback*—people need to know how well they are doing.
- *Reward results*—don't let accomplishments pass unnoticed.

STUDY GUIDE

19.2 How do thought processes and decisions affect motivation to work?

Be Sure You Can . . .

- explain the role of social comparison in Adams's equity theory

- apply the equity theory to explain how people with felt negative inequity behave

- differentiate the terms *expectancy*, *instrumentality*, *valence*

- explain the implications of Vroom's expectancy equation, $M = E \times I \times V$

- explain Locke's goal-setting theory

- describe the fit between goal-setting theory and MBO

Define the Terms

Expectancy

Instrumentality

Valence

Rapid Review

- Adams's equity theory recognizes that social comparisons take place when rewards are distributed in the workplace.

- In equity theory, any sense of inequity is considered a motivating state that causes a person to behave in ways that can reduce the perceived inequity.

- Vroom's expectancy theory states that motivation = expectancy × instrumentality × valence.

- Managers using expectancy theory are advised to make sure rewards are achievable (maximizing expectancies), predictable (maximizing instrumentalities), and individually valued (maximizing valence).

- Locke's goal-setting theory emphasizes the motivational power of goals that are specific and challenging, as well as set through participatory means.

- The joint goal-setting process in Management by Objectives provides a framework for managers to apply goal setting theory in practice.

Reflect/React

1. Is it against human nature to work harder in response to perceived positive inequity?

2. Can a person with low expectancy ever be motivated to work hard at a task?

3. Will goal-setting theory work if the goals are fixed and only the means are open for discussion?

The theories discussed so far focus on people satisfying needs, resolving felt inequities, and/or pursuing positive expectancies and task goals. Instead of looking within the individual to explain motivation in these ways, *reinforcement theory* takes a different approach. It views human behavior as determined by its environmental consequences.

• Operant Conditioning Influences Behavior by Controlling Its Consequences

The premises of reinforcement theory rely on what E. L. Thorndike called the **law of effect**: People generally repeat behavior that results in a pleasant outcome, and avoid behavior that results in an unpleasant outcome.[16] Psychologist B. F. Skinner used this notion to popularize the concept of **operant conditioning**. This is the process of applying the law of effect to influence behavior by manipulating its consequences.[17] You may think of operant conditioning as learning by reinforcement.

Positive reinforcement strengthens or increases the frequency of desirable behavior by making a pleasant consequence contingent on its occurrence. *Example:* A manager nods to express approval to someone who makes a useful comment during a staff meeting. **Negative reinforcement** increases the frequency of or strengthens desirable behavior by making the avoidance of an unpleasant consequence contingent on its occurrence. *Example:* A manager who has nagged a worker every day about tardiness does not nag when the worker comes to work on time.

Punishment decreases the frequency of or eliminates an undesirable behavior by making an unpleasant consequence contingent on its occurrence. *Example:* A manager issues a written reprimand to an employee whose careless work creates quality problems. **Extinction** decreases the frequency of or eliminates an undesirable behavior by making the removal of a pleasant consequence contingent on its occurrence. *Example:* After observing that co-workers are providing social approval to a disruptive employee, a manager counsels co-workers to stop giving this approval.

Figure 19.3 shows how managers might apply these four reinforcement strategies in the work setting. In this case the supervisor's goal is to improve work quality as part of a total quality management program. Notice that both positive and negative reinforcement strategies strengthen desirable behavior when it occurs. Punishment and extinction strategies weaken or eliminate undesirable behaviors.

Figure 19.3	How do managers apply reinforcement strategies to influence work behavior?

To strengthen quality work, a supervisor might use positive reinforcement by praising the individual, or negative reinforcement by no longer complaining to him about poor quality work. To discourage poor quality work, a supervisor might use extinction (withholding things that are positively reinforcing such outcomes) or punishment (associating the poor-quality work with unpleasant results for the individual).

The **law of effect** states that behavior followed by pleasant consequences is likely to be repeated; behavior followed by unpleasant consequences is not.

Operant conditioning is the control of behavior by manipulating its consequences.

Positive reinforcement strengthens a behavior by making a desirable consequence contingent on its occurrence.

Negative reinforcement strengthens a behavior by making the avoidance of an undesirable consequence contingent on its occurrence.

Punishment discourages a behavior by making an unpleasant consequence contingent on its occurrence.

Extinction discourages a behavior by making the removal of a desirable consequence contingent on its occurrence.

• Positive Reinforcement Connects Desirable Behavior with Pleasant Consequences

MANAGEMENT TIPS

Guidelines for positive reinforcement

Positive Reinforcement:
- Clearly identify desired work behaviors.
- Maintain a diverse inventory of rewards.
- Inform everyone what must be done to get rewards.
- Recognize individual differences when allocating rewards.
- Follow the laws of immediate and contingent reinforcement.

Among the reinforcement strategies, positive reinforcement deserves special attention. It should be part of any manager's motivational strategy. In fact, it should be part of our personal life strategies as well—as parents working with our children, for example.

A popular business example of positive reinforcement is found with Mary Kay Cosmetics. The legendary pink Cadillac prize for top performers is a classic case. Over the years and in various versions, right up to convertibles and SUVs, this has provided tremendous motivation for Mary Kay's sales force. Of course, the prizes are always awarded with great ceremony at gala celebrations.[18]

Whether we are talking about pink cadillacs, pay, praise, or any other positive reinforcers, two laws govern the process. The *law of contingent reinforcement* states: For a reward to have maximum reinforcing value, it must be delivered only if the desired behavior is exhibited. The *law of immediate reinforcement* states: The more immediate the delivery of a reward after the occurrence of a desirable behavior, the greater the reinforcing value of the reward. *Management Tips* presents several useful guidelines for using these laws for positive reinforcement.

One of the ways to mobilize the power of positive reinforcement is through a process known as **shaping**. This is the creation of a new behavior by the positive reinforcement of successive approximations to it. The timing of positive reinforcement can also make a difference in its impact. A *continuous reinforcement schedule* administers a reward each time a desired behavior occurs. An *intermittent reinforcement schedule* rewards behavior only periodically. In general, continuous reinforcement will likely elicit a desired behavior more quickly than will intermittent reinforcement. Also, behavior acquired under an intermittent schedule will be more permanent than will behavior acquired under a continuous schedule.

Shaping is positive reinforcement of successive approximations to the desired behavior.

• Punishment Connects Undesirable Behavior with Unpleasant Consequences

As a reinforcement strategy, punishment attempts to eliminate undesirable behavior by making an unpleasant consequence contingent with its occurence. To punish an employee, for example, a manager may deny a valued reward, such as verbal praise or merit pay, or administer an unpleasant outcome, such as a verbal reprimand or pay reduction. Like positive reinforcement, punishment can be done poorly or it can be done well. All too often, it is done both too frequently and poorly. If you look again at *Management Tips* you'll find advice on how to best handle punishment when it is necessary as a reinforcement strategy.

Perhaps this discussion of punishment raises other questions in your mind. The use of reinforcement techniques in work settings has produced many success stories of improved safety, decreased absenteeism and tardiness, and increased productivity.[19] But, there are still debates over both the results and the ethics of controlling human behavior.

Some people worry that use of operant conditioning principles ignores the individuality of people, restricts their freedom of choice, and fails to recognize that people can be motivated by things other than extrinsic rewards. Others agree that reinforcement involves the control of behavior, but argue that control is part of every manager's job. The ethical issue, they say, isn't whether to use reinforcement principles, but whether we use them well in the performance context of the organization.

Even as research continues, the value of reinforcement in combination with the insights of the other motivation theories discussed in this module seems undeniable.[20]

PACESETTERS

Entrepreneur's ideas about hard work just too good to fail.

"I have this deep passion for entrepreneurs and what they do and what they add to society," says Charles Schwab. He should. As founder and chairman of the financial services firm, Charles Schwab, he employs over 16,000 people. He started the $4 billion firm with an investment of $100,000 in 1975. Schwab learned the values of hard work and commitment early in life. When growing up he was dyslexic, but didn't know it. Believing that he "had to work harder than the other kids," he did just that. He also says that a sense of humility is an ever-present reminder that you can always try to do better. He strives to create a work environment in which employees work hard and are treated with respect, the same as customers. Says Schwab: "People love working because when they go home at night, they can feel good about themselves."

Charles Schwab, *founder and chairman, Charles Schwab*

Be Sure You Can . . .

- explain the law of effect and operant conditioning

- illustrate how positive reinforcement, negative reinforcement, punishment, and extinction can influence work behavior

- explain the reinforcement technique of shaping

- describe how managers can use the laws of immediate and contingent reinforcement when allocating rewards

Define the Terms

Extinction

Law of effect

Negative reinforcement

Operant conditioning

Positive reinforcement

Punishment

Shaping

Rapid Review

- Reinforcement theory views human behavior as determined by its environmental consequences.

- The law of effect states that behavior followed by a pleasant consequence is likely to be repeated; behavior followed by an unpleasant consequence is unlikely to be repeated.

- Managers use strategies of positive reinforcement and negative reinforcement to strengthen desirable behaviors.

- Managers use strategies of punishment and extinction to weaken undesirable work behaviors.

- Positive reinforcement and punishment both work best when applied according to the laws of contingent and immediate reinforcement.

Reflect/React

1. Is operant conditioning a manipulative way to influence human behavior?

2. When is punishment justifiable as a reinforcement strategy?

3. Is it possible for a manager, or parent, to only use positive reinforcement?

MODULE
19

TEST PREP
Take the complete set of Module 19 quizzes online!

Multiple Choice

1. Maslow's progression principle stops working at the level of _____ needs.
   (a) growth **(b)** self-actualization **(c)** achievement **(d)** self-esteem

2. Lower-order needs in Maslow's hierarchy correspond to _____ needs in ERG theory.
   (a) growth **(b)** affiliation **(c)** existence **(d)** achievement

3. A worker high in need for _____ power in McClelland's theory tries to use power for the good of the organization.
   (a) position **(b)** expert **(c)** personal **(d)** social

4. In the _____ theory of motivation, an individual who feels underrewarded relative to a co-worker might be expected to reduce his or her work efforts in the future.
   (a) ERG **(b)** acquired needs **(c)** two-factor **(d)** equity

5. Which of the following is a correct match?
   (a) McClelland—ERG theory **(b)** Skinner—reinforcement theory **(c)** Vroom—equity theory **(d)** Locke—expectancy theory

6. In Herzberg's two-factor theory, base pay is considered a/an _____ factor.
   (a) hygiene **(b)** satisfier **(c)** equity **(d)** higher-order

7. The expectancy theory of motivation says that: motivation = expectancy × _____ × _____.
   (a) rewards/valence **(b)** instrumentality/valence **(c)** equity/instrumentality **(d)** rewards/valence

8. When a team member shows strong ego needs in Maslow's hierarchy, the team leader should find ways to link this person's work on the team task with _____.
   (a) compensation tied to group performance
   (b) individual praise and recognition for work well done
   (c) lots of social interaction with other team members
   (d) challenging individual performance goals

9. When someone has a high and positive "expectancy" in expectancy theory of motivation, this means that the person _____.
   (a) believes he or she can meet performance expectations **(b)** highly values the rewards being offered **(c)** sees a relationship between high performance and the available rewards **(d)** believes that rewards are equitable

10. The law of _____ states that behavior followed by a positive consequence is likely to be repeated, whereas behavior followed by an undesirable consequence is not likely to be repeated.
    (a) reinforcement **(b)** contingency **(c)** goal setting **(d)** effect

Short Response

11. What preferences does a person high in the need for achievement bring to the workplace?

12. Why is MBO a way to apply goal-setting theory?

13. What are three ways a worker could reduce the discomforts of perceived negative inequity over a pay raise?

14. How can shaping be used to encourage desirable work behaviors?

Integration & Application

I overheard a conversation between two Executive MBA students. One was telling the other: "My firm just contracted with Musak to have mood music piped into the offices at various times of the workday." The other replied: "That's a waste of money; there should be better things to do if the firm is really interested in increasing motivation and performance."

Questions: Is the second student right or wrong, and why?

SELF-ASSESSMENT
Student Engagement Survey

INSTRUCTIONS *Use the following scale to indicate the degree to which you agree with the following statements:*

1—No agreement
2—Weak agreement
3—Some agreement
4—Considerable agreement
5—Very strong agreement

1 Do you know what is expected of you in this course?
2 Do you have the resources and support you need to do your coursework correctly?
3 In this course, do you have the opportunity to do what you do best all the time?
4 In the last week, have you received recognition or praise for doing good work in this course?
5 Does your instructor seem to care about you as a person?
6 Is there someone in the course who encourages your development?
7 In this course, do your opinions seem to count?
8 Does the mission/purpose of the course make you feel your study is important?
9 Are other students in the course committed to doing quality work?
10 Do you have a best friend in the course?
11 In the last six sessions, has someone talked to you about your progress in the course?
12 In this course, have you had opportunities to learn and grow?

SCORING AND INTERPRETATION

Score the instrument by adding up all your responses. A score of 0–24 suggests you are "actively disengaged" from the learning experience; a score of 25–47 suggests you are "moderately engaged"; a score of 48–60 indicates you are "actively engaged."

This instrument is a counterpart to a survey used by the Gallup Organization to measure the "engagement" of American workers. The Gallup results are surprising—indicating that up to 19 percent of U.S. workers are actively disengaged, with the annual lost productivity estimated at some $300 billion per year. One has to wonder: What are the costs of academic disengagement by students?

PATHWAYS to WileyPLUS

CASE SNAPSHOT

Go online to read this case!

The Red Cross: But Can They Help Themselves?

After facing criticism for its response to Hurricane Katrina, its head recently resigned, citing irreconcilable differences with a board of directors she claimed was operating by yesterday's strategies. The board disagrees. Who must change for the Red Cross to survive?

MODULE 19 Online Interactive Learning Resources

Skill Builder
• Initiative

Experiential Exercises
• Why Do We Work?
• Compensation and Benefits Debate

Team Project
• CEO Pay

Money isn't everything;

Motivational Dynamics

Best Buy's CEO, Bradbury H. Anderson, is an unusual example in a business world where big CEO paychecks often attract criticism. What did he do? Instead of taking hundreds of thousands of stock options as part of his annual salary, he distributed them to lower-level workers. "I'm not trying to do a great thing," he said: "I'm just going to do what's appropriate for a leader."[1] Although Anderson's salary plus bonus was still over $3 million for the year, it's still a story worth considering. Most CEOs who can afford it, don't share the wealth this way.

Just how far does pay go in influencing motivation? When does the extreme pay of the CEO or other higher-ups become a turn-off for lower

the job counts too

levels? What else, besides pay, counts highly as a "turn-on" for most people?[2] Would your list match these top items found in a Harris Poll: Having control over your work, being able to use your talents and skills, having your work appreciated?

These are all good questions. And, there are a lot of interesting things happening as well-intentioned managers try to answer them.

When a Sun Microsystems executive talks about a group of workers that is 15 percent more productive than others in the company, would you guess that he's talking about "virtual workers," ones who work largely from home offices?[3]

And what do you think happened when a team at Chubb insurance was asked to take on more performance responsibility? They agreed. But only in return for having more control over their work schedules. Some chose to work compressed weeks and others took flexible hours. One team member says that they all planned the work and "really pulled together." They also speeded insurance claims processing and reduced the team's absenteeism rate.[4]

→ MODULE GUIDE

 20.1 What is the link between motivation, performance, and rewards?

- Motivation is influenced by both extrinsic and intrinsic rewards.
- Merit pay is a type of pay-for-performance system.
- Bonuses and profit sharing plans link pay with performance.
- Employee stock ownership ties financial rewards to firm performance.

 20.2 How do job designs and work schedules influence motivation?

- Job simplification builds narrow, routine, and repetitive jobs.
- Job rotation and job enlargement increase task variety in job content.
- Job enrichment expands job content with self-management responsibilities.
- Self-managing teams are a form of job enrichment for groups.
- Alternative work schedules offer flexibility in job context.
- Contingency and part-time work have pluses and minuses.

20.1 What Is the Link Between Motivation, Performance, and Rewards?

One way to integrate many of the insights from motivation theories discussed in the previous module is with the model shown in Figure 20.1. It shows motivation influencing effort that, when combined with appropriate individual abilities and organizational support, leads to performance.[5] And when rewards for performance are perceived as equitable and reinforcing, satisfaction and motivation are both increased.

Can you see the integration here? Does this model seem to depict the ways you would expect motivation, performance, and rewards to fit together?

| Figure 20.1 | How can the various motivation theories be combined in an integrated model of motivational dynamics at work? |

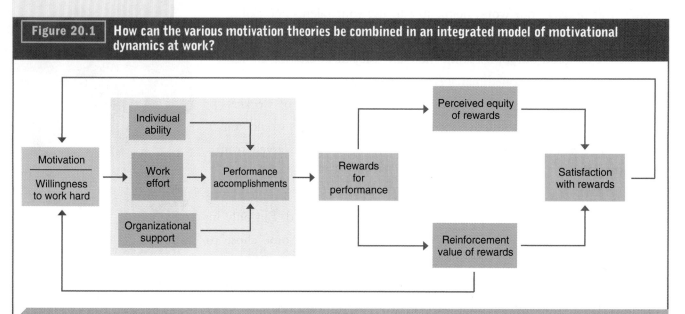

In this integrated model, individual performance is a function of ability, support, and effort. Motivation predicts effort. Motivation is usually higher when extrinsic rewards for performance are both given according to reinforcement principles and also perceived as equitable. Motivation should also be higher when job performance creates intrinsic rewards that are self-satisfying.

• Motivation Is Influenced by Both Extrinsic and Intrinsic Rewards

An **extrinsic reward** is provided by someone else.

If you describe a work setting as "motivating," you probably envision one rich in rewards, right? While this is true, we also need to recognize that there are different types of rewards out there and that they can mean quite different things depending on how they are administered. And, some rewards may be more clearly linked with performance than others.

Extrinsic rewards are externally administered; one person gives them to another.[6] The most common examples are pay raises and bonuses, promotions, time off, special assignments, office fixtures, awards, verbal praise, and recognition. **Intrinsic rewards**, by contrast, are self-administered and occur naturally as we work.[7] Examples are the sense of control and skill utilization reported in the Harris poll results in the module opener.

An **intrinsic reward** occurs naturally during job performance.

A **performance-contingent reward** is linked directly to job performance.

A **performance-contingent reward** is one that is received in direct correlation to one's performance. Because intrinsic rewards occur naturally as we do our jobs, you can argue that they are always performance contingent. An air traffic controller, for example, says: "I don't know of anything I'd rather be doing. I love working the airplanes." At a small copper kettle manufacturer in northern Ohio, a maker of timpani drum bowls says: "It gets in your blood and you can't get rid of it. It's something you can create with your hands and no one else can."[8]

Extrinsic rewards are a somewhat different story. Depending on who is giving them out and how, they may or may not be performance contingent. And when they are not, the motivational impact on performance has to be questioned. You've probably heard or even made this complaint in one of your jobs. It's also an issue in criticisms of CEO pay. Not only do some consider it too high on the average, many CEOs seem to do well even when their companies do poorly[9]. What is your reaction upon learning that: a Honeywell CEO once received some $54 million in compensation the same year that his firm laid off 11,600 workers worldwide; the CEO of Cendant Corp. took home $133 million in a year that his firm lost 21 percent of its value?[10]

• Merit Pay Is a Type of Pay-for-Performance System

Pay! It may be that no other work issue receives as much attention. And when it comes to handling pay increases, there is no doubt that the trend in industry today is toward "merit."[11]

If you are part of a **merit pay** system, your pay increases will be performance contingent; they will be based on some assessment of how well you perform. This notion fits well with the equity, expectancy, and reinforcement theories discussed in the previous module.[12] Merit pay plans are supposed to recognize and positively reinforce high performers. They are also supposed to put low performers on notice, hopefully encouraging them to do better in the future, or perhaps leave.

Merit pay systems make a lot of sense in principle, but they can also run into difficulties. A survey reported by the *Wall Street Journal* found that only 23 percent of employees believed they understood their companies' reward systems.[13] Think about the possible problems. Who assesses performance? Suppose the employee doesn't agree with the assessment? Is the system fair and equitable to everyone involved? Is there enough money available to make the merit increases meaningful for those who receive them?

A good merit pay system will be able to handle these questions and more. For sure it will be based on a solid foundation of agreed-upon and well-defined performance measures. At Applebee's International, Inc., the restaurant chain, for example, managers know that part of their merit pay will be determined by what percentage of their best workers are retained. In an industry known for high turnover, Applebee's wants to retain its best workers. The company makes this a high priority goal for managers, and makes their pay increases contingent on how well they do.[14] In terms of clear performance measures this system is on target. But even this system can break down if Applebee's managers don't perceive that it is administered in a fair, consistent, and credible fashion.

Merit pay awards pay increases in proportion to performance contributions.

Bonus pay plans provide one-time payments based on performance accomplishments.

• Bonuses and Profit Sharing Plans Link Pay with Performance

There's a bit more to the Applebee's story. If you are one of the employees that managers want to retain, you might be on the receiving end of "Applebucks"—small cash bonuses that are given to reward performance and raise loyalty to the firm.[15] This is a modest example of a another pay-for-performance approach—the "bonus." How would you like to someday receive a letter like this one, once sent to two top executives by Amazon.com's chairman Jeff Bezos? "In recognition and appreciation of your contributions," his letter read, "Amazon.com will pay you a special bonus in the amount of $1,000,000."[16] Not bad for a performance incentive!

Bonus pay plans provide one-time or lump-sum payments to employees based on the accomplish-

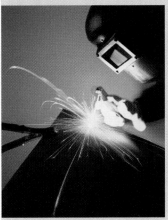

NEWSLINE

How to make pay-for-performance pay off At Lincoln Electric, long known for its innovative approach to employee compensation, a pay-for-performance system includes a low base salary topped by bonuses tied to company profitability and individual performance ratings. To promote quality and impart a sense of responsibility, the company holds employees accountable for each piece of work they produce. Pieces are "signed," or marked, which allows tracing of defective ones back to the worker. Managers also note rejects and returns on employees' merit ratings, which also directly impact year-end bonuses. Lincoln's system isn't for everyone, and it's certainly not problem-free. The firm still faces hard questions about its unique approach to incentives and how well it fits with the demands of globalization. For example, when Lincoln embarked on international expansion that affected its profitability, domestic workers complained. They felt things beyond their control, like the costs of the firm's globalization drive, were threatening their bonuses.

Reflect: Does a pay-for-performance system such as Lincoln's appeal to you? Suppose you had the choice between a job that paid a straight salary and one that was straight commission? Which would you prefer and why?

ment of specific performance targets or some other extraordinary contribution, such as an idea for a work improvement. Bonuses have been most common at the executive level, but many companies now use them more extensively across levels.[17] And whereas some bonus systems award bonuses to individuals, others award them to everyone in the group or division responsible for high performance. Home Depot focuses at the store level. The firm paid out $90 million in cash bonuses in one year to employees in stores that met special financial goals.[18]

Another pay-for-performance approach is **profit sharing**. It distributes to employees a proportion of net profits earned by the organization in a performance period. At the marketing services firm Valassis Communications Inc., a member of *Fortune's* 100 Best Companies to Work For, every employee from the press operator right up to CEO is eligible for profit sharing that runs from 10 to 25 percent of pay. Vatex America, an apparel manufacturer, distributes 10 percent of pretax profits to employees each month and an additional amount at the end of the year. The exact share depends on an individual's monthly attendance, tardiness, and performance as rated by supervisors.[19]

Gain-sharing plans extend the profit-sharing concept by allowing groups of employees to share in any savings or "gains" realized through their efforts to reduce costs and increase productivity. The classic example of gain sharing is the Scanlon plan, which usually results in distributing 75 percent of gains to workers, with the company keeping the remaining 25 percent. At East Alabama Medical Center, another of *Fortune's* 100 Best Companies, a gain-sharing plan focuses attention on the mission of caring for people. It rewards employees with gain-sharing compensation for meeting patient satisfaction and financial goals. The CEO distributes the checks at a special annual ceremony.[20]

• Employee Stock Ownership Ties Financial Rewards to Firm Performance

Chances are that if you go to work for private industry you'll have a chance to participate in yet another pay-for-performance approach that is very popular today: stock ownership. Starbucks uses this as part of its recipe—not for coffee, but for rewards and performance. The company offers employees **stock options** linked to their base pay.[21] Such options give the owner the right to buy shares of stock at a future date at a fixed price. This means that they gain financially the more the stock price rises above the original option price. However, they lose this gain if the stock price ends up lower.

The expectation is that employees with stock options will be highly motivated to do their best so that the firm performs well and its stock price increases. The Hay Group reports that the most admired U.S. companies are also ones that offer stock options to a greater proportion of their workforces.[22] Their use seems to have a positive impact at Starbucks. The firm's employees use the phrase "bean-stocking it" when they find ways to reduce costs or increase sales.

Employee stock ownership plans take this notion a step further by helping people purchase stock in their employing companies. The assumption, as with stock options, is that stock ownership will motivate employees to work hard so that the company stays successful.

At Anson Industries, a Chicago construction firm, this is played out to the extreme – almost every employee is an owner.[23] Only employees can own Anson stock, and 95 percent do so. But employees can sell their shares only for things like medical emergencies, downpayments on homes, and retirement planning. An administrative assistant bought 9,000 shares over 30 years and now finds them worth close to $700,000; a benefits manager accumulated $500,000 worth over her career. She says it did make a difference in her job performance: "You have a different attitude. . . everyone here has the same attitude because it's our money."

Profit sharing distributes to employees a proportion of net profits earned by the organization.

Gain sharing plans allow employees to share in cost savings or productivity gains realized by their efforts.

Stock options give the right to purchase shares at a fixed price in the future.

STUDY GUIDE

20.1 What is the link between motivation, performance, and rewards?

Be Sure You Can . . .

- construct an integrative model of motivation that includes ideas of the content, process, and reinforcement theories

- differentiate extrinsic and intrinsic rewards

- explain the concept of performance-contingent rewards

- describe bonuses, profit sharing, gain sharing, and stock options as pay-for-performance systems

Define the Terms

Bonus pay

Extrinsic rewards

Gain sharing

Intrinsic rewards

Merit pay

Performance-contingent reward

Profit sharing

Stock options

Rapid Review

- An integrative model of motivational dynamics draws together the insights of the needs, equity, expectancy, and reinforcement theories.

- Extrinsic rewards like pay are provided by a supervisor acting for the organization.

- Intrinsic rewards, like a sense of achievement, come directly from the work experience itself.

- Merit pay is a type of performance-contingent reward where one's pay increase is tied directly to performance accomplishments.

- Incentive compensation programs, such as bonuses, gain sharing, and profit sharing, allow workers to benefit financially from improved organizational profits and productivity.

Reflect/React

1. How can you modify Figure 20.1 to make it better fit with your work experiences?

2. Would you be willing to have your entire annual pay increase based on merit?

3. Should it be mandatory that all employees have the possibility of stock ownership in their employers?

Job design is the allocation of specific work tasks to individuals and groups.

Remember the module subtitle: Money isn't everything; the job counts too! When we move beyond pay as a motivational concern, **job design** has to be considered highly important.

If you really think about it, why can't all jobs be designed to meet two goals: high job performance and high job satisfaction? To do this, however, a job would have to be a good fit between the needs and talents of the individual, and the task goals and requirements of the organization. And as you might expect, just what constitutes a good fit is going to vary from one individual and situation to the next.

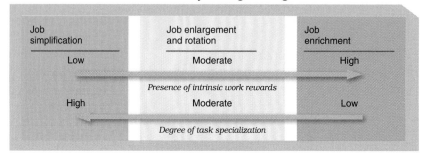

A continuum of job-design strategies.

• Job Simplification Builds Narrow, Routine, and Repetitive Jobs

Job simplification employs people in clearly defined and very specialized tasks.

Herzberg's two-factor theory was discussed in the previous module. He would not be a fan of **job simplification**. This job design approach comes to us from Taylor's Scientific Management principles described in Module 3. It puts people to work on well-defined, highly specialized and standardized tasks. The automobile assembly line is a classic example; service work in fast-food restaurants is another. What other examples can you think of?

Simplified jobs are narrow in *job scope*, the number and variety of different tasks a person performs. Many people around the world earn their living working in these types of jobs.[24] Most likely the athletic shoes you wear, your jeans, and your electronic goods are all made this way. And increasingly you'll find as much of this work as possible being done by computer-guided machines. In fact, the most extreme form of job simplification is **automation**, or the total mechanization of a job. You may not realize it, but robots most likely played a big role in building the car that you're driving.

Automation is the total mechanization of a job.

The logic of job simplification is straightforward. Workers in simplified jobs need only a limited set of skills. They should master the job quicker and be able to consistently perform well as they do the same tasks over and over again. However, things don't always work out this well. Although simplified jobs appeal to some people, others dislike the structured and repetitive tasks. Instead of being highly productive they might actually drive up costs through absenteeism and turnover, and as boredom and alienation result in poor performance.

But before you are too quick to dismiss this job design approach, consider the case of Cindy Vang. She works on an assembly line for Medtronics, Inc. Her job is in a dust-free room where she makes a specialized medical component. She is certified on five of 14 job skills in her department. At any given time, however, she performs only one of them, for example, feeding small devices by tweezers into special containers. Some might view her job as tedious work without much challenge. But Vang says: "I like it." Importantly, she notes that the job doesn't interfere with her home life with a husband and three sons. She meets her economic needs through a low-stress job and comfortable work environment.[25]

• Job Rotation and Job Enlargement Increase Task Variety in Job Content

One way to move beyond simplification in job design is to broaden the scope through *horizontal loading*—having the individual perform tasks associated with earlier and later stages in the workflow. This can be done through **job rotation** that increases task variety by periodically shifting workers between jobs involving different task assignments. Managers often use it for training, so that people understand both multiple jobs and how their jobs relate to others.

Vertical Loading

Move planning and controlling in from above

Horizontal Loading

Move tasks in from earlier in workflow

Job Design

... expands job scope

Move tasks in from later in workflow

Move out work that can be done at lower levels

... increases job depth

Another approach to horizontal loading is through **job enlargement**. This increases task variety by combining two or more tasks that separate workers previously handled. Most often, these are tasks done immediately before or after the work performed in the original job.

What would Herzberg say about job rotation and job enlargement? Well, he's still not real happy. He would argue that just adding more variety to low content tasks isn't very satisfying or motivational. He wants something more.

• Job Enrichment Expands Job Content with Self-Management Responsibilities

"If you want people to do a good job," says Herzberg, you have to "give them a good job to do."[26] He goes on to argue that this is best done through **job enrichment**, the practice of expanding job content to create more opportunities for higher-order need satisfaction. In contrast to job enlargement and rotation, job enrichment focuses not just on job scope but also on *job depth*—the extent to which the individual, not the supervisor, performs task planning and evaluating duties. This is called *vertical loading* of job content by building more self-management into job designs.

Modern management theory values job enrichment and its motivating potential. However, in true contingency fashion, it recognizes that job enrichment may not work for everyone. This perspective is reflected in the core characteristics model developed by J. Richard Hackman and his associates. It offers a way for managers to design jobs that best fit the needs of both the people doing them and the organization.[27]

The core characteristics model approaches job design with a focus on five "core" job characteristics: skill variety, task identity, task significance, autonomy, and job feedback. A job that scores high on these characteristics is considered enriched. Can you think of any specific jobs that might score high or low in this model?

Job rotation increases task variety by periodically shifting workers between different jobs.

Job enlargement increases task variety by combining into one job two or more tasks previously assigned to separate workers.

Job enrichment increases job depth by adding work planning and evaluating duties normally performed by the supervisor.

PACESETTERS

Meet the craftswomen of the world.

Did you know that women, by themselves, support one-quarter of the world's families? Paola Gianturco didn't, until she heard the news from the United Nations Fourth World Conference on Women, held in China. Since then she has traveled the world to learn more about the struggles of third-world women entrepreneurs. She met Muslim mirror embroiderers in a poor Indian village in the state of Gujarat, found women knitters in Bolivian cooperatives blessing loan money with confetti and beer, and watched Zulu women in South Africa weave baskets that later sold under a common brand name. Gianturco helps support women entrepreneurs through the Crafts Center, a nonprofit in Washington, D.C., with the mission "to improve the lives of the world's poor, especially women, by helping them develop sustainable micro enterprises, while preserving their cultures, beliefs, and environments."

Paola Gianturco, *director, Crafts Center*

How to Enrich Jobs by Improving Core Characteristics

Form natural units of work   Make sure that the tasks people perform logically relate to one another and provide a clear and meaningful task identity.

Combine tasks   Expand job responsibilities by pulling together into one larger job a number of smaller tasks previously done by others.

Establish client relationships   Put people in contact with others who, as clients inside and/or outside the organization, use the results of their work.

Open feedback channels   Provide opportunities for people to receive performance feedback as they work and to learn how performance changes over time.

Practice vertical loading   Give people more control over their work by increasing their authority to perform the planning and controlling previously done by supervisors.

Members of **self-managing teams** make many decisions about how they do their work.

Skills-based pay compensates workers by the number of job-relevant skills they master.

As shown in the *Exhibit – How to Enrich Jobs By Improving Core Characteristics*, job satisfaction and job performance are influenced by the impact of the core characteristics on a person's psychological states, including the perceived: meaningfulness of the work, responsibility for the outcomes, and knowledge of results. But don't forget, the core characteristics approach is also a contingency model that recognizes that not everyone will be a good fit for a highly enriched job. Those who are expected to respond most favorably are likely to have strong growth needs, appropriate job knowledge and skills, and be otherwise satisfied with the job context.

• Self-Managing Teams Are a Form of Job Enrichment for Groups

In a growing number of organizations, the focus of job design is shifting from the individual to the group. One of the popular developments in this area is with **self-managing work teams**. These teams reflect redesigned jobs, to allow the workers to create a high degree of task interdependence and the authority to make many decisions about how they go about doing their work.[28] As such, you might think of this as a form of job enrichment for groups.

As Figure 20.2 shows, self-managing teams operate with participative decision making, shared tasks, and the responsibility for many of the managerial tasks performed by supervisors in more traditional settings. The self-management responsibilities include planning and scheduling work, training members in various tasks, sharing tasks, meeting performance goals, ensuring high quality, and solving day-to-day operating problems. In some settings, the team's authority may even extend to hiring and firing members.

A key feature of self-managing teams is *multitasking*, in which team members each develop the skills to perform several different jobs. This creates yet another alternative for incentive pay. **Skills-based pay** compensates workers according to the number of

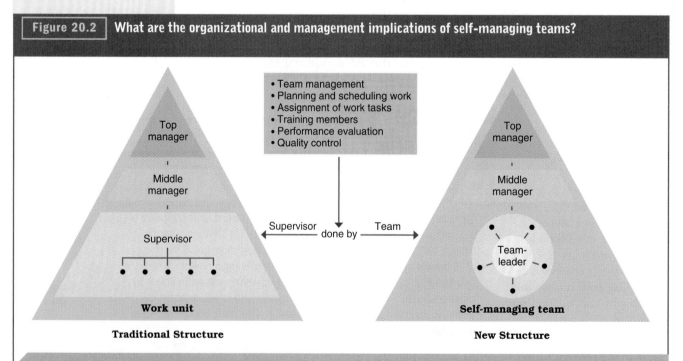

| Figure 20.2 | What are the organizational and management implications of self-managing teams? |

Members of self-managing teams make decisions together on team membership, task plans and job assignments, training and performance evaluations, and quality control. Because they essentially manage themselves in these ways, they no longer need a traditional supervisor or department head. Instead, the team leader performs this role with the support of team members. The team leader and team as a whole report to the next higher level of management and are held collectively accountable for performance results.

job-relevant skills they master. It is common in self-managing teams where part of the "self-management" includes training and certification of co-workers in job skills. It also reinforces the concept of continuous learning. Wouldn't you want to acquire more skills and knowledge if you knew your company would reward you for it?

• Alternative Work Schedules Offer Flexibility in Job Context

Not only is the content of jobs changing for people in today's workplace, the context is changing too. One significant development is the emergence of alternative ways for people to schedule their work time.[29] As more and more workers struggle to balance their work and family responsibilities, opportunities for flexibility in work schedules can be highly valued and motivational.

A **compressed workweek** allows a worker to complete a full-time job in less than the standard five days of 8-hour shifts.[30] Its most common form is the "4–40," that is, accomplishing 40 hours of work in four 10-hour days. This is found at USAA, a diversified financial services company that has ranked among the 100 best companies to work for in America. A large part of the firm's San Antonio workforce is on a four-day schedule, with some working Monday through Thursday, and others working Tuesday through Friday.[31]

Although compressed workweeks can cause scheduling problems, possible customer complaints, and even union objections, the benefits are there as well. USAA reports improved morale, as well as lower overtime costs, less absenteeism, and decreased use of sick leave.

The term **flexible working hours**, also called *flextime*, describes any work schedule that gives employees some choice in daily work hours. A typical flextime schedule offers choices of starting and ending times, while still putting in a full workday. Some people may start earlier and leave earlier, while others do the opposite. The flexibility provides opportunities to attend to personal affairs such as medical appointments, home emergencies, and children's school schedules.

Sample flexible working hours schedule

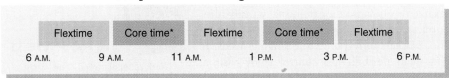

| Flextime | Core time* | Flextime | Core time* | Flextime |

6 A.M.   9 A.M.   11 A.M.   1 P.M.   3 P.M.   6 P.M.

Flexible hours help organizations attract and retain those talented employees with complicated personal responsibilities. These include dual-career couples, single parents with child-care responsibilities, and employees who are caring for elderly parents. Is such flexibility high on your list of desirable job attributes?

All top 100 companies in *Working Mother* magazine's list of best employers for working moms offer flexible scheduling. Reports indicate that flexibility in dealing with non-work obligations reduces stress and unwanted job turnover.[32] The women's sports apparel company Athleta, for example, attributes its low turnover rate compared with the industry average to flexible scheduling.

Another work scheduling alternative is **job sharing**, where two or more persons split one full-time job. This often involves each person working one-half day, but it can also be done on weekly or monthly sharing arrangements. Both the employees and organizations benefit when talented people who cannot devote a full day to work are kept or brought back into the workforce.

Then there is remote work, virtual offices, or work at home.[33] Whatever you call it, many people do some form of **telecommuting**. They spend at least a portion of scheduled work hours outside the office linked with co-workers, customers, and bosses by a variety of advanced information technologies. And, it's popular. Estimates are that 27 percent of American workers will spend at least one day a month working at home by 2008.[34]

When asked what they like, telecommuters report increased productivity, fewer distractions, the freedom to be their own boss, and the benefit of having more

A **compressed workweek** allows a worker to complete a full-time job in less than five days.

Flexible working hours give employees some choice in daily work hours.

Job sharing splits one job between two people.

Telecommuting involves using IT to work at home or outside the office.

time for themselves. But there are potential negatives as well. Some telecommuters report working too much, having less time to themselves, difficulty separating work and personal life, and having less time for family.[35] One says: "You have to have self-discipline and pride in what you do, but you also have to have a boss that trusts you enough to get out of the way."[36] Management Tips offers several guidelines for how to make telecommuting work for you.[37]

• Contingency and Part-Time Work Have Pluses and Minuses

The growing use of temporary workers is another striking employment trend.[38] **Part-time work** is done on any schedule less than the standard 40-hour workweek and where the individual is not designated as a full-time employee.

Part-time work is temporary employment for less than the standard 40-hour workweek.

Part-time and temporary workers now constitute some 30 percent of the U.S. workforce; over 90 percent of firms surveyed by the American Management Association use them.[39] No longer limited to the traditional areas of clerical services, sales personnel, and unskilled labor, these workers serve an increasingly broad range of employer needs. It is now possible to hire on a part-time basis everything from executive support, such as a chief financial officer, to such special expertise as engineering, computer programming, and market research.[40]

Contingency workers are employed on a part-time and temporary basis to supplement a permanent workforce.

Many employers have come to rely on part-timers who work as **contingency workers**. Sometimes called *permatemps*, they supplement the full-time workforce working part-time only and somewhat permanently. Companies like this because they can usually easily hire, contract, and terminate part-time or contingency workers in response to changing needs. It gives them flexibility to control labor costs and deal with economic cycles.

But there is a possible dark side to part-time and contingency work as well. Employers usually treat part-time and contingency workers as different from the full-timers. Companies may pay temporary workers less and restrict or deny eligibility for important benefits, such as health care and life insurance. They are also typically left on their own to set up pension plans. The next time you read or hear about this in the news, give it some thought. The trend toward hiring part-time and contingency workers may be good for business, but is it good for society?

STAY INFORMED

Work schedule trends and preferences:

- Flextime ranks #1 in desired job supports.
- 12% of U.S. workers do some remote work.
- 70% of Agilent's workers are remote at least some of the time.
- 33% of women and 28% of men would like part-time work if they could afford it.
- 58% of retiring baby boomers would like to work part-time.

STUDY GUIDE

20.2 How do job designs and work schedules influence motivation?

Be Sure You Can . . .

- differentiate job simplification, enlargement, and rotation

- list and describe the five core job characteristics

- explain the relationship between these characteristics and job enrichment

- explain how a person's growth needs and skills can affect their responses to enriched jobs

- describe a self-managing team

- differentiate compressed work week, flexible working hours, and job sharing

- explain the pros and cons of part-time work

Define the Terms

Automation

Compressed workweek

Contingency workers

Flexible working hours

Job design

Job enlargement

Job enrichment

Job rotation

Job simplification

Job sharing

Part-time work

Self-managing team

Skill-based pay

Telecommuting

Rapid Review

- Jobs are ideally designed so workers enjoy high levels of both job performance and job satisfaction.

- Job simplification creates jobs with well-defined tasks with many routine operations, such as the typical assembly-line job.

- Job enlargement allows individuals to perform a broader range of tasks; job rotation allows individuals to shift among different jobs of similar skill levels.

- Job enrichment builds jobs that have more self-management responsibilities, including planning and controlling of the work.

- The core characteristics model of job design analyzes jobs according to five core characteristics: skill variety, task identity, task significance, autonomy, and feedback.

- Alternative work schedules can help organizations respond better to individual needs and personal circumstances; they include the compressed workweek, flextime, job sharing, telecommuting, and part-time or contingency work.

Reflect/React

1. Is job simplification only good for people who have little career ambition?

2. Would you expect someone to want more pay if their job is enriched?

3. Is it inevitable that employees will abuse flextime and telecommuting work schedules?

Multiple Choice

1. In the integrated model of motivation presented in this module, people will be satisfied with rewards only if they are _____.
(a) perceived as equitable **(b)** intrinsic **(c)** meeting growth needs **(d)** improving on hygiene factors

2. Both Barry and Marissa are highly motivated college students. Knowing this I can expect them to be _____ in my class.
(a) hard working **(b)** high performing **(c)** highly satisfied **(d)** highly dissatisfied

3. A _____ pay plan is performance contingent because it awards bonuses based on cost savings or productivity increases that workers help to generate for their employers.
(a) merit **(b)** gain sharing **(c)** profit sharing **(d)** skills-based

4. If a manager redesigns a job through vertical loading, she would most likely _____.
(a) move tasks from earlier in the workflow into the job
(b) move tasks from later in the workflow into the job
(c) move higher level or managerial responsibilities into the job **(d)** raise the standards for high performance

5. Which job design strategy allows workers to shift among a variety of jobs requiring essentially the same skills?
(a) Job simplification **(b)** Job enlargement **(c)** Job rotation **(d)** Job sharing

6. According to the core characteristics model of job design, people will be most likely to find an enriched job motivating if they _____.
(a) receive stock options **(b)** have ability and support **(c)** experience vertical loading **(d)** are satisfied with the job context

7. Workers who are on a compressed workweek schedule typically work _____ .
(a) 40 hours in 4 days **(b)** remotely from home **(c)** part-time **(d)** a flexible day

8. Job _____ is where two workers split one job on a mutually arranged work schedule.
(a) rotation **(b)** sharing **(c)** enrichment **(d)** compression

9. When a job allows a person to do a complete unit of work, for example, process an insurance claim from point of receipt from the customer to point of final resolution for the customer, it would be considered high on which core characteristic?
(a) Task identity **(b)** Task significance **(c)** Task autonomy **(d)** Feedback

10. Automation is the most extreme form of _____ in job design.
(a) vertical loading **(b)** horizontal loading **(c)** task identity **(d)** simplification

Short Response

11. What is the difference between bonus, gain sharing, and stock options as pay-for-performance plans?

12. Why are self-managing teams called job enrichment for groups?

13. Why is a person's growth-need strength included as a moderator variable in the core characteristics model?

14. Why might an employer not want to offer employees the option of working on a compressed workweek schedule?

Integration & Application

Rick Solloway is frustrated with one of his employees. Jon wasn't performing up to expectations and has a bad attitude. Rick says: "There's a certain number of people who, despite everything you try, just don't work out. I'm going to let him go and look for a replacement."

Questions: Be a "good conscience" advisor to Rick; help him to double-check this decision before implementing it. What questions would you ask him to make sure that he really has done everything possible to find a good motivational fit between Jon and the job Rick is asking him to perform?

INSTRUCTIONS *Complete this inventory by circling the number that indicates the extent to which you agree or disagree with each of the following statements.*

1 How much time do you spend on nonwork-related activities such as taking care of family, spending time with friends, participating in sports, enjoying leisure time?
Almost none/never 1 2 3 4 5 Very much/always

2 How often do family duties and nonwork responsibilities make you feel tired out?
Almost none/never 1 2 3 4 5 Very much/always

3 How often do you feel short of time for family-related and nonwork activities?
Almost none/never 1 2 3 4 5 Very much/always

4 How difficult is it for you to do everything you should as a family member and friend to others?
Almost none/never 1 2 3 4 5 Very much/always

5 I often feel that I am being run ragged, with not enough time in a day to do everything and do it well.
Completely disagree 1 2 3 4 5 Completely agree

6 I am given entirely too much work to do.
Strongly disagree 1 2 3 4 5 Strongly agree

7 How much conflict do you feel there is between the demands of your job and your family, and nonwork activities life?
Not at all/never 1 2 3 4 5 A lot/very often

8 How much does your job situation interfere with your family life?
Not at all/never 1 2 3 4 5 A lot/very often

9 How much does your family life and nonwork activities interfere with your job?
Not at all/never 1 2 3 4 5 A lot/very often

SCORING AND INTERPRETATION

Work-life conflict is defined as "a form of interrole conflict in which the role pressures from the work and family nonwork domains are mutually noncompatible in some respect." Demands of one role make it difficult to satisfy demands of the others.

Family Demand Score: Total items #1, #2, #3, #4 and divide by 4.
Work Demand Score: Total items #5, #6 and divide by 2.
Work-Family Conflict Score: Total items #7, #8, #9 and divide by 3.

PATHWAYS to WileyPLUS

CASE SNAPSHOT

Go online to read this case!

Starbucks: Gigantic. . . and Getting Bigger Every Day

What's a coffee giant to do when it's already on every street corner? Starbucks is trying to revitalize its brand by diversifying its product offerings and making the shift from coffee joint to lifestyle lounge. But is the company overreaching? And will consumers take the bait?

MODULE 20 | **Online Interactive Learning Resources**

Skill Builder
- Self-Efficacy

Experiential Exercises
- The Best Job Designs
- Contingency Workforce

Team Project
- Unleashing Human Potential

Teams and Teamwork

• Pacesetters

The real power of any group is in the mix of members

• Management Tips

Seven sins of deadly meetings

• Newsline

Working through the Web can supercharge group work

• Self-Assessment

Team Leader Skills

• Case Snapshot

Steve Jobs

Great teams are everywhere. Do you remember films like Toy Story, A Bug's Life, Monsters Inc., and Finding Nemo? These popular animated films share a common heritage: Pixar Animation Studios. To create the best animated films, Pixar's leadership, including CEO Steven Jobs of Apple Computer fame, knows it can be only as good as the talents of its workforce. The firm does its best to attract great people and enthuse them with a challenging, satisfying, and rewarding workplace—one where teams are paramount. The website declares: "Pixar provides an environment that is irresistible in its professional challenges, creative output and open, collaborative spirit."[1]

be better than one

Check research on success in the NBA. Scholars find that both good and bad basketball teams win more the longer the players have been together. Why? A "teamwork effect" creates wins because players know each other's moves and playing tendencies.

Shift to the hospital operating room. Scholars noticed an interesting pattern: the same heart surgeons had differing death rates for similar procedures when performed in different hospitals.

Why? Upon investigating further they found that results were better in locations where the surgeons did more operations. Why? The researchers claim it's because the doctors had more time working together with the surgery teams—anesthesiologists, nurses, and other surgical technicians. They say it's not only the surgeon's skills that count; the skills of the team and the time spent working together count too.[2]

Is there any doubt that groups and teams can have a performance edge?[3]

➔ MODULE GUIDE

 21.1 Why is an understanding of teams so important?

- Formal and informal groups are building blocks of organizations.
- Organizations use a variety of committees, task forces, and cross-functional teams.
- Virtual teams are increasingly common in organizations.
- Teams offer synergy and other benefits to their members and the organization.
- Teams can also suffer from common performance problems.

 21.2 What are the foundations of successful teamwork?

- Teams need the right members and inputs to be effective.
- Teams must use the right processes to be effective.
- Teams move through different stages of development.
- Team performance is affected by norms and cohesiveness.
- Team performance is affected by task and maintenance roles.
- Team performance is affected by use of communication networks.
- Team performance is affected by use of decision-making methods.
- Team performance suffers when groupthink leads to bad decisions.

The opening examples seem to confirm the module subtitle: Two heads can be better than one. But the key word is *can*. We all know that although teams can be great, they're often not. And how often have you heard someone declare: "A camel is an elephant put together by a committee"?

So let's start this discussion realistically. On one level there seems little to debate; groups and teams have a lot to offer organizations. But at another level, you sometimes wonder if the extra effort is really worth it. Teams can be more pain than gain. There's a lot to learn about them and about their roles in organizations if we are to participate in and help lead teams for real performance gains.[4]

A **team** is a small group of people with complementary skills who work together to accomplish shared goals while holding each other mutually accountable for performance results.[5] Teams are essential to organizations of all types and sizes. Many tasks are well beyond the capabilities of individuals alone.[6] And in this sense, **teamwork**, people actually working together to accomplish a shared goal, is a major high-performance asset.[7]

> A **team** is a collection of people who regularly interact to pursue common goals.

> **Teamwork** is the process of people actively working together to accomplish common goals.

> A **formal group** is officially recognized and supported by the organization.

• Formal and Informal Groups Are Building Blocks of Organizations

A **formal group** is officially designated for a specific organizational purpose. You'll find formal groups described by different labels—such as *departments* (e.g., market research department), *work units* (e.g., audit unit), *teams* (e.g., customer service team), or *divisions* (e.g., office products division). You'll also see them identified on organization charts as headed by supervisors, managers, department heads, team leaders and the like.

Roles managers play in teams

| Supervisor | Network facilitator | Helpful participant | External coach |

These formal groups are basic building blocks of organization structures. Some people, in fact, describe organizations as interlocking networks of groups in which managers and leaders play "linking pin" roles.[8] This means that they serve both as head of one work group and as a subordinate member in the next-higher-level one.

The informal structure of an organization also consists of **informal groups**. They emerge from natural or spontaneous relationships among people. Some are *interest groups* whose members pursue a common cause, such as a women's career network. Some are *friendship groups* that develop for a wide variety of personal reasons, including shared hobbies and other nonwork interests. Others are *support groups* where members basically help one another do their jobs.

> An **informal group** is unofficial and emerges from relationships and shared interests among members.

• Organizations Use a Variety of Committees, Task Forces, and Cross-Functional Teams

You will find many types of formal groups operating in organizations.[9] A **committee** brings together people outside of their daily job assignments to work in a small team for a specific purpose. The task agenda is specific and ongoing. For example, an organization may have standing committees for diversity and compensation.[10] A designated head or chairperson typically leads the committee and is held accountable for its performance.

> A **committee** is designated to work on a special task on a continuing basis.

Project teams or task forces bring together people from various parts of an organization to work on common problems, but on a temporary rather than continuing basis. Project teams, for example, might be formed to develop a new product or service, redesign an office layout, or provide specialized consulting for a client.[11] A task force might be formed to address employee retention problems. Management Tips offers tips for holding project and task force meetings.[12]

The **cross-functional team**, whose members come from different functional units, is indispensable to organizations that emphasize adaptation and horizontal integration.[13] Members of cross-functional teams are supposed to work together on specific problems or tasks, sharing information and exploring new ideas. They are expected to help knock down the "walls" that otherwise separate departments and people in the organization. At Tom's of Maine, for example, the company uses "Acorn Groups"—symbolizing the fruits of the stately oak tree—to help launch new products. These groups bring together members of all departments to work on new ideas from concept to finished product. The goal is to minimize problems and maximize efficiency through cross-departmental cooperation.[14]

Another development is use of **employee involvement teams**. These groups of workers meet on a regular basis, with the goal of applying their expertise and attention to continuous improvement. A popular form of employee involvement team is the **quality circle**, a group of workers that meets regularly to discuss and plan specific ways to improve work quality.[15] After receiving special training in problem solving, team processes, and quality issues, members of the quality circle try to suggest ways to raise productivity through quality improvements.

Self-managing work teams were discussed in the previous module as an example of job enrichment for groups. You should recall that the members of these teams make a lot of group decisions, share tasks, and take on supervisory responsibilities.[16] This takes the notion of group work to the extreme. And with the growing popularity of self-managing teams you have to ask an important question: Are you ready to share in the responsibilities for high-performance team leadership?[17]

• Virtual Teams Are Increasingly Common in Organizations

A vice president for human resources at Marriott once called electronic meetings "the quietest, least stressful, most productive meetings you've ever had."[18] She was talking about a type of group that is increasingly common in today's organizations: the **virtual team**.[19] This is a group of people who work together and solve problems through computer-mediated rather than face-to-face interactions.

As you probably well know, the constant emergence of new technologies is making virtual collaboration both easier and more common. At home it may be MySpace or Facebook; at the office it's likely to be group blogs, editable websites called "wikis," and various types of online meeting resources.[20] In terms of potential advantages, the virtual environment allows group work by people who may be located at great distances from one another. It offers cost and time efficiencies. And it can help reduce interpersonal problems that might otherwise occur when a team is dealing with controversial issues.[21] Discussions and information shared among team members also can be easily stored online for continuous updating and access.[22]

Are there any downsides to virtual groups? For sure there can be problems, and often they occur for the same reasons as in other groups.[23] Members of virtual teams can have difficulties establishing good working relationships. The lack of face-to-face interaction limits the role of emotions and nonverbal cues in the communication process, perhaps depersonalizing relations among team members.[24] Yet as more people have experience in online forums, and with effort and sound management, teams working in virtual space rather than face-to-face are proving their performance potential.[25]

A **project team** or **task force** is convened for a specific purpose and disbands after completing its task.

A **cross-functional team** operates with members who come from different functional units of an organization.

An **employee involvement team** meets on a regular basis to help achieve continuous improvement.

A **quality circle** is a team of employees who meet periodically to discuss ways of improving work quality.

Members of a **self-managing work team** have the authority to make decisions about how they share and complete their work.

Members of a **virtual team** work together and solve problems through computer-based interactions.

Characteristics of High-Performance Teams

- **Clear, elevating goals**
- **Results-driven structure**
- **Competent team members**
- **Unified commitments**
- **Collaborative climate**
- **Standards of excellence**
- **External support and recognition**
- **Principled leadership**

• Teams Offer Synergy and Other Benefits to Their Members and the Organization

When it comes to the performance contributions of groups of any type, **synergy** is the creation of a whole that exceeds the sum of its parts. When teams perform well, it's because of synergy, the pooling of individual talents and efforts to create extraordinary results.[26] This is the force behind the module opening examples—creativity at Pixar Studios, successful heart surgeries, and more winning basketball games.

Teams are not only good for organizations, they are also good for their members.[27] Just as in life overall, being part of a work team or informal group can strongly influence our attitudes and behaviors. The personal relationships can help people do their jobs better—making contacts, sharing ideas, responding to favors, and bypassing roadblocks. And, being part of a team often helps satisfy important needs that may be difficult to meet in the regular work setting or life overall. In teams one can find social relationships, a sense of security and belonging, and emotional support.

Synergy is the creation of a whole greater than the sum of its individual parts.

• Teams Can Also Suffer from Common Performance Problems

Notwithstanding all this positive talk, however, we all know that working in groups isn't always easy or productive. Problems not only happen, they occur quite frequently.[28] One of the most troublesome is **social loafing**—the presence of "free-riders" who slack off and allow other team members to do the work.[29] For whatever reason, perhaps in the absence of spotlight on personal performance, individuals sometimes work less hard, not more hard, when they are part of a group.

Social loafing is the tendency of some people to avoid responsibility by free-riding in groups.

What can you do, as a team leader, when someone is free-riding? You might take actions to make individual contributions more visible, reward individuals for their contributions, make task assignments more interesting, and keep group size small so that free-riders are more visible to peer pressure and leader evaluation.[30] And if you've ever considered free-riding, think again. You may get away with it in the short term, but your reputation will suffer much longer.

Other common problems of teams include personality conflicts and differences in work styles that antagonize others and disrupt relationships and accomplishments. Sometimes group members withdraw from active participation due to uncertainty over tasks or battles about goals or competing visions. Ambiguous agendas or ill-defined problems can also cause fatigue and loss of motivation when teams work too long on the wrong things, having little to show for it.

Finally, not everyone is always ready to do group work. This might be due to lack of motivation, but it may also stem from conflicts with other work deadlines and priorities. Low enthusiasm for group work may also result from perceptions of poor team organization or progress, as well as by meetings that seem to lack purpose. These and other difficulties can easily turn the great potential of teams into frustration and failure.

NEWSLINE

Working through the Web can supercharge group work More and more organizations are tapping the great potential of the Web to supercharge groups and teamwork. The brand identity and design firm, R. Bird & Company, Inc., uses a novel

software product called Basecamp. Members participating in project teams and task forces log in, post and share information, and monitor deadlines in virtual space; no face-to-face meetings are required. Basecamp works like a Google homepage; members with login identities access private Web pages and are able to post messages, link files, modify to-do lists, track progress according to milestones, and more. It's a bit like a workaday version of MySpace or Facebook, things that have proven themselves valuable in the informal networks of the Web. Now, these technologies are being put to work as part of an organization's group structure, linking people virtually as needed and desired across the limitations of physical distance.

Reflect: In what ways are you already using and participating in virtual groups? What types of collaborative software are you presently familiar with? Can you see how continuing developments in Web space will change the way you work in the future?

Be Sure You Can . . .

- define team and team work

- differentiate formal and informal groups

- explain how committees, task forces, and cross-functional teams operate

- describe the roles managers play in teams

- explain the potential advantages and disadvantages of virtual teams

- explain synergy and the benefits of teams

- discuss social loafing and other potential problems of teams

Define the Terms

Committee	Self-managing work teams
Cross-functional team	
Employee involvement team	Social loafing
	Synergy
Formal group	Task force
Informal group	Team
Project team	Teamwork
Quality circle	Virtual team

Rapid Review

- A team consists of people with complimentary skills working together for shared goals and holding each other accountable for performance.

- Organizations use a variety of committees, task forces, project teams, cross-functional teams, and employee involvement teams to accomplish special tasks and coordinate across functions.

- Self-managing teams allow team members to perform many tasks previously done by supervisors, while virtual teams use computers to link members across time and space.

- Teams benefit organizations by providing for synergy that allows the accomplishment of tasks that are beyond individual capabilities alone.

- Social loafing and other problems can limit the performance of teams.

- Teams can suffer from social loafing when a member slacks off and lets others do the work.

Reflect/React

1. Do committees and task forces do better work when they are given short deadlines?

2. Are there some things that just shouldn't be done using virtual instead of face-to-face teams?

3. Why do people in groups often tolerate social loafers?

An **effective team** achieves high levels of task performance, membership satisfaction, and future viability.

So far we've really been talking about the presence of teams in organizations. Now it's time to talk about the teamwork that can make them successful. Look at Figure 21.1. It diagrams a team as an open system that, like the organization itself, transforms a variety of inputs through teamwork into outputs.[31] It also shows that an **effective team** should be accomplishing three output goals—task performance, member satisfaction, and team viability.[32]

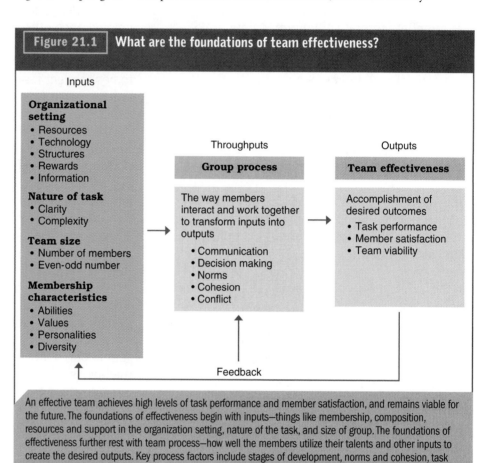

Figure 21.1 | **What are the foundations of team effectiveness?**

An effective team achieves high levels of task performance and member satisfaction, and remains viable for the future. The foundations of effectiveness begin with inputs—things like membership, composition, resources and support in the organization setting, nature of the task, and size of group. The foundations of effectiveness further rest with team process—how well the members utilize their talents and other inputs to create the desired outputs. Key process factors include stages of development, norms and cohesion, task and maintenance activities, communication, and decision making.

The first outcome of an effective team is a high level of *task performance*. When you are on a team, ask: Did we accomplish our tasks and meet expectations? The second outcome of an effective team is *member satisfaction*. Ask: Are we individually and collectively pleased with our participation in the process? The third outcome of an effective team is *viability for future action*. Ask: Is this team capable of working successfully together again in the future?[33]

• Teams Need the Right Members and Inputs to Be Effective

The foundations for team effectiveness are set when a team is formed. The better the inputs, we can argue, the more likely that the team will achieve success. One of the most important inputs of any group is the *team composition*. This is the mix of abilities, skills, backgrounds, and experiences of the members. For anyone creating a team, furthermore, this represents one of the most important decisions to be made: Just who should be on the team?

In the ideal world, managers carefully form teams by choosing members whose talents and interests fit well with the job to be done. If you were in charge of a new team, wouldn't you want to select members this way? Some interesting research by scholars at Northwestern University sheds light on what might be called the "recipe for success."

Luis Nuñes Amaral, Robert McCormick, and Brian Uzzi found that the most creative teams include a mix of experienced people and those who haven't worked together before.[34] The experienced members, or incumbents, have the connections; the newcomers add fresh thinking.

This research introduces the role of diversity in team membership. And the conclusion is that diversity is good, even essential, in terms of creativity and high performance. But Uzzi makes an important point. He says, "Gender, race and ethnicity are proxies for the kind of diversity we're talking about—diversity of background, training and experience."[35] When team members are too homogeneous along these lines, he says that people may feel quite comfortable with one another but that their teams tend to underperform.

What are your experiences on this issue? Do you seem to get along better in teams whose members are homogeneous? Have you encountered problems on teams whose members are diverse and heterogeneous?

Diverse teams do have more complications and it may take some time to work through them. But along with the complications of diversity also come special opportunities. Diverse teams expand the variety of talents, ideas, perspectives, and experiences available for problem solving. In the international arena, for example, research indicates that culturally diverse work teams have more difficulty learning how to work well together than do culturally homogeneous ones.[36] But after mastering the challenges of learning how to work well with one another, the diverse teams eventually prove to be more creative than the homogeneous ones.

There are other important inputs that also influence team effectiveness. One is the *nature of the task* itself. Clearly defined tasks make it easier for team members to combine their work efforts. Complex tasks require more information exchange and intense interaction than do simpler tasks. Predictably, the *organizational setting* makes a difference. A key issue here is support—how well the organization supports the team in terms of information, material resources, technology, organization structures, available rewards, and even physical space. Having support, as we have all probably experienced, can make a big difference in how well we perform in groups and individually.

Team size also makes a difference. Size affects how members work together, handle disagreements, and reach agreements. The number of potential interactions increases geometrically as teams increase in size, which congests communications. So how big should a team be? In general, teams larger than six or seven members can be difficult to manage for the purpose of creative problem solving. When voting is required, you should also remember that teams with odd numbers of members help to prevent ties.

![Diversity & team performance chart]

Diversity & team performance

Effective team
Process gains > losses

Ineffective team
Process losses > gains

Critical zone

Team performance (vertical axis)

Time together in team (horizontal axis)

• Teams Must Use the Right Processes to Be Effective

Although having the right inputs available to a team is important, it does not guarantee effectiveness. **Group process** counts too. This is the heart of teamwork—the way the members of any team actually work together as they transform inputs into outputs. Also called *group dynamics*, the process aspects of any group or team include how members get to know each other, develop expectations and loyalty, communicate, handle conflicts, and make decisions.

As the Team Effectiveness Equation indicates, a positive process takes full advantage of group inputs; the gains enhance team effectiveness. But any problems with group process can quickly drain energies and create losses that reduce effectiveness. This is what occurs, for example, when team members have difficulty managing diversity. When the internal dynamics fail in any way, team effectiveness can quickly suffer. Haven't you been on teams where people seemed to spend more time dealing with personality conflicts than with the task?

Group process is the way team members work together to accomplish tasks.

Team Effectiveness Equation

Team effectiveness = Quality of inputs × (Process gains − Process losses)

• Teams Move through Different Stages of Development

Research suggests that five distinct phases occur in the life cycle of any team.[37] An effective team moves through these stages smoothly and with proper attention to the process challenges at each point of development.

First comes the *forming stage of team development*, one of initial task orientation and interpersonal testing. For example, new members likely ask: "What can or does the team offer me?" "What will they ask me to contribute?" "Can my efforts serve the task needs of the team while also meeting my needs?" In this stage, people begin to identify with other members and with the team itself. They focus on getting acquainted, establishing interpersonal relationships, discovering what is considered acceptable behavior, and learning how others perceive the team's task.

The *storming stage of team development* is a period of high emotionality. Tension often emerges between members over tasks and interpersonal concerns. There may be periods of conflict, outright hostility, and even infighting as individuals try to impose their preferences on others. But, with progress, this is also the stage where members clarify task agendas and begin to understand one another's interpersonal styles. Attention begins to shift toward obstacles that may impede task accomplishment; team members start looking for ways to meet team goals while also satisfying individual needs. Failures in the storming stage can prove to be a lasting liability, but success sets a strong foundation for future effectiveness.

Cooperation is an important issue for teams in the *norming stage of team development*. At this point, members of the team begin to coordinate their efforts as a working unit and tend to operate with shared rules of conduct. The team feels a sense of leadership, with each member starting to play useful roles. Most interpersonal hostilities give way to a precarious balancing of forces as norming builds initial integration. Members are likely to develop initial feelings of closeness, a division of labor, and a sense of shared expectations. This helps protect the team from disintegration, while processes continue to develop.

Teams in the *performing stage of team development* are more mature, organized, and well functioning. This is a stage of total integration in which team members often creatively deal with both complex tasks and any interpersonal conflicts. The team operates with a clear and stable structure, members are motivated by team goals, and the team scores high on the criteria of team maturity shown in the figure.[38]

The *adjourning stage of team development* is the final stage for temporary committees, task forces, and project teams. Here, team members prepare to achieve closure and disband, ideally with a sense that they have accomplished important goals. As you may have experienced yourself, after working intensely with others for a period of time, breaking up the close relationships actually can be quite emotional.

• Team Performance Is Affected by Norms and Cohesiveness

Have you ever felt pressure, subtle or not, from other group members when you do something wrong—come

Assessing the maturity of a team	Very poor			Very good	
1. Trust among members	1	2	3	4	5
2. Feedback mechanisms	1	2	3	4	5
3. Open communications	1	2	3	4	5
4. Approach to decisions	1	2	3	4	5
5. Leadership sharing	1	2	3	4	5
6. Acceptance of goals	1	2	3	4	5
7. Valuing diversity	1	2	3	4	5
8. Member cohesiveness	1	2	3	4	5
9. Support for each other	1	2	3	4	5
10. Performance norms	1	2	3	4	5

late to a meeting, fail to complete an as-signed task, or act out of character? What you are experiencing is related to group **norms**, or behaviors expected of team members.[39] A norm is a rule or standard that guides behavior. When vi-olated, team members are usually pres-sured to conform; in the extreme, vio-lating a norm can result in expulsion from the group or social ostracism.

There are any number of norms oper-ating in a group at any given time. Dur-ing the forming and storming stages of development, for example, norms often focus on expected attendance and levels

A **norm** is a behavior, rule, or stan-dard expected to be followed by team members.

of commitment. By the time the team reaches the performing stage, norms have formed around adaptability, change, and desired levels of achievement. And without doubt one of the most important norms for any team is the *performance norm*. It defines the level of work effort and performance that team members are expected to contribute.

Not surprisingly, teams with positive performance norms are likely to be more suc-cessful in accomplishing their tasks than those with negative performance norms. But how do you build teams with the right norms? Actually, there are a number of things leaders can and should do.[40] They range from acting as a positive role model, to bringing in members who fit the norms, to holding meetings to discuss and agree on norms.

Whether the team members will accept and conform to norms is largely deter-mined by **cohesiveness**, the degree to which members are attracted to and motivated to remain part of a team.[41] Members of a highly cohesive team value their member-ship. They try to conform to norms and behave in ways that meet the expectations of other members, and they get satisfaction from doing so. In this way, at least, a highly cohesive team is good for its members. But, does the same hold true for team per-formance?

Cohesiveness is the degree to which members are attracted to and motivated to remain part of a team.

Figure 21.2 shows that when the performance norm of a team is positive, high cohe-sion and the resulting conformity to norms benefits team performance. This is a best-case scenario for both a team leader or manager and the organization. When the per-formance norm is negative in a cohesive team, however, high conformity to the norm creates a worst-case scenario. Team performance suffers because members restrict their efforts to conform with the low-performance norm.

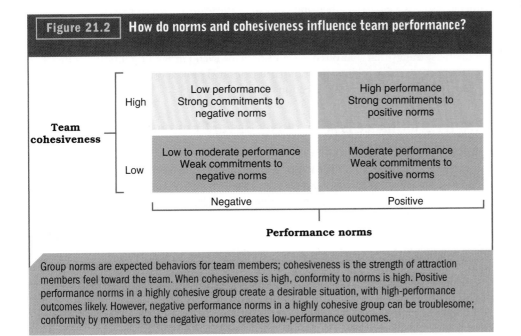

| Figure 21.2 | How do norms and cohesiveness influence team performance? |

Group norms are expected behaviors for team members; cohesiveness is the strength of attraction members feel toward the team. When cohesiveness is high, conformity to norms is high. Positive performance norms in a highly cohesive group create a desirable situation, with high-performance outcomes likely. However, negative performance norms in a highly cohesive group can be troublesome; conformity by members to the negative norms creates low-performance outcomes.

What are the implications of this complex relationship between norms and cohesiveness? Basically it boils down to this: Each of us should be aware of what can be done to build both positive norms and high cohesiveness in our teams. In respect to cohesiveness, this means such things as keeping team size as small as possible, working to gain agreements on team goals, increasing interaction among members, rewarding team outcomes rather than individual performance, introducing competition with other teams, and increasing homogeneity among team members.

• Team Performance Is Affected by Task and Maintenance Roles

A **task activity** is an action taken by a team member that directly contributes to the group's performance purpose.

Research on the group process identifies two types of activities that are essential if team members are to work well together over time.[42] **Task activities** contribute directly to the team's performance purpose; **maintenance activities** support the emotional life of the team as an ongoing social system. Although you might expect that these are things that team leaders or managers should be doing, this is only partially correct. In fact, all team members should share the responsibilities for task and maintenance leadership.

A **maintenance activity** is an action taken by a team member that supports the emotional life of the group.

Distributed leadership roles in teams

Team leaders provide task activities	Team leaders provide maintenance activities
• Initiating • Elaborating • Information sharing • Opinion giving • Summarizing	• Gatekeeping • Following • Encouraging • Harmonizing • Reducing tension

Team leaders avoid disruptive activities

• Being aggressive   • Competing
• Blocking   • Withdrawal
• Self-confessing   • Horsing around
• Seeking sympathy   • Seeking recognition

The concept of *distributed leadership in teams* makes every member continually responsible for both recognizing when task or maintenance activities are needed and taking actions to provide them. Leading through task activities involves making an effort to define and solve problems and advance work toward performance results. Without the relevant task activities such as initiating agendas and sharing information, teams have difficulty accomplishing their objectives. Leading through maintenance activities, such as encouraging others and reducing tensions, helps strengthen and perpetuate the team as a social system.

A **decentralized communication network** allows all members to communicate directly with one another.

Both task and maintenance activities stand in distinct contrast to the dysfunctional or *disruptive behaviors* that team leaders and effective members should avoid. These include the obvious, things that you often see and perhaps even engage in yourself—things like agressiveness, excessive joking, and nonparticipation. Think about this the next time one of your groups is drifting in the direction of ineffectiveness.

• Team Performance Is Affected by Use of Communication Networks

Teams can use the different communication networks shown in Figure 21.3 as they work and interact together.[43] In a **decentralized communication network**, all members communicate directly with one another. Sometimes called the *all-channel* or *star* structure, this arrangement works well for tasks that require lots of creativity, information processing, and problem solving. When tasks are less demanding, members can often divide up the work and then simply coordinate the final results using a **centralized communication network**, sometimes called the *wheel* or *chain* structure.

In a **centralized communication network**, communication flows only between individual members and a hub or center point.

When teams break into subgroups, either on purpose or because members are experiencing issue-specific disagreements, the resulting interaction pattern may create a *restricted communication network*. Left unmanaged, this structure can deteriorate to the point where subgroups fail to adequately communicate with one another and even engage in antagonistic relations.

Figure 21.3 | What communication networks are used in teams?

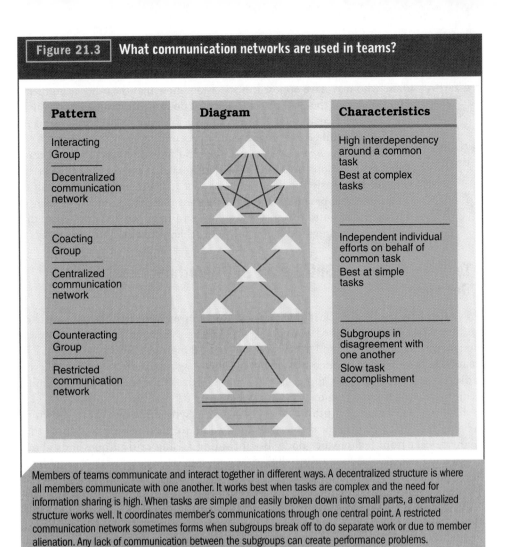

Pattern	Diagram	Characteristics
Interacting Group Decentralized communication network		High interdependency around a common task Best at complex tasks
Coacting Group Centralized communication network		Independent individual efforts on behalf of common task Best at simple tasks
Counteracting Group Restricted communication network		Subgroups in disagreement with one another Slow task accomplishment

Members of teams communicate and interact together in different ways. A decentralized structure is where all members communicate with one another. It works best when tasks are complex and the need for information sharing is high. When tasks are simple and easily broken down into small parts, a centralized structure works well. It coordinates member's communications through one central point. A restricted communication network sometimes forms when subgroups break off to do separate work or due to member alienation. Any lack of communication between the subgroups can create performance problems.

• Team Performance Is Affected by Use of Decision-Making Methods

The best teams don't limit themselves to just one **decision-making** method. In true contingency-management fashion, they choose and use methods that best fit the problems at hand.[44] Edgar Schein, a respected scholar and consultant, describes how teams can make decisions by at least six different methods.[45]

In *decision by lack of response*, one idea after another is suggested without any discussion taking place. When the team finally accepts an idea, all alternatives have been bypassed and discarded by simple lack of response rather than by critical evaluation. In *decision by authority rule*, the leader, manager, committee head, or some other authority figure makes a decision for the team. Although time efficient, the quality of the decision depends on whether the authority figure has the necessary information; its implementation depends on how well other team members accept the top-down approach. In *decision by minority rule*, two or three people dominate or "railroad" the team into making a mutually agreeable decision. How often have you heard: "Does anyone object? Okay, let's go ahead with it."

One of the most common ways teams make decisions, especially when early signs of disagreement arise, is *decision by majority rule*. This method is consistent with a democratic political system, but is often used without awareness of its potential problems. The very process of voting can create coalitions; that is, some people will be "winners" and others will be "losers." In all likelihood, you've been on the losing side at times. How did it feel? If you're like me, it may have made you feel left out, unenthusiastic about supporting the majority decision, and even hoping for a future chance to win.

Decision making is the process of making choices among alternative courses of action.

Teams are often encouraged to try for *decision by consensus*. This is where full discussion leads to most members favoring one alternative, with the other members agreeing to support it. After reaching a consensus, even those who may have opposed the decision know that the other team members listened to their concerns. Consensus doesn't require unanimity, but it does require that team members are able to argue, engage in reasonable conflict, and still get along with and respect one another.[46]

A *decision by unanimity* may be the ideal state of affairs. Here, all team members agree on the course of action to take. This is a logically perfect method for decision making in teams, but it is also extremely difficult to attain in actual practice. One of the reasons that teams sometimes turn to authority decisions, majority voting, or even minority decisions is the difficulty of managing the team process to achieve consensus or unanimity.

• Team Performance Suffers When Groupthink Leads to Bad Decisions

How often have you held back stating your views in a meeting, agreed to someone else's position when it really seemed wrong, or went along with a boss's suggestions even though you disagreed?[47] If and when you do these things you are likely involved in **groupthink**, the tendency for members of highly cohesive groups to lose their critical evaluative capabilities.[48] It tends to occur when teams strive for consensus or unanimity, seeking agreements and trying to avoid disagreements.[49]

Groupthink is a tendency for highly cohesive teams to lose their evaluative capabilities.

Teams experiencing groupthink often display the symptoms like those shown in the Exhibit. They act this way because they want to avoid doing anything that might detract from feelings of goodwill—including raising critical questions about a suggested course of action. But when everyone publicly agrees with a suggestion while privately having serious doubts about it, groupthink occurs. The result is often a bad decision.

Psychologist Irving Janis ties a variety of well-known historical blunders to groupthink, including the lack of preparedness of U. S. naval forces for the Japanese attack on Pearl Harbor, the Bay of Pigs invasion under President Kennedy, and the many roads that led to U. S. involvement in Vietnam. In all likelihood, it is present all too often, in any team, at any level, in all sorts of organizations.

When and if you encounter groupthink or believe your group is headed in that direction, Janis suggests a number of things leaders might do to avoid or minimize the groupthink effects. These include assigning one member to act as a critical evaluator or 'devil's advocate' during each meeting; creating sub teams to work on the same issues and then share their findings; bringing in outsiders to offer viewpoints on group processes and decisions; holding a 'second chance' meeting after an initial decision is made; and, being purposely absent from some meetings to let the group deliberate on its own.

EXHIBIT

Symptoms of Groupthink

Illusions of invulnerability   Members assume that the team is too good for criticism or beyond attack.

Rationalizing unpleasant and disconfirming data   Members refuse to accept contradictory data or to thoroughly consider alternatives.

Belief in inherent group morality   Members act as though the group is inherently right and above reproach.

Stereotyping competitors as weak, evil, and stupid   Members refuse to look realistically at other groups.

Applying direct pressure to deviants to conform to group wishes   Members refuse to tolerate anyone who suggests the team may be wrong.

Self-censorship by members   Members refuse to communicate personal concerns to the whole team.

Illusions of unanimity   Members accept consensus prematurely, without testing its completeness.

Mind guarding   Members protect the team from hearing disturbing ideas or outside viewpoints.

Be Sure You Can . . .

- list the outputs of an effective team

- identify inputs that influence team effectiveness

- discuss how diversity influences team effectiveness

- list five stages of group development

- explain how norms and cohesion influence team performance

- list ways to build positive norms and to change cohesiveness

- illustrate task, maintenance, and disruptive activities in teams

- describe how groups use decentralized and centralized communication networks

- discuss the different ways groups make decisions

- list the symptoms of groupthink

Define the Terms

Centralized communication network	Effective team
	Group process
Cohesiveness	Groupthink
Decentralized communication network	Maintenance activity
	Norm
Decision making	Task activity

Rapid Review

- An effective team achieves high levels of task performance, member satisfaction, and team viability.

- Important team input factors include the membership characteristics, nature of the task, organizational setting, and group size,

- A team matures through various stages of development, including forming, storming, norming, performing, and adjourning.

- Norms are the standards or rules of conduct that influence the behavior of team members; cohesion is the attractiveness of the team to its members.

- In highly cohesive teams, members tend to conform to norms; the best situation for a manager or leader is a team with positive performance norms and high cohesiveness.

- Distributed leadership occurs when team members step in to provide helpful task and maintenance activities and discourage disruptive activities.

- Effective teams make use of alternative communication networks and decision-making methods to best complete tasks.

- Groupthink is a tendency of members of highly cohesive teams to lose their critical evaluative capabilities and make poor decisions.

Reflect/React

1. What happens if a team can't get past the storming stage?

2. Why would a manager ever want to reduce the cohesion of a work group?

3. Is groupthink found only in highly cohesive teams, or could it exist in precohesive ones?

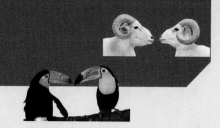

Multiple Choice

1. When a group of people is able to achieve more than what its members could by working individually, this is called _____.
   (a) distributed leadership **(b)** consensus **(c)** team viability **(d)** synergy

2. A "quality circle" is an example of how organizations try to use _____ groups for performance advantage.
   (a) virtual **(b)** informal **(c)** employee involvement **(d)** self-managing

3. An effective team is defined as one that achieves high levels of task performance, member satisfaction, and _____.
   (a) resource efficiency **(b)** team viability **(c)** group consensus **(d)** creativity

4. In the open-systems model of teams, the _____ is an important input factor.
   (a) communication network **(b)** decision-making method **(c)** performance norm **(d)** diversity of membership

5. A basic rule of team dynamics might be stated this way: The greater the _____ in a team, the greater the conformity to norms.
   (a) membership diversity **(b)** cohesiveness **(c)** task clarity **(d)** competition among members

6. Groupthink is most likely to occur in teams that are _____.
   (a) large in size **(b)** diverse in membership **(c)** high performing **(d)** highly cohesive

7. A team performing very creative and unstructured tasks is most likely to succeed using _____.
   (a) a decentralized communication network **(b)** decisions by majority rule **(c)** decisions by minority rule **(d)** more task than maintenance activities

8. Members of a team tend to become more motivated and better able to deal with conflict during the _____ stage of team development.
   (a) forming **(b)** norming **(c)** performing **(d)** adjourning

9. A _____ decision is one in which all members agree on the course of action to be taken.
   (a) consensus **(b)** unanimous **(c)** majority **(d)** synergy

10. The best way to try and increase the cohesiveness of a team would be to _____.
    (a) start competition with other groups **(b)** add more members **(c)** reduce isolation from other groups **(d)** increase the heterogeneity of members

Short Response

11. What are the major differences among a task force, employee involvement group, and a self-managing team?

12. How can a manager influence team performance by modifying group inputs?

13. How do cohesiveness and performance norms together influence team performance?

14. What are two symptoms, and two possible remedies, of groupthink?

Integration & Application

Mariel Martinez has just been appointed manager of a production team operating the 11 P.M. to 7 A.M. shift in a large manufacturing firm. An experienced manager, Mariel is pleased that the team members seem to really like and get along well with one another, but she notices that they also appear to be restricting their task outputs to the minimum acceptable levels.

Questions: How might Mariel improve this situation?

PATHWAYS to WileyPLUS

WILEY PLUS

CASE SNAPSHOT

Go to online to read this case!

Steve Jobs: Creative Control
This leader revived Apple with his emphasis on design and demand for innovation. He prefers creative approaches to problem solving and allows it room to develop within the corporate culture.

MODULE 21 — Online Interactive Learning Resources

Skill Builder
• Team Contributions

Experiential Exercises
• After Meeting Project Review
• Work Team Dynamics

Team Project
• Superstars on the Team

Self-Assessment
• Empowering Others

Conflict and Negotiation

For baseball fans this is old news. But it's worth a look.

When Theo Epstein, only 31 years old and considered a baseball "wonder-kid," resigned as General Manager of the World-Champion Boston Red Sox, it caught a lot of people by surprise. Many thought he'd be building a dynasty, not resigning. What's the story here?

Part of the answer rests with the changing nature of the general manager role. The job has moved from the superplayer/manager role into the corporate executive role, and with this shift teams have been hiring younger GMs like Epstein. They bring a new look and approach to the office, described by one player's agent as: "They speak the language of CEO-dom." But in the mix, they also can create and become embroiled in conflict.

always easy

Some wonder if Epstein left because the Boston club's owners wouldn't give him the autonomy he wanted to run the team. He just refers to "complexities." One of the owners called it a "difference" in management opinion.[1] We'd probably call it an irresolvable conflict.

And when it comes to conflict, what about Epstein's "youth;" how well did it play in the baseball establishment? Do we have a case of Generation X (aged 25–40) running into difficulties when working for Baby Boomers (aged 55+)? Are the value differences so extreme that conflicts are inevitable?

Baby Boomers are known for their work ethic, being loyal to their employers, choosing work over family if need be. Gen-Xers are considered more skeptical and value interests other than work. And, interestingly, they are also likely to change jobs more often.[2]

We might say that "generational" complications are inevitable in one's work and career. Are they part of your experience? And, how well prepared are you if such complications someday create conditions for conflict between yourself and co-workers or supervisors?

➔ MODULE GUIDE

 22.1 What should we know about dealing with conflict?

- Conflicts can occur over substantive or emotional issues.
- Conflicts can be both functional and dysfunctional.
- Organizations have many sources of potential conflict.
- People use different interpersonal conflict management styles.
- Managers can use structural approaches to deal with conflicts in organizations.

 22.2 How can we negotiate successfully?

- Negotiation is a process of reaching agreement.
- Negotiation can be approached in distributive or integrative ways.
- Integrative agreements require commitment, trust, and information.
- Successful negotiation should meet high ethical standards.
- Negotiators should guard against common negotiation pitfalls.
- Mediation and arbitration are forms of third-party negotiations.

The Red Sox owners have probably mulled this situation over more than once; Epstein likely has too. But for us it's just another example of a fact of organizational life—conflict. Among your interpersonal skills, the ability to deal with conflicts is critical. Managers and leaders, just as owners of baseball clubs, spend a lot of time dealing with it. But *conflict* is one of those words like *communication* or *power*. We use it a lot, but rarely think it through to the specifics.

In management, the term **conflict** refers to disagreements among people. And in our experiences, it can emerge or form around two quite different types of issues–substantive and emotional.[3]

• Conflicts Can Occur over Substantive or Emotional Issues

If Theo Epstein and the Red Sox owners really did disagree over the amount of control he would have to run the ball club, this was a case of **substantive conflict**. These conflicts involve disagreements over such things as goals and tasks, the allocation of resources, the distribution of rewards, policies and procedures, and job assignments. You are in a substantive conflict with someone when, for example, each of you wants to solve a problem by following a different strategy.

If Epstein and the owners clashed over personality and value differences, this was a case of **emotional conflict**. These conflicts result from feelings of anger, distrust, dislike, fear, and resentment, as well as relationship problems. You know this form of conflict as a clash of personalities or emotions, when you don't want to agree with another person just because you don't like or are angry with him.

What do you think happened in the Red Sox case? My guess is that the conflict was both substantive and emotional. And when the two get intertwined, it gets very complicated and difficult to resolve them.

Most people encounter substantive and emotional conflicts almost every day. Many are minor and pass quickly; others are more major, perhaps very upsetting and even consuming enormous amounts of our time and energies. But we shouldn't fear these conflicts. Rather we really need to understand and learn how to best deal with them.

In fact, not all conflict is bad, and the absence of conflict isn't always good. As the saying goes, a smooth ride isn't always the best ride; the absence of conflict can sometimes be a signal that something is wrong. Can you imagine yourself in a managerial situation where you need to stimulate conflict, not reduce it?

• Conflicts Can Be Both Functional and Dysfunctional

Take a look at Figure 22.1. It shows the inverted U curve of the conflict intensity and performance relationship. Notice that although conflict at the extremes is harmful, conflict in the middle region is beneficial.

Conflict of moderate intensity can be constructive, offering the potential to actually improve performance. This **functional conflict** stimulates us toward greater work efforts, more creativity in problem solving, and even to cooperate more with others. It helps keep things in check, and to make sure that alternatives are carefully considered in decision making, and often provides the creative edge that makes the difference between "okay" and "really great" performance.

We know the destructive side of conflict as well. You probably recognize **dysfunctional conflict** best when it overloads you physically or mentally, making it hard to concentrate or make real progress on goals. Perhaps you've been in groups where a few people get into emotional conflicts that seem never ending. Their intensity spills over to affect everyone, making it harder to work together and even creating tendencies for the group to just do the bare minimum to get by.

Conflict is a disagreement over issues of substance and/or an emotional antagonism.

Substantive conflict involves disagreements over goals, resources, rewards, policies, procedures, and job assignments.

Emotional conflict results from feelings of anger, distrust, dislike, fear, and resentment as well as from personality clashes.

> **What to Do When You Need to Create Conflict**
>
> - Get more people involved to create greater diversity of viewpoints.
> - Play or have others play the "devil's advocate" role to challenge existing ways.
> - Create a sense of competition that encourages different ideas and suggestions.
> - Change the structure by forming subgroups to work on the same tasks.

Functional conflict is constructive and helps boost task performance.

Dysfunctional conflict is destructive and hurts task performance.

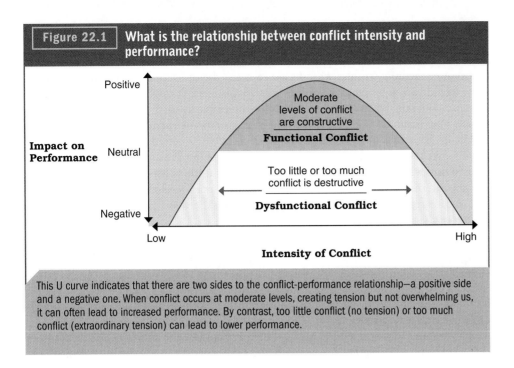

| Figure 22.1 | What is the relationship between conflict intensity and performance? |

This U curve indicates that there are two sides to the conflict-performance relationship—a positive side and a negative one. When conflict occurs at moderate levels, creating tension but not overwhelming us, it can often lead to increased performance. By contrast, too little conflict (no tension) or too much conflict (extraordinary tension) can lead to lower performance.

But remember, again, that too little conflict also can be dysfunctional. Perhaps this has happened to you in teams where nobody wanted to disagree with a suggestion that, if you admitted it, just wasn't very good. This lack of substantive conflict can cause groupthink, promote complacency, and result in the loss of a creative, high-performance edge.

• Organizations Have Many Sources of Potential Conflict

As the *Exhibit–Sources of Conflicts in Organizations* shows, the workplace is a natural home for conflict. Its sources rest with role ambiguities, resource scarcities, task interdependencies, and more. Even unresolved prior conflicts are breeding grounds for more conflict in the future. And the types of conflicts that can involve us are also many and varied. Some of the conflicts are internal ones where we own all or part of the conflict experience. Others are due in large part to our group memberships, or roles in the organization structure.

Do you recognize, for example, when you are experiencing *intrapersonal conflicts*? These are conflicts caused by incompatible goals or expectations. *Approach–approach conflict* occurs when a person must choose between two positive and equally attractive alternatives—perhaps a job transfer to another city versus having a network of close friends and family in the current location. *Avoidance–avoidance conflict* occurs when a person must choose between equally unattractive alternatives. For example, you might one day face either losing your job or accepting a job transfer to a faraway town. *Approach–avoidance conflict* occurs when a person faces a choice with both positive and negative aspects, such as taking a higher-paying job that will require excessive work time.

Of course you're familiar with the dynamics and anxieties caused by *interpersonal conflict* between individuals. Sometimes these are substantive, such as disagreements between supervisors and subordinates over a performance evaluation. Other times they are purely emotional, resting with personality differences.

EXHIBIT

Sources of conflicts in organizations

Role ambiguities   When people aren't sure what they are supposed to do, conflict with others is likely; task uncertainties increase odds of working at cross-purposes at least some of the time.

Resource scarcities   When people have to share resources with one another and/or when they have to compete with one another for resources, the conditions are ripe for conflict.

Task interdependencies   When people must depend on others doing things first before they can do their own jobs, conflicts often occur; dependency on others creates anxieties and other pressures.

Competing objectives   When people work on objectives that are competing, conflict is a natural byproduct; win-lose conditions pit people against one another.

Structural differentiation   When people work in parts of the organization where structures, goals, time horizons, and even staff compositions are very different, conflict is likely with other units.

Unresolved prior conflicts   When conflicts go unresolved, they remain latent and often reemerge in the future as the basis for conflicts over the same or related matters.

The same possibilities evidence themselves as *intergroup conflict* that occurs between representatives of different groups. For example, can you imagine the conflict between members of the marketing department, who want to quickly satisfy a customer's order, and those in manufacturing, who decide to delay the order because of other priorities? How would you, as a manager, work to resolve this issue? It might be addressed by creating cross-functional teams and task forces for interdepartmental coordination, or seeking greater integration through a team or matrix organization structure.

Finally, if we look at the organization as a whole we can often spot *interorganizational conflict* that takes place between organizations. These are the conflicts senior executives have to deal with as they manage the boundary relationships between their organizations and the external environment. For example, conflict may develop between business firms and outside regulators or consumer advocacy groups, between labor unions and the employers of their members, and even between nations.

• People Use Different Interpersonal Conflict Management Styles

With all this potential for conflict in and around organizations, how do people deal with it? Interpersonally, people respond to conflict through different combinations of cooperative and assertive behaviors.[4]

Think about how you tend to behave when in conflict with someone else. In terms of *cooperativeness*, do you often try to satisfy the other person's needs and concerns? Or are you uncooperative? In terms of *assertiveness*, do you act assertively to satisfy your own needs and concerns? Or are you nonassertive when facing conflict? Figure 22.2 shows that different combinations of cooperative and assertive behaviors result in five conflict management styles—avoidance, accommodation, competition, compromise, and collaboration.[5]

In **avoidance**, everyone withdraws and pretends that conflict doesn't really exist, hoping that it will simply go away. **Accommodation** plays down differences and highlights similarities and areas of agreement. Peaceful coexistence through recognition of common interests is the goal. In reality, such smoothing may ignore the real essence of a conflict.

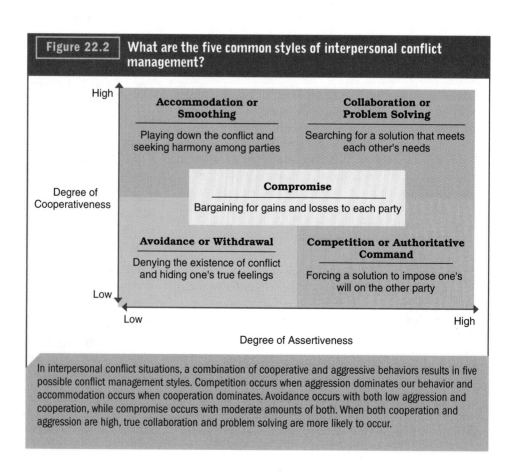

Figure 22.2 | **What are the five common styles of interpersonal conflict management?**

Degree of Cooperativeness — High / Low

Accommodation or Smoothing
Playing down the conflict and seeking harmony among parties

Collaboration or Problem Solving
Searching for a solution that meets each other's needs

Compromise
Bargaining for gains and losses to each party

Avoidance or Withdrawal
Denying the existence of conflict and hiding one's true feelings

Competition or Authoritative Command
Forcing a solution to impose one's will on the other party

Degree of Assertiveness — Low / High

In interpersonal conflict situations, a combination of cooperative and aggressive behaviors results in five possible conflict management styles. Competition occurs when aggression dominates our behavior and accommodation occurs when cooperation dominates. Avoidance occurs with both low aggression and cooperation, while compromise occurs with moderate amounts of both. When both cooperation and aggression are high, true collaboration and problem solving are more likely to occur.

Both avoidance and accommodation create **lose-lose conflict**; no one achieves her or his true desires. And the underlying reasons for conflict often remain unresolved, only to recur in the future.

In **competition**, one party wins through superior skill or outright domination. A common form in managerial situations is authoritative command, where a higher-level supervisor simply dictates a solution to subordinates. **Compromise** occurs through trade-offs, where each party to the conflict gives up and gains something of value. These are both forms of **win-lose conflict** where each party strives to gain at the other's expense. But whenever one party loses something, antecedents may be set for future conflicts.

Unlike the prior methods, **collaboration** tries to find and address the problem and reconcile the real differences underlying a conflict. As you would expect, it is often the most effective conflict management style. It is a form of **win-win conflict** that tries to resolve things to the mutual benefit of all conflicting parties. The process depends on the willingness of all parties to dig in, confront the issues, and openly and honestly discuss them. When effective, collaboration eliminates the underlying causes of a conflict and creates win-win outcomes.

Management Tips shows when each of the five conflict management styles might be useful.[6] Most of us probably use each at least some of the time. But we should make good choices, being sure to fit our style to the requirements of each unique conflict situation.[7] It's also worth remembering that unresolved or suppressed conflicts often sow the seeds for future conflicts. Only true **conflict resolution**, characteristic of the collaborative style, eliminates the underlying causes of a conflict in ways that should prevent similar conflicts in the future.

• Managers Can Use Structural Approaches to Deal with Conflicts in Organizations

Most managers will tell you that not all conflict management in groups and organizations can be resolved at the interpersonal level. Think about it. Aren't there likely to be times when personalities and emotions prove irreconcilable? In such cases a structural approach to conflict management can often help.

Take the case of conflict that really traces to a resource issue—someone or some group doesn't have enough, or two parties have to share from a common pool. The structural solution is to *make more resources available* to everyone. Although costly and not always possible, this is a straightforward way to resolve resource-driven conflicts.

In **lose-lose conflict** no one achieves his or her true desires and the underlying reasons for conflict remain unaffected.

Competition or authoritative command uses force, superior skill, or domination to win a conflict.

Compromise occurs when each party to the conflict gives up something of value to the other.

In **win-lose conflict** one party achieves its desires and the other party does not.

Collaboration or problem solving involves working through conflict differences and solving problems so everyone wins.

In **win-win conflict** the conflict is resolved to everyone's benefit.

Conflict resolution is the removal of the substantial and/or emotional reasons for a conflict.

MANAGEMENT TIPS

When to use conflict management styles

- Collaboration and problem solving is preferred to gain true conflict resolution when time and cost permit.
- Avoidance may be used when an issue is trivial, when more important issues are pressing, or when people need to cool down temporarily and regain perspective.
- Authoritative command may be used when quick and decisive action is vital or when unpopular actions must be taken.
- Accommodation may be used when issues are more important to others than to yourself or when you want to build "credits" for use in later disagreements.
- Compromise may be used to arrive at temporary settlements of complex issues or to arrive at expedient solutions when time is limited.

International agency promotes labor rights worldwide

The International Labour Organization, known in the news as the ILO, is the only surviving entity from the 1919 Treaty of Versailles, which formed the League of Nations, the precursor to the United Nations. The ILO describes its mission as the "promotion of social justice and internationally recognized labor rights." In its report, "Time for Equality at Work", the ILO notes that

work discrimination based on a person's religion, skin color, and gender occurs every day around the world. It also states that the elimination of such discrimination is essential to advance the values of human dignity, individual freedom, social justice, and social cohesion. The ILO maintains that the elimination of discrimination will not happen just because governments want it to happen; everyone—employers and workers—is responsible for championing equality at work.

Reflect: The ILO seems to advocate engaging in positive conflict in behalf of human rights. What is your record of stepping forward to challenge discrimination? Are you willing to speak out for equality in the workplace?

When people are stuck in conflict and just can't seem to appreciate one another's points of view, *appealing to higher-level goals* can sometimes focus their attention on one mutually desirable outcome. The appeal to higher goals offers a common frame of reference for analyzing differences and reconciling disagreements.

When appeals to higher goals don't work, it may be that *changing the people* is necessary. That is, a manager may need to replace or transfer one or more of the conflicting parties to eliminate the conflict. And when the people can't be changed, they may have to be separated by *altering the physical environment*. Sometimes it is possible to rearrange facilities, workspace, or workflows to physically separate conflicting parties and decrease opportunities for contact with one another.

Organizations also use a variety of *integrating devices* to help in managing conflicts between groups. These approaches include assigning people to formal liaison roles, convening special task forces, setting up cross-functional teams, and even switching to the matrix form of organization.

By *changing reward systems* it is sometimes possible to reduce conflicts driven by competition for rewards. An example is shifting rewards to the group level as a way of reinforcing teamwork and reducing tendencies of team members to compete with one another.

By *changing policies and procedures*, organizations may redirect behavior in ways that minimize the likelihood of known conflict-prone situations. Finally, by *training in interpersonal skills*, organizations can help prepare people to communicate and work more effectively in situations where conflict is likely.

> *Two co-workers may have different beliefs, but at crunch time, they should be able to work together for the good of the company.*
>
> R. Roosvelt Thomas, **AUTHOR AND DIVERSITY CONSULTANT**

22.1 What should we know about dealing with conflict?

Be Sure You Can . . .

- differentiate substantive and emotional conflict

- differentiate functional and dysfunctional conflict

- list and give examples of four levels of conflict in and around organizations

- explain the common causes of conflict in organizations

- explain the conflict management styles of avoidance, accommodation, competition, compromise, and collaboration

- discuss the structural approaches to conflict management

Define the Terms

Accommodation	Dysfunctional conflict
Avoidance	Emotional conflict
Collaboration	Functional conflict
Competition	Lose-lose conflict
Compromise	Substantive conflict
Conflict	Win-lose conflict
Conflict resolution	Win-win conflict

Rapid Review

- Interpersonal conflict occurs as disagreements between people over substantive or emotional issues.

- Moderate levels of conflict can be functional for performance, stimulating effort and creativity.

- Too little conflict is dysfunctional when it leads to complacency.

- Too much conflict is dysfunctional when it overwhelms us.

- Conflict in and around organizations occurs at the intrapersonal, interpersonal, intergroup, and interorganizational levels.

- Tendencies toward cooperativeness and assertiveness create the interpersonal conflict management styles of avoidance, accommodation, compromise, competition, and collaboration.

- Conflict in organizations can also be managed through structural approaches that involve changing people, goals, resources, or work arrangements.

Reflect/React

1. Is substantive or emotional conflict more difficult for people to handle?

2. Is the absence of conflict always a problem?

3. When is it better to avoid conflict rather than directly engage it?

Put yourself in the following situations. How would you behave, and what would you do? *Situation*: Your employer offers you a promotion, but the pay raise being offered is disappointing. *Situation*: You have enough money to order one new computer for your department, but two of your subordinates really need one.[8]

• Negotiation Is a Process of Reaching Agreement

These are but two examples of the many work situations that lead to **negotiation**—the process of making joint decisions when the parties involved have alternative preferences, perhaps to the point of outright conflict. Stated a bit differently, negotiation is a way of reaching agreement.[9]

People negotiate over salary, merit raises, performance evaluations, job assignments, work schedules, work locations, and many other considerations. Nothing could serve you better than learning some basic negotiating skills to deal with these and similar situations in the future. The learning begins by recognizing two goals in the negotiation process—substance goals and relationship goals.

Substance goals in negotiation focus on outcomes. They relate to what is being negotiated—the pay raise or who gets the computer, for example. **Relationship goals** in negotiation focus on the people issues and processes. They are tied to the way people work together while negotiating and how they will be able to work together again in the future.

It's a mistake to weight either substance or process over the other; both are important. It's rare that we can be satisfied to get what we want while damaging relationships in the process. But by the same token, how often do you want to sacrifice what you want just to preserve a relationship?

• Negotiation Can Be Approached in Distributive or Integrative Ways

A negotiation is considered effective when it resolves issues of substance while maintaining or even improving working relationships among the negotiating parties.[10] Effective negotiation usually scores well on quality, cost, and harmony criteria. One test for an effective negotiation is the question: "Now that it's over, am I and is the other party willing to implement the decision and follow through as agreed?"[11]

The way each party approaches a negotiation can significantly impact its results.[12] In the book *Getting to Yes*, Roger Fisher and William Ury describe **distributive negotiation** as a process in which each party focuses mainly on staking out claims for certain preferred outcomes. In *hard distributive negotiation* things become highly competitive as each party focuses on narrow self-interests, trying to gain from losses by the other. As you might expect, these win-lose conditions often damage working relationships. In *soft distributive negotiation* one party basically backs off and accepts a loss, perhaps just "to get things over with." But when one party acts accommodative, it may be done with underlying resentment and little personal conviction.

Fisher and Ury really don't like distributive negotiation; they see the pitfalls and recognize its limitations. They advocate an alternative known as **integrative negotiation**, often called *principled negotiation*. This approach takes more of a win-win orientation that considers the interests of all parties. The goal is an outcome that is based on the merits of individual claims, and that serves each party's desires as much as possible. Ideally, no one should lose in an integrative negotiation, and relationships shouldn't be harmed.

When asked by an interviewer to illustrate how the integrative approach to negotiation differs from a distributive one, William Ury gave this example.[13] A union worker presents a manager with a list of requests. The manager says: "That's your solution, now what's the problem?" The union worker responds with a list of problems. The manager says: "Well, I can't give you *that* solution, but I think we can solve your problem this way." Can you see the manager's attempt to be "integrative" here?

Negotiation is the process of making joint decisions when the parties involved have different preferences.

Substance goals in negotiation focus on outcomes.

Relationship goals in negotiation focus on people's relationships and interpersonal processes.

Distributive negotiation focuses on win-lose claims made by each party for certain preferred outcomes.

> **Four Criteria of Effective Negotiation**
>
> 1. **Quality**—getting a "wise" agreement satisfactory to all sides
> 2. **Cost**—being efficient, using minimum resources and time
> 3. **Harmony**—acting to strengthen rather than weaken relationships
> 4. **Implementation**—gaining real commitments to live up to agreements

Integrative negotiation uses a win-win orientation to reach solutions acceptable to each party.

• Integrative Agreements Require Commitment, Trust, and Information

➡ **Fisher and Ury's Four Rules for Integrative Negotiation**

1. Separate the people from the problem.
2. Focus on interests, not on positions.
3. Generate many alternatives before deciding what to do.
4. Insist that results be based on some objective standard.

It isn't easy to gain integrative agreements; Fisher and Ury don't deny that fact. Rather, they offer the four rules in the accompanying box as starting points for moving in an integrative rather than distributive direction.[14] Commitment to the process, proper attitudes, and good information are all necessary foundations for integrative agreements. Each negotiating party must be willing to trust, share information with, and ask reasonable questions of the other.

Integrative agreements are more likely when each party knows both what it really wants and what the other wants. Consider Figure 22.3, which introduces a typical case of labor–management negotiations over wage terms in a new contract.[15]

Look first at the figure and case from the labor union's perspective. The union negotiator has told her management counterpart that the union wants a new wage of $15.00 per hour. This expressed preference is the union's initial offer. However, she also has in mind a minimum reservation point of $13.25 per hour. This is the lowest wage rate that she will accept for the union.

Now look from the perspective of the management negotiator. He has a different perspective. His initial offer is $12.75 per hour, with $13.75 per hour representing his maximum reservation point.

Classic two-party negotiation defines the **bargaining zone** as the distance between one party's minimum reservation point and the other party's maximum reservation point. In this example, the bargaining zone of $13.25 per hour to $13.75 per hour is a "positive" one, since the reservation points of the two parties overlap. There is room for true negotiation. If, however, the union's minimum reservation point exceeded the management's maximum reservation point, no room would exist for bargaining.

A key task for any negotiator is to discover each party's reservation points. That's the only way to really know if a positive bargaining zone exists. If it does, negotiations can proceed effectively. Otherwise, negotiations will stall until either one party or the other, or both, are willing to modify the original stance.

A **bargaining zone** is the area between one party's minimum reservation point and the other party's maximum reservation point.

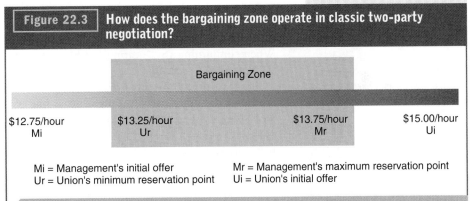

| Figure 22.3 | How does the bargaining zone operate in classic two-party negotiation? |

Mi = Management's initial offer
Ur = Union's minimum reservation point
Mr = Management's maximum reservation point
Ui = Union's initial offer

The bargaining zone in a negotiation is set by the difference in the minimum and maximum reservation points of the negotiating parties. In this example of a salary negotiation, and even though each would like a better deal, the union representatives know that they would accept a wage offer as low as $13.25 an hour (their minimum reservation point) and the management representatives know they would pay as much as $13.75 an hour (their maximum reservation point). Within these two extremes lies the bargaining zone—each party would settle on a wage between $13.25 and $13.75. Outside of this zone, each party is prepared to walk away without an agreement.

By the way, one of the most important negotiations we ever have with our employers is over our starting salary.[16] Will you be well prepared and able to find the bargaining zone?

• Successful Negotiation Should Meet High Ethical Standards

In the midst of negotiations like the one just described it may be easy to drift off into manipulative, deceitful, and even dishonest behaviors. This may be especially true when negotiators let substance goals override any concerns for relationship goals. Haven't you seen or read about people who seemed more interested in "getting just a bit more" or getting as much as they can than in reaching what Fisher and Ury would call a truly integrative agreement?

What about honor, one's sense of ethics? Does it fall by the wayside in the quest to win? In business situations does an undue emphasis on profits or personal gain motivate unethical negotiating behavior?

As we have said so many times in this book, there is no substitute for ethical behavior. Keep this in mind in negotiation situations. Watch for tendencies in yourself and in others to do unethical things and then try to explain them away with inappropriate rationalizing: "It was really unavoidable," "Oh, it's harmless," "The results justify the means," or "It's really quite fair and appropriate."[17]

In **mediation** a neutral party tries to help conflicting parties improve communication to resolve their dispute.

In **arbitration** a neutral third party issues a binding decision to resolve a dispute.

These excuses for questionable behavior are morally and organizationally unacceptable. Long-run losses may follow ill-gotten short-run gains. Negotiators using unethical tactics often incur lasting legacies of distrust, disrespect, and dislike. Someone who acts unethically in a negotiation may get what he or she wants, but ends up paying the price when targeted for "revenge" in later negotiations.

• Negotiators Should Guard against Common Negotiation Pitfalls

At this point I think you'll agree that the negotiation process can be very complex. Even the best-intentioned negotiators can fail. Sometimes we get trapped and do the wrong things not because of ethical lapses, but because we don't recognize and act to avoid common negotiating errors or pitfalls.

The first negotiation pitfall is the *myth of the "fixed pie."* This assumes that in order for you to gain, the other person must give something up. Negotiating under this belief fails to recognize that we can sometimes either expand or better utilize the pie to everyone's advantage. A second negotiation error is *nonrational escalation of conflict*. The negotiator in this case becomes committed to previously stated demands and allows personal needs for enhancing ego and saving face to exaggerate the perceived importance of satisfying them.

The third common negotiating error or pitfall is *overconfidence and ignoring the other's needs*. The negotiator becomes overconfident, believes that his or her position is the only correct one, and fails to see the needs of the other party and the merits in its position. The fourth error is *too much telling and too little hearing*. When committing the "telling" problem, parties to a negotiation don't really make themselves understood to each other. When committing the "hearing" problem, they fail to listen sufficiently well to understand what each is saying.[18]

The next time you're involved in a negotiation that is not going well, stop to consider if you, or the other party, is caught up in one of these negotiation pitfalls. They're not ideas; they're real. They're also likely to trap you someday if your guard isn't up.

• Mediation and Arbitration Are Forms of Third-Party Negotiations

For any of the reasons just discussed, and more, it may not always be possible to achieve integrative agreements. And when disputes reach the point of impasse, third-party approaches are often the next best choice for resolving things.

Mediation involves a neutral third party who tries to improve communication between negotiating parties and keep them focused on relevant issues. The mediator generally does not issue a ruling or make a decision, but often takes an active role in discussions. This may include making suggestions in an attempt to move the parties toward agreement.

Arbitration, such as salary arbitration in professional sports, is a stronger form of dispute resolution. It involves a neutral third party, the arbitrator, who acts as a "judge" and issues a binding decision. This usually includes a formal hearing in which the arbitrator listens to both sides and reviews all facets of the case before making a ruling.

Some organizations formally provide for a process called *alternative dispute resolution*. This approach utilizes mediation and arbitration, but only after direct attempts to negotiate agreements between the conflicting parties has failed. Often an ombudsperson, or designated neutral third party who listens to complaints and disputes, plays a key role in the process.

PACESETTERS

Conflict and negotiation are center stage when nations meet

On any given day, United Nations Secretary General Kofi A. Annan has his hands full. Full of conflict and negotiation, that is. The UN, committed by mission to preserving peace through international cooperation and collective security, is often center stage when members of the community of 189 nations have disagreements with one another. Part of Annan's task is to help them peacefully resolve conflicts, and together advance harmony and progress throughout the world. One of his priorities is a Global Compact supporting human rights, labor, and the environment. The compact is designed to unite them in practices "enabling all the world's people to share the benefits of globalization and embedding the global market in values and practices that are fundamental to meeting socio-economic needs." He is also concerned about rallying resources to fight poverty around the world. A current initiative is to get developing countries to share ideas and knowledge to build strengths in less developed ones. And, of course, he's dealing with budget problems at the UN, the oil-for-food scandal, and the problem of how to find ways for the international community to help out in Iraq even with disagreements with the U.S. and Great Britain over the war.

Kofi A. Annan, *Secretary General, United Nations.*

Be Sure You Can . . .

- differentiate substance and relationship goals in negotiation

- explain distributive and integrative negotiation

- explain the role of the bargaining zone in negotiation

- discuss the ethical challenges of negotiation

- list potential negotiation pitfalls

- differentiate between mediation and arbitration in dispute resolution

Define the Terms

Arbitration

Bargaining zone

Distributive negotiation

Integrative negotiation

Mediation

Negotiation

Relationship goals

Substance goals

Rapid Review

- Negotiation is the process of making decisions and reaching agreement in situations in which the participants have different preferences.

- Effective negotiation occurs when both substance goals (dealing with outcomes) and relationship goals (dealing with processes) are achieved.

- The distributive approach to negotiation emphasizes win-lose outcomes; the integrative approach, or principled negotiation approach, emphasizes win-win outcomes.

- Ethical problems in negotiation can arise when people become manipulative and dishonest in trying to satisfy their self-interests at any cost.

- Participants in negotiations sometimes fall prey to pitfalls like the myth of the fixed pie, irrational escalation, overconfidence, and too much telling with too little hearing.

- When negotiations are at an impasse, third-party approaches such as mediation and arbitration offer alternative and structured ways for dispute resolution.

Reflect/React

1. If you have a good relationship with someone, are you likely to give in too easily when negotiating?

2. Is it possible to completely avoid distributive negotiation?

3. What can you do when the person you are negotiating with seems trapped by the myth of the fixed pie?

Multiple Choice

1. A conflict is most likely to be functional and have a positive impact on group performance when it is _____.
(a) based on emotions **(b)** resolved by arbitration **(c)** caused by resource scarcities **(d)** of moderate intensity

2. When a manager points out that two persons in conflict should agree on higher-level goals and then work backward from there to resolve the conflict, this is an example of a/an _____ approach to conflict management.
(a) avoidance **(b)** structural **(c)** accommodation **(d)** distributive

3. The interpersonal conflict management style with the greatest potential for true conflict resolution is _____.
(a) compromise **(b)** competition **(c)** smoothing **(d)** collaboration

4. When people are highly cooperative but not very assertive in a conflict situation, the likelihood is that they will be using which conflict management style?
(a) avoidance **(b)** authoritative **(c)** smoothing **(d)** collaboration

5. If you are in a situation where you must choose between an attractive job transfer to another city and having a great network of friends and family in your current location, you might experience _____ conflict.
(a) lose-lose **(b)** approach–avoidance **(c)** approach–approach **(d)** interorganizational

6. If you are an observer in a labor–management negotiation and notice that each side is taking a competitive stance, staking out its claims for desired outcomes, the likelihood is that this negotiation is _____ in nature.
(a) intrapersonal **(b)** principled **(c)** approach–avoidance **(d)** distributive

7. The criteria of an effective negotiation include high quality, low cost, and _____.
(a) harmony **(b)** timeliness **(c)** efficiency **(d)** personal gain

8. The distance between one party's minimum reservation point and the other party's maximum reservation point in a negotiation over salary is called the _____.
(a) bargaining zone **(b)** zone of indifference **(c)** fixed pie effect **(d)** escalation point

9. When a negotiator becomes committed to previously stated demands and becomes concerned about saving face by not compromising on them, a negotiation error known as _____ is occurring.
(a) overconfidence **(b)** poor ethics **(c)** irrational exuberance **(d)** nonrational escalation

10. When a professional baseball player reaches an impasse negotiating for a contract renewal with his present club, the matter is often referred to _____ where an outside person acts as a judge and makes the decision for them.
(a) arbitration **(b)** alternative dispute resolution **(c)** mediation **(d)** principled negotiation

Short Response

11. What interpersonal styles create lose-lose and win-lose outcomes in conflict management?

12. Why is conflict of moderate intensity considered functional?

13. What is the difference between substance and relationship goals in negotiation?

14. How does arbitration differ from mediation?

Integration & Application

When Professor Kraham received her teaching assignments for Spring Semester from the Department Head, she was surprised. Instead of teaching her normal load of one management course and one organizational behavior course, she was given two strategic management courses. She will have to do a lot of extra work preparing for the strategic management classes and this is going to leave less time available for the research she needs to complete to stay on track for promotion and tenure. She is determined to raise the issue with the Department Head and try to negotiate a better teaching schedule.

Questions: What type of conflict is Professor Kraham experiencing in this situation? What suggestions would you give her for how to negotiate with the Department Head in a way that will result in an integrative agreement?

INSTRUCTIONS *In the space to the left of each of the following statements, write the number from the following scale that indicates how likely you are to respond that way in a conflict situation.*
1 = very unlikely   2 = unlikely   3 = likely   4 = very likely

1 I am usually firm in pursuing my goals.

2 I try to win my position.

3 I give up some points in exchange for others.

4 I feel that differences are not always worth worrying about.

5 I try to find a position that is intermediate between the other person's and mine.

6 In approaching negotiations, I try to be considerate of the other person's wishes.

7 I try to show the logic and benefits of my positions.

8 I always lean toward a direct discussion of the problem.

9 I try to find a fair combination of gains and losses for both of us.

10 I attempt to work through our differences immediately.

11 I try to avoid creating unpleasantness for myself.

12 I try to soothe the other person's feelings and preserve our relationship.

13 I attempt to get all conerns and issues immediately out in the open.

14 I sometimes avoid taking positions that would create controversy.

15 I try not to hurt others' feelings.

SCORING

Total your scores for items 1, 2, 7; enter that score here [*Competing* = _____]. Total your scores for items 8, 10, 13; enter that score here [*Collaborating* = _____]. Total your scores for items 3, 5, 9; enter that score here [*Compromising* = _____]. Total your scores for items 4, 11, 14; enter that score here [*Avoiding* = _____]. Total your scores for items 6, 12, 15; enter that score here [*Accommodating* = _____].

INTERPRETATION

Research indicates that each conflict management style has a role to play in management. But the best overall conflict management approach is collaboration; only it can lead to problem solving and true conflict resolution. Consider any patterns that may be evident in your scores and think about how to best handle the conflict situations in which you become involved.

PATHWAYS to WileyPLUS

CASE SNAPSHOT

Go online to read this case!

Research in Motion/Blackberry: From Growing Tall to Nearly Squashed: The Rise and Almost Fall of Research in Motion

Research in Motion (RIM) has produced perhaps the most successful portable e-mail device to date. But a recently settled lawsuit disputed its patent for wireless e-mail and threatened to disrupt RIM's hold on the market.

MODULE 22 Online Interactive Learning Resources

Skill Builder
• Relationship Management

Experiential Exercise
• Feedback and Assertiveness

Team Project
• Negotiating Salaries

Change can be your

Innovation and Organizational Change

When a group of Japanese students drove their car out of Tokyo one day, that event hardly seemed remarkable. But when they arrived some 900 kilometers later on the northern island of Hokkaido, Mitsubishi's president considered it a notable feat. The students' car, powered by a new engine technology, had made the trip without refueling! In fact, the gas tank still had fuel to spare. This was an important breakthrough. Company engineers had long studied the problem without successfully solving it. Finally, through a lot of hard work, information sharing, problem solving, and learning, they found the answer.[1]

best friend

It may have seemed unremarkable, too, when a group of Motorola engineers, designers, and marketers met in a Chicago office. But it became the innovation lab Moto City, a new home away from coroporate headquarters and its bureaucracy. Their task was simple but challenging: Come up with a better cell phone. What they created together was the Motorola Razr; 12.5 million sold the first year on the market.[2]

Novel answers to perplexing problems continuously move people, organizations, and societies ahead in our dynamic world. Wouldn't it be nice if all of society's institutions, business, government, and nonproft alike, were continuously upgrading services, creating new products, and helping to make our world a better place?

As Harvard scholars Michael Beer and Nitin Nohria observe: "The new economy has ushered in great business opportunities and great turmoil. Not since the Industrial Revolution have the stakes of dealing with change been so high. Most traditional organizations have accepted, in theory at least, that they must either change or die."[3]

➔ MODULE GUIDE

 23.1 What are the roles of innovation and change in organizations?

- Creativity and innovation are sources of competitive advantage.
- Innovative organizations share many common characteristics.
- Organizations pursue both transformational and incremental changes.
- Change in organizations can move from top down, bottom up, or both.

 23.2 How do managers lead the processes of organizational change?

- Adaptive organizations need change leaders, not status quo managers.
- Unfreezing, changing, and refreezing are three phases of planned change.
- Managers use force-coercion, rational persuasion, and shared power change strategies.
- Change leaders identify and deal positively with resistance to change.
- Organization development is a way of building sustainable capacities for change.

Creativity is the generation of a novel idea or unique approach that solves a problem or crafts an opportunity.

Innovation is the process of taking a new idea and putting it into practice.

Process innovations result in better ways of doing things.

Product innovations result in new or improved goods or services.

Commercializing innovation turns ideas into economic value added.

As a corporate leader looking toward the future, John Chambers, CEO of Cisco Systems, says: "Companies that are successful will have cultures that thrive on change even though change makes most people uncomfortable."[4] What about you? Are you quick to embrace new ideas, ways, and opportunities? Or, are you more comfortable with habit, preferring things as they are rather than as they might be?

• Creativity and Innovation Are Sources of Competitive Advantage

In his book *The Circle of Innovation*, consultant Tom Peters warns managers against getting too comfortable with past accomplishments. He points them, instead, toward innovating as the best way to gain competitive advantage.[5] And the best place to start is with all the creative potential that exists in an organization's workforce, the intellectual capital we have spoken about so much in this book.

Creativity is the generation of a novel idea or unique approach to solving performance problems or exploiting performance opportunities.[6] It is one of our greatest personal assets, even though it may be too often unrecognized by us and by others. We exercise creativity every day in lots of ways—solving problems at home, building something for the kids, or even finding ways to pack too many things into too small a suitcase. But what about creativity at work, on the job? Can we say the same?

Creativity is a driver of **innovation**, the process of developing new ideas and putting them into practice.[7] Management consultant Peter Drucker calls innovation "an effort to create purposeful, focused change in an enterprise's economic or social potential."[8] Said a bit differently, it is the act of converting new ideas into usable applications with positive economic or social consequences. And if you stop and think about it, your desktop, briefcase, or backpack are probably full of examples of innovations that enrich your life.

Innovation in and by organizations mostly occurs in two broad forms. **Process innovations** result in better ways of doing things; **product innovations** result in new or improved goods and services. But regardless of its type, innovation occurs only when a creative new idea is moved all the way from the point of invention to the point of actual application or use. In business this is known as **commercializing innovation**—the process of turning new ideas into products or processes that can increase profits through greater sales or reduced costs.[9]

At companies like Apple, Nike, and 3M Corporation, commercializing innovation is a way of life; it's part of the business model. In any given year, for example, the likelihood is that 3M will generate over one-third of its revenues from products that didn't exist four years ago. And it owes its success to the imagination of employees like Art Fry. You probably don't know him, but you know the product he helped create. Fry is the person whose creativity turned a 3M adhesive that "wasn't sticky enough" into the blockbuster product known worldwide as Post-It Notes®.

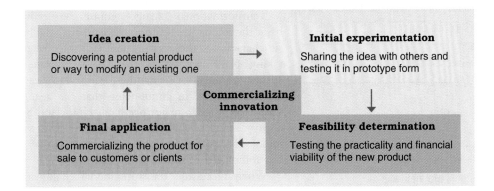

• Innovative Organizations Share Many Common Characteristics

Innovative organizations like 3M tend to share certain features in common.[10] In highly innovative organizations the *corporate strategy and culture support innovation*. The strategies of the organization, the visions and values of senior management, and the framework of policies and expectations emphasize an innovation spirit. Organizations discourage innovation when cultures are intolerant of differences and risk adverse, valuing conformity more than creativity. Johnson & Johnson's former CEO James Burke believes that managers should eliminate risk-averse climates and replace them with organizational cultures in which innovation is a norm. He once said: "I try to give people the feeling that it's okay to fail, that it's important to fail."[11]

In highly innovative organizations, *organization structures support innovation*. Bureaucracy is an enemy of innovation. More and more large organizations are trying to break its confines by taking advantage of horizontal designs, team structures, and "innovation labs" like Motorola's Moto City featured in the opener. *Business Week* describes the innovative structures this way: "Instead of assembly line, think swarming beehive. Teams of people from different disciplines gather to focus on a problm. They brainstorm, tinker and toy with different approaches."[12]

In highly innovative organizations, *top management supports innovation*. Top management isolation can kill innovation by isolating senior executives and making lower levels fearful of making mistakes. But at 3M, for example, many top managers have been innovation leaders and product champions in the company's past. They know what it's like and they make sure to hire people whose values, attitudes, and skills align with innovation goals. They mainstream people in critical innovation roles, and they tolerate criticisms and differences of opinion as these roles are played out.[13] They also understand that success doesn't always come in a straight line, admitting that mistakes are often part of the innovation process. A Toro Company CEO once held a party for a group of engineers whose new molding technique didn't work in lawn mowers. Why? He wanted to honor the risk they had taken. Later, they discovered the technique could be successfully used in other Toro products.[14]

> **Critical Innovation Roles in Organizations**
>
> - **Idea generators**—provide new insights and discoveries.
> - **Information gatekeepers**—stay abreast of outside developments.
> - **Product champions**—advocate for new products or processes.
> - **Project managers**—keep innovation projects on track.
> - **Innovation leaders**—keep innovation values, goals visible.

• Organizations Pursue Both Transformational and Incremental Changes

Innovation is only one part of the story when it comes to organizations keeping up with the times. Look at the big U.S. automakers. They're struggling and in some cases it's not because they don't have the right ideas, it's because they can't rally the organization around them. In other words, they have difficulty creating organizational change.

And when it comes to organizational change, many would probably argue that only major, frame-breaking, radical change can save the legacy companies like GM and Ford. They are talking about **transformational change** that results in a major and comprehensive redirection of the organization.[15]

Transformational change results in a major and comprehensive redirection of the organization.

Transformational change requires leadership from the top because its purpose is to alter the basic character of the organization. Consider what's taking place at FEMA, the U.S. government agency criticized for its handling of the Hurricane Katrina disaster. In announcing that the agency was going to get a major overhaul, Homeland Security Secretary Michael Chertoff said: "We will retool FEMA, maybe even radically, to increase our ability to deal with catastrophic events."[16]

When successful, transformational change results in fundamental shifts in strategies, culture, structures, and even the underlying sense of organizational purpose or mission. As you might expect, this type of change is intense, highly stressful, and very complex to achieve. Management Tips offers several lessons learned from studies of large-scale transformational change in business.[17] But be cautious as you think about it; reports are that as many as 70 percent or more of large-scale change efforts actually fail.[18] Getting back to FEMA, only time will tell if the agency achieves the change goals set by Michael Chertoff.

There is another more modest, frame-*bending*, side to organizational change. This is **incremental change**, that which tweaks and nudges existing systems and practices to better align them with emerging problems and opportunities. The intent isn't to break and remake the system, but to move it forward through continuous improvements.

Leadership of incremental change focuses on building on existing ways of doing things with the goal of doing them better in the future. Common incremental changes in organizations involve new products, new processes, new technologies, and new work systems. You might think of this in the context of a good total quality management program, one where the search is always on for better ways and higher performance.

One shouldn't get the idea, by the way, that incremental change is somehow inferior to transformational change. Rather, most would argue that both are important; incremental changes keep things tuned up (like the engine on a car) in between transformations (when the old car is replaced with a new one). I'll bet, for example, that your college or university is continually updating courses and modifying curricula—incremental change. I'll bet, too, that it only occasionally eliminates entire majors and departments to replace them with new and different ones—transformational change.

Incremental change bends and adjusts existing ways to improve performance.

• Change in Organizations Can Move from Top Down, Bottom Up, or Both

As you might expect from this discussion, there is no "one best way" about organizational change. The forces and directions affecting it come from all over, and are inside and outside of the organization. But one thing for sure is that top managers have a special responsibility to read the environment and understand the organization well enough to know when change is needed. And then, they're supposed to step in and provide the leadership to accomplish it.

In **top-down change**, senior managers initiate changes with the goal of comprehensive impact on the organization and its performance capabilities. But one of the reasons so many change efforts fail is that a lot of them are badly implemented.[19] And one of the reasons for poor implementation is top management failure to build commitments within the workforce so that most everyone actively supports and follows through with change goals. The result is a lot of wasted time, organizational resources, and opportunities.

The high failure rate of large-scale changes makes it quite clear that you can't simply mandate change from the top. Instead, successful change requires the support of others throughout the organization. This is really just good management, another application of the participatory planning and group decision-making issues we discussed in earlier modules. Change programs have little chance of success without the support of those who must implement them. And the best way to build these commitments is to involve them in the change planning.

In **top-down change**, the change initiatives come from senior management.

In **bottom-up change**, the initiatives for change come from any and all parts of the organization, not just top management. If you think about it, this type of change is essential in terms of adapting day-to-day operations, systems, processes, and technologies to the changing requirements of work. This is where an empowered workforce brings the full value of its creativity and intellectual capital to the table.

Managers facilitate bottom-up change through their commitments to delegation, involvement, and participation. A good example occurred at Johnson Controls, Inc., where Jason Moncer was given the nickname "Mr. Kaizen" by his co-workers.[20] The nickname refers to a Japanese practice of continuous improvement. Moncer earned it by offering many ideas for changes in his work area. At his plant, workers contributed over 200 suggestions that the company implemented in just one year alone. In other words, when the workers talk at Johnson Controls, managers listen.

Putting top-down and bottom-up change together probably offers organizations the best of both worlds. In fact, this was the approach taken by GE's former CEO Jack Welch when he first took the top job. Welch, concerned about GE's performance, began an aggressive top-down restructuring that led to major workforce cuts and a trimmer organization structure. Once underway, however, he created a structure for bottom-up change driven by employee involvement. He called the program Work-Out.[21]

In GE's Work-Out sessions, employees confronted their managers in a "town meeting" format. The manager sat or stood in front listening to suggestions from subordinates about removing performance obstacles and improving operations. Welch expected the managers to respond immediately to the suggestions, and to try to implement as many of them as possible. From the top, Welch initiated the Work-Out program to drive organizational change from the bottom up.

In **bottom-up change**, change initiatives come from all levels in the organization.

" *I keep my ears open. I work at building a reputation for being receptive.* "

Marissa Mayer, DIRECTOR OF CONSUMER WEB PRODUCTS, GOOGLE

23.1 What are the roles of innovation and change in organizations?

Be Sure You Can . . .

- explain the importance of creativity in organizations

- list steps in the process of commercializing innovation

- list and explain characteristics of innovative organizations

- identify the critical innovation roles in organizations

- differentiate transformational and incremental change

- discuss the pros and cons of top-down change and of bottom-up change

Rapid Review

- Innovation is a process that turns creative ideas into products or processes that benefit organizations and their customers.

- Highly innovative organizations tend to have supportive cultures, strategies, structures, staffing, and top management.

- Transformational change makes radical changes in organizational directions; incremental change makes continuing adjustments to existing ways and practices.

- Top-down change is initiated by senior management; bottom-up change is initiated by empowered persons working at all organizational levels.

Define the Terms

Bottom-up change

Commercializing innovation

Creativity

Incremental change

Innovation

Process innovations

Product innovations

Top-down change

Transformational change

Reflect/React

1. Can a creative person prosper in an organization that isn't very innovative?

2. What difference does a leader make in terms of how innovative an organization becomes?

3. When is it better to pursue incremental rather than transformational change?

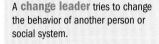

23.2 How Do Managers Lead the Processes of Organizational Change?

Like many other new CEOs, when Angel Martinez became head of Rockport Company he wanted to change traditional ways of doing things and increase the company's future competitiveness. But instead of embracing the changes he sponsored, employees resisted. Martinez said they "gave lip service to my ideas and hoped I'd go away."[22]

After Bank of America announced a large quarterly operating loss, its new CEO at the time, Samuel Armacost, complained that managers seemed more interested in taking orders than initiating change. He said: "I came away quite distressed from my first couple of management meetings. Not only couldn't I get conflict, I couldn't even get comment. They were all waiting to see which way the wind blew."[23]

• Adaptive Organizations Need Change Leaders, Not Status Quo Managers

Martinez and Armacost were trying, if not succeeding, to be **change leaders**. These are managers who act as *change agents*, who take leadership responsibility for changing the existing pattern of behavior of another person or social system.[24] In theory, every manager should act as a change leader. But the reality is, as the prior examples suggest, that there is a substantial tendency toward the status quo—accepting things as they are and not wanting to change.

Most of us do tend to act habitually and in stable ways over time. And you have to admit there is a certain comfort to that—driving the same route to work, having the same morning coffee routine, and so forth. We may not want to change, even when circumstances require it.

As a manager and change leader you have to recognize and deal with such tendencies, in yourself and in others. The responsibilities of change leadership include being willing to question the status quo, staying alert to situations or to people needing change, being open to good ideas and opportunities, and being ready and able to support new ways of doing things.

> A **change leader** tries to change the behavior of another person or social system.

Change leaders versus status quo managers	
Change leaders	**Status quo managers**
• Confident of ability • Willing to take risks • Seizes opportunity • Expects surprise • Makes things happen	• Threatened by change • Bothered by uncertainty • Prefers predictability • Supports the status quo • Waits for things to happen

• Unfreezing, Changing, and Refreezing Are Three Phases of Planned Change

The issues of status quo tendencies and the risks of complacency led Kurt Lewin, a noted psychologist, to describe **planned change** as a process with three phases: *unfreezing*—preparing a system for change; *changing*—making actual changes in the system; and *refreezing*—stabilizing the system after change.[25]

Planned change has little chance for long-term success unless people are open to doing things differently. **Unfreezing** is the stage in which managers help others to develop, experience, and feel a real need for change. The goal here is to get people to view change as a way of solving a problem or taking advantage of an opportunity. Some might call this the "burning bridge" phase, arguing that in order to get people to jump off a bridge, you might just have to set it on fire. Managers can simulate the burning bridge by engaging people with facts and information that communicate the need for change—environmental pressures, declining performance, and examples of alternative approaches. And as you have probably experienced, conflict can help people to break old habits and recognize new ways of thinking about or doing things.

> **Planned change** aligns the organization with anticipated future challenges.

> **Unfreezing** is the phase during which a situation is prepared for change.

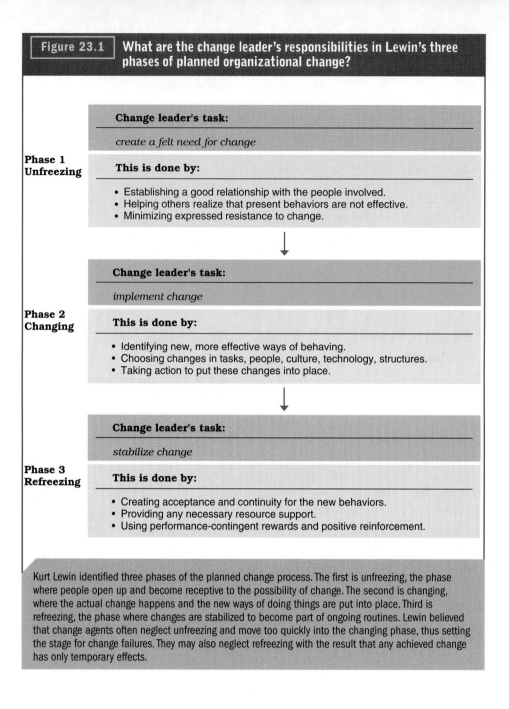

Figure 23.1 What are the change leader's responsibilities in Lewin's three phases of planned organizational change?

Phase 1 Unfreezing

Change leader's task:

create a felt need for change

This is done by:

- Establishing a good relationship with the people involved.
- Helping others realize that present behaviors are not effective.
- Minimizing expressed resistance to change.

Phase 2 Changing

Change leader's task:

implement change

This is done by:

- Identifying new, more effective ways of behaving.
- Choosing changes in tasks, people, culture, technology, structures.
- Taking action to put these changes into place.

Phase 3 Refreezing

Change leader's task:

stabilize change

This is done by:

- Creating acceptance and continuity for the new behaviors.
- Providing any necessary resource support.
- Using performance-contingent rewards and positive reinforcement.

Kurt Lewin identified three phases of the planned change process. The first is unfreezing, the phase where people open up and become receptive to the possibility of change. The second is changing, where the actual change happens and the new ways of doing things are put into place. Third is refreezing, the phase where changes are stabilized to become part of ongoing routines. Lewin believed that change agents often neglect unfreezing and move too quickly into the changing phase, thus setting the stage for change failures. They may also neglect refreezing with the result that any achieved change has only temporary effects.

Changing is the phase where a planned change actually takes place.

Refreezing is the phase at which change is stabilized.

The **changing** phase is where actual change takes place. Ideally these changes are planned in ways that give them the best opportunities for success, having maximum appeal and posing minimum difficulties for those being asked to make them.[26] Although this phase should follow unfreezing in Lewin's model, he believes it is often started too early. When change takes place before people and systems are ready for it, the likelihood of resistance and change failure is much greater. In this sense Lewin might liken the change process to building a house; you need to put a good foundation in place before you begin the framing.

As shown in Figure 23.1, the final stage in the planned change process is **refreezing**. Here, the focus is on stabilizing the change to make it as long lasting as needed. Linking change with rewards, positive reinforcement, and resource support all help with refreezing. Of course, in today's dynamic environments there may not be a lot time for refreezing before things are ready to change again. You may well find that refreezing in Lewin's sense probably gives way quite often to a phase of evaluating and reassessing. We begin preparing for or undertaking more change even while trying to take full advantage of the present one.

• Managers Use Force-Coercion, Rational Persuasion, and Shared Power Change Strategies

When it comes to actually moving people and systems to change, the issue boils down to change strategy. Figure 23.2 summarizes three common change strategies—force-coercion, rational persuasion, and shared power. Each should be understood and most likely used by all change leaders.[27]

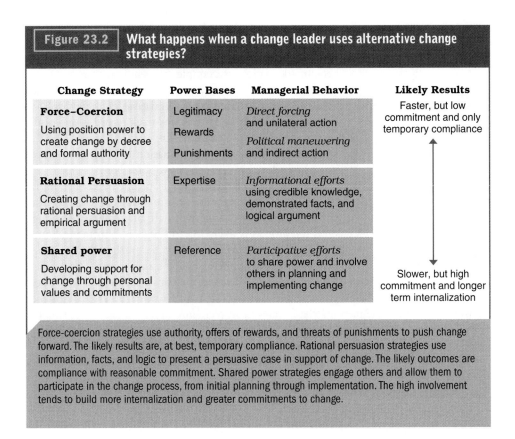

Figure 23.2	What happens when a change leader uses alternative change strategies?

Change Strategy	Power Bases	Managerial Behavior	Likely Results
Force–Coercion Using position power to create change by decree and formal authority	Legitimacy Rewards Punishments	*Direct forcing* and unilateral action *Political maneuvering* and indirect action	Faster, but low commitment and only temporary compliance ↕ Slower, but high commitment and longer term internalization
Rational Persuasion Creating change through rational persuasion and empirical argument	Expertise	*Informational efforts* using credible knowledge, demonstrated facts, and logical argument	
Shared power Developing support for change through personal values and commitments	Reference	*Participative efforts* to share power and involve others in planning and implementing change	

Force-coercion strategies use authority, offers of rewards, and threats of punishments to push change forward. The likely results are, at best, temporary compliance. Rational persuasion strategies use information, facts, and logic to present a persuasive case in support of change. The likely outcomes are compliance with reasonable commitment. Shared power strategies engage others and allow them to participate in the change process, from initial planning through implementation. The high involvement tends to build more internalization and greater commitments to change.

A **force-coercion strategy** uses the power bases of legitimacy, rewards, and punishments as the primary inducements to change.[28] In a *direct forcing* strategy, the change agent takes direct and unilateral action to command that change take place. This involves the exercise of formal authority or legitimate power, offering special rewards and/or threatening punishment. In *political maneuvering*, the change agent works indirectly to gain special advantage over other persons to force the change. This involves bargaining, obtaining control of important resources, forming alliances, or granting favors.

One thing to remember is that most people will probably respond to force-coercion in a limited way, and most likely out of fear of punishment or hope for a reward. The result is usually temporary compliance with the change agent's desires; the new behavior continues only so long as the opportunity for rewards and punishments exists. This is why force-coercion may be most useful as an unfreezing strategy. It can help to break people from old habits and create some impetus to try new ones.

An example of how force-coercion can help unfreeze a situation is the example of General Electric's Work-Out program, discussed earlier.[29] Jack Welch started Work-Out to create a forum for active employee empowerment. But he made participation mandatory from the start; he used his authority to force employees to participate. And he was confident in doing so because he believed that, once started, the program would prove valuable enough to survive and prosper on its own. It did.

An alternative to force-coercion is the **rational persuasion strategy**, attempting to bring about change through persuasion backed by special knowledge, information, facts, and

A **force-coercion strategy** pursues change through formal authority and/or the use of rewards or punishments.

A **rational persuasion strategy** pursues change through empirical data and rational argument.

Why people may resist change

Fear of the unknown   not understanding what is happening or what comes next

Disrupted habits   feeling upset to see the end of the old ways of doing things

Loss of confidence   feeling incapable of performing well under the new ways of doing things

Loss of control   feeling that things are being done "to" you rather than "by" or "with" you

Poor timing   feeling overwhelmed by the situation or that things are moving too fast

Work overload   not having the physical or psychic energy to commit to the change

Loss of face   feeling inadequate or humiliated because it appears that the old ways weren't good ways

Lack of purpose   not seeing a reason for the change and/or not understanding its benefits

A **shared power strategy** pursues change by participation in assessing change needs, values, and goals.

rational argument. The likely outcome of rational persuasion is compliance with reasonable commitment. This is actually the strategy that you learn and practice so much in school, when writing reports and making formal presentations on group projects. And you'll do a lot of it in the real world as well. But, as you fully realize, the strategy is dependent on very good facts and information, as well as the change agent's ability to communicate them persuasively.

The persuasive power in this strategy works best when the change agent has credibility as an expert. But the credibility can also be gained from external consultants or experts, or by case examples, demonstration projects, or benchmarks. Ford, for example, has sent managers to Disney World to learn about customer loyalty, hoping to stimulate them to lead customer-service initiatives of their own.[30] A Ford vice president says, "Disney's track record is one of the best in the country as far as dealing with customers." In this sense the power of rational persuasion is straightforward: If it works for Disney, why can't it work for Ford?

A **shared power strategy** engages people in a collaborative process of identifying values, assumptions, and goals from which support for change will naturally emerge. Although slow, the process is likely to yield high commitment. Sometimes called a *normative reeducative strategy*, this approach relies on empowerment and participation. The change leader works together with others as a team to develop the consensus needed to support change. This requires being comfortable and confident in allowing others to influence decisions that affect the planned change and its implementation. And because it entails a high level of involvement, this strategy is often quite time consuming. But shared power can deliver major benefits in terms of longer-lasting and internalized change.

The great power of the shared power strategy lies with unlocking the creativity and experience of people within the system. Unfortunately, many managers hesitate to use it for fear of losing control or of having to compromise on important organizational goals. However, Harvard scholar Teresa M. Amabile points out that managers and change leaders can share power regarding choice of means and processes, even if they can't debate the goals. "People will be more creative," she says, "if you give them freedom to decide how to climb particular mountains. You needn't let them choose which mountains to climb."[31]

• Change Leaders Identify and Deal Positively with Resistance to Change

The chapter subtitle says that "change can be your best friend." At this point, however, we should probably add: "but only if you deal with resistance in the right ways." When people resist change, they are most often defending something important to them that now appears threatened.

The *Exhibit – Why People May Resist Change* probably contains some familiar items. Surely you've seen some or all of these forms of change resistance in your own experience. And honestly now, haven't you also been a resistor at times? When you were, how did the change leader or manager respond? How do you think they should have responded?

It is tempting to view resistance to change as something that must be overcome or defeated. But this mindset can easily cause problems. Perhaps a better way is to view resistance as feedback, as a source of information about how people view the change and its impact on them. Armed with this feedback, a good change leader should be able to achieve a better fit among the change, the situation, and the people involved.

When managers changed the work schedules at ON Semiconductor's Rhode Island plant, for example, it didn't seem like a very big deal to them. But to the workers, it was significant enough to bring about an organizing attempt by the Teamster's Union. When management delved into the issues, they found that workers viewed changes in weekend work schedules as threatening to their personal lives. With inputs from the workers, however, the managers resolved the problem satisfactorily.[32]

Researchers have found that once resistance appears in organizations, managers try to deal with it in various ways, and some of their choices are better than others.[33] *Education and communication* uses discussions, presentations, and demonstrations to educate people about a change before it happens. *Participation and involvement* allows others to contribute ideas and help design and implement the change. *Facilitation and support* provides encouragement and training, channels for communicating problems and complaints, and ways of helping to overcome performance pressures. *Negotiation and agreement* offers incentives to those who are actively resisting or ready to resist, trying to make trade-offs in exchange for cooperation.

Although very different, each of the prior strategies for dealing with resistance to change has a role to play in organizations. Two other approaches, also found in management practice, are considerably more risky and prone to negative side effects. Change leaders who use *manipulation and cooptation* try to covertly influence resistors by providing information selectively and structuring events in favor of the desired change. When they use *explicit and implicit coercion*, they try to force resistors to accept change by threatening them with a variety of undesirable consequences if they do not go along as asked. Would you agree that most people don't like to be on the receiving end of these strategies?

 Checkpoints for Successful Change

- **Benefit**—make sure people involved see a clear advantage in the change.
- **Compatibility**—keep the change as close as possible to existing values and experiences.
- **Simplicity**—make the change as easy as possible to understand and use.
- **Triability**—allow people to try the change step-by-step, making adjustments as they go.

• Organization Development Is a Way of Building Sustainable Capacities for Change

Sometimes members of organizations should take time out, sit together, and systematically reflect on strengths and weaknesses, performance accomplishments and failures, and the future. And, they should take collective responsibility for initiating and making any needed changes.

One way to ensure that this happens is through a process known as **organization development (OD)**. This is a comprehensive and participatory approach designed to build capacity for self-directed and continuing long-run organizational change.[34] Two goals are pursued simultaneously in organization development. The *outcome goals of OD* focus on making specific changes to improve performance. The *process goals of OD* focus on making people more capable of working together to continue making changes as needed.

It's the second goal that most differentiates organization development from other change efforts. In fact you might think of OD as a form of "planned change plus." The "plus" means that change is accomplished in such a way that organization members develop a capacity for continued self-renewal. That is, OD tries to achieve change in ways that help organization members become more active and self-reliant in their ability to make future changes on their own initiatives.

Although it often involves the assistance of a consultant with special training, all managers can and should include OD in their change leadership agendas. To begin the OD process successfully, any consultant or facilitator must first *establish a working relationship* with members of the organization. The next step is *diagnosis*—gathering and analyzing data to assess the situation and set appropriate change objectives. Because the members do this together, unfreezing takes place as they identify areas where actions need to be taken.

Organization development is a comprehensive, participatory way for self-directed and continuing long-run organizational change.

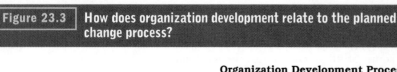

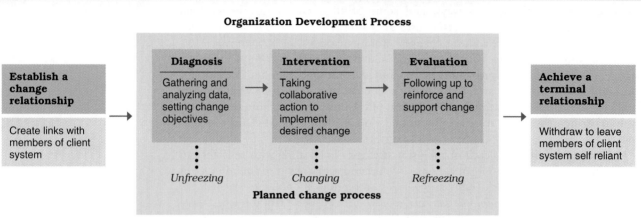

Organization development is a unique approach to planned change that tries to simultaneously create positive change (outcome goal) and leave everyone involved more capable of creating future changes (process goal). Often done with the help of a consultant or trained facilitator, OD engages organization members in a process of diagnosis, intervention, and evaluation that corresponds to unfreezing, changing, and refreezing in Lewin's model. Because the diagnosis is data-based and the process is participatory, OD can be described as using the rational persuasion and shared power strategies of planned change.

Diagnosis is followed by active *intervention*, taking steps to improve the functioning of individuals, groups, and the organization as a whole. Also essential to any OD effort is *evaluation*. This is the examination of the process to determine whether things are proceeding as desired and whether further action is needed. Eventually, the OD consultant or facilitator should *achieve a terminal relationship* that leaves the organization and its members able to function on their own. If OD has been well done, the system and its members should be better prepared to manage their ongoing need for self-renewal, change, and development.

You should get a sense from this discussion that organization development is both data-based and participatory. The data gathering can be done in several ways. Interviews are common, as are written surveys of employee attitudes and perceptions. Many such "climate" or "morale" questionnaires have been tested for reliability and validity, and some even have norms available that provide comparative data from other organizations.

As shown in Figure 23.3, organizational development it is a potent combination of the rational persuasion and shared power change strategies. While engaged in the OD process, organization members work together to gather data on organizational functioning, analyze it, decide what needs to be changed, and make commitments to actually follow through with the desired changes.

This is very powerful stuff indeed.

> *Innovation is deviation. If you don't create an environment where people can deviate from defined processes, they can't innovate.*
>
> Christian Belady, DISTINGUISHED TECHNOLOGIST AT HEWLETT-PACKARD

STUDY GUIDE

23.2 How do managers lead the processes of organizational change?

Be Sure You Can . . .

- list Lewin's phases of planned change

- discuss a change leader's responsibilities for each phase

- explain the force-coercion, rational persuasion, and shared power change strategies

- discuss the pros and cons of each change strategy

- list reasons why people resist change

- identify strategies for dealing with resistance to change

- explain outcome and process goals of OD

Define the Terms

Change leader

Changing

Force-coercion strategy

Organization development

Planned change

Rational persuasion strategy

Refreezing

Shared power strategy

Unfreezing

Rapid Review

- Change leaders are change agents who take responsibility for helping to change the behavior of people and organizational systems.

- Lewin's three phases of planned change are unfreezing (preparing a system for change), changing (making a change), and refreezing (stabilizing the system with a new change in place).

- Successful change agents understand the force-coercion, rational persuasion, and shared power change strategies, and the different outcomes likely to follow the use of each.

- People resist change for a variety of reasons, including fear of the unknown and force of habit; this resistance can be a source of feedback that can help improve the change process.

- Effective change agents deal with resistance positively and in a variety of ways, including education, participation, facilitation, manipulation, and coercion.

- Organization development is a comprehensive and participatory approach to change that involves organization members in a data-based process of diagnosis, intervention, and evaluation.

Reflect/React

1. Is there any role today for status quo managers in organizations?

2. Can the refreezing phase of planned change ever be completed in today's dynamic environment?

3. Should managers avoid the force-coercion change strategy altogether?

Multiple Choice

1. Product innovations create new goods or services for customers, while _____ innovations create new ways of doing things in the organization.
   (a) content **(b)** process **(c)** quality **(d)** task

2. When organizations use total quality management approaches such as quality circles to try and generate ideas for continuous improvement, this is an example of _____ change.
   (a) incremental **(b)** transformational **(c)** radical **(d)** top-down

3. The innovation process isn't really successful in an organization until a new idea is _____.
   (a) tested as a prototype **(b)** proven to be financially feasible **(c)** put into practice **(d)** discovered or invented

4. A manager using a force-coercion strategy is most likely relying on _____ power to bring about the planned change.
   (a) expertise **(b)** reference **(c)** position **(d)** information

5. The most participative of the planned change strategies is _____.
   (a) negotiation and agreement **(b)** rational persuasion
   (c) shared power **(d)** education and communication

6. When one deals with resistance by trying to covertly influence others, offering only selective information and/or structuring events in favor of the desired change, this is an example of _____.
   (a) rational persuasion **(b)** manipulation and cooptation
   (c) negotiation **(d)** facilitation

7. In organization development _____ goals pursue improved performance and _____ goals pursue greater capacity for self-sustaining change.
   (a) unfreezing/refreezing **(b)** empirical/rational
   (c) outcome/process **(d)** top-down/bottom-up

8. The responses most likely to be associated with use of a force-coercion change strategy are best described as _____.
   (a) internalized behaviors **(b)** compliance behaviors
   (c) cooptation behaviors **(d)** cooperative behaviors

9. Organization development's attempt to involve people in deciding how and why to change things for themselves is most consistent with the _____ strategy of planned change.
   (a) shared power **(b)** political maneuvering **(c)** direct forcing **(d)** negotiation and agreement

10. Which stage of the organization development process is most similar to the unfreezing phase in Lewin's model?
    (a) diagnosis **(b)** intervention **(c)** evaluation
    (d) termination

Short Response

11. What are the advantages and disadvantages of top-down and bottom-up change?

12. How does a manager's responsibilities for change leadership vary among Lewin's three phases of planned change?

13. What are the major differences in the potential outcomes of force-coercion, rational persuasion, and shared power strategies of planned change?

14. What does the statement "OD is planned change plus" mean?

Integration & Application

One of the common experiences new college graduates have in their first jobs is that they "spot things that need to be changed." They are just full of new ideas, and they are ready and quick to challenge existing ways of doing things. They are enthusiastic and well-intentioned. But, more often than most probably expect, their new bosses turn out to be skeptical, not too interested, or even irritated. And their co-workers who have been in place for some time may feel and act the same.

Questions: What is the new employee to do? One option is to just forget it and take an "I'll just do my job" approach. Let's reject that. But, then, how can you in your next new job be an effective change leader? How can you use change strategies and deal with resistance from your boss and co-workers in a manner that creates for you a reputation as someone with good ideas for positive change?

SELF-ASSESSMENT
Empowering Others

INSTRUCTIONS *Think of times when you have been in charge of a group—this could be a full-time or part-time work situation, a student work group, or whatever. Complete the following questionnaire by recording how you feel about each statement according to this scale:*

1 = Strongly disagree   2 = Disagree   3 = Neutral
4 = Agree   5 = Strongly agree

When in charge of a group, I find that:

1 Most of the time other people are too inexperienced to do things, so I prefer to do them myself.

2 It often takes more time to explain things to others than to just do them myself.

3 Mistakes made by others are costly, so I don't assign much work to them.

4 Some things simply should not be delegated to others.

5 I often get quicker action by doing a job myself.

6 Many people are good only at very specific tasks and so can't be assigned additional responsibilities.

7 Many people are too busy to take on additional work.

8 Most people just aren't ready to handle additional responsibilities.

9 In my position, I should be entitled to make my own decisions.

SCORING

Total your responses: enter the score here [_____].

INTERPRETATION

This instrument gives an impression of your *willingness to delegate*. Possible scores range from 9 to 45. The lower your score, the more willing you appear to be to delegate to others. Willingness to delegate is an important managerial characteristic: It is essential if you—as a manager—are to "empower" others and give them opportunities to assume responsibility, exercise self-control in their work, and have influence in change situation.

PATHWAYS to WileyPLUS

CASE SNAPSHOT

Go online to read this case!

Kate Spade, Inc.: From Bags to Riches

How did this company go from dining-room table venture to a phenomenally adored fashion brand in just a handful of years? Will the brand sustain its focus on fashion accessories, or, like other companies experiencing consistent and large growth, will it be tempted to diversify? Could doing so dilute its brand image?

MODULE 23   Online Interactive Learning Resources

Skill Builder
• Strength and Energy

Experiential Exercises
• Creative Solutions
• Force-Field Analysis

Team Project
• Innovation Audit

Module 1

1. b
2. d
3. a
4. c
5. a
6. d
7. c
9. b
10. b
11. Prejudice involves holding a negative stereotype or irrational attitude toward a person who is different from one's self. Discrimination occurs when such prejudice leads to decisions that adversely affect the other person in their job or in their advancement opportunities at work or in their personal lives.
12. Global outsourcing of labor involves contracting for services or employing persons in foreign countries where wages are lower than in the home country. This outsourcing means that fewer workers will be employed in jobs at home. When local jobs are eliminated or not created because of the outsourcing, the result is job migration—the shifting of jobs from the home country to another country.
13. The "free agent economy" is one where there is a lot of job-hopping and people work for several different employers over a career, rather than just one. This relates not only to the preferences the individuals but also the nature of organizational employment practices. As more organizations reduce the hiring of full-time workers in favor of more part-timers and independent contractors, this creates fewer long-term job opportunities for potential employees. Thus they become "free agents" who sell their services to difference employers on a part-time and contract basis.
14. An open system interacts with its environment to obtain resources that are used to produce finished goods and services. These should be products that are valued by customers; purchases by loyal customers provide revenues that help support the acquisition of resources to continue the input–throughput–output cycle. However, an open system is only customer driven when it actively listens to customers and concerns and then tries to provide them with products that are best fit with their needs and desires. When customer feedback is neglected, the open system may survive in the short run but it will have a difficult time surviving in the long run. An example could be the auto-makers who fail to produce vehicles that satisfy changing customer tastes, such as high fuel efficiency, and lose market share to others who listen better to customers and keep offering new options, such as hybrid engines.

Integration & Application Your answer to this question should show a clear understanding of the following concepts and how they can be applied to a real-world example: open system, value chain, and customer-driven organization. Make sure you both define these terms and give good examples for them.

Module 2

1. d
2. c
3. c
4. b
5. b
6. c
7. b
8. a
9. d
10. c
11. The direction in managerial work is toward acting as a "coach" and "facilitator" of others in their work. This means that the manager is concerned with supporting and helping others to do well in their jobs.
12. Planning sets the objectives or targets that one hopes to accomplish. Controlling measures actual results against the planning objectives or targets, and makes any corrections necessary to better accomplish them. Thus, planning and controlling work together in the management process, with planning setting the stage for controlling.
13. You can spot a low quality of work life environment through such signs or symptoms as: People don't receive a lot of respect from higher-level managers, they complain that their pay is unfair and that they have limited opportunities to learn new skills, they don't show a lot of pride in their work, and they work in unsafe or unhealthy or just unpleasant work conditions.
14. You will typically find that top managers are more oriented toward the external environment than the first-level or lower level managers. This means top managers must be alert to trends, problems, and opportunities that can affect the performance of the organization as a whole. The first-line or lower manager is most concerned with the performance of his or her immediate work unit, and managing the people and resources of the unit on an operational day-to-day basis. Top management is likely to be more strategic and long term in orientation.

Integration & Application I consider myself "effective" as a manager if I can help my work unit achieve high performance and the persons in it to achieve job satisfaction. In terms of skills and personal development, the framework of essential management skills offered by Katz is a useful starting point. At the first level of management, technical skills are important and I would feel capable in this respect. However, I would expect to learn and refine these skills even more through my work experiences. Human skills, the ability to work well with other people, will also be very important. Given the diversity anticipated for this team, I will need good human skills and I will have to keep improving my capabilities in this area. One area of consideration here is emotional intelligence, or my ability to understand how the emotions of myself and others influence work relationships. I will also have a leadership responsibility to help others on the team develop and utilize these skills so that the team itself can function effectively. Finally, I would expect opportunities to develop my conceptual or analytical skills in anticipation of higher level appointments. In terms of personal development I should recognize that the conceptual skills will increase in importance relative to the technical skills as I move upward in management responsibility, while the human skills are consistently important.

Module 3

1. a
2. b
3. c
4. a
5. c
6. c
7. d
8. b
9. a
10. a
11. You can see Scientific Management principles operating everywhere from UPS delivery, to fast-food restaurants, to order-fulfillment centers. In each case the workers are trained to perform highly specified job tasks that are

carefully engineered to be the most efficient. Their supervisors try to keep the process and workers well supported. In some cases the workers may be paid on the basis of how much work they accomplish in a time period, such as a day or week. The basic principles are to study the job, identify the most efficient job tasks and train the workers, and then support and reward the workers for doing them well.

12. According to the deficit principle, a satisfied need is not a motivator of behavior. The social need, for example, will only motivate if it is deprived or in deficit. According to the progression principle, people move step by step up Maslow's hierarchy as they strive to satisfy their needs. For example, esteem need becomes activated only after the social need is satisfied. Maslow also suggests, however, that the progression people stops operating at the level of self-actualization; the more this need is satisfied the stronger it gets.

13. The Hawthorne Effect occurs when people singled out for special attention tend to perform as expected. An example would be giving a student a lot of personal attention in class with the result that he or she ends up studying harder and performing better. This is really the same thing as McGregor's notion of the self-fulfilling prophesy with the exception that he identified how it works to both the positive and the negative. When managers, for example, have positive assumptions about people they tend to treat them well and the people respond in ways that reinforce the original positive thinking. This is a form of Hawthorne Effect. McGregor also pointed out that negative self-fulfilling prophesies result when managers hold negative assumptions about people and behavior accordingly.

14. Contingency thinking takes an "if—then" approach to situations. It seeks to modify or adapt management approaches to fit the needs of each situation. An exam-

ple would be to give more customer contact responsibility to workers who want to satisfy social needs at work, while giving more supervisory responsibilities to those who want to satisfy their esteem or ego needs.

Integration & Application A bureaucracy operates with a strict hierarchy of authority, promotion based on competency and performance, formal rules and procedures, and written documentation. Enrique can do all of these things in his store. However, he must be careful to meet the needs of the workers and not to make the mistake identified by Argyris—failing to treat them as mature adults. While remaining well organized, there is room for the store manager to help workers meet higher order esteem and self-fulfillment needs, as well as to exercise autonomy under Theory Y assumptions. Enrique must also be alert to the dysfunctions of bureaucracy that appear when changes are needed or when unique problems are posed or when customers want to be treated personally. The demands of these situations clash with the ways of bureaucracies that are set up to handle routine work efficiently and impersonally, with and emphasis on rules, procedures and authority.

Module 4

1. a
2. c
3. d
4. a
5. c
6. b
7. c
8. b
9. a
10. a
11. Distributive justice means that everyone is treated the same, that there is no discrimination based on things like age, gender, sexual orientation. An example would be a man and a woman who both apply for the same job. A man-

ager violates distributive justice if interviews only the man and not the woman as well, or vice versa. Procedural justice means that rules and procedures are fairly followed. For example, a manager violates distributive justice if she punishes one person for coming to work late while ignoring late behavior by another person with whom she regularly plays golf.

12. The "spotlight questions" for double-checking the ethics of a decision are: "How would I feel if my family finds out?" "How would I feel if this were published in the local newspaper?"

13. Bosses are in positions of power vis-à-vis those who report to them. "Bad bosses" can use this power in ways that can move subordinates in the direction of unethical behavior. Examples would be requests to do things that are against organizational policy or even illegal, such as padding the boss's expense reports, with the implicit threat that if the individual doesn't do what the boss asks, he or she will suffer negative consequences. Bosses may also inadvertently move people toward unethical behavior when they set performance goals that are so high and difficult that the individual believes the only way he or she can meet them is to do something that is unethical. Bosses intentionally or unintentionally can abuse power and influence their subordinates in these and other ways.

14. The rationalizations include believing that: (1) the behavior is not really illegal; (2) the behavior is really in everyone's best interests; (3) no one will find out; and (4) the organization will protect you.

Integration & Application If the manager adopts a position of cultural relativism, there will be no perceived problem in working with the Tanzanian firm. The justification would be that as long as it is operating legally in Tanzania, that makes everything okay. The absolutist position would hold that the contract should not be taken because the factory conditions are unacceptable at home and therefore are unacceptable anywhere. The cultural relativism position can be criticized because it makes it easy to do business in places where people are not treated well; for example, the absolutist position can be criticized as trying to impose one's values on people in a different cultural context.

Module 5

1. a
2. c
3. b
4. d
5. d
6. a
7. a
8. b
9. c
10. d

11. The classical view of corporate social responsibility presents the case against corporate social responsibility. It argues that concerns for socially responsible behavior divert attention from a firm's primary duties to earn profits for its owners. The argument against social responsibility holds that it reduces profits by raising business costs; it also diverts the business from its primary purpose and gives it too much social power in the community.

12. The "virtuous circle" concept of social responsibility holds that social responsibility practices do not hurt the bottom line and often help it; when socially responsible actions result in improved financial performance, this encourages more of the same actions in the future—a virtuous circle being created.

13. When a board of directors is exercising its responsibilities for corporate governance, it will make sure that the top management is running the firm in the best interests of the owners, that everything is done legally, that all financial transactions are proper, and that any compensation and rewards to the management are justifiable.

14. An immoral manager acts unethically and may do illegal things intentionally to realize some personal gain; an amoral manager does these things without considering their ethical/legal consequences or implications.

Integration & Application When Kraft executives decided to stop some of its advertising to children, it had already been criticized publicly for doing this type of advertising. Thus it is reacting to criticism in this situation, not acting proactively ahead of it. If we were to place their decision on the social responsibility strategy framework in the module, it would be accommodative. It might be borderline proactive in the sense that it is acting in ways that will incur at least some short-run losses of sales, so the executives could be considered to be trying to stake out a leadership position within the industry on this issue. There would be no doubt about the strategy being proactive if they had done this before public criticism occurred.

Module 6

1. c
2. a
3. a
4. b
5. a
6. a
7. d
8. d
9. c
10. a

11. An approach of valuing diversity shows through leadership a commitment to helping people understand their differences, often through education and training programs. An approach of managing diversity, according to Roosevelt Thomas, is a step beyond in that it is where the leadership commits to changing the culture of the organization to empower everyone and create a fully inclusive environment where human resources are respected and fully utilized.

12. There are numbers of subcultures that form in organizations and can become the source of perceived differences as people work with one another across subculture boundaries. Examples of common organizational subcultures include those based on age, gender, profession, and work function. If younger workers stereotype older workers as uncreative and less ambitious, a team consisting of an age mix of members might experience some difficulties. This illustrates an example of problems among generational subcultures.

13. Organizations are power structures, and the way people view and respond to power differences in organizations can be very significant in how they operate. In a national culture where power distance is high, there would be a tendency in organizations to respect persons of authority—perhaps defer to them, use job titles and formal greetings, and refrain from challenging their views in public meetings. In a low or moderate power distance culture, by contrast, there might be more informality in using first names without job titles and being more casual in relationships and even in public disagreements with views expressed by senior people.

14. The cultural orientation of assertiveness would be important in a corporation's global training because it has a lot to do with how people are likely to handle relationships. A culture that runs high in assertiveness would include societal tendencies toward confrontation and "tough" stances as people in disagreements might deal with one another. In a low-assertiveness culture the tendency would be toward modesty and less aggressiveness. When representatives of these different cultures work together, they could have problems dealing with conflict; the high-assertive culture person would appear "pushy" to the other, while the low assertiveness culture person's behavior might be misinterpreted as a lack of concern. When good problem solving is the goal, these persons might need help understanding one another so that issues are resolved and not just left open.

Integration & Application The friend must recognize that the cultural differences between the United States and Japan may affect the success of group-oriented work practices such as quality circles and work teams. The United States was the most individualistic culture in Hofstede's study of national cultures; Japan is much more collectivist. Group practices such as the quality circle and teams are natural and consistent with the Japanese culture. When introduced into a more individualistic culture, these same practices might cause difficulties or require some time for workers to get used to. At the very least, the friend should proceed with caution, discuss ideas for the new practices with the workers before making any changes, and then monitor the changes closely so that adjustments can be made to improve them as the workers gain familiarity with them and have suggestions of their own.

Module 7

1. d
2. d
3. b
4. a
5. b
6. a
7. c
8. c
9. d
10. a
11. In a joint venture the foreign corporation and the local corporation each own a portion of the firm—e.g., 75% and 25%. In a wholly owned subsidiary the foreign firm owns the local subsidiary in its entirety.

12. The relationship between an MNC and a host country should be mutually beneficial. Sometimes, however, host countries complain that MNCs take unfair advantage of them and do not include them in the benefits of their international operations. The complaints against MNCs include taking excessive profits out of the host country, hiring the best local labor, not respecting local laws and customs, and dominating the local economy. Engaging in corrupt practices is another important concern.

13. If a Senator says she favors "protectionism" in international trade, it basically means that she wants to make sure that domestic American firms are protected against foreign competitors. In other words, she doesn't want foreign companies coming into America and destroying through competition the local firms. Thus, she wants to protect them in some ways such as imposing import tariffs on the foreign firms' products or imposing legal restrictions on them setting up businesses in America.

14. Currency risk in international business involves the rise and fall of currencies in relationship with one another. For an American company operating in Japan, currency risk involves the value of the Dollar vis-à-vis the Yen. When the Dollar falls relative to the Yen (requiring more of them to buy 1 Yen), it means that buying products and making investments in Japan will be more costly; the "risk" of this eventuality needs to be planned for when entering business relationships in foreign countries. Political risk is the potential loss in one's investments in foreign countries due to wars or political changes that might threaten the assets. An example would be a Socialist government coming into power and deciding to "nationalize" or take over ownership of all foreign companies.

Integration & Application This issue of MNC vs. transnational is growing in importance. When a large global company like Ford or IBM is strongly associated with a national identity, the firm might face risk in international business when foreign consumers or governments are angry at the firm's home country; they might stop buying its products or make it hard for them to operate. When the MNC has a strong national identity, its home constituents might express anger and create problems when the firm makes investments in creating jobs in other countries. Also, when the leadership of the MNC views itself as having one national home, it might have a more limited and even ethnocentric approach to international operations. When a firm operates as a transnational, by contrast, it becomes a global citizen and, theoretically, at least is freed from some potential problems identified here. Because a transnational views the world as its home, furthermore, its workforce and leadership is more likely to be globally diverse and have broad international perspectives on the company and its opportunities.

Module 8

1. a
2. b
3. b
4. a
5. a
6. b
7. a
8. c
9. c
10. a
11. Entrepreneurship is rich with diversity. It is an avenue for business entry and career success that is pursued by many women and members of minority groups. Data show almost 40 percent of U.S. businesses are owned by women. Many report leaving other employment because they had limited opportunities. For them, entrepreneurship made available the opportunities for career success that they lacked. Minority-owned businesses are one of the fastest-growing sectors, with the growth rates highest for Hispanic-owned, Asian-owned, and African-American–owned businesses in that order.

12. The three stages in the life cycle of an entrepreneurial firm are birth, breakthrough, and maturity. In the birth stage, the leader is challenged to get customers, establish a market, and find the money needed to keep the business going. In the breakthrough stage, the challenges shift to becoming and staying profitable and managing growth. In the maturity stage, a leader is more focused on revising/maintaining a good business strategy and more generally managing the firm for continued success and possibly more future growth.

13. The limited partnership form of small business ownership consists of a general partner and one or more "limited partners." The general partner(s) play an active role in managing and operating the business; the limited partners do not. All contribute resources of some value to the partnership for the conduct of the business. The advantage of any partnership form is that the partners may share in profits, but their potential for losses is limited by the size of their original investments.

14. A venture capitalist is an individual or group of individuals that invests money in new start-up companies and gets a portion of ownership in return. The goal is to sell their ownership stakes in the future for a profit. An angel investor is a type of venture capitalist, but on a smaller and individual scale. This is a person who invests in a new venture, taking a share of ownership, and also hoping to gain profit through a future sale of the ownership.

Integration & Application The friend is right—it takes much forethought and planning to prepare the launch of a new business venture. In response to the question of how to ensure that you are really being customer-focused in the new start-up, I would ask and answer the following questions to frame my business model with a strong customer orientation. "Who are my potential cus-

tomers? What market niche am I shooting for? What do the customers in this market really want? How do these customers make purchase decisions? How much will it cost to produce and distribute my product/service to these customers? How much will it cost to attract and retain customers?" Following an overall executive summary, which includes a commitment to this customer orientation, I would address the following areas in writing up my initial business plan. The plan would address such areas as company description—mission, owners, and legal form—as well as an industry analysis, product and services description, marketing description and strategy, staffing model, financial projections with cash flows, and capital needs.

Module 9

1. b
2. c
3. a
4. c
5. d
6. a
7. b
8. c
9. c
10. c
11. An optimizing decision represents the absolute "best" choice of alternatives. It is selected from a set of all known alternatives. A satisficing decision selects the first alternative that offers a "satisfactory" choice, not necessarily the absolute best choice. It is selected from a limited or incomplete set of alternatives.

12. A risk environment is one in which things are not known for sure—all the possible decision alternatives, all the possible consequences for each alternative, but they can be estimated as probabilities. For example, if I take a new job with a new employer, I can't know for certain that it will turn out as I expect; but I could be 80% sure that I'd like the new responsibilities, or only 60% sure

that I might get promoted within a year. In an uncertain environment things are so speculative that it is hard to even assign such probabilities.

13. A manager using systematic thinking is going to approach problem solving in a logical and rational fashion. The tendency will be to proceed in a linear step-by-step manner, handling one issue at a time. A manager using intuitive thinking will be more spontaneous and open in problem solving. He or she may jump from one stage in the process to the other and deal with many different things at once.

14. Escalating commitment is the tendency of people to keep investing in a previously chosen course of action, continuing to pursue it, even though it is not working. This is a human tendency to try and make things work by trying harder, investing more time, effort, resources, etc. In other words, I have decided in the past to pursue this major in college; I can't be wrong, can I? The feedback from my grades and course satisfaction suggests it isn't working; but I'm doing it now so I just need to make it work right. I'll just stick with it and see if things eventually turn out okay. In this example, I am making a decision to continue with the major that is most likely an example of escalating commitment.

Integration & Application This is what I would say. On the question of whether a group decision is best or an individual decision is best the appropriate answer is probably: It all depends on the situation. Sometimes one is preferable to the other; each has its potential advantages and disadvantages. If you are in a situation where the problem being addressed is unclear, the information needed to solve it is uncertain, and you don't have a lot of personal expertise, the group approach to decision making is probably best. Group decisions offer advantages like bringing

more information and ideas to bear on a problem; they often allow for more creativity; and, they tend to build commitments among participants to work hard to implement any decisions reached. On the other hand, groups can be dominated by one or more members and they can take a lot of time making decisions. Thus, when time is short the individual decision is sometimes a better choice. However, it is important that you, as this individual, are confident that you have the information needed to solve the problem or can get it before making your decision.

Module 10
1. d
2. a
3. b
4. d
5. c
6. a
7. d
8. b
9. c
10. a

11. The five steps in the formal planning process are: (1) Define your objectives, (2) determine where you stand relative to objectives, (3) develop premises about future conditions, (4) identify and choose among action alternatives to accomplish objectives, and (5) implement action plans and evaluate results.

12. Planning facilitates controlling because the planning process sets the objectives and standards that become the basis for the control process. If you don't have objectives and standards, you have nothing to compare actual performance with; consequently, control lacks purpose and specificity.

13. Contingency planning essentially makes available optional plans that can be quickly implemented if things go wrong with the original plan. Scenario planning is a longer term form of contingency planning that tries to project several future scenarios that might

develop over time and to associate each scenario with plans for best dealing with it.

14. Participation is good for the planning process in part because it brings to the process a lot more information, diverse viewpoint, and potential alternatives than would otherwise be available if just one person or a select group of top managers are doing the planning. Furthermore and very importantly, through participation in the planning process people develop an understanding of the final plans and the logic used to arrive at them, and they develop personal commitments to trying to follow-through and work hard to make implementation of the plans successful.

Integration & Application Benchmarking is the use of external standards to help evaluate one's own situation and develop ideas and directions for improvement. Curt and Rich are both right to a certain extent about its potential value for them. Rich is right in suggesting that there is a lot to learn by looking at what other bookstores are doing really well. The bookstore owner/manager might visit other bookstores in other towns which are known for their success. By observing and studying the operations of those stores and then comparing her store to them, the owner/manager can develop plans for future action. Curt is also right in suggesting that there is a lot to be learned potentially from looking outside the bookstore business. They should look at things like inventory management, customer service, facilities in other settings—not just bookstores; they should also look outside their town as well as within it.

Module 11
1. a
2. a
3. d
4. b

5. b

6. c

7. c

8. d

9. a

10. a

11. The Army's "after-action review" takes place after an action or activity has been completed. This makes it a form of "feedback" control. The primary purpose is to critique the action/activity and try to learn from it so that similar things in the future can be done better and so that the people involved can be best trained.

12. Quality circles bring together persons from various parts of the work place with a common commitment to quality improvements. They meet regularly to discuss quality results and options, and to try and maintain a continuous improvement momentum in their work areas. The members may receive special quality training. The members are expected to actively serve as quality champions in their work areas and to work with team members to come up with continuous quality improvements.

13. A progressive discipline system works by adjusting the discipline to fit the severity and frequency of the inappropriate behavior. In the case of a person who comes late to work, for example, progressive discipline might involve a verbal warning after three late arrivals, a written warning after five, and a pay-loss penalty after seven. In the case of a person who steals money from the business, there would be immediate dismissal after the first such infraction.

14. The just-in-time inventory approach reduces the carrying costs of inventories. It does this by trying to have materials arrive at a work station just in time to be used. When this concept works perfectly, there are no inventory carrying costs. However, even if it is imperfect and some inventory ends up being stockpiled it should still be less than that which would otherwise be the case.

Integration & Application I would begin the speech by describing MBO as an integrated planning and control approach. I would also clarify that the key elements in MBO are objectives and participation. Any objectives should be clear, measurable, and time-defined. In addition, these objectives should be set with the full involvement and participation of the employees; they should not be set by the manager and then told to the employees. Given this, I would describe how each business manager should jointly set objectives with each of his or her employees and jointly review progress toward their accomplishment. I would suggest that the employees should work on the required activities while staying in communication with their managers. The managers, in turn, should provide any needed support or assistance to their employees. This whole process could be formally recycled at least twice per year.

Module 12

1. a

2. b

3. b

4. c

5. a

6. b

7. c

8. a

9. c

10. d

11. A corporate strategy sets long-term direction for an enterprise as a whole. Functional strategies set directions so that business functions such as marketing and manufacturing support the overall corporate strategy. A corporate strategy sets long-term direction for an enterprise as a whole. Functional strategies set directions so that business functions such as marketing and manufacturing support the overall corporate strategy.

12. If you want to sell at lower prices than competitors and still make a profit, you have to have lower operating costs (profit = revenues − costs). Also, you have to be able to operate at lower costs in ways that are hard for your competitors to copy. This is the point of a cost leadership strategy—always seeking ways to lower costs and operate with greater efficiency than anyone else.

13. A Question Mark in the BCG matrix has a low market share in a high growth industry. This means that there is a lot of upside potential, but for now it is uncertain whether or not you will be able to capitalize on it. Thus, hard thinking is required. If you are confident the recommended strategy is growth; if you aren't it would be retrenchment, to allow resources to be deployed into more promising opportunities.

14. Strategic leadership is the ability to enthuse people to participate in continuous change, performance enhancement, and the implementation of organizational strategies. The special qualities of the successful strategic leader include the ability to make trade-offs, create a sense of urgency, communicate the strategy, and engage others in continuous learning about the strategy and its performance responsibilities.

Integration & Application A SWOT analysis is useful during strategic planning. It involves the analysis of organizational strengths and weaknesses, and of environmental opportunities and threats. Such a SWOT analysis in this case would help frame Kim's thinking about the current and future positioning of her store, particularly in respect to possible core competencies and competitive opportunities and threats. Then she can use Porter's competitive strategy model for further strategic refinements. This involves the possible use of three alternative strategies: differentiation, cost leadership, and focus. In this situation, the larger department store seems better positioned to follow the cost leadership strategy. This means that Kim may want to consider the other two alternatives. A differentiation strategy would involve trying to distinguish Kim's products from those of the larger store. This might involve a "made in America" theme or an emphasis on leather or canvas or some other type of clothing material. A focus strategy might specifically target college students and try to respond to their tastes and needs rather than those of the larger community population. This might involve special orders and other types of individualized service for the college student market.

Module 13

1. b
2. c
3. b
4. a
5. b
6. c
7. b
8. a
9. c
10. d
11. An organization chart depicts the formal structure of the organization. This is the official picture or the way things are supposed to be. However, the likelihood is that an organization chart quickly becomes out of date in today's dynamic environments. So one issue is whether or not the chart one is viewing actually depicts the current official structure. Second, there is a lot more to the way things work in organizations than what is shown in the organization chart. People are involved in a variety of informal networks that create an informal structure. It operates as a shadow lying above or behind the formal structure and also influences operations. Both the formal structure and informal structure must be understood; at best an organization chart helps with understanding the formal one.
12. There are two major ways that informal structures can be good for organizations. First, they can help get work done efficiently and well. When people know one another in informal relationships, they can and often do use these relationships as part of their jobs. Sometimes an informal contact makes it a lot easier to get something done or learn how to do something than the formal linkages displayed on an organization chart. Second, being part of informal groups is an important source of potential need satisfaction. Being in an informal network or group can satisfy needs in ways that one's job can't sometimes and add considerably to the potential satisfactions of the work experience.
13. The product structure organizes work around a product; the division or unit would be headed by a product manager or executive. The geographical structure organizes work by area or location; different geographical regions would be headed by regional managers or executives.
14. The matrix structure is organized in a traditional functional fashion in the vertical dimension. For example, a business might have marketing, human resources, finance, and manufacturing functions. On the horizontal dimension, however, it is organized divisionally in a product or project fashion, with a manager heading up each special product or project. Members from the functional departments are assigned to permanent cross-functional teams for each product or project. They report vertically to their functional bosses and horizontally to their product/project bosses. This two-boss system is the heart of the matrix organization.

Integration & Application A network structure often involves one organization "contracting out" aspects of its operations to other organizations that specialize in them. The example used in the text was of a company that contracted out its mailroom services. Through the formation of networks of contracts, the organization is reduced to a core of essential employees whose expertise is concentrated in the primary business areas. The contracts are monitored and maintained in the network to allow the overall operations of the organization to continue even though they are not directly accomplished by full-time employees. There are many possibilities for doing something similar in a university. In one model, the core staff would be the faculty. They would be supported by a few administrators who managed contracts with outsourcing firms for things like facilities maintenance, mail, technology support, lawns maintenance, food services, housing services, and even things like development, registrar and student affairs. Another model would have the administrators forming a small core staff who contract out for the above and, in addition, for faculty who would be hired "as needed" and on contracts for specific assignments.

Module 14

1. b
2. c
3. b
4. b
5. b
6. c
7. c
8. d
9. a
10. b
11. Today's organizations are able to maintain centralization of control while still decentralizing a lot of operational decision making because of the great advantages of information technology. With the right information, systems management stays immediately informed of performance results and can step in to make corrections as necessary. This allows them to release more decision-making authority, knowing that they will know quickly if things are going wrong.

12. An organic design tends to be quicker and more flexible because it is very strong in lateral communication and empowerment. People at all levels are talking to one another and interacting as they gather and process information and solve problems. They don't wait for the vertical structure and "bosses" to do these things for them. This means that as the environment changes they are more likely to be on top of things quickly. It also means that when problems are complex and difficult to solve, they will work with multiple people in various parts of the organization to best deal with them.

13. When subsystems are highly differentiated they tend to need more sophisticated integrating mechanisms. Many organizations find the use of liaison roles, task forces, teams, and the matrix organization helpful under these circumstances.

14. Value-based management means that the manager and leader act with a consistent and clear commitment to espoused values. Their values are clear and well communicated. Through their actions they live up to the values. No one doubts their integrity since there is no inconsistency between what they say and what they do, and their values serve as positive models for others in the organization.

Integration & Application Organizations today are operating in often complex, changing, and difficult decision environments. They also tend to operate with the benefit of the latest information technology and information systems. In this situation they are able to operate with fewer staff personnel since the information needs of the organization tend to be met by managers using their information technology to stay informed and communicate with one another. They also need fewer middle managers and can operate with fewer management levels because this information processing capability is built into all work roles. In the past the staff and middle managers served as information processors for other parts of the organization. Now IT makes this less necessary. Also, with the emphasis today on human capital and talent it makes sense for organizations to allow individuals through delegation of authority to use their talents and exercise initiative in their jobs. They need less-direct supervision; delegation gives them the freedom to use their talents and intellects to best do their jobs. Under these conditions, again, fewer management levels are necessary.

Module 15

1. a
2. b
3. c
4. b
5. b
6. b
7. a
8. d
9. a
10. d

11. Orientation activities introduce a new employee to the organization and the work environment. This is a time when the individual may develop key attitudes and when performance expectations will also be established. Good orientation communicates positive attitudes and expectations and reinforces the desired organizational culture. It formally introduces the individual to important policies and procedures that everyone is expected to follow.

12. Mentoring is when a senior and experienced individual adopts a newcomer or more junior person with the goal of helping him or her develop into a successful worker. The mentor may or may not be the individual's immediate supervisor. The mentor meets with the individual and discusses problems, shares advice, and generally supports the individual's attempts to grow and perform. Mentors are considered very useful for persons newly appointed to management positions.

13. Any performance assessment approach should be both valid and reliable. To be valid it must measure accurately what it claims to measure—whether that is some aspect of job performance or personal behavior. To be reliable it must deliver the same results consistently—whether applied by different raters to the same person or when measuring the same person over time. Valid and reliable assessments are free from bias and as objective as possible.

14. The graphic rating scale simply ask a supervisor to rate an employee on an established set of criteria, such as quantity of work or attitude toward work. This leaves much room for subjectivity and debate. The behaviorally anchored rating scale asks the supervisor to rate the employee on specific behaviors that had been identified as positively or negatively affecting performance in a given job. This is a more specific appraisal approach and leaves less room for debate and disagreement.

Integration & Application As Sy's supervisor, you face a difficult but perhaps expected human resource management problem. Not only is Sy influential as an informal leader, he also has considerable experience on the job and in the company. Even though he is experiencing performance problems using the new computer system, there is no indication that he doesn't want to work hard and continue to perform for the company. Although retirement is an option, Sy may also be transferred, promoted, or simply terminated. The latter response seems unjustified and may cause legal problems. Transferring Sy, with his agreement, to another position could be a positive move; promoting Sy to a supervisory position in which his experience and networks would be useful is another possibility. The key in this situation seems to be moving Sy out so that a computer-literate person can take over the job, while continuing to utilize Sy in a job that better fits his talents. Transfer and/or promotion should be actively considered both in his and in the company's interest.

Module 16

1. b
2. b
3. a
4. d
5. a
6. c
7. c
8. a
9. a
10. b
11. Position power is based on reward, coercion or punishment, and legitimacy or formal authority. Managers, however, need to have more power than that made available to them by the position alone. Thus, they have to develop personal power through expertise and reference. This personal power is essential in helping managers get things done beyond the scope of their position power alone.
12. Leadership situations are described by Fiedler according to: Position power—how much power the leader has in terms of rewards, punishments, and legitimacy; Leader–member relations—the quality of relationships between the leader and followers; Task structure—the degree to which the task is clear and well defined, or open ended and more ambiguous. Highly favorable situations are high in position power, have good leader–member relations, and have structured tasks; highly unfavorable situations are low in position power, have poor leader–member relations, and have unstructured tasks.
13. According to House's path-goal theory, the following combinations are consistent with successful leadership. Participative leadership

works well, for example, when performance incentives are low and people need to find other sources of need satisfaction. Through participation the leader gains knowledge that can help identify important needs and possible ways of satisfying them other than through the available performance incentives. Directive leadership works well, for example, when people aren't clear about their jobs or goals. In these cases the leader can step in and provide direction that channels their efforts toward desired activities and outcomes.
14. Servant leadership is basically other-centered and not self-centered. A servant leader is concerned with helping others to perform well so that the organization or group can ultimately do good things for society. The person who accepts the responsibilities of servant leadership is good at empowering others so that they can use their talents while acting independently to do their jobs in the best possible ways.

Integration & Application In his new position, Marcel must understand that the transactional aspects of leadership are not sufficient to guarantee him long-term leadership effectiveness. He must move beyond the effective use of task-oriented and people-oriented behaviors and demonstrate through his personal qualities the capacity to inspire others. A charismatic leader develops a unique relationship with followers in which they become enthusiastic, highly loyal, and high achievers. Marcel needs to work very hard to develop positive relationships with the team members. He must emphasize in those relationships high aspirations for performance accomplishments, enthusiasm, ethical behavior, integrity and honesty in all dealings, and a clear vision of the future. By working hard with this agenda and by allowing his personality to positively express itself in the team setting, Marcel should make continuous progress as an effective and moral leader.

Module 17

1. b
2. a
3. c
4. b
5. c
6. b
7. d
8. b
9. a
10. c
11. The manager's goal in active listening is to help the subordinate say what he or she really means. To do this, the manager should carefully listen for the content of what someone is saying, paraphrase or reflect back what the person appears to be saying, remain sensitive to nonverbal cues and feelings, and not be evaluative.
12. Well intentioned managers can make bad decisions when they base decisions on bad information. Because of the manager's position of authority in the organization, those below him or her may be reluctant to communicate upward information that they believe the manager doesn't want to hear. Thus, they may filter the information to make it as agreeable to the manager as possible. As a result of this filtering of upward communication the manager may end up with poor or incomplete information and subsequently make bad decisions.
13. The four major errors in giving constructive feedback would be: 1) being general rather than specific, 2) choosing a poor time, 3) including in the message irrelevant things, 4) overwhelming the receiver with too much information at once.
14. Ethnocentrism is when a person views his or her own culture as superior to others. It can interfere with cross-cultural communication when the ethnocentrism leads the person to ignore cultural signals that indicate his or her behavior is inappropriate or offensive by local cultural standards. With the ethnocentric attitude of cultural superiority, the individual is inclined not

to change personal ways or display the sensitivity to local cultural ways that are necessary to effective communication.

Integration & Application Glenn can do a number of things to establish and maintain a system of communication with his employees and for his department store branch. To begin, he should, as much as possible, try to establish a highly interactive style of management based upon credibility and trust. Credibility is earned through building personal power through expertise and reference. With credibility, he might set the tone for the department managers by using MBWA—"managing by wandering around." Once this pattern is established, trust will build between him and other store employees, and he should find that he learns a lot from interacting directly with them. Harold should also set up a formal communication structure, such as bimonthly store meetings, where he communicates store goals, results, and other issues to the staff, and in which he listens to them in return. An e-mail system whereby Glenn and his staff could send messages to one another from their workstation computers would also be beneficial.

Module 18
1. c
2. d
3. b
4. b
5. d
6. a
7. a
8. b
9. d
10. c
11. All the Big Five personality traits are relevant to the workplace. To give some basic examples, consider the following. Extroversion suggests whether or not a person will reach out to relate and work well with others. Agreeableness suggests whether or not a person is open to the ideas of others and willing to go along with group decisions. Conscientiousness suggests whether someone can be depended on to meet commitments and perform agreed-upon tasks. Emotional stability suggests whether or not someone will be relaxed and secure, or uptight and tense, in work situations. Openness suggests whether someone will be open to new ideas or resistant to change.

12. The Type A personality is characteristic of people who bring stress on themselves by virtue of personal characteristics. These tend to be compulsive individuals who are uncomfortable waiting for things to happen, who try to do many things at once, and who generally move fast and have difficulty slowing down. Type A personalities can be stressful for both the individuals and the people around them. Managers must be aware of Type A personality tendencies in their own behavior and among others with whom they work. Ideally, this awareness will help the manager take precautionary steps to best manage the stress caused by this personality type.

13. The halo effect occurs when a single attribute of a person, such as the way he or she dresses, is used to evaluate or form an overall impression of the person. Selective perception occurs when someone focuses in a situation on those aspects that reinforce or are most consistent with his or her existing values, beliefs, or experiences.

14. Job satisfaction is an attitude that reflects how people feel about their jobs, work settings and the people with whom they work. A typical job satisfaction survey might ask people to respond to questions about their pay, co-worker relationships, quality of supervisor, nature of the work setting and the type of work they are asked to do. These questions might be framed with a scale ranging from "very satisfied" to "not satisfied at all" for each question or job satisfaction dimension.

Integration & Application Scott needs to be careful. Although there is modest research support for the relationship between job satisfaction and performance, there is no guarantee that simply doing things to make people happier at work will cause them to be higher performers. Scott needs to take a broader perspective on this issue and his responsibilities as a manager. He should be interested in job satisfaction for his therapists and do everything he can to help them to experience it. But he should also be performance oriented and understand that performance is achieved through a combination of skills, support and motivation. He should be helping the therapists to achieve and maintain high levels of job competency. He should also work with them to find out what obstacles they are facing and what support they need – things that perhaps he can deal with in their behalf. All of this relates as well to research indications that performance can be a source of job satisfaction. And finally, Scott should make sure that the therapists believe they are being properly rewarded for their work since rewards are shown by research to have an influence on both job satisfaction and job performance.

Module 19
1. b
2. c
3. d
4. d
5. b
6. a
7. b
8. b
9. a
10. d
11. People high in need for achievement will prefer work settings and jobs in which they have (1) challenging but achievable goals, (2) individual responsibility, and (3) performance feedback.
12. MBO is a structured approach to joint goal-setting and perform-

ance review by a manager or team leader and subordinates or team members. This offers a direct application of goal-setting theory. Participation of both manager and subordinate in goal setting offers an opportunity to choose goals to which the subordinate will respond and which also will serve the organization. Furthermore, through goal setting, the manager and individual subordinates can identify performance standards or targets. Progress toward these targets can be positively reinforced by the manager. Such reinforcements can serve as indicators of progress to someone with high need for achievement, thus responding to their desires for performance feedback.

13. When perceived inequity exists and individual might: 1–quit the job, 2–speak with the boss to try and increase rewards to the point where the inequity no longer exists, 3–decide to reduce effort to the level that seems consistent with the rewards being received.

14. Shaping encourages the formation of desirable work behaviors by rewarding successive approximations to those behaviors. In this sense, the behavior doesn't have to be perfect to be rewarded–it just has to be moving in the right direction. Over time and with a change of reinforcement scheduling from continuous to intermittent such rewards can end up drawing forth the desired behavior.

Integration & Application The use of Muzak would be considered improvement in a hygiene factor under Herzberg's two-factor theory. Thus it would not be a source of greater work motivation and performance. Herzberg suggests that job content factors are the satisfiers or motivators. Based in the job itself, they represent such things as responsibility, sense of achievement, and feelings of growth. Job context factors are considered sources of dissatisfaction. They are found in the job

environment and include such things as base pay, technical quality of supervision, and working conditions. Whereas improvements in job context such as introduction of Muzak make people less dissatisfied, improvements in job content are considered necessary to motivate them to high-performance levels.

Module 20

1. a
2. a
3. b
4. c
5. c
6. d
7. a
8. b
9. a
10. d
11. A bonus is a special monetary reward given in recognition of a performance achievement. Gain sharing is a system where the employee receives a reward calculated as a percentage of the "gain" they have helped to create through increased productivity. Stock options are rights to purchase stock at a later point in time at a price set earlier, with the anticipation that the employee will work hard to cause the stock price to rise and thus receive a greater financial benefit when his or her options are exercised in the future.
12. Because self-managing teams take on the supervisory functions of planning and controlling they become a form of job enrichment for groups. This would be an example of "vertical loading" in which the elimination of the supervisory role and the transferring of its responsibilities into the group itself create a self-management situation that is a form of job enrichment.
13. Growth-need strength helps determine which individuals are good candidates for job enrichment. A person high in growth-need strength seeks higher-order satisfaction of ego and self-fulfill-

ment needs at work. These are needs to which job enrichment can positively respond. A person low in growth-need strength may not respond well to the demands and responsibilities of an enriched job.

14. The compressed workweek, or 4–40 schedule, offers employees the advantage of a three-day weekend. However, it can cause problems for the employer in terms of ensuring that operations are covered adequately during the normal five workdays of the week. Labor unions may resist, and the compressed workweek will entail more complicated work scheduling. In addition, some employees find that the schedule is tiring and can cause family adjustment problems.

Integration & Application It might be easy for Rick to say that the person has a bad attitude and should be replaced. But why is the attitude negative? Are there work-related causes for it and could these causes be corrected through some effort by Rick? Does the person have valuable talents and experience that should be saved and that could offer major performance opportunities if the bad attitude situation was corrected? Rick can start by talking with the person and observing him or her to try and understand better the needs that he or she has at work and how these needs are being met or thwarted. Rick should also be trying to understand the person's skills and how they relate to the job that he or she is being asked to perform. Ideally, Rick should be trying to find a good "fit" between the individual's needs and talents and the job and work context. To the extent that he can discover the ideal fit and try to create it he may well find that a valuable employee has been retained with a positive attitude for the future.

Module 21

1. d
2. c
3. b
4. d
5. b
6. d
7. a
8. c
9. b
10. a

11. In a task force members are brought together to work on a specific assignment. The task force usually disbands when the assignment is finished. In an employee involvement group, perhaps a quality circle, members are brought together to work on an issue or task over time. They meet regularly and always deal with the same issue/task. In a self-managing team, the members of a formal work group provide self-direction. They plan, organize, and evaluate their work, share tasks, and help one another develop skills; they may even make hiring decisions. A true self-managing team does not need the traditional "boss" or supervisor, since the team as a whole takes on the supervisory responsibilities.

12. Input factors can have a major impact on group effectiveness. In order to best prepare a group to perform effectively, a manager should make sure that the right people are put in the group (maximize available talents and abilities), that these people are capable of working well together (membership characteristics should promote good relationships), that the tasks are clear, and that the group has the resources and environment needed to perform up to expectations.

13. A group's performance can be analyzed according to the interaction between cohesiveness and performance norms. In a highly cohesive group, members tend to conform to group norms. Thus, when the performance norm is positive and cohesion is high, we can expect everyone to work hard to support the norm—high performance is likely. By the same token, high cohesion and a low performance norm will act similarly—low performance is likely. With other combinations of norms and cohesion, the performance results will be more mixed.

14. The book lists several symptoms of groupthink along with various strategies for avoiding groupthink. For example, a group whose members censure themselves to refrain from contributing "contrary" or "different" opinions and/or whose members keep talking about outsiders as "weak" or the "enemy" may be suffering from groupthink. This may be avoided or corrected, for example, by asking someone to be the "devil's advocate" for a meeting and by inviting-in an outside observer to help gather different viewpoints.

Integration & Application Mariel is faced with a highly cohesive group whose members conform to a negative or low-performance norm. This is a difficult situation that is ideally resolved by changing the performance norm. In order to gain the group's commitment to a high-performance norm, Mariel should act as a positive role model for the norm. She must communicate the norm clearly and positively to the group. She should not assume that everyone knows what she expects of them. She may also talk to the informal leader and gain his or her commitment to the norm. She might carefully reward high-performance behaviors within the group. She may introduce new members with high-performance records and commitments. And she might hold group meetings in which performance standards and expectations are discussed, with an emphasis on committing to new high-performance directions. If attempts to introduce a high-performance norm fail, Mariel may have to take steps to reduce group cohesiveness so that individual members can pursue higher-performance results without feeling bound by group pressures to restrict their performance.

Module 22

1. d
2. b
3. d
4. c
5. b
6. d
7. a
8. a
9. d
10. a

11. Lose-lose outcomes arise from the conflict management styles of avoiding and accommodating. Win-lose outcomes arise from competing and compromising.

12. Conflict of moderate intensity is often functional because it creates a level of tension or anxiety that causes people to work with greater creativity, to work harder and to be more persistent. Without any conflict people might become complacent and believe that what they are currently doing or achieving is sufficient, even though things could be done better. When conflict is to high the anxieties and stresses might overload people and make it difficult for them to stay on task and achieve performance goals.

13. In a negotiation, both substance and relationship goals are important. Substance goals relate to the content of the negotiation. A substance goal, for example, may relate to the final salary agreement between a job candidate and a prospective employer. Relationship goals relate to the quality of the interpersonal relationships among the negotiating parties. Relationship goals are important because the negotiating parties most likely have to work together in the future. For example, if relationships are poor after a labor–management negotiation, the likelihood is that future problems will occur.

14. Arbitration and mediation are both third-party approaches to conflict resolution. However, arbitration involves the third party acting as a judge who actually gives a "ruling" as to how a conflict situation is to be resolved. The mediator, by contrast, works with and listens to the conflicting parties while trying to help them find agreement, but without issuing a binding ruling on the case.

Integration & Application This is a typical interpersonal conflict between a person and their boss, one caused by a disagreement over the substance of the work that the person is being assigned. There is no indication that there are any emotional disagreements or issues involved. One possible way to deal with the situation is for the instructor to ask for a meeting with the department head to discuss her teaching assignment. This meeting might be opened by expressing her support for the department's teaching goals and needs, but also expressing concern for her own time and areas of expertise. If the faculty member and/or the department head can get the conversation initially focused on the department's goals and needs this would provide an overall goal context within which to discuss the problem and hopefully resolve it. By focusing first on the higher-level goal shared in common it might be possible to find ways to meet the needs of the department while still meeting the needs of the instructor, or at least coming close enough so that she is willing to give her courses her best. This is a form of problem solving in which the two work together to meet their respective individual needs but always referring back to the higher-level goal on which they both agree whenever the discussion gets bogged down.

Module 23

1. b
2. a
3. c
4. c
5. c
6. b
7. c
8. b
9. a
10. a

11. Top down change has the advantage of top management commitment to the change process. It can also utilize the power vested in top management to push the change and unfreeze the lower-level systems to accept it. Bottom up change has the advantage of lower-level commitment to the change process. This means these levels are likely to unfreeze themselves and push for changes that seem meaningful to them and to their work.

12. Lewin's three phases of planned change are unfreezing, changing and refreezing. In terms of the change leadership challenges the major differences in attention would be as follows: unfreezing—preparing a system for change; changing—moving or creating change in a system; and refreezing—stabilizing and reinforcing change once it has occurred.

13. In general, managers can expect that others will be more committed and loyal to changes that are brought about through shared power strategies. Rational persuasion strategies can also create enduring effects if they are accepted.

Force-coercion strategies tend to have temporary effects only.

14. The statement that "OD equals planned change plus" basically refers to the fact that OD tries both to create change in an organization and to make the organization members capable of creating such change for themselves in the future.

Integration & Application In any change situation, it is important to remember that successful planned change occurs only when all three phases of change—unfreezing, changing, and refreezing—have been taken care of. Thus, I would not rush into the changing phase. Rather, I would work with the people involved to develop a felt need for change based on their ideas and inputs as well as mine. Then I would proceed by supporting the changes and helping to stabilize them into everyday routines. I would also be sensitive to any resistance and respect that resistance as a signal that something important is being threatened. By listening to resistance, I would be in a position to better modify the change to achieve a better fit with the people and the situation. Finally, I would want to take maximum advantage of the shared power strategy, supported by rational persuasion, and with limited use of force-coercion (if it is used at all). By doing all of this, I would like my staff to feel empowered and committed to constructive improvement through planned change. Throughout all of this I would strive to perform to the best of my ability and gain trust and credibility with everyone else; in this way I would be a positive role model for change.

Glossary

360° feedback Performance review that includes superiors, subordinates, peers, and even customers in the appraisal process.

A

accommodation Plays down differences and highlights similarities to reduce conflict.

accommodative strategy Business strategy that accepts social responsibility and tries to satisfy economic, legal, and ethical criteria.

accountability The requirement to show performance results to a supervisor.

active listening System of listening that helps the source of a message say what he or she really means.

affirmative action An effort to give preference in employment to women and minority group members.

after-action review A review device that identifies lessons learned in a completed project, task force, or special operation.

agreeableness Being good-natured, cooperative, and trusting.

anchoring and adjustment heuristic Adjustment of a previously existing value or starting point to make a decision.

angel investor A wealthy individual willing to invest in return for equity in a new venture.

arbitration A neutral third party issues a binding decision to resolve a dispute.

assessment center Examination of how job candidates handle simulated work situations.

attitude A predisposition to act in a certain way.

authoritarianism The degree to which a person defers to authority and accepts status differences.

autocratic leadership style Leadership style characterized by unilateral command-and-control behavior.

automation The total mechanization of a job.

availability heuristic Use of readily available information to assess a current situation.

avoidance Behavior pretending that a conflict doesn't really exist.

B

B2B business strategy Use of IT and Web portals to link organizations vertically in supply chains.

B2C business strategy Use of IT and Web portals to link businesses with customers.

bargaining zone The area between one party's minimum reservation point and the other party's maximum reservation point.

BATNA The best alternative to a negotiated agreement.

BCG matrix Device that analyzes business opportunities according to market growth rate and market share.

behavioral decision model Device that describes decision making with limited information and bounded rationality.

behaviorally anchored rating scale Rating scale that uses specific descriptions of actual behaviors to rate various levels of performance.

benchmarking Use of external comparisons to gain insights for planning.

best practices Methods that lead to superior performance.

biculturalism A situation wherein minority members adopt characteristics of majority cultures in order to succeed.

bona fide occupational qualifications Employment criteria justified by capacity to perform a job.

bonus pay plan Incentive plan that provides one-time payments based on performance accomplishments.

bottom-up change Change initiatives that come from all levels in the organization.

breakeven analysis Device that calculates the point at which sales revenues cover costs.

breakeven point Where revenues = costs; losses end and profits begin.

budget A plan that commits resources to projects or activities.

bureaucracy A rational and efficient form of organization founded on logic, order, and legitimate authority. It emphasizes formal authority, rules, order, fairness, and efficiency.

business plan Plan that describes the direction for a new business and the financing needed to operate it.

business strategy Plan that identifies how a division or strategic business unit will compete in its product or service domain.

C

career development System by which a person manages how he or she grows and progresses in a career.

career planning The process of matching career goals and individual capabilities with opportunities for their fulfillment.

centralized communication network System in which communication flows only between individual members and a hub or center point.

certain environment Decision environment that offers complete information on possible action alternatives and their consequences.

change leader Person who tries to change the behavior of another person or social system.

changing The phase where a planned change actually takes place.

charismatic leader Person who develops special leader–follower relationships and inspires followers in extraordinary ways.

child labor The full-time employment of children for work otherwise done by adults.

classical decision model Device that describes decision making with complete information.

coaching Situation in which an experienced person offers performance advice to a less-experienced person.

code of ethics A formal statement of values and ethical standards.

coercive power The capacity to punish or withhold positive outcomes as a means of influencing other people.

cognitive dissonance Discomfort felt when attitude and behavior are inconsistent.

cohesiveness The degree to which members are attracted to and motivated to remain part of a team.

collaboration Working through conflict differences and solving problems so everyone wins.

collective bargaining The process of negotiating, administering, and interpreting a labor contract.

commercializing innovation Process that turns ideas into economic value added.

committee Unit or team designated to work on a special task on a continuing basis.

communication The process of sending and receiving symbols with meanings attached.

comparable worth System of comparison that holds that persons performing jobs of similar importance should receive comparable pay.

competition Conflict management style that uses force, superior skill, or domination to "win" a conflict.

competitive advantage An advantage that comes from operating in successful ways that are difficult to imitate.

compressed workweek Employee management system that allows a worker to complete a full-time job in less than five days.

compromise Situation that occurs when each party to the conflict gives up something of value to the other.

conceptual skill The ability to think analytically and solve complex problems.

concurrent control Control method that focuses on what happens during the work process.

conflict A disagreement over issues of substance and/or an emotional antagonism.

conflict resolution The removal of the substantial and/or emotional reasons for a conflict.

conscientiousness Being responsible, dependable, and careful.

constructive stress A positive influence on effort, creativity, and diligence in work.

contingency planning Planning method that identifies alternative courses of action to take when things go wrong.

contingency thinking Planning method that tries to match management practices with situational demands.

contingency workers Persons employed on a part-time and temporary basis to supplement a permanent workforce.

controlling The process of measuring performance and taking action to ensure desired results.

core competency A special strength that gives an organization a competitive advantage.

core values Beliefs and values shared by organization members.

corporate governance Oversight of a company's management by a board of directors.

corporate social responsibility The obligation of an organization to serve its own interests and those of its stakeholders.

corporate strategy A chosen long-term direction for the total enterprise.

corporation A legal entity that exists separately from its owners.

corruption Using illegal practices to further one's business interests.

cost-benefit analysis Comparison between the costs and benefits of each potential course of action.

cost leadership strategy A type of competitive strategy that seeks to operate with lower costs than competitors.

creativity The generation of a novel idea or unique approach that solves a problem or crafts an opportunity.

crisis An unexpected problem that can lead to disaster if not resolved quickly and appropriately.

critical-incident technique System of keeping a log of someone's effective and ineffective job behaviors.

cross-functional team Unit bringing together members from different functional departments.

cultural etiquette Use of appropriate manners and behaviors in cross-cultural situations.

cultural intelligence The ability to adapt to new cultures.

cultural relativism Philosophy that suggests there is no one right way to behave; cultural context determines ethical behavior.

culture A shared set of beliefs, values, and patterns of behavior common to a group of people.

culture shock The confusion and discomfort that a person experiences when in an unfamiliar culture.

currency risk Possible loss because of fluctuating exchange rates.

customer-driven organization Organization that focuses its resources, energies, and goals on satisfying the needs of customers.

customer structure System of organization that groups together people and jobs that serve the same customers or clients.

D

debt financing Borrowing money that must be repaid over time with interest.

decentralization The location of decision authority is closer to lower organizational levels.

decentralized communication network Communication system that allows all members to communicate directly with one another.

decision A choice among possible alternative courses of action.

decision-making process Process that begins with identification of a problem and ends with evaluation of implemented solutions.

defensive strategy Seeking protection by doing the minimum legally required.

delegation Process by which managers transfer authority and responsibility to positions below them.

democratic leadership style Leadership style that encourages participation with an emphasis on both task accomplishment and development of people.

departmentalization The process of grouping together people and jobs into work units.

destructive stress A negative influence on one's performance.

differentiation The degree of difference between subsystems in an organization.

differentiation strategy Business strategy wherein the company offers products that are unique and different from the competition.

discipline The act of influencing behavior through reprimand.

discrimination A situation that occurs when someone is denied a job or job assignment for non-job-relevant reasons.

distributive justice Management style that focuses on treating people the same regardless of personal characteristics.

distributive negotiation Arbitration style that focuses on "win–lose" claims made by each party for certain preferred outcomes.

diversity Describes the variety of race, gender, age, and other individual differences in a group of employees.

divestiture Selling off parts of the organization to refocus attention on core business areas.

division of labor People and groups performing different jobs.

divisional structure Grouping together of people working on the same product, in the same area, or with similar customers.

downsizing Intentional decrease in the size of operations.

dysfunctional conflict Destructive conflict that hurts task performance.

E

e-business strategy Business strategy that uses the Internet to gain competitive advantage.

ecological fallacy System of thought that assumes that a generalized cultural value applies equally well to all members of the culture.

economic order quantity Inventory management technique that places new orders when inventory levels fall to predetermined points.

effective communication Communication in which the receiver fully understands the intended meaning.

effective team Group that achieves high levels of task performance, membership satisfaction, and future viability.

efficient communication Communication that occurs at minimum cost.

emotional conflict Conflict that results from feelings of anger, distrust, dislike, fear, and resentment as well as from personality clashes.

emotional intelligence The ability to manage ourselves and our relationships effectively.

emotional stability Being relaxed, secure, and unworried.

employee involvement team Group that meets on a regular basis to help achieve continuous improvement.

empowerment Management philosophy that allows others to gain power and achieve influence within the organization.

entrepreneur Person willing to pursue opportunities in situations that others view as problems or threats.

entrepreneurship Dynamic, risk-taking, creative, growth-oriented behavior.

equal employment opportunity The right to employment and advancement without regard to race, sex, religion, color, or national origin.

equity financing Financial transaction involving the exchange of ownership shares for outside investment monies.

escalating commitment The continuation of a course of action even though it is not working.

ethical behavior Actions that are "right" or "good" in the context of a governing moral code.

ethical dilemma A situation that although offering potential benefit or gain is also unethical.

ethical framework See "**code of ethics**"

ethical imperialism An ethical outlook that attempts to impose ethical standards on other cultures.

ethical leadership A leadership approach that values integrity and appears to others to be "good" and "right" by moral standards.

ethics Set moral standards of what is "good" and "right" behavior.

ethics mindfulness Enriched awareness that leads to consistent ethical behavior.

ethics training Training to help people understand the ethical aspects of decision making and to incorporate high ethical standards into their daily behavior.

ethnocentrism The belief that one's membership group or subculture is superior to all others.

expatriate worker A person who lives and works in a foreign country.

expectancy A person's belief that working hard will result in high task performance.

expert power The capacity to influence other people because of specialized knowledge.

exporting Selling local products abroad.

external control Control of internal functions through direct supervision or administrative systems.

extinction Behavioral learning that discourages a behavior by making the removal of a desirable consequence contingent on its occurrence.

extrinsic reward Beneficial outcome provided by someone else.

extroversion Being outgoing, sociable, and assertive.

F

family business Business owned and controlled by members of a family.

family business feud Conflict between family members over how the business is run.

feedback The process of telling someone else how you feel about something that person did or said.

feedback control A type of control that takes place after completing an action.

feedforward control A type of control that ensures clear directions and needed resources before the work begins.

filtering The intentional distortion of information to make it more favorable to the recipient.

first-mover advantage Benefits from being first to exploit a niche or enter a market.

flexible working hours Adjustable timetable that gives employees some choice in daily work hours.

focused cost leadership strategy Business strategy that seeks the lowest costs of operations within a special market segment.

focused differentiation strategy Business strategy that offers a unique product to a special market segment.

force-coercion strategy Business strategy that pursues change through formal authority and/or the use of rewards or punishments.

forecasting Attempts to predict the future.

foreign subsidiary A local operation completely owned by a foreign firm.

formal group A group officially recognized and supported by the organization.

formal structure The official structure of the organization.

framing error Solving a problem in the context perceived.

franchising A firm pays a fee for rights to use another company's name and operating methods.

free-agent economy Economy in which people change jobs more often, and many work on independent contracts with a shifting mix of employers.

functional chimneys problem A lack of communication and co-ordination across functions.

functional conflict Constructive conflict that helps boost task performance.

functional strategy Strategy that guides activities within one specific area of operations.

functional structure Organizational scheme that groups together people with similar skills who perform similar tasks.

fundamental attribution error Outlook that overestimates internal factors and underestimates external factors as influences on someone's behavior.

G

general environment The overall combination of cultural, economic, legal-political, and educational conditions.

general partnership Form of legal organiztion in which two or more owners share the management and risk of a business.

geographical structure Organizational system that groups together people and jobs performed in the same location.

glass ceiling A hidden barrier to the advancement of women and minorities.

glass ceiling effect An invisible barrier limiting career advancement of women and minorities.

global economy Economic conditions in which resources, markets, and competition are worldwide in scope.

global manager A manager who is culturally aware and informed on international affairs.

global outsourcing Contracting for work that is performed by workers in other countries.

global sourcing Purchase of materials or services around the world for local use.

globalization The worldwide process of growing interdependence of resource flows, product markets, and business competition.

globalization strategy Business strategy that adopts standardized products and advertising for use worldwide.

graphic rating scale Visual scale that uses a checklist of traits or characteristics to evaluate performance.

group process The way team members work together to accomplish tasks.

groupthink A tendency for highly cohesive teams to lose their evaluative capabilities.

growth strategy Business strategy involving expansion of the organization's current operations.

growth-need strength The desire to achieve psychological growth in one's work.

h

halo effect The tendency to use one attribute to develop an overall impression of a person or situation.

Hawthorne effect The tendency of persons singled out for special attention to perform as expected.

hierarchy of objectives Lower-level objectives help to accomplish higher-level ones.

high-context culture Culture that relies heavily on nonverbal and situational cues as well as spoken or written words in communication.

higher-order needs Esteem and self-actualization needs in Maslow's hierarchy.

human resource management The process of attracting, developing, and maintaining a high-quality workforce.

human resource planning Planning that analyzes staffing needs and identifies actions to fill those needs.

human skill The ability to work well in cooperation with other people.

hygiene factors Factors that eliminate job dissatisfaction but don't motivate, such as working conditions, interpersonal relations, organizational policies, and salary.

I

immoral manager A manager who acts unethically.

importing The process of acquiring products abroad and selling them in domestic markets.

impression management An attempt to create desired perceptions in the eyes of others.

inclusivity The degree to which the organization is open to anyone who can perform a job

incremental change Change that slowly bends and adjusts existing methods to improve performance.

independent contractors Persons who are hired on temporary contracts and are not part of the organization's permanent workforce.

individualism–collectivism The degree to which a society emphasizes individuals and their self-interests.

individualism view Ethical system in which ethical behavior advances long-term self-interests.

informal group A group that is unofficial and emerges from relationships and shared interests among members.

informal structure The set of unofficial relationships among an organization's members.

information competency The ability to gather and use information to solve problems.

initial public offering An initial selling of shares of stock to the public at large.

innovation The process of taking a new idea and putting it into practice.

input standard Standardized measure of work efforts that go into a performance task.

instrumental values Preferences regarding the means to desired ends.

instrumentality A person's belief that various outcomes will occur as a result of task performance.

integration The level of coordination achieved between subsystems in an organization.

integrative negotiation Negotiation approach that uses a "win-win" orientation to reach solutions acceptable to each party.

integrity Honesty, credibility, and consistency in putting values into action.

intellectual capital The collective brainpower or shared knowledge of a workforce.

interactional justice The degree to which others are treated with dignity and respect.

interactive leadership Leadership style strong on motivating, communicating, listening, and relating positively to others.

internal control Belief that control of one's life comes through self-discipline and self-control.

international business Business that conducts commercial transactions across national boundaries.

intrinsic reward Reward that occurs naturally during job performance.

intuitive thinking Problem-solving style that approaches problems in a flexible and spontaneous fashion.

ISO certification Form that verifies an organization meets international quality standards.

J

job burnout Physical and mental exhaustion from work stress.

job design The allocation of specific work tasks to individuals and groups.

job enlargement Modification of a position that increases task variety by combining into one job two or more tasks previously assigned to separate workers.

job enrichment Modification of a position that increases job depth by adding work planning and evaluating duties normally performed by the supervisor.

job migration The movement of jobs that occurs when global outsourcing shifts from one country to another.

job rotation Modification of a position that increases task variety by periodically shifting workers between different jobs.

job satisfaction The degree to which an individual feels positive about a job and work experience.

job simplification Employs people in clearly defined and very specialized tasks.

job sharing Splits one job between two people.

joint venture Business unit that operates in a foreign country through co-ownership with local partners.

just-in-time scheduling Inventory management system that routes materials to workstations "just in time" for use.

justice view The belief that ethical behavior treats people impartially and fairly.

K

knowledge workers Employees who use their minds and intellects as critical assets to employers.

L

labor contract A formal agreement between a union and employer about the terms of work for union members.

labor union An organization that deals with employers on the workers' collective behalf.

laissez-faire leadership style Leadership style that is low on both task and people concerns.

law of effect Behavioral law that states that behavior followed by pleasant consequences is likely to be repeated; behavior followed by unpleasant consequences is not.

leadership The process of inspiring others to work hard to accomplish important tasks.

leadership style The recurring pattern of behaviors exhibited by a leader.

leading The process of arousing enthusiasm and inspiring efforts to achieve goals.

learning organization An organization that continuously changes and improves, using the lessons of experience.

legitimate power The capacity to influence other people by virtue of formal authority, or the rights of office.

licensing agreement Transaction in which one firm pays a fee for rights to make or sell another company's products.

lifelong learning A continuous learning process from daily experiences.

limited liability corporation (LLC) A hybrid business form combining advantages of the sole proprietorship, partnership, and corporation.

limited liability partnership (LLP) A business form in which there are both general partners and limited liability partners.

locus of control The extent to which one believes that what happens is within one's control.

long-range plans Business plans that cover three years or more.

lose-lose conflict A conflict in which no one achieves his or her true desires and the underlying reasons for conflict remain unaffected.

low-context culture A culture that emphasizes communication via spoken or written words.

lower-order needs Physiological, safety, and social needs in Maslow's hierarchy.

M

Machiavellianism The degree to which someone uses power manipulatively.

maintenance activity An action taken by a team member that supports the emotional life of the group.

management The process of planning, organizing, leading, and controlling the use of resources to accomplish performance goals.

management by exception System that focuses attention on substantial differences between actual and desired performance.

management by objectives (MBO) System in which managers and employees jointly define goals for every unit of an organization and use them to monitor progress.

management by walking around (MBWA) System in which managers spend time out of their offices, meeting and talking with workers at all levels.

manager A person who supports and is responsible for the work of others.

managing diversity Building an inclusive work environment that allows everyone to reach his or her potential.

masculinity–femininity The degree to which a society values assertiveness and materialism.

matrix structure Structure that combines functional and divisional approaches to emphasize project or program teams.

mechanistic design Organizational design that is bureaucratic, using a centralized and vertical structure.

mediation Situation in which a neutral party tries to help conflicting parties improve communication to resolve their dispute.

mentoring Process in which early career employees are assigned as protégés to more senior employees.

merit pay Awards pay increases in proportion to performance contributions.

middle manager Person who oversees the work of large departments or divisions.

mission The organization's reason for existence in society.

mixed message Miscommunication that results when words communicate one message while actions, body language, or appearance communicate something else.

modeling Management style that uses personal behavior to demonstrate performance expected of others.

monochronic culture Culture in which people tend to do one thing at a time.

moral absolutism Ideology that suggests ethical standards apply absolutely across all cultures.

moral manager Person who manages in an ethical manner.

moral-rights view Ideology that believes that ethical behavior respects and protects fundamental rights.

motivation The level, direction, and persistence of effort expended at work.

multicultural organization An organization that is based on pluralism and operates with inclusivity and respect for diversity.

multidomestic strategy Business strategy that customizes products and advertising to best fit local needs.

multinational corporation (MNC) A business with extensive international operations in more than one foreign country.

multiperson comparison Diagnostic tool that compares one person's performance with that of others.

N

necessity-based entrepreneurship Building of new ventures because of a lack of other employment options.

need An unfulfilled physiological or psychological desire.

need for achievement The desire to do something better, to solve problems, or to master complex tasks.

need for affiliation The desire to establish and maintain good relations with people.

need for power The desire to control, influence, or be responsible for other people.

negative reinforcement Psychological technique that strengthens a behavior by making the avoidance of an undesirable consequence contingent on its occurrence.

negotiation The process of making joint decisions when the parties involved have different preferences.

network structure Business structure that uses IT to link with networks of outside suppliers and service contractors.

noise Any disturbance that interferes with the transmission, receipt, or feedback of a message.

nonprogrammed decision Specific solution crafted for a unique problem.

nonverbal communication Communication that takes place through gestures and body language.

norm A behavior, rule, or standard expected to be followed by team members.

O

objectives Specific results that one wishes to achieve.

observable culture The culture an observer can see and hear when walking around an organization.

obstructionist strategy Business strategy that avoids social responsibility and reflects mainly economic priorities.

open system System that transforms resource inputs from the environment into product outputs.

openness Being curious, receptive to new ideas, and imaginative.

operant conditioning The control of behavior by manipulating its consequences.

operating objectives Specific results that organizations try to accomplish.

operational plan A plan that identifies activities to implement strategic goals.

optimizing decision The alternative giving the absolute best solution to a problem.

organic design Business design that is adaptive, using a decentralized and horizontal structure.

organization A collection of people working together in a division of labor to achieve a common purpose.

organization chart Chart that describes the arrangement of work positions within an organization.

organization development A comprehensive, participatory way for self-directed and continuing long-run organizational change.

organization structure A system of tasks, reporting relationships, and communication linkages.

organizational behavior The study of individuals and groups in organizations.

organizational citizenship Demonstration of behaviors that are the "extras" people do to go the extra mile in their work.

organizational culture A system of shared beliefs and values guiding behavior.

organizational design The process of configuring organizations to meet environmental challenges.

organizational purpose The reason for the existence of the organization; usually to provide society with useful goods or services.

organizational subcultures Groupings of people based on shared demographic and job identities.

organizing The process of assigning tasks, allocating resources, and coordinating work activities.

orientation Process of familiarizing new employees with jobs, co-workers, and organizational policies and services.

output standard Measurement of performance results in terms of quantity, quality, cost, or time.

P

part-time work Temporary employment for less than the standard 40-hour workweek.

participatory planning Planning that includes the persons who will be affected by plans and/or who will implement them.

partnership When two or more people agree to contribute resources to start and operate a business together.

perception The process of organizing and interpreting sensory information.

performance appraisal The process of formally evaluating performance and providing feedback to a job holder.

performance contingent reward A reward linked directly to job performance.

performance effectiveness An output measure of task or goal accomplishment.

performance efficiency An input measure of resource cost associated with goal accomplishment.

performance opportunity A situation that offers the possibility of a better future, if the right steps are taken.

performance threat A situation where something is wrong or likely to be wrong.

personal wellness The pursuit of a personal-health promotion program.

personality The profile of characteristics making a person unique from others.

persuasion The act of presenting a message in a manner that causes others to support it.

plan A statement of intended means for accomplishing objectives.

planned change System of change that aligns the organization with anticipated future challenges.

planning The process of setting objectives and determining how to accomplish them.

policy A standing plan that communicates broad guidelines for decisions and action.

political risk The possible loss of investment in or control over a foreign asset because of instability and political changes in the host country.

political-risk analysis Trend analysis that forecasts how political events may impact foreign investments.

polychronic culture A culture in which people accomplish many different things at once.

positive reinforcement A means of strengthening a behavior by making a desirable consequence contingent on its occurrence.

power The ability to get someone else to do something you want done or to make things happen the way you want.

power distance The degree to which a society accepts unequal distribution of power.

prejudice The display of negative, irrational attitudes toward women or minorities.

proactive strategy Business strategy that meets all the criteria of social responsibility, including discretionary performance.

problem solving Identifying difficulties and taking action to resolve them.

procedural justice An approach to justice that focuses on the fair application of policies and rules.

procedure A rule that precisely describes actions to take in specific situations.

process innovation New system of action that results in a better way of doing things.

process reengineering Systemic analysis of work processes to design new and better ones.

product innovation Change to a product that results in new or improved goods or services.

product structure System of organization that groups together people and jobs working on a single product or service.

productivity The quantity and quality of work performance, with resource utilization considered.

programmed decision Application of a solution from past experience to a routine problem.

progressive discipline Disciplinary approach that ties reprimands to the severity and frequency of misbehavior.

project One-time activity that has clear beginning and end points.

project management Oversight of a project that ensures the timely and correct accomplishment of project activities.

project plan Diagram of a project that specifies activities, resources, and timetables.

project team or task force A group convened for a specific purpose that disbands after completing its task.

projection Misperception of others that assigns personal attributes to other individuals.

protectionism Tariffs and favorable treatments that protect domestic firms from foreign competition.

proxemics The study of how people use interpersonal space.

punishment Negative outcome that discourages a behavior by making an unpleasant consequence contingent on its occurrence.

Q

quality circle A small group of employees that meets regularly to discuss ways of improving work quality.

quality of work life The overall quality of human experiences in the workplace.

R

rational persuasion strategy Means of pursuing change through empirical data and rational argument.

realistic job preview A recruiting approach that provides job candidates with all pertinent information about a job and organization.

recruitment A set of activities designed to attract a qualified pool of job applicants.

referent power The capacity to influence other people because of their desire to identify personally with you.

refreezing The phase at which change is stabilized.

reliability Situation in which a selection device gives consistent results over repeated measures.

representativeness heuristic Device that assesses the likelihood of an occurrence using a stereotyped set of similar events.

restructuring Change of business strategy that reduces the scale/or mix of operations.

retrenchment strategy Business strategy that changes operations to correct weaknesses.

reward power The capacity to offer something of value as a means of influencing other people.

risk environment Business environment lacks complete information but offers probabilities of the likely outcomes for possible action alternatives.

S

satisficing decision A decision that chooses the first satisfactory alternative that presents itself.

satisfier factor Positive factor found in job content, such as a sense of achievement, recognition, responsibility, advancement, or personal growth.

scenario planning Business plan that identifies alternative future scenarios and makes plans to deal with each.

scientific management Management style that emphasizes careful selection and training of workers and supervisory support.

selection Choosing whom to hire from a pool of qualified job applicants.

selective perception The tendency to define problems from one's own point of view.

self-fulfilling prophecy A situation that occurs when a person acts in ways that confirm another's expectations.

self-management The ability to understand oneself, exercise initiative, accept responsibility, and learn from experience.

self-managing team Team in which the members make many decisions about how they share, plan and do their work.

self-monitoring The degree to which someone is able to adjust behavior in response to external factors.

self-serving bias Perception of events that underestimates internal factors and overestimates external factors as influences on someone's behavior.

servant leadership Leadership style that emphasizes serving others, helping them use their talents to help organizations best serve society.

shamrock organization Organizational structure that operates with a core group of full-time long-term workers supported by others who work on contracts and part-time.

shaping Positive reinforcement of successive approximations to the desired behavior.

shared power strategy A strategy that pursues change by participation in assessing change needs, values, and goals.

short-range plan Business plan that covers a year or less.

skill-based pay Pay structure that compensates workers by the number of job-relevant skills they master.

small business A business with fewer than 500 employees that is independently owned and operated and does not dominate its industry.

social entrepreneurship Business approach that seeks novel ways to solve pressing social problems.

social loafing The tendency of some people to avoid responsibility by "free-riding" in groups.

social responsibility audit Device that assesses an organization's accomplishments in areas of social responsibility.

socialization Orientation program that systematically influences the expectations, behavior, and attitudes of new employees.

sole proprietorship An individual pursuing business for a profit.

specific environment Limited business environment that includes only the people and groups with whom an organization interacts.

stakeholders People and institutions most directly affected by an organization's performance.

stereotype Misperception of others that assigns attributes commonly associated with a group to an individual.

stock options Give the right to purchase shares at a fixed price in the future.

strategic alliance Two or more organizations join together in partnership to pursue an area of mutual interest.

strategic intent Business strategy that focuses organizational energies on achieving a compelling goal.

strategic management The process of formulating and implementing strategies.

strategic leadership Leadership style that inspires people to implement organizational strategies.

strategic plan Business plan focused on identifying long-term directions for the organization.

strategy A comprehensive plan guiding resource allocation to achieve long-term organization goals.

strategy formulation The process of creating strategies.

strategy implementation The process of putting strategies into action.

stress A state of tension experienced by individuals facing extraordinary demands, constraints, or opportunities.

stretch goals Performance targets that employees must work extra hard and stretch to reach.

strong cultures Clear, well defined, and widely shared among members.

substantive conflict Conflict that involves disagreements over goals, resources, rewards, policies, procedures, and job assignments.

subsystem A smaller component of a larger system.

succession plan Plan that describes how the leadership transition and related financial matters will be handled.

succession problem The issue of who will run the business when the current head leaves.

supply chain management Inventory management system that uses information technology to link suppliers and purchasers in cost-efficient ways.

sustainable development Approach to business development that meets the needs of the present without hurting future generations.

sweatshop Manufacturing plant that employs workers at very low wages, for long hours, and in poor working conditions.

SWOT analysis Device that examines organizational strengths and weaknesses and environmental opportunities and threats.

synergy The creation of a whole greater than the sum of its individual parts.

system A collection of interrelated parts working together for a purpose.

systematic thinking Decision-making style that approaches problems in a rational and analytical fashion.

T

task activity An action taken by a team member that directly contributes to the group's performance purpose.

task force A temporary team put together to solve a specific problem, usually involving several departments.

team A collection of people who regularly interact to pursue common goals.

team structure Organizational system that uses permanent and temporary cross-functional teams to improve lateral relations.

teamwork The process of people actively working together to accomplish common goals.

technical skill The ability to use expertise to perform a task with proficiency.

telecommuting Use of IT to allow employees to work from outside the office.

terminal values Preferences about desired end states.

Theory X A theory stating that people dislike work, lack ambition, are irresponsible, and prefer to be led.

Theory Y A theory stating that people are willing to work, accept responsibility, and are self-directed and creative.

time orientation The degree to which a society emphasizes short-term or long-term goals.

top manager A manager who guides the performance of the organization as a whole or of one of its major parts.

top-down change Style of change in which change initiatives come from senior management.

total quality management Management style that commits to quality objectives, continuous improvement, and doing things right the first time.

transactional leadership Leadership style that directs the efforts of others through tasks, rewards, and structures.

transformational change Type of change resulting in a major and comprehensive redirection of the organization.

transformational leadership Leadership style that is inspirational and arouses extraordinary effort and performance.

transnational corporation An MNC that operates worldwide on a borderless basis.

transnational strategy Business strategy that seeks efficiencies of global operations with attention to local markets.

Type A personality Personality oriented toward extreme achievement, impatience, and perfectionism.

U

uncertain environment Business environment that lacks so much information it is difficult to assign probabilities to the likely outcomes of alternatives.

uncertainty avoidance The degree to which a society tolerates risk and uncertainty.

unfreezing The phase during which a situation is prepared for change.

utilitarian view Philosophy that states ethical behavior delivers the greatest good to the most people.

V

valence The value a person assigns to work-related outcomes.

validity Scores on a selection device have consistently, demonstrated links with future job performance.

value-based management Management style that actively develops, communicates, and enacts shared values.

value chain A sequence of activities through which organizations transform inputs into outputs.

values Broad beliefs about what is appropriate behavior.

venture capitalists People who make large investments in new ventures in return for an equity stake in the business.

vertical integration The acquisition by an organization of its suppliers or distributors.

virtual organization Information technologies are used to operate a shifting network of alliances.

virtual team Team in which the members work together and solve problems through computer-based interactions.

virtuous circle When corporate social responsibility leads to improved financial performance that leads to more social responsibility.

W

whistleblower Person who exposes the misdeeds of others in organizations.

win-lose conflict A conflict in which one party achieves its desires and the other party does not.

win-win conflict A conflict resolved to everyone's benefit.

work sampling Recruitment device that evaluates applicants as they perform actual work tasks.

workforce diversity Description for the range of differences among workers in gender, race, age, ethnic culture, ablebodiness, religious affiliation, and sexual orientation.

workplace privacy The right to privacy while at work.

workplace rage Aggressive behavior toward co-workers or the work setting.

World Trade Organization (WTO) A global institution to promote free trade and open markets around the world.

Z

zero-based budget Budget structure that allocates resources as if each budget was brand new.

Module 1

[1] Information from a Hudson Global Resources report in "The Future is Funky," *Irish Independent* (December 9, 2004), p. 3.

[2] The founding story of The Container Store is available at www.containerstore.com.

[3] See the discussion by Terry Thomas, John R. Schermerhorn, Jr., and John W. Dinehart, "Strategic Leadership of Ethical Behavior in Business," *Academy of Management Executive*, vol. X (2004), pp. 56–68.

[4] See Diya Gullapalli, "Living with Sarbanes-Oxley," *Wall Street Journal* (October 17, 2005), pp. R1, R3.

[5] Richard W. Judy and Carol D'Amico (eds.), *Workforce 2020: Work and Workers for the 21st Century* (Indianapolis: Hudson Institute, 1997).

[6] Johnson & Johnson corporate website, Credo section: www.jnj.com.

[7] See Judith Burns, "Everything You Wanted to Know About Corporate Governance . . . But Didn't Know How to Ask," *Wall Street Journal* (October 27, 2003), pp. R1, R7.

[8] Bruce Meyrson, "Former WorldCom Directors to Pay $18 Million from Own Pocket in Investor Settlement," *Associated Press State & Local Wire* (January 7, 2005).

[9] See Thomas L. Friedman, *The World Is Flat: A Brief History of the Twenty-First Century* (New York: Farrar, Straus and Giroux, 2005).

[10] Kenichi Ohmae's books include *The Borderless World: Power and Strategy in the Interlinked Economy* (New York: Harper, 1989); *The End of the Nation State* (New York: Free Press, 1996); *The Invisible Continent: Four Strategic Imperatives of the New Economy* (New York: Harper, 1999) and *The Next Global Stage: Challengers and Opportunities in Our Borderless World* (Upper Saddle River, N.J.: Wharton School Publishing, 2005).

[11] This example is from Friedman, op cit., pp. 208–209.

[12] For a discussion of globalization, see Thomas L. Friedman, *The Lexus and the Olive Tree: Understanding Globalization* (New York: Bantam Doubleday Dell, 2000); John Micklethwait and Adrian Woolridge, *A Future Perfect: The Challenges and Hidden Promise of Globalization* (New York: Crown, 2000); and Alfred E. Eckes, Jr., and Thomas W. Zeiler, *Globalization and the American Century* (Cambridge, UK: Cambridge University Press, 2003).

[13] Christy Lilly, "Rocky Boots CEO Explains Outsourcing," *Connections* (Ohio University College of Business, 2005), p. 6.

[14] Andrea Hopkins, "Outsourcing Causes 9% of U.S. Layoffs," *Reuters.com* (June 10, 2004).

[15] *Workforce 2000: Work and Workers for the 21st Century* (Indianapolis: Towers Perrin/Hudson Institute, 1987).

[16] For trends in population demographics see "Losing Ground," *Business Week* (November 21, 2005), p. 122.

[17] Judy and D'Amico, op cit.

[18] See Richard D. Bucher, *Diversity Consciousness: Opening Our Minds to People, Cultures, and Opportunities* (Upper Saddle River, NJ: Prentice-Hall, 2000).

[19] See, for example, Yochi J. Dreazen and Jess Bravin, "Bias Suit Against Microsoft Aims at 'Flat' Workplace," *Wall Street Journal* (January 4, 2001), p. A10.

[20] Information from "Racism in Hiring Remains, Study Says," *Columbus Dispatch* (January 17, 2003), p. B2.

[21] Information for Stay Informed from Patricia M. Flynn and Susan M. Adams, "Women on Board," *BizEd* (September/October 2004), pp. 34–39: "Gender Pay Gap," *The Columbus Dispatch* (January 2,

2005), p. F1; and Carol Hymowitz, "Too Many Women Fall for Stereotypes of Selves, Study Says," *Wall Street Journal* (October 24, 2005), p. B1; and "The New Diversity," *Wall Street Journal* (November 14, 2005), pp. R1, R3; "Breaking into the Boardroom," *Wall Street Journal* (March 27, 2006), p. B3.

[22] For discussions of the glass ceiling effect, see Ann M. Morrison, Randall P. White, and Ellen Van Velso, *Breaking the Glass Ceiling* (Reading, MA: Addison-Wesley, 1987); Anne E. Weiss, *The Glass Ceiling: A Look at Women in the Workforce* (New York: Twenty First Century, 1999); and Debra E. Meyerson and Joyce K. Fletcher, "A Modest Manifesto for Shattering the Glass Ceiling," *Harvard Business Review* (January/February 2000).

[23] For background, see Taylor Cox, Jr., "The Multicultural Organization," *Academy of Management Executive*, vol. 5 (1991), pp. 34–47; and *Cultural Diversity in Organizations: Theory, Research and Practice* (San Francisco: Berrett-Koehler, 1993).

[24] Judith B. Rosener, "Women Make Good Managers, So What?" *Business Week* (December 11, 2000), p. 24.

[25] Charles O'Reilly III and Jeffrey Pfeffer, *Hidden Value: How Great Companies Achieve Extraordinary Results with Ordinary People* (Boston: Harvard Business School Press, 2000), p. 2.

[26] Thomas A. Stewart, *Intellectual Capital: The Wealth of Organizations* (New York: Bantam, 1998).

[27] Dave Ulrich, "Intellectual Capital = Competency × Commitment," *Harvard Business Review* (Winter, 1998), pp. 15–26.

[28] Max DePree's books include *Leadership Is an Art* (New York: Dell, 1990) and *Leadership Jazz* (New York: Dell, 1993). See also Herman Miller's home page at www.hermanmiller.com.

[29] See Peter F. Drucker, *The Changing World of the Executive* (New York: T.T. Times Books, 1982), and *The Profession of Management* (Cambridge, MA: Harvard Business School Press, 1997); and Francis Horibe, *Managing Knowledge Workers: New Skills and Attitudes to Unlock the Intellectual Capital in Your Organization* (New York: Wiley, 1999).

[30] Daniel Pink, A Whole New Mind: Moving from the Information Age to the Conceptual Age (New York: Riverhead Books, 2005).

[31] See Tom Peters, "The Brand Called You," *Fast Company* (August/September 1997), p. 83.

[32] Charles Handy, *The Age of Unreason* (Cambridge, MA: Harvard Business School Press, 1990).

[33] Peters, op cit.

[34] Developed from Peters, op cit. (2000).

[35] Robert Reich, "The Company of the Future," *Fast Company* (November 1998), pp. 124+.

[36] For an overview of organizations and organization theory, see W. Richard Scott, *Organizations: Rational, Natural and Open Systems,* 4th ed. (Englewood Cliffs, NJ: Prentice-Hall, 1998).

[37] James Collins and Jerry Porras, *Built to Last* (New York: Harper Business, 1994).

[38] Chris Nuttall, "Google Eyes On Its Piece of the Pi," *Financial Times* (August 20/21, 2005), p. 8.

[39] Jeffrey Abrahams, *Mission Statement Book* (Berkeley, CA: Ten Speed Press, 1999).

[40] Excerpts from Ben & Jerry's corporate website: www.ben&jerrys.com.

[41] For a discussion of organizations as systems, see Scott, op cit. and Lane Tracy, *The Living Organization* (New York: Quorum Books, 1994).

[42] Micheline Maynard, "So Southwest Is Mortal After All," *New York Times* (October 16, 2005), pp. 3.1–3.4.

[43] Jeffrey F. Rayport and Bernard J. Jaworski, *Harvard Business Review* (December 2004), p. 55.

[44] Tom Peters, "The New Wired World of Work," *Business Week* (August 28, 2000), pp. 172–73.

[45] Developed in part from Jay A. Conger, *Winning 'em Over: A New Model for Managing in the Age of Persuasion* (New York: Simon & Schuster, 1998), pp. 180–181; Stewart D. Friedman, Perry Christensen, and Jessica DeGroot, "Work and Life: The End of the Zero-Sum Game," *Harvard Business Review* (November/December 1998), pp. 119–129; Chris Argyris, "Empowerment: The Emperor's New Clothes," *Harvard Business Review* (May/June 1998), pp. 98–105; and John A. Byrne, "Management by Web," *Business Week* (August 28, 2000), pp. 84–98.

[46] Friedman, op cit., p. 469.

Information from Jamie Smyth, "Xerox's Chief Copies Good Practices Not Past Mistakes," Irish Times (March 21, 2003), p. 24; William M. Bulkeley, "Running the Show," Wall Street Journal (November 8, 2004), p. R3; and Hymowitz, op cit., 2005.

Information from Daniel Akst, "Room at the Top for Improvement," Wall Street Journal (October 26, 2004), p. D8.

See *Outcome Measurement Project*, Phase I and Phase II Reports (St. Louis: American Assembly of Collegiate Schools of Business, 1986 and 1987).

Module 2

[1] "Monster.com Growth Continues with 8 Million Job Seeker Accounts; Monster.com Dominates the Online Career Space, Ranked #1 According to Media Metrix," *Business Wire* (June 20, 2000). See also www.monster.com; and, Jeanette Borzo, "More Over, Monster", *The Wall Street Journal* (June 19, 2006) p. R12.

[2] Information from *Wall Street Journal* (September 21, 2005), p. R4.

[3] David Whitford, "A Human Place to Work," *Fortune* (January 8, 2001), pp. 108–20.

[4] See examples in Carol Hymowitz, "As Managers Climb, They Have to Learn How to Act the Parts," *Wall Street Journal* (November 14, 2005), p. B1.

[5] For a perspective on the first-level manager's job, see Leonard A. Schlesinger and Janice A. Klein, "The First-Line Supervisor: Past, Present and Future," pp. 370–82, in Jay W. Lorsch (ed.), *Handbook of Organizational Behavior* (Englewood Cliffs, NJ: Prentice-Hall, 1987). Research reported in "Remember Us?" *Economist* (February 1, 1992), p. 71.

[6] For a discussion see Marcus Buckingham, "What Great Managers Do," *Harvard Business Review* (March, 2005), Reprint R0503D.

[7] Carol Hymowitz, "Should CEOs Tell Truth About Being in Trouble, Or Is That Foolhardy? *Wall Street Journal* (February 15, 2005), p. B1; see also Ben Elgin, "Can Anyone Save HP?" *Business Week* (February 21, 2005), pp. 28–35.

[8] Stewart D. Friedman, Perry Christensen, and Jessica De Groot, "Work and Life: The End of the Zero-Sum Game," *Harvard Business Review* (November December 1998), pp. 119–29.

[9] Alan M. Webber, "Danger: Toxic Company," *Fast Company* (November 1998), pp. 152+.

[10] Mintzberg, op cit. (1973/1997), p. 30.

[11] See, for example, John R. Veiga and Kathleen Dechant, "Wired World Woes: www.help," *Academy of Management Executive*, vol. 11 (August 1997), pp. 73–79.

[12] Mintzberg, op cit. (1973/1997), p. 60.

[13] For research on managerial work see Morgan W. McCall, Jr., Ann M. Morrison, and Robert L. Hannan, *Studies of Managerial Work: Results and Methods. Technical Report #9* (Greensboro, NC: Center for Creative Leadership, 1978), pp. 7–9. See also John P. Kotter, "What Effective General Managers Really Do," *Harvard Business Review* (November/December 1982), pp. 156–57.

[14] For a classic study see Thomas A. Mahoney, Thomas H. Jerdee, and Stephen J. Carroll, "The Job(s) of Management," *Industrial Relations*, vol. 4 (February 1965), pp. 97–110.

[15] This running example is developed from information from "Accountants Have Lives, Too, You Know," *Business Week* (February 23, 1998), pp. 88–90; Silvia Ann Hewlett and Carolyn Buck Luce, "Off-Ramps and On-Ramps: Keeping Talented Women on the Road to Success," *Harvard Business Review* (March, 2005), reprint #9491; and the Ernst & Young website: www.ey.com.

[16] Information on women and men leaving jobs from Sylvia Ann Hewlett and Carolyn Buck Luce, "Off-Ramps and On-Ramps," *Harvard Business Review* (March 2005), Reprint R0503B.

[17] See Mintzberg, op cit. (1973/1997); and Henry Mintzberg, "Covert Leadership: The Art of Managing Professionals," *Harvard Business Review* (November/December 1998), pp. 140–147; and, Jonathan Gosling and Henry Mintzberg, "The Five Minds of a Manager," *Harvard Business Review* (November 2003), pp. 1–9.

[18] See Mintzberg, op cit. (1973/1997); and Henry Mintzberg, "Covert Leadership: The Art of Managing Professionals," *Harvard Business Review* (November/December 1998), pp. 140–147; and, Jonathan Gosling and Henry Mintzberg, "The Five Minds of a Manager," *Harvard Business Review* (November 2003), pp. 1–9.

[19] This incident is taken from John P. Kotter, "What Effective General Managers Really Do," *Harvard Business Review* (November/December 1982), pp. 156–157.

[20] Ibid.

[21] Robert L. Katz, "Skills of an Effective Administrator," *Harvard Business Review* (September/October 1974), p. 94.

[22] Hendrie Weisinger, *Emotional Intelligence at Work* (San Francisco: Jossey-Bass, 2000).

[23] See Daniel Goleman's books *Emotional Intelligence* (New York: Bantam, 1995) and *Working with Emotional Intelligence* (New York: Bantam, 1998); and his articles "What Makes a Leader," *Harvard Business Review* (November/December 1998), pp. 93–102, and "Leadership That Makes a Difference," *Harvard Business Review* (March/April 2000), pp. 79–90, quote from p. 80.

[24] Quotes from "Insuring Success for the Road," *BizEd* (March/April 2005), p. 19.

[25] Henry Mintzberg, "The Manager's Job: Folklore and Fact," *Harvard Business Review*, vol. 53 (July/August 1975), p. 61. See also his book *The Nature of Managerial Work* (New York: Harper & Row, 1973, and HarperCollins, 1997).

John A. Byrne, "Letter From the Editor," Fast Company (April, 2005), p. 14.

Information from Una McCaffrey, "The Man Who's Seen it All Favours a Flat Structure of Management," Irish Times (June 10, 2005), p. 32.

Module 3

[1] For a timeline of twentieth-century management ideas see "75 Years of Management Ideas and Practices: 1922–1997," *Harvard Business Review*, supplement (September/October 1997).

[2] Pauline Graham, *Mary Parker Follett—Prophet of Management: A Celebration of Writings from the 1920s* (Boston: Harvard Business School Press, 1995).

[3] See Peter F. Drucker, "Looking Ahead: Implications of the Present," *Harvard Business Review* (September/October, 1997), pp. 18–32.

[4] A thorough review and critique of the history of management thought, including management in ancient civilizations, is provided by Daniel A. Wren, *The Evolution of Management Thought*, 4th ed. (New York: Wiley, 1993).

[5] For a timeline of major people and themes see "75 Years of Management," op.cit.

[6] For a sample of this work see Henry L. Gantt, *Industrial Leadership* (Easton, MD: Hive, 1921; Hive edition published in 1974); Henry C. Metcalfe and Lyndall Urwick (eds.), *Dynamic Administration: The Collected Papers of Mary Parker Follett* (New York: Harper & Brothers, 1940); James D. Mooney, *The Principles of Administration*, rev. ed. (New York: Harper & Brothers, 1947); Lyndall Urwick, *The Elements of Administration* (New York: Harper & Brothers, 1943) and *The Golden Book of Management* (London: N. Neame, 1956).

[7] References on Taylor's work are from Frederick W. Taylor, *The Principles of Scientific Management* (New York: W. W. Norton, 1967), originally published by Harper & Brothers in 1911. See Charles W. Wrege and Amedeo G. Perroni, "Taylor's Pig-Tale: A Historical Analysis of Frederick W. Taylor's Pig Iron Experiments," *Academy of Management Journal*, vol. 17 (March 1974), pp. 6–27, for a criticism; see Edwin A. Lock, "The Ideas of Frederick W. Taylor: An Evaluation," *Academy of Management Review*, vol. 7 (1982), p. 14, for an examination of the contemporary significance of Taylor's work. See also the biography, Robert Kanigel, *The One Best Way* (New York: Viking, 1997).

[8] Kanigel, op cit.

[9] A. M. Henderson and Talcott Parsons (eds. and trans.), *Max Weber: The Theory of Social Economic Organization* (New York: Free Press, 1947).

[10] Ibid., p. 337.

[11] Available in the English language as Henri Fayol, *General and Industrial Administration* (London: Pitman, 1949); subsequent discussion relies on M. B. Brodie, *Fayol on Administration* (London: Pitman, 1949).

[12] M. P. Follett, *Freedom and Coordination* (London: Management Publications Trust, 1949).

[13] Information from "Honesty Top Trait for Chair," *Columbus Dispatch* (January 15, 2003), p. G1.

[14] The Hawthorne studies are described in detail in F. J. Roethlisberger and William J. Dickson, *Management and the Worker* (Cambridge, MA: Harvard University Press, 1966); and G. Homans, *Fatigue of Workers* (New York: Reinhold, 1941). For an interview with three of the participants in the relay-assembly test-room studies, see R. G. Greenwood, A. A. Bolton, and R. A. Greenwood, "Hawthorne a Half Century Later: 'Relay Assembly Participants Remember,'" *Journal of Management*, vol. 9 (1983), pp. 217–31.

[15] The criticisms of the Hawthorne studies are detailed in Alex Carey, "The Hawthorne Studies: A Radical Criticism," *American Sociological Review*, vol. 32 (1967), pp. 403–16; H. M. Parsons, "What Happened at Hawthorne?" *Science*, vol. 183 (1974), pp. 922–32; and B. Rice, "The Hawthorne Defect: Persistence of a Flawed Theory," *Psychology Today*, vol. 16 (1982), pp. 70–74. See also Wren, op cit.

[16] This discussion of Maslow's theory is based on Abraham H. Maslow, *Eupsychian Management* (Homewood, IL: Richard D. Irwin, 1965); and Abraham H. Maslow, *Motivation and Personality*, 2nd ed. (New York: Harper & Row, 1970).

[17] Douglas McGregor, *The Human Side of Enterprise* (New York: McGraw-Hill, 1960).

[18] See Gary Heil, Deborah F. Stevens, and Warren G. Bennis, *Douglas McGregor on Management: Revisiting the Human Side of Enterprise* (New York: Wiley, 2000).

[19] Chris Argyris, *Personality and Organization* (New York: Harper & Row, 1957).

[20] Information on attitude survey in the federal bureaucracy from David E. Rosenbaum, "Study Ranks Homeland Security Dept. Lowest in Morale, *New York Times* (October 16, 2005), p. 17.

[21] The ideas of Ludwig von Bertalanffy contributed to the emergence of this systems perspective on organizations. See his article, "The History and Status of General Systems Theory," *Academy of Management Journal*, vol. 15 (1972), pp. 407–426. This viewpoint is further developed by Daniel Katz and Robert L. Kahn in their classic book, *The Social Psychology of Organizations* (New York: Wiley, 1978). For an integrated systems view, see Lane Tracy, *The Living Organization* (New York: Quorum Books, 1994). For an overview, see W. Richard Scott, *Organizations: Rational, Natural, and Open Systems*, 4th ed. (Upper Saddle River, NJ: Prentice-Hall, 1998).

[22] See discussion by Scott, op cit., pp. 66–68.

[23] For an overview, see Scott, op cit., pp. 95–97.

[24] Peter Senge, *The Fifth Discipline* (New York: Harper, 1990).

[25] This example is from Marjorie Kelly, "Iphigene's Song: How Family Mission Provides an Ethical Compass," *Business Ethics* (Fall 2005), p. 6. Quote from "How Good Is Google?" The Economist (November 1, 2003). See also John Battelle, The Search: How Google and Its Rivals Rewrote the Rules of Business and Transformed Our Culture (New York: Penguin, 2005). For additional information from its corporate website, go to www.google.com/corporate/history.html. Information from Larry Page and Sergey Brin, Founders, Google, Inc., pp. 22–25.

Nilekani Quote: *Business Week*, April 24, 2006.

Drucker Quote: *Business Week*, November 28, 2005.

Module 4

[1] "Ebbers sentenced to 25 years," retrieved from CNN online: money.cnn.com/2005/07/13.

[2] Headline from *The Irish Times* (June 20, 2005), p. 14; see also Mark Maremont, "Tyco Ex-Officials Get Jail Terms, Big Fines," *Wall Street Journal* (September 20, 2005), pp. C1, C4.

[3] See the discussion by Terry Thomas, John W. Dienhart, and John R. Schermerhorn, Jr., "Leading Toward Ethical Behavior in Business," *Academy of Management Executive*, vol. 18 (May 2004), pp. 56–66.

[4] See the discussion by Lynn Sharpe Paine, "Managing for Organizational Integrity," *Harvard Business Review* (March/April 1994), pp. 106–117.

[5] Desmond Tutu, "Do More Than Win," *Fortune* (December 30, 1991), p. 59.

[6] Ibid.

[7] For an overview, see Linda K. Trevino and Katherine A. Nelson, *Managing Business Ethics*, 3rd ed. (New York: Wiley, 2003).

[8] Information from Sue Shellenbarger, "How and Why We Lie at the Office: From Pilfered Pens to Padded Accounts," *Wall Street Journal* (March 24, 2005), p. D1.

[9] Milton Rokeach, *The Nature of Human Values* (New York: Free Press, 1973). See also W. C. Frederick and J. Weber, "The Values of Corporate Executives and Their Critics: An Empirical Description and Normative Implications," in W. C. Frederick and L. E. Preston (eds.), *Business Ethics: Research Issues and Empirical Studies* (Greenwich, CT: JAI Press, 1990).

[10] See Gerald F. Cavanagh, Dennis J. Moberg, and Manuel Velasquez, "The Ethics of Organizational Politics," *Academy of Management Review*, vol. 6 (1981), pp. 363–74; Justin G. Locknecker, Joseph A. McKinney, and Carlos W. Moore, "Egoism and Independence: Entrepreneurial Ethics," *Organizational Dynamics* (Winter 1988), pp. 64–72; and Justin G. Locknecker, Joseph A. McKinney, and Carlos W. Moore, "The Generation Gap in Business Ethics," *Business Horizons* (September/October 1989), pp. 9–14.

[11] Raymond L. Hilgert, "What Ever Happened to Ethics in Business and in Business Schools," *The Diary of Alpha Kappa Psi* (April 1989), pp. 4–8.

[12] Jerald Greenburg, "Organizational Justice: Yesterday, Today, and Tomorrow," *Journal of Management*, vol. 16 (1990), pp. 399–432; and Mary A. Konovsky, "Understanding Procedural Justice and Its Impact on Business Organizations," *Journal of Management*, vol. 26 (2000), pp. 489–511.

[13] Interactional justice is described by Robert J. Bies, "The Predicament of Injustice: The Management of Moral Outrage," in L. L. Cummings & B. M. Staw (eds.), *Research in Organizational Behavior*,

vol. 9 (Greenwich, CT: JAI Press, 1987), pp. 289–319. The example is from Carol T. Kulik & Robert L. Holbrook, "Demographics in Service Encounters: Effects of Racial and Gender Congruence on Perceived Fairness," *Social Justice Research*, vol. 13 (2000), pp. 375–402.

[14] The United Nations' Universal Declaration of Human Rights is available online at: http://www.un.org/Overview/rights.html.

[15] Robert D. Haas, "Ethics—A Global Business Challenge," *Vital Speeches of the Day* (June 1, 1996), pp. 506–509.

[16] Thomas Donaldson, "Values in Tension: Ethics Away from Home," *Harvard Business Review*, vol. 74 (September/October 1996), pp. 48–62.

[17] Thomas Donaldson and Thomas W. Dunfee, "Towards a Unified Conception of Business Ethics: Integrative Social Contracts Theory," *Academy of Management Review*, vol. 19 (1994), pp. 252–85.

[18] Developed from Donaldson, op cit.

[19] Reported in Barbara Ley Toffler, "Tough Choices: Managers Talk Ethics," *New Management*, vol. 4 (1987), pp. 34–39. See also Barbara Ley Toffler, *Tough Choices: Managers Talk Ethics* (New York: Wiley, 1986).

[20] See discussion by Trevino and Nelson, op cit., pp. 47–62.

[21] Information from Steven N. Brenner and Earl A. Mollander, "Is the Ethics of Business Changing?" *Harvard Business Review*, vol. 55 (January/February 1977).

[22] This research is summarized by Archie Carroll, "Pressure May Force Ethical Hand," *BGS International Exchange* (Fall 2004), p. 5.

[23] Ibid.

[24] Ibid.

[25] Saul W. Gellerman, "Why 'Good' Managers Make Bad Ethical Choices," *Harvard Business Review*, vol. 64 (July/August, 1986), pp. 85–90.

[26] Survey results from Del Jones, "48% of Workers Admit to Unethical or Illegal Acts," *USA Today* (April 4, 1997), p. A1.

[27] See, for example, David Bielo, "MBA Programs for Social and Evironmental Stewardship," *Business Ethics* (Fall 2005), pp. 22–28.

[28] Alan L. Otten, "Ethics on the Job: Companies Alert Employees to Potential Dilemmas," *Wall Street Journal* (July 14, 1986), p. 17; and "The Business Ethics Debate," *Newsweek* (May 25, 1987), p. 36.

[29] See "Whistle-Blowers on Trial," *Business Week* (March 24, 1997), pp. 172–78; and "NLRB Judge Rules for Massachusetts Nurses in Whistle-Blowing Case," *American Nurse* (January/February 1998), p. 7.

[30] For a review of whistleblowing, see Marcia P. Micelli and Janet P. Near, *Blowing the Whistle* (Lexington, MA: Lexington Books, 1992); see also Micelli and Near, "Whistleblowing: Reaping the Benefits," *Academy of Management Executive*, vol. 8 (August 1994), pp. 65–72.

[31] Information from Ethics Resource Center, "Major Survey of America's Workers Finds Substantial Improvements in Ethics": www.ethics.org/releases/nr_20030521_nbes.html.

[32] Information from James A. Waters, "Catch 20.5: Mortality as an Organizational Phenomenon," *Organizational Dynamics*, vol. 6 (Spring 1978), pp. 3–15.

[33] Robert D. Gilbreath, "The Hollow Executive," *New Management*, vol. 4 (1987), pp. 24–28.

[34] Information from "Gifts of Gab: A Start-up's Social Conscience Pays Off," *Business Week* (February 5, 2001), p. F38.

[35] Developed from recommendations of the Government Accountability Project reported in "Blowing the Whistle without Paying the Piper."

[36] See Marc Gunther, "Can Factory Monitoring Ever Really Work?" *Business Ethics* (Fall 2005), p. 12.

[37] Information from corporate website: www.gapinc.com/community-sourcing/vendor_conduct.htm.

Information from "Designs in Afghanistan" and "Cleaner Water, Better Future," *BizEd* (September/October 2004), pp. 29, 32.

Information from Thomas Teal, "Not a Fool, Not a Saint," *Fortune* (November 11, 1996), pp. 201–204; quote from Shelley Donald Coolidge, Christian Science Monitor (March 28, 1996).

Adapted from James Weber, "Management Value Orientations: A Typology and Assessment," International Journal of Value Based Management, vol. 3, no. 2 (1990), pp. 37–54.

Donaldson Quote: *Associated Press*, April 5, 1997.

Module 5

[1] Robert Reich, *The Future of Success* (New York: Knopf, 2001), p. 7.

[2] Reich, op cit.

[3] Information from Tom's of Maine website: www.tomsofmaine.com/about. Although Colgate-Palmolive Co. bought the company in early 2006, Tom Chappell stated that his firm's business philosophy would not change.

[4] Information from "Ivory Tower: How an MBA Can Bend Your Mind," *Business Week* (April 1, 2002), p. 12.

[5] See Thomas Donaldson and Lee Preston, "The Stakeholder Theory of the Corporation," *Academy of Management Review*, vol. 20 (January 1995), pp. 65–91.

[6] For a discussion of "profits with principles," see Ira A. Jackson and Jane Nelson, "Values-Driven Performance: Seven Strategies for Delivering Profits with Principles," *Ivey Business Journal* (November/December 2004), pp. 1–8.

[7] For a good review see Robert H. Miles, *Managing the Corporate Social Environment* (Englewood Cliffs, NJ: Prentice-Hall, 1987).

[8] Ken Stammen, "Firm Takes Day Off to Give Back to Community," *The Columbus Dispatch* (October 9, 2004), p. E1.

[9] Examples from "Teaching Notes: From IBM Science and Math Teachers," *Business Week* (October 3, 2005); "Googling for Charity," *Business Week Online* (October 28, 2005); "100 Best Corporate Citizens for 2004," www.*business-ethics.com* (retrieved November 1, 2005).

[10] Information from "The Socially Correct Corporate," *Fortune* special advertising section (July 24, 2000), pp. S32–S34; Joseph Pereiva, "Doing Good and Doing Well at Timberland," *Wall Street Journal* (September 9, 2003), pp. B1, B10.

[11] The "compliance–conviction" distinction is attributed to Mark Goyder in Martin Waller, "Much Corporate Responsibility Is Box-Ticking," *The Times Business* (July 8, 2003), p. 21.

[12] Archie B. Carroll, "A Three-Dimensional Model of Corporate Performance," *Academy of Management Review*, vol. 4 (1979), pp. 497–505. Carroll's continuing work in this area is most recently reported in Mark S. Schwartz and Archie B. Carroll, "Corporate Social Responsibility: A Three Domain Approach, "*Business Ethics Quarterly*, vol. 13 (2003), pp. 503–530.

[13] The historical framework of this discussion is developed from Keith Davis, "The Case For and Against Business Assumption of Social Responsibility," *Academy of Management Journal* (June 1973), pp. 312–22; Keith Davis and William Frederick, *Business and Society: Management: Public Policy, Ethics*, 5th ed. (New York: McGraw-Hill, 1984). This debate is discussed by Joel Makower in *Putting Social Responsibility to Work for Your Business and the World* (New York: Simon & Schuster, 1994), pp. 28–33. See also "Civics 101," *Economist* (May 11, 1996), p. 61.

[14] The Friedman quotation is from Milton Friedman, *Capitalism and Freedom* (Chicago: University of Chicago Press, 1962); the Samuelson quotation is from Paul A. Samuelson, "Love That Corporation," *Mountain Bell Magazine* (Spring 1971). Both are cited in Davis, op. cit.

[15] Davis and Frederick, quoted in op. cit.

[16] Davis, op cit.

[17] See James K. Glassman, "When Ethics Meet Earnings," *International Herald Tribune* (May 24–25, 2003), p. 15; Simon Zaydek,

"The Path to Corporate Social Responsibility," *Harvard Business Review* (December 2004), pp. 125–132.

[18] See Makower, op cit. (1994), pp. 71–75; and Sandra A. Waddock and Samuel B. Graves, "The Corporate Social Performance–Financial Performance Link," *Strategic Management Journal* (1997), pp. 303–319.

[19] Elizabeth Gatewood and Archie B. Carroll, "The Anatomy of Corporate Social Response," *Business Horizons*, vol. 24 (September/October 1981), pp. 9–16.

[20] Zaydek, op cit.

[21] Ibid.

[22] Carol Hymowitz, "Asked to Be Charitable, More CEOs Seek to Aid Their Businesses as Well," *Wall Street Journal* (February 22, 2005), p. B1.

[23] Zaydek, op cit.

[24] Information from "17th Annual Business Ethics Awards," *Business Ethics* online: http://www.business-ethics.com/whats_new/annual.html (retrieved November 3, 2005).

[25] Judith Burns, "Everything You Wanted to Know About Corporate Governance . . . But Didn't Know to Ask," *Wall Street Journal* (October 27, 2003), p. R6.

[26] See for example, "Pay for Performance Report," Institute of Management and Administration (December 2003); "Good News: You're Fired," *Newsweek* (July 25, 2005), p. 48.

[27] "Warming to Corporate Reform," *Wall Street Journal* (October 25, 2005), p. R2.

[28] Archie B. Carroll, "In Search of the Moral Manager," *Business Horizons* (March/April 2001), pp. 7–15.

[29] Thomas, Schermerhorn, and Dinehart, op cit.

[30] Sarah Ellison, "Why Kraft Decided to Ban Some Food Ads to Children," *Wall Street Journal* (October 31, 2005), pp. A1, A13.

See Joel Makower, *Putting Social Responsibility to Work for Your Business and the World* (New York: Simon & Schuster, 1994), pp. 17–18.

Information from John McManus, "Coffee Entrepreneur Is Wide Awake to Africa's Problems," *The Irish Times* (July 15, 2005), p. 24.

Information from www.cepaa.org/AboutSAI/.

Peter B. Vail, *Managing as a Performance Art: New Ideas for a World of Chaotic Change* (San Francisco: Jossey-Bass, 1989), pp. 8–9. Used by permission.

Module 6

[1] See Carol Hymowitz, "The New Diversity," *Wall Street Journal* (November 14, 2005), pp. R1, R3, and Joi Preciphs, "Moving Ahead . . .but Slowly," *Wall Street Journal* (November 14, 2005), p. R3, and "Changing Mix," *Wall Street Journal* (November 14, 2005), p. R3.

[2] Quote from "The Winners," *Working Mother Magazine* online (retrieved October 10, 2005 from www.workingmother.com).

[3] Information and quotes from "Japan's Diversity Problem," *Wall Street Journal* (October 24, 2005), pp. B1, B5.

[4] "Beyond the Balance Sheet," *Forbes* online (retrieved October 2, 2005, from www.forbes.com).

[5] Lee Gardenswartz and Anita Rowe, *Managing Diversity: A Complete Desk Reference and Planning Guide* (Chicago: Irwin, 1993).

[6] R. Roosevelt Thomas, Jr., *Beyond Race and Gender* (New York: AMACOM, 1992), p. 10; see also R. Roosevelt Thomas, Jr., "From 'Affirmative Action' to 'Affirming Diversity,'" *Harvard Business Review* (November/December 1990), pp. 107–17; R. Roosevelt Thomas, Jr., with Marjorie I. Woodruff, *Building a House for Diversity* (New York: AMACOM, 1999).

[7] "The Conundrum of the Glass Ceiling," *The Economist* (July 23, 2005), p. 64.

[8] Information from Hymowitz, op cit., p. R3.

[9] Carol Stephenson, "Leveraging Diversity to Maximum Advantage: The Business Case for Appointing More Women to Boards," *Ivey Business Journal* (September/October 2004), Reprint # 9B04TE03, pp. 1–8.

[10] Points in the business case box are from The Honourable Donald H. Oliver, "Achieving Results Through Diversity: A Strategy for Success," *Ivey Business Journal* (March/April, 2005), Reprint # 9B05TB09, pp. 1–6.

[11] Thomas Kochan, Katerina Bezrukova, Robin Ely, Susan Jackson, Aparna Joshi, Karen Jehn, Jonathan Leonard, David Levine, and David Thomas, "The Effects of Diversity on Business Performance: Report of the Diversity Research Network," reported in SHRM Foundation Research Findings (retrieved from www.shrm.org/foundation/findings.asp). Full article published in *Human Resource Management* (2003).

[12] Oliver, op cit.

[13] Gardenswartz and Rowe, op cit., p. 220.

[14] Taylor Cox, Jr., *Cultural Diversity in Organizations* (San Francisco: Berrett Koehler, 1994).

[15] See Anthony Robbins and Joseph McClendon III, *Unlimited Power: A Black Choice* (New York: Free Press, 1997), and Augusto Failde and William Doyle, *Latino Success: Insights from America's Most Powerful Latino Executives* (New York: Free Press, 1996).

[16] Information from "Demographics: The Young and the Restful," *Harvard Business Review* (November 2004), p. 25.

[17] "Many U.S. Employees Have Negative Attitudes to their Jobs, Employers and Top Managers," The Harris Poll #38 (May 6, 2005), available from www.harrisinteractive.com; and "U. S. Job Satisfaction Keeps Falling, The Conference Board Reports Today (February 25, 2005; retrieved from www.conference-board.org).

[18] Mayo Clinic, "Workplace Generation Gap: Understand Differences Among Colleagues" (July 6, 2005; retrieved from http://www.cnn.com/HEALTH/library/WL/00045.html).

[19] Developed from ibid.

[20] Information in "Stay Informed" based on "The Conundrum of the Glass Ceiling," *The Economist* (July 23, 2005), pp. 63–65.

[21] Stephanie N. Mehta, "What Minority Employees Really Want," *Fortune* (July 10, 2000), pp. 181–86.

[22] Ibid. See also "The 50 Women to Watch: 2005," *Wall Street Journal* (October 31, 2005), pp. R1–R11.

[23] Thomas, op cit. Minifigure developed op.cit. 1992, p. 28.

[24] Amy Chozick, "Beyond the Numbers," *Wall Street Journal* (November 14, 2005), p. R4.

[25] Thomas, op cit. (1992), p. 17.

[26] Information from "100 Best Corporate Citizens," *Business Ethics* online (retrieved from www.business-ethics.com, November 1, 2005).

[27] Thomas, op cit. (1992), p. 17.

[28] Thomas and Woodruff, op cit. (1999), pp. 211–226.

[29] Survey reported in "The Most Inclusive Workplaces Generate the Most Loyal Employees," *Gallup Management Journal* (December 2001; retrieved from http://gmj.gallup.com/press_room/release.asp?i?117).

[30] "Diversity Today: Corporate Recruiting Practices in Inclusive Workplaces," *Fortune* (June 12, 2000), p. S4.

[31] For a good overview see Richard D. Lewis, *The Cultural Imperative: Global Trends in the 21st Century* (Yarmouth, ME: Intercultural Press, 2002); and Martin J. Gannon, *Understanding Global Cultures* (Thousand Oaks, CA: Sage, 1994).

[32] Based on Barbara Benedict Bunker, "Appreciating Diversity and Modifying Organizational Cultures: Men and Women at Work," in Suresh Srivastva and David L. Cooperrider (eds.), *Appreciative Management and Leadership: The Power of Positive Thought and Action in Organizations* (San Francisco: Jossey-Bass, 1990), pp. 127–149.

[33] Examples reported in Neil Chesanow, *The World-Class Executive* (New York: Rawson Associates, 1985).

[34] P. Christopher Earley and Elaine Mosakowski, "Toward Cultural Intelligence: Turning Cultural Differences Into Workplace Advantage," *Academy of Management Executive*, vol. 18 (2004), pp. 151–157.

[35] See Gary P. Ferraro, "The Need for Linguistic Proficiency in Global Business," *Business Horizons* (May/June 1996), pp. 39–46; quote from Carol Hymowitz, "Companies Go Global, but Many Managers Just Don't Travel Well," *Wall Street Journal* (August 15, 2000), p. B1.

[36] Edward T. Hall, *The Silent Language* (New York: Anchor Books, 1959);

[37] Edward T. Hall, *Beyond Culture* (New York: Doubleday, 1976).

[38] Edward T. Hall, *Hidden Differences* (New York: Doubleday, 1990).

[39] Geert Hofstede, *Culture's Consequences* (Beverly Hills, CA: Sage, 1984), and, *Culture's Consequences: Comparing Values, Behaviors, Institutions and Organizations Across Nations,* 2nd Edition (Thousand Oaks, CA: Sage, 2001). See also Michael H. Hoppe, "An Interview with Geert Hofstede," *Academy of Management Executive,* Vol. 18 (2004), pp. 75–79.

[40] Geert Hofstede and Michael H. Bond, "The Confucius Connection: From Cultural Roots to Economic Growth," *Organizational Dynamics,* vol. 16 (1988), pp. 4–21.

[41] This dimension is explained more thoroughly by Geert Hofstede et al., *Masculinity and Femininty: The Taboo Dimension of National Cultures* (Thousand Oaks, CA.: Sage, 1998).

[42] Information for "Stay Informed" from "The Conundrum of the Glass Ceiling," *The Economist* (July 23, 2005), p. 634, and, "Japan's Diversity Problem," *The Wall Street Journal* (October 24, 2005), pp. B1, B5.

[43] "Japan's Diversity Problem," op. cit.

[44] See Hofstede and Bond, op cit.

[45] See Geert Hofstede, *Culture and Organizations: Software of the Mind* (London: McGraw-Hill, 1991).

[46] Robert J, House, Paul J. Hanges, Mansour Javidan, Peter W. Dorfman, and Vipin Gupta (Editors), *Culture, Leadership and Organizations: The GLOBE Study of 62 Societies* (Thousand Oaks, CA: Sage Publications, Inc., 2004).

[47] This summary is based on Ibid, and Mansour Javidan, P. Dorfman, Mary Sully de Luque, and Robert J. House, "In the Eye of the Beholder: Cross Cultural Lessons in Leadership from Project GLOBE," *Academy of Management Perspectives,* (February, 2006), pp. 67–90.

[48] For additional cultural models and research see the summary in House, op cit., as well as: Fons Trompenaars, *Riding the Waves of Culture: Understanding Cultural Diversity in Business* (London: Nicholas Brealey Publishing, 1993); Harry C. Triandis, *Culture and Social Behavior* (New York: McGraw-Hill, 1994); Steven H. Schwartz, "A Theory of Cultural Values and Some Implications for Work," *Applied Psychology: An International Review,* Vol. 48 (1999), pp. 23–47; Martin J. Gannon, *Understanding Global Cultures,* 3rd Edition (Thousand Oaks, CA: Sage, 2004).

Information from "Furnishing Good Benefits Along with Sofas," BizNewOrleans online (March 28, 2004), retrieved from: www.biznewsorleans.com (November 8, 2005); and, Kerry Capell, "IKEA," *Business Week* (November 14, 2005), pp. 96–105.

Information from Marjorie Valbrun, "More Muslims Claim They Suffer Job Bias," *The Wall Street Journal* (April 15, 2003), pp. B1,B8.

Items for the WV Cultural Awareness Quiz selected from a longer version by James P. Morgan, Jr., and published by University Associates, 1987. Used by permission.

Module 7

[1] Information on hour wage costs reported in "Breaking a Taboo, High Fashion Starts Making Goods Overseas," *Wall Street Journal* (September 27, 2005), pp. A1, A10.

[2] Quotes from www.limited.com/feature.jsp and www.limited.com/who/index.jsp. See also Les Wexner, "How I Conquered the Women's Retail Clothing Industry (and an Ulcer), *Fortune Small Business* (September 2003), pp. 40–43.

[3] See Kenichi Ohmae, *The Borderless World: Power and Strategy in the Interlinked Economy* (New York, Harper, 1989), and *The Evolving Global Economy* (Cambridge, MA: Harvard Business School Press, 1995). For a good overview and examples of developments in the global economy, see Thomas L. Friedman, *The World Is Flat: A Brief History of the Twenty-First Century* (New York: Farrar, Straus & Giroux, 2005).

[4] For a discussion of globalization, see two books by Thomas L. Friedman: *The Lexus and the Olive Tree: Understanding Globalization* (New York: Bantam Doubleday Dell, 2000), and, *The World Is Flat: A Brief History of the Twenty-First Century* (New York: Farrar, Straus & Giroux, 2005).

[5] Paul Wilson, "Foreign Companies Big Employers in Ohio," *Columbus Dispatch* (December 26, 2005), p. F6.

[6] Quote from John A. Byrne, "Visionary vs. Visionary," *Business Week* (August 28, 2000), p. 210.

[7] See, for example, information on global IT outsourcing from "2005 Global IT Outsourcing Study," Diamond Cluster Report, retrieved from www.globaloutsourcing.org (November 12, 2005).

[8] First reported in *Business Week* (February 29, 1988), pp. 63–66; further information on corporate website: www.falconproducts.com/.

[9] Developed from Anthony J. F. O'Reilly, "Establishing Successful Joint Ventures in Developing Nations: A CEO's Perspective," *Columbia Journal of World Business* (Spring 1988), pp. 65–71; and "Best Practices for Global Competitiveness," *Fortune* (March 30, 1998), pp. S1–S3, special advertising section.

[10] Whipp and Inoue, op cit.

[11] "Starbucks Wins Trademark Case," *The Economic Times*, Bangalore (January 3, 2006), p. 8.

[12] Karby Leggett, "U.S. Auto Makers Find Promise—and Peril—in China," *Wall Street Journal* (June 19, 2003), p. B1; "Did Spark Spark a Copycat?" *Business Week* (February 7, 2005), p. 64.

[13] Many newspapers and magazines publish annual lists of the world's largest multinational coporations. *Fortune's* annual listing is available from www.fortune.com.

[14] See Peter F. Drucker, "The Global Economy and the Nation-State," *Foreign Affairs*, vol. 76 (September/October 1997), pp. 159–71.

[15] Adapted from R. Hall Mason, "Conflicts between Host Countries and Multinational Enterprise," *California Management Review*, vol. 17 (1974), pp. 6, 7.

[16] Data on national corruption scores from "Tainted by Corruption," *Wall Street Journal* (January 27, 2005), p. A2.

[17] Marc Gunther, "Can Factory Monitoring Ever Really Work?," *Business Ethics* (Fall 2005), p. 12.

[18] "An Industry Monitors Child Labor," *New York Times* (October 16, 1997), pp. B1, B9; and Rugmark International website: www.rugmark.de.

[19] See Simon Zadek, "The Path to Corporate Responsibility," *Harvard Business Review* (December 2004), pp. 125–130; and information at corporate website: www.nikebiz.com/labor/toc_monitoring.html.

[20] See, for example, Peter Marsh, "The Country Prince Comes of Age," *Business Life* August 9, 2005), p. 9.

[21] For a perspective on the role of women in expatriate managerial assignments, see Marianne Jelinek and Nancy J. Adler, "Women: World-Class Managers for Global Competition," *Academy of Management Executive* (February 1988), pp. 11–19.

[22] See J. Stewart Black and Hal B. Gregersen, "The Right Way to Manage Expats," *Harvard Business Review* (March/April 1999), Reprint #99201.

[23] See Robert B. Reich, "Who Is Them?" *Harvard Business Review* (March/April 1991), pp. 77–88.

[24] Carol Hymowitz, "The New Diversity," *Wall Street Journal* (November 14, 2005), p. R1.

Information from Andrew Morse, "Running the Show," *Wall Street Journal* (October 31, 2005), pp. R5, R6.

Information from Mark Niquette, "Honda's 'Bold Move' Paid Off," *Columbus Dispatch* (November 16, 2002), pp. C1, C2.

Developed from "Is Your Company Really Global?," *Business Week* (December 1, 1997).

Lafley Quote: *The Wall Street Journal*, March 29, 2006.

Module 8

[1] Information from "Got Spanish?" *Business Week Frontier* (August 14, 2000), p. F12; and "Cultivating Creativity," Interview by National Association of Female Executives (August 2000): www.nafe.com.

[2] Information from "Women Business Owners Receive First-Ever Micro Loans via the Internet," *Business Wire* (August 9, 2000); Jim Hopkins, "Non-Profit Loan Group Takes Risks on Women in Business," *USA Today* (August 9, 2000), p. 2B; and "Women's Group Grants First Loans to Entrepreneurs," *Columbus Dispatch* (August 10, 2000), p. B2.

[3] Speech at the Lloyd Greif Center for Entrepreneurial Studies, Marshall School of Business, University of Southern California, 1996.

[4] This list is developed from Jeffry A. Timmons, *New Venture Creation: Entrepreneurship for the 21st Century* (New York: Irwin/McGraw-Hill, 1999), pp. 47–48; and Robert D. Hisrich and Michael P. Peters, *Entrepreneurship*, 4th ed. (New York: Irwin/McGraw-Hill, 1998), pp. 67–70.

[5] Information from the corporate websites and from The Entrepreneur's Hall of Fame: www.ltbn.com/halloffame.html.

[6] For a review and discussion of the entrepreneurial mind, see Timmons, op.cit., pp. 219–225.

[7] Timothy Butler and James Waldroop, "Job Sculpting: The Art of Retaining Your Best People," *Harvard Business Review* (September/October 1999), pp. 144–152.

[8] See the review by Hisrich and Peters, op. cit.; and Paulette Thomas, "Entrepreneurs' Biggest Problems and How They Solve Them," *Wall Street Journal Reports* (March 17, 2003), pp. R1, R2.

[9] "Smart Talk: Start-Ups and Schooling," *Wall Street Journal* (September 7, 2004), p. B4.

[10] *Paths to Entrepreneurship: New Directions for Women in Business* (New York: Catalyst, 1998), and Eve Hayek, "Report Shatters Myths About U.S. Women's Equality" (October 1, 2005); both available on the National Foundation for Women Business Owners website: www.nfwbo.org/key.html.

[11] Data in Stay Informed from ibid.; and "Smart Talk: Start-Ups and Schooling," *Wall Street Journal* (September 7, 2004), p. B4.

[12] National Foundation for Women Business Owners, *Women Business Owners of Color: Challenges and Accomplishments* (1998).

[13] Data reported by Karen E. Klein, "Minority Start Ups: A Measure of Progress," *Business Week* (August 25, 2005; retrieved from www.businessweekonline); "Adam Aichols," N.Y. Leads Boom in Hispanic Business, New York Daily News (March 21, 2006).

[14] David Bornstein, *How to Change the World: Social Entrepreneurs and the Power of New Ideas* (Oxford, U.K.: Oxford University Press, 2004).

[15] See Laura D'Andrea Tyson, "Good Works—With a Business Plan," *Business Week* (May 3, 2004, retrieved from Business Week Online, November 14, 2005, at www. businessweek.com).

[16] Information from "Chapter 2," *Kellogg* (Winter 2004), p. 6.

[17] *The Facts About Small Business 1999* (Washington, DC: U.S. Small Business Administration, Office of Advocacy).

[18] See U.S. Small Business Administration website: www.sba.gov; and *Statistical Abstract of the United States* (Washington, DC: U.S. Census Bureau, 1999).

[19] "Small Business Expansions in Electronic Commerce," U.S. Small Business Administration, Office of Advocacy (June 2000).

[20] Information from Will Christensen, "Rod Spencer's Sports-Card Business Has Migrated Cyberspace Marketplace," *Columbus Dispatch* (July 24, 2000), p. F1.

[21] Discussion based on "The Life Cycle of Entrepreneurial Firms," in Ricky Griffin (ed.), *Management*, 6th ed. (New York: Houghton Mifflin, 1999), pp. 309–310; and Neil C. Churchill and Virginia L. Lewis, "The Five Stages of Small Business Growth," *Harvard Business Review* (May/June 1993), pp. 30–50.

[22] See U.S. Small Business Administration website: www.sba.gov.

[23] George Gendron, "The Failure Myth," *Inc.* (January 2001), p. 13.

[24] Based on Norman M. Scarborough and Thomas W. Zimmerer, *Effective Small Business Management* (Englewood Cliffs, NJ: Prentice-Hall, 2000), pp. 25–30; and Scott Clark, "Most Small-Business Failures Tied to Poor Management," *Business Journal* (April 10, 2000).

[25] Information reported in "The Rewards," *Inc. State of Small Business* (May 20–21, 2001), pp. 50–51.

[26] Data reported by The Family Firm Institute: www.ffi.org/looking/factsfb.html.

[27] Conversation from the case "Am I My Uncle's Keeper?" by Paul I. Karofsky (Northeastern University Center for Family Business) and published at www.fambiz.com/contprov.cfm? ContProvCode=NECFB&ID=140.

[28] *Survey of Small and Mid-Sized Businesses: Trends for 2000* (Arthur Andersen, 2000).

[29] Ibid.

[30] Developed from William S. Sahlman, "How to Write a Great Business Plan," *Harvard Business Review* (July/August 1997), pp. 98–108.

[31] Marcia H. Pounds, "Business Plan Sets Course for Growth," *Columbus Dispatch* (March 16, 1998), p. 9; see also firm website: www.calcustoms.com.

[32] Standard components of business plans are described in many text sources, such as Linda Pinson and Jerry Jinnett, *Anatomy of a Business Plan: A Step-by-Step Guide to Starting Smart, Building the Business, and Securing Your Company's Future*, 4th ed. (Dearborn Trade, 1999), and Scarborough and Zimmerer, op. cit.; and on websites such as American Express Small Business Services, Business Town.com., and BizplanIt.com.

[33] "You've Come a Long Way Baby," *Business Week Frontier* (July 10, 2000).

Instrument adapted from Norman M. Scarborough and Thomas W. Zimmerer, *Effective Small Business Management*, 3rd ed. (Columbus: Merrill, 1991), pp. 26–27. Used by permission.

Features:

Pacesetters-Information from David J. Dent, "The Next Black Power Movement: The Boom in African-American Entrepreneurship Isn't Just a Business Story. It's Also a Logical Extension of the Civil Rights Struggle. Here's Why," *Fortune Small Business* (May 2, 2003), www.fortune.com/fortune/smallbusiness/articles/0, 15114, 449148, 00.html.

Newsline-Information from Scott Williams, "Program to Help Firms Enter the Internet Marketplace," *Hispanic Business* (August 2000); and information on the program website: www.usmcoc.org(retrieved November 14, 2005).

Module 9

[1] "They Don't Teach This in B-School," *Business Week* (September 19, 2005), pp. 46–47.

[2] Peter F. Drucker, "Looking Ahead: Implications of the Present," *Harvard Business Review* (September/October 1997), pp. 18–32. See

also Shaker A. Zahra, "An Interview with Peter Drucker," *Academy of Management Executive*, vol. 17 (August 2003), pp. 9–12.

3 Henry Mintzberg, *The Nature of Managerial Work* (New York: HarperCollins, 1997).

4 "Why Drucker Still Matters," *Business Week* (November 28, 2005), p. 100.

5 For a good discussion, see Watson H. Agor, *Intuition in Organizations: Leading and Managing Productively* (Newbury Park, CA: Sage, 1989); Herbert A. Simon, "Making Management Decisions: The Role of Intuition and Emotion," *Academy of Management Executive*, vol. 1 (1987), pp. 57–64; Orlando Behling and Norman L. Eckel, "Making Sense Out of Intuition," *Academy of Management Executive*, vol. 1 (1987), pp. 57–64; Orlando Behling and Norman L. Eckel, "Making Sense Out of Intuition," *Academy of Management Executive*, vol. 5 (1991), pp. 46–54.

6 See Hugh Courtney, Jane Kirkland, and Patrick Viguerie, "Strategy Under Uncertainty," *Harvard Business Review* (November/December 1997), pp. 67–79.

7 See George P. Huber, *Managerial Decision Making* (Glenview, IL: Scott, Foresman 1975). For a comparison, see the steps in Xerox's problem-solving process as described in David A. Garvin, "Building a Learning Organization," *Harvard Business Review* (July/August 1993), pp. 78–91, and the Josephson model for ethical decision making described at www.josephsoninstitute.org/MED/MED-4sevensteppath.htm.

8 Joseph B. White and Lee Hawkins, Jr., "GM Cuts Deeper in North America," *Wall Street Journal* (November 22, 20005), p. A3. See also Rick Wagoner, "A Potrait of My Industry," *Wall Street Journal* (December 6, 2005), p. A20.

9 Peter F. Drucker, *Innovation and Entrepreneurship: Practice and Principles* (New York: Harper & Row, 1985).

10 White and Hawkins, op cit.

11 For a sample of Simon's work, see Herbert A. Simon, *Administrative Behavior* (New York: Free Press, 1947); James G. March and Herbert A. Simon, *Organizations* (New York: Wiley, 1958); Herbert A. Simon, *The New Science of Management Decision* (New York: Harper, 1960).

12 This presentation is based on the work of R. H. Hogarth, D. Kahneman, A. Tversky, and others, as discussed in Max H. Bazerman, *Judgment in Managerial Decision Making*, 3rd ed. (New York: Wiley, 1994).

13 Barry M. Staw, "The Escalation of Commitment to a Course of Action," *Academy of Management Review*, vol. 6 (1981), pp. 577–587; and Barry M. Staw and Jerry Ross, "Knowing When to Pull the Plug," *Harvard Business Review*, vol. 65 (March/April 1987), pp. 68–74.

14 The classic work is Norman R. Maier, "Assets and Liabilities in Group Problem Solving," *Psychological Review*, vol. 74 (1967), pp. 239–249.

15 Information from Bart Boehlert, "Kate Spade and Her Hip Handbags," *Urban Desires* (1996), http://desires.com/2.1/Style/Spade/spade.html; "Kate and Andy Spade," *Fortune Small Business* (September 2003), pp. 51–57; and company website: www.katespade.com.

16 For scholarly reviews, see Dean Tjosvold, "Effects of Crisis Orientation on Managers' Approach to Controversy in Decision Making," *Academy of Management Journal*, vol. 27 (1984), pp. 130–138; and Ian I. Mitroff, Paul Shrivastava, and Firdaus E. Udwadia, "Effective Crisis Management," *Academy of Management Executive*, vol. 1 (1987), pp. 283–292.

17 Developed from Anna Muoio, "Where There's Smoke It Helps to Have a Smoke Jumper," *Fast Company*, vol. 33, p. 290.

18 Josephson, op. cit.

19 See also Gerald F. Cavanagh, *American Business Values*, 4th ed. (Upper Saddle River, NJ: Prentice-Hall, 1998).

AIM Survey (El Paso, TX: ENFP Enterprises, 1989). Copyright ©1989 by Weston H. Agor. Used by permission.

Features:

Pacesetters-Information from George Anders, "What a Racket: 'Overgrips' Launch Ex-IBMer's New Career," *Wall Street Journal* (October 4, 2005), pp. A17, A19.

Newsline-Example from Carol Hymowitz, "Middle Managers Are Unsung Heroes on Corporate Stage," *Wall Street Journal* (September 19, 2005), p. B1.

Module 10

1 Information from corporate website: www.kinkos.com/about_us.

2 Joseph B. White and Lee Hawkins, Jr., "GM Cuts Deeper in North America," *Wall Street Journal* (November 22, 20005), p. A3.

3 For the CEO's perspective on General Motors and the U.S. automobile industry, see Rick Wagoner, "A Portrait of My Industry," *Wall Street Journal* (December 6, 2005), p. A20.

4 *Eaton Corporation Annual Report*, 1985.

5 See Paul Ingrassia, "The Right Stuff," *Wall Street Journal* (April 8, 2005), p. D5.

6 Henry Mintzberg, "The Manager's Job: Folklore and Fact," *Harvard Business Review*, vol. 53 (July/August 1975), pp. 54–67; and Henry Mintzberg, "Planning on the Left Side and Managing on the Right," *Harvard Business Review*, vol. 54 (July/August 1976), pp. 46–55.

7 For a classic study, see Stanley Thune and Robert House, "Where Long-Range Planning Pays Off," *Business Horizons*, vol. 13 (1970), pp. 81–87. For a critical review of the literature, see Milton Leontiades and Ahmet Teel, "Planning Perceptions and Planning Results," *Strategic Management Journal*, vol. 1 (1980), pp. 65–75; and J. Scott Armstrong, "The Value of Formal Planning for Strategic Decisions," *Strategic Management Journal*, vol. 3 (1982), pp. 197–211. For special attention to the small business setting, see Richard B. Robinson Jr., John A. Pearce II, George S. Vozikis, and Timothy S. Mescon, "The Relationship between Stage of Development and Small Firm Planning and Performance," *Journal of Small Business Management*, vol. 22 (1984), pp. 45–52; and Christopher Orphen, "The Effects of Long-Range Planning on Small Business Performance: A Further Examination," *Journal of Small Business Management*, vol. 23 (1985), pp. 16–23. For an empirical study of large corporations, see Vasudevan Ramanujam and N. Venkatraman, "Planning and Performance: A New Look at an Old Question," *Business Horizons*, vol. 30 (1987), pp. 19–25.

8 Quote from Stephen Covey and Roger Merrill, "New Ways to Get Organized at Work," *USA Weekend* (February 6/8, 1998), p. 18. Books by Stephen R. Covey include: *The 7 Habits of Highly Effective People: Powerful Lessons in Personal Change* (New York: Fireside, 1990), and Stephen R. Covey and Sandra Merril Covey, *The 7 Habits of Highly Effective Families: Building a Beautiful Family Culture in a Turbulent World* (New York: Golden Books, 1996).

9 "McDonald's Tech Turnaround," *Harvard Business Review* (November 2004), p. 128.

10 Quotes from *Business Week* (August 8, 1994), pp. 78–86.

11 See William Oncken, Jr., and Donald L. Wass, "Management Time: Who's Got the Monkey?" *Harvard Business Review*, vol. 52 (September/October 1974), pp. 75–80, and featured as an HBR classic, *Harvard Business Review* (November/December 1999).

12 For more on the long term, see Danny Miller and Isabelle Le Breton-Miller, *Managing for the Long Run* (Cambridge, MA: Harvard Business School Press, 2005).

13 See Elliot Jaques, *The Form of Time* (New York: Russak & Co., 1982). For an executive commentary on his research, see Walter Kiechel III, "How Executives Think," *Fortune* (December 21, 1987), pp. 139–144.

14 See Henry Mintzberg, "Rounding Out the Manager's Job," *Sloan Management Review* (Fall 1994), pp. 1–25.

15 Excerpts in sample sexual harassment policy from American Express's advice to small businesses at www.americanexpress.com (retrieved November 21, 2005).

16 Information from "Avoiding a Time Bomb: Sexual Harassment," *Business Week*, Enterprise issue (October 13, 1997), pp. ENT20–21.

17 For a thorough review of forecasting, see J. Scott Armstrong, *Long-Range Forecasting*, 2nd ed. (New York: Wiley, 1985).

18 Forecasts in Stay Informed from "Long-Term Forecasts on EIU Country Data and Market Indicators & Forecasts," *The Economist* Intelligence Unit, www.eiu.com (retrieved November 21, 2005).

19 The scenario-planning approach is described in Peter Schwartz, *The Art of the Long View* (New York: Doubleday/Currency, 1991); and Arie de Geus, *The Living Company: Habits for Survival in a Turbulent Business Environment* (Boston, MA: Harvard Business School Press, 1997).

20 Ibid.

21 See, for example, Robert C. Camp, *Business Process Benchmarking* (Milwaukee: ASQ Quality Press 1994); Michael J. Spendolini, *The Benchmarking Book* (New York: AMACOM, 1992); and Christopher E. Bogan and Michael J. English, *Benchmarking for Best Practices: Winning Through Innovative Adaptation* (New York: McGraw-Hill, 1994).

22 "How Classy Can 7-Eleven Get?" *Business Week* (September 1, 1997), pp. 74–75; and Kellie B. Gormly, "7-Eleven Moving Up a Grade," *Columbus Dispatch* (August 3, 2000), pp. C1–C2.

Source: Suggested by a discussion in Robert E. Quinn, Sue R. Faerman, Michael P. Thompson, and Michael R. McGrath, *Becoming a Master Manager: A Contemporary Framework* (New York: Wiley, 1990), pp. 75–76.

Features:

Pacesetters-Information from "Skype: How a Startup Harnessed the Hoopla," *Business Week* (September 26, 2005), 35.

Newsline-Information from Peter Burrows and Manjeet Kripalani, "Cisco: Sold on India," *Business Week* (November 28, 2005), pp. 50–51.

Module 11

1 T. J. Rodgers, with William Taylor and Rick Foreman, "No Excuses Management," *World Executive's Digest* (May 1994), pp. 26–30.

2 Rob Cross and Lloyd Baird, "Technology Is Not Enough: Improving Performance by Building Institutional Memory," *Sloan Management Review* (Spring 2000), p. 73.

3 "The Renewal Factor: Friendly Fact, Congenial Controls," *Business Week* (September 14, 1987), p. 105.

4 Example from George Anders, "Management Guru Turns Focus to Orchestras, Hospitals," *Wall Street Journal* (November 21, 2005), pp. B1, B5.

5 Information from Leon E. Wynter, "Allstate Rates Managers on Handling Diversity," *Wall Street Journal* (October 1, 1997), p. B1.

6 Information from Kathryn Kranhold, "U.S. Firms Raise Ethics Focus," *Wall Street Journal* (November 28, 2005), p. B4.

7 Information from Raju Narisetti, "For IBM, a Groundbreaking Sales Chief," *Wall Street Journal* (January 19, 1998), pp. B1, B5.

8 Based on discussion by Harold Koontz and Cyril O'Donnell, *Essentials of Management* (New York: McGraw-Hill, 1974), pp. 362–365; see also Cross and Baird, op.cit.

9 Information from Louis Lee, "I'm Proud of What I've Made Myself Into—What I've Created," *Wall Street Journal* (August 27, 1997), pp. B1, B5; and Jim Collins, "Bigger, Better, Faster," *Fast Company*, vol. 71 (June 2003), p. 74.

10 See Dale D. McConkey, *How to Manage by Results*, 3rd ed. (New York: AMACOM, 1976); Stephen J. Carroll, Jr., and Henry J. Tosi, Jr., *Management by Objectives: Applications and Research* (New York: Macmillan, 1973); and Anthony P. Raia, *Managing by Objectives* (Glenview, IL: Scott, Foresman, 1974).

11 For a discussion of research on MBO, see Carroll and Tosi, op.cit.; Raia, op.cit; and Steven Kerr, "Overcoming the Dysfunctions of MBO," *Management by Objectives*, vol. 5, no. 1 (1976). Information in part from Dylan Loeb McClain, "Job Forecast: Internet's Still Hot," *New York Times* (January 30, 2001), p. 9.

12 McGregor, op.cit.

13 The work on goal setting and motivation is summarized in Edwin A. Locke and Gary P. Latham, *Goal Setting: A Motivational Technique That Works!* (Englewood Cliffs, NJ: Prentice-Hall, 1984).

14 The "hot stove rules" are developed from R. Bruce McAfee and William Poffenberger, *Productivity Strategies: Enhancing Employee Job Performance* (Englewood Cliffs, NJ: Prentice-Hall, 1982), pp. 54–55. They are originally attributed to Douglas McGregor, "Hot Stove Rules of Discipline," in G. Strauss and L. Sayles (eds), *Personnel: The Human Problems of Management* (Englewood Cliffs, NJ: Prentice-Hall, 1967).

15 For basic readings on quality control, see See Joseph M. Juran, *Quality Control Handbook*, 3rd ed. (New York: McGraw-Hill, 1979) and "The Quality Trilogy: A Universal Approach to Managing for Quality," in H. Costin (ed.), *Total Quality Management* (New York: Dryden, 1994); W. Edwards Deming, *Out of Crisis* (Cambridge, MA: MIT Press, 1986) and "Deming's Quality Manifesto," *Best of Business Quarterly*, vol. 12 (Winter 1990–1991), pp. 6–101; Howard S. Gitlow and Shelly J. Gitlow, *The Deming Guide to Quality and Competitive Position* (Englewood Cliffs, NJ: Prentice-Hall, 1987); Juran, op cit. (1993); and Rafael Aguay, *Dr. Deming: The American Who Taught the Japanese About Quality* (New York: Free Press, 1997).

16 See Edward E. Lawler III, Susan Albers Mohrman, and Gerald E. Ledford, Jr., *Employee Involvement and Total Quality Management: Practices and Results in Fortune 1000 Companies* (San Francisco: Jossey-Bass, 1992).

17 The exhibit is based on Philip B. Crosby, *Quality Is Free* (New York: McGraw-Hill, 1979); *The Eternally Successful Organization* (New York: McGraw-Hill, 1988); and *Quality Is Still Free: Making Quality Certain in Uncertain Times* (New York: McGraw-Hill, 1995).

18 Edward E. Lawler III and Susan Albers Mohrman, "Quality Circles After the Fad," *Harvard Business Review* (January/February 1985), pp. 65–71.

19 Quotes from Arnold Kanarick, "The Far Side of Quality Circles," *Management Review*, vol. 70 (October 1981), pp. 16–17.

20 See the description of Wal-Mart's supply chain strengths in Thomas L. Friedman, *The World Is Flat: A Brief History of the Twenty-First Century* (New York: Farrar, Straus & Giroux, 2005), pp. 128–136.

21 "Gauging the Wal-Mart Effect," *Wall Street Journal* (December 3–4, 2005), p.l A9.

Information from Adelle Waldman, "Behind-the-Scenes Arts Work," *Wall Street Journal* (September 20, 2005), p. B6.

Information on the Mumbai *dabawallas* is widely available through various Internet sources. See, for example, "Learning from the Dabbawallas," *The Hindu* (August 3, 2004).

Instrument from Julian P. Rotter, "External Control and Internal Control," *Psychology Today* (June 1971), p. 42. Used by permission.

Holmes Quote: *The American Law Review*, 1872.

Module 12

1 Information from "Starbucks: Making Values Pay," *Fortune* (September 29, 1997), pp. 261–272; Howard Schultz and Dori Jones Yang, *Pour Your Heart into It* (San Francisco: Hyperion, 1997); and www.starbucks.com.

2 Jim Collins, "Bigger, Better, Faster," *Fast Company*, vol. 71 (June 2003), p. 74.

3 For a recent biography of Henry Ford, see Steven Watts, *The People's Tycoon: Henry Ford and the American Century* (New York: Knopf, 2005).

4 Information and quotes from Marcia Stepanek, "How Fast Is Net Fast?" *Business Week E-Biz* (November 1, 1999), pp. EB52–EB54.

5 Strategic challenges facing the U.S. automobile industry are described by Rick Wagoner, "A Portrait of My Industry," *Wall Street Journal* (December 6, 2005), p. A20.

[6] Keith H. Hammond, "Michael Porter's Big Ideas," *Fast Company* (March 2001), pp. 150–156.

[7] Gary Hamel and C. K. Prahalad, "Strategic Intent," *Harvard Business Review* (May/June 1989), pp. 63–76.

[8] Information from "Gauging the Wal-Mart Effect," *Wall Street Journal* (December 3–4, 2005), p. A9.

[9] The four grand strategies were originally described by William F. Glueck, *Business Policy: Strategy Formulation and Management Action*, 2nd ed. (New York: McGraw-Hill, 1976).

[10] Michael A. Hitt, R. Duane Ireland, and Robert E. Hoskisson, *Strategic Management: Competitiveness and Globalization* (Minneapolis: West, 1997), p. 197.

[11] See William McKinley, Carol M. Sanchez, and A. G. Schick, "Organizational Downsizing: Constraining, Cloning, Learning," *Academy of Management Executive*, vol. 9 (August 1995), pp. 32–44.

[12] Kim S. Cameron, Sara J. Freeman, and A. K. Mishra, "Best Practices in White-Collar Downsizing: Managing Contradictions," *Academy of Management Executive*, vol. 4 (August 1991), pp. 57–73.

[13] This strategy classification is found in Hitt et al., op. cit.; the attitudes are from a discussion by Howard V. Perlmutter, "The Tortuous Evolution of the Multinational Corporation," *Columbia Journal of World Business*, vol. 4 (January/February 1969).

[14] Data in Stay Informed from "How Central Europe's Workers Stack Up," *Business Week* (December 12, 2005), p. 51.

[15] See Michael E. Porter, "Strategy and the Internet," *Harvard Business Review* (March 2001), pp. 63–78.

[16] Information from Michael Rappa, *Business Models on the Web* (www.ecommerce.ncsu.edu/business_models.html. February 6, 2001).

[17] Peter F. Drucker, *Management: Tasks, Responsibilities, Practices* (New York: Harper & Row, 1973), p. 122.

[18] See Laura Nash, "Mission Statements—Mirrors and Windows," *Harvard Business Review* (March/April 1988), pp. 155–156; James C. Collins and Jerry I. Porras, "Building Your Company's Vision," *Harvard Business Review* (September/October 1996), pp. 65–77; and James C. Collins and Jerry I. Porras, *Built to Last: Successful Habits of Visionary Companies* (New York: Harper Business, 1997).

[19] Gary Hamel, *Leading the Revolution* (Boston, MA: Harvard Business School Press, 2000), pp. 72–73.

[20] Collins and Porras, op cit.

[21] Peter F. Drucker's views on organizational objectives are expressed in his classic books: *The Practice of Management* (New York: Harper & Row, 1954), and *Management: Tasks, Responsibilities, Practices* (New York: Harper & Row, 1973). For a more recent commentary, see his article, "Management: The Problems of Success," *Academy of Management Executive*, vol. 1 (1987), pp. 13–19.

[22] C. K. Prahalad and Gary Hamel, "The Core Competencies of the Corporation," *Harvard Business Review* (May/June 1990), pp. 79–91; see also Hitt et al., op. cit., pp. 99–103.

[23] For a discussion of Michael Porter's approach to strategic planning, see his books *Competitive Strategy* and *Competitive Advantage*, and his article, "What Is Strategy?" *Harvard Business Review* (November/December, 1996), pp. 61–78; and Richard M. Hodgetts' interview "A Conversation with Michael E. Porter: A Significant Extension Toward Operational Improvement and Positioning," *Organizational Dynamics* (Summer 1999), pp. 24–33.

[24] See Michael E. Porter, *Competitive Strategy: Techniques for Analyzing Industries and Competitors* (New York: Free Press, 1980), and *Competitive Advantage: Creating and Sustaining Superior Performance* (New York: Free Press, 1986).

[25] Information from www.polo.com.

[26] For more on GE and Jeffrey Immelt, see "The Immelt Revolution," *Business Week* (March 28, 2005), pp. 64–73.

[27] Richard G. Hammermesh, "Making Planning Strategic," *Harvard Business Review*, vol. 64 (July/August 1986), pp. 115–120; and Richard G. Hammermesh, *Making Strategy Work* (New York: Wiley, 1986).

[28] See Gerald B. Allan, "A Note on the Boston Consulting Group Concept of Competitive Analysis and Corporate Strategy," Harvard Business School, Intercollegiate Case Clearing House, ICCH9-175-175 (Boston: Harvard Business School, June 1976).

[29] R. Duane Ireland and Michael A. Hitt, "Achieving and Maintaining Strategic Competitiveness in the 21st Century," *Academy of Management Executive*, vol.13 (1999), pp. 43–57.

[30] Porter, op cit., 2001.

Source: Joseph A. Devito, *Messages: Building Interpersonal Communication Skills*, 3rd ed. (New York: HarperCollins, 1996), referencing William Haney, *Communicational Behavior: Text and Cases*, 3rd ed. (Homewood, IL: Irwin, 1973). Reprinted by permission.

Features:

Pacesetters-Information from Michael S. Malone, "Meet Meg Whitman," *Wall Street Journal* (March 16, 2005), p. A24; "Running the Show," *Wall Street Journal* (October 31, 2005), p. R24.

Newsline-Information from "Based in New Jersey, Thriving in Bulgaria," *Business Week* (December 12, 2005), p. 54; and "How Central Europe's Workers Stack Up," *Business Week* (December 12, 2005), p. 51.

Charan Quote: *Business Week,* May 29, 2006.

Haas Quote: *Harvard Business Review*, September-October, 2005.

Module 13

[1] Information from Richard Teitelbaum, "The Wal-Mart of Wall Street," *Fortune* (October 13, 1997), pp. 128–130; and "Edward Jones: The Last Not-Com Brokerage," *Industry Standard* (August 7, 2000); online: www.thestandard.com/article/display/0.1151.17432.000.html.

[2] See, for example, Charles O'Reilly III and Jeffrey Pfeffer, *Hidden Value: How Great Companies Achieve Extraordinary Results with Ordinary People* (Boston: Harvard Business School Press, 2000); Jeffrey Pfeffer and John F. Veiga, "Putting People First for Organizational Success," *Academy of Management Executive*, vol. 13 (May 1999), pp. 37–48; Jeffrey Pfeffer, *The Human Equation: Building Profits by Putting People First* (Boston: Harvard Business School Press, 1998); Jeffrey Pfeffer, "When It Comes to 'Best Practices'—Why Do Smart Organizations Occasionally Do Dumb Things?" *Organizational Dynamics*, vol. 25 (Summer 1996), pp. 33–44; and, Michael Beer, "How to Develop an Organization Capable of Sustained High Performance: Embrace the Drive for Results—Capability Development Paradox," *Organizational Dynamics*, vol. 29 (spring 2001), pp. 233–247.

[3] Henry Mintzberg and Ludo Van der Heyden, "Organigraphs: Drawing How Companies Really Work," *Harvard Business Review* (September/October 1999), pp. 87–94.

[4] Ibid.

[5] The classic work is Alfred D. Chandler, *Strategy and Structure* (Cambridge, MA: MIT Press, 1962).

[6] See Alfred D. Chandler, Jr., "Origins of the Organization Chart," *Harvard Business Review* (March/April 1988), pp. 156–157.

[7] See David Krackhardt and Jeffrey R. Hanson, "Informal Networks: The Company Behind the Chart," *Harvard Business Review* (July/August 1993), pp. 104–111.

[8] See Kenneth Noble, "A Clash of Styles: Japanese Companies in the U.S.," *New York Times* (January 25, 1988), p. 7.

[9] For a discussion of departmentalization, see H. I. Ansoff and R. G. Bradenburg, "A Language for Organization Design," *Management Science*, vol. 17 (August 1971), pp. B705–B731; Mariann Jelinek, "Organization Structure: The Basic Conformations," in Mariann Jelinek, Joseph A. Litterer, and Raymond E. Miles (eds.), *Organizations by Design: Theory and Practice* (Plano, TX: Business Publications, 1981), pp. 293–302; Henry Mintzberg, "The Structuring of Organizations," in James Brian Quinn, Henry Mintzberg, and Robert M. James (eds.), *The Strategy Process: Concepts, Contexts, and Cases* (Englewood Cliffs, NJ: Prentice-Hall, 1988), pp. 276–304.

[10] Robert L. Simison, "Jaguar Slowly Sheds Outmoded Habits," *Wall Street Journal* (July 26, 1991), p. A6; and Richard Stevenson, "Ford

Helps Jaguar Get Back Old Sheen," *International Herald Tribune* (December 14, 1994), p. 11.

[11] These alternatives are well described by Mintzberg , op cit.

[12] Excellent reviews of matrix concepts are found in Stanley M. Davis and Paul R. Lawrence, *Matrix* (Reading, MA: Addison-Wesley, 1977); Paul R. Lawrence, Harvey F. Kolodny, and Stanley M. Davis, "The Human Side of the Matrix," *Organizational Dynamics*, vol. 6 (1977), pp. 43–61; and Harvey F. Kolodny, "Evolution to a Matrix Organization," *Academy of Management Review*, vol. 4 (1979), pp. 543–553.

[13] Davis and Lawrence, op cit.

[14] Susan Albers Mohrman, Susan G. Cohen, and Allan M. Mohrman, Jr., *Designing Team-Based Organizations* (San Francisco: Jossey-Bass, 1996).

[15] See Glenn M. Parker, *Cross-Functional Teams* (San Francisco: Jossey-Bass, 1995).

[16] Information from William Bridges, "The End of the Job," *Fortune* (September 19, 1994), pp. 62–74; Alan Deutschman, "The Managing Wisdom of High-Tech Superstars," *Fortune* (October 17, 1994), pp. 197–206.

[17] See the discussion by Jay R. Galbraith, "Designing the Networked Organization: Leveraging Size and Competencies," in Susan Albers Mohrman, Jay R. Galbraith, Edward E. Lawler III and Associates, *Tomorrow's Organizations: Crafting Winning Strategies in a Dynamic World* (San Francisco: Jossey-Bass, 1998), pp. 76–102. See also Rupert F. Chisholm, *Developing Network Organizations: Learning from Practice and Theory* (Reading, MA: Addison-Wesley, 1998).

[18] See Jerome Barthelemy, "The Seven Deadly Sins of Outsourcing," *Academy of Management Executive*, vol. 17 (2003), pp. 87–98.

[19] See the collection of articles by Cary L. Cooper and Denise M. Rousseau (eds.), *The Virtual Organization: Vol. 6, Trends in Organizational Behavior* (New York: Wiley, 2000).

Source: Developed from Joseph A. Raelin, *The Clash of Cultures, Managers and Professionals* (Boston: Harvard Business School Press, 1986).

Features:

Pacesetters-For more information see the AceNet website: www.acenetworks.org.

Shapiro Quote: *Harvard Business Review*, January-February, 1997.

Module 14

[1] Information from www.kpmg.com.

[2] For a discussion of organization theory, see W. Richard Scott, *Organizations: Rational, Natural, and Open Systems*, 4th ed. (Upper Saddle River, NJ: Prentice-Hall, 1998).

[3] For a classic work see Jay R. Galbraith, *Organizational Design* (Reading, MA: Addison Wesley, 1977).

[4] David Van Fleet, "Span of Management Research and Issues," *Academy of Management Journal*, vol. 26 (1983), pp. 546–552.

[5] Information for Stay Informed from Tim Stevens, "Winning the World Over," *Industry Week* (November 15, 1999).

[6] See George P. Huber, "A Theory of Effects of Advanced Information Technologies on Organizational Design, Intelligence, and Decision Making," *Academy of Management Review*, vol. 15 (1990), pp. 67–71.

[7] Developed from Roger Fritz, *Rate Your Executive Potential* (New York: Wiley, 1988), pp. 185–186; Roy J. Lewicki, Donald D. Bowen, Douglas T. Hall, and Francine S. Hall, *Experiences in Management and Organizational Behavior*, 3rd ed. (New York: Wiley, 1988), p. 144.

[8] Max Weber, *The Theory of Social and Economic Organization*, A. M. Henderson, trans., and H. T. Parsons (New York: Free Press, 1947). For classic treatments of bureaucracy, see also Alvin Gouldner, *Patterns of Industrial Bureaucracy* (New York: Free Press, 1954); and

Robert K. Merton, *Social Theory and Social Structure* (New York: Free Press, 1957).

[9] Tom Burns and George M. Stalker, *The Management of Innovation* (London: Tavistock, 1961), republished (London: Oxford University Press, 1994). See also Wesley D. Sine, Hitoshi Mitsuhashi, and David A. Kirsch, "Revisiting Burns and Stalker": Formal structure and New Ventore performance in Emerging Economic Scenarios, *Academy of Management Journal*, vol. 49 (2006), pp. 121–132.

[10] See Henry Mintzberg, *Structure in Fives: Designing Effective Organizations* (Englewood Cliffs, NJ: Prentice-Hall, 1983).

[11] "What Ails Microsoft?" *Business Week* (September 26, 2005), p. 101.

[12] "Should Microsoft Break Up, on Its Own?" *Wall Street Journal* (November 26–27, 2005), p. B16.

[13] See, for example, Jay R. Galbraith, Edward E. Lawler III, and Associates, *Organizing for the Future* (San Francisco: Jossey-Bass, 1993); and Susan Albers Mohrman, Jay R. Galbraith, Edward E. Lawler III, and Associates, *Tomorrow's Organizations: Crafting Winning Strategies in a Dynamic World* (San Francisco: Jossey-Bass, 1998).

[14] Peter Senge, *The Fifth Discipline: The Art and Practice of the Learning Organization* (New York: Doubleday, 1994).

[15] See Rosabeth Moss Kanter, *The Changing Masters* (New York: Simon & Schuster, 1983). Quotation from Rosabeth Moss Kanter and John D. Buck, "Reorganizing Part of Honeywell: From Strategy to Structure," *Organizational Dynamics*, vol. 13 (Winter 1985), p. 6.

[16] Paul R. Lawrence and Jay W. Lorsch, *Organizations and Environment* (Boston: Division of Research, Graduate School of Business Administration, Harvard University, 1967).

[17] See Jay R. Galbraith, op.cit., and Susan Albers Mohrman, "Integrating Roles and Structure in the Lateral Organization," chapter 5 in Jay R. Galbraith, Edward E. Lawler III, and Associates, *Organizing for the Future* (San Francisco: Jossey-Bass Publishers, 1993).

[18] Michael Hammer and James Champy, *Reengineering the Corporation: A Manifesto for Business Revolution*, rev. ed. (New York: Harper Business, 1999).

[19] Michael Hammer, *Beyond Reengineering* (New York: Harper Business, 1997).

[20] Ibid., p. 5; see also the discussion of processes in Gary Hamel, *Leading the Revolution* (Boston, MA: Harvard Business School Press, 2000).

[21] Hammer, op cit. (1997), pp. 28–30.

[22] Edgar H. Schein, "Organizational Culture," *American Psychologist*, vol. 45 (1990), pp. 109–119. See also Schein's *Organizational Culture and Leadership*, 2nd ed. (San Francisco: Jossey-Bass, 1997); and *The Corporate Culture Survival Guide* (San Francisco: Jossey-Bass, 1999).

[23] James Collins and Jerry Porras, *Built to Last* (New York: Harper Business, 1994).

[24] Schein, op.cit. (1997); Terrence E. Deal and Alan A. Kennedy, *Corporate Cultures: The Rites and Rituals of Corporate Life* (Reading, MA: Addison-Wesley, 1982); and Ralph Kilmann, *Beyond the Quick Fix* (San Francisco: Jossey-Bass, 1984).

[25] In their book *Corporate Culture and Performance* (New York: Macmillan, 1992), John P. Kotter and James L. Heskett make the point that strong cultures have the desired effects over the long term only if they encourage adaptation to a changing environment. See also Collins and Porras, op cit. (1994).

[26] This is a simplified model developed from Schein, op cit. (1997).

[27] James C. Collins and Jerry I. Porras, "Building Your Company's Vision," *Harvard Business Review* (September/October 1996), pp. 65–77.

[28] Reported in Jenny C. McCune, "Making Lemonade," *Management Review* (June, 1997), pp. 49–53.

Source: John F. Veiga and John N. Yanouzas, *The Dynamics of Organization Theory: Gaining a Macro Perspective* (St. Paul, MN: West, 1979), pp. 158–60. Used by permission.

Features:

Newsline-Information from Simon London, "Enterprise Drives Home the Service Ethic," *Financial Times* (June 2, 2003), p. 7.

Pacesetters-Information from "At lears, a Great Communicator," *Business Week* (October 31, 2005), pp. 50, 51.

Module 15

[1] Information from "Many U.S. Employees Have Negative Attitudes to Their Jobs, Employers and Top Managers," Harris Poll #38 (May 6, 2005), retrieved from www.harrisinteractive.com.

[2] Information on Great Place to Work Institute at www.greatplace-towork.com.

[3] Information and quotes from corporate website: www.working-woman.com.

[4] List in box from "The Winners: Best Companies for Women of Color 2005," Working Mother Media, retrieved from www.working-mother.com.

[5] See Jeffrey Pfeffer, *The Human Equation: Building Profits by Putting People First* (Boston: Harvard University Press, 1998).

[6] Jeffrey Pfeffer and John F. Veiga, "Putting People First for Organizational Success," *Academy of Management Executive*, vol. 13 (May 1999), pp. 37–48.

[7] Ibid.; and Pfeffer, op.cit. See also James N. Baron and David M. Kreps, *Strategic Human Resources: Frameworks for General Managers* (New York: Wiley, 1999).

[8] Quotes from Kris Maher, "Human-Resources Directors Are Assuming Strategic Roles," *Wall Street Journal* (June 17, 2003), p. B8.

[9] For a discussion of affirmative action, see R. Roosevelt Thomas, Jr., "From 'Affirmative Action' to 'Affirming Diversity,'" *Harvard Business Review* (November/December 1990), pp. 107–117.

[10] See the discussion by David A. DeCenzo and Stephen P. Robbins, *Human Resource Management*, 6th ed. (New York: Wiley, 1999), pp. 66–68 and 81–83.

[11] Ibid., pp. 77–79.

[12] See, for example, Randall Smith, "African-American Broker Sues Alleging Bias at Merrill Lynch," *Wall Street Journal* (December 1, 2005), p. C3.

[13] See Frederick S. Lane, *The Naked Employee: How Technology Is Compromising Workplace Privacy* (New York: Amacon, 2003).

[14] Quote from George Myers, "Bookshelf," *Columbus Dispatch* (June 9, 2003), p. E6.

[15] For reviews see Richard B. Freeman and James L. Medoff, *What Do Unions Do?* (New York: Basic Books, 1984); Charles C. Heckscher, *The New Unionism* (New York: Basic Books, 1988); and Barry T. Hirsch, *Labor Unions and the Economic Performance of Firms* (Kalamazoo, MI: W.E. Upjohn Institute for Employment Research, 1991).

[16] Data for Stay Informed from U. S. Bureau of Labor Statistics, "Union Members Summary," news release (January 27, 2005), retrieved from www.bls.gov/cps/; and, "Negative Attitudes to Labor Unions Show Little Change in Last Decade," Harris Poll #68 (August 31, 2005), retrieved from www.harrisinteractive.com. See also Robert Guy Matthews and Kris Maher, "Labor's PR Problem," *Wall Street Journal* (August 15, 2005), pp. B1, B4; and, Kris Maher, "The New Union Worker," *Wall Street Journal* (September 27, 2005), p. B1.

[17] Yochi J. Dreazen, "Percentage of U.S. Workers in a Union Sank, to Record Low of 13.5% Last Year," *Wall Street Journal* (January 19, 2001), p. A2.

[18] The company view on challenges facing the U.S. automobile industry are described by Rick Wagoner, "A Portrait of My Industry," *Wall Street Journal* (December 6, 2005), p. A20.

[19] Quote from William Bridges, "The End of the Job," *Fortune* (September 19, 1994), p. 68

[20] See Sarah E. Needleman, "Initial Phone Interviews Do Count," *The Wall Street Journal* (February 7, 2006), p. 29.

[21] See John P. Wanous, *Organizational Entry: Recruitment, Selection, and Socialization of Newcomers* (Reading, MA: Addison-Wesley, 1980), pp. 34–44.

[22] Josey Puliyenthuruthel, "How Google Searches for Talent," *Business Week* (April 11, 2005), p. 52.

[23] Quote from Ronald Henkoff, "Finding, Training, and Keeping the Best Service Workers," *Fortune* (October 3, 1994), pp. 110–122.

[24] This involves the social information processing concept as discussed in Gerald R. Salancik and Jeffrey Pfeffer, "A Social Information Processing Approach to Job Attitudes and Task Design," *Administrative Science Quarterly*, vol. 23 (June 1978); pp. 224–253.

[25] Dick Grote, "Performance Appraisal Reappraised," *Harvard Business Review Best Practice* (1999), Reprint F00105.

[26] See Larry L. Cummings and Donald P. Schwab, *Performance in Organizations: Determinants and Appraisal* (Glenview, IL: Scott, Foresman, 1973).

[27] For a good review, see Gary P. Latham, Joan Almost, Sara Mann, and Celia Moore, "New Developments in Performance Management," *Organizational Dynamics*, vol. 34, no. 1 (2005), pp. 77–87.

[28] See Mark R. Edwards and Ann J. Ewen, *360-Degree Feedback: The Powerful New Tool for Employee Feedback and Performance Improvement* (New York: AMACOM, 1996).

Source: Developed in part from Robert E. Quinn, Sue R. Faerman, Michael P. Thompson, and Michael R. McGrath, *Becoming a Master Manager: A Contemporary Framework* (New York: Wiley, 1990), p. 187. Used by permission.

Features:

Newsline-Information from Sue Shellenbarger, "Gray Is Good: Employers Make Efforts to Retain Older Workers," *Wall Street Journal* (December 1, 2005), p. D1.

Peacesetters-Information from Tom Matthews, "Queen of the Corporate Jungle," *Columbus Dispatch* (October 23, 2005), pp. E1, E2.

Module 16

[1] Information and quotes from Sharon Shinn, "Luv, Colleen," *BizEd* (March/April 2003), pp. 18–23; corporate website: www.southwestairlines.com; "We Weren't Just Airborne Yesterday," http://www.tfly.swa.com/about_swa/airborne.html; quote from http://www.kelleher.html (11/24/2000).

[2] Abraham Zaleznick, "Leaders and Managers: Are They Different?" *Harvard Business Review* (May/June 1977), pp. 67–78.

[3] Tom Peters, "Rule #3: Leadership Is Confusing as Hell," *Fast Company* (March 2001), pp. 124–140.

[4] Quotations from Marshall Loeb, "Where Leaders Come From," *Fortune* (September 19, 1994), pp. 241–242; Genevieve Capowski, "Anatomy of a Leader: Where Are the Leaders of Tomorrow?" *Management Review* (March 1994), pp. 10–17. For additional thoughts, see Warren Bennis, *Why Leaders Can't Lead* (San Francisco: Jossey-Bass, 1996).

[5] See Steven Kerr, "How Can Organizations Best Prepare People to Lead and Manage Others?" *Academy of Management Executive*, vol. 18 (2004), pp. 118–142.

[6] Rosabeth Moss Kanter, "Power Failure in Management Circuits," *Harvard Business Review* (July/August 1979), pp. 65–75.

[7] The classic treatment of these power bases is John R. P. French Jr. and Bertram Raven, "The Bases of Social Power," in Darwin Cartwright (ed.), *Group Dynamics: Research and Theory* (Evanson, IL: Row, Peterson, 1962), pp. 607–613.

[8] For managerial applications of this basic framework, see Gary Yukl and Tom Taber, "The Effective Use of Managerial Power," *Personnel*, vol. 60 (1983), pp. 37–49; and Robert C. Benfari, Harry E. Wilkinson, and Charles D. Orth, "The Effective Use of Power," *Business*

Horizons, vol. 29 (1986), pp. 12–16. Gary A. Yukl, *Leadership in Organizations*, 4th ed. (Englewood Cliffs, NJ: Prentice-Hall, 1998), includes "information" as a separate, but related, power source.

[9] The early work on leader traits is well represented in Ralph M. Stogdill, "Personal Factors Associated with Leadership: A Survey of the Literature," *Journal of Psychology*, vol. 25 (1948), pp. 35–71. See also Edwin E. Ghiselli, *Explorations in Management Talent* (Santa Monica, CA: Goodyear, 1971); and Shirley A. Kirkpatrick and Edwin A. Locke, "Leadership: Do Traits Really Matter?" *Academy of Management Executive* (1991), pp. 48–60.

[10] See also John W. Gardner's article, "The Context and Attributes of Leadership," *New Management*, vol. 5 (1988), pp. 18–22; John P. Kotter, *The Leadership Factor* (New York: Free Press, 1988); and Bernard M. Bass, *Stogdill's Handbook of Leadership* (New York: Free Press, 1990).

[11] Kirkpatrick and Locke, op cit. (1991).

[12] This terminology comes from the classic studies by Kurt Lewin and his associates at the University of Iowa. See, for example, K. Lewin and R. Lippitt, "An Experimental Approach to the Study of Autocracy and Democracy: A Preliminary Note," *Sociometry*, vol. 1 (1938), pp. 292–300; K. Lewin, "Field Theory and Experiment in Social Psychology: Concepts and Methods," *American Journal of Sociology*, vol. 44 (1939); and K. Lewin, R. Lippitt, and R. K. White, "Patterns of Aggressive Behavior in Experimentally Created Social Climates," *Journal of Social Psychology*, vol. 10 (1939), pp. 271–301.

[13] Robert R. Blake and Jane Srygley Mouton, *The New Managerial Grid III* (Houston: Gulf Publishing, 1985).

[14] For a good discussion of this theory, see Fred E. Fiedler, Martin M. Chemers, and Linda Mahar, *The Leadership Match Concept* (New York: Wiley, 1978); Fiedler's current contingency research with the cognitive resource theory is summarized in Fred E. Fiedler and Joseph E. Garcia, *New Approaches to Effective Leadership* (New York: Wiley, 1987).

[15] See, for example, Robert J. House, "A Path-Goal Theory of Leader Effectiveness," *Administrative Sciences Quarterly*, vol. 16 (1971), pp. 321–338; Robert J. House and Terrence R. Mitchell, "Path-Goal Theory of Leadership," *Journal of Contemporary Business* (Autumn 1974), pp. 81–97; the path-goal theory is reviewed by Bass, op cit., and Yukl, op cit. A supportive review of research is offered in Julie Indvik, "Path-Goal Theory of Leadership. A Meta-Analysis," in John A. Pearce II and Richard B. Robinson Jr. (eds.), *Academy of Management Best Paper Proceedings* (1986), pp. 189–192.

[16] See the discussions of path-goal theory in Yukl, op cit.; and Bernard M. Bass, "Leadership: Good, Better, Best," *Organizational Dynamics* (Winter 1985), pp. 26–40.

[17] Survey data in Stay Informed box from Gallup Leadership Institute, *Briefings Report 2005-01* (Lincoln, NE: University of Nebraska-Lincoln); "The Stat," *Business Week* (September 12, 2005), p. 16; and, "U.S. Job Satisfaction Keeps Falling, The Conference Board Reports Today," The Conference Board (February 28, 2005), retrieved from www.conference-board.org.

[18] Among the popular books addressing this point of view are Warren Bennis and Burt Nanus, *Leaders: The Strategies for Taking Charge* (New York: Harper Business 1997); Max DePree, *Leadership Is an Art*, op cit.; Kotter, *The Leadership Factor*, op cit.; Kouzes and Posner, *The Leadership Challenge*, op cit.

[19] The distinction was originally made by James McGregor Burns, *Leadership* (New York: Harper & Row, 1978) and was further developed by Bernard Bass, *Leadership and Performance Beyond Expectations* (New York: Free Press, 1985) and Bernard M. Bass, "Leadership: Good, Better, Best," *Organizationational Dynamics* (Winter 1985), pp. 26–40. See also Bernard M. Bass, "Does the Transactional-Transformational Leadership Paradigm Transcend Organizational and National Boundaries?" *American Psychologist*, vol. 52 (February 1997), pp. 130–139.

[20] See the discussion in Bass, op cit., 1997.

[21] This list is based on Kouzes and Posner, op cit.; Gardner, op cit.

[22] Daniel Goleman, "Leadership That Gets Results," *Harvard Business Review* (March/April 2000), pp. 78–90. See also his books *Emotional*

Intelligence (New York: Bantam Books, 1995) and *Working with Emotional Intelligence* (New York: Bantam Books, 1998).

[23] Daniel Goleman, "What Makes a Leader?" *Harvard Business Review* (November/December 1998), pp. 93–102.

[24] Goleman, op cit. (1998).

[25] Daniel Goleman, Annie McKee, Richard E. Boyatsis, *Primal Leadership: Realizing the Power of Emotional Intelligence* (Boston, MA: Harvard Business School Press, 2002).

[26] Ibid., p. 3.

[27] Information from "Women and Men, Work and Power," *Fast Company*, issue 13 (1998), p. 71.

[28] Jane Shibley Hyde, "The Gender Similarities Hypothesis," *American Psychologist*, vol. 60, no. 6 (2005), pp. 581–592.

[29] A. H. Eagley, S. J. Daran, and M. G. Makhijani, "Gender and the Effectiveness of Leaders: A Meta-Analysis," *Psychological Bulletin*, vol. 117 (1995), pp. 125–145.

[30] Research on gender issues in leadership is reported in Sally Helgesen, *The Female Advantage: Women's Ways of Leadership* (New York: Doubleday, 1990); Judith B. Rosener, "Ways Women Lead," *Harvard Business Review* (November/December 1990), pp. 119–125; and Alice H. Eagley, Steven J. Karau, and Blair T. Johnson, "Gender and Leadership Style Among School Principals: A Meta Analysis," *Administrative Science Quarterly*, vol. 27 (1992), pp. 76–102; Jean Lipman-Blumen, *Connective Leadership: Managing in a Changing World* (New York: Oxford University Press, 1996); Alice H. Eagley, Mary C. Johannesen-Smith, and Marloes L. van Engen, "Transformational, Transactional and Laissez-Faire Leadership: A Meta-Analysis of Women and Men, *Psychological Bulletin*, vol. 124, no. 4, (2003), pp. 569–591; and Carol Hymowitz, "Too Many Women Fall For Stereotypes of Selves, Study Says," *Wall Street Journal* (October 24, 2005), p. B.1.

[31] Data reported by Rochelle Sharpe, "As Women Rule," *Business Week* (November 20, 2000), p. 75.

[32] Eagley, et al., op cit.; Hymowitz, op cit.; Rosener, op cit.; Vroom, op cit.

[33] Rosener, op cit. (1990).

[34] See research summarized by Stephanie Armour, "Do Women Compete in Unhealthy Ways at Work?" *USA Today* (December 30, 2005), pp. B1–B2.

[35] Quote from "As Leaders, Women Rule," *Business Week* (November 20, 2000), pp. 75–84. Rosabeth Moss Kanter is the author of *Men and Women of the Corporation*, 2nd ed. (New York: Basic Books, 1993).

[36] Hyde, op cit.; Hymowitz, op cit.

[37] For debate on whether some transformational leadership qualities tend to be associated more with female than male leaders, see "Debate: Ways Women and Men Lead," *Harvard Business Review* (January/February 1991), pp. 150–160.

[38] "Many U.S. Employees Have Negative Attitudes to Their Jobs, Employers and Top Managers," Harris Poll #38 (May 6, 2005), retrieved from www.harrisinteractive.com.

[39] Information from "The Stat," *Business Week* (September 12, 2005), p. 16.

[40] See Terry Thomas, John R. Schermerhorn, Jr., and John W. Dienhart, "Strategic Leadership of Ethical Behavior in Business," *Academy of Management Executive*, vol. 18 (May 2004), pp. 56–66.

[41] Doug May, Adrian Chan, Timothy Hodges, and Bruce Avolio, "Developing the Moral Component of Authentic Leadership," *Organizational Dynamics*, vol. 32, (2003), pp. 247–260.

[42] Peter F. Drucker, "Leadership: More Doing than Dash," *Wall Street Journal* (January 6, 1988), p. 16.

[43] "Information from Southwest CEO Puts Emphasis on Character," *USA Today* (September 26, 2004), retrieved from www.usatoday/money/companies/management on December 12, 2005.

[44] Robert K. Greenleaf and Larry C. Spears, *The Power of Servant Leadership: Essays* (San Francisco: Berrett-Koehler, 1996).

[45] Jay A. Conger, "Leadership: The Art of Empowering Others," *Academy of Management Executive*, vol. 3 (1989), pp. 17–24.

[46] Max DePree, "An Old Pro's Wisdom: It Begins with a Belief in People," *New York Times* (September 10, 1989), p. F2; Max DePree, *Leadership Is an Art* (New York: Doubleday, 1989); David Woodruff, "Herman Miller: How Green Is My Factory," *Business Week* (September 16, 1991), pp. 54–56; and Max DePree, *Leadership Jazz* (New York: Doubleday, 1992).

[47] Lorraine Monroe, "Leadership Is About Making Vision Happen— What I Call 'Vision Acts,'" *Fast Company* (March 2001), p. 98; School Leadership Academy website: www.lorrainemonroe.com.

[48] Greenleaf and Spears, op cit., p. 78.

Source: Questionnaire by W. Warner Burke, Ph.D. Used by permission.

Features:

Pacesetters-Information from Keith H. Hammonds, "The Monroe Doctrine," *Fast Company* (October, 1999); and www.lorrainemonroe.com.

Newsline-Information and quotes from "An American Sage," *Wall Street Journal* (November 14, 2005), p. A22; Scott Thurm and Joann S. Lublin, "Peter Drucker's Legacy Includes Simple Advice: It's All About People," *Wall Street Journal* (November 14, 2005), pp. B1, B3; and John A. Byrne, "The Man Who Invented Management," *Business Week* (November 28, 2005), pp. 96–106.

Module 17

[1] Quotes from *Business Week* (July 8, 1991), pp. 60–61; for additional information see center's website: www.ccl.org.

[2] See Mintzberg, op cit., Kotter, op. cit.

[3] Henry Mintzberg, *The Nature of Managerial Work* (New York: Harper & Row, 1973).

[4] John P. Kotter, "What Effective General Managers Really Do," *Harvard Business Review*, vol. 60 (November/December 1982), pp. 156–157; and *The General Managers* (New York: Macmillan, 1986).

[5] "Relationships Are the Most Powerful Form of Media," *Fast Company* (March 2001), p. 100.

[6] Information from American Management Association, "The Passionate Organization Fast-Response Survey" (September 25–29, 2000), and organization website: http://www.amanet.org/aboutama/index.htm.

[7] Survey information from "What Do Recruiters Want?" *BizEd* (November/December 2002), p. 9; "Much to Learn, Professors Say," *USA Today* (July 5, 2001), p. 8D; and AMA Fast-Response Survey, "The Passionate Organization" (September 26–29, 2000).

[8] Jay A. Conger, *Winning 'Em Over: A New Model for Managing in the Age of Persuasion* (New York: Simon & Schuster, 1998), pp. 24–79.

[9] This discussion developed from ibid.

[10] Quotations from John Huey, "America's Most Successful Merchant," *Fortune* (September 23, 1991), pp. 46–59; see also Sam Walton and John Huey, *Sam Walton: Made in America: My Story* (New York: Bantam Books, 1993).

[11] *Business Week* (February 10, 1992), pp. 102–108.

[12] See Robert H. Lengel and Richard L. Daft, "The Selection of Communication Media as an Executive Skill," *Academy of Management Executive*, vol. 2 (August 1988), pp. 225–232.

[13] See Eric Matson, "Now That We Have Your Complete Attention," *Fast Company* (February/March 1997), pp. 124–132.

[14] David McNeill, *Hand and Mind: What Gestures Reveal about Thought* (Chicago: University of Chicago Press, 1992).

[15] Tom Peters and Nancy Austin, *A Passion for Excellence* (New York: Random House, 1985).

[16] This discussion is based on Carl R. Rogers and Richard E. Farson, "Active Listening" (Chicago: Industrial Relations Center of the University of Chicago, n.d.).

[17] Information from Carol Hymowitz, "Managers See Feedback from Their Staffers as Most Valuable," *Wall Street Journal* (August 22, 2000), p. B1.

[18] A useful source of guidelines is John J. Gabarro and Linda A. Hill, "Managing Performance," Note 9-96-022 (Boston, MA: Harvard Business School Publishing, n.d.).

[19] Information from Esther Wachs Book, "Leadership for the Millennium," *Working Woman* (March 1998), pp. 29–34.

[20] Information from Hilary Stout, "Self-Evaluation Brings Change to a Family's Ad Agency," *Wall Street Journal* (January 6, 1998), p. B2.

[21] A classic work on proxemics is Edward T. Hall's book, *The Hidden Dimension* (Garden City, NY: Doubleday, 1986).

[22] Mirand Wewll, "Alternative Spaces Spawning Desk-Free Zones," *Columbus Dispatch* (May 18, 1998), pp. 10–11.

[23] Information from Susan Stellin, "Intranets Nurture Companies from the Inside," *New York Times* (January 21, 2001), p. C4.

[24] Developed from *Working Woman* (November 1995), p. 14; and Elizabeth Weinstein, "Help! I'm Drowing in E-Mail!" *Wall Street Journal* (January 10, 2002), pp. B1, B4; Erin White, "The Jungle," *Wall Street Journal* (November 2, 2004), p. B8.

[25] Alison Overholt, "Intel's Got (Too Much) Mail," *Fortune* (March, 2001), pp. 56–58.

[26] Data in Stay Informed from "Privacy Special Report," *PC Computing* (March 2000), p. 88.

[27] Example from Heidi A. Schuessler, "Social Studies Class Finds How Far E-Mail Travels," *New York Times* (February 22, 2001), p. D8.

[28] Information from Carol Hymowitz, "More American Chiefs Are Taking Top Posts at Overseas Concerns," *Wall Street Journal* (October 17, 2005), p. B1

[29] Information from Ben Brown, "Atlanta Out to Mind Its Manners," *USA Today* (March 14, 1996), p. 7.

Source: From Douglas T. Hall, Donald D. Bowen, Roy J. Lewicki, and Francine S. Hall, *Experiences in Management and Organizational Behavior*, 2nd ed. (New York: Wiley, 1985). Used by permission.

Features:

Pacesetter-Information from ibid., and www.sony.com/SCA/bios/stringer.

Newsline-Information from Bruce Nussbaum, "Innovation as a Team Sport," *Business Week* (October 24, 2005), p. 144; and " 'Mosh Pits' of Creativity," *Business Week* (November 7, 2005), pp. 98–99.

Module 18

[1] Max DePree, "An Old Pro's Wisdom: It Begins with a Belief in People," *New York Times* (September 10, 1989), p. F2; Max DePree, *Leadership Is an Art* (New York: Doubleday, 1989); David Woodruff, "Herman Miller: How Green Is My Factory," *Business Week* (September 16, 1991), pp. 54–56; and Max DePree, *Leadership Jazz* (New York: Doubleday, 1992).

[2] See M. R. Barrick and M. K. Mount, "The Big Five Personality Dimensions and Job Performance: A Meta-Analysis," *Personnel Psychology*, vol. 44 (1991), pp. 1–26.

[3] For a sample of research see G. M. Hurtz and J. J. Donovan, "Personality and Job Performance: The Big Five Revisited," *Journal of Applied Psychology*, vol. 85 (2000), pp. 869–879; and, T. A. Judge and R. Ilies, "Relationship of Personality to Performance Motivation: A Meta-Analytic Review," *Journal of Applied Psychology*, vol. 87 (2002), pp. 797–807.

[4] This discussion based in part on John R. Schermerhorn, Jr., James G. Hunt, and Richard N. Osborn, *Organizational Behavior,* Ninth Edition (New York: John Wiley & Sons, 2005), pp. 54–60.

[5] J. B. Rotter, "Generalized Expectancies for Internal versus External Control of Reinforcement," *Psychological Monographs*, vol. 80 (1966), pp. 1–28.

[6] T. W. Adorno, E. Frenkel-Brunswick, D. J. Levinson, and R. N. Sanford, *The Authoritarian Personality* (New York: Harper & Row, 1950).

[7] Niccolo Machiavelli, *The Prince*, trans. George Bull (Middlesex, UK: Penguin, 1961).

[8] I. Briggs-Myers, *Introduction to Type* (Palo Alto, CA: Consulting Psychologists Press, 1980). For management applications and research, see William L. Gardner and Mark J. Martinko, "Using the Myers-Briggs Type Indicator to Study Managers: A Literature Review and Research Agenda," *Journal of Management*, vol. 22 (1996), pp. 45–83.

[9] See M. Snyder, *Public Appearances/Private Realities: The Psychology of Self-Monitoring* (New York: Freeman, 1987).

[10] Daniel Goleman, "Leadership That Gets Results," *Harvard Business Review* (March/April 2000), pp. 78–90. See also his books *Emotional Intelligence* (New York: Bantam Books, 1995) and *Working with Emotional Intelligence* (New York: Bantam Books, 1998).

[11] See Arthur P. Brief, Randall S. Schuler, and Mary Van Sell, *Managing Job Stress* (Boston: Little, Brown, 1981), pp. 7, 8.

[12] The classic work is Meyer Friedman and Ray Roseman, *Type A Behavior and Your Heart* (New York: Knopf, 1974).

[13] Sue Shellenbarger, "Do We Work More or Not? Either Way, We Feel Frazzled," *Wall Street Journal*, (July 30, 1997), p. B1.

[14] See, for example, "Desk Rage," *Business Week* (November 27, 2000), p. 12.

[15] See Hans Selye, *Stress in Health and Disease* (Boston: Butterworth, 1976).

[16] Carol Hymowitz, "Can Workplace Stress Get *Worse*?" *Wall Street Journal* (January 16, 2001), pp. B1, B3.

[17] See Steve M. Jex, *Stress and Job Performance* (San Francisco: Jossey-Bass, 1998).

[18] The extreme case of "workplace violence" is discussed by Richard V. Denenberg and Mark Braverman, *The Violence-Prone Workplace* (Ithaca, NY: Cornell University Press, 1999).

[19] See Daniel C. Ganster and Larry Murphy, "Workplace Interventions to Prevent Stress-Related Illness: Lessons from Research and Practice," chapter 2 in Cooper and Locke (eds.), *Industrial and Organizational Psychology: Linking Theory with Practice* (Malden, MA: Blackwell Business, 2000); Jonathan D. Quick, Amy B. Henley, and James Campbell Quick, "The Balancing Act—At Work and at Home," *Organizational Dynamics*, vol. 33 (2004), pp. 426–437.

[20] Data in Stay Informed from "Michael Mandel, "The Real Reasons You're Working So Hard," *Business Week* (October 3, 2005), pp. 60–70; "Many U.S. Employees Have Negative Attitudes to Their Jobs, Employers and Top Managers," The Harris Poll #38 (May 6, 2005), retrieved from www.harrisinteractive.com.

[21] Information from "Last Week's Top Story," *The Columbus Dispatch* (December 11, 2005), p. F1.

[22] See H. R. Schiffman, *Sensation and Perception: An Integrated Approach*, 3rd ed. (New York: Wiley, 1990).

[23] Information from "Misconceptions About Women in the Global Arena Keep Their Numbers Low," Catalyst study: www.catalystwomen.org/home.html.

[24] The classic work is Dewitt C. Dearborn and Herbert A. Simon, "Selective Perception: A Note on the Departmental Identification of Executives," *Sociometry*, vol. 21 (1958), pp. 140–144. See also, J. P. Walsh, "Selectivity and Selective Perception: Belief Structures and Information Processing", *Academy of Management Journal*, vol. 24 (1988), pp. 453–470.

[25] Quote from Sheila O'Flanagan, "Underestimate Casual Dressers at Your Peril," *The Irish Times* (July 22, 2005).

[26] See William L. Gardner and Mark J. Martinko, "Impression Management in Organizations," *Journal of Management* (June 1988), pp. 332–343.

[27] Sandy Wayne and Robert Liden, "Effects of Impression Management on Performance Ratings," *Academy of Management Journal* (February 2005), pp. 232–252.

[28] Information and quote from Joann S. Lublin, "How One Black Woman Lands Her Top Jobs: Risks and Networking," *Wall Street Journal* (March 4, 2003), p. B1.

[29] Martin Fishbein and Icek Ajzen, *Belief, Attitude, Intention and Behavior: An Introduction to Theory and Research* (Reading, MA: Addison-Wesley, 1973).

[30] See Leon Festinger, *A Theory of Cognitive Dissonance* (Palo Alto, CA: Stanford University Press, 1957).

[31] For an overview see Paul E. Spector, *Job Satisfaction* (Thousand Oaks, CA: Sage, 1997); Timothy A. Judge and Allan H. Church, "Job Satisfaction: Research and Practice," chapter 7 in Cary L. Cooper and Edwin A. Locke (eds.), op cit.(2000); Timothy A. Judge, "Promote Job Satisfaction Through Mental Challenge," chapter 6 in Edwin A. Locke (ed.), *The Blackwell Handbook of Principles of Organizational Behavior* (Malden, MA: Blackwell, 2004).

[32] Information in Stay Informed from Linda Grant, "Happy Workers, High Returns," *Fortune* (January 12, 1998), p. 81; Judge, op cit. (2002); "U.S. Employees More Dissatisfied With Their Jobs," Associated Press (February 28, 2005), retrieved from www.msnbc.com; "U.S. Job Satisfaction Keeps Falling, The Conference Board Reports Today," The Conference Board (February 28, 2005), retrieved from www.conference-board.org.

[33] Data reported in "When Loyalty Erodes, So Do Profits," *Business Week* (August 13, 2001), p. 8.

[34] Dennis W. Organ, *Organizational Citizenship Behavior: The Good Soldier Syndrome* (Lexington, MA: Lexington Books, 1988).

[35] See Mark C. Bolino and William H. Turnley, "Going the Extra Mile: Cultivating and Managing Employee Citizenship Behavior," *Academy of Management Executive*, vol. 17 (August 2003), pp. 60–67.

[36] These relationships are discussed in Charles N. Greene, "The Satisfaction-Performance Controversy," *Business Horizons*, vol. 15 (1982), pp. 31; Michelle T. Iaffaldano and Paul M. Muchinsky, "Job Satisfaction and Job Performance: A Meta Analysis," *Psychological Bulletin*, vol. 97 (1985), pp. 251–273.

[37] This discussion follows conclusions in Judge, op cit. (2004). For a summary of the early research see Iaffaldano and Muchinsky, op cit.

Self Assessment: Adapted from R.W. Bortner, "A Short Rating scale as a Potential Measure of Type A Behavior", *Journal of Chronic Diseases*, vol. 22 (1966), pp.87–91. Used by permission.

Features:

Newsline-Information from Carol Hymowitz, "Teamwork Fosters Faster Solutions Than Going Solo," *The Wall Street Journal* (September 20, 2005), p. B6.

Pacesetters-Information and quotes from "Panera CEO's Recipe: Learn from the Past, Anticipate Trends," *Wall Street Journal* (June 10, 2003), p. B1; Carolyn Walkup, "Ron Shaich," *Nation's Restaurant News* (October 2004).

Harrington Quote: *The Wall Street Journal*, May 18, 2006.

Module 19

[1] Information and quotes from Julie Flaherty, "A Parting Gift from the Boss Who Cared," *New York Times* (September 28, 2000), pp. C1, C25; Business Wire Press Release, "Employees of the Butcher Company Share over $18 Million as Owner Shares Benefits of Success" (September 21, 2000).

[2] See Abraham H. Maslow, *Eupsychian Management* (Homewood, IL: Richard D. Irwin, 1965); Abraham H. Maslow, *Motivation and Personality*, 2nd ed. (New York: Harper & Row, 1970). For a research perspective, see Mahmoud A. Wahba and Lawrence G. Bridwell, "Maslow Reconsidered: A Review of Research on the Need Hierarchy," *Organizational Behavior and Human Performance*, vol. 16 (1976), pp. 212–240.

[3] Clayton P. Alderfer, *Existence, Relatedness, and Growth* (New York: Free Press, 1972).

[4] Developed originally from a discussion in Edward E. Lawler III, *Motivation in Work Organizations* (Monterey, CA: Brooks/Cole Publishing, 1973), pp. 30–36.

[5] The complete two-factor theory is in Frederick Herzberg, Bernard Mausner, and Barbara Block Synderman, *The Motivation to Work*, 2nd ed. (New York: Wiley, 1967); Frederick Herzberg, "One More Time: How Do You Motivate Employees?" *Harvard Business Review* (January/February 1968), pp. 53–62, and reprinted as an *HBR classic* (September/October 1987), pp. 109–120.

[6] Critical reviews are provided by Robert J. House and Lawrence A. Wigdor, "Herzberg's Dual-Factor Theory of Job Satisfaction and Motivation: A Review of the Evidence and a Criticism," *Personnel Psychology*, vol. 20 (Winter 1967), pp. 369–389; Steven Kerr, Anne Harlan, and Ralph Stogdill, "Preference for Motivator and Hygiene Factors in a Hypothetical Interview Situation," *Personnel Psychology*, vol. 27 (Winter 1974), pp. 109–124. See also Frederick Herzberg, "Workers' Needs: The Same around the World," *Industry Week* (September 21, 1987), pp. 29–32.

[7] For a collection of McClelland's work, see David C. McClelland, *The Achieving Society* (New York: Van Nostrand, 1961); "Business Drive and National Achievement," *Harvard Business Review*, vol. 40 (July/August 1962), pp. 99–112; David C. McClelland, *Human Motivation* (Glenview, IL: Scott, Foresman, 1985); David C. McClelland and Richard E. Boyatsis, "The Leadership Motive Pattern and Long-Term Success in Management," *Journal of Applied Psychology*, vol. 67 (1982), pp. 737–743.

[8] David C. McClelland and David H. Burnham, "Power Is the Great Motivator," *Harvard Business Review* (March/April 1976), pp. 100–110.

[9] Information in Stay Informed from "CEO Pay: Sky High Gets Even Higher," *CNN Money* (August 30, 2005), retrieved from www.money.cnn.com. Suggested by Victoria Richebacher.

[10] See, for example, J. Stacy Adams, "Toward an Understanding of Inequity," *Journal of Abnormal and Social Psychology*, vol. 67 (1963), pp. 422–436; J. Stacy Adams, "Inequity in Social Exchange," in vol. 2, L. Berkowitz (ed.), *Advances in Experimental Social Psychology* (New York: Academic Press, 1965), pp. 267–300.

[11] See, for example, J. W. Harder, "Play for Pay: Effects of Inequity in a Pay-for-Performance Context," *Administrative Science Quarterly*, vol. 37 (1992), pp. 321–335.

[12] Victor H. Vroom, *Work and Motivation* (New York: Wiley, 1964; republished by Jossey-Bass, 1994).

[13] The work on goal-setting theory is well summarized in Edwin A. Locke and Gary P. Latham, *Goal Setting: A Motivational Technique That Works!* (Englewood Cliffs, NJ: Prentice Hall, 1984). See also Edwin A. Locke, Kenneth N. Shaw, Lisa A. Saari, and Gary P. Latham, "Goal Setting and Task Performance 1969–1980," *Psychological Bulletin*, vol. 90 (1981), pp. 125–152; Mark E. Tubbs, "Goal Setting: A Meta-Analytic Examination of the Empirical Evidence," *Journal of Applied Psychology*, vol. 71 (1986), pp. 474–483; and Terence R. Mitchell, Kenneth R. Thompson, and Jane George-Falvy, "Goal Setting: Theory and Practice," chapter 9 in Cary L. Cooper and Edwin A. Locke (eds.), *Industrial and Organizational Psychology: Linking Theory with Practice* (Malden, MA: Blackwell Business, 2000), pp. 211–249.

[14] Gary P. Latham and Edwin A. Locke, "Self-Regulation Through Goal Setting," *Organizational Behavior and Human Decision Processes*, vol. 50 (1991), pp. 212–247.

[15] Edwin A. Locke, "Guest Editor's Introduction: Goal-Setting Theory and Its Applications to the World of Business," *Academy of Management Executive*, vol. 18, no. 4 (2004), pp. 124–125.

[16] E. L. Thorndike, *Animal Intelligence* (New York: Macmillan, 1911), p. 244.

[17] B. F. Skinner, *Walden Two* (New York: Macmillan, 1948); *Science and Human Behavior* (New York: Macmillan, 1953); *Contingencies of Reinforcement* (New York: Appleton-Century-Crofts, 1969).

[18] For the Mary Kay story and philosophy see Mary Kay Ash, *Mary Kay on People Management* (New York: Warner Books, 1985); and Jim Underwood, *More Than a Pink Cadillac: Mary K Inc.'s 9 Leadership Keys to Success* (New York: McGraw-Hill, 2003).

[19] For a good review, see Lee W. Frederickson (ed.), *Handbook of Organizational Behavior Management* (New York: Wiley-Interscience, 1982); Fred Luthans and Robert Kreitner, *Organizational Behavior Modification* (Glenview, IL: Scott-Foresman, 1985); and Andrew D. Stajkovic and Fred Luthans, "A Meta-Analysis of the Effects of Organizational Behavior Modification on Task Performance 1975–95," *Academy of Management Journal*, vol. 40 (1997), pp. 1122–1149.

[20] Edwin A. Locke, "The Myths of Behavior Mod in Organizations," *Academy of Management Review*, vol. 2 (October 1977), pp. 543–553.

Source: This survey was developed from a set of "Gallup Engagement Questions" presented in John Thackray, "Feedback for Real," *Gallup Management Journal* (March 15, 2001), retrieved from http://gmj.gallup.com/management_articles/employee_engagement/article.asp?i=238&p=1, June 5, 2003; data reported from James K. Harter, "The Cost of Disengaged Workers," Gallup Poll (March 13, 2001).

Features:

Newsline-Information from Eleena De Lisser, "Start-Up Attracts Staff with a Ban on Midnight Oil," *Wall Street Journal* (August 23, 2000), pp. B1, B6; and corporate website: www.ipswitch.com.

Pacesetters-Information from "Charles Schwab," *Fortune Small Business* (September, 2003), pp. 104–115.

Module 20

[1] Information from Joann S. Lublin, "A Few Share the Wealth," *Wall Street Journal* (December 12, 2005), p. B1.

[2] Information for Stay Informed from "Three Factors Appear to Have Big Impact on Job Satisfaction," The Harris Poll #74 (December 20, 2000), retrieved from www.harrisinteractive.com.

[3] Information from Michelle Conlin, "The Easiest Commute of All," *Business Week* (December 12, 2005), pp. 78–80.

[4] Information from Sue Shellenbarger, "Flextime: Employers Try New Policies for Alternative Schedules," *Wall Street Journal* (November 17, 2005), p. D1.

[5] The Individual Performance Equation and its management and research implications are discussed in William L. Gardner and John R. Schermerhorn, Jr., "Strategic Operational Leadership and the Management of Supportive Work Environments," in Robert L. Phillips and James G. Hunt (eds.), *Leadership: A Multi-Organizational-Level Perspective* (Beverly Hills, CA: Sage, 1992); Thomas N. Martin, John R. Schermerhorn, Jr., and Lars L. Larson, "Motivational Consequences of a Supportive Work Environment," in M. L. Maehr and C. Ames (eds.), *Advances in Motivation and Achievement: Motivation Enhancing Environments*, vol. 6 (Greenwich, CT: JAI Press, 1989); John R. Schermerhorn, Jr., "Team Development of High Performance Management," *Training & Development Journal*, vol. 40 (1986), pp. 38–41; and John R. Schermerhorn, Jr., William L. Gardner, and Thomas N. Martin, "Management Dialogues: Turning on the Marginal Performer," *Organizational Dynamics* (Summer 1990), pp. 47–59.

[6] For a comprehensive treatment of extrinsic rewards, see Bob Nelson, *1001 Ways to Reward Employees* (New York: Workman Publishing, 1994).

[7] For a research perspective, see Edward Deci, *Intrinsic Motivation* (New York: Plenum, 1975); Edward E. Lawler III, "The Design of Effective Reward Systems," in Jay W. Lorsch (ed.), *Handbook of Organizational Behavior* (Englewood Cliffs, NJ: Prentice-Hall, 1987), pp. 255–271.

[8] Example from Frank Hinchey, "Tops in Copper," *Columbus Dispatch* (August 27, 2000), pp. G1, G2.

[9] See "The WSJ 350: A Survey of CEO Compensation," *The Wall Street Journal* (April 10, 2006).

[10] As CEO Pay Rockets Higher, Shareholders Urge Companies to Share the Rewards More Widely," report by *Responsible Wealth* (April 5, 2000), "CEO's Cash In, But How Many are Worth $100 million?" *USA Today* (April 19, 2006), p. 10A; www.responsiblewealth.org/press/CEO_shareholder.html.

[11] See Kaja Whitehouse, "More Companies Offer Packages Linking Pay Plans to Performance," *Wall Street Journal* (December 13, 2005), p. B6.

[12] Information from David Whitford, "A Human Place to Work," *Fortune* (January 8, 2001), pp. 108–20.

[13] Whitehouse, op cit.

[14] Erin White, "How to Reduce Turnover," *Wall Street Journal* (November 21, 2005), p. B5.

[15] White, op cit.

[16] Information from Susan Pulliam, "New Dot-Com Mantra: 'Just Pay Me in Cash, Please,'" *Wall Street Journal* (November 28, 2000), p. C1.

[17] Opdyke, op cit.

[18] Whitehouse, op cit.

[19] Amanda Bennett, "Paying Workers to Meet Goals Spreads, but Gauging Performance Proves Tough," *Wall Street Journal* (September 10, 1991), p. B1; "Pay to Live On, Stock to Grow On," *Fortune* (January 8, 2001), p. 151.

[20] See Carl F. Frost, John H. Wakeley, and Robert A. Ruh, *The Scanlon Plan for Organizational Development* (Lansing, MI: Michigan State University Press, 1996).

[21] Jeffrey Pfeffer and John F. Veiga, "Putting People First for Organizational Success," *Academy of Management Executive*, vol. 13 (May 1999), pp. 37–48.

[22] Information from www.intel.com and "Stock Ownership for Everyone," Hewitt Associates (November 27, 2000), www.hewitt.com/hewitt/business/talent/subtalent/con_bckg_global.htm.

[23] Information from Andrew Blackman, "You're the Boss," *Wall Street Journal* (April 11, 2005), p. R5.

[24] For a thought-provoking discussion of this issue, see Ben Hamper, *Rivethead: Tales from the Assembly Line* (New York: Warner, 1991).

[25] Information from David Whitford, "A Human Place to Work," *Fortune* (January 8, 2001), pp. 108–120.

[26] See Frederick Herzberg, Bernard Mausner, and Barbara Block Synderman, *The Motivation to Work*, 2nd ed. (New York: Wiley, 1967). The quotation is from Frederick Herzberg, "One More Time: Employees?" *Harvard Business Review* (January/February 1968), pp. 53–62, and reprinted as an HBR Classic in (September/October 1987), pp. 109–120.

[27] For a complete description of the core characteristics model, see J. Richard Hackman and Greg R. Oldham, *Work Redesign* (Reading, MA: Addison-Wesley, 1980).

[28] See, for example, Paul S. Goodman, Rukmini Devadas, and Terri L. Griffith Hughson, "Groups and Productivity: Analyzing the Effectiveness of Self-Managing Teams," chapter 11 in John R. Campbell and Richard J. Campbell, *Productivity in Organizations* (San Francisco: Jossey-Bass, 1988); Jack Orsbrun, Linda Moran, Ed Musslewhite, and John H. Zenger, with Craig Perrin, *Self-Directed Work Teams: The New American Challenge* (Homewood, IL: BusinessOne/Irwin, 1990); Dale E. Yeatts and Cloyd Hyten, *High Performing Self-Managed Work Teams* (Thousand Oaks, CA: Sage, 1997).

[29] Barney Olmsted and Suzanne Smith, *Creating a Flexible Workplace: How to Select and Manage Alternative Work Options* (New York: American Management Association, 1989).

[30] See Allen R. Cohen and Herman Gadon, *Alternative Work Schedules: Integrating Individual and Organizational Needs* (Reading, MA: Addison-Wesley, 1978), p. 125; Simcha Ronen and Sophia B. Primps, "The Compressed Work Week as Organizational Change: Behavioral and Attitudinal Outcomes," *Academy of Management Review*, vol. 6 (1981), pp. 61–74.

[31] Information from Lesli Hicks, "Workers, Employers Praise Their Four-Day Workweek," *Columbus Dispatch* (August 22, 1994), p. 6.

[32] Business for Social Responsibility Resource Center: www.bsr.org/resourcecenter (January 24, 2001); Anusha Shrivastava, "Flextime is now key Benefit for Mom-Friendly Employers," *Columbus Dispatch* (September 23, 2003), p. C2; Sue Shellenbarger, "Number of Women Managers Rises," *Wall Street Journal* (September 30, 2003), p. D2.

[33] "Networked Workers," *Business Week* (October 6, 1997), p. 8; and Diane E. Lewis, "Flexible Work Arrangements as Important as Salary to Some," *Columbus Dispatch* (May 25, 1998), p. 8.

[34] Christopher Rhoads and Sara Silver, "Working at Home Gets Easier," *Wall Street Journal* (December 29, 2005), p. B4.

[35] For a review see Wayne F. Cascio, "Managing a Virtual Workplace," *Academy of Management Executive*, vol. 14 (2000), pp. 81–90.

[36] Quote from Phil Porter, "Telecommuting Mom Is Part of a National Trend," *Columbus Dispatch* (November 29, 2000), pp. H1, H2.

[37] These guidelines are collected from a variety of sources, including: The Southern Calfornia Telecommuting Partnership: www.socalcommute.org/telecom.htm; ISDN Group; www.isdnzone.com/telcom/tips.

[38] Data in Stay Informed from Michelle Conlin, "The Easiest Commute of All," *Business Week* (December 12, 2005), pp. 78–80; Shellenbarger, op cit., 2005; "Huge Gap in US CEO/Worker Pay," *Financial Times* (June 22, 2006), p. 4

[39] See "Report on the American Workforce 1999" (Washington: U.S. Bureau of Labor Statistics); "1999 AMA Survey of Contingent Workers" (New York: American Management Association, 1999).

[40] Data and example from Sue Shellenbarger, "Employees Are Seeking Fewer Hours; Maybe Bosses Should Listen," *Wall Street Journal* (February 21, 2001), p. B1.

Source: Based on Nini Yang, Chao. D. Chen, Jaepil Choi, and Yimin Zou, "Sources of Work-Family Conflict: A Sino-U.S. Comparison of the Effects of Work and Family Demands," *Academy of Management Journal*, vol. 43, no. 1, pp. 113–123.

Source: Reprinted by permission from J. R. Hackman and G. R. Oldham. *The Job Diagnostic Survey: An Instrument for the Diagnosis of Jobs and the Evaluation of Job Redesign Projects, Technical Report 4* (New Haven, CT: Yale University, Department of Administrative Sciences, 1974).

Features:

Newsline-See *Restoring Competitive Luster to American Industry: An Agenda for Success* (Cleveland, OH: Lincoln Electric Company), Barnaby J. Feder, "Carrots, Sticks, and Growing Pains," *International Herald Tribune* (September 8, 1994), pp. 9, 10; corporate website: www.lincolnelectric.com.

Pacesetters-Information from www.craftscenter.org/about/board.

Module 21

[1] Information from Brent Schlender, "Pixar's Fun House," *Fortune* (July 23, 2001); corporate website: http://www.pixar.com.

[2] Information from Scott Thurm, "Teamwork Raises Everyone's Game," *Wall Street Journal* (November 7, 2005), p. B7.

[3] Ibid.

[4] See, for example, Edward E. Lawler III, Susan Albers Mohrman, and Gerald E. Ledford Jr., *Employee Involvement and Total Quality Management: Practices and Results in Fortune 1000 Companies* (San Francisco: Jossey-Bass, 1992); Susan A. Mohrman, Susan A. Cohen and Monty A. Mohrman, *Designing Team-based Organizations: New Forms for Knowledge Work* (San Francisco: Jossey-Bass, 1995).

[5] Jon R. Katzenbach and Douglas K. Smith, *The Wisdom of Teams: Creating the High Performance Organization* (Boston: Harvard Business School Press, 1993).

[6] See Edward E. Lawler III, *From the Ground Up: Six Principles for Building the New Logic Corporation* (San Francisco: Jossey-Bass, 1996), pp. 131?.

7 Data from Lynda C. McDermott, Nolan Brawley, and William A. Waite, *World-Class Teams: Working Across Borders* (New York: Wiley, 1998), p. 5; Survey reported in "Meetings Among Top Ten Time Wasters," *San Francisco Business Times* (April 7, 2003); www.bizjournals.com/sanfrancisco/stories/2003/04/07/daily21.html.

8 The "linking pin" concept is introduced in Rensis Likert, *New Patterns of Management* (New York: McGraw-Hill, 1962).

9 See discussion by Susan G. Cohen and Don Mankin, "The Changing Nature of Work," in Susan Albers Mohrman, Jay R. Galbraith, Edward E. Lawler III, and Associates, *Tomorrow's Organization: Crafting, Winning Capabilities in a Dynamic World* (San Francisco: Jossey-Bass, 1998), pp. 154–178.

10 Information from "Diversity: America's Strength," special advertising section, *Fortune* (June 23, 1997); American Express corporate communication (1998).

11 See Susan D. Van Raalte, "Preparing the Task Force to Get Good Results," *S.A.M. Advanced Management Journal*, vol. 47 (Winter 1982), pp. 11–16; Walter Kiechel III, "The Art of the Corporate Task Force," *Fortune* (January 28, 1991), pp. 104–106.

12 Developed from Eric Matson, "The Seven Sins of Deadly Meetings," *Fast Company* (April/May 1996), p. 122.

13 Mohrman et al., op cit.

14 Information from Jenny C. McCune, "Making Lemonade," *Management Review* (June 1997), pp. 49–53.

15 For a good discussion of quality circles, see Edward E. Lawler III and Susan A. Mohrman, "Quality Circles After the Fad," *Harvard Business Review*, vol. 63 (January/February 1985), pp. 65–71; Edward E. Lawler III and Susan Albers Mohrman, "Employee Involvement, Reengineering, and TQM: Focusing on Capability Development," in Mohrman, et al. (1998), pp. 179–208.

16 See, for example, Paul S. Goodman, Rukmini Devadas, and Terri L. Griffith Hughson, "Groups and Productivity: Analyzing the Effectiveness of Self-Managing Teams," chapter 11 in John R. Campbell and Richard J. Campbell, *Productivity in Organizations* (San Francisco: Jossey-Bass, 1988); Jack Orsbrun, Linda Moran, Ed Musslewhite, and John H. Zenger, with Craig Perrin, *Self-Directed Work Teams: The New American Challenge* (Homewood, IL: Business One Irwin, 1990); Dale E. Yeatts and Cloyd Hyten, *High Performing Self-Managed Work Teams* (Thousand Oaks, CA: Sage, 1997).

17 Information in box from Carl E. Larson and Frank M. J. LaFasto, *Teamwork: What Must Go Right/What Can Go Wrong* (San Francisco: Sage, 1989).

18 William M. Bulkeley, "Computerizing Dull Meetings Is Touted as an Antidote to the Mouth That Bored," *Wall Street Journal* (January 28, 1992), pp. B1, B2.

19 See Wayne F. Cascio, "Managing a Virtual Workplace," *Academy of Management Executive*, vol. 14 (2000), pp. 81–90.

20 Robert D. Hof, "Teamwork, Supercharged," *Business Week* (November 21, 2005), pp. 90–92.

21 See Sheila Simsarian Webber, "Virtual Teams: A Meta-Analysis," http://www.shrm.org/foundation/findings.asp.

22 Cascio, op cit.

23 See Stacie A. Furst, Martha Reeves, Benson Rosen, and Richard S. Blackburn, "Managing the Life Cycle of Virtual Teams," *Academy of Management Executive*, vol. 18, no. 2 (2004), pp. 6–11.

24 R. Brent Gallupe and William H. Cooper, "Brainstorming Electronically," *Sloan Management Review* (Winter 1997), pp. 11–21; Cascio, op cit.

25 Cascio, op cit.

26 Harold J. Leavitt, "Suppose We Took Groups More Seriously," in Eugene L. Cass and Frederick G. Zimmer (eds.), *Man and Work in Society* (New York: Van Nostrand Reinhold, 1975), pp. 67–77.

27 Ibid.

28 See Marvin E. Shaw, *Group Dynamics: The Psychology of Small Group Behavior*, 2nd ed. (New York: McGraw-Hill, 1976); Leavitt, op cit.

29 A classic work is Bib Latane, Kipling Williams, and Stephen Harkins, "Many Hands Make Light the Work: The Causes and Consequences of Social Loafing," *Journal of Personality and Social Psychology*, vol. 37 (1978), pp. 822–832.

30 John M. George, "Extrinsic and Intrinsic Origins of Perceived Social Loafing in Organizations," *Academy of Management Journal* (March 1992), pp. 191–202; and W. Jack Duncan, "Why Some People Loaf in Groups While Others Loaf Alone," *Academy of Management Executive*, vol. 8 (1994), pp. 79–80.

31 Ibid.; Lawler et al., op cit., 1998.

32 For a review of research on group effectiveness, see J. Richard Hackman, "The Design of Work Teams," in Jay W. Lorsch (ed.), *Handbook of Organizational Behavior* (Englewood Cliffs, NJ: Prentice-Hall, 1987), pp. 315–342; and J. Richard Hackman, Ruth Wageman, Thomas M. Ruddy, and Charles L. Ray, "Team Effectiveness in Theory and Practice," Chapter 5 in Cary L. Cooper and Edwin A. Locke, *Industrial and Organizational Psychology: Linking Theory with Practice* (Malden, MA: Blackwell, 2000).

33 For a discussion of effectiveness in the context of top management teams, see Edward E. Lawler III, David Finegold, and Jay A. Conger, "Corporate Boards: Developing Effectiveness at the Top," in Mohrman, op cit. (1998), pp. 23–50.

34 "Dream Teams," *Northwestern* (Winter 2005), p. 10; Matt Golosinski, "Teamwork Takes Center Stage," *Northwestern* (Winter 2005), p. 39.

35 Golosinski, op cit., p. 39.

36 See Warren Watson, "Cultural Diversity's Impact on Interaction Process and Performance," *Academy of Management Journal*, vol. 16 (1993); and Christopher Earley and Elaine Mosakowski, "Creating Hybrid Team Structures: An Empirical Test of Transnational Team Functioning," *Academy of Management Journal*, vol. 5 (February 2000), pp. 26–49.

37 J. Steven Heinen and Eugene Jacobson, "A Model of Task Group Development in Complex Organizations and a Strategy of Implementation," *Academy of Management Review*, vol. 1 (1976), pp. 98–111; Bruce W. Tuckman, "Developmental Sequence in Small Groups," *Psychological Bulletin*, vol. 63 (1965), pp. 384–399; Bruce W. Tuckman and Mary Ann C. Jensen, "Stages of Small-Group Development Revisited," *Group & Organization Studies*, vol. 2 (1977), pp. 419–427.

38 See, for example, Edgar Schein, *Process Consultation* (Reading, MA: Addison-Wesley, 1988); and Linda C. McDermott, Nolan Brawley, and William A. Waite, *World-Class Teams: Working Across Borders* (New York: Wiley, 1998).

39 For a good discussion, see Robert F. Allen and Saul Pilnick, "Confronting the Shadow Organization: How to Detect and Defeat Negative Norms," *Organizational Dynamics* (Spring 1973), pp. 13–16.

40 See Schein, op cit., pp. 76–79.

41 Marvin E. Shaw, *Group Dynamics: The Psychology of Small Group Behavior* (New York: McGraw-Hill, 1976).

42 A classic work in this area is K. Benne and P. Sheets, *Journal of Social Issues*, vol. 2 (1948), pp. 42–47; see also Likert, op cit., pp. 166–169; Schein, op cit. pp. 49–56.

43 Based on John R. Schermerhorn Jr., James G. Hunt, and Richard N. Osborn, *Organizational Behavior*, 7th ed. (New York: Wiley, 2000), pp. 345–346.

44 Victor H. Vroom and Arthur G. Jago, *The New Leadership: Managing Participation in Organizations* (Englewood Cliffs, NJ: Prentice Hall, 1988); Victor H. Vroom, "A New Look in Managerial Decision-Making," *Organizational Dynamics* (Spring 1973), pp. 66–80; Victor H. Vroom and Phillip Yetton, *Leadership and Decision-Making* (Pittsburgh: University of Pittsburgh Press, 1973).

45 Schein, op cit., pp. 69–75.

46 See Kathleen M. Eisenhardt, Jean L. Kahwajy, and L. J. Bourgeois III, "How Management Teams Can Have a Good Fight," *Harvard Business Review* (July/August 1997), pp. 77–85.

[47] Michael A. Roberto, "Why Making the Decisions the Right Way Is More Important Than Making the Right Decisions," *Ivey Business Journal* (September/October 2005), pp. 1–7.

[48] See Irving L. Janis, "Groupthink," *Psychology Today* (November 1971), pp. 43–46; and *Victims of Groupthink*, 2nd ed. (Boston: Houghton Mifflin, 1982).

[49] See also Michael Harvey, M. Ronald Buckley, Milorad M. Novicevic, and Jonathon R. B. Halbesleben, "The Abilene Paradox After Thirty Years: A Global Perspective," *Organizational Dynamics*, vol. 33 (2004), pp. 215–226.

Source: Developed from Lynda McDermott, Nolan Brawley, and William Waite, *World-Class Teams: Working across Borders* (New York: Wiley, 1998).

Features:

Newsline-This example is from Hof, op cit. Information from James Hannah, "Exec Touts Rigorous Retreats," *Columbus Dispatch* (October 8, 2000), p. G2.

Pacesetters-Information from Carol Hymowitz, "Managers Err if They Limit Their Hiring to People Just Like Them," *Wall Street Journal* (October 12, 2004), p. B1.

Module 22

[1] Information from Stefan Fatsis and Jon Weinbach, "Front-Office Fireworks," *Wall Street Journal* (November 7, 2005), pp. B1, B8.

[2] See Loretta Chao, "What GenXers Need to Be Happy," *Wall Street Journal* (November 29, 2005), p. B6; and Mayo Clinic, "Workplace Generation Gap: Understand Differences Among Colleagues," retrieved from www.MayoClinic.com.

[3] Richard E. Walton, *Interpersonal Peacemaking: Confrontations and Third-Party Consultation* (Reading, MA: Addison-Wesley, 1969), p. 2.

[4] See Kenneth W. Thomas, "Conflict and Conflict Management," in M. D. Dunnett (ed.), *Handbook of Industrial and Organizational Behavior* (Chicago: Rand McNally, 1976), pp. 889–935.

[5] See Robert R. Blake and Jane Strygley Mouton, "The Fifth Achievement," *Journal of Applied Behavioral Science*, vol. 6 (1970), pp. 413–427; and Alan C. Filley, *Interpersonal Conflict Resolution* (Glenview, IL: Scott, Foresman, 1975).

[6] See Alan C. Filley, *Interpersonal Conflict Resolution* (Glenview, IL: Scott, Foresman, 1975; and L. David Brown, *Managing Conflict at Organizational Interfaces* (Reading, MA: Addison-Wesley, 1983).

[7] This discussion is based on Filley, op cit.

[8] Portions of this treatment of negotiation originally adapted from John R. Schermerhorn Jr., James G. Hunt, and Richard N. Osborn, *Managing Organizational Behavior*, 4th ed. (New York: Wiley, 1991), pp. 382–387. Used by permission.

[9] See Bert Spector, "An Interview with Roger Fisher and William Ury," *Academy of Management Executive*, vol. 18 (2004), pp. 101–112.

[10] See Roger Fisher and William Ury, *Getting to Yes: Negotiating Agreement Without Giving In* (New York: Penguin, 1983); James A. Wall, Jr., *Negotiation: Theory and Practice* (Glenview, IL: Scott, Foresman, 1985); and William L. Ury, Jeanne M. Brett, and Stephen B. Goldberg, *Getting Disputes Resolved* (San Francisco: Jossey-Bass, 1997).

[11] Danny Ertel, "Getting Past Yes: Negotiating as if Implementation Mattered," *Harvard Business Review* (November 2004), pp. 60–68.

[12] Fisher and Ury, op cit.

[13] Example from Spector, op cit., p. 105.

[14] Ibid.; see also Spector, op cit.

[15] Developed from Max H. Bazerman, *Judgment in Managerial Decision Making*, 4th ed. (New York: Wiley, 1998), chapter 7.

[16] Information in Stay Informed reported in "Salary Talks," *Columbus Dispatch* (November 22, 2005), and http://www.womendontask.com/stats.html.

[17] Roy J. Lewicki and Joseph A. Litterer, *Negotiation* (Homewood, IL: Irwin, 1985).

[18] Fisher and Ury, op cit.

Source: Adapted from Thomas-Kilmann, *Conflict Mode Instrument*. Copyright © 1974, Xicom, Inc., Tuxedo, NY 10987. Used by permission.

Features:

Newsline-Information from ILO website: http://www.ilo.org/public/english/index.htm and http://www.ilo.org/public/english/standards/decl/publ/ reports/report4.htm.

Pacesetters-Information from the United Nations website: www.un.org/News/ ossg/sg/pages/sg_biography.html (February 22, 2001).

Thomas Quote: *The Wall Street Journal*, November14, 2005.

Module 23

[1] Information from "On the Road to Innovation," in special advertising section, "Charting the Course: Global Business Sets Its Goals," *Fortune* (August 4, 1997).

[2] Information from "'Mosh Pits' of Creativity," *Business Week* (November 7, 2005), pp. 98–99.

[3] Michael Beer and Nitin Nohria, "Cracking the Code of Change," *Harvard Business Review* (May/June 2000), pp. 133–141.

[4] Quote from John A. Byrne, "Visionary vs. Visionary," *Business Week* (August 28, 2000), p. 210.

[5] Tom Peters, *The Circle of Innovation* (New York: Knopf, 1997).

[6] See, for example, Roger von Oech, *A Whack on the Side of the Head* (New York: Warner Books, 1983) and *A Kick in the Seat of the Pants* (New York: Harper & Row, 1986).

[7] See Peter F. Drucker, "The Discipline of Innovation," *Harvard Business Review* (November/December 1998), pp. 3–8.

[8] Peter F. Drucker, *Management: Tasks, Responsibilities, and Practices* (New York: Harper & Row, 1973), p. 797.

[9] Based on Edward B. Roberts, "Managing Invention and Innovation," *Research Technology Management* (January/February 1988), pp. 1–19, and Hamel, op cit. See also Gary Hamel, *Leading the Revolution* (Boston, MA: Harvard Business School Press, 2000), pp. 293–295.

[10] This discussion is stimulated by James Brian Quinn, "Managing Innovation Controlled Chaos," *Harvard Business Review*, vol. 63 (May/June 1985).

[11] Kenneth Labich "The Innovators," *Fortune* (June 6, 1988), pp. 49–64.

[12] "'Mosh Pits' of Creativity," *Business Week* (November 7, 2005), p. 99.

[13] See Roberts, op cit.

[14] Example from *Fortune* (December 1991), pp. 56–62; additional information from corporate website: www.toro.com.

[15] For a discussion of alternative types of change, see David A. Nadler and Michael L. Tushman, *Strategic Organizational Design* (Glenview, II: Scott, Foresman, 1988); John P. Kotter, "Leading Change: Why Transformations Efforts Fail," *Harvard Business Review* (March/April 1995), pp 59–67; and W. Warner Burke, *Organization Change* (Thousand Oaks, CA: Sage, 2002).

[16] "FEMA to See Radical Change Homeland Security Chief Says," *Columbus Dispatch* (December 21, 2005), p. A5.

[17] Based on Kotter, op. cit.

[18] Beer and Nohria, op cit.; and "Change Management, An Inside Job," *Economist* (July 15, 2000), p. 61.

[19] Beer and Nohria, op cit.; and "Change Management, An Inside Job," *Economist* (July 15, 2000), p. 61.

[20] Reported in Robert Rose, "Kentucky Plant Workers Are Cranking Out Good Ideas," *Wall Street Journal* (August 13, 1996), p. B1.

[21] Beer & Nohria, op. cit.

[22] Reported in Carol Hymowitz, "Task of Managing Changes in Workplace Takes a Careful Hand," *Wall Street Journal* (July 1, 1997), p. B1.

[23] Reported in G. Christian Hill and Mike Tharp, "Stumbling Giant—Big Quarterly Deficit Stuns BankAmerica, Adds Pressure on Chief," *Wall Street Journal* (July 18, 1985), pp. 1–16.

[24] For an overview see W. Warner Burke, *Organization Change: Theory and Practice* (Thousand Oaks, CA: Sage, 2002).

[25] Kurt Lewin, "Group Decision and Social Change," in G. E. Swanson, T. M. Newcombm and E. L. Hartley (eds.), *Readings in Social Psychology* (New York: Holt, Rinehart, 1952), pp. 459–473.

[26] Criteria in box based on Everett C. Rogers, *Communication of Innovations*, 3rd Ed. (New York: Free Press, 1993).

[27] This discussion is based on Robert Chin and Kenneth D. Benne, "General Strategies for Effecting Changes in Human Systems," in Warren G. Bennis, Kenneth D. Benne, Robert Chin, and Kenneth E. Corey (eds.), *The Planning of Change*, 3rd ed. (New York: Holt, Rinehart, 1969), pp. 22–45.

[28] The change agent descriptions here and following are developed from an exercise reported in J. William Pfeiffer and John E. Jones, *A Handbook of Structured Experiences for Human Relations Training*, vol. 2 (La Jolla, CA: University Associates, 1973).

[29] Ram N. Aditya, Robert J. House, and Steven Kerr, "Theory and Practice of Leadership: Into the New Millennium," chapter 6 in Cary L. Cooper and Edwin A. Locke, *Industrial and Organizational Psychology: Linking Theory with Practice* (Malden, MA: Blackwell, 2000).

[30] Information from Mike Schneider, "Disney Teaching Execs Magic of Customer Service," *Columbus Dispatch* (December 17, 2000), p. G9.

[31] Teresa M. Amabile, "How to Kill Creativity," *Harvard Business Review* (September/October 1998), pp. 77–87.

[32] Sue Shellenbarger, "Some Employers Find Way to Ease Burden of Changing Shifts," *Wall Street Journal* (March 25, 1998), p. B1.

[33] John P. Kotter and Leonard A. Schlesinger, "Choosing Strategies for Change," *Harvard Business Review*, vol. 57 (March/April 1979); 109–112.

[34] Overviews of organization development are provided by David L. Bradford and W. Warner Burke (eds.), *Reinventing Organization Development* (San Francisco: Pfeiffer, 2005); W. Warner Burker *Organization Development: A Normative View* (Reading, MA: Addison-Wesley, 1987); William, Rothwell, Roland Sullivan, and Gary N. McLean, *Practicing Organization Development* (San Francisco: Jossey-Bass, 1995); and Wendell L. French and Cecil H. Bell Jr., *Organization Development*, 6th ed. (Englewood Cliffs, NJ: Prentice-Hall, 1998).

Source: Questionnaire adapted from L. Steinmetz and R. Todd, *First Line Management*, 4th ed. (Homewood, IL: BPI/Irwin, 1986), pp. 64–67. Used by permission.

Features:

Pacesetters-Information from "Managing Google's Idea Factory," *Business Week* (October 3, 2005), pp. 88–90; "Google Wants All Your Business," *Business Week* (December 19, 2005), p. 77.

Newsline-Information from Stephen H. Wildstrom, "Video iPod, I Love You," *Business Week* (November 7, 2005), p. 20; "Voices of Innovation," *Business Week* (December 12, 2005), p. 22.

Mayer Quote: *Business Week*, October 3, 2005.

Belady Quote: *The Columbus Dispatch*, March 27, 2006.

Photo Credits

Chapter 1
Page 2: Melanie Stetson Freeman/ Getty Images News and Sport Services. **Page 3:** Pat Bennett/Alamy Images. **Page 4:** Rolf Vennenbernd/ dpa/Landov LLC. **Page 15:** Jacques Alexandre/Age Fotostock America, Inc.

Chapter 2
Page 16: ©AP/Wide World Photos. **Page 17:** VCL/Taxi/Getty Images, Inc. **Page 20:** Stockbyte/Getty Images. **Page 31:** David Rae Morris/ Bloomberg News/Landov LLC.

Chapter 3
Page 32: Courtesy Urwick Archive, PowerGen Library, Henley Management College. **Page 33:** Jan Tove Johansson/ Taxi/Getty Images. **Page 47:** ©Apple Computer, Inc.

Chapter 4
Page 48: Rick Maiman/Bloomberg News/Landov LLC. **Page 49:** Bartee Photography/Age Fotostock American, Inc. **Page 56:** ©Polaris Images. **Page 63:** Hugh Threlfall/ Alamy Images.

Chapter 5
Page 65: Tim Davis/Stone/Getty Images. **Page 72:** ©AP/Wide World Photos. **Page 77:** Courtesy Burt's Bees, Inc.

Chapter 6
Page 78: Ken Usami/Photodisc/Getty Images, Inc. **Page 79:** Jeffrey Becom/Lonely Planet Images/Getty Images. **Page 86:** ©AP/Wide World Photos. **Page 93:** Courtesy MySpace.com.

Chapter 7
Page 94: Stuart O Sullivan/Getty Images. **Page 95:** Greg Stott/Masterfile. **Page 107:** Courtesy Toyota Motor Corp.

Chapter 8
Page 108: Garry Hunter/Stone/Getty Images. **Page 109 (top):** Tim Davis/ Stone/Getty Images. **Page 109 (bottom):** ©AP/Wide World Photos. **Page**

110: Sebastian D Souza/AFP/ Getty Images News and Sport Services. **Page 111 (top left):** ©AP/Wide World Photos. **Page 111 (top right):** ©AP/Wide World Photos. **Page 112:** Courtesy Room to Read. **Page 117:** Courtesy United States-Mexico Chamber of Commerce. **Page 121:** Jay Freis/The Image Bank/Getty Images.

Chapter 9
Page 122: Courtesy NOAA. **Page 123:** Isabelle Rozenbaum/Age Fotostock America, Inc. **Page 127:** Courtesy Norfolk Sourthern Corp. **Page 137:** Stockbyte/Getty Images.

Chapter 10
Page 138: Courtesy FedEx Kinko's Office and Print Services.**Page 139:** GK Hart/Vikki Hart/The Image Bank/Getty Images. **Page 147:** Courtesy Cisco Systems, Inc. **Page 151:** ©2006 by Skype Ltd.

Chapter 11
Page 152: Indranil Mukherjee/AFP/ Getty Images News and Sport Services. **Page 153:** Andrea Sperling/ Taxi/Getty Images. **Page 157:** ©AP/ Wide World Photos. **Page 165:** Alan King/Alamy Images.

Chapter 12
Page 166: Etienne de Malglaive/ Gamma-Presse, Inc. **Page 167:** Tim Flach/Stone/Getty Images. **Page 169:** STR/AFP/Getty Images/Getty Images News and Sport Services. **Page 181:** ©Dunkin Brands.

Chapter 13
Page 182: Courtesy Edward Jones. **Page 183:** Bob Anderson/Masterfile. **Page 186:** Tom Hussey/Workbook Stock/Getty Images. **Page 197:** Courtesy mozilla.org.

Chapter 14
Page 198: David Stoecklein/Corbis Images. **Page 199:** Renee Lynn/ Stone/Getty Images, Inc. **Page 201:** Courtesy Enterprise Rent-A-Car.

Page 211: Sion Touhig/ Getty Images News and Sport Services.

Chapter 15
Page 212: Courtesy Working Mother Magazine. **Page 213:** DAJ/Getty Images, Inc. **Page 216:** Vanderlei Almeida/AFP/ Getty Images News and Sport Services. **Page 225:** ©AP/Wide World Photos.

Chapter 16
Page 226: Courtesy Wieck Southwest Airlines. **Page 227:** Art Wolfe/Stone/ Getty Images. **Page 236:** Alan Levenson/Time Life Pictures/Getty Images News and Sport Services. **Page 239:** REUTERS/Kim Stallknecht /Landov LLC.

Chapter 17
Page 240: Garry Gay/Photographer s Choice/Getty Images. **Page 241:** Digital Vision/Getty Images. **Page 244:** Ranald Mackechnie/The Image Bank/Getty Images. **Page 253:** Photo by Mark Robert Halper provided courtesy of MySpace.com.

Chapter 18
Page 254: Nick White/Digital Vision/Getty Images. **Page 255:** Art Wolfe/Stone/Getty Images, Inc. **Page 263:** Liane Cary/Age Fotostock America, Inc. **Page 269:** Joel Saget/AFP/Getty Images News and Sport Services.

Chapter 19
Page 270: Lightscapes/Age Fotostock America, Inc. **Page 271:** Manoj Shah/The Image Bank/Getty Images. **Page 275:** Darrem Robb/Getty Images. **Page 285:** Mark Wiens/Masterfile.

Chapter 20
Page 286: Rusty Jarrett/Getty Images News and Sport Services. **Page 287:** Alberto Biscaro/Masterfile. **Page 289:** Jonathan Knowles/Photonica/Getty Images. **Page 299:** Reuters/Landov LLC.

Name Index

Organization Index